GOD
THE
REDEEMER

WHAT THE
BIBLE SAYS
ABOUT
GOD
THE
REDEEMER

Jack Cottrell

College Press Publishing Company, Joplin, Missouri

Scripture quotations,
unless otherwise noted,
are from the
NEW AMERICAN STANDARD BIBLE

Copyright © 1987
College Press Publishing Company
Second Printing, 1991

Library of Congress Catalog Card Number: 87-070449
International Standard Book Number: 0-89900-254-4

Table of Contents

PREFACE

. . . The gravest question before the Church is always God Himself, and the most portentous fact about any man is not what he at a given time may say or do, but what he in his deep heart conceives God to be like. . . .

A right conception of God is basic not only to systematic theology but to practical Christian living as well. It is to worship what the foundation is to the temple; where it is inadequate or out of plumb the whole structure must sooner or later collapse. I believe there is scarcely an error in doctrine or a failure in applying Christian ethics that cannot be traced finally to imperfect and ignoble thoughts about God.

The heaviest obligation lying upon the Christian Church today is to purify and elevate her concept of God until it is once more worthy of Him—and of her. In all her prayers and labors this should have first place.

These words of A.W. Tozer[1] express my own heart-felt conviction, the conviction that has helped me to see this writing project through to its completion in this present volume. About three and one-half years ago I began to write the study on God for College Press' "What the Bible

---

1. A.W. Tozer, *The Knowledge of the Holy* (London: James Clarke & Co., 1965), pp. 9, 10, 12.

Says About" series. At that time I did not know that it would take this long to complete or require this many volumes. But at last it is finished, and this present title can be considered as the last of a three-volume set under the general title of *The Doctrine of God*. Volume One is *God the Creator*; Volume Two is *God the Ruler*; and now this one is *God the Redeemer*. My prayer is that they will serve to glorify God and edify his people.

As in the other two volumes, here I have quoted from the New American Standard Bible except as noted. At times I have modified the form of the text (not the content) by converting poetic form into prose and by not following the all-capital-letters policy for *LORD* (where it translates the name *Yahweh* in the Old Testament) and for New Testament quotations from the Old Testament.

I owe a very special word of thanks to two people whose valuable assistance has expedited the production of this volume. My friend and former student Mark Morse has graciously provided the computer equipment (hardware and software) used in writing this book (a first-time experience for me). Also, Kenneth Craycraft, my Graduate Assistant at Cincinnati Christian Seminary, has devoted many, many hours of tedious labor toward the proof-reading and indexing of this work. I am humbly grateful for their help.

Finally I joyfully dedicate this volume to the three people who are God's best gifts to me: my three children—Russell, Cathleen, and Susan. To me they are my Jedidiah ("Beloved of the Lord," II Sam. 12:25), my Hephzibah ("My delight is in her," Isa. 62:4), and my Abigail ("A father's joy," I Sam. 25:3).

1

INTRODUCTION

The first volume in this series emphasized God as Creator; the second volume emphasized God as Sovereign. The focal point of this present work is that God is Savior. R. E. O. White is correct in saying that when the Bible refers to God as Savior and Redeemer, "it emphasizes a quality and initiative in Yahweh as fundamental as creatorhood [and] sovereignty."[1] These three basic designations of God (Creator; Sovereign or Ruler; Savior or Redeemer) represent the three major aspects of his work: creation, providence, and redemption.[2] Without diminishing the importance of the first two in any way, we may confidently say that the last of these is the dominant theme of the Bible, both in the Old Testament and in the New. "Yahweh is the saving

---

1. R. E. O. White, "Savior," *Evangelical Dictionary of Theology*, ed. Walter A. Elwell (Grand Rapids: Baker Book House, 1984), p. 975.
2. In this work, unless specifically noted, we shall use the words *salvation* and *redemption* interchangeably; the same applies to *Savior* and *Redeemer*. Technically speaking the words are not exactly equivalent. *Salvation* is the more general term, with *redemption* connoting a specific form which salvation may take.

God," as Claus Westermann says.[3] As another puts it, "The creed of Israel is, in brief, 'Yahweh saves'."[4] In the New Testament the name is changed but the creed is the same: "Jesus saves."

> The dominant note of the New Testament is salvation. Jesus proclaimed the gospel, the good news of the saving purpose of God. That name, given to its first four books, might rightly be the title of the New Testament as a whole. Its theme is the good news of God's coming in Christ for the salvation of men . . . . The Church saw as its first task the proclamation of this word of salvation.[5]

We must agree with W. N. Clarke: "The glory of Christianity is salvation."[6]

If it is true that modern man has less and less use for God as such, it is also true that those who acknowledge him at all are less and less inclined to think of him as Savior. One reason for this is the diminished concept of sin in the modern world. "The modern man is not concerned with sin," says Rall.[7] Of course he recognizes that the world is filled with evils, failures, social ills, and conflicts of all kinds; but he just does not want to think of them as *sin*. This is because *sin* connotes a wrongdoing for which one is responsible *before God*, and modern man does not want to see himself in this light. He will take his evil and his failures to sociologists and psychologists, but not to God.[8] As Karl Menninger points out in his book, *Whatever Became of Sin?*, "In all of the laments and reproaches made by our seers and prophets, one misses any mention of 'sin,' a word which used to be a veritable watchword of prophets."[9] A problem may be "evil, disgraceful, corrupt, prejudicial,

---

3. Claus Westermann, *What Does the Old Testament Say About God?*, ed. Friedemann W. Golka (Atlanta: John Knox Press, 1979), p. 27.
4. T. B. Kilpatrick, "Salvation (Christian)," *Encyclopedia of Religion and Ethics*, ed. James Hastings (New York: Charles Scribner's Sons, 1929), XI:112.
5. Harris Franklin Rall, *Religion as Salvation* (Nashville: Abingdon-Cokesbury Press, 1953), p. 87.
6. William Newton Clarke, *The Christian Doctrine of God* (New York: Charles Scribner's Sons, 1909), p. 212.
7. H. F. Rall, *Religion as Salvation*, p. 51.
8. Ibid., pp. 51-52, 57.
9. Karl Menninger, *Whatever Became of Sin?* (New York: Hawthorn Books, 1973), p. 13.

harmful," but never sinful, says Menninger.[10] The significance of this is obvious: without a sense of sin, there can be no real sense of God as Savior.

Boniface Willems points out another reason for the contemporary loss of the Saviorhood of God. "The sense of the need of redemption seems to have lost much of its keenness through the general process of secularization," he says.[11] A century of unprecedented growth in scientific knowledge has given modern man a sense of self-sufficiency; he feels capable of meeting his needs from his own resources. As Rall sums up this idea,

> . . . Once man stood in fear of nature and its incalculable forces, and even more of the world of evil spirits; so he sought supernatural aid. Science revealed to modern man a world of order; invention and engineering put into his hands the means of control. With these instruments he could now conquer disease and want and make nature his servant. Science was the new messiah, and man was his own savior. . . .[12]

Thus even apart from the lack of a sense of sin, even the more concrete needs of contemporary man do not generate within him an inclination to call upon God as Savior.

All of this, of course, simply underlines the urgency of the theme of this volume, that the true God—the God of the Bible—is our Savior and Redeemer. This is still the heart of the Christian message.

THE LANGUAGE OF REDEMPTION

The Bible is filled with what we may call the language of redemption. It uses several important Hebrew and Greek words to express this aspect of the work of God. Some of these words convey the more general concept of salvation, while others speak more specifically of redemption. In this section we will simply survey the biblical use of these words in order to show how pervasive is the concept that God is our Savior and our Redeemer.

---

10. Ibid., p. 17.
11. Boniface A. Willems, *The Reality of Redemption* (New York: Herder and Herder, 1970), p. 7.
12. H. F. Rall, *Religion as Salvation*, pp. 88-89.

God Our Savior

A number of words in both the Old and New Testaments speak of God's work of salvation or deliverance in general. These words may also be used in secular or non-theological contexts, but their predominant application is to God. They describe for us a God whose very nature is to save his people and whose saving activity is faithful and persistent.

Yāsha'

The most common Hebrew word which expresses the salvation concept is the verb yāsha', along with its derivatives. There is nothing unusual about this word; it simply means "to save, deliver, help, rescue, preserve." The following are just a few examples of the way it is used of God's work. "My shield is with God, who saves the upright in heart" (Ps. 7:10). "Now I know that the Lord saves His anointed; He will answer him from His holy heaven, with the saving strength of His right hand" (Ps. 20:6). "And the Lord their God will save them in that day as the flock of His people" (Zech. 9:16). "For I am with you," declares the Lord, "to save you" (Jer. 30:11). "Moreover, I will save you from all your uncleanness" (Ezek. 36:29). "But I will have compassion on the house of Judah and deliver them" (Hosea 1:7).

One form of this word is often translated as the English noun *Savior*. It is most often applied to God, even by God himself: "For I am the Lord your God, the Holy One of Israel, your Savior" (Isa. 43:3). "And all flesh will know that I, the Lord, am your Savior, and your Redeemer, the Mighty One of Jacob" (Isa. 49:26; cf. 60:16). God's people address him as Savior. David praises him thus: "My God, my rock, in whom I take refuge; my shield and the horn of my salvation, my stronghold and my refuge; my savior, Thou dost save me from violence" (II Sam. 22:3). He adds this prayer: "Wondrously show Thy lovingkindness, O Savior of those who take refuge at Thy right hand" (Ps. 17:7). The prophets also address God thus: "Truly, Thou art a God who hides Himself, O God of Israel, Savior!" (Isa. 45:15). Jeremiah refers to him as "Thou Hope of Israel, its Savior in time of distress" (Jer. 14:8).

While the term *savior* is sometimes used of human beings with reference to temporal deliverance (cf. Judg. 3:9, 15; Neh. 9:27), God

12

alone is the ultimate Savior who brings lasting salvation. He says, "I, even I, am the Lord; and there is no savior besides me" (Isa. 43:11). "And there is no other God besides Me, a righteous God and a Savior; there is none except Me" (Isa. 45:21). "Yet I have been the Lord your God since the land of Egypt; and you were not to know any god except Me, for there is no savior besides Me" (Hosea 13:4).

See also Psalm 106:21 and Isaiah 63:8.

Sōzō

The New Testament counterpart to *yāsha'* is the Greek word *sōzō*, which also means "to save." Other important forms of the word are *sōtēria* ("salvation") and *sōtēr* ("Savior"). Titus 3:5 is an example of how *sōzō* is used: "He saved us, not on the basis of deeds which we have done in righteousness, but according to His mercy, by the washing of regeneration and renewing by the Holy Spirit." The title *sōtēr* or "Savior" is used twenty-four times in the New Testament, both for God (eight times) and for Jesus Christ (sixteen times). Mary's song of praise begins, "My soul exalts the Lord, and my spirit has rejoiced in God my Savior" (Luke 1:46-47). Paul declares that God "is the Savior of all men, especially of believers" (I Tim. 4:10). The Pastoral Epistles often refer to "God our Savior" (I Tim. 1:1; 2:3; Titus 1:3; 2:10; 3:4; see Jude 25).

Throughout the New Testament Jesus Christ is referred to as our Savior. Paul says that from the seed of David "God has brought to Israel a Savior, Jesus" (Acts 13:23). At his birth the angels said, "For today in the city of David there has been born for you a Savior, who is Christ the Lord" (Luke 2:11). This was "the appearing of our Savior Christ Jesus" (II Tim. 1:10). After his death and resurrection he was exalted to God's right hand "as a Prince and a Savior" (Acts 5:31). Looking ahead to his second coming, "we eagerly wait for a Savior, the Lord Jesus Christ" (Phil. 3:20; cf. Titus 2:13). He is "the Savior of the body," the church (Eph. 5:23), and in a real sense "the Savior of the world" (I John 4:14; John 4:42). "Christ Jesus our Savior" gives us grace and peace (Titus 1:4) and the Holy Spirit (Titus 3:6). Jesus Christ is called our "Lord and Savior" (II Peter 1:11; 2:20; 3:2, 18) as well as our "God and Savior" (Titus 2:13; II Peter 1:1). The language of salvation applies equally to

13

God the Father and God the Son.[13]

Other Terms

Three other terms for God's saving work are used less frequently but still deserve to be mentioned. One is the Hebrew *nātsal*, which means "to deliver." An example of its use is Psalm 34:19, "Many are the afflictions of the righteous; but the Lord delivers him out of them all." Similarly Psalm 72:12 says, "For he will deliver the needy when he cries for help." Another word is *'āzar*, which means "to help." The Psalmist uses this word in referring to God as his helper: "Hear, O Lord, and be gracious to me; O Lord, be Thou my helper" (Ps. 30:10). Also, "God is my helper; the Lord is the sustainer of my soul" (Ps. 54:4). A New Testament word used fairly often is *ruomai*, meaning "to save, to deliver." It is used in Romans 11:26 (quoting Isa. 59:20): "The Deliverer will come from Zion, He will remove ungodliness from Jacob."

"A God of Deliverances"

Taking all of the above words into consideration, especially the Hebrew *yāsha'*, we are overwhelmed by the constant and consistent references to God as the God of salvation. The writers practically identify him with salvation, as in Isaiah 12:2, "Behold, God is my salvation, I will trust and not be afraid." In his post-exodus song Moses said, "The Lord is my strength and song, and He has become my salvation" (Ex. 15:2). The Psalmist refers to the Lord as "the God who is our salvation" (Ps. 68:19). "He only is my rock and my salvation" (Ps. 62:2, 6); "the Lord is my light and my salvation" (Ps. 27:1). "Make haste to help me, O Lord, my salvation!" (Ps. 38:22).

Salvation is seen as having its origin in God. Jonah's prayer concludes with these words of confidence: "Salvation is from the Lord" (Jonah 2:9). "Surely, in the Lord our God is the salvation of Israel," says Jeremiah 3:23. "The salvation of the righteous is from the Lord; He is their strength in time of trouble" (Ps. 37:39). This is David's personal faith: "My soul waits in silence for God only; from Him is my

---

13. See chapter three below for a more complete discussion of the doctrine of the Trinity.

14

salvation. . . . On God my salvation and my glory rest" (Ps. 62:1, 7).

Salvation is spoken of as God's possession: "Salvation belongs to the Lord" (Ps. 3:8). It is "the salvation of the Lord" (Lam. 3:26), "the salvation of our God" (Ps. 98:3; Isa. 52:10). Passages too numerous to list refer to "Thy salvation" (e.g., Ps. 18:35; 40:10) and "His salvation" (e.g., I Chron. 16:23; Isa. 25:9). God claims it as "My salvation" (e.g., Ps. 91:16; Isa. 56:1). See Psalm 50:23; Luke 3:6; Acts 28:28.

The biblical writers can scarcely think of God without thinking of salvation. They refer to him as the "God of my salvation" (Ps. 25:5; 27:9; 51:14; 88:1; Micah 7:7; Hab. 3:18), the "God of our salvation" (I Chron. 16:35; Ps. 65:5; 79:9; 85:4), "the God of your salvation" (Isa. 17:10), and "the God of his salvation" (Ps. 24:5). Yahweh is "the Rock of his [my, our] salvation" (Deut. 32:15; Ps. 89:26; 95:1). Such a thought can only bring praise: "The Lord lives, and blessed be my rock; and exalted be the God of my salvation" (Ps. 18:46).

In the New Testament this salvation is attributed specifically to Jesus Christ. He is "the source of eternal salvation" (Heb. 5:9). In him "the grace of God has appeared, bringing salvation to all men" (Titus 2:11). We may obtain "salvation through our Lord Jesus Christ" (I Thes. 5:9), for "salvation . . . is in Christ Jesus" (II Tim. 2:10). Acts 4:12 makes this exclusive: "And there is salvation in no one else; for there is no other name under heaven that has been given among men, by which we must be saved."

No wonder the Psalmist cries out, "God is to us a God of deliverances" (Ps. 68:20). This is the very essence of his being.

God Our Redeemer

God is not only our Savior; he is our Redeemer. In ordinary usage these words are properly used interchangeably, but technically there is an important distinction between them. *Redemption* is a more specific term and usually carries an important connotation not necessarily found in the general term *salvation*. It is the idea of rescuing or setting free by paying some kind of price. Such a meaning is found in several important biblical words which describe the work of God our Redeemer.

Gā'al

The most significant of these words is the Hebrew *gā'al*, meaning "to set free, to liberate, to redeem." Such a meaning can be clearly seen in

15

the way the word was used to refer to some very specific social and religious duties among the Hebrews. For instance, it was used to describe a worshiper's act of redeeming an item that he had consecrated as holy to the Lord, such as a house or a field. If he wanted to redeem it, he had to pay a price equal to six-fifths of the value of the item (Lev. 27:15, 19). The same could be done with the first-born of unclean animals, which by divine law were to be dedicated to God but could not be used for sacrifice (Lev. 27:11-13). By paying the price, the animal's original owner could redeem it or buy it back.

The word *gā'al* takes on special meaning when it is used for the act of redeeming someone (or his property) who had to sell himself into slavery (or sell his property) because of debts or extreme poverty. If the person himself became financially able, then he was allowed to redeem himself. But if this was not possible, then it was the right (or even the duty) of the nearest relative to pay the price to redeem what had been forfeited. See Leviticus 25:25ff. The following verses are a concise example of this practice:

> . . . Now if the means of a stranger or of a sojourner with you becomes sufficient, and a countryman of yours becomes so poor with regard to him as to sell himself to a stranger who is sojourning with you, or to the descendants of a stranger's family, then he shall have redemption right after he has been sold. One of his brothers may redeem him, or his uncle, or his uncle's son, may redeem him, or one of his blood relatives from his family may redeem him; or if he prospers, he may redeem himself (Lev. 25:47-49).

What is significant about this is that a participle form of this verb – the word *gō'ēl* – came to be used of one's relatives, especially of the near-relative who had the responsibility of redemption. Sometimes it is translated as just "kinsfolks" or "relatives" (I Kings 16:11). In contexts where redemption is in view, some have begun to translate it as "kinsman-redeemer" (e.g., the New International Version). The best example of this is the book of Ruth, where Boaz is called the *gō'ēl* (kinsman-redeemer) of Naomi and Ruth (Ruth 2:20). By purchasing a piece of family property, Boaz was able not only to acquire the property but to redeem Ruth from widowhood. She became his wife and they had a son, an ancestor of David and of Jesus. Though Ruth was only the daughter-in-law of Naomi, Naomi considered the child to be one of

16

her own family. Thus the other women said to Naomi, "Blessed is the Lord who has not left you without a *gō'ēl*," a redeemer or kinsman-redeemer (Ruth 4:14). Some see this nuance as part of the very root meaning of the word: "The primary meaning of this root is to do the part of a kinsman and thus to redeem his kin from difficulty or danger."[14] "The *gō'ēl* rescues that which was forfeited and restores justice to those who are not in a position to help themselves."[15]

This is the term that is used extensively in the Old Testament to refer to God's redemptive work. Especially in the Psalms and the prophets we read that "God is Israel's Redeemer who will stand up for his people and vindicate them. There may be a hint of the Father's near kinship or ownership in the use of this word. . . . God, as it were, redeems his sons from a bondage worse than slavery."[16] This is one of the words used to refer to God's delivering Israel from Egypt: "I am the Lord, and I will bring you out from under the burdens of the Egyptians, and I will deliver you from their bondage. I will also redeem you with an outstretched arm and with great judgments" (Exodus 6:6). The Psalmist reflects upon this great redemption: "Thou hast by Thy power redeemed Thy people" (Ps. 77:15). Isaiah adds, "In His love and in His mercy He redeemed them" (Isa. 63:9). The Lord himself comforts his people with these words: "Do not fear, for I have redeemed you; I have called you by name; you are Mine!" (Isa. 43:1).

Most significantly, God takes upon himself the name of *Gō'ēl*, the Redeemer. "'I will help you,' declares the Lord, 'and your Redeemer is the Holy One of Israel'" (Isa. 41:14). In similar contexts where he promises redemption, God names himself as the *Gō'ēl*. He is "the Lord your Redeemer, the Holy One of Israel" (Isa. 43:14; 48:17); "the Lord, the King of Israel and his Redeemer, the Lord of hosts" (Isa. 44:6); "the Lord, your Redeemer, and the one who formed you from the womb" (Isa. 44:24); "our Redeemer, the Lord of hosts . . . , the Holy One of Israel" (Isa. 47:4); "the Lord, the Redeemer of Israel, and its Holy One"

---

14. R. Laird Harris, "*gā'al*," *Theological Wordbook of the Old Testament*, ed. R. Laird Harris et al. (Chicago: Moody Press, 1980), I:144.

15. Colin Brown, "Redemption," section on λύω (part), *The New International Dictionary of New Testament Theology*, ed. Colin Brown (Grand Rapids: Zondervan, 1978), III:178.

16. R. Laird Harris, "*gā'al*," p. 144.

17

(Isa. 49:7); "your Redeemer, the Mighty One of Jacob" (Isa. 49:26; 60:16); "the Lord your Redeemer" (Isa. 54:8). "Their Redeemer is strong, the Lord of hosts is His name; He will vigorously plead their case" (Jer. 50:34). Twice this designation is accompanied by the reference to God as a rock: "And they remembered that God was their rock, and the Most High God their Redeemer" (Ps. 78:35); he is "my rock and my Redeemer" (Ps. 19:14). As someone has said, "God is the reliable protector who never wavers."[17] Twice the idea of God as a near-relative is included in the text: "For your husband is your Maker, whose name is the Lord of hosts; and your Redeemer is the Holy One of Israel, who is called the God of all the earth" (Isa. 54:5). "Thou, O Lord, art our Father, our Redeemer from of old is Thy name" (Isa. 63:16). One use of the term is definitely Messianic: "And a Redeemer will come to Zion" (Isa. 59:20, cited of Jesus in Rom. 11:26). Some think that Job 19:25 also refers to the Messiah: "I know that my Redeemer lives, and at the last He will take His stand on the earth."

Without a doubt God's description of himself as *Gō'ēl* takes us to the very heart of his nature. E. M. B. Green sums up the significance of it in this way:[18]

> . . . Certainly the *gō'ēl* metaphor was ascribed to God to stress his kinship with his people Israel and his gracious love to them. But it also emphasizes that the carrying out of the kinsman's function by the Lord cost him as dear as it did the human kinsman who had to pay a ransom price.

Though the idea of a ransom price is not always evident in the Old Testament contexts, it is certainly inherent in the terminology and thus forms a fitting background for the New Testament teaching that God's own Son was the price he paid for our redemption.

Lutroō

This leads to our discussion of the main New Testament term cor-

---

17. Helmer Ringgren, "*gā'al*," *Theological Dictionary of the Old Testament*, revised edition, ed. G. J. Botterweck and Helmer Ringgren, tr. John T. Willis (Grand Rapids: Eerdmans, 1977), II:355.
18. E. M. B. Green, *The Meaning of Salvation* (Philadelphia: Westminster Press, 1965), p. 31.

responding to *gā'al*, namely, *lutroō*, along with its derivatives. In its most common grammatical form its basic meaning is "to ransom, to redeem, to rescue." Barclay says, "The whole background of the word is 'captivity'. It has always got to do with rescuing, redeeming, liberating, ransoming a man or a thing from some hostile power which has him or it in its possession."[19] It "expresses the 'redeeming', 'rescuing' of a man from a power or a situation which has him in its grip and from which he is powerless to free himself."[20] It is used in Titus 2:14, which says that Christ "gave Himself for us, that He might redeem us from every lawless deed." The idea of a ransom price is clearly seen in I Peter 1:18-19, "Knowing that you were not redeemed with perishable things like silver or gold from your futile way of life inherited from your forefathers, but with precious blood, as of a lamb unblemished and spotless, the blood of Christ."

The participle form of this verb is used frequently in the Septuagint to translate *gō'ēl* when referring to God as Redeemer. A cognate form *(lutrōtēs)*, meaning "deliverer," is used in Acts 7:35 in reference to Moses.

Though used only twice in the New Testament, the word *lutron* is very significant. It is the word Jesus used when he said, "The Son of Man did not come to be served, but to serve, and to give His life a ransom for many" (Matt. 20:28; cf. Mark 10:45). Its meaning is drawn from the rich Old Testament background of the concept of redemption, of the ransom price paid to set someone free from bondage, from slavery, or from some kind of obligation. Barclay says that "always it is a price and a payment which releases [a man] from a debt and a liability which otherwise he would have been bound to satisfy."[21] When used of Jesus it means this, says Barclay,[22]

> . . . that Jesus Christ by his life and by his death released man from an obligation, a liability and a debt which otherwise he would have been bound to pay, and delivered him from a bondage and a slavery, by paying the purchase price of freedom which he himself could never have paid.

19. William Barclay, *New Testament Words* (Philadelphia: Westminster Press, 1974), p. 193.
20. Ibid., p. 194.
21. Ibid., p. 190.
22. Ibid., p. 192.

19

A related word, *antilutron*, is used in I Tim. 2:6, which says that Jesus "gave Himself as a ransom for all."

Other Terms

Several other important terms convey the idea of God's work as a work of redemption. The first is the Hebrew word *pādāh*, which is nearly synonymous with *gā'al* and means "to redeem, ransom, rescue." Procksch says, "It is used especially of freeing from bondage or imprisonment under an alien power."[23] An example is Psalm 31:5, "Into Thy hand I commit my spirit; Thou hast ransomed me, O Lord, God of truth." Psalm 130:7-8 says, "O Israel, hope in the Lord; for with the Lord there is lovingkindness, and with Him is abundant redemption. And He will redeem Israel from all his iniquities." God says, "Indeed, I brought you up from the land of Egypt and ransomed you from the house of slavery" (Micah 6:4). In the following passages *pādāh* and *gā'al* are used synonymously: "For the Lord has ransomed Jacob, and redeemed him from the hand of him who was stronger than he" (Jer. 31:11). "I will ransom them from the power of Sheol; I will redeem them from death" (Hosea 13:14).

Another word is *kāpar* (or *kāphar)*, which means "to make atonement, pardon, forgive." It is used especially in the book of Leviticus with reference to the sacrifices and offerings used in temple worship. It includes the idea of atoning by offering a substitute. It is used of God in Psalm 78:38, "But He, being compassionate, forgave their iniquity, and did not destroy them." Another form of the word, *kōpēr* (or *kōphēr)*, serves as a noun and is equivalent to *lutron*. It means "ransom," as in Isaiah 43:3, "For I am the Lord your God, the Holy One of Israel, your Savior; I have given Egypt as your ransom, Cush and Seba in your place."

Two other New Testament words must also be included here, namely, *agorazō* and *exagorazō*. They come from the word *agora* ("marketplace") and mean "to buy in the marketplace, to purchase, to redeem." They are used in crucial passages explaining Christ's redeeming work. I Corinthians 6:20 says that "you have been bought with a

---

23. O. Procksch, "λύω," *Theological Dictionary of the New Testament*, ed. Gerhard Kittel, tr. Geoffrey W. Bromiley (Grand Rapids: Eerdmans, 1967), IV:333.

price." This price is set forth in the song of praise to the Lamb in Revelation 5:9, "Worthy art Thou to take the book, and to break its seals; for Thou wast slain, and didst purchase for God with Thy blood men from every tribe and tongue and people and nation." *Exagorazō* is used in Galatians 4:5, which says that God sent his Son "in order that He might redeem those who were under the Law, that we might receive the adoption as sons." "Christ redeemed us from the curse of the Law, having become a curse for us" (Gal. 3:13).

All of the words surveyed here in connection with God as Redeemer, including the major terms *gā'al* and *lutroō*, are significant in their emphasis on God's paying a price to set us free. Colin Brown's words apply here, that "the redeeming activity of God" is "the use of his power in the service of his love and faithfulness which redeems from bondage." Also, it is "liberation from slavery . . . and the reclaiming by Yahweh into his rightful ownership of 'the people of his possession'."[24] Even when the concept of a ransom price is not explicit, the idea of the costliness of our redemption is there. What Green says of the three Hebrew words applies to all of the words discussed here:[25]

> It is surely no accident that three words . . . which in normal usage denote what can only be called a ransom or substitutionary idea, should be applied to God in his redeeming activity. . . . What, however, the use of these words does most forcibly suggest is that God's salvation is a very costly matter to him. Despite the dangers, the writers in both Testaments take the risk of using such language of God, lest we should ever assume about God's salvation, what Renan said of his forgiveness, *"C'est son metier"*. It is not God's obligation to deliver us. Salvation springs from costly grace.

The Redeemed of the Lord

In concluding this section on the language of redemption, it is appropriate to note that the people of the Lord are sometimes described simply as the ones whom he has redeemed. "Let the redeemed of the Lord say so, whom He has redeemed from the hand of the adversary"

---

24. Colin Brown, "Redemption," section on λύτρον (part), *The New International Dictionary of New Testament Theology*, III:192-193.
25. E. M. B. Green, *The Meaning of Salvation*, pp. 32-33.

Ps. 107:2). "And they will call them, 'The holy people, the redeemed of the Lord'" (Isa. 62:12). "And the ransomed of the Lord will return, and come with joyful shouting to Zion" (Isa. 35:10); Isaiah 51:11 is similar. The following passage sums up the work of the Savior and the joy of the saved: "Blessed are you, O Israel; who is like you, a people saved by the Lord, who is the shield of your help, and the sword of your majesty!" (Deut. 33:29).

SALVATION IS HIS NAME

The essence and character of God as Savior and Redeemer are seen not only in the vocabulary of salvation as discussed above, but also in his very name. This is true of the name *Yahweh* in the Old Testament, as well as the name *Jesus* in the New Testament. The connection with salvation is evident in both of these names, as well as in some of the other titles applied to Jesus.

Yahweh

The Old Testament saints knew the God of Abraham, Isaac and Jacob as *Elohim* (God) and *Adonai* (Lord), but these were not names in the strict sense of the word. God's "proper name" (his "given" name, as we might call it) was *Jehovah* or *Yahweh*. The exact spelling and pronunciation are not known to us today. Most seem to prefer *Yahweh* (or *YHWH*, to correspond to the four letters of the Hebrew word), though *Jehovah* still finds frequent use because of certain hymns and Bible versions. Though we may wish it were otherwise, we will probably not be able to settle these matters in this life.

It is important, however, that we try to understand the meaning and significance of this name. The point here is that this wonderful name, the most glorious and majestic name in the universe, embodies the marvelous truth that our God is a God of salvation. As Bavinck says, "It is especially in the name *Yhwh* that the Lord reveals himself as the God of grace."[26]

The etymology or origin of this name is not at all certain, though most connect it in some way with the Hebrew verb *hāyāh*, "to be, to ex-

---

26. Herman Bavinck, *The Doctrine of God*, ed. and tr. William Hendriksen (Grand Rapids: Eerdmans, 1951), p. 103.

ist, to become."[27] This seems warranted by Exodus 3:14, where God is replying to Moses' question about his name: "And God said to Moses, 'I AM WHO I AM'; and He said, 'Thus you shall say to the sons of Israel, 'I AM has sent me to you.'" Sometimes this is taken to mean that God's name is meant to emphasize his aseity or eternity or self-existence.[28]

But there is no agreement on this point. Some argue whether. the name *Yahweh* is from the qal or the hiphil form of the verb. If it is hiphil, as Freedman argues,[29] then God's name has a causative significance and means "He who creates," not "He who is"; and the name in Exodus 3:14 should read, "I create whatever I create." Others disagree strongly with this reconstruction, citing the fact that there is no known example of the verb *hāyāh* in the hiphil form. They prefer something like the simple "I AM" or "He is," based on the qal form of the verb.[30]

But even at this, the exact meaning of the name is not pinned down, since the tense of the verb may still be argued, and the larger context of Exodus 3:14 must be considered.[31] Some put it in a future tense, "I will be what I will be," and connect it with Exodus 6:2-8, emphasizing God's faithfulness therefrom.[32] As Bavinck sums up this view,[33]

> . . . The One who appears to Moses is not a new or a strange God, but is the God of the fathers, the Unchangeable the Immutable One, the Faithful One, the eternally Self-consistent One, the One who never leaves

---

27. R. Laird Harris questions this connection between the name and the verb, and suggests that the name is an old word of unknown origin which sounded something like the verb *hāyāh* in Moses' day. See his editorial note in the article by J. Barton Payne, "*hāwāh*," *Theological Wordbook of the Old Testament*, ed. R. Laird Harris et al.(Chicago: Moody Press, 1980), I:210-211.

28. See Jack Cottrell, *What the Bible Says About God the Creator* (Joplin, Mo.: College Press, 1983), p. 248. See also Carl F.H. Henry, *God, Revelation and Authority, Vol. II: God Who Speaks and Shows, Fifteen Theses, Part One* (Waco, Texas: Word Books, 1976, pp. 213-15.

29. D. N. Freedman, "*YHWH*" (part), *Theological Dictionary of the Old Testament*, ed. G. J. Botterweck and Helmer Ringgren, tr. David E. Green (Grand Rapids: Eerdmans, 1986), V:513ff.

30. J. Barton Payne, "*hāwāh*," p. 211. See also Carl Henry, *God, Revelation and Authority*, II:218-219.

31. See the excellent discussion of suggested alternatives in Carl Henry, *God, Revelation and Authority*, II:213-225.

32. Herman Bavinck, *The Doctrine of God*, pp. 105-106.

33. Ibid., p. 106.

or forsakes his people but ever seeks his own and ever saves them, who is unchangeable in his grace, in his love, in his succor, who will be what he is, since he ever remaineth himself. . . .

Still others take Exodus 3:12 as the key to understanding the meaning of *Yahweh*. Here the Lord declares his most frequent covenant promise, "Certainly I will be with you." Payne says this shows that verse 14 should be read as "I am present is what I am," and that *Yahweh* means "faithful presence."[34] "It connotes God's nearness, his concern for man, and the revelation of his redemptive covenant."[35] Carl Henry comments thus: "On this view YAHWEH emphasizes his living active presence, responsive to the needs of Moses and his people, in whose behalf he is redemptively ready to intervene."[36]

This view is very attractive, and I am inclined to accept it, but not on the basis of etymology as much as on context and on the general biblical use of God's name. R. Laird Harris cautions, "As to the meaning of the name, we are safer if we find the character of God from his works and from the descriptions of him in the Scripture rather than to depend on a questionable etymology of his name."[37] It may well be that this name did not bear the connotation of salvation at first, but that it acquired its redemptive significance under Moses, as Payne suggests.[38] Without negating any transcendent ontological or metaphysical connotations that may be present in the name, as Henry says, we may nevertheless understand *Yahweh* as including from this point on "the pledge of redemptive presence."[39] Henry's comments are much to the point: "In our view, YAHWEH is the revelation of the Eternal, the independent sovereign of all, who pledges in free grace to come to the redemptive rescue of his chosen people. *The God who is,* who is *eternally there,* will personally manifest his redemptive presence in Israel's midst." This

---

34. J. Barton Payne, "*hāwāh*," p. 212.

35. Ibid.

36. Carl F. H. Henry, *God, Revelation and Authority,* II:219.

37. R. Laird Harris, editorial note in J. Barton Payne, "*hāwāh*," p. 211.

38. J. Barton Payne, "*hāwāh*," p. 212. Bavinck says, "At this time God gives an entirely new meaning to an old name, a meaning which before this time would not have been understood" (*The Doctrine of God,* p. 107).

39. Carl F. H. Henry, *God, Revelation and Authority,* II:220.

name reveals God as "the divine redemptive intervener," as the "redemptive Deliverer," as the "Covenantal Redeemer."[40]

Thus the very name of God brings us into the sphere of salvation. We cannot think of him without thinking of him as Savior and Redeemer. Girdlestone puts it well:[41]

> . . . God's personal existence, the continuity of His dealings with man, the unchangeableness of His promises, and the whole revelation of His redeeming mercy, gather round the name *Jehovah*. "Thus saith *Jehovah*," not "thus saith *Elohim*," is the general introduction to the prophetic messages. It is as *Jehovah* that God became the Saviour of Israel, and as *Jehovah* He saves the world; and this is the truth embodied in the name of *Jesus*, which is literally *Jehovah*-Saviour.

This leads us into our consideration of the names of Jesus.

Jesus

However we may understand the pre-existence of Jesus and his incarnation, strictly speaking Jesus of Nazareth did not exist until he was conceived by the Holy Spirit in the womb of his mother Mary. The divine Logos, the second person of the Trinity, who became incarnate as Jesus, had always existed as God and with God (John 1:1). It was the eternal Logos who participated in the work of creation (John 1:3) and who has participated in the works of divine providence since that time. The work which the Logos performs in the person of Jesus of Nazareth, however, is salvation—no more, no less. The very thought of Jesus should bring with it the thought of salvation. This was his purpose, his rationale, his reason for being.

This should be evident to us from the very meaning of his name, *Jesus*. The angel who announced the Savior's birth to Joseph said, "You shall call His name Jesus, for it is He who will save His people from their sins" (Matt. 1:21). The name is equivalent to the Hebrew name *Joshua*, which was formed by combining *Yahweh* and *yāsha'* for the literal meaning of "Jehovah-Savior," as Girdlestone says, or

---

40. Ibid., pp. 219-224.
41. Robert B. Girdlestone, *Synonyms of the Old Testament* (Grand Rapids: Eerdmans, 1951 reprint of 1897 ed.), p. 38.

"Yahweh our Help" or "Yahweh is salvation." Commenting on the meaning of *Joshua*, Philo said that it means "Salvation is of the Lord."[42] This is the name chosen by God himself to be borne by his incarnate Son, ever to remind us that he and he alone is the source of our salvation (Acts 4:12). As Henry says, "When the early Christians spoke the name JESUS, they expressed their awareness that the MESSIAH embodies Yahweh's promised salvation."[43]

Several other appellations applied to Jesus convey the concept of salvation also. The title *Kurios*, usually translated "Lord," is one of the most common New Testament designations for Jesus, especially after his resurrection from the dead. With few exceptions Paul reserves this title for the risen Christ. What makes this significant is that in the Septuagint this is the word that is regularly used in the place of (not as a strict translation of) the divine name, *Yahweh*. Over 6,150 times *Kurios* replaces *Yahweh* as the name for God. Whatever else this may mean, this much is clear: when the early Christians familiar with the Septuagint (such as Paul) called Jesus *Kurios*, they could not help but identify him with Yahweh, the God of salvation.

It is often pointed out that Jesus took for himself the divine name "I AM" as set forth in Exodus 3:14, with all its redemptive significance. Sometimes the evidence for this is exaggerated,[44] but a few statements of Jesus seem to confirm this point. First is his remarkable claim, "Truly, truly, I say to you, before Abraham was born, I AM" (John 8:58). There was little reason for Jesus to use the present tense unless he was making the special point of identifying himself with the divine name. Also significant are such passages as John 8:24, where Jesus says, "Unless you believe that I am *He*, you shall die in your sins." The word *He* has been added by the translators; Jesus' literal statement is "Unless you believe that I AM, you shall die in your sins." The same is true in John 8:28, "When you lift up the Son of Man, then you will know that I AM." See also John 13:19, "From now on I am telling you before it comes to

---

42. K. H. Rengstorf, "Jesus Christ," *The New International Dictionary of New Testament Theology*, ed. Colin Brown (Grand Rapids: Zondervan, 1976), II:332.

43. Carl F. H. Henry, *God, Revelation and Authority*, II:230.

44. See, for example, the passages cited by Carl Henry (*God, Revelation and Authority*, II:228-229): "I AM the Bread of Life"; "I AM the Light of the world"; "I AM the door"; and others like these. This need not be understood as anything more than ordinary grammatical usage.

pass, so that when it does occur, you may believe that I AM." Such statements seem to be calculated to make us think of Jesus as Yahweh, the God of salvation.

One other name for Jesus demands our attention, the one used in Isaiah 7:14 as quoted in Matthew 1:23, "'Behold, the virgin shall be with child, and shall bear a Son, and they shall call His name Immanuel,' which translated means, 'GOD WITH US.'" This is usually understood to mean that in the person of Jesus Christ, God is present among us. This immediately causes us to think once again of Exodus 3:12-14, where God's name embodies his redemptive presence among his people: "Present is what I am." Relating this to the name *Immanuel*, Carl Henry says, "The Gospels offer us, in a word, YAHWEH unchangeably faithful to his covenant engagement, the present I AM, the incarnate God."[45] But there is another connotation to *Immanuel*: God is with us rather than against us; he is with us, for us, on our side. This is the very reason he wants to save us, the very reason he became incarnate in Jesus of Nazareth. He is not our enemy; he does not want to see us perish, even though as sinners we deserve it. He is *with us*; he wants to help us; he wants to save and redeem us. His very name declares it.

REDEMPTION AND CREATION

The concept of redemption and the nature of God's work as Redeemer cannot be understood except against the background of creation. The first volume in this series, *What the Bible Says About God the Creator*, has already discussed God's work of creation and his nature as Creator. Included there was a brief discussion of one aspect of the relation between creation and redemption.[46] Here we must explore in further detail the question of how these two works of God are related. In brief, we must assert the essential unity of the creative and redeeming activity of God, but we must be careful not to exaggerate and misrepresent this unity.

False Unity

It has been quite common, especially in this Darwinian era, to em-

---

45. Ibid., pp. 227-228.
46. Jack Cottrell, *What the Bible Says About God the Creator*, pp. 171-191.

phasize the idea that creation and redemption are a unity in the sense that they are simply two stages in God's one original plan for the universe. "The work of creation is one with the work of redemption," says Regin Prenter.[47] "Creation is the beginning of redemption, and redemption is the consummation of creation."[48] The terms thus are practically interchangeable; one can say it either way: creation is the first step of redemption, or redemption is the second step of creation.

N. M. Wildiers points out that at least since the Middle Ages, two contrasting views on this subject have been advanced. He describes the Thomist view, which draws a sharp distinction between creation and redemption, as follows:[49]

> . . . In the original plan for the world (the order of creation) no provision was made for an Incarnation of the Word. If the first human being had not sinned, the Incarnation would not have taken place. The Incarnation was "decreed" only after man had sinned, and so it derived entirely from that circumstance. To restore the primal world order—blighted by sin—the Son of God was born into this world as a man in order to set the human race once more upon the path to its ultimate destiny. In this account of things the link between Christ and the world is merely accidental. No Fall, no Incarnation. . . .

Over against this view is one called the Scotist interpretation, which sees Christ and the incarnation as part of God's original plan for his creation. As Wildiers describes it,[50]

> . . . Right from the beginning—that is to say, quite independently of the Fall—the whole creation was planned with the God-man in view. Even if man had not sinned, the Word would have become man; for the truth is that Christ is the supreme revelation of God in this world and the masterpiece of God's creation. . . . The Incarnation was contained,

---

47. Regin Prenter, *Creation and Redemption*, tr. Theodor I. Jensen (Philadelphia: Fortress Press, 1967), p. 208.
48. Ibid., p. 200.
49. N. M. Wildiers, *An Introduction to Teilhard de Chardin*, tr. Hubert Hoskins (New York: Harper & Row, 1968), pp. 130-131. This is essentially the view which I defended in *What the Bible Says About God the Creator*, pp. 179ff.
50. Ibid., pp. 131-132.

therefore, in the original plan of creation. The Fall introduced only an accidental change in this: the God-man, who had been conceived as the goal and crown of the whole created order, would also through his sufferings and death act as the redeemer of all mankind.

It seems that much of the modern theological world has opted for the Scotist interpretation, in one form or another. For example, it is quite common in Neo-orthodoxy, a representative of which is Hendrikus Berkhof. Berkhof notes that what is called the Thomist view above is the traditional view, i.e., that creation was quite sufficient in and of itself, and "it was only due to the fall that God had to open up an entirely different way to eternal life" through Jesus Christ. Thus "Christ is the 'emergency measure' through which God brings creation back in line." "Salvation thus serves the order of creation." However, says Berkhof, "historical criticism has put an end to this type of thinking." We now understand the Bible to portray "creation as the first of the series of God's redemptive deeds." It has an introductory relation to salvation; it is "the preamble and pointer to salvation." Creation simply prepared the way for the coming of Christ: "The world was created in view of Jesus Christ; God would not have created the world if not in connection with his coming and exaltation."[51]

Another example of this view is the Roman Catholic scientist and theologian, Pierre Teilhard de Chardin, who tried to combine a totally evolutionary cosmology with a mystical Christology. The whole creation, he said, is progressing toward a Christologically-defined goal or "Omega point"; Jesus of Nazareth was simply an important step on the way toward that goal. As Georges Crespy puts it, "In Teilhard's perspective the incarnation is not motivated . . . by the necessity of repairing and restoring" a creation harmed by the alien forces of sin. Rather, "the goal of the incarnation . . . appears only in its relationship to the global process of cosmogenesis,"[52] i.e., in relation to processes inherent in the universe since its beginning. Included in these processes

---

51. Hendrikus Berkhof, *Christian Faith: An Introduction to the Study of the Faith*, tr. Sierd Woudstra (Grand Rapids: Eerdmans, 1979), pp. 166-168. See *What the Bible Says About God the Creator*, pp. 177-179, for a brief discussion of other Neo-orthodox theologians (Barth, Brunner, and Thielicke).

52. Georges Crespy, *From Science to Theology: An Essay on Teilhard de Chardin*, tr. George H. Shriver (Nashville: Abingdon Press, 1968), p. 86.

is the presence of evil itself, which cannot be separated from a world that is being created via evolution rather than instantaneously. Christ's redeeming work can be called a kind of liberation, but this must be carefully understood, as Francisco Bravo notes: "Liberation is not the reparation of an *accident* which occurred in creation. On the contrary, it is the overcoming of a *substantial* evil which affects creation because of creation's very nature. The Word became incarnate to bring creation to fulfillment, not just to excise a tumor from it."[53] According to Teilhard, creation, incarnation and redemption are just three aspects of a single mystery, three indissolubly linked acts that are successive degrees of a single process.[54]

A final example of this view is Regin Prenter, who views creation itself as a kind of redemption. He sees the initial creation described in Genesis as God's dualistic struggle against the powers of chaos, death and destruction. God is victorious and overcomes these powers, thus making way for life. This is followed by a kind of continuing creation, however, since these negative forces continue to try to reassert themselves. Thus, says Prenter, "creation is God's continually ongoing struggle against the powers of destruction."[55] This creation continues throughout the Old Testament in such events as the exodus from Egypt and the restoration from Babylon.[56] Redemption through Christ, then, is just another stage in this work of creation. Prenter calls it the "second creation" and "the consummation of the creation of the world." He says, "It is the same creative work which is being carried forward,"[57] i.e., the struggle against chaos. As he further explains,[58]

. . . We are not able to explain how God's struggle against and victory over the powers of chaos in the first creation could be followed by a new rebellion on the part of the very powers which had just been vanquished and which in the beginning had wanted to lay God's work of creation waste. We know only that in the world in which we live God's creative will is at the same time his redemptive will. As God through his unceasing struggle against the powers of chaos carries his work of creation forward,

---

53. Francisco Bravo, *Christ in the Thought of Teilhard De Chardin*, tr. Cathryn B. Larme (Notre Dame: University of Notre Dame Press, 1967), p. 62.

54. Ibid., pp. 62-63.

55. Regin Prenter, *Creation and Redemption*, p. 194.

56. Ibid., p. 195.

57. Ibid., p. 197.

58. Ibid., p. 200.

he is also active in the special covenant or salvation history subduing the rebellious powers of destruction, which are at work after (and through the agency of) the first creation. And these two activities, creation and redemption, go hand in hand from the very beginning. Both are a struggle against the same enemy with the same end in view: the final consummation of God's creative work and the final destruction of all the powers of chaos.

Views such as these of Berkhof, Teilhard and Prenter present what I believe is a false unity between the works of creation and redemption. They all speak of a kind of *continuity* between them, i.e., the latter is a kind of continuation of the former. Redemption in a sense builds upon the prior work of creation, lifting it to a higher level. The entire process is seen as a single, uninterrupted program of God, whose plan to redeem was just as ultimate as—if not actually prior to—his plan to create.

The Intervening Fall

The basic reason why there is so much misunderstanding of the proper relationship between creation and redemption is because there is a widespread rejection of the biblical fact of the Fall into sin as pictured in Genesis 3. According to Scripture, the Fall was a singular historical event that took place after the creation and interrupted the continuity of the on-going world. The whole course of history was altered from its intended path and goal. The human race along with the whole of nature was placed under the curse and consequences of sin (Rom. 5:12ff.; 8:19-23). God's purpose for creation thus cannot be achieved within the scope of God's creating work alone.

It is this Fall that made redemption necessary, not to continue a process of creation already begun and still in progress, but to arrest and correct a process of deterioration that threatened to abort the whole purpose for creation. Redemption is not the continuation of creation, but the correction of the Fall. As such it restores or reinstates God's original purpose for the creation by turning it back toward its proper goal. Thus the key word is not *continuation* but *restoration*. God's purpose for creation will be achieved, but only through redemption. Their unity lies in a common source (God) and a common goal; but they represent two different means of achieving the goal, not two stages of the same means.

Generally speaking, however, modernistic theology lacks any con-

31

cept of an intervening Fall. Under the influence of destructive biblical criticism and the theory of evolution, it usually rejects the historicity of Genesis 3. Sin does not have a specific origin, but is seen as a necessary dimension of an evolving universe. Prenter's view is a good example of this. He sees the story of Adam as a kind of paradigm for every individual. *We* did not sin in Adam; *he* sins in every one of us. The story of the Fall repeats itself over and over again; each of us has his own "fall." "We do not conceive of the primitive state and the fall as unique phenomena in the past, but as rationally incomprehensible contradictions which wrestle with each other in man's existence so long as both God and sin have a hold upon him."[59]

This kind of reconstruction of the data concerning the Fall of Adam and Eve inevitably leads to a similar reconstruction of the relation between creation and redemption, as discussed above. This shows how important it is to maintain a proper view of the historicity of the events described in the early chapters of Genesis. One cannot reject the reality of the Fall and leave the rest of the Bible intact.

At this point we should also note the extravagance of the statement by Langdon Gilkey, that "the ideas of creation and redemption are mutually dependent in the most intimate way; neither one can be made intelligible, or even affirmed, without the other."[60] We must seriously question this so-called mutual dependence between creation and redemption, as if the existence of the one somehow *requires* the existence of the other. Theoretically speaking, at least, creation does not depend upon redemption nor require it for its own existence; it is capable of existing independently with a full integrity of its own. It is only the intervening fact of the Fall that has *made* it dependent upon redemption for rescue and restoration. On the other hand, redemption *is* inherently dependent upon creation for its reality, meaningfulness and justification. On this point I can agree with Gilkey. This leads us into our next section.

Redemption Presupposes Creation

We cannot speak of redemption without presupposing creation.

---

59. Ibid., pp. 254-256.
60. Langdon Gilkey, *Maker of Heaven and Earth* (Garden City, N.Y.: Doubleday Anchor, 1965), p. 249.

This is true for several reasons. In the first place, biblical redemption is redemption from sin, and sin itself is a meaningful concept only in light of the fact of creation. What is sin? It is the transgression of the law of God the Creator (I John 3:4). But what gives God the right to lay down absolute laws for us to obey? The right of ownership based on creation (Ps. 24:1-2). And what makes us obligated to obey those laws? The fact that we are his creatures.[61] As Gilkey rightly says, "Sin can only be understood in relation to the structural necessities of man's nature as a creature of God. For this reason the idea of creation is an unavoidable presupposition for the Christian interpretation of sin."[62] "For it is only if God can validly claim us as His own, that He can righteously judge us for our rebellion against Him."[63]

A second reason why redemption presupposes creation also relates to the ownership factor mentioned above. The one who creates acquires all the rights and responsibilities of ownership over that which he creates. This takes on a special meaning in light of the concept of redemption as discussed earlier in this chapter. The owner of a thing has the right to redeem that thing back to himself if it has become estranged from him for some reason. By paying the proper price, he can retrieve that which is by right his own possession. Or viewed from the perspective of the nature of a *gō'ēl*, the nearest kinsman of one in bondage may pay the price to redeem that relative and set him free. This is where creation and redemption intertwine. God redeems those whom he has created. As our rightful owner, he buys us back after we have sold ourselves into slavery to sin. As our nearest relative, our Creator-Father as Kinsman-Redeemer pays the price that sets us free.

This relationship is seen in God's redemption of Israel from exile in Babylon. Referring to the exodus from Egypt as a kind of figurative creation of Israel as a people for his own possession, he then declares that he will redeem (from Babylon) what he has created.

> But now, thus says the Lord, your Creator, O Jacob, and He who formed you, O Israel, "Do not fear, for I have redeemed you; I have call-

---

61. See Jack Cottrell, *What the Bible Says About God the Creator*, pp. 163-164.
62. Langdon Gilkey, *Maker of Heaven and Earth*, pp. 228-229.
63. Ibid., p. 280.

ed you by name; you are Mine! . . . Bring My sons from afar, and My daughters from the ends of the earth, everyone who is called by My name, and whom I have created for My glory, whom I have formed even whom I have made." (Isa. 43:1-7; cf. 14-21)

"Remember these things, O Jacob, and Israel, for you are My servant; I have formed you, you are My servant, O Israel, you will not be forgotten by Me. I have wiped out your transgressions like a thick cloud, and your sins like a heavy mist. Return to Me, for I have redeemed you." Shout for joy, O heavens, for the Lord has done it! Shout joyfully, you lower parts of the earth; break forth into a shout of joy, you mountains, O forest, and every tree in it; for the Lord has redeemed Jacob and in Israel He shows forth His glory. Thus says the Lord, your Redeemer, and the one who formed you from the womb, "I, the Lord, am the maker of all things, stretching out the heavens by Myself, and spreading out the earth all alone . . . . It is I who says of Jerusalem, 'She shall be inhabited!' and of the cities of Judah, 'They shall be built.' And I will raise up her ruins again." (Isa. 44:21-26)

What is true of God as the figurative Creator of the nation of Israel is also true of God as the literal Creator of the whole world. All the people of the earth are his created family, and he has paid the price of redemption for them all (Titus 2:11; I Tim. 4:10; I John 4:14). What he has created, he has redeemed. (I.e., he has made redemption available to all and has offered it to all, but not all are willing to receive it. The scope of redemption accomplished is not the same as the scope of redemption applied.)

I am not denying that someone other than the Creator could attempt to rescue or to save those in need of deliverance, but such salvation would not be *redemption* in the strict sense of the word. Redemption is the right and the privilege only of the Creator.[64]

There is one other reason why redemption presupposes creation, namely, only the Creator has the *power* to redeem the world from the predicament into which it has fallen. This is a point well made by Langdon Gilkey. The evil that threatens our world takes three forms, says Gilkey: fate, sin, and death; but the gospel of redemption is that God has defeated evil in all of its forms.[65] How is God able to do this?

---

64. I would not go so far as Procksch, who speaks of "a bond of kinship which commits God to the duty of redemption" ("λύω," p. 330). Whether speaking of Israel or the world, I cannot say that God had a *duty* to redeem it.

65. Langdon Gilkey, *Maker of Heaven and Earth*, pp. 247-248.

Because—and *only* because—he is the Creator, the Maker of heaven and earth. Specifically, "the unconditioned nature of God as Creator is required for the Gospel victory over each one of the three guises of evil."[66] In the first place, men fear that they are but pawns subject to the blind forces of *fate*. But such a state would exist only in a deterministic universe where God himself were in the grip of such forces. And this is not the case. The fact of creation negates such blind determinism and shows that God is in control. If God promises us redemption through Christ, we know that he is able to provide it and that nothing can hinder him—because he is the Creator. "Only a creator of all can be the guardian of man's destiny."[67]

In the second place, says Gilkey, only the Creator is able to redeem us from *sin*. How does anyone except the Creator have the right to forgive someone who transgresses the law? Just as the Creator alone has the right to judge us for breaking the law, he alone has the right to pardon us for doing so.[68]

Finally, and perhaps most significantly, only God the Creator can deliver us from the power of *death*. "Here above all," says Gilkey, "the unconditioned creative power of God is needed if we are to hope for victory. . . . Only if God has at first brought us into being out of nothingness, can He at the end bring us into life after death."[69] The prominence of resurrection as the essence of redemption cannot go unnoticed in the pages of the New Testament. Salvation includes both resurrection of the spirit or soul by the power of the Holy Spirit in Christian baptism (Rom. 6:3-5; Col. 2:12), and resurrection of the body at the second coming (Rom. 8:10-11). Do we comprehend the magnitude of this phenomenon called "resurrection from the dead"? Do we

---

66. Ibid., p. 278.
67. Ibid., pp. 278-279.
68. Ibid., pp. 280-281. Gilkey bases this right on God's transcendence over his own law, as an aspect of his general transcendence as Creator. Since God in a sense stands "beyond the law," he is free to have mercy on those who defy it. I disagree with this reasoning, mainly because the Bible does not present it in this way. God does not transcend his own law in the sense that he can just ignore it or set it aside even in the interests of his own mercy. But he *is* Lord over his own law to the extent that he can provide a substitute for sinful man to receive the punishment required by that law. Thus Gilkey is right in principle, but wrong in the specific explanation of the principle. He does not do justice to the biblical teaching concerning the necessity of the cross (Rom. 3:26).
69. Ibid., p. 283.

understand the infinite power required to accomplish it? In showing us that our God is able to bring to pass whatever he pleases, Romans 4:17 says that God is the one "who gives life to the dead and calls into being that which does not exist." The only thing comparable to resurrection is creation from nothing! Only the one who created life can recreate life and make those who are dead alive again. Rall is correct when he says, "Life is the key word for our understanding of salvation. Just as sin means death, so salvation means life. . . . This is salvation, God's gift of life: life at its fullest and highest, life of body and spirit, . . . life consummated in another world. Salvation is life."[70] And only the Lord of creation is the Lord of life.

We have stressed the point that redemption presupposes creation in several ways. The following lengthy but pithy quotation from Gilkey sums up the importance of this idea:[71]

> In the case of every major promise of the Gospel, therefore, the unconditioned power of God the Creator stands as the foundation on which Christian confidence is based. As a response to this Gospel, Christian life is a life of trust in God; it is the commitment of the spirit to God, because in God is known to lie the ultimate security and fulfillment of that spirit. The Gospel, therefore, would be able to make no meaningful promise, and Christian faith would be a delusion, unless the God who is proclaimed there were the Creator and source of all finitude, unconditioned and transcendent in His being and eternal in His existence. The transcendent majesty of God is not just an abstraction dear to the theologian's mind; it is the sole ground of faith and trust for all who believe with Luther that God is a "mighty fortress," and for all who through faith in Him look forward to the fulfillment of His promises. The idea of creation provides, therefore, the only framework in which the Christian Gospel can be preached effectively and believed intelligibly. The knowledge of God that we have in historical revelation is, it is true, the sole basis for our understanding of the purpose and meaning of creation. But the God revealed there as our Lord and Savior is inescapably He who infinitely transcends His creation in power and glory, and so who must be understood, not only as a personal Father, but also as the self-existent ground of all being.

---

70. H. F. Rall, *Religion as Salvation*, p. 92.
71. Langdon Gilkey, *Maker of Heaven and Earth*, pp. 284-285.

The Redeemer Is the Creator

A point that is implicit if not explicit in the preceding discussion is that the same God who created this world is the one who has redeemed it. The Redeemer is the Creator. According to Gilkey, "This theological conjunction is perhaps the most fundamental affirmation of the Old and the New Testaments." Indeed, "The identity of God the Creator and God the Redeemer, of the almighty power of existence with the love of Christ, is the theological axis of the Gospel of good news."[72] By this we know not only that the Redeemer has the power to accomplish his intended salvation, but also that the all-powerful Creator himself is benevolent and not hostile toward us. What could be more tragic than a would-be redeemer who is impotent to save? What could be more dreadful than an omnipotent creator who has no concern for his creatures' welfare?

Such images are not unknown. One of the strongest rivals to early Christianity was Gnosticism, whose cosmology included just such a bifurcation of deities. The supreme god was identified with all goodness and was even described with such titles as Light, Life, Spirit, Father, and the Good. He is the one from whom salvation may be sought. The god who created the world, however, was thought to be totally different. Known as the Demiurge, this "monstrous and benighted archon (lord) of the nether powers" created chiefly "to satisfy his ambition, vanity, and lust for dominion." Misguided and pitiable at best, he was more often pictured as an evil and hostile figure marked by pride, ignorance and malevolence.[73] This dualism of evil creator and benevolent savior was faced and fought by the Christian apologists of the second century, especially Irenaeus.[74]

Perhaps the worst example of this Gnostic heresy was Marcion, who deliberately tried to restructure Christianity to conform with his dualistic presuppositions. The basic feature of his system was his absolute distinction between the evil creator-god of the Old Testament and the Loving Father of the New Testament, as represented by Jesus Christ. As

72. Ibid., p. 250.

73. Hans Jonas, "Gnosticism," *The Encyclopedia of Philosophy*, ed. Paul Edwards (New York: Macmillan, 1967), III:337-338.

74. See J. N. D. Kelly, *Early Christian Doctrines*, revised edition (San Francisco: Harper & Row, 1978), p. 86.

described by Harold O. J. Brown,[75]

> . . . The creator of this world is alien to the true God and alien to spiritual man. He is the Yahweh of the Old Testament, a wild god, one who can rage, make mistakes, and repent, one who knows nothing of grace, but only strict justice. This God is responsible for the misery of man; and he gave us the Old Testament with all its features . . . .

On the other hand, Christ came "to save us from the God of wrath, in whose clutches we presently languish," and to show us "the unknown God of love," the supreme deity who is a good and spiritual Father.[76]

Gilkey maintains that one of the main purposes of the three main early Christian creedal statements (Apostles', Nicene, Chalcedonian) was to affirm the "fundamental conjunction of creation and redemption through the one Lord of all," in direct opposition to the Gnostic heresy. Their message was that "it is the God who created all things that is at work for our salvation. The great message of early preaching and theology alike was that in the person and loving deeds of Jesus Christ, God the Creator and Lord had revealed Himself."[77] Gilkey also believes that this need to find both power and love in the same God is what underlies the formulation of the classical doctrine of the Trinity. It enables us to say that "God the Creator is love," i.e., we can affirm "the astounding union in God of creative power and redeeming love."[78]

Recognizing that the Redeemer is the Creator also helps us to bring the entire scope of redemption into perspective. Sometimes we picture God as sending his Son into the world to save our souls or spirits out of this world for eternal fellowship with himself. This is partially true, of course (1 Peter 1:9), but it is not the whole truth. We are saved not *from* creation, but *along with* creation. A God who is interested in saving *only*

---

75. Harold O. J. Brown, *Heresies* (Garden City, N.Y.: Doubleday, 1984), p. 61.

76. Ibid., pp. 61, 64.

77. Langdon Gilkey, *Maker of Heaven and Earth*, pp. 250-251. This interpretation of the creeds is much to be preferred to that of John Reumann, who thinks they represent "a certain tension between creation and redemption" by assigning creation to God the Father and redemption to God the Son. (*Creation and New Creation* [Minneapolis: Augsburg, 1973], p. 8)

78. Langdon Gilkey, *Maker of Heaven and Earth*, pp. 251-253. We must question Gilkey's unspoken assumption in this connection, namely, that God is known as loving and gracious *only* in Jesus Christ. Surely we cannot ignore the abundant Old Testament teaching that Yahweh the Creator is also a loving and merciful Redeemer.

our souls is more like the supreme deity of the Gnostics than the God of the Bible. Our Redeemer is the Creator of the whole world, and thus he has an intrinsic interest in and love for everything in it, whether it be material or spiritual. Thus his redemption includes the whole cosmos (Rom. 8:19-23; II Pet. 3:13). This means that our bodies as well as our souls are redeemed (Rom. 8:23).

This theme has been expounded by some under the rubric, "The Cosmic Christ," based on an exposition of Colossians 1:15-20.[79] The thesis is that "Christ came not only to individuals, but to the whole universe, and that His work is significant for the whole of creation. . . . The farthest parts of the universe were related in some positive way to the Redeeming Act."[80] Now, this concept is quite acceptable when correctly understood, but in some ecumenical circles it has been seriously distorted into a basis for believing in universal salvation where even pagans and unbelievers are assumed to be "anonymous Christians." John Reumann surveys this idea and rightly dismisses it as a false exegesis of Scripture.[81]

Old Creation, New Creation

A final point regarding the relation between redemption and creation is the fact that God's redemptive activity is sometimes described in creation terminology.[82] As noted above, the redemption of Israel from Egyptian bondage is described as an act of creation when God refers to himself as Israel's Creator and Maker (Isa. 43:1; 45:11), and when he refers to Israel itself as a people whom he has formed, created, and made (Isa. 43:7). This is a figurative use of terms. The formation of the nation of Israel was not a literal act of creation, and God's redemptive activity in the Old Testament should not be described as a kind of "continuing creation," as if it were somehow in continuity with the metaphysical creation of Genesis 1.[83] Nor should it be labeled "new

---

79. See Allan D. Galloway, *The Cosmic Christ* (London: Nisbet & Co., 1951).

80. Ibid., p. 55.

81. John Reumann, *Creation and New Creation*, pp. 48-56.

82. See Jack Cottrell, *What the Bible Says About God the Creator*, p. 139.

83. This is contrary to John Reumann's discussion of the Old Testament data about God's redemptive activity among the Israelites under the heading, "Creation Continues— Redemptively" (*Creation and New Creation*, ch. III, pp. 57-82).

creation,"[84] a term which the Bible reserves for the redemptive work of Christ alone. The Old Testament redemptive events could be called "new acts of (figurative) creation," but not "acts of new creation." Redemption through Christ as new creation is a theme that occurs frequently in the New Testament. The specific term *kainē ktisis*, which may be translated either as "new creation" or as "new creature," occurs only twice. II Corinthians 5:17 says that "if any man is in Christ, he is a new creature; the old things passed away; behold, new things have come." Galatians 6:15 says, "For neither is circumcision anything, nor uncircumcision, but a new creation." These passages seem to be referring specifically to the tremendous change that takes place in the individual when he accepts Christ as Savior and is regenerated through the Holy Spirit. The reference to "newness of life" in Romans 6:4 is similar. Ephesians 2:10 says that the Christian has been "created in Christ Jesus," an expression undoubtedly referring to the new creation and not to Genesis 1. Ephesians 4:24 says that the "new self . . . has been created in righteousness and holiness of the truth," which in context is comparing our redemptive renewal with the original creation of man in God's image (see Col. 3:10). The first Adam/second Adam comparison between Adam and Christ also identifies Christ as the beginning of a new creation (I Cor. 15:45-47).

Christians have already begun to experience the new creation. We live as new creatures in the midst of the "old creation." But even this old creation, though presently still suffering under the effects of the Fall, will at the second coming experience its own renewal. This is truly "cosmic redemption," and is described thus by Paul in Romans 8:19-22,

> . . . For the anxious longing of the creation waits eagerly for the revealing of the sons of God. For the creation was subjected to futility, not of its own will, but because of Him who subjected it, in hope that the creation itself also will be set free from its slavery to corruption into the freedom of the glory of the children of God. For we know that the whole creation groans and suffers the pains of childbirth together until now.

This cosmic renewal is foretold in Isaiah 65:17, where Yahweh promises, "For behold, I create new heavens and a new earth; and the

---

84. Contrary to Norman Young, *Creator, Creation and Faith* (Philadelphia: Westminster Press, 1976), pp. 66ff.

former things shall not be remembered or come to mind." He adds these words in Isaiah 66:22, that "the new heavens and the new earth which I make will endure before Me." II Peter 3:10-12 describes the eschatological purging of the universe by fire, and then the promise from Isaiah is recalled: "But according to His promise we are looking for new heavens and a new earth, in which righteousness dwells" (II Peter 3:13). This was the subject of John's final, climactic revelation: "And I saw a new heaven and a new earth" (Rev. 21:1).

Thus the new creation, though begun, is not yet completed; its completion is the object of our hope. Ephesians 1:7 says that "we have redemption through His blood, the forgiveness of our trespasses"; this is a present possession. Romans 8:23 says that we still await "the redemption of our body." It is quite appropriate to refer to both the present and the future aspects of the new creation as *redemption*, as these passages do. It is arbitrary to call the first phase *reconciliation* and the last phase *redemption*, as Karl Barth does.[85]

The main point of this whole section on redemption and creation has been to emphasize how intimately connected these two themes are in the Bible, and how we must understand them both individually and in their relationships to one another if we are to have a proper knowledge of the God of the Bible, who is the God of Abraham and the God of our Lord Jesus Christ.

REDEMPTION AND PROVIDENCE

Since the second volume in this series dealt with the biblical doctrine of providence,[86] it is fitting that a few comments be made about the relation of this doctrine to redemption. In the most general sense of the word, providence is the broad scope of God's continuing, post-creation activity in relation to the on-going world. In this sense even the works of redemption might be subsumed under providence.

---

85. "Reconciliation as the restoration of the communion of sinful men with God in Christ is certainly complete," says Barth. "But redemption is reconciliation without qualification" and thus "is more than reconciliation. For redemption in its true sense we *wait*. And Redeemer in this true, strict sense is Jesus Christ in his second coming—not before and not otherwise." (Karl Barth, "Church and Culture," in *Theology and Church: Shorter Writings 1920-1928*, tr. Louise P. Smith [London: SCM Press, 1962], p. 348).

86. Jack Cottrell, *What the Bible Says About God the Ruler* (Joplin, Mo.: College Press, 1984).

It is important to make a distinction between these two concepts, however. Redemption is a part of God's activity in the on-going world, but it is a very special kind of activity. We may say that basically God's redemptive work includes everything that he does to accomplish "the eternal purpose which He carried out in Christ Jesus our Lord" (Ephesians 3:11). Whatever God has done, is doing, or will do—directly or indirectly—to bring about the salvation of mankind is a part of his redemptive activity. Much of this work, especially that which falls into the category of the indirect, would also be included under the heading of providence. The most prominent example of this would be God's dealings with the nation of Israel in Old Testament times. God's working among the Israelites did not in itself accomplish our redemption, but it was related to it as the means by which God prepared for the coming of the Redeemer. On the other hand, the redemptive work accomplished directly by both Jesus Christ and the Holy Spirit usually would not be thought of as providence at all. Here we are thinking of Jesus' virgin conception, the incarnation itself, the life of Jesus as such, his miracles, the atonement, the resurrection, the outpouring of the Spirit at Pentecost, the supernatural application of redemption to the individual believer (forgiveness, regeneration), the indwelling and empowerment of the Spirit, the inspiration of the Bible, and other such miraculous or supernatural activities that make salvation a reality. These are not works of providence but works of redemption. Even some Old Testament phenomena fall into this category, e.g., theophanies, special revelation, and miracles.

At the other end of the spectrum, there are many works of providence that could in no way be considered redemptive. The works of God that fall under the heading of general providence (i.e., his general oversight of nature and history) have no redemptive purpose. Even many of the things that we call special providence do not have redemption in view, e.g., acts of judgment upon the nations related to Israel in the Old Testament, and the answers to most prayers.

Somewhere in between those works of God which are purely providential and those that are purely redemptive are those works that overlap both categories. Their ultimate purpose is redemptive, but they are accomplished by providential means. One example, as noted above, is God's providential dealings with Israel in Old Testament times. Another example is the opening of doors for the preaching of the gospel in New Testament times. The point here is that God may use providential means to carry out his redemptive purposes.

In the context of this book, when we speak of redemption, ordinarily we will be thinking of that work accomplished by Jesus in his death, resurrection, ascension, and intercession at God's right hand. Other aspects may be in view at times; but when they are, they will usually be specifically identified.

THE PLAN OF THIS BOOK

The rest of this book will proceed as follows. In the next chapter we will follow the pattern already established in the other two volumes and examine alternatives to redemption found in world philosophies and religions. Again we will stress the uniqueness of the biblical doctrine of redemption, just as we stressed the uniqueness of biblical creation and biblical providence.

At this point we will deviate from the pattern already announced[87] and adhered to in the previous volumes, namely, first presenting a description of the work of God, then examining the nature of God as required by and illuminated by that work. In relation both to creation and providence, this is what was done. After describing the nature of creation *ex nihilo*, the first volume then included several chapters exploring God's nature in light of creation. Likewise the second volume offered several chapters explaining the work of providence (including miracles) before explaining God's nature as Sovereign Ruler. In this volume, however, it seems best to delay the summary of God's saving work until the basic biblical data concerning essential aspects of God's nature have been set forth. In this case it seems that we can best understand the nature of redemption if we understand the nature of the God who is working the works that bring it about.

Thus the next few chapters will discuss various aspects of the nature of God that are especially relevant to the doctrine of salvation. First there is a chapter on the Trinity. This appears at this point because it seems that the reality of God as three-in-one is not fully revealed and does not become fully relevant until we come to the New Testament work of redemption. This work cannot be rightly understood, however,

---

87. Jack Cottrell, *What the Bible Says About God the Creator*, p. 44.

unless we understand the concept of the Trinity (at least, insofar as our finite minds are able to understand it).

The next chapter deals with the justice or righteousness of God as his basic consistency of character in dealing with his creatures. We stress the point that God's justice includes both his love and his holiness, as over against the tendency to gloss over the holiness (wrath, judgment) aspect. The next two chapters deal more specifically with these two sides of God's nature. Under the general heading of the holiness of God we also include the study of his law and wrath. Then under the general heading of the love of God we will also discuss the concepts of mercy, patience, and grace.

At this point comes the chapter on the work of redemption. Following a survey of the Old Testament background, we concentrate on what God has done in the person of Jesus Christ, particularly in his atonement and resurrection. An important point is how the work of Jesus demonstrates the righteousness of God, i.e., how God remains true both to his holiness and love while saving us from our sins.

The last chapter of the book returns to one final aspect of the nature of God that is seen most clearly in reference to his work of redemption, i.e., his faithfulness. This includes a study of the attribute of immutability. After rejecting extremes on both sides, we conclude that the concept of immutability is best understood in relation to God's faithfulness and truth.

2

ALTERNATIVES TO REDEMPTION

In his book *Religion as Salvation* H. R. Rall lamented in the early 1950s that "the idea of religion as salvation has not had much place in the modern world." Contemporary man sees his needs to be of a more immanent and material nature, and he sees himself as capable of meeting them from his own resources. Thus salvation, says Rall, belongs to an "extinct ideology."[1]

These observations are certainly correct, as long as one defines salvation in the narrow sense found in the Bible, i.e., as being saved by a divine Redeemer from the consequences of sin committed against God himself. But salvation is seldom defined so narrowly. Even Rall's comment that "salvation means help from a higher power"[2] is too general. In fact, the concept of salvation may be and often is understood in a *very* general sense – so general that it applies to secular philosophies and non-Christian religions as well as to Christianity. Here is one exam-

---

1. Harris Franklin Rall, *Religion as Salvation* (Nashville: Abingdon-Cokesbury Press, 1953, 1953), pp. 5-6.
2. Ibid., p. 88.

ple: "Salvation stands for the attainment of the end of man, however this end may be conceived of (heaven, happiness, God, *nirvana*, nothingness, the future, mankind, man, and so on)."[3] Another understanding is that it refers to the promise of release from undesirable conditions.[4] Charles Braden relates it to "man's attempt to achieve enduring satisfaction."[5] Surely with definitions as broad as these, the concept of salvation will never become outmoded. It has been and will continue to be an aspect of every world view, philosophy and religion.

The same does not apply, however, to the concept of redemption. While we may use the terms *redemption* and *salvation* somewhat interchangeably, it is more proper to distinguish between them. The former is a much more specific idea and cannot be given the broad connotations that may be attached to the latter. Some of the writers participating in the symposium *Types of Redemption*, for example, felt compelled to substitute the word *salvation* instead. After being assigned the topic, "Redemption in Ancient Egypt and Early Christianity," S. G. F. Brandon noted that he would "exchange the word 'Redemption' for that of 'Salvation'. For 'Redemption' naturally suggests a buying-back or repurchase of somebody or something owned by another." Though such a concept is found in Christianity, he said, it does not occur in ancient Egyptian soteriology.[6] Although some do not interpret redemption this precisely,[7] Brandon is quite correct; and his comment points up one of

---

3. R. Panikkar, "The Myth of Incest as Symbol for Redemption in Vedic India," *Types of Redemption*, ed. R. J. Zwi Werblowsky and C. J. Bleeker (Leiden: E. J. Brill, 1970), p. 130.

4. See G. Scholem, "Opening Address," *Types of Redemption*, ed. R. J. Zwi Werblowsky and C. J. Bleeker (Leiden: E. J. Brill, 1970), p. 8.

5. Charles S. Braden, *Man's Quest for Salvation* (Chicago: Willett, Clark & Company, 1941), p. ix.

6. S. G. F. Brandon, "Redemption in Ancient Egypt and Early Christianity," *Types of Redemption*, ed. R. J. Zwi Werblowsky and C. J. Bleeker (Leiden: E. J. Brill, 1970), p. 36.

7. For example, R. Panikkar is quite correct in distinguishing between redemption and salvation, but he defines the former much too loosely as "a certain regaining of a lost state" or possibly "that process by which man acquires his ultimate status by means of the intervention of an extra-individual factor" ("The Myth of Incest," p. 130). The definition "to rescue and to deliver from bondage" gets closer to the precise meaning but still omits the concepts of a buying-back and a purchase price (Henry H. Presler, "Indian Aborigine Contributions to Hindu Ideas of Mukti Liberation," *Types of Redemption*, ed. R. J. Zwi Werblowsky and C. J. Bleeker [Leiden: E. J. Brill, 1970], p. 145).

the main purposes of this chapter, namely, to demonstrate the glorious uniqueness of the Biblical concept of redemption. The fact is that the idea of redemption as taught in the Old and New Testaments does not occur in *any* world religion or philosophy, Egyptian or otherwise.

If we are speaking of salvation understood in its broadest sense, however, this is not the case. The concept of salvation is quite common and occurs in practically every system of belief, ancient and contemporary. Just about everyone senses a gap between the actual and the ideal (however understood), and at the same time has some kind of plan for closing that gap. That is his concept of salvation.

The purpose of this chapter is to set forth a selected sampling of concepts of salvation. This is being done not just to increase understanding of these various views, but also to highlight the uniqueness of the Biblical idea of redemption, as noted above. When these non-Christian views are compared and contrasted with Scriptural teaching on the subject, it will be very clear that the former are distinct and non-acceptable *alternatives* to the latter.

Deciding how to outline the material for this chapter was not an easy task, since there are so many different distinctions to be made between concepts of salvation and so many different ways to categorize them.[8] For example, salvation may be understood in religious terms, or it may be a purely secular concept. Also, it may be a purely spiritual concept, or it may be material in nature, or some of both. (Even some ostensibly religious ideas of salvation are mainly material.) Also, the salvation may be other-worldly (e.g., achieved in heaven), or it may be thought of as solely within this world, or it may be some of both. Again, salvation may be thought of as something experienced only by the individual, or it may apply only to whole communities or society in general, or it may have both individual and societal implications. Another perspective is whether salvation is oriented to the past, as the regaining of something that was lost; or whether it is oriented to the present, as the immediate realization of an ideal state; or whether it looks to the future, as a promised possession to be received later. Another aspect of salvation is the

---

8. Two useful summaries of the various ways of distinguishing salvation concepts are the following: Charles S. Braden, *Man's Quest for Salvation*, ch. I, "Types of Salvation Ideas"; and Millard J. Erickson, *Christian Theology* (Grand Rapids: Baker Book House, 1985), III:888-891.

means by which a person is saved. Does he save himself (by knowledge, works, or self-effort of another kind), or is he saved by something or someone outside himself? Another question is whether salvation applies only to people or whether it embraces the whole cosmos as well. With reference to people, another question is whether all or only some will be saved.

A very significant distinction is whether salvation is vertical, horizontal or internal. That is, does it have to do with our relation to God, with our relation to other people, or with our own inner selves?[9] For the main sections of this chapter, I have chosen to use this categorization, beginning with some major views of salvation which see it as mainly individual in nature, as having to do with some problem that exists within a person's own individual existence. The problem is not always strictly internal but does involve a problem that is strictly personal and is not derived from breached relationships either with other people or with God. The second major category includes views of salvation which see it as mainly a horizontal adjustment of some kind, i.e., as the correction of some basic rupture of human interrelationships. Finally we will examine those views which interpret salvation as dealing primarily with a problem that exists between man and God himself. These views are surprisingly few in number when compared with the others.

H. F. Rall sums up the main aspects listed above thus: "The basic questions as to the meaning of salvation may be put in three simple phrases: from what, to what, by what."[10] The first of these three questions asks about the nature of the circumstances *from which* one is saved. The Christian may immediately reply that we are saved from sin, which is true; but this is not a universally accepted idea. In fact it is one of the rarest of views. Other possibilities are that we are saved from finitude, suffering, physical existence, death, hell, the cycle of reincarnation, bondage, oppression, and alienation. The second question asks, "*To what* are we saved?" We could say forgiveness of sins and peace with God, but again this would be a minority view. Answers heard more often would include happiness, bliss, heaven, eternal life, abundant life, well-being, freedom or liberation, union with the divine

---

9. Regarding this last distinction, see Millard Erickson, *Christian Theology*, III:889.
10. Harris Franklin Rall, *Religion as Salvation*, p. 91.

being, a higher state of being or consciousness, reconciliation, annihilation, and *nirvana*.[11] The last question concerns the agent *by which* we are saved. Are we saved by something that we ourselves can accomplish, e.g., faith, repentance, knowledge, external rituals, sacrifices, good character or morals, decisions, magic, mystical technique, or asceticism? Or are we saved by some agent other than ourselves, such as fate, the proletarian revolution, a divine or quasi-divine hero, or God's grace?

These three basic questions—from what, to what, and by what—will form the framework for our examination of individual religious or philosophical views of salvation.

SALVATION AS SELF-FULFILLMENT

The first group of alternatives to redemption are those views which see man's basic problem as internal or personal. The idea is that something about man's own nature is not right, and that this has resulted in undesirable consequences for him already or that it will in the future. Salvation is thus some kind of change or adjustment in our being or thinking or acting that will eliminate the deficiency in our nature (along with its bad results) and enable us to be everything that we are supposed to be or can be or already are. It enables us to close the gap between our real and our ideal existence and thus achieve self-fulfillment.

Traditional Eastern Religions

We begin our survey with a look at the views of salvation in two of the oldest continuously-existing religions, Hinduism and Buddhism. These two systems of thought are very similar in many ways, mainly because Buddhism arose in India against the background of Hinduism. Though they differ in terminology and in some significant details, their basic frameworks are much the same. Both preach the salvation of self-fulfillment or self-realization.

Hinduism

Hinduism as a general religious system is divided into a number of

---

11. I am not implying that none of these elements is actually included in salvation; some of them definitely are.

sects which differ somewhat on certain details pertaining to salvation;[12] but generally speaking there are two main approaches, which some call the philosophical and the religious views.[13] There are only one or two points on which they differ enough to make it worth mentioning; these will be identified at the appropriate places.

Hinduism is basically a pantheistic monism, which means it believes that there is only one kind of true existence or being, and that this being is all divine.[14] This is true of man's inner soul or true self. Only this part of man has real existence; nothing else, including the body and the mind, is a part of the true essence of man. The true inner essence, though, is divine in nature. Some Hindus think that each individual self is actually identical with Brahman (God) in the fullest sense of the word; others look upon these selves as having emanated out of Brahman, thus being numerically separate from him though of the very same divine essence. (This is one of the differences that affect somewhat the doctrine of salvation, as will be noted below.) In either case the essential self bears all the marks of divinity; it is eternal and indestructible and immutable. It is quite free from all the limitations, changes and experiences that befall both the body and the mind.[15]

At this point we may begin to identify the basic problem from which we must be saved, according to Hinduism. Even though the true self is one with God, it *does not know* this to be the case. It has forgotten or is otherwise ignorant of its real nature. Thus it can be said that no matter what else is wrong with us, the basic problem is *ignorance*. As T. R. V. Murti says, "All our troubles are due to ignorance, primarily ignorance of oneself."[16] That is, we are ignorant of the fact that we actually are divine. Instead we think of ourselves as being identical with the bodies which we can see and touch. When the self commits this tragic error of

---

12. Satis Chandra Chatterjee distinguishes twelve chief types of religious thought within Hinduism ("Hindu Religious Thought," *The Religion of the Hindus*, ed. Kenneth W. Morgan [New York: Ronald Press, 1953], p. 207).

13. A. S. Geden, "Salvation (Hindu)," *Encyclopedia of Religion and Ethics*, ed. James Hastings (New York: Charles Scribner's Sons, 1921), XI:133.

14. See Jack Cottrell, *What the Bible Says About God the Creator* (Joplin, Mo.: College Press, 1983), pp. 82-86.

15. Henry H. Presler, "Indian Aborigine Contributions," p. 147.

16. T. R. V. Murti, "The Concept of Freedom as Redemption," *Types of Redemption*, ed. R. J. Zwi Werblowsky and C. J. Bleeker (Leiden: E. J. Brill, 1970), p. 217.

identifying itself with the body, "it forgets that it is really divine and behaves like a finite, limited, and miserable creature."[17]

As a result of confusing itself with the body, the self falls from its "supreme aloofness" and becomes a part of the phenomenal world, the world of sense experience. It becomes "entangled in the empirical world,"[18] and thus becomes subject to all the pain and suffering and distress that exist here. It does no good to hope for deliverance by death, for the Hindu doctrine of *karma* guarantees that the soul will remain entrapped in its bondage to material existence and suffering. *Karma* is the inviolable law of moral causation; it means that all one's actions earn certain consequences, good or bad, and one must remain in the world until those consequences have worked themselves out. If these merited results are not experienced in this life, then one will be reborn or reincarnated into another life (body) so that his *karma* will not be thwarted. The only problem is that while one is waiting for these results to come upon him, he himself is becoming further and further entangled in the world and is making more and more bad decisions, thus increasing his karmic debt even further.

Thus one becomes locked into a seemingly endless cycle of rebirth or transmigration known as *samsara*. This is the Hindu equivalent to hell. Zaehner describes it thus:[19]

> . . . For the Hindu, life in space and time is without beginning and, unless the way of liberation is found, without end too; and eternal life in *this* sense becomes a crushing burden in its endless, pointless, senseless repetitiveness; and as the twin doctrines of *karma* and *samsara* developed, the revulsion against never-ending life through never-ending death in a manifestly imperfect world became more and more extreme. . . .

We must remember, though, that such suffering is not man's basic problem; it is merely the result of a deeper problem, namely, ignorance of one's true self. "The problem is principally cognitive," as Murti says.[20]

Having discerned the nature of the problem, we now turn to the

---

17. S. C. Chatterjee, "Hindu Religious Thought," p. 241.
18. Henry H. Presler, "Indian Aborigine Contributions," pp. 147-148.
19. R. C. Zaehner, *Hinduism*, 2 ed. (New York: Oxford University Press, 1966), p. 61.
20. T. R. V. Murti, "The Concept of Freedom as Redemption," p. 217.

Hindu concept of the nature of salvation itself, known as *mukti* or *moksha*. On the most immediate level salvation is release, freedom or liberation from suffering, from the world itself, and from the damning cycle of death and rebirth. "For the individual self the highest good of life is liberation from bondage to the flesh, a state of complete and absolute cessation of all pain and misery."[21] *Moksha* denotes "deliverance from bondage to the world and its fetters which is the desired and ideal end of the Hindu religious life."[22]

Such emancipation is possible even in this life once one comes to know his true self. He can enjoy a sense of freedom from this world "by the more or less complete suppression of the desires and faculties of the body, by mechanical devices, ascetic or other, for controlling the bodily passions."[23] By no longer identifying himself with his body, "he is not deceived by the world which still appears before him. He has no desire for the world's objects and is, therefore, not affected by the world's misery. He is in the world and yet out of it."[24]

Full salvation, however, comes only through total escape from the world. Once one is totally free from the wheel of reincarnation and thus from material existence as such, his true and pure self is reunited in oneness with the pure essence of the supreme Brahman. For those Hindus who hold that each self is completely identical with the totality of Brahman, this does not involve any real change except in one's knowledge and experience of himself. For those who hold that individual selves are emanations from Brahman, there is the experience of being rejoined with God without necessarily losing one's sense of individual existence.[25] Using some of the figures taken from Hindu Scriptures, Zaehner says that "the liberated soul is like a fish in the sea, permeated within and without with water, or it is like a maggot in a fig, enveloped by the fig, living on it, and almost of the same texture as it."[26]

We come now to the crucial question, *by what* is one saved in Hindu thought? Here we find one of the principal divergences among the

---

21. S. C. Chatterjee, "Hindu Religious Thought," p. 219.

22. A. S. Geden, "Salvation (Hindu)," p. 132.

23. Ibid., p. 133.

24. S. C. Chatterjee, "Hindu Religious Thought," p. 242.

25. See A.S. Geden, "Salvation (Hindu)," pp. 134-135.

26. R. C. Zaehner, *Hinduism*, pp. 78-79.

Hindus themselves. Here is where the so-called philosophical and religious schools of thought differ considerably. In brief the former believes that a man can be saved only by his own self-effort, notably knowledge; the latter believes that man is helped in his quest for salvation by the grace of God. The former view is the dominant one.

In theory it should be possible for one to save himself simply by the law of *karma*. By doing more and more good works, and by progressively overcoming the influences of the body through more and more intense asceticism, it should be possible to finally nullify all the negative karmic results, even if it takes countless millions of reincarnations. The sad truth, however, is that this does not happen; works alone are not enough. As Presler says, morality may "enable a sunken individual to struggle up to the surface of his plight, but not to get out of it."[27] This is why works alone, though usually identified as a way of escape for Hindus, is called a subordinate, inferior, tedious, and less sure way.[28]

But there is another way of escape, a more sure way, in fact the only way according to the philosophical or Sankaran school; and that way is *knowledge*. "The perfect way, the path chosen by the wise, which supersedes all other ways, is through knowledge."[29] This follows naturally from the fact that man's basic problem is ignorance. If ignorance of his true state is the source of all of man's ills, then he can overcome these ills by achieving knowledge of his true state. As Presler says, "The main escape route is through the intellect."[30] This is truly salvation by knowledge.

What is the object of this saving knowledge? The object is one's true self. As Chatterjee says, "What is absolutely necessary for liberation is the light of true knowledge about the self."[31] This means first of all that we recognize that the body is not to be thought of as the real self. Then it means that we acknowledge that the self is actually and already one with Brahman, that it is divine. As we can see, this act of knowing is not

---

27. Henry H. Presler, "Indian Aborigine Contributions," p. 150. See also R. C. Zaehner, *Hinduism*, p. 126.
28. A. S. Geden, "Salvation (Hindu)," p. 135.
29. Ibid., p. 134.
30. Henry H. Presler, "Indian Aborigine Contributions," p. 151.
31. S. C. Chatterjee, "Hindu Religious Thought," p. 209.

simply a present condition required for receiving some future salvation; it is in effect realizing that one is already "saved." It is not achieving or acquiring something that one did not already have; it is simply acknowledging something that is an existing fact.[32] This is why the Hindu way of salvation is called *self-realization*: one realizes the nature of his true self.

There seems to be more to this way of salvation than mere cognition, however. Self-realization is not just an act; it is a process. It is the process of realizing more and more completely and directly our oneness with Brahman. Murti speaks of it as "the progressive realization of the pure self as distinct from the body."[33] This is not accomplished without effort and much spiritual discipline. As Zaehner says, the way of knowledge "in practice means the attainment of *moksha* by rigorous self-discipline."[34] In addition to instruction from the sacred writings, "this saving knowledge has to be attained through control of the passions, purification of the body and mind, and the practice of meditation and concentration."[35] This includes mystical practices such as Yoga.[36]

It is obvious that the way of knowledge does not by any means exclude works; it is hardly salvation by "knowledge alone." Be that as it may, whether we are speaking of the way of works alone or the way of knowledge also, we are speaking of salvation by self-effort. Whatever the nature of the saving activity, it is accomplished by the individual himself. As Presler says, "Man himself, and not any extraneous power, is responsible for his own emancipation."[37] He breaks the fetters by his own efforts. "Each prisoner effects his own freedom, or remains bound. Freedom is the result of self-effort. *Mukti* means liberation by self-striving."[38] Chatterjee puts it thus: "It is man himself who is responsible for his bondage because it is his ignorance about the reality of the self that has caused it. So it lies in man's power to liberate himself by means of a penetrating insight into, and a clear realization of, the nature of his

32. A. S. Geden, "Salvation (Hindu)," p. 135.
33. T. R. V. Murti, "The Concept of Freedom as Redemption," p. 218.
34. R. C. Zaehner, *Hinduism*, p. 139.
35. S. C. Chatterjee, "Hindu Religious Thought," pp. 210, 220, 242.
36. Ibid., pp. 210, 221.
37. Henry H. Presler, "Indian Aborigine Contributions," p. 148.
38. Ibid., p. 146.

self."[39]

But this is not the whole story. Another strand of Hindu thought introduces a third way of salvation, the more religious way. In addition to the ways of works and knowledge, according to the Bhagavad-Gita, one may be saved by the way of *bhakti*, or loving devotion to God, who rewards his devotees with saving grace.

In philosophical Hinduism there is a noticeable lack of any reference to God as any kind of power outside ourselves who helps us to be saved. Salvation is by self-realization of our own Godhood. At most God may be thought of as the source of the revelation of the knowledge that saves,[40] but this would be true only in a kind of figurative sense in philosophical thought. It is only in the way of *bhakti* that God becomes personally and actively involved in man's salvation through various incarnations of himself. He simply asks that men surrender to him in absolute faith, love and devotion. For those who do, "God actively helps the soul to liberation by the exercise of his grace. . . . God leads the souls not only to liberation, the 'state of Brahman', but also to participation in himself—he 'causes them to enter' him. He in return loves the soul and asks to be loved by it."[41] According to some, God even bestows the power to love him as he desires.[42] Perhaps most important of all, this complete devotion brings forgiveness of sins. "A firm faith in Brahman destroys all sins of man and renders him perfectly pure."[43] For devotees of Siva, "once one had confessed oneself Siva's slave, all sins, even the slaying of a Brahman or a cow, would be wiped out."[44]

This is certainly different from the ways of works and knowledge; but we should note that despite the references to grace, there still seems

---

39. S. C. Chatterjee, "Hindu Religious Thought," p. 210.

40. See T. R. V. Murti, "The Concept of Freedom as Redemption," pp. 216, 220. He says that "the Grace of God is accepted by most Indian religions for revelation of the real." Also, God "may and does show us the way to achieve freedom. That is his grace." K. Sivaraman also seems to equate God's grace with his self-revelation, saying that "the bestowal of revelatory grace is *moksha*" ("The Meaning of *Moksha* in Contemporary Hindu Thought and Life," *Living Faiths and Ultimate Goals*, ed. S. J. Samartha [Geneva: World Council of Churches, 1974], p. 10; see also pp. 3, 6, 9).

41. R. C. Zaehner, *Hinduism*, p. 126.

42. S. C. Chatterjee, "Hindu Religious Thought," p. 251.

43. Ibid.

44. R. C. Zaehner, *Hinduism*, p. 130. See also Charles S. Braden, *Man's Quest for Salvation*, pp. 36-37. He speaks of a devotee of Krishna who "feels borne down by a sense of guilt for sin" and "falls back on the mercy of God."

to be an element of works even in the way of *bhakti*. Geden says that in the *bhakti* system, *moksha* is still "a goal to be reached by endeavour."[45] When a man demonstrates his devotion to God by keeping himself constantly engaged in the service and worship of God, by devoting his body and mind to the cause of truth and goodness, and by studying the holy scriptures, this pleases God. "Being thus pleased, God gives His grace to the man who loves Him."[46] "We are constantly to remember Him, meditate on Him, and serve and worship Him. One who is thus devoted to the Supreme Self, heart and soul, and is resigned to Him in all humility and meekness, receives His grace and overcomes the lure of the world."[47] Thus it seems that there is a real sense in which God gives his grace to those who *deserve* it by their near-perfect lives. This is still quite different from the free grace of Yahweh, the God of our Lord Jesus Christ.

Braden notes, however, that the followers of the *bhakti* way have argued among themselves as to what part the soul plays in its own salvation. They have developed two points of view, he says, one called the "cat way" and the other the "monkey way." He explains,[48]

> . . . One held that in the process man takes no part beyond that of complete surrender to God, just as a kitten does nothing when it is being carried to safety by the mother cat; it resigns itself wholly to the mother who carries it in her mouth. The other held that just as the baby monkey, while being carried by the mother, clings to her with its own hands and arms, so the soul cooperates with God in its own salvation; the soul must play an active part in its own redemption.

Whether this gets any closer to the Christian concept of grace may be a matter of dispute. What will be clear later, however, is that no matter how much the sincere follower of *bhakti* speaks of grace, there is still a vital element missing from his system that makes it a vain and futile hope for salvation.

Buddhism

Buddhism is the child of early Hinduism and thus shares many of

---

45. A. S. Geden, "Salvation (Hindu)," p. 135.
46. S. C. Chatterjee, "Hindu Religious Thought," p. 228.
47. Ibid., p. 256. See also p. 251: God gives grace to those who are pure in heart.
48. Charles S. Braden, *Man's Quest for Salvation*, p. 39.

the latter's concepts. Its cosmology is usually monistic but not necessarily pantheistic, since Buddhism is thought by many to be non-theistic. Ultimate reality, the Absolute, is one; and every individual's true self is identified with this one Absolute.

Also like Hinduism, two main approaches to salvation have been developed in Buddhism. The original and more philosophical one seems to retain the essence of Buddha's own teaching, which was salvation by self-effort. This is called the Hinayana school of Buddhism, or sometimes the Theravada school (its main surviving sect). The later and more religious school, called Mahayana, introduced the concept of a savior who offers salvation by grace. The parallel with Hinduism is quite striking.

Both groups share the same basic cosmology summarized above.

"Buddha's religion has been founded as a religion of salvation," notes H. Dumoulin. It "gives an answer to man's first religious question, to the question of salvation."[49] The spirit of Buddha is "the spirit to save all people by any and all means." Buddha himself vowed "to save all people."[50] What did he hope to save them from? Here the answer is similar in many ways to Hinduism. Man's immediate problem is suffering, which is the result of existing in the world. To exist is to suffer: this is the first of Buddha's "four noble truths." The state of misery and sorrow and suffering is known as *dukkha*. As in Hinduism, the problem is compounded by the law of *karma* and the hopeless cycle of death and reincarnation. "The law of cause and effect is universal; each man must carry his own burden of sin and must go along to its retribution."[51]

At this point appears one of the teachings most characteristic of Buddhism, which is the second of the "four noble truths." It is the idea that all suffering springs from desire, lust or craving. Buddha is reported to have said in a sermon, "Now this, monks, is the noble truth of the cause of pain: the craving, which tends to rebirth, combined with

---

49. H. Dumoulin, "Grace and Freedom in the Way of Salvation in Japanese Buddhism," *Types of Redemption*, ed. R. J. Zwi Werblowsky and C. J. Bleeker (Leiden : E. J. Brill, 1970), p. 98.

50. *The Teaching of Buddha*, 265 revised ed. (Tokyo: Buddhist Promoting Foundation, 1982), pp. 28, 32.

51. Ibid., p. 194.

pleasure and lust, finding pleasure here and there; namely the craving for passion, the craving for existence, the craving for non-existence."[52] Such desire is directed mostly toward things of this world, which are by their very nature transitory and temporal and thus unable to satisfy.

Underlying this ubiquitous craving, however, is an even more basic problem, which is the real cause of suffering because it is the cause of the craving itself. This ultimate villain, as in Hinduism, is ignorance. Desires are truly evil, "but man is ignorant of the truth of these desires and so he becomes attached to them. This, Buddha concludes, is the cause of all human suffering." In other words, "suffering originates in attachment, attachment originates in craving, and craving originates in ignorance."[53]

Man misunderstands the true nature of things. "This misunderstanding is called, in Buddhist terminology, illusion or bewilderment, which is inherent in human nature; this illusion is *avdiya* or ignorance of the true nature of existence."[54] Especially, it is an ignorance of the true self, the false identification of the body with the self. The Buddhist teacher Sariputta said that the deceived person "looks upon his body as his self, thinking that his self consists of body or that his body is in his self or that his self is in his body, being possessed by the thought, 'I am body, body is mine.'" Both the body and the consciousness of such a person become altered, and through the change and alteration "grief, lamentation, pain, dejection, and despair arise."[55] Such a person simply does not understand that only the Absolute exists and that all particular existences, including his own, are not ultimately real. "In our loss of the perception of the Void and our conviction that particular things are finally real, we come to believe in the separate, isolated reality of some enduring self within us for which we plan and hope great things."[56] We

---

52. *The Teachings of the Compassionate Buddha*, ed. E. A. Burtt (New York: New American Library, 1955), p. 30.

53. Fumio Masutani, *A Comparative Study of Buddhism and Christianity*, 7 ed. (Tokyo: Bukkyo Dendo Kyokai, 1967), p. 15.

54. Teruji Ishizu, "The Basis of the Idea of Redemption in Japanese Religions," *Types of Redemption*, ed. R. J. Zwi Werblowsky and C. J. Bleeker (Leiden: E. J. Brill, 1970), p. 94.

55. *The Teachings of the Compassionate Buddha*, p. 99.

56. Douglas A. Fox, *Buddhism, Christianity, and the Future of Man* (Philadelphia: Westminster Press, 1972), p. 50.

forget that our true self is one with the Absolute.

There is some disagreement as to the true nature of the self and even of the Absolute in Buddhist thought. The question is whether the Absolute has real existence or whether it is a kind of nothingness or void. If it is the latter, then the true self of man has no real existence either. This no-self or no-soul doctrine (called *anatta*) does seem to be present in Buddhist thought. "The non-existence of self is the ultimate truth," says Ishizu.[57] Buddha did not speak of the soul as an ontological entity; he spoke of individuals as "personalities." Each personality is a complex or bundle of *skandhas*, which are the various states or functions that make us who we are. These *skandhas* are feeling, sense-perception, conscience, and intelligence. "Thus there is really no self or soul but only the ever changing *skandhas*."[58] "The no-self doctrine," says Ninian Smart, "implies both that living beings have no eternal souls and that there is no cosmic Self. . . . The concept of an underlying self is superfluous and erroneous."[59] Or as another puts it, all beings are egoless. "But people fail to grasp this truth of life. They are apt to think that there exists 'I,' fixed and immutable."[60] Such ignorance leads to craving and thus to suffering.

Given this concept of man's basic problem, the nature of salvation itself (what one is saved *to*) should be obvious. Salvation is freedom or escape from *dukkha*, that is, from the cycle of rebirth and existence in this world with all its craving and consequent suffering. The third of the "four noble truths" is the fact that such escape is possible: desire may be eliminated. Braden says that this is the "gospel" of Buddhism. "It was to the proclamation of this truth that the Buddha gave his forty years of itinerant evangelism. Suffering is a terrible fact of human life; it finds its cause in craving or desire; but the situation is not therefore hopeless, for it is possible to destroy desire and thus destroy suffering."[61]

---

57. Teruji Ishizu, "The Basis of the Idea of Redemption," p. 93.

58. Charles S. Braden, *Man's Quest for Salvation*, pp. 53-55. Also Gaius Glenn Atkins and Charles S. Braden, *Procession of the Gods*, 3 ed. (New York: Harper & Brothers, 1948), pp. 182-184.

59. Ninian Smart, "Buddhism," *The Encyclopedia of Philosophy*, ed. Paul Edwards (New York: Macmillan, 1967), I:417.

60. Fumio Masutani, *A Comparative Study*, p. 46.

61. Charles S. Braden, *Man's Quest for Salvation*, p. 66.

Freedom from suffering can be partly experienced even in this life as a state of well-being derived from conquering all desires.[62] A Buddhist psalm says,[63]

> All passion have I put away, and all
> Ill will for ever have I rooted out;
> Illusion utterly has passed from me;
> Cool am I now. Gone out all fire within.

The ultimate salvation, however, is total escape from this-worldly existence, or "emancipation from the cycle of birth and death which is part of the transience of the universe."[64] This is the final state of *Nirvana*. It means that the self is freed to be what it truly is anyway, namely, one with the Absolute. The exact nature of *Nirvana* is a point of dispute. Those who favor the no-soul doctrine say that it means extinction of the individual self in the sense of a flame's being put out. Others see it simply as absorption into the Absolute in the sense of a small flame's being united with a larger one. In the latter sense a person does not lose his being but only his existence as a particular being. As Fox describes it, "*Nirvana* is the state of having died to the vulnerable particular self and its clamorous demands and of having found oneself to be the Universal Self, no less. *Nirvana* is the extinction of the flickering candle of particularity in the golden glow of unquenchable Being."[65] We need not decide which interpretation of *Nirvana* is correct; in either case there is unqualified deliverance from *dukkha*, which is the essence of salvation.

This leads to the last question, namely, *by what* is a person saved, according to Buddhism? The answer is stated in the last of the "four noble truths," which says that the only way to the cessation of pain and suffering is to follow the "eightfold path." The first step on the "eightfold path" is, naturally, right belief or true knowledge of the nature of the self and of suffering. This is what we would expect, given the fact that ignorance is the underlying cause of man's problems. Thus a key concept

---

62. See C. A. F. Rhys Davids, "Salvation (Buddhist)," *Encyclopedia* of Religion and Ethics, ed. James Hastings (New York: Charles Scribner's Sons, 1921), XI:110.

63. *The Teachings of the Compassionate Buddha*, p. 75.

64. Masao Abe, "Buddhist *Nirvana*: Its Significance in Contemporary Thought and Life," *Living Faiths and Ultimate Goals*, ed. S. J. Samartha (Geneva: World Council of Churches, 1974), p. 18.

65. Douglas A. Fox, *Buddhism, Christianity, and the Future of Man*, p. 88.

for Buddhism is *enlightenment.* Buddha himself is called "the Perfectly Enlightened One,"[66] and his teaching (called the *dharma*) is the means to the salvation of others.[67] In one sense this means that faith is the way of deliverance, since it requires one to have faith in Buddha's teaching. "Those who listen to His teachings are free from the delusions and the miseries of life. 'People can not be saved by relying on their own wisdom,' He said, 'and through faith they must enter into my teaching.'"[68] Some see this as not an invitation to blind faith in Buddha but as an invitation to exercise one's reasoning powers just as Buddha has done. Thus the key to salvation is "man's reasoning power."[69]

Whether derived by faith or reason, right knowledge is still the way of salvation. This involves especially right knowledge of oneself. As de Silva remarks, for Buddhism "man's chief problem is with himself, and as such, redemption or salvation is found in the resolution of the problem of selfhood."[70]

As in Hinduism, however, knowledge alone as a simple cognitive act will not lead to Nirvana. It must be followed and accompanied by a life of thorough self-discipline. Knowledge saves, but it is only the first step of the "eightfold path." The other seven steps are right intention or aspiration, right speech, right action or conduct, right livelihood, right effort, right mindfulness, and right concentration.[71] The goal of the entire system, of course, is to eliminate craving or greed, to arrive at a proper mental state. "The point of the teachings is to control your own mind. Keep your mind from greed," and this will prevent suffering. "A man's mind may make him a Buddha, or it may make him a beast. Misled by error, one becomes a demon; enlightened, one becomes a Buddha. Therefore control your mind and do not let it deviate from the right path."[72]

Thus, at least for original Buddhism, salvation is completely a matter of self-effort; one is saved by his own works. It all comes down to this,

---

66. *The Teaching of Buddha,* p. 14.
67. Ibid., p. 30.
68. Ibid., p. 70. See Charles S. Braden, *Man's Quest for Salvation,* p. 62.
69. Fumio Masutani, *A Comparative Study,* p. 51.
70. Lynn A. de Silva, *Creation, Redemption, Consummation in Christian and Buddhist Thought* (Chiengmai: Thailand Theological Seminary, 1964), p. 34.
71. *The Teachings of the Compassionate Buddha,* p. 30.
72. *The Teaching of Buddha,* pp. 20,22.

says Braden: "Salvation is won not through the aid of any power outside oneself, but by sheer self-effort. A way is set forth by the Buddha,
but he who would achieve the goal must by his own unaided effort
follow that way. . . . The Buddha saves no one."[73] "Man is his own
saviour," says de Silva.[74] "It is I that can save myself and bring happiness to myself," as Masutani sums it up. "In the way of Buddha, the
ultimate refuge was to be sought in oneself and nowhere else."[75] He
continues,[76]

> . . . What we can rely on is ourselves only. Without beseeching God,
> or invoking God's aid, we can only depend on our inner light, on the
> teaching of Buddha, and on the encouragement from those who are
> walking the same way. Tremendous effort is needed to overcome the
> disturbing desire and win the ultimate peace, following this path. . . . Only
> sustained effort and diligence can win the victory.

Buddha's last words were supposedly, "Work out your own freedom
with diligence."[77]

This is classical Buddhism, that of the Hinayana or Theravada
school. But we must now discuss the later development called the
Mahayana school, which is comparable in some ways to the *bhakti*
aspect of Hinduism. Those who follow the Mahayana way repudiate the
idea of salvation by "self power" and depend wholly on "Other Power,"
or a power outside themselves.[78] This power resides in the person and
work of a particular Buddha named Amithaba or Amida (and perhaps
even in some others like him). "He is genuinely a savior Buddha and all
who call upon his name are saved."[79] How has he achieved this role of
savior? The story is that when Amida began his quest for Buddhahood,
he took forty-six (or forty-eight) vows, the chief one of which was that
all the merit and knowledge he would acquire would be made available
to others so that they too might be saved. He even renounced his own
right to Buddhahood so that more merits might be shared with others.
"He shuns retiring into the final state of nirvana, though fully entitled to
it, preferring, by his own free choice, to toil for even the lowest of beings
for ages. He is actuated by this motiveless altruism from the very start of

---

73. Charles S. Braden, *Man's Quest for Salvation*, p. 72.
74. Lynn A. de Silva, *Creation, Redemption, Consummation*, p. 63.
75. Fumio Masutani, *A Comparative Study*, pp. 52-53.
76. Ibid., pp. 56-57.
77. Ibid., p. 57.
78. H. Dumoulin, "Grace and Freedom," pp. 98-99.
79. Charles S. Braden, *Man's Quest for Salvation*, p. 76.

his career." This is, Murti continues, "a free phenomenalizing act of grace and compassion."[80] The end result is a vast accumulation of superabundant merits which may be transferred to those who turn to Amida.[81]

What is the result of this transfer of merit? Geden sums it up thus: "By mere faith in Amida the greatest sinner is delivered from the power and penalty of his sins, and secures entrance into the heaven of eternal bliss."[82] It is salvation from *sin*. Sinners are destined to ages of punishment, but "if these wicked men recite the holy name of Amida Buddha with singleness of mind, all the sins which would have destined them to the evil world will be cleared away."[83] For those who call upon his name, he will "expiate, at every mentioning of the name, the sins which lead to rebirth during eighty million aeons."[84] On the positive side, the transfer of merit ushers one into a blissful heaven or paradise called the Pure Land. Whether there is still a *Nirvana* to be achieved beyond this is a matter of dispute among Buddhists.

The final question is *how* this transfer of merits, with its resultant expiation of sins and gift of paradise, is received by the individual. Two conditions have been mentioned in quotations above, namely, (1) faith, and (2) calling on the name of Amida. These represent two different schools of Mahayana thought. In the earlier school, called Pure Land Buddhism, salvation was a matter of faith in Buddha and his vow, or "the total surrender of the believer to the salvific Vow of Amida Buddha."[85] But it was still necessary to express this faith by naming the name of Amida ten times, a practice called *Nembutsu*. This is based on the Buddha's own vow, which supposedly included these words: "Though I attain Buddhahood, I shall never be complete until people with sincere faith endeavor to be reborn in my land by repeating my name in sincere faith ten times and actually do succeed in this rebirth."[86]

80. T. R. V. Murti, "The Concept of Freedom as Redemption," p. 221.

81. Charles S. Braden, *Man's Quest for Salvation*, p. 76; Teruji Ishizu, "The Basis of the Idea of Redemption," pp. 94-95.

82. A. S. Geden, "Salvation (Hindu)," p. 136.

83. *The Teaching of Buddha*, pp. 216-218.

84. Charles S. Braden, *Man's Quest for Salvation*, p. 78. He is citing a popular Buddhist sacred writing called Sukhavati Vyuha.

85. H. Dumoulin, "Grace and Freedom," p. 99.

86. *The Teaching of Buddha*, p. 204. See p. 218: "Those who are thus able to recite the holy name, when they come to the end of life, will be met by Amida Buddha. . .

In practice the *Nembutsu* was an act of self-exertion and was often accompanied by meditation. Thus some felt that even this was too much like salvation by works. So another school, called True Pure Land Buddhism, arose near the beginning of the thirteenth century through the efforts of Honen and his disciple Shinran. According to Honen, just one invocation of Amida's name from a sincere heart is sufficient for salvation; anything more smacks of works. But Shinran said that even this is self-exertion or works; faith in Amida and faith alone is all that is needed to be saved, and even this faith is a gift of Amida. This is sometimes called "Shinran's gospel of pure grace." Dumoulin sums it up: "The all-efficiency of the Original Vow of Amida Buddha regarding human faith is the center of Shinran's teaching. It is not the Nembutsu practice but faith that flows from Amida's name, which assures salvation."[87]

Thus we see that Buddhism, like Hinduism, includes more than one approach to salvation. Each contains a philosophical approach that emphasizes salvation by knowledge but is a thorough-going salvation by one's own works with little or no help from an outside source including God. But each also contains a religious approach that attributes salvation to a savior outside oneself who offers grace to those who will receive it. Though the conditions for receiving it often included works, there have been some in each group that made it a free gift conditioned only on faith. These last two approaches to salvation—bhakti Hinduism and True Pure Land Buddhism—are thought by many to be equivalent to the Christian doctrine of redemption through Jesus Christ. They are touted as having a doctrine of grace just the same as Christianity. Whether this is so or not will be discussed later when we set forth the Bible's teaching on the work of God our Redeemer.

Ancient Middle-Eastern Religions

Another category of self-fulfillment concepts of salvation is the ancient religions of the Middle East. These are of importance to us because of their juxtaposition in time and space with Christianity. Those that ex-

---

and will be led . . . into the Buddha's land, where they will be born in all purity of the white lotus."

87. H. Dumoulin, "Grace and Freedom," p. 102. See pp. 99-102.

isted before Christ are sometimes cited by unbelieving critics as the source of certain Christian beliefs and practices. Others are well known to us because they existed alongside Christianity and assimilated some Biblical concepts into their own systems. Here we will examine only two of these, each of which is a clear-cut doctrine of personal salvation through self-fulfillment. In each case a savior-figure is involved, as was typical of most middle-eastern religions of that day. Nevertheless in each case salvation is still the result of one's own works, which was also typical.

The Egyptian Cult of Osiris

The first example to be examined is the Egyptian cult of Osiris, which can be traced back to the third millennium B.C. It dominated Egyptian beliefs concerning salvation until well into the Christian era. It is also a prime example of what are usually called the "mystery religions" of the Middle East, most of which bear some similarities to Osirian religion.

As was generally the case in the mystery religions, the major problem addressed by the cult of Osiris was death and the after-life. It appears that the Egyptian people were obsessed by death and the desire for immortality. Osiris apparently provided the solution to the problem. As Brandon says, "Osiris was the Egyptian saviour, and it was from death or the consequences of death that he saved his faithful."[88] Their concern was mainly with physical death; they wanted some assurance that they would live on in a pleasant after-life.

This assurance was provided by Osiris, who according to Egyptian mythology was an ancient king who was killed unjustly by his brother Set. When his body was found floating in the Nile, it was rescued by his wife Isis who, along with her sister, used various means to halt the process of decay. Then by a miraculous act (either by Isis or by the sun-god Re), Osiris was raised from the dead to a life among the gods. Here he accused his murderer Set before a tribunal of the gods, and he was vindicated while Set was condemned. Osiris then assumed his own place among the divine pantheon.[89] His role as savior was won by his having

---

88. S. G. F. Brandon, "Redemption in Ancient Egypt," p. 36.
89. Ibid., pp. 37-38.

experienced resurrection himself and by his being vindicated before the divine tribunal. After a while he also assumed the role of judge of the dead, but this is not directly related to his saving activity.

Despite the fact that Osiris is looked upon as a savior, the Egyptians had no concept of grace or redemption from sin. In fact they had a very pronounced belief in salvation by works. A person's character and deeds in this life are what ultimately determine whether he survives death and has a pleasant eternity. How is this related to Osiris' role as savior? The answer seems to lie in the fact that the person who dies has two hurdles to cross before his salvation is assured. One is death itself; the other is a kind of post-mortem judgment. It is with reference to the first that Osiris plays his major part. According to the myth, his bodily decay had been reversed, and he had been raised back to life. In imitation of this, the Egyptians developed the technique and ritual of embalming. The whole thing had a religious significance. It was meant to be a re-enactment of Osiris' experience. Through the principle of sympathetic magic the deceased was thought to become united with or identified with Osiris in his death and resurrection, and thus experience resurrection himself. As Brandon says, "We may safely conclude that the Egyptians believed that the saving efficacy of this Osirian mortuary ritual ultimately stemmed from the divine saviour himself, whose primordial experience made such salvation possible."[90] Obviously this aspect of salvation was not accomplished by the person's works but depended only on the proper performance of the ritual and the power of Osiris.

The second soteriological hurdle is quite a different story, however. After resurrection had occurred, the person still had to appear before some kind of tribunal to be judged according to the works done in his lifetime. Some of the early Pyramid Texts suggest that the people feared the possibility that someone might come forward to accuse them of wrongdoing and that they would have to face either justification or condemnation. The basis for judgment seems to have been the person's works. For example, the following was written of a deceased king: "He desires that he may be justified . . . through that which he has done." This seems to be a concept of justification by works.[91] The kind of works

---

90. Ibid., p. 39.
91. S. G. F. Brandon, *The Judgment of the Dead* (New York: Charles Scribner's

they had in mind may be seen from the following selections from a declaration of innocence inscribed on the tomb of a nobleman: "I built a house, I set up the doors. I dug a lake, and I planted trees. The king praised me. . . . I gave bread to the hungry, clothing to the naked, I ferried him who had no boat."[92]

Interestingly, Osiris becomes involved in this judgment in two ways. First, there developed the concept of a kind of ritual participation with Osiris in his own justification before the divine tribunal. Just as the gods had vindicated him while condemning his murderer Set, so does the dead and risen devotee share in Osiris' justification. At first this seems to have been limited to kings only, but later became the privilege of the common man also. Whatever effect this vicarious justification was supposed to have, it stemmed from the magical mortuary ritual and not from any particular devotion to Osiris during one's life. The fact is, though, that this shared justification did not seem to preclude a decisive judgment based on a person's own deeds.[93]

This leads to the second way in which Osiris becomes involved in the judgment of the dead: not as advocate or mediator for the accused, but as a kind of presiding judge. This seems somewhat inconsistent with his role as savior, especially since during the judgment process his saving powers seem to be totally irrelevant. At this point it all depends upon the deeds and character of the one being judged.

The judgment process seems to have consisted of two major events, the first of which was the defendant's declaration of his own innocence before the gods. In these declarations or confessions there is no appeal to Osiris for aid or for salvation; the individual's plea is based solely upon his claim to an upright life. His first declaration is made before Osiris himself and consists of a long list of "I have nots": e.g., I have not committed iniquity against men; I have not ill-treated animals; I have not impoverished a poor man; I have not caused weeping; I have not killed; I have not had sexual relations with a boy; I have not added to the weights of the balance; I have not captured the birds of the gods; I have not deflected water in its season; and many more, concluding with

Sons, 1967), p. 9.
   92. Ibid., p. 15.
   93. Ibid., pp. 10, 21-23. See also Brandon,. "Redemption in Ancient Egypt," pp. 42-43.

the protestation, "I am pure. I am pure. I am pure. I am pure."[94] The second declaration is made before a tribunal of forty-two deities. Each one is addressed and identified in turn, and receives a claim of innocence with regard to a particular wrong-doing. Then follows a speech in which the defendant asserts his righteousness and in effect declares that the gods therefore owe him salvation. "I come to you, without evil, having committed no deceit, without iniquity within me, without an hostile witness against me. I have done nothing," he says. "I did that of which men speak, that in which the gods rejoice. . . . I have given bread to the hungry, water to the thirsty, clothing to the naked, a boat to him that had none. I have made provision for divine offerings and for the offerings to the blessed dead. Save me, therefore, and protect me!"[95]

This phase of the judgment is followed by a second, in which the heart of the accused is weighed in a balance against a feather which symbolizes truth. The point seems to be a test to see whether he was telling the truth in his declarations of innocence.[96] If he passes the test, he is ushered into heaven. However, if he does not, his fate is indicated in various papyrus paintings of the balance scale judgment. Included is a figure described as "a fearsome hybrid monster, made up of the parts of a crocodile, a lion, and a hippopotamus. It is named Am-mut, the 'eater of the dead'; its function is obvious."[97]

This is the essence of the Egyptian concept of salvation. Despite the presence of a savior-god whose benefits could be tapped through ritual magic, the real source of salvation was the individual himself through his own works. As Brandon says, the idea seems to be that "a happy after-life was not to be obtained only by the practice of ritual magic, but that it must be deserved by the moral quality of one's life on earth."[98]

Gnosticism

The second example of ancient middle-eastern doctrines of salvation as self-fulfillment is the religion of the Gnostics, especially in the post-apostolic era when it had actually adopted certain Christian terms

---

94. S. G. F. Brandon, *The Judgment of the Dead*, pp. 31-33.
95. Ibid., pp. 33-34.
96. Ibid., p. 40.
97. Ibid., p. 29.
98. Ibid., p. 41.

and concepts into its system. Like the Egyptians, the Gnostics had a savior; those who were loosely called Christian Gnostics identified this savior with Jesus. In the final analysis, however, the Gnostics of all stripes taught salvation by *gnōsis* or knowledge.

Salvation was definitely the main concern of Gnosticism. Its very name suggests that its primary interest was in knowledge; but as Nygren points out, it was a very specific kind of knowledge: "knowledge of the Way of salvation, of the mysterious formulae and passwords which give the soul access to the higher world and bring about its perfect union with the Divine." Nygren cites Clement of Alexandria as saying that *gnōsis* is knowledge of "who we are and what we have become; whence we are and whither we come; whither we hasten, whence we are redeemed; what our birth is and what our rebirth." Clearly then, says Nygren, "the centre of the Gnostic outlook is . . . the problem of salvation." He adds, "Gnosticism is thus, in the strictest sense, a *Way of salvation*; Gnosis is salvation technique."[99]

According to Gnosticism the main problem, the condition from which man needs to be saved, is ontological. That is to say, it has to do with the circumstances of his existence, a state of being whose origin was not of his own making. On the surface the problem sounds very similar to the Hindu and Buddhist view: man's spirit or true self is essentially divine but has become entrapped in the world of matter; its basic need is to escape from this world and to be reunited to pure divinity. The difficulty is that it is not even aware of its plight: "In its unredeemed state the spirit, so far from its source and immersed in soul and flesh, is unconscious of itself, benumbed, asleep, or intoxicated by the poison of the world—in brief, it is ignorant."[100]

Even though these details are very similar to Hinduism and Buddhism, the Gnostic system as a whole is fundamentally different from these religions of the Far East. Whereas the latter are strictly monistic, Gnosticism is based on a dualistic cosmology.[101] In the pantheism

---

99. Anders Nygren, *Agape and Eros*, tr. Philip S. Watson (Philadelphia: Westminster Press, 1953), pp. 293-294, 297.

100. Hans Jonas, "Gnosticism," *The Encyclopedia of Philosophy*, ed. Paul Edwards (New York: Macmillan, 1967), III:340.

101. See Jack Cottrell, *What the Bible Says About God the Creator* (Joplin, Mo.: College Press, 1983), pp. 57-59.

of the Hindus, for example, the material world is either just an illusion or is an aberrant emanation from deity itself. Man's entrapment in a body is itself the result of ignorance or wrong thinking; thus right thinking will deliver him. For dualists such as the Gnostics it is not the same. The world itself is quite real but has been created by an evil deity (the Demiurge). After creating the world, he and six other sinister powers proceeded to create man for the express purpose of imprisoning particles of the divine substance of the good deity in this world of hostile matter. Thus each human being finds himself in a state of "basic evil": his spirit is a little portion of deity but has been separated from its source and true home by being entrapped in a material body.[102]

Thus the problem is not as easily solved in Gnosticism as in Hinduism or Buddhism. In the latter, just being awakened to the nature of his true identity (oneness with the Absolute) enables one to overcome his ignorance and realize that identity. For the Gnostics it is more complicated, since their prison has its own independent reality and is the product of evil, hostile powers. One cannot escape it by retreating into the pure recesses of one's mind or true self; rather, the spirit must almost literally fight its way through an obstacle course that exists by virtue of the way the material universe was created. As Jonas describes it, this world "is like a vast prison whose innermost dungeon is the earth . . . . Around and above it, the cosmic spheres are ranged like concentric enclosing shells." Some Gnostics put the number of these shells at seven; others made it as high as 365. The problem is that, even at death, the divine spirit that longs to return to its native home must pass through all these hostile spheres, each one of which is guarded by its own ruler.[103] Such a thing is possible, but only if the spirit knows all the proper passwords, so to speak.

So the key to salvation is knowledge—not only a knowledge of one's true identity as divine and of the fact of his imprisonment in matter, but also a knowledge of the cosmos and of the secret formulas which ensure passage out of it and back to his true home. This is, as Jonas says, "salvation by gnosis."[104] It is not a matter of good works

---

102. Hans Jonas, "Gnosticism," pp. 338-339.
103. Ibid., p. 339.
104. Ibid., p. 340.

and ethical living; in fact, some Gnostics were quite antinomian. And as H.O.J. Brown points out, even those who did stress a high level of morality did so for the purpose of minimizing bodily distractions rather than of pleasing God.[105] The whole emphasis was on knowledge; they sought "salvation by the path of enlightenment."[106]

This need for very special knowledge is what leads to the Gnostic idea of a divine savior. For how can our poor imprisoned spirits ever know the secrets of salvation except through *revelation* from the heavenly Father himself? But because the transcendent God cannot deign to enter the mundane cosmos, he sends a messenger of only slightly lesser authority to bring this revelation to his entrapped children. This messenger "penetrates the barriers of the spheres, outwits the archons [rulers of the spheres], awakens the spirit from its earthly slumber, and imparts to it the saving knowledge from without."[107] The so-called Christian Gnostics identified this messenger with Jesus Christ. Thus they called Jesus their savior, but with a meaning entirely different from that of the Bible. As they saw it, "God the Father sent Christ, the firstborn aeon known as Nous (not Logos), to free the souls of the spiritual from the power of the base creative angels who hold them prisoner in vile physical bodies."[108]

Thus the role of the savior in Gnostic thought is that of *revealer only*. Once he has brought the needed information, his task is complete. It is then up to the individual to accept it and use it to save himself. Nygren has some very perceptive comments on this system of the Gnostics:[109]

> . . . Salvation means nothing but the deliverance of the spirit from the toils of matter. Furthermore, Christ is not, in Gnosticism, Saviour in the full Christian sense. He is rather Teacher and Revealer of the Gnostic secrets and Forerunner on the Gnostic Way of salvation. His task is to awaken rather than, strictly speaking, to save. Power to ascend to the Divine life exists already in the imprisoned human spirit; it only needs to be awakened and made effective. Not that the Gnostic preaches mere self-salvation; he is too well aware of man's helplessness for that, and

---

105. Harold O. J. Brown, *Heresies* (Garden City, N.Y.: Doubleday, 1984), p. 49.
106. Ibid., p. 59.
107. Hans Jonas, "Gnosticism," p. 340.
108. H. O. J. Brown, *Heresies*, p. 59.
109. Anders Nygren, *Agape and Eros*, p. 301.

without the Saviour and the message from above no salvation would be possible. On the other hand, the Saviour fulfils much the same function as the beauty of the sensible world in Platonism. In both cases it is a question of setting in motion the possibilities already present in the human spirit, but unable to function without such external stimulus. We might most accurately say that *the task of the Gnostic Saviour is that of Forerunner and Example for the self-salvation of the human spirit.*

Thus the Gnostic way of salvation also turns out to be salvation by self-effort or by one's own works. Revealed knowledge, necessitating a "savior," is an essential prerequisite; but the salvation of each individual is actually in his own hands. He must find the knowledge deposited by the divine messenger[110] and retain it until death; then he must use the secret names and formulas and incantations to pass through the series of spheres that separate him from heaven. Thus, as Nygren points out, *"through its own instrumentality"* the spirit ascends to the heavenly world.[111]

We have examined two religions from the same part of the world in which Christianity arose and whose doctrines of salvation initially appear to resemble that of the Bible, especially in their inclusion of a divine figure who is thought of as a savior. But as we have seen, both Osiris and the Gnostic savior have a very limited responsibility when it comes to providing salvation for mankind. Their saving activities fall far short of what we actually need and of what has been provided by Jesus our Lord. In the final analysis neither the Egyptian nor the Gnostic way of salvation is salvation by God; the fulfillment of one's proper and desired destiny must be achieved by the individual through his own efforts.

Secular Philosophies

We will examine just two other examples of the concept of salvation through self-fulfillment, both of them in the area of secular philosophy. The point here is to show that salvation in the broadest sense is not a pursuit limited to religious world views but is a concern of non-religious thought systems as well. Obviously in the latter kind of philosophy there

---

110. Here is the justification for Gnosticism as a religion. The Gnostics presented themselves as the guardians of the secret knowledge; they offered to share it with converts.

111. Ibid., p. 302.

will be no appeal to God; so we would expect that whatever kind of salvation is delineated, it will be something that man accomplishes for himself.

The two examples discussed here are classical Hellenistic philosophy (which we will call Hellenism) and Existentialism. Both view salvation as self-fulfillment or self-realization, i.e., as the process by which the individual compensates for some inner or personal lack and becomes everything that he can or should be. The discussion of each view will be brief and quite general, without focusing on any one particular philosopher. Only a general impression is sought.

Hellenism

By Hellenism we are referring mainly to the great pre-Christian philosophers such as Socrates, Plato and Aristotle. The ways in which these and other Greek philosophers described the human predicament and human need were not at all uniform, but they did seem to agree that the most immediate problem is ignorance. Whatever the ultimate goal being sought, whether it be a return to the Platonic realm of Ideas or the experience of Aristotelian *eudaimonia* (well-being), the means of achieving it is right knowledge. More precisely the means is the proper exercise of human reason, or the practice of philosophy.

J. H. Randall says of these men, "At first, the philosophers taught a religion founded on reason, not revelation. This is the great glory of the Hellenistic Schools, that they taught a rational religion, a liberal religion."[112] He refers to the Greek philosophers preceding the Skeptics as "men seeking personal peace and freedom by intellectual methods, by thinking, by finding the truth."[113] G. L. Prestige suggests that the Gnostics themselves derived their "salvation by knowledge" theme from the great Greek schools of philosophy.[114] As another puts it, in Greek philosophy salvation is accomplished "by man's self-mastery through autonomous reason."[115]

---

112. John Herman Randall, Jr., *Hellenistic Ways of Deliverance and the Making of the Christian Synthesis* (New York: Columbia University Press, 1970), p. 12.

113. Ibid., p. 56.

114. G. L. Prestige, *Fathers and Heretics* (London: S.P.C.K., 1963), p. 35.

115. Werner Foerster, "σώζω, etc." (part), *Theological Dictionary of the New Testament*, ed. Gerhard Friedrich, tr. Geoffrey W. Bromiley (Grand Rapids: Eerdmans, 1971), VII:1002.

An example is Plato. Nygren notes how Plato agreed with some of the ancient mystery religions concerning the nature of salvation: "For both of them salvation means the deliverance of the soul from the prison-house of the body and the senses, and its restoration to its original heavenly home." But they differ as to the means to this end. For the mysteries it was ritual and ceremony; for Plato it was "through philosophy."[116] Plato thought that "there is a hope for the philosophic soul of escaping from the wheel of reincarnation."[117] His praise for the philosopher knew no bounds. In his view, "the true life for man is thus the philosophic life or the life of wisdom, since it is only the philosopher who attains true universal science and apprehends the rational character of Reality." In his ideal society, philosophers would be kings, since it is their responsibility to apprehend the Ideal and to try to model their own lives and the lives of others according to the pattern.[118] Like most of the Greeks he and his teacher Socrates believed in what is called "the primacy of the intellect." Virtue and knowledge are the same, they said; if a person *knows* what is right, he will then naturally *do* what is right.[119] Thus all the problems of man's behavior and destiny can be solved by the philosophical discernment of what is right.

One statement concerning Aristotle shows his concurrence with the above: "It is in the exercise of reason, then, and in the exercise of that reason concerning the noblest objects, that man's complete happiness is found."[120]

Thus in Hellenism, if anyone deserved the title of "savior," it was the philosopher. In fact some did refer to them as saviors.[121] But they were neither divine nor divinely sent; they were simply doing what any human being theoretically has the capacity to do. That salvation is by philosophical reasoning is just another way of saying that salvation is by human self-effort; man saves himself by his own works.

---

116. Anders Nygren, *Agape and Eros*, p. 167.

117. Frederick Copleston, *A History of Philosophy, Volume I: Greece and Rome, Part I*, new revised ed. (Garden City, N.Y.: Doubleday Image, 1962), p. 240.

118. Ibid., pp. 224-225.

119. Ibid., pp. 129, 245.

120. Frederick Copleston, *A History of Philosophy, Volume I: Greece and Rome, Part II*, new revised ed. (Garden City, N.Y.: Doubleday Image, 1962), p. 90.

121. Werner Foerster, "σώζω," p. 1007.

Existentialism

Our second example is Existentialism. This is a rather broad framework of thought originating mostly with Soren Kierkegaard in the nineteenth century. The basic framework has been employed by theistic philosophers and even by certain so-called Christian theologians, but it has also been developed by those who are non-religious or even atheistic. Here we are considering Existentialism in its latter or secular form, though much of what is said could also apply to theistic Existentialism.

As the very name implies, this philosophy is concerned with existence, namely, the meaning of the existence of the individual person. The key term is *authenticity*. The existentialist asks, what does it mean to exist authentically? In a sense we have come full circle, because in essence this is the very same question the Hindu is asking, i.e., what is the nature of the true self? The purpose of existentialist philosophy is to enable a person to exist truly and authentically.

The nature of man's problem is that each one of us simply finds himself existing in this world in rather arbitrary circumstances without a clue as to why we are or who we are, and with a host of built-in limitations that keep us from actualizing the sense of freedom that we find within ourselves. This situation is given different names; it is our facticity, our thrownness, our givenness. As John Macquarrie expresses it, "No one has chosen to be. He simply finds himself in existence. We discover ourselves, so to speak, as free existents in the midst of a world of things."[122] He gives this explanation of Heidegger's concept of thrownness:[123]

> . . . Man is thrown into existence, each one is thrown into his own particular existential situation. From the human point of view, it is rather like the throw of a dice. Just as you may throw a three or a six, so in life you may come up American or Vietnamese, white or black, affluent or destitute, ill-natured or good-natured, intelligent or stupid. There is no known reason why the throw should be one way rather than another. . . .

---

122. John Macquarrie, *Existentialism* (Philadelphia: Westminster Press, 1972), p. 148.
123. Ibid., p. 149.

Some existentialists would use the word *absurd* to describe this situation: existence is absurd.[124]

The thrownness itself might not be so bad if it were not for the "radical finitude" that comes with it. "I have been born into this particular historical situation in this particular society, and all kinds of forces are operating in the situation and in the society to shape my life and to limit what I can become."[125] Here is the basic source of inauthentic existence: most of us let ourselves be molded by the external influences around us. We yield to pressure; we "go along with the crowd"; we conform. We become slaves to tradition and routine. We do not act; we react. We make no real decisions from within ourselves. Such action without decision, according to the existentialist, is less than human:[126]

> The emphasis placed on decision often leads the existentialists to a corresponding depreciation of action in which the element of conscious, even agonizing, decision is not apparent. Habit and custom, traditional and routine ways of doing things, are criticized as falling below the level of truly human action. . . .

Since this is not authentic existence, there is a radical gap between the self that is and the self that could be and should be; in other words one is alienated from his true self. "For the existentialist, alienation is understood chiefly in inward terms. It is the existent's alienation from his own deepest being. He is not himself but simply a cipher in the mass-existence of the crowd or a cog in the industrial system or whatever it may be."[127]

From this it is obvious that the "saved state" or the state of authentic existence is achieved when a person resists the constant pressures to conform and takes his destiny into his own hands and begins to make his own decisions from his own free choices. People "become truly themselves only to the extent that they freely choose themselves," as Macquarrie puts it. "Existence is authentic to the extent that the existent has taken possession of himself and, shall we say, has molded himself in

---

124. Alasdair MacIntyre, "Existentialism," *The Encyclopedia of Philosophy*, ed. Paul Edwards (New York: Macmillan, 1967), III:148.

125. John Macquarrie, *Existentialism*, p. 148; see p. 150.

126. Ibid., pp. 145-146.

127. Ibid., p. 160.

his own image."[128] In this way he asserts his freedom, even in the face of his facticity or thrownness. The actualizing of freedom is essential to authentic existence; "there is no humanity without freedom."[129]

The means to such "salvation," i.e., the means to authentic existence, should be quite clear. It is nothing other than the *act of choosing*. Simply by making his own decision, by choosing his own course of action, one begins to live authentically. By asserting himself he becomes himself. "The existentialist, then, insists on action, for only in action does existence attain concreteness and fullness."[130] Whatever a person chooses, as long as he himself is actually doing the choosing, what he is really choosing is *himself*. "It is out of its decisions that the self emerges."[131] Macquarrie sums it up thus: "An act of will or decision seems to be at the center of every existentialist idea of human wholeness. . . . To gather up the whole self into a concentrated act of will is really and authentically to become oneself and to be rescued from the scattering and dissolution of the self in trivial concerns and in the crowd."[132] As another says, "If any single thesis could be said to constitute the doctrine of existentialism, it would be that the possibility of choice is the central fact of human nature." When people choose, "it is their choices that bring whatever nature they have into being."[133]

This point needs to be made very clear: it is not the content of the choice that is important, but rather the choosing itself. "Existentialism does not supply a content, or rather it permits many contents. But it is concerned more with the intensity and passion of our decisions than with their actual content."[134] This does not mean that all existentialists are totally indifferent to the content of their or others' choices. It is simply to say that Existentialism does not make it its business to dictate particular choices.

Though it is a secular philosophy, Existentialism is a classic example of self-fulfillment through self-effort. By his own decisions and actions a

---

128. Ibid., p. 161.
129. Ibid., p. 141. MacIntyre says, "For existentialism all the important possibilities of human life are bound up with the fact of human freedom" ("Existentialism," p. 149).
130. John Macquarrie, *Existentialism*, p. 136.
131. Ibid., p. 145.
132. Ibid., pp. 169-170.
133. Alasdair MacIntyre, "Existentialism," p. 149.
134. John Macquarrie, *Existentialism*, p. 171.

person *rescues* himself (Macquarrie's word; see above at note 132) from inauthenticity or lostness.

Conclusion

In this section we have surveyed quite a variety of concepts of salvation, but they all have certain things in common. They are all concerned with problems related to an individual's own personal existence, whether that problem be described as suffering, ignorance, death, or self-alienation. In most cases the problems are not moral or spiritual in origin but rather are ontological. This means that they are rooted in the very nature of existence rather than being caused by personal sins. For those versions of Hinduism (*bhakti*) and Buddhism (Mahayana) that do speak of sins, such sins are not conceived of as violations of the will of a personal and sovereign God. (This point will be discussed later.)

Another point which these views have in common is their emphasis on salvation by one's own efforts, usually in the form of knowledge or works or both. Sometimes a personal savior is involved, but either his work is not decisive (as with Osiris) or it is simply a prerequisite to the individual's own self-efforts (as with the Gnostic savior). The savior-figures in *bhakti* Hinduism and Mahayana Buddhism (especially its True Pure Land form) seem to be more than this, but later discussion will show why they fall short of actually being able to provide salvation to sinners.

SALVATION AS THE HEALING OF SOCIETY

Since the nineteenth century Western society has become increasingly secularized as more and more people have felt less and less need for God in their lives. In the latter part of the twentieth century this trend has spread even to Christendom itself, with large segments of it attempting to reorient their mission around this-worldly concerns while weaning themselves from God. All of this has resulted in some rather serious changes in the concept of salvation. G. Scholem has made these perceptive remarks:[135]

. . . When religion undergoes, as it does so often and so visibly in our

---

135. G. Scholem, "Opening Address," p. 11.

days, the process of secularisation, that is to say when it is interpreted in apparently irreligious terms, we encounter a very characteristic shifting of emphasis: what was formerly taken as a state of redemption, especially in its messianic connotations, by now becomes the condition in which alone true human experience is possible. The unredeemed state is no longer worthy to be called human. The redeemed state is where human experience starts. . . .

This is very true. The new concepts of salvation in our secular age seem to prefer terminology such as humanization instead. In his unsaved state man is enduring a less-than-human existence; salvation is whatever enables him to be fully human. (We have already seen this to be the case in the secular philosophy of Existentialism.)

Secularization brings about other changes in men's thinking about salvation as well. For one thing, it takes the emphasis away from the supernatural or the after-life or an other-worldly kind of salvation, and focuses attention instead upon a salvation that can be accomplished within our own space and time. This change seems to lead almost inevitably to another, namely, a concentration upon the needs of society as a whole rather than the needs of the individual. As long as one can sing "this world is not my (final) home," he can put up with the irritations and injustices and persecutions that exist in it. But once a person begins to think that this world is the only one that mankind will ever have, he begins to think about how it can be made into the very best possible place, i.e, a kind of utopia or paradise on earth if possible.

This last thought is what distinguishes the contents of this section from that of the previous section (and the one to follow). Here we are turning from concepts of salvation that deal with personal fulfillment to those concepts that see salvation mainly as the healing of interpersonal relationships, with the immediate goal being to change the whole of society. This does not mean that personal fulfillment is ignored, but rather that it is usually seen as a kind of by-product or inevitable result of the healing of society. Man's basic problems are not seen as arising from within individuals as much as from social institutions and structures that have become distorted and inverted and have gone out of control. Thus the concern for salvation is focused primarily upon society as a whole.

The contents of this section will include two completely secular (even atheistic) philosophies, namely, Marxism and Secular Humanism; followed by three movements from within Christendom that have focused mainly on societal salvation, namely, Liberalism, Secular Theology, and Liberation Theology.

Marxism

No world view could be more secular or this-worldly than Marxism. As such it is a perfect example of the point made by Scholem noted above, that when world views become secularized their concepts of salvation are couched in terms of humanization. Thus does the Marxist Ajit Roy, speaking of "A Marxist View of Liberation," say that it is a matter of "man's fulfilment," an effort to "enable the proletarian masses to really live as men."[136] He cites an early comment by Karl Marx, that the oppressed and unliberated worker "no longer feels himself to be really active in any but his animal functions—eating, drinking, procreating at most in his dwelling and in dressing-up, etc.; and in his human functions he no longer feels himself to be anything but an animal."[137] Thus does an unjust society condemn "vast masses of the population to an animal existence," says Roy, until liberation occurs. And then, "for the first time, man, in a certain sense, is finally marked off from the rest of the animal kingdom and emerges from animal to really human conditions of existence."[138] A major theme in Marxist philosophy is "the new man."[139]

In view of this, Marxism would seem to be a self-fulfillment philosophy and as such would be similar to the concepts of salvation discussed in the previous section. This is true in the sense that Marxism looks ahead to a time when all men will be changed, fulfilled and humanized. But the real problem as well as its solution, according to classical Marxism, does not lie in the individual but in an "evil" society. Hence its main concern is to "redeem" the structures of society as a whole. As Hans Küng says, "Soviet communism starts out from the

---

136. Ajit Roy, "A Marxist View of Liberation," *Living Faiths and Ultimate Goals*. ed. S.J. Samartha (Geneva: World Council of Churches, 1974), pp. 56-57.

137. Karl Marx, *Economic and Philosophical Manuscripts of 1844* (Moscow, p. 73), cited by Roy, "A Marxist View of Liberation," p. 57.

138. Ajit Roy, "A Marxist View of Liberation," pp. 58-59.

139. See Carl F.H. Henry, *God, Revelation and Authority, Volume IV: God Who Speaks and Shows, Fifteen Theses, Part Three* (Waco: Word Books, 1979), pp. 578ff.; also Klaus Bockmuehl, *The Challenge of Marxism: A Christian Response* (Downers Grove, Ill.: InterVarsity Press, 1980), Part Four, "Creating the New Man."

assumption that the world is evil and needs 'redemption.'"[140] Communism, says John C. Bennett, sees itself "as an absolute movement of redemption in history," as the movement that "will bring redemption from all social evil."[141]

Marxism describes man's basic ills in terms of alienation. Man is alienated from himself; classes of men are alienated from each other. The result is that most people live in a state of bondage. The basic cause of this alienation and bondage is economic and in today's world can be traced to one economic system in particular, namely, capitalism. Under the capitalistic system the means of producing goods for resale (i.e., land, raw materials, tools, factories, machinery—in short, capital) are the privately-owned property of one group (the "capitalists"), while another group (the "proletariat") provides the labor for producing the goods. As Marxists see it, "the capitalistic form of property" is "the modern root of all evil."[142]

Under this system the initial problem is that man is alienated from himself; he experiences "estrangement from himself . . . as a result of oppressive social and economic systems."[143] This happens when a worker spends his labor (which is a part of himself) making a product; but because the means of production belong to someone else, his product is taken away from him and sold. This might not be so bad if all the money received from the sale were then given to the worker as his just wage, but the problem is actually compounded because the product is usually sold for much more money than the worker receives for his wage (i.e., "surplus value"). "When, therefore, the owner takes that object as surplus value, he robs the workman of his very *self*. He *alienates* a part of the workman's being."[144]

A more tangible result is another form of alienation, that between whole classes of men. The class of workers becomes alienated from the capitalistic class. Their relationship is one of oppression and exploita-

---

140. Hans Küng, *Does God Exist? An Answer for Today*, tr. Edward Quinn (Garden City, N.Y.: Doubleday, 1980), p. 241.

141. John C. Bennett, *Christianity and Communism Today* (New York: Association Press, 1960), pp. 81-82.

142. Ibid., p. 28.

143. Ibid., p. 100.

144. Lester DeKoster, *Communism and Christian Faith* (Grand Rapids: Eerdmans, 1962), p. 32.

tion; by claiming all products and pocketing all surplus value, capitalists are robbing the workers of their very being. This is looked upon as a form of bondage: "man's subjugation by man through the division of the community into two classes; one class exploiting and oppressing the other."[145] Such exploitation is "the great original sin."[146] This sin is not the kind for which particular individuals may be held responsible; it is an evil that exists in the very fabric of society. Thus it is society, and not necessarily this or that individual, that must be saved.[147]

What, then, is the nature of salvation according to Marxism? In simple terms, it is the abolition of capitalism, especially the private ownership of the means of production. "From the form of private ownership of productive means, mankind must move to the form of common ownership of those means. That transition is, in Marxism, salvation."[148] According to Karl Marx's dialectical understanding of history, it is inevitable that this will happen. He interpreted all of modern history as a series of necessary transitions from one economic system to another. It began with a primitive form of communism, but then fell into a series of successive exploitative systems: first slavery, then serfdom, then capitalism. (The common basis for exploitation in each case is the private ownership of the means of production.) But capitalism is the end of the line for this type of economic system. The next inevitable transition will be to socialism and then to pure communism, where the means of production are owned in common and exploitation ceases. Thus the historical process ends where it began, namely, with communism as an economic system.[149] DeKoster sums it up thus:[150]

> . . . The original sin occurred when man fell from the communal life of the nomadic tribe by acknowledging the right to private property in the means of production. From this sin followed all the evils of exploitation and struggle. Redemption from social evil can occur only when the original sin is undone, the private ownership of productive means is

---

145. Ajit Roy, "A Marxist View of Liberation," p. 56.

146. F. J. Sheed, *Communism and Man* (New York: Sheed & Ward, 1949), p. 86.

147. Lester DeKoster, *Communism and Christian Faith*, p. 44.

148. Ibid.

149. James D. Bales, *Communism: Its Faith and Fallacies* (Grand Rapids: Baker Book House, 1962), pp. 81ff.

150. Lester DeKoster, *Communism and Christian Faith*, p. 42.

destroyed, and man is thus reunited with reality in the common possession of these means. Then only will exploitation cease, the dialectic come
to an end, and man be enabled to enjoy the fruits of his own labor.

Thus for Marxism salvation is an earthly paradise of which all men
partake (at least those who are still living when it arrives). The basis for
the utopian conditions is the abolition of private ownership. When this
happens the same class both owns and works. Since there is only one
class, the basis for class struggle is removed. In this "classless society,"
there are no more oppression and exploitation. Justice and peace
prevail, and evil is done away. "A temporal heaven would have been
brought to earth."[151]   Küng describes it as[152]

> . . . a kingdom of freedom and of human self-realization, where—
> despite all individual peculiarities—there is in principle no inequality or op-
> pression of human beings, classes and nations, where the exploitation of
> men by men has come to an end, so that the state can lose its political
> function as controlling power and religion becomes superfluous.

Most significantly, man's own nature undergoes a moral change. Instead of being motivated by selfishness, greed, and envy, man will
selflessly and joyously and voluntarily work not just to meet his own
basic needs but to serve the needs of others. All this results from the
change in the social order. As Henry says, "According to the Marxist-
Leninist outlook, this altruistic new man would arise spontaneously,
once the communist society appeared, and would devote all energies to
the common good."[153]

What is the means by which this salvation will be achieved? Here is a
bit of a paradox in Marxist theory. On the one hand it is emphasized that
this will inevitably occur as the result of the unstoppable dialectical flow
of history. At the same time, the working class is urged to take matters
into their own hands and force the change. This seems to be the domi-

---

151. Ibid., p. 34.
152. Hans Küng, *Does God Exist?*, p. 247.
153. Carl F. H. Henry, *God, Revelation and Authority*, IV:579. See also Hans
Küng, *Does God Exist?*, p. 249. According to Klaus Bockmuehl, in recent years some
Marxists have come to realize that the revolution may not take place until at least some individuals are changed first, putting their ego-dominated pasts behind them and putting the
interests of humanity before their own (*The Challenge of Marxism*, pp. 127ff.).

nant emphasis. In other words, if salvation comes, it will be brought about by man himself. Man achieves his own liberation through the "revolutionary reorganization of society."[154]

Specifically, the working class will be the agent of liberation, and revolution will be its means. "The redeemer is the proletariat," says DeKoster.[155] "It is from this class that Marx expects salvation by way of revolt to come; the proletariat is the 'suffering savior' of Marxist 'theology.'"[156] Bales quotes an anonymous Marxist source as saying, "We know there are powerful forces at work, which, given a little shove, will bring about the changes mankind so deeply yearns for."[157] This "little shove" is revolution, which as Bales notes is an essential part of the dialectal advance.[158] Thus Communists see themselves as "the only group in history who wage revolution not to exploit any group but to free all of mankind."[159]

Thus does Marxism present itself as a system of salvation. "The proletariat has a messianic mission to free the world from bondage to poverty and to ignorance. . . . The communist earthly paradise is the heaven for which they work."[160]

Secular Humanism

Another significant view of social salvation is modern Secular Humanism. Over the years the term *humanism* has been applied to a number of different movements and philosophies. Here we are concerned only with the one to which the term *secular* is usually attached, the one whose world view is set forth in the "Humanist Manifesto II" and is most often associated with the American Humanist Association. It will be referred to simply as Humanism.

Humanism is a materialistic, this-worldly philosophy. A leading Humanist, Corliss Lamont, lists ten central propositions of Humanism, the very first of which is that it "believes in a naturalistic metaphysics or attitude toward the universe that considers all forms of the supernatural

---

154. Ajit Roy, "A Marxist View of Liberation," p. 56.
155. Lester DeKoster. *Communism and Christian Faith.* p. 42.
156. Ibid., p. 13.
157. James D. Bales. *Communism*, p. 102.
158. Ibid., p. 135.
159. Ibid., p. 121.
160. Ibid., p. 191.

as myth; and that regards Nature as the totality of being." Whatever future man has is confined to this world: "Humanism definitely places the destiny of man within the very broad limits of this natural world."[161]

In this sense Humanism is no less secular than Marxism, but it lacks a deterministic philosophy of history such as that worked out by Marx. It does not see a particular future as inevitable, but it does have an ideal that it urges all men to work for. This is referred to in "Humanist Manifesto II" as "a secular society on a planetary scale."[162] Humanism does assume that we are in the midst of an evolutionary process, but it is not the very specialized economic evolution envisioned by Marx. It is the more ordinary biological and social evolution so widely accepted by modern man.

Given this evolutionary framework, Humanism interprets man's current predicament not in terms of a Fall from some prior ideal state (such as the Garden of Eden or primitive communism) but in terms of unfulfilled potential. Mankind is not so much enduring some kind of radical evil as it is facing the possibility of failing to achieve what it has the capacity to achieve. The significant advances in the evolution of human intelligence and the tremendous progress in the sciences put man into the position of being able to direct his own future evolution and to develop a paradise on earth.

This potential paradise is described in guarded yet optimistic terms. Lamont refers to it as "an enduring citadel of peace and beauty upon this earth."[163] The 1933 "Humanist Manifesto I" says, "The goal of humanism is a free and universal society in which people voluntarily and intelligently cooperate for the common good."[164] This older manifesto endorsed socialism as a part of this ideal society,[165] but the later one (1973) makes it clear that this is not to be understood as an endorsement of Communism.[166] In any case Humanism believes it is possible for man "to create a higher civilization of world dimensions," in

161. Corliss Lamont, *The Philosophy of Humanism*, 5 ed. (New York: Frederick Ungar, 1965), pp. 12-13, 107.

162. *Humanist Manifestos I and II* (Buffalo: Prometheus Books, 1973), p. 15.

163. Corliss Lamont, *The Philosophy of Humanism*, p. 14.

164. *Humanist Manifestos I and II*, p. 10.

165. Ibid.

166. Ibid., pp. 17, 23.

Lamont's words.[167]

The only problem is that man does not seem to be living up to his potential. He is not rolling up his sleeves and accepting the responsibility for engineering a program for "satisfying survival." [168] Instead he seems to be more content to place himself in the hands of non-existent supernatural beings, thus squandering opportunities and jeopardizing the possibilities for the future that actually exist. Thus, according to Humanism, trusting in "God" is one of the biggest obstacles to progress today. Here is what the "Manifesto" says:[169]

> . . . Humanists still believe that traditional theism, especially faith in the prayer-hearing God, assumed to love and care for persons, to hear and understand their prayers, and to be able to do something about them, is an unproved and outmoded faith. Salvationism, based on mere affirmation, still appears as harmful, diverting people with false hopes of heaven hereafter. Reasonable minds look to other means for survival.

Also, the "Manifesto" condemns those who "flee in despair from reason and embrace irrational cults and theologies of withdrawal and retreat." It finds belief in the supernatural "either meaningless or irrelevant to the question of the survival and fulfillment of the human race." Even when redefined in modern terms, such beliefs "often perpetuate old dependencies and escapisms; they easily become obscurantist, impeding the free use of the intellect." Traditional religions "inhibit humans from helping themselves or experiencing their full potentialities."[170]

The solution to man's problems and the only hope for any kind of future salvation, says Humanism, lie within the hands of man alone. Man must be his own savior. The second manifesto says very clearly, "Humans are responsible for what we are or will become. No deity will save us; we must save ourselves."[171] Lamont says that human beings are "the masters of their own destiny."[172] He continues,[173]

---

167. Corliss Lamont, *The Philosophy of Humanism*, p. 283.
168. *Humanist Manifestos I and II*, p. 15.
169. Ibid., p. 13.
170. Ibid., pp. 14, 16.
171. Ibid., p. 16.
172. Corliss Lamont, *The Philosophy of Humanism*, p. 13.
173. Ibid., p. 109.

As for the future, it is up to the human race to work out its own destiny upon this globe. Humanism denies that there is any overarching fate, either in the form of a Divine Providence or a malignant Satanism, that is either helping or hindering man's progress and well-being. . . . To a significant degree [human beings] are the moulders of their own fate and hold in their own hands the shape of things to come.

For the Humanist this is not just a "have to" situation; it is a matter of "can do." Humanists are very optimistic and confident about man's ability to save himself. Lamont says, "Humanism, having its ultimate faith in man, believes that human beings possess the power or potentiality of solving their own problems, through reliance primarily upon reason and scientific method applied with courage and vision."[174] The first manifesto said, "Man is at last becoming aware that he alone is responsible for the realization of the world of his dreams, that he has within himself the power for its achievement. He must set intelligence and will to the task."[175] Like Marxism, Humanism's main arena for its "saving" activity is society as a whole. And like Marxism, it too is confident that a changed society will result in fulfillment for all individuals. It does not look for immortal salvation, of course, but for an environment where "self-actualization" is possible, where one can find the "whole person fulfilled." "The ultimate goal should be the fulfillment of the potential for growth in each human personality."[176]

Christian Liberalism

We switch now from a discussion of two secular concepts of social salvation to an examination of three movements from within Christendom itself. The first of these is Christian Liberalism, a term which refers to the fairly distinct school of theology that traces its origin to Schleiermacher and Ritschl and which dominated the scene during the last quarter of the nineteenth and the first quarter of the twentieth centuries. Though it may be called theistic, it rejected the concept of a transcendent God and denied any sharp distinction between the natural and the

---

174. Ibid., p. 13.
175. *Humanist Manifestos I and II*, p. 10.
176. Ibid., pp. 14, 16, 18.

supernatural. God as Immanent Spirit is present in all of life.

Though some allowance was made for individual immortality, this was not a main concern and was often treated agnostically. The main emphasis was on the kind of salvation that involves mankind as a whole and can take place in this world. While some Liberals were more "evangelical" than others, the movement as a whole was much closer to Humanism than to orthodox Christianity. In fact it is plausible to see Humanism as Liberalism carried to its logical conclusions.

As with Humanism, mankind's basic problem as seen by Liberalism must be defined in terms of man's evolutionary background. Liberals accepted the Darwinian hypothesis and interpreted man as being in the process of development. He has climbed beyond the animal stage and is now a creature of spirit. The problem, however, is that his spirit is still weak, and the vestiges of his animal nature often overpower it. This causes him to engage in behavior that we call sin, and this is a real threat to man's future development. Kenneth Cauthen sums this point up very clearly:[177]

> . . . Certain underlying themes appear repeatedly in the writings of liberal thinkers. Man is universally viewed as a being who has emerged out of nature through a process of evolution. Yet, man is superior to nature. His basic problem is how he can achieve the greatest possible development of his moral and spiritual capacities in light of the obstacles to this fulfillment which confront him by virtue of his connections with the world of nature. . . .

This explains the "basic liberal conviction" concerning the origin of sin, that it "arises out of the inability of the spirit to master the non-moral impulses of the body. Sin is a kind of weakness by which the will is overpowered and its consent given to the surging passions of the animal nature."[178] An example of this idea is Walter Rauschenbusch, foremost representative of Liberalism's "social gospel." Explaining the nature of sin, he points out that we are equipped with powerful appetites that overwhelm us, ignorance that causes us to make mistakes, and instincts that become rampant and overgrown, trampling our inward freedom.

---

177. Kenneth Cauthen, *The Impact of American Religious Liberalism* (New York: Harper & Row, 1962), p. 159.
178. Ibid., p. 119.

We have high ideals but are weighted down by inertia. "This sensual equipment, this ignorance and inertia, out of which our moral delinquencies sprout, are part of our human nature." They make us more liable to pity than condemnation.[179]

Rauschenbusch is not denying that we sin, but he thinks of sin not so much as an insult to God as a violation of our responsibilities to one another. Traditional theology errs in treating sin as "a private transaction between the sinner and God." Sin is essentially selfishness, and that means selfishness toward other men. "The sinful mind, then, is the unsocial and anti-social mind." Real rebellion against God is cheating one's neighbor and oppressing the poor.[180]

This leads into one other very important aspect of Liberalism's analysis of human sin and the human predicament. Not only is sin on the part of individuals mainly anti-social behavior, says Rauschenbusch; it can be and often is a characteristic of social *institutions*. Whole communities and collective aspects of human life can be corrupted so that the institution itself is evil and thus corrupts those individuals who are a part of it or are influenced by it. Rauschenbusch calls these "the super-personal forces of evil." These may include such things as governments, trade unions, and political organizations. These are not necessarily evil in themselves but may become so when selfishness and greed prevail over the interests and needs of all men.[181] "When these super-personal forces are based on an evil principle, or directed toward an evil purpose, or corrupted by some controlling group interest which is hostile to the common good, they are sinners of sublimer mould, and they block the way of redemption."[182]

What, then, is the nature of salvation according to Liberalism? It is the moral transformation of individuals and of society as a whole. For individuals it is the victory of spirit over nature, the conquest of the animal impulses that constantly nag us. As Cauthen says, "Salvation is viewed as the triumph of moral personality over the lower impulses of

---

179. Walter Rauschenbusch, *A Theology for the Social Gospel* (New York: Macmillan, 1918), pp. 45-46.

180. Ibid., pp. 46-50.

181. Ibid., pp. 69ff.

182. Ibid., p. 110.

the body and the mechanisms of the physical environment."[183] It is an ethical, moral, internal change of heart rather than a change in one's legal status before God. In traditional terms, it is sanctification rather than justification. W.A. Brown, a Liberal, explains: "From the point of view of the individual experience, we defined salvation as the substitution of the outgoing for the self-centred life. . . . The history of redemption is the history of mankind's progressive victory over selfishness and distrust."[184]

More significant, however, is the social aspect of salvation, the transformation of the whole of society. This was the theme that was dear to the heart of all Liberals, especially those most closely associated with the "social gospel." They trusted the immanent forces of evolution to be on their side and to be bringing about the Kingdom of God through the historical process. Cauthen describes Shailer Mathews' view thus: "Salvation is the notion of an evolutionary process in which spiritual forces are gradually overcoming the forces of nature. The cosmos itself is on the side of progress. Sin is being gradually sloughed off as moral personality comes to dominate the impulses inherited from the animals."[185] Brown says it this way: "From the point of view of history, salvation is the process by which the divine ideal is realized in society through the establishment of the kingdom of God among men."[186] Liberals believed very strongly that the Kingdom of God could be established upon the earth in the sense of an immanent and universal moral paradise. This was their faith, and this was their goal. "Their interest, while not discounting or denying but even looking forward with some eagerness to salvation in another and better world, is nevertheless concerned mainly with making the good life possible in the here and now."[187] Rauschenbusch says that the "social gospel" is mainly interested in "redeeming the historical life of humanity from the social wrongs which now pervade it . . . . Its chief interest is concentrated on

---

183. Kenneth Cauthen, *The Impact of American Religious Liberalism*, pp. 53, 159, 211.

184. William Adams Brown, *Christian Theology in Outline* (New York: Charles Scribner's Sons, 1906), p. 320.

185. Kenneth Cauthen, *The Impact of American Religious Liberalism*, p. 161.

186. William Adams Brown, *Christian Theology in Outline*, pp. 315-316.

187. Charles S. Braden, *Man's Quest for Salvation*, p. 219.

those manifestations of sin and redemption which lie beyond the individual soul."[188] This includes the salvation of the super-personal forces.[189]

One last question remains, namely, how will this moral transformation be accomplished? Particularly, what is the role of Jesus Christ in the Liberal view of salvation? After all, we are working here within the Christian tradition. Jesus must function in some way as Savior. Exactly what is that function? The answer is that Jesus' saving work can be almost altogether subsumed under the general category of *revelation*. Whatever he did, in life or in death, was a revelation of the ideal human character and as such teaches us and inspires us to live the same kind of life that he did. This is how he saves us. "The essence of salvation in liberal thought is moral transformation whereby the personality is integrated around the ideals of Christ."[190] He does not merely teach us these ideals; by the example of his own life and death he *inspires* us to follow in his steps. The cross itself is interpreted in terms of moral influence. Speaking of the atonement, Brown says that "its saving efficacy consists in its moral influence in arousing repentance and faith."[191] As Braden puts it, salvation is won "through a sincere following of Christ who supremely by his life, culminating in his death on the cross, has shown man the way to God."[192]

If this is the extent of Christ's saving work, then it should be obvious that the real means to salvation is man himself. Christ may show the way and may inspire us with his example, but the actual accomplishment of salvation is in our own hands. This is true especially in view of the fact that salvation is interpreted primarily in terms of moral transformation (rather than, for instance, the legal satisfaction of the penalty for sin). Christ may help us by his teaching and example, but the real work of transforming our own lives and society itself—i.e., salvation—is something we have to do for ourselves. If this is the case, we may wonder how Liberal Christianity differs from the many non-Christian and even secular views of salvation that we have already examined. We

---

188. Walter Rauschenbusch, *A Theology for the Social Gospel*, p. 95.
189. Ibid., pp. 110ff.
190. Kenneth Cauthen, *The Impact of American Religious Liberalism*, p. 53.
191. William Adams Brown, *Christian Theology in Outline*, p. 365.
192. Charles S. Braden, *Man's Quest for Salvation*, p. 220.

may even wonder, as far as his work is concerned, how much different the Liberals' Jesus is from the Gnostics' savior-god. Each of them served as a means of revelation, and what they revealed is but a starting point from which man must work out his own salvation. We may even wonder whether the Liberals' conception of Jesus is as sublime as the Buddhists' view of Amida. Whether the latter can really provide what he offers is a question to be discussed later, but at least he *offers* to remove man's sins by means of his own vicarious merits.

In short, Liberalism leaves us with still another system of salvation by self-effort, whether that salvation be concerned with individuals or with society as a whole.

Secular Theology

The contemporary counterpart of Liberalism is Secular Theology, a name we shall use for that current of thought within Christendom that springs from the influence of Dietrich Bonhoeffer, who coined or inspired such expressions as "a world come of age," "religionless Christianity," and "learning to live without God, before God." Drawing also on the work of Bultmann and Tillich, the Anglican bishop John A. T. Robinson gave Secular Theology to the masses with his popular 1963 book, *Honest to God*.[193]

The Secular Theologians (or Secularists, for short) would agree wholeheartedly with Gustave Todrank's judgment that "the Christian myth of salvation is obsolete for the twentieth century."[194] Though they retain Christian terminology, they have abandoned its traditional content. Their approach to theology in general and to salvation in particular is really very similar to that of Liberalism, or even to Humanism except for the theistic and Christian references. Their emphasis is only secondarily on individual salvation and mainly on the conversion of society as a whole. And as the very name *Secular* suggests, the arena of their concern is this world only. As Todrank notes, "One aspect of the current revolution in Christianity is an obvious transition from the otherworldly to the this-worldly," a transition which has had "revolutionary conse-

---

193. John A. T. Robinson, *Honest to God* (London: SCM Press, 1963).

194. Gustave H. Todrank, *The Secular Search for a New Christ* (Philadelphia: Westminster Press, 1969), p. 29.

quences, one of which is the notion of salvation without immortality."[195] Todrank's own goal is to set forth a "secular christian salvation," one derived from a "modified this-worldly approach."[196]

The Secularists interpret mankind's "lostness" in much the same way as the others discussed in this section, namely, we are not experiencing the fullness of our humanity. The race as a whole is not living up to its full potential as human beings. Todrank says that the Secularists have "become distressingly aware of the enormous gap between life as it is and life as it ought to be."[197] Paul Lehmann agrees: "Man has lost the secret of his humanity and the key to the meaning of his life and of the world in which he cannot help but live it out."[198] The essence of this lost humanity is the corruption of interpersonal relationships, the dissolution of fellowship, or what Lehmann calls "destroyed community."[199] Its most obvious manifestations are the widespread oppression, exploitation and degradation suffered by the poor and powerless at the hands of the selfish and greedy. Such conditions are not just the result of sinful individuals but are due to corrupt social institutions such as governments and economic systems.

From this is should not be difficult to discern what the saved state would be like, according to Secularists. It is an earthly society in which everyone is able to live a fully human life. Key words are self-fulfillment, humanization, and maturity. In an article entitled "What Does Salvation Mean to Christians Today?" David Jenkins gives the answer: "To be human." He says that "being human as the gift of God refers not only to what Christians *do* mean by salvation today. It is also in accordance with what Christians *ought* to mean by salvation today." It is "the gift of God to men so that they might be all that they might be."[200] Paul Lehmann paraphrases the question "What shall I do to be saved?" as "What shall I do to be what I am?"[201]

---

195. Ibid., p. 23.

196. Ibid., pp. 33, 41.

197. Ibid., p. 159.

198. Paul L. Lehmann, *Ethics in a Christian Context* (New York: Harper & Row, 1963), p. 96.

199. Ibid., p. 97.

200. David Jenkins, "What Does Salvation Mean to Christians Today?", *Living Faiths and Ultimate Goals*, ed. S. J. Samartha (Geneva: World Council of Churches, 1974), p. 34.

201. Paul Lehmann, *Ethics in a Christian Context*, p. 155.

Lehmann describes salvation in terms of *maturity*. He says[202] that it is

> . . . the power to be what man has been created and purposed to be. It is the power to be and to stay human, that is, to attain wholeness or maturity. For maturity is the full development in a human being of the power to be truly and fully himself in being related to others who also have the power to be truly and fully themselves. The Christian *koinonia* is the foretaste and the sign in the world that God has always been and is contemporaneously doing what it takes to make and to keep human life human. . . .

"In short, maturity is salvation."[203] In Jenkins' words, "Salvation is, ultimately, the giving of God Himself to men so that their humanity is infinitely filled and fulfilled."[204] It is "profound satisfaction and transforming fulfillment."[205]

All of this could be understood quite Biblically if it were meant to include the complete maturity of the redeemed man, body and spirit, in heaven. This is not what Secularists mean by fulfillment, however. They are speaking of this earthly life only. When Todrank says that "salvation refers to that total life orientation which makes for the most and the best creative well-being,"[206] he is speaking of *material* well-being. Willems says that it is the church's task to "bring about the presence of salvation and redemption in the world" by helping all men "to realize earthly values."[207] Colin Williams explains "the new secular hope" as the hope for "the participation of all men in a truly human existence in this world," by which he means "real participation in the material benefits of this life." It is the hope for "human participation in the fruits of the natural world of creation," or for "free participation for all in a meaningful human existence now."[208]

---

202. Ibid., p. 101.
203. Ibid., p. 99.
204. David Jenkins, "What Does Salvation Mean . . . ?", p. 36.
205. Gustave Todrank, *The Secular Search*, p. 36.
206. Ibid., pp. 46-47.
207. Boniface A. Willems, *The Reality of Redemption* (New York: Herder and Herder, 1970), p. 121.
208. Colin W. Williams, *What in the World?* (New York: National Council of the Churches of Christ, 1964), pp. 50-51.

This will happen when all men accept one another in full fellowship or *koinonia*. Thus salvation is a relational or social concept. Salvation simply means fellowship, says Willems. It means "allowing the other to approach us," or "the acceptance and reverence of the otherness of our fellows."[209] Lehmann says God is working to bring about a "new humanity." The "divinely willed order of life" is for man "to be himself in being related to his fellow man." The essence of this saved state is *koinonia* or community or fellowship.[210]

Now we must ask the question, how is this salvation to be accomplished? By what means can mankind be redeemed and a "new humanity" created? The Secularist unhesitatingly says that God is the one who will accomplish this, indeed, who *is* accomplishing it at this very moment, in our very world, under our very noses. To this we might be tempted to reply that we are aware of the work God is doing through his church in the world. But this is the very thing the Secularist does *not* mean. God is not working through the so-called "religious" institutions, as we might expect, but rather he is working through *secular* means, *secular* movements, *secular* organizations, and *secular* events. Here is the key to understanding Secular Theology: whatever is happening in the secular history of this world to enable all men to enjoy earthly life to its fullest is interpreted as the redemptive work of God. What others of us would call providence, Secularists call redemption.[211] What others of us would call the permissive will of God, the Secularists in effect call his purposive and preceptive will.[212] And the "will of God" (to use Lehmann's favorite phrase) is "to make and to keep human life human." The will of God "is what God is doing in the world to achieve the humanity of man, i.e., human maturity."[213] "What God is doing in the world to make and to keep human life human is to bring about human maturity; in other words, to bring to pass a new humanity."[214]

---

209. Boniface Willems, *The Reality of Redemption*, pp. 20-21.
210. Paul Lehmann, *Ethics in a Christian Context*, pp. 85, 97, 124.
211. Colin Williams notes this objection to the Secularists' concept of God's working in the world, an objection that arose even from among the participants in the World Council of Churches. Those who raised this objection were in the minority, however. (*What in the World?*, p. 32ff.)
212. See especially Paul Lehmann, *Ethics in a Christian Context*, pp. 74-81.
213. Ibid., pp. 248-249.
214. Ibid., p. 117.

"What God is doing in the world is setting up and carrying out the conditions for what it takes to keep human life human. The fruit of this divine activity is human maturity, the wholeness of every man and of all men in the new humanity."[215]

Although God is the one who is working redemptively in the world through various secular means, it is the task of the church to *identify* those places in the world where God is at work (to make and keep human life human) and to *join in* his activity. These are the words of Harvey Cox: "The church is first of all a responding community, a people whose task it is to discern the action of God in the world and to join in His work."[216] "God is always one step ahead of man," says Cox,[217] which means that it is God who initiates the work in the secular realm and leaves it up to the church to find out about it and participate. Cox likes the image that compares the work of God with a "floating crap game," with the church being in the role of the confirmed gambler whose major compulsion upon arising each day is to "know where the action is" so he can run there and "dig it."[218] Lehmann refers to this as the "appraisal of and obedience to what God is doing in the world."[219]

But how can we know which world events are "God's works" and which are not? Here is where Jesus Christ enters in, according to Secular Theology. He provides our understanding of what God is doing in the world.[220] He is "the revelation of God in and through whom all other apprehensions of God's activity are to be criticized and comprehended."[221] As Harvey Cox says, "The key to locating the action is, of course, that the same God who was there yesterday is present in the action today. To locate today's action we need to know the lead actor, and this actor has disclosed himself in the life of Jesus."[222] So our ministry, says Cox, "is simply the continuation of Jesus' ministry."[223]

---

215. Ibid., p. 124.

216. Harvey Cox. *The Secular City*. revised ed. (New York: Macmillan, 1966), p. 91.

217. Ibid., p. 100.

218. Ibid., p. 108.

219. Paul Lehmann. *Ethics in a Christian Context*. p. 81.

220. David Jenkins, "What Does Salvation Mean . . . ?", p. 36.

221. Paul Lehmann, *Ethics in a Christian Context*, p. 89.

222. Harvey Cox. *The Secular City*. p. 109.

223. Ibid.

Now we come to the heart of the Secularist view of salvation. Just how is Jesus' ministry understood by Cox and others? "But what is the character of Jesus' ministry?" Cox asks. He answers his own question by quoting Luke 4:18-19, Jesus' own words: "The Spirit of the Lord is upon Me, because He anointed Me to preach the gospel to the poor. He has sent Me to proclaim release to the captives, and recovery of sight to the blind, to set free those who are downtrodden, to proclaim the favorable year of the Lord." Cox sums up Jesus' task thus: "He was to announce the arrival of the new regime. He was to personify its meaning. And he was to begin distributing its benefits."[224] This is vitally important for our understanding of secular salvation: these words of Jesus are taken as the essence of redeeming activity, and they are interpreted in a completely material and secular sense rather than spiritual. Thus in Secular Theology we have the "social gospel" *redivivus*. The saving work of God is "social change," as Cox says.[225] It is "politics," says Lehmann. God "is the God of politics," he says, and his will is "a clear and concrete matter of politics." And politics is simply that activity required "to make and keep human life *human* in the world."[226]

The concept of politics is understood quite broadly here. As Kliever explains it,[227]

. . . We speak of God in a political way when we place ourselves where the restoring, reconciling activity of God is going on, where the proper relationship between people is appearing or trying to appear. Speaking of God politically is more than pledging "one nation under God"—it is creating one nation under God "with liberty and justice for all.". . .

It is what Jenkins calls "the present struggles to be human, that is, to achieve freedom from oppression, from physical degradation and from being overwhelmed in an environment seemingly out of control."[228] What are some specific examples? Paul Lehmann cites the efforts of a

---

224. Ibid., pp. 109-110.
225. Ibid., p. 91.
226. Paul Lehmann, *Ethics in a Christian Context*, pp. 82-85.
227. Lonnie D. Kliever, *The Shattered Spectrum: A Survey of Contemporary Theology* (Atlanta: John Knox Press, 1981), p. 32.
228. David Jenkins, "What Does Salvation Mean . . . ?", p. 35.

disciple of Gandhi to redistribute wealth in his native land of India as an example of what God is doing in the world.[229] Another example would be any efforts towards desegregation or solving the racial crisis.[230] Another major example would be the liberation movements of Latin America, which Williams calls "secular conversion." We can see "Christ's redeeming work" in these movements, "where the masses are at last awakening and turning from despair to hope and from resignation under injustice to a determination to build a society where all men will have a new dignity and a freer participation in a more truly human community." Since this is what God is doing, this is what Christians ought to be doing also.[231]

Such is the Secularists' view of salvation. It can be characterized as immanent, materialistic, and social. Although there is much emphasis on "what God is doing," it seems that in the final analysis this salvation will be accomplished by human efforts at social revolution. It makes no difference who is doing this work, whether it be Marxists, other atheists, Hindus, Catholics, or Christians. As far as the nature of the salvation is concerned, it is difficult if not impossible to distinguish between the Secularists' version and that of the Humanists (or even the Marxists). The Secularist may comfort his conscience by attributing this work to God, but we can hear the Humanists and Marxists in Latin America saying, "Fine, fine, if you say so; now let's just keep on doing what we are doing." For in the end it is man who does it. It is another example of salvation by self-effort.

Liberation Theology

There is no sharp line of demarcation between Secular Theology and Liberation Theology. The latter has developed by natural progression out of the former, with the intermediate stage being something called the Theology of Hope. Today the Theologians of Hope to a large degree have been assimilated into Liberation Theology; thus we need not devote a separate section to them.

In many ways Liberation Theology simply echoes Secular

---

229. Paul Lehmann, *Ethics in a Christian Context*, p. 156.
230. Ibid., p. 152; Colin Williams, *What in the World?*, p. 46.
231. Colin Williams, *What in the World?*, pp. 31, 52.

Theology, but there are at least three main differences between them. First of all, Liberation Theology more openly espouses "universal salvation" as far as God and eternity are concerned, so that this whole aspect of salvation can be set aside as irrelevant for mankind today. If anyone persists in pressing the question about immortality and the after-life, the Liberationist can simply reply that that has been taken care of and no one should worry about it. Thus all our attention can be turned to the more immediate problem of social revolution, which is the only aspect of salvation that really matters. For example, the Liberationist Gustavo Gutierrez speaks of the presence of grace in all people, whether they are conscious of it or not. He mentions the currently popular concepts of "anonymous Christianity" and "Christendom without the name," i.e., the independence of salvation from Christian faith. He affirms that "all men are in Christ efficaciously called to communion with God." All things have been saved in Christ.[232] Clark Pinnock gives a good summary of this view of Gutierrez:[233]

> . . . Although Gutierrez features salvation centrally in his theology, he errs greatly in his exposition of it, one mistake leading to another. He begins with the universalistic assumption that all men now participate in Christ and will finally be saved. Therefore, evangelism is quite superfluous to his concerns. Men do not need to be, since they have already been, justified by faith. The unevangelized do not need to hear the Gospel because they can open themselves to God apart from it. . . .
>
> Holding this view, that all human beings will finally be saved, Gutierrez is free to concentrate exclusively on the mundane and intrahistorical form salvation takes. . . .

A second difference between Secular Theology and Liberation Theology is that the latter makes much more open use of Marxist terms and concepts. In fact one of the strongest criticisms usually made of Liberationists is that they sound more Marxist than Christian.

A third difference is that Liberation Theology much more openly espouses revolution—even violent revolution—as a legitimate means for

---

232. Gustavo Gutierrez, *A Theology of Liberation*, tr. Caridad Inda and John Eagleson (Maryknoll, N.Y.: Orbis Books, 1973), p. 71. See also pp. 150-152.

233. Clark H. Pinnock, "Liberation Theology: the Gains, the Gaps," *Christianity Today* (January 16, 1976), 20:14.

redeeming society. Of course, this also indicates its affinity with Marxism, for which revolution is a standard tool. It also indicates how far it has diverged from the Liberal "social gospel," which relied on evolution rather than revolution.

Although Liberation Theology often is taken very broadly to include the Black Liberation and Women's Liberation movements, our attention here will be directed mostly toward Third World Liberationism.

The Liberationists' analysis of the human predicament focuses on concrete, this-worldly forms of oppression, exploitation and bondage, and these almost exclusively in terms of economics. As Erickson puts it, "The basic problem of society is the oppression and exploitation of the powerless classes by the powerful."[234] As another says, "*Class* oppression is viewed as the underlying source and model of all other forms of human bondage."[235]

The main object of concern is not personal sin but social sin, particularly the sin of economic oppression and economic inequality. As Gutierrez explains,[236]

> . . . In the liberation approach sin is not considered as an individual, private, or merely interior reality—asserted just enough to necessitate a "spiritual" redemption which does not challenge the order in which we live. Sin is regarded as a social, historical fact, the absence of brotherhood and love in relationships among men, the breach of friendship with God and with other men, and, therefore, an interior, personal fracture. When it is considered in this way, the collective dimensions of sin are rediscovered. . . . Sin is evident in oppressive structures, in the exploitation of man by man, in the domination and slavery of peoples, races, and social classes. Sin appears, therefore, as the fundamental alienation, the root of a situation of injustice and exploitation. . . .

If this sounds Marxian, it is no accident; we have already noted the relationship that exists here. Carl Henry well says, "Marxian analysis of class struggle and proposed Marxian solutions are accepted as gospel."[237]

What *is* the solution, according to Liberation Theology? In a word,

---

234. Millard Erickson, *Christian Theology*, III:892.
235. Lonnie Kliever, *The Shattered Spectrum*, p. 86.
236. Gustavo Gutierrez, *A Theology of Liberation*, p. 175.
237. Carl F. H. Henry, *God, Revelation and Authority*, IV:558.

liberation. "The salvation of Christ," says Gutierrez, "is a radical liberation from all misery, all despoliation, all alienation." It takes place in those historical situations "where men and social classes struggle to liberate themselves from the slavery and oppression to which other men and social classes have subjected them."[238] The result must be nothing less than a full transformation of society, a new social order, an earthly Kingdom of God where justice and freedom are possessed by all.

Thus the liberation efforts must focus primarily on the sinful structures of society. As Núñez describes it, "The problem is social, and the solution has to be given on the collective plane. It is not simply a matter of the salvation of individuals, but of the transformation of society."[239] Of particular concern are the economic structures, especially the allegedly oppressive nature of capitalism. For example, Jose Miranda makes an elaborate attempt to show how the Bible condemns capitalism and defends socialism in *Marx and the Bible*.[240] Economic equality is the key to paradise.[241] Gutierrez characterizes the prevailing attitude among Liberationists thus:[242]

> . . . Only a radical break from the status quo, that is, a profound transformation of the private property system, access to power of the exploited class, and a social revolution that would break this dependence would allow for the change to a new society, a socialist society—or at least allow that such a society might be possible.

The Liberationist concept of utopia, he says, involves "a new social consciousness" and "a social appropriation . . . of the means of production."[243]

Gutierrez summarizes the essence of Liberation Theology in these words:[244]

---

238. Gustavo Gutierrez, *A Theology of Liberation*, p. 178.
239. Emilio A. Núñez C., *Liberation Theology*, tr. Paul E. Sywulka (Chicago: Moody Press, 1985), p. 176.
240. Jose Miranda, *Marx and the Bible: A Critique of the Philosophy of Oppression*, tr. John Eagleson (Maryknoll, N.Y.: Orbis Books, 1974).
241. Carl Henry notes that for Liberation Theology, socialism is the true liberator, not God. (*God, Revelation and Authority*, IV:561)
242. Gustavo Gutierrez, *A Theology of Liberation*, pp. 26-27.
243. Ibid., p. 237.
244. Ibid., p. 307.

The theology of liberation attempts to reflect on the experience and meaning of the faith based on the commitment to abolish injustice and to build a new society; this theology must be verified by the practice of that commitment, by active, effective participation in the struggle which the exploited social classes have undertaken against their oppressors. Liberation from every form of exploitation, the possibility of a more human and more dignified life, the creation of a new man—all pass through this struggle.

Thus Liberation Theology promises "a new society" and "a new man." It allows every man to be fully human. As Roger Haight says, it portrays salvation "as identical with a process of humanization," which means "a movement toward a greater degree of human freedom, the essence of what it means to be human."[245] Liberation means freedom, and freedom means humanness.

There remains the question of how this saving liberation is to be accomplished. The answer is much the same as that of Secular Theology except for the emphasis on revolution. Credit is given to God for being at work in history. Jesus is understood mainly as revelation, as an example of the kind of freedom it is possible to achieve on this earth. As Haight says, "Salvation appears in the way Jesus lived his life." He came to create God's Kingdom on earth; it was "a process that was exemplified and effected in Jesus' actual historical doings. Jesus is a revelation from God" that human history can be meaningful.[246] He says further,[247]

. . . In Jesus one sees a human existence that is meaningful. And were it generalized or extended out into the social sphere of public history, the result would be a just social order, constituted by just social relationships, where the lives of the suffering and oppressed would be attended to through the institutions that human beings create. Jesus thus reveals that meaningful history is possible, that is, it has a possible and not an inherent or necessary meaning, through God's power to the extent that human beings are willing to accept and live in God's power.

This simply means that Jesus showed us what to do; now it is up to us to

---

245. Roger Haight, *An Alternative Vision: An Interpretation of Liberation Theology* (New York: Paulist Press, 1985), pp. 38-39.
246. Ibid., p. 134.
247. Ibid.

do it. "For the salvation revealed by Jesus Christ to become real it must be historically actualized" by our imitating his example.[248]

This brings us back to familiar ground. In the final analysis man himself is his own savior, his own liberator. He saves himself and the world by his participation in the class struggle. Becoming socially and politically active is the equivalent of conversion. "By working, transforming the world, breaking out of servitude, building a just society, and assuming his destiny in history, man forges himself," says Gutierrez.[249] Violence may be a legitimate means as long as it is being used by the oppressed to achieve their liberation.[250] Whatever the means, we create our own salvation history (comparable to the Exodus) when we join the struggle, for "the struggle for a just society is in its own right very much a part of salvation history."[251] A Chinese theologian has carried this thought to its logical extreme by suggesting that Mao Tse-tung's New China is a prime example of contemporary salvation history. "Is the 'salvation' we have seen in New China going to be the norm determining the shape and content of man's search for what it means to be human? Is New China going to be the main instrument in the appearance of a new world order in which the salvation of man is to have its fulfilment?" he asks.[252] And why should it not be, from the standpoint of Liberationists? Is this not the very thing they are seeking in Latin America and other parts of the world? And does this not perfectly illustrate the point that "salvation by liberation" is indeed a work of man's own hands?

Conclusion

In considering alternatives to the Biblical concept of redemption, we have surveyed in this section some of the major examples of salvation as the healing of society; and again it seems that we have come full circle. We began this section with an examination of Marxism's concept of salvation, and moved from there to Humanism and then to three movements from within Christendom itself. The last of these, Liberation

---

248. Ibid., pp. 135-136.
249. Gustavo Gutierrez, *A Theology of Liberation*, p. 159.
250. See ibid., pp. 109, 126 (n. 41).
251. Ibid., p. 168.
252. Choan-seng Song, "New China and Salvation History—A Methodological Enquiry," *Living Faiths and Ultimate Goals*, ed. S. J. Samartha (Geneva: World Council of Churches, 1974), p. 72.

Theology, has been found to be preaching the same gospel as Marxism; and this theology is little different in principle from the other Christian movements discussed here, being a logical successor to Liberalism and Secular Theology. It seems that once the seeds of secularization have sprouted and matured, no matter what ground they were sown in, the fruit is remarkably similar. The goal for each of the movements examined here, secular or Christian, is a this-worldly paradise in which the enjoyment of material things is a primary value. Since sin is principally a matter of corrupt social structures, salvation itself concentrates on changing these structures. For individuals salvation means living a fully human life in the paradise created thereby. Where Jesus Christ has any role at all, he is seen as a revealer, a teacher, an example, a way-shower. Most significantly, the basic means for achieving salvation in each case is man's own works. In this connection Walter Kasper's comments apply quite well to all the views grouped together here and are an appropriate conclusion to this section:[253]

> We encounter this hope in a secularized form in the various modern utopian visions, among which the faith in evolutionary progress and the revolutionary utopianism of Marxism with its coming kingdom of freedom have been the most influential. Both of these assume that man must take his destiny into his own hands and be the author of his own happiness. When its radical implications are accepted, this modern idea of human autonomy excludes in principle any idea of a mediator and therefore any idea of a redemption that is not a self-redemption and self-liberation by man himself. . . .

SALVATION AS ACCEPTANCE BY GOD

The final category of views that are alternatives to the Biblical doctrine of redemption deals with those views that see salvation as the healing of a breach between man and God. Some of the views already discussed have included concepts of deity, but none of them have identified the essence of man's problem as focusing on his relationship with the deity. They have seen the problem either as something internal within man or as a breach of interpersonal, societal relationships. Here,

---

253. Walter Kasper, *The God of Jesus Christ*, tr. Matthew J. O'Connell (New York: Crossroad Publishing Co., 1984), p. 159.

though, the basic problem is man's relationship with God.

The views discussed in this section assume not only that there is a breach between man and God, but that this breach is unnatural and has been caused by man. Specifically, it has been caused by man's sin against the will and law of God as personal Creator and Law-giver. This is contrary to most of the views already discussed, which see man's problem as something arising not out of his own choice but out of his very nature or being (e.g., ignorance, finitude) or out of the circumstances in which he finds himself (e.g., victimized by unjust social structures). In these other views, when sin is discussed at all, it is usually redefined or even figuratively applied. Most significantly, it is never seen primarily as a breach between God and man. Even when salvation includes the notion of being forgiven of one's sins by the deity (as in *bhakti* Hinduism and True Pure Land Buddhism), the sins are not sins committed against the deity himself.

Thus the two views to be discussed here are quite different from anything dealt with thus far. And it is no accident that both of these views have originated from within the context of Biblical religion and have a doctrine of God ultimately derived from Biblical revelation: the God of Abraham, the personal Creator and Law-giver of the Old Testament. These two views are Judaism and Islam.[254]

Judaism

First to be discussed is Judaism, which must be distinguished from Old Testament religion as such. Although the Old Testament is still the sacred book for serious Jews, its religious teachings can be fully appreciated and understood only in the light of New Testament revelation. Because the latter is rejected by Judaism, its understanding of the Old Testament itself will at worst be distorted and at best be incomplete. Its doctrine of salvation in particular suffers significantly because of this. Also, much of the doctrinal content of Judaism is derived not from the Old Testament but from rabbinical tradition as recorded in such writings as the Midrash and the Talmud.

---

254. Noss says that Muhammad "relied heavily upon Jewish and Christian tradition for his conception of the relation of God to men," but still he gave Allah "an Arabian character and personality" (John B. Noss, *Man's Religions* [New York: Macmillan, 1949], p. 709).

We may distinguish also between two separate aspects of Judaism's concept of salvation, the national and the personal. The national hope was especially strong in the intertestamental period after the Jews had come under Roman rule. This hope was drawn from Old Testament examples and promises of a deliverer to be sent by God to rescue his people from bondage. Many of the Jews interpreted this to mean that a messiah would come and deliver them from Roman oppression and set up an earthly kingdom in which the Jews would be favored. Thus their national salvation "belonged to the age to come, when God's Messiah had arisen, driven the Romans from the Holy Land, and ruled in peace and justice from Jerusalem. This, of course, was the characteristic messianic belief . . . of first-century Palestine." It was shared by Pharisees, Essenes and Zealots alike, the Sadducees being an exception.[255]

Our main concern here, however, is the Judaistic concept of personal salvation. As was already pointed out in the introduction to this section, Judaism understands man's problem to be separation or alienation from God, caused by his own sin. Its glory is the Torah, God's holy law given to man. As long as the Torah is obeyed, man remains in fellowship with God. But when the law is violated, sinful man becomes estranged from God and is no longer worthy of fellowship.

For the Jew, then, the saved state is fellowship with God or acceptance by God. For the sinner it means the forgiveness of sins and a reinstatement in God's favor. The main concern is knowing that one's present relationship with God is in good order. "Salvation, in its eschatological sense of deliverance from punishment or assurance of eternal life hereafter, means less to the Jew than to some others."[256]

By what means does the Jew hope to be accepted by God? "The chief stress is laid upon works," as Joseph says.[257] This is true in two ways. First, "the chief, practically the sole, way to divine acceptance lies through obedience," and second, "in the case of sin, through repentance."[258] Regarding this first idea, a man tries to keep himself in God's

---

255. E. M. B. Green, *The Meaning of Salvation* (Philadelphia: Westminster Press, 1965), p. 71. See the entire discussion, pp. 55ff.

256. Morris Joseph, "Salvation (Jewish)," *Encyclopedia of Religion and Ethics*, ed. James Hastings (New York: Charles Scribner's Sons, 1921), XI:138.

257. Ibid., p. 140.

258. Ibid.

favor by obeying the law. In this sense the law or Torah itself is an aid to salvation because it shows one how to earn God's good will. "The guarantee of salvation" lies in "the obedient and devout life."[259] Green shows that this idea arose as early as the second century B.C. with "the beginning of the Jewish doctrine of merit, the idea that if you kept the Law, you could put God in your debt." He points out how "good works are taught as the way of salvation" in the Apocrypha.[260] Joseph says, "This life, with all its strenuous, health-giving activities," is "man's one sure chance of justifying himself, of redeeming himself, in God's sight. So he must take this life and make it as good as he can. If he is to be 'saved' hereafter, he must save himself here—save himself by living the worldly life in worthy fashion."[261] Some Jews have accepted the idea of a treasury of merit whereby the extra merits of the fathers (e.g., Abraham, Isaac, Jacob) might be transferred to one's own account. Ordinarily, however, says Joseph, the Jew is reluctant to put his trust in this ancestral merit; "all the time he has felt, and known, that his moral salvation was, in the last resort, mainly, if not exclusively, dependent upon himself."[262] "We are thrown back, then, upon works as the essential condition of salvation."[263]

But what happens when a man sins, as he always does? Then, as Green says, he "is cast back upon God's mercy as the real ground of his confidence. God is . . . 'the gracious one'. He will save."[264] But how does one win God's mercy and forgiveness? As stated above, by repentance. It must be noted, however, that repentance itself "is essentially good works; it is a change of temper issuing in the changed, the reformed, life."[265] This includes works of penance for one's sins, and it also includes suffering and tribulation. "Tribulation, too, is an aid to expiation"; it atones for sin. And since death is the supreme tribulation, it "expiates every sin."[266] Thus even in forgiveness the emphasis is on

---

259. Ibid., p. 141.
260. E. M. B. Green, *The Meaning of Salvation*, p. 64.
261. Morris Joseph, "Salvation (Jewish)," p. 138.
262. Ibid., pp. 144-145.
263. Ibid., p. 143.
264. E. M. B. Green, *The Meaning of Salvation*, p. 64.
265. Morris Joseph, "Salvation (Jewish)," p. 143.
266. Ibid., p. 144.

man's works; he must deserve to be forgiven. As Joseph says,[267]

> . . . The divine grace plays a certain part in it, but the chief part, by common consent, is performed by the man himself. In the case of sin—and all men are sinners in various degree—expiation by repentance and suffering is the condition precedent to acceptance by God; and if that essential condition is satisfied, forgiveness and reconciliation follow as a matter of course. . . .

It is said here that grace plays a part in man's salvation, and that must be acknowledged. It is "the one external saving power," the crown of all other means of salvation.[268] Grace helps the sinner to repent, and grace leads to God's "acceptance of repentance as the sinner's expiation."[269] Whatever man cannot do on his own, grace makes up the difference. "Crowning all the means of salvation, and completing their effectiveness, is the divine mercy, which compensates for human deficiencies and supplements human merits."[270] Here is where faith plays a part, since we must believe that there is a God and that he will forgive as promised.

But works and repentance are still the key to salvation; "the good life is the one saving force, according to Judaism."[271] As already noted above, man is mainly if not exclusively dependent upon himself. Grace plays a part, but the chief part is that of man. "No superhuman ally is needed by the atoning soul. The forces in the sinner's own breast suffice. If they are marshalled in their full strength, they are all-powerful. . . . For the Jew contrition, supplication, and more important still, the contrite life suffice for salvation."[272]

Thus in Judaism there is a great advance over the views considered earlier with regard to a proper understanding of the problem from which man needs salvation, but there is very little advance with regard to the means of receiving salvation. The grace of God is acknowledged and invoked, but is compromised by the notion that man must perform works

---

267. Ibid., p. 138.
268. Ibid., p. 146.
269. Ibid., pp. 138, 146.
270. Ibid., p. 146.
271. Ibid., p. 142.
272. Ibid., p. 138.

that make him worthy of that grace.

Islam

The last alternative to redemption to be discussed here is Islam's view of salvation. Some wonder whether this religion even has such a doctrine. If so, "the idea of redemption is certainly not a central one in Islam" and "is, on the whole, quite alien to the Qur'an." One possible reason is the idea that by just being a member of the Muslim community one attains salvation. Another possibility is the thought that man's in-born religiousness makes salvation so easy. Whatever the reason, says Lazarus-Yafeh, "it seems that Islam . . . felt no need for redemption and therefore did not develop this notion." Whatever references there are must be "marginal, transitory and certainly not essential to Islam."[273]

This view is probably a bit extreme; for even though the word itself does not occur with frequency, the Muslim does see a difference between being saved and being lost. There is something to be saved from, and something to be saved to. The idea is definitely there.

Concerning that from which man needs to be saved, the Muslim believes wholeheartedly in sin, the wrath of Allah, and eternal punishment for the lost. He believes in a sovereign, personal God who has revealed his law to mankind. When man sins and disobeys that law, separation from God ensues.[274] He becomes guilty and liable to punishment. If he dies unsaved, he suffers the tortures of hell forever. The Koran (or Qur'an) describes their fate thus:[275]

> . . . And they who believe not, shall have garments of fire fitted unto them: boiling water shall be poured on their heads; their bowels shall be dissolved thereby, and also their skins; and they shall be beaten with maces of iron. So often as they shall endeavour to get out of hell, because of the anguish of their torments, they shall be dragged back into the same; and their tormentors shall say unto them, Taste ye the pain of burning (22:20-21).

---

273. Hava Lazarus-Yafeh, "Is There a Concept of Redemption in Islam?", *Types of Redemption*, ed. R. J. Zwi Werblowsky and C. J. Bleeker (Leiden: E. J. Brill, 1970), pp. 168, 172, 180.

274. Hasan Askari, "Unity and Alienation in Islam," *Living Faiths and Ultimate Goals*, ed. S. J. Samartha (Geneva: World Council of Chuches, 1974), p. 51.

275. Citations from the Koran are from the translation by George Sale (London: Frederick Warne and Co., 1890). Sale provides no verse divisions.

The emphasis on the after-life is very strong in Islam, and thus the concept of salvation is quite other-worldly. Because the basic problem is sin against Allah, the basic element in salvation is forgiveness and acceptance by him. Sin is understood more in terms of a legal offense than an inner corruption; thus its main effect is to consign the soul to hell. Salvation from sin, then, is mainly salvation from post-mortem punishment. As Sell says, "Thus it is not so much escape from the power of sin in this life as escape from its punishment hereafter that is implied in the term 'salvation.'"[276] On the positive side, of course, this means access to heaven, which is seen as a paradise filled with physical comforts and bliss. Here is just one of the many descriptions given by the Koran:

> . . . As to those who believe and do good works, we will not suffer the reward of him who shall work righteousness to perish: for them are prepared gardens of eternal abode, which shall be watered by rivers; they shall be adorned therein with bracelets of gold, and shall be clothed in green garments of fine silk and brocades; reposing themselves therein on thrones. O how happy a reward, and how easy a couch! (18:29-30)

The most important question is how one can attain to such a reward. The answer is that a person receives it by a combination of faith and works, as the first line in the previous quotation says: it is for "those who believe and do good works." Faith is first and most important. God has had mercy on man in his ignorance and has sent him a series of prophets, culminating in Muhammad, to instruct and guide him. Thus man's foremost responsibility is to accept God and his prophets (especially Muhammad) and their teaching (especially the Koran). The one absolutely essential confession of faith is "There is no God but Allah, and Muhammad is his prophet." Failure to believe in Allah and Allah alone is the one unforgivable sin. A Muslim who does believe may commit all sorts of sins and be cast into hell because of them, but he will not have to stay there eternally. For him it is only a kind of purgatory; sooner or later he will be declared fit for heaven and ushered into it. Thus "no Moslem is ultimately lost."[277] The result is, as Brandon says,

---

276. Edward Sell, "Salvation (Muslim)," *Encyclopedia of Religion and Ethics*, ed. James Hastings (New York: Charles Scribner's Sons, 1921), XI:149.
277. Ibid.; see also Charles S. Braden, *Man's Quest for Salvation*, p. 232.

that Islam "has made a proper faith in God, rather than moral virtue, the supreme criterion for salvation at the Last Judgment."[278]

At the same time no Muslim wants to go to Hell, even for a temporary period. Hence he is concerned with how to go directly to heaven. Here is where works become necessary in addition to faith. He must perfect his faith by his works. "Man is to be saved by his own works."[279] The emphasis falls on ritual works rather than everyday moral conduct. The five main requirements (called the five pillars of Islam) are (1) reciting the confession of faith; (2) praying five daily prayers; (3) fasting, especially during Ramadan; (4) giving the required alms; and (5) making a pilgrimage to Mecca. "The pilgrimage to Mecca is a sure means of salvation," says Sell.[280] Another sure means, though not a requirement, is being slain as a martyr in battle for Islam.[281] All works earn merits or demerits, and "at the judgment every man stands on his own merits before Allah."[282]

The Muslim concept of the final judgment includes a great balance scales in which merits and demerits are weighed against one another. If the good deeds are heavier, the individual goes to Paradise; if the evil deeds are heavier, he goes to Hell. Realizing their shortcomings, many Muslims say extra prayers and make extra pilgrimages just to earn extra merit, in hopes of accumulating enough to tip the scales in their favor at least 50.1%. "And the doing of these deeds is very meritorious. In the day of judgment they will be weighed in God's balance and will help to cancel the evil deeds which are placed in the other pan of the balance."[283] In this way, says Miller, a person is "required to earn God's favor and forgiveness by works of merit."[284]

There is still one catch to all of this, and that is the fact that Islam is a deterministic religion.[285] Even the one who has believed and done

---

278. S. G. F. Brandon. *The Judgment of the Dead.* p. 148.

279. Edward Sell, "Salvation (Muslim)." p. 149.

280. Ibid.

281. William McElwee Miller, *A Christian's Response to Islam* (Nutley, N.J.: Presbyterian and Reformed, 1977), p. 56.

282. Charles S. Braden, *Man's Quest for Salvation.* p. 242.

283. William Miller, *A Christian's Response to Islam,* pp. 57, 82; S. G. F. Brandon, *The Judgment of the Dead,* p. 141.

284. William Miller, *A Christian's Response to Islam,* p. 85.

285. See Jack Cottrell, *What the Bible Says About God the Ruler* (Joplin, Mo: College Press, 1984), pp. 69-71.

good works can never be sure what God will decide in his case, "as it depends ultimately on the arbitrary decree of God concerning him."[286] Since the final decision is arbitrary, one "can only hope for the mercy of God, hope that the angels or the Prophet will intercede for him in the last day, and he will be saved from hell."[287]

Nevertheless a person must proceed as if it were all up to him. After receiving initial guidance from God via the Koran, he must do his best to work out his own salvation. No savior is needed or provided. Muhammad is rarely referred to as Savior, and even then his role is that of a teacher or revealer.[288] Jesus is considered a great prophet (though now superseded by Muhammad), but not a Redeemer.[289]

In the final analysis the Muslim notion of salvation boils down to this, according to Miller: "Believe in God and in his Apostle Muhammad, and do what God requires, and if God so wills he will accept you."[290] Braden gives this summary: "Moslem salvation may be characterized in the main as otherworldly, with escape from hell and the eternal bliss of paradise as the final goal. The method of attaining it is in orthodox Islam a combination of faith and works."[291]

CONCLUSION

Outside the sphere of revelation, one's conception of the nature of man's primary predicament dictates the conception of salvation (and often the conception of God). It seems that the basic problem is usually described in one of three ways (or in a combination thereof): as ignorance, as weakness, or as sin. Usually this is limited to the first two. Within the sphere of revelation, the third one becomes prominent.

In our survey of the alternatives to redemption we have found a number of world views that diagnose man's basic problem as ignorance. This was seen to be the case with classical Hinduism and Buddhism and with Gnosticism, for example. We have also found some world views

---

286. Edward Sell, "Salvation (Muslim)," p. 149.
287. William Miller, *A Christian's Response to Islam*, p. 83.
288. Ibid., pp. 80, 82.
289. Hava Lazarus-Yafeh, "Is There a Concept of Redemption in Islam?", pp. 171-172.
290. William Miller, *A Christian's Response to Islam*, p. 81.
291. Charles S. Braden, *Man's Quest for Salvation*, p. 225.

that see the problem as some kind of ontological weakness. An example is Egyptian religion, where death itself was the obstacle; another is Existentialism, which focuses on man's finitude. Sometimes there is a combination of ignorance and weakness. Christian Liberalism might be cited as an example, the weakness stemming from man's evolutionary past and contributing to the ignorance.

In such concepts of salvation, if God has any role at all, that role is to provide *knowledge* to offset the ignorance and *power* to dispel the weakness. Sometimes a mediator between God and man is posited, but usually not. Gnosticism is an example that involves a mediator (to bring the necessary knowledge), but it should be emphasized that the necessity for such a mediator is ontological rather than ethical. I.e., it was not man's sins that separated man from God, but the material world itself. It was not sin but mere matter that repelled the supreme deity and caused him to send a representative. Another example of a system with a mediator is Liberalism, which of course sees Jesus of Nazareth in this role. He came to provide knowledge through his teaching and example, and to provide power for holy living also through his example of service and sacrifice.

The one thing missing in all these views is a solid conception of sin. For example, Murti says of Hinduism that it has a consciousness of suffering and pain where Christianity and Judaism have a corresponding consciousness of sin.[292] Zaehner agrees, saying that Hinduism speaks of salvation "not from moral guilt but from the human condition as such."[293] In Egypt the death problem was physical only, and not a spiritual death that separates one from God. For the Existentialist, man's flaw is not moral but ontological.[294] Brown notes, "Gnosticism places the source of evil in the order of nature, i.e., in the materiality of bodily existence, not in the moral order."[295]

As this statement shows, some will use the term *evil* but not *sin*. For example, speaking of Secular Theology, Todrank speaks freely of "salvation from evil," with evil being defined as anything that obstructs or destroys the salvation process. But sin is another thing altogether.

---

292. T. R. V. Murti, "The Concept of Freedom," p. 214.
293. R. C. Zaehner, *Hinduism*, p. 138.
294. John Macquarrie, *Existentialism*, p. 159.
295. Harold O. J. Brown, *Heresies*, p. 60.

The Christian church, he says, through the ages "has been neurotically preoccupied with sin." He suggests that anyone who would commit a sinful act (as he defines it) would have to be psychologically ill, and thus there really is no sin for which anyone is morally responsible.[296]

Still others will use the word *sin*, but will simply redefine it. For example, Ishizu says that for Buddhism sin is not sin committed toward a personal God, whose wrath it arouses. Sin is seen as simply not fully understanding the non-existence of the self; it is ignorance of the true nature of existence; it is basically illusion.[297]

Without a properly defined doctrine of sin, no world view will ever be able to formulate a concept of salvation that is true or that will meet man's true needs. Such philosophies and religions may speak of some type of salvation, but they can never speak of redemption, nor can they provide a Redeemer.

But some of the groups surveyed here do speak of sin and make this one of the main problems if not *the* main problem which stands between man and salvation. This usually makes a significant difference in the way these groups think about salvation and about God's role in it. However, as has already been seen above, just the fact that someone uses the term *sin* does not mean that he is using it in the Biblical sense. Even when sin is thought of as a moral wrong that comes from the heart of man, it still is not sin in the full sense of the word unless it is seen as sin *against God*, as a violation of the will of a personal God and an offense against him. Unfortunately, several of the world views that think of man as sinner do not think of him as sinning against God. This is true of *bhakti* Hinduism and True Pure Land Buddhism. Sins may be committed against oneself or against other people, but not against God. Buddhism does not even have a clear concept of God. Amida Buddha, who offers forgiveness for sins, is not the one sinned against, nor is he a mediator between the sinner and the offended one. In neither case do we find divine holiness violated, a sense of divine wrath, or any need for atonement or reconciliation between God and man. Both religions do have savior-figures who offer forgiveness, but the question is, what right do they have to make such an offer? And even if they do have the right,

---

296. Gustave Todrank, *The Secular Search*, pp. 148, 151-152.
297. Teruji Ishizu, "The Basis of the Idea of Redemption," p. 95.

on what basis is such forgiveness provided? Can one man's (Amida's) extra good works—even if he might have any—truly make up for someone else's sins?

Similar criticisms might be offered against the three Christian movements discussed here, Liberalism, Secular Theology and Liberation Theology. As we saw, for these groups sin is basically against other people and only indirectly against God. It is also a part of the impersonal societal structures in which we exist. Thus there is a noticeable lack of emphasis on the wrath of God and no true atonement. Jesus is Revealer, not Redeemer.

But when we come to Judaism and Islam, we do seem to find concepts of sin that are more consistent with the Biblical teaching. They do seem to view sin as an offense against God, requiring his forgiveness. But still they do not have a sound view of redemption. Why not? Because in addition to a proper view of sin, one must have a proper view of God fully to understand what is required to forgive man's sins and reinstitute fellowship between God and man. And these religious groups, whose view of God is basically sound in so many ways, still lack a full understanding of the wrath of God and especially of his grace.

What we are saying here is that there are two keys to a sound understanding of redemption. First, one must have a proper view of sin, namely, as an offense against God himself. It must be seen as a breaking of the law of God, who himself must be seen as one who had the right to lay down such a law in the first place and has the right to hold man responsible for breaking it. Such a view of sin and law are possible only if this world and man have been created *ex nihilo* by an omnipotent and sovereign God. This is one of the main reasons why a proper view of redemption will not be found outside the circle of Biblical revelation, namely, because there is no understanding of *ex nihilo* creation outside this circle.[298]

The second key to a sound understanding of redemption is a proper view of the nature of God himself, particularly a right understanding of his wrath and his grace. Without a proper perception of the wrath of God as an essential aspect of his holiness, the role and work of Jesus

---

298. See Jack Cottrell, *What the Bible Says About God the Creator*, chs. two and three, and pp. 163ff.

will never be correctly understood. Only when we see the meaning of the wrath of God will we see why a Mediator between God and sinful man is required. Man's need for a Mediator is based neither in metaphysics nor in epistemology; neither our weakness nor our ignorance *required* a Mediator. It is sin alone, understood as an offense against God, that made the mediation of Christ necessary. Because of our sins we are the objects of God's holy wrath; it is his *wrath* that requires the Mediator.

At the same time, we must have a proper perception of the grace of God as an essential aspect of his love in order to understand the nature of Christ's redemptive work. We must see that only the *grace* of God could provide the Mediator. The wrath of God requires it, and his grace provides it. Only within this framework can we understand what it means to say that God is our *Redeemer*. Without this, men and philosophies and religions may continue to speak of salvation, but they cannot properly speak of redemption. Nor can they properly speak of salvation by grace through faith. As we have seen, most of them do not even attempt to do so, but quite openly make salvation a matter of man's own works. Those who do speak of grace, notably *bhakti* Hinduism and True Pure Land Buddhism, do not have any basis for doing so because they have no true Mediator in the sense of a Sin-bearer.

Indeed, all the views of salvation discussed in this chapter are truly *alternatives* to redemption; they are not authentic concepts of redemption. Such is found only in Biblical Christianity. Only the God of the Bible, the God of Abraham and the God of our Lord Jesus Christ, is a Redeemer.

3

THE TRINITY

Why should the doctrine of the Trinity be dealt with at this point? Why was it not discussed in the volume on creation, or the one on providence? Because the trinitarian nature of God becomes relevant and becomes known to us only in relation to God's work of redemption. Of course, all three persons of the divine nature were involved in the pre-redemptive works of creation and providence, but it was not necessary for God to explain his threeness until the work of redemption itself was accomplished. This is because the three persons of the Trinity are not equally involved in the work, or works, of redemption. Only God the Son becomes incarnate and accomplishes that for which human nature is required. Only God the Spirit is poured out on Pentecost to be the regenerating and sanctifying power within God's people. Along with this "division of labor" related to the redeeming process comes the unfolding knowledge of the fact of the Trinity.

Others have tried to ground our knowledge of the Trinity in different aspects of God's nature or works. Augustine said that an analysis of the fact that God is love should lead to trinitarian conclusions, for love requires a lover, a loved one, and love itself.[1] R. C. Neville suggests that creation can provide a general model for interpreting the Trinity.[2] Karl Barth says that the Trinity is known through an analysis of the fact of revelation itself, in which, he says, there are three aspects: the One who reveals, the act or manner of his revealing, and the result of his revealing. Thus we have the Revealer, the Revelation, and the Revealedness.[3]

All efforts to derive the Trinity from anything but the work of redemption are speculative, however. Warfield is surely correct in saying that "the revelation of the Trinity was incidental to, and the inevitable effect of, the accomplishment of redemption." That is, it was the redemptive work itself that made the Trinity known: the incarnation of God the Son and the outpouring of the Holy Spirit. The word revelation alluding to and explaining the Trinity follows naturally and necessarily upon the work itself.[4] He continues,[5]

> . . . The doctrine of the Trinity, in other words, is simply the modification wrought in the conception of the one only God by His complete revelation of Himself in the redemptive process. It necessarily waited, therefore, upon the completion of the redemptive process for its revelation, and its revelation, as necessarily, lay complete in the redemptive process.

A concept implicit in the above discussion is that the fact of the Trinity can be known only through special revelation. It is not available through general revelation, through rational speculation, or through religious experience. Religious liberalism, having repudiated word revelation, refers often to the so-called original "Trinity of experience" which was displaced by the "Trinity of speculation" in the third and fourth centuries of the Christian era. The idea is that the earliest

---

1. Augustine, "On the Trinity," VIII.x. See B. B. Warfield, "The Biblical Doctrine of the Trinity," *Biblical and Theological Studies*, by B. B. Warfield, ed. Samuel G. Craig (Nutley, N.J.: Presbyterian and Reformed, 1952), pp. 25-26.

2. Robert C. Neville, "Creation and the Trinity," *Theological Studies* (1969), 30:3ff.; see Edmund J. Fortman, *The Triune God: A Historical Study of the Doctrine of the Trinity* (Grand Rapids: Baker Book House, 1982), p. 289.

3. Karl Barth, *Church Dogmatics. Volume I: The Doctrine of the Word of God. Part 1*, tr. G. T. Thomson (Edinburgh: T. & T. Clark, 1936), pp. 339-340.

4. B. B. Warfield, "The Biblical Doctrine of the Trinity," p. 33.

5. Ibid.

disciples experienced God in a three-fold way, which caused them to think of God as a three-fold being. This reconstruction of the origin of trinitarian thinking is itself speculation, however, and its usual purpose is to give credence to a modalistic concept of the Trinity, the inadequacy of which will be shown below. The fact remains that special revelation alone can account for the only concept of the Trinity that is worthy of the name and that sets Christianity apart from the other religious systems of the world.

Many have tried to undermine the uniqueness of Christianity by discerning so-called trinities or triads in pagan religions and secular philosophies. For example, William Fulton cites the triune grouping of Brahma, Siva and Visnu in Hinduism; that of Osiris, Isis and Horus in Egyptian religion; Plotinus' One, One-Many and One-and-Many; and Comte's Great Being, Great Medium and Great Fetish.[6] Albert Knudson lists some others, such as Anu, Enlil and Ea among the Sumerians; Sin, Shamash and Ishtar among the Babylonians; and Uranos, Kronos and Zeus among the Romans. But he rightly says that all of these differ radically from the Christian Trinity; any resemblance is superficial.[7] Buswell emphatically agrees: "There is only one Triune God among all the religions of the world. Indeed there are triads everywhere to be found, but these many instances of threeness and oneness are not logically comparable in any true sense with the doctrine of the Trinity."[8]

Some object to the doctrine of the Trinity as such simply because the term *trinity* is not found in the Bible. It is true that there is no Biblical word corresponding to the English word *trinity*. In the King James Version the term *Godhead* appears three times, in Acts 17:29, Romans 1:20, and Colossians 2:9. Some associate this word with the concept of the Trinity, but without warrant. It never has the connotation of Trinity. In Acts 17:29 it translates *theios*, an adjective meaning "divine." It is used without a noun and means simply "the divine one, the deity." In

---

6. William Fulton, "Trinity," *Encyclopedia of Religion and Ethics*, ed. James Hastings (New York: Charles Scribner's Sons, 1922), XII:458.

7. Albert C. Knudson, *The Doctrine of God* (Nashville: Abingdon-Cokesbury Press, 1930), pp. 370-371. Warfield agrees: "None of these triads has the slightest resemblance to the Christian doctrine of the Trinity" ("The Biblical Doctrine of the Trinity," p. 23).

8. James Oliver Buswell, Jr., *A Systematic Theology of the Christian Religion* (Grand Rapids: Zondervan, 1962), I:102.

Romans 1:20 it translates *theiotēs,* which is the noun form of the above adjective and means "divine being, deity." In Colossians 2:9 the word is *theotēs,* a noun derived from *theos* ("God") meaning "deity, divinity, divine nature." The earliest uses of the actual words for "Trinity" occur in the latter part if the second century, when Theophilus uses the Greek term and Tertullian uses the Latin term.[9]

Thus we acknowledge that the actual term is a post-Biblical word. This does not mean that the *concept* of the Trinity is not to be found in Scripture, however. I affirm with Warfield that it is a "genuinely Scriptural doctrine." As he puts it, "The doctrine of the Trinity lies in Scripture in solution; when it is crystallized from its solvent it does not cease to be Scriptural, but only comes into clearer view."[10] In this chapter we are seeking to do just that, i.e., bring the doctrine of the Trinity into clearer view.

THE REVELATION OF GOD'S THREENESS

When we say that the Trinity is known to us only in relation to God's redemptive work, this in itself directs our attention to the New Testament as the primary source for our knowledge of this doctrine. While the Old Testament provides some hints that are consistent with trinitarian thought, we would never come to this conclusion if the Old Testament were our sole source of knowledge of God. As Warfield says, "It is a plain matter of fact that none who have depended on the revelation embodied in the Old Testament alone have ever attained to the doctrine of the Trinity."[11] Thus if we are to uncover the Biblical data on this matter, we must begin with the New Testament.

The Deity of Christ in the New Testament

The one specific fact that makes it impossible for us to avoid the doctrine of the Trinity is the New Testament teaching on the deity of Christ.

---

9. Theophilus, "To Autolycus," II:15, tr. Marcus Dods, *The Ante-Nicene Fathers,* ed. Alexander Roberts and James Donaldson (New York: Charles Scribner's Sons, 1913), II:101; and Tertullian, "Against Praxeas," II, tr. Peter Holmes, *The Ante-Nicene Fathers,* ed. Alexander Roberts and James Donaldson (New York: Charles Scribner's Sons, 1908), III:598. The work by Tertullian is the first work devoted to the doctrine of the Trinity.
10. B. B. Warfield, "The Biblical Doctrine of the Trinity," p. 22.
11. Ibid., p. 29.

If Scripture did not portray Jesus of Nazareth as God in the flesh, the question of the Trinity would never have arisen. The same is true to a lesser extent of its portrayal of the Holy Spirit as a divine person. Thus if anyone wants to know where the Bible says anything about a Trinity, this is it: "the whole mass of evidence which the New Testament provides of the Deity of Christ and the Divine personality of the Holy Spirit." In a word, "Jesus Christ and the Holy Spirit are the fundamental proof of the doctrine of the Trinity."[12]

In this section we will survey the New Testament's teaching on Christ's deity.

Divine Titles

First of all, several of the titles ascribed to Jesus in the New Testament imply his deity. Perhaps the most significant of these is the title "Lord" (*Kurios* in Greek), which is used for Jesus almost five hundred times. This was a common title for pagan deities,[13] but more important is its relation to Old Testament usage. In most extant manuscripts of the Septuagint (the Greek Old Testament), *kurios* is the word which appears in place of Yahweh, the divine name itself. (Some manuscripts retain the four Hebrew letters of the name, YHWH.) This means that the title "Lord" is used over six thousand times in reference to Yahweh, and never for pagan deities and idols. Thus any Jew who knew his Old Testament in its Septuagint form would have associated this title immediately with the one true God. This is certainly the case with the Apostle Paul and other New Testament writers, who frequently quote from the Septuagint version of the Old Testament.

It is significant, then, that the New Testament writers use this title so frequently – in Paul's case almost exclusively – for Jesus. There is no way that they could have applied this title to Christ in its religious sense without in their minds identifying him with Yahweh. When the early Christians confessed "Jesus is Lord" (Romans 10:9; I Cor. 12:3), they were confessing belief in his deity. As Wainwright says, "There are indications that Christians consciously transferred the title from God to Christ in such a way as to suggest that Christ was almost identical with

---

12. Ibid., p. 35.
13. Arthur W. Wainwright, *The Trinity in the New Testament* (London: S.P.C.K., 1962), p. 77.

God."[14]

Another title with divine implications is "Son of Man." Though many throughout Christian history have used this title to represent the human nature of Jesus (in tandem with "Son of God" to represent his divine nature), in all probability it points to Jesus' deity. This is said in view of the content usually given to this title in New Testament times. The apocryphal Book of Enoch applies it to a supernatural, heavenly figure who judges men and angels on the day of judgment. Daniel 7:13-14 depicts the Son of Man as a heavenly figure appearing before the throne of the Ancient of Days to receive an eternal kingdom and universal worship. Thus it was used as a title of transcendent, divine glory. Significantly, this is the title Jesus applies most often to himself. When he does so, as Stauffer says, he "claims for himself all the heavenly majesty of this Son of Man," since this "is just about the most pretentious piece of self-description that any man in the ancient East could possibly have used!"[15] Vos calls this the "greatest and most celestial of all titles."[16] Cullmann agrees that "the statement 'Jesus is the Son of Man' is primarily an exalted declaration of majesty, not a title of humiliation."[17]

One other title with divine content is "Son of God." In pagan circles this was a common title for deities,[18] but again the most significant factor is the way the Jews themselves understood this expression. On two occasions when Jesus referred to God as his Father, the Jews accused him of blasphemy and wanted to kill him, because he "was calling God His own Father, making Himself equal with God" (John 5:18; see John 10:33, 36). In neither case did Jesus deny his identity as Son of God, nor did he object to equating this with a claim to deity. At his trial he was asked, "Are You the Son of God, then?" his answer was affirmative (Luke 22:70). Again he was accused of blasphemy and thought worthy of death, as the Jews said to Pilate, "We have a law, and by that law He

14. Ibid., p. 89.
15. Ethelbert Stauffer, *New Testament Theology*, tr. John Marsh (London: SCM Press, 1955), pp. 108-109.
16. Geerhardus Vos, *The Self-Disclosure of Jesus*, ed. Johannes Vos (Grand Rapids: Eerdmans, 1954), p. 254.
17. Oscar Cullmann, *The Christology of the New Testament*, revised ed., tr. Shirley C. Guthrie and Charles A. M. Hall (Philadelphia: Westminster Press, 1959), p. 177.
18. A. W. Wainwright, *The Trinity in the New Testament*, p. 173.

ought to die because He made Himself out to be the Son of God" (John 19:7). It is apparent from incidents such as these that Jesus' reference to himself as the Son of God was taken to be a claim to deity. Such was the content of this title. As Wainwright says, "Of all the titles which describe Jesus' interaction with God, 'Son of God' is best fitted to express the idea of Jesus' divinity."[19]

Jesus is Lord; Jesus is the Son of Man; Jesus is the Son of God. Each of these titles in its own way testifies to the divine nature of Jesus Christ.

Divine Works

In the New Testament Jesus is described as performing works that only God has the power or prerogative to do. He is seen first of all as Creator of the universe. Colossians 1:16 says, "For by Him all things were created . . . all things have been created by Him and for Him." John 1:3 says of the Logos who became incarnate in Jesus of Nazareth, "All things came into being by Him; and apart from Him nothing came into being that has come into being." First Corinthians 8:6 and Hebrews 1:2 tell us the same thing. What is the point of these passages? Nothing less than to identify Jesus as the Creator, as God himself.[20]

Scripture also attributes the work of providence to Jesus. Colossians 1:17 says that "in Him all things hold together." Hebrews 1:3 says he "upholds all things by the word of His power." Such a work as this, i.e., preserving in existence all that has been created from nothing, is a work of which only the Sovereign Creator is capable. Jesus is thus identified as divine.

Salvation, too, is a divine work; and this work is attributed to Jesus. We have already noted in the first chapter how he is called "Savior" sixteen times in the New Testament. Of special significance is his authority to forgive sins (Mark 2:10), a claim the Jews equated with blasphemy, for "who can forgive sins but God alone?" (Mark 2:7). Jesus never denied that this was something that only God has the authority to do; he just performed a miracle to show that he had such divine authority.

The works of creation, providence and salvation are truly the works

---

19. Ibid., p. 172.

20. See Jack Cottrell, *What the Bible Says About God the Creator* (Joplin, Mo.: College Press, 1983), pp. 138-139, 184.

of God, but they are works in which Jesus shares. This can only mean that he himself is God.

He Is Called God

A third line of evidence concerning the deity of Christ is the fact that he is specifically called God in several New Testament passages. All of these are disputed in one way or another by those who deny Christ's deity, of course, but the best exegesis shows that they refer to Jesus and testify to his divine nature. The first is John 1:1, "In the beginning was the Word, and the Word was with God, and the Word was God." The Word (*Logos*) is identified with Jesus in verse 14, establishing his divinity. Efforts to limit the last clause in John 1:1 to something less than full deity destroy themselves against the requirements of Greek grammar, especially Colwell's Rule.[21]

Another passage is John 20:28, where Thomas, upon seeing the risen Christ for the first time, exclaims, "My Lord and my God!" This would be the most blatant blasphemy if Jesus were not indeed God, and Jesus himself would be guilty of it for not immediately rejecting such ascriptions. But Jesus does not rebuke Thomas; instead he commends all those who would come to share this conviction.

Another passage in the Johannine literature is I John 5:20, "And we know that the Son of God has come, and has given us understanding, in order that we might know Him who is true, and we are in Him who is true, in His Son Jesus Christ. This is the true God and eternal life." Who is here being called "true God"? The nearest antecedent to the demonstrative pronoun ("this," *houtos*) is "His Son Jesus Christ," who is also identified as "eternal life" here and in I John 1:2. Jesus is the true God.

In Romans 9:5 the Apostle Paul concludes a list of the privileges accorded the Jews with a doxological blessing: "Whose are the fathers, and from whom is the Christ according to the flesh, who is over all, God blessed forever. Amen." Some try to place a period either after "flesh" or after "over all," thus making the doxology a separate statement referring to God the Father rather than to Christ. Bruce Metzger has shown

---

21. E. C. Colwell, "A Definite Rule for the Use of the Article in the Greek New Testament," *Journal of Biblical Literature* (January 1933), 52:13. See Edmond C. Gruss, *Apostles of Denial* (Grand Rapids: Baker Book House, 1970), pp. 115-119.

that such efforts do not succeed,[22] and that the translation above is true to the original intention of Paul. Jesus Christ himself is the one who is "God blessed forever."

Other passages referring directly to Jesus as God are Titus 2:13, "Looking for the blessed hope and the appearing of the glory of our great God and Savior, Christ Jesus"; Hebrews 1:8, "But of the Son He says, 'Thy throne, O God, is forever and ever'"; and II Peter 1:1, which refers to "the righteousness of our God and Savior, Jesus Christ."

Equality with God

Many other passages do not specifically refer to Jesus as God, but in just as forceful a way ascribe to him full equality with God. John 5:23 is such a passage. Here Jesus himself says that the Father has given all judgment to the Son, "in order that all may honor the Son, even as they honor the Father." The key words are "even as" (*kathōs*), which indicate that the Son is to receive equal honor with the Father.

Another passage that should be noted is Galatians 1:1, "Paul, an apostle (not sent from men, nor through the agency of man, but through Jesus Christ, and God the Father, who raised Him from the dead)." Here Paul clearly distinguishes Jesus from the category of men and at the same time coordinates him with God the Father as the source of his apostleship. The fact that there is only one preposition makes the coordination even closer.

One of the strongest testimonies to the deity of Christ is Philippians 2:6, which says that "although He existed in the form of God," he "did not regard equality with God a thing to be grasped." Speaking of his pre-incarnate state, Paul says Christ was "in the form of God" (*en morphē theou*). The term *morphē*, translated "form," should not be understood as form over against content. In fact the word more nearly means the very content of a thing, the sum of those characteristics which make a thing precisely what it is. So here it means the sum of those characteristics which make God *God*. That Christ existed "in the form of God" means that he possessed all the qualities and attributes of deity. This fact is reinforced by the expression "equality with God."

---

22. Bruce M. Metzger. "The Punctuation of Rom. 9:5," *Christ and Spirit in the New Testament*, ed. Barnabas Lindars and Stephen Smalley (Cambridge: University Press, 1973), pp. 95-112.

Equality with God was something Christ did not have to grasp after because it was inalienably his by nature; it was something he did not have to jealously cling to because he could never lose it. In his incarnation he gave up neither the form of God nor equality with God; he "emptied Himself" temporarily only of the prerogatives connected with being fully divine (verse 7).[23]

Colossians 2:9 states simply, "For in Him all the fulness of Deity dwells in bodily form." We could not ask for a more clear and straightforward affirmation of Christ's deity. Our Savior in his human nature ("bodily form") has the totality of Godhood within him; it is impossible for him to be more divine than he is. Warfield says it means that "everything that enters into Godhead and constitutes it Godhead, dwells in Him."[24]

Another passage indicating equality between Christ and God the Father is Hebrews 1:3, which says that "He [the Son] is the radiance of His [the Father's] glory and the exact representation of His nature." David Wells says that these expressions "make an unmistakable assertion of divinity." The latter one especially "has the idea . . . of conveying the exact reality of God." It "does not have the connotation of a pale representation, but such a precise replica that it conveyed the essential nature of the thing."[25] Thus are Father and Son set forth as being fully equal.

Finally we should note how the book of Revelation coordinates the work of the Father and the work of the Lamb in their heavenly glory. The day of judgment is the great day of "their wrath" (6:17). The saved have both the Lamb's name and the Father's name on their foreheads (14:1). God and the Lamb have one throne (22:1), and together they are the temple and the light of heaven (21:22-23). Eternity is ascribed to each. In 1:8 God the Father says, "I am the Alpha and the Omega, . . . who is and who was and who is to come." In 22:13 Jesus says, "I am the Alpha and the Omega, the first and the last, the beginning and the end." That each receives worship will be noted below.

---

23. See the excellent discussion of this passage in George Lawlor. *When God Became Man* (Chicago: Moody Press, 1978).

24. B. B. Warfield, "The Biblical Doctrine of the Trinity," p. 47.

25. David F. Wells, *The Person of Christ* (Westchester, Ill.: Crossway Books, 1984), pp. 54, 188 (n. 55).

Jesus Is Worshiped

In view of the abundant data concerning Christ's deity already noted, we should not be surprised to see that he is worshiped along with the Father. Neither men (Acts 10:25-26) nor angels (Rev. 19:10; 22:8-9) rightly receive worship. The angel exhorts John to "worship God" (Rev. 22:9). Yet we have already seen how Jesus asks us to honor him even as we honor the Father (John 5:23), and how he received the sincere worship of the Apostle Thomas (John 20:28). Philippians 2:10-11 says that those who worship the Son bring glory to the Father. Some believe that I Timothy 3:16 and Philippians 2:6-11 were early Christian hymns honoring Christ. Romans 9:5; II Timothy 4:18; and II Peter 3:18 are doxologies of praise to him. The book of Revelation pictures the heavenly hosts giving explicit worship to the Lamb (5:8-11). They say, "Worthy is the Lamb that was slain to receive power and riches and wisdom and might and honor and glory and blessing" (5:12). Then follows perhaps the most irrefutable evidence of the deity of Christ in all of Scripture, as "every created thing" (a category in which Christ is *not* included) offers worship to the Father *and the Lamb* identically: "To Him who sits on the throne, and to the Lamb, be blessing and honor and glory and dominion forever and ever" (5:13).

Jesus Is Yahweh

We have already seen how the title "Lord" relates Jesus with Yahweh of the Old Testament. There are other connections that are even more direct. In a number of instances New Testament writers apply to Jesus Christ specific Old Testament passages that speak unequivocally of Yahweh. For example, Matthew 3:3 says that Isaiah 40:3 is talking of John the Baptist's ministry as the forerunner of the Messiah: "Make ready the way of the Lord, make His paths straight!" But Isaiah 40:3 speaks specifically of Yahweh: "Clear the way for the LORD in the wilderness; make smooth in the desert a highway for our God."[26] The same is true of Malachi 3:1, where Yahweh says, "Behold, I am going to send My messenger, and he will clear the way before Me." In Mat-

---

26. In many versions of the Bible, when the word *LORD* appears in all capital letters in the Old Testament, it stands for *YHWH* in the original.

thew 11:10, however, the Holy Spirit sees fit to change *Me* to *You*, thus showing that the specific reference is to Jesus: "Behold, I send My messenger before Your face, who will prepare Your way before You."

Other passages are equally insistent that Old Testament references to Yahweh are speaking of Jesus Christ. Hebrews 1:10-12 quotes Psalm 102:25-27 and applies it to our Savior, thus ascribing to him Yahweh's work of creation and attribute of eternality. Joel 2:32 is especially significant: "And it will come about that whoever calls on the name of the LORD will be delivered." The New Testament quotes this passage on two occasions and refers it to Christ (Acts 2:21, 36; Rom. 10:9, 13). Similar comparisons can be made between Psalm 68:18 and Ephesians 4:6-8; between Isaiah 45:23 and Philippians 2:10-11 (see Rom. 14:11); between Deuteronomy 10:17 and Revelation 17:14, 19:16; between Psalm 34:8 and I Peter 2:3; between Isaiah 8:14 and I Peter 2:5-8; and between Psalm 24:7-10 and I Corinthians 2:8.

After surveying passages such as these and many others, Christopher Kaiser says, "We conclude that Jesus is identified with Yahweh, the God of Israel, in virtually all the strata of the New Testament, early as well as late."[27] This does not mean that Jesus *alone* is Yahweh, but that Yahweh of the Old Testament *includes* Jesus, along with the Father and the Spirit.

Jesus Is Distinct from the Father

This leads to a final comment regarding the New Testament data about the deity of Christ. We have seen a number of lines of evidence all leading to the same inescapable conclusion, namely, that Jesus truly is divine; he is God. But we should also note that he is always pictured as *distinct* from God the Father (and God the Spirit). This is what made it necessary for the early Christians to explore more fully the concept of the Trinity.

The Deity of the Holy Spirit in the New Testament

The identity of the Holy Spirit is not the main problem relating to the Trinity, simply because the issue of the identity of Jesus in relation to the

---

27. Christopher B. Kaiser, *The Doctrine of God: An Historical Survey* (Westchester, Ill.: Crossway Books, 1982), p. 35.

Father is so much more prominent in the New Testament. But once the issue has been raised with reference to Jesus, it can not be escaped with reference to the Spirit, either. Although the references to the Spirit's divine nature are relatively few, they do force us to ask how he is related to the Father and the Son.

Although the personhood of the Spirit is not the main point here, we must briefly summarize the principal evidences for this fact, so that we may understand that we are speaking of a personal being who is distinct from the Father and the Son. First, in John 14:16 Jesus says that when he goes away, the Father will send the disciples "another Helper." The term *Helper* means also a counselor or an advocate, and is a distinctly personal concept (just as terms like *lawyer* and *minister* and *professor* denote persons to us today). Also, Jesus says this one will be "another" helper. Here he uses the Greek word *allos*, which means "another of the same kind" (rather than *heteros*, "another of a different kind"). The Spirit is personal, just as Jesus is personal.

Some other familiar lines of evidence for the personhood of the Spirit are as follows: (1) He is placed in juxtaposition with other persons (Matt. 28:19; Acts 15:28). (2) He does the kinds of things that persons do. He uses his mind (Rom. 8:27; I Cor. 2:10-11); he makes decisions (Acts 13:2; 15:28); he speaks (John 16:13-14; Acts 8:29; I Tim. 4:1); he teaches (John 14:16, 26; I Cor. 2:13); he experiences emotions or feelings (Isa. 63:10; Eph. 4:30). (3) He can be treated like a person. He can be lied to (Acts 5:3), tempted (Acts 5:9), blasphemed (Matt. 12:31), and insulted (Heb. 10:29).

The more immediately relevant point is that the Holy Spirit is a *divine* person. These divine characteristics are attributed to him: eternality (Heb. 9:14), omniscience (I Cor. 2:10-11), omnipresence (Ps. 139:7-10), and perhaps omnipotence (Ps. 104:30; Zech. 4:6). Also, Jesus says that the only truly unforgivable sin is blasphemy against the Holy Spirit (Matt. 12:31-32). However difficult it may be to understand exactly what this sin is, this point is clear: how such a sin could be unforgivable is incomprehensible unless the Spirit is divine. Another point is that in Acts 5:3-4 the Holy Spirit seems to be specifically identified with God. Verse 3 says that Ananias lied to the Holy Spirit, and verse 4 repeats this idea thus: "You have not lied to men, but to God." Another strong indication of deity is the way the Spirit is included in the many trinitarian formulas and statements that will be set forth in the next section.

These are the kinds of references to the Holy Spirit that cause Christians to raise the question of the Trinity (instead of just a "Binity," or one God in two persons). The answer to the question must deal not only with the New Testament's references to the deity of Christ but also with its references to the deity of the Spirit.

Trinitarian Passages in the New Testament

Another aspect of New Testament data that point toward the doctrine of the Trinity is the numerous trinitarian passages that speak of Father, Son and Spirit together. In almost every case the subject is the salvation they have provided and continue to provide to those who believe. In many cases the individual works of each person of the Trinity are the main emphasis, but a critical presupposition of this point is that all three are vitally involved in the salvation process. Seeing them mentioned together in this way naturally leads us to think in trinitarian terms.

Several passages seem rather formalized and probably suggest a pattern of speaking and teaching that was already in existence by the time their respective New Testament books were written. The baptismal formula in Matthew 28:19 is the most well known and most influential of these: "Go therefore and make disciples of all the nations, baptizing them in the name of the Father and the Son and the Holy Spirit." This passage reflects oneness as well as threeness, since only *one name* is mentioned. This indicates an essential equality as well as equal significance in the bestowing of salvation. The connecting of this formula with the universal experience of Christian baptism insured that the question of the Trinity would continue to be in the forefront of theological thinking until it could be resolved in a relatively satisfying manner.

Two formula-like passages occur in the Corinthian letters. One is II Corinthians 13:14, "The grace of the Lord Jesus Christ, and the love of God, and the fellowship of the Holy Spirit, be with you all." Such a concise benediction is eminently suitable for occasions of formal and informal piety and was no doubt used thus in the first-century church. It too would keep trinitarian faith alive and well among Christians. The other Corinthian passage is more didactic than devotional, but it is well calculated to emphasize the unity of the threefold source of spiritual gifts: "Now there are varieties of gifts, but the same Spirit. And there are

130

varieties of ministries, and the same Lord. And there are varieties of effects, but the same God who works all things in all persons" (I Cor. 12:4-6). The obvious parallelism calls specific attention to the Trinity.

One other passage may be cited as probably being deliberately worded to emphasize the Trinity, namely, I Peter 1:2, which says that the saints are chosen "according to the foreknowledge of God the Father, by the sanctifying work of the Spirit, that you may obey Jesus Christ and be sprinkled with His blood." Here all three persons of the Trinity are named as having individually unique roles in our salvation. From the very beginning Christians have understood themselves to be redemptively related not just to an abstract deity but to the three persons who are the one true and living God.

There are many other trinitarian passages in the New Testament, but more often than not the grouping of Father, Son and Spirit together seems more incidental to the writer's main point than deliberately calculated to impress the concept of the Trinity upon our minds. But this kind of secondary allusion to the threeness of God is significant in itself. It indicates how natural it was for the Christian mind already to be thinking in trinitarian terms without having to justify it, explain it, or apologize for it. The threefold source of our salvation was already accepted and taken for granted.

Most of these incidental passages occur in Paul's letters. Several of them will now be listed without comment.

> Now I urge you, brethren, by our Lord Jesus Christ and by the love of the Spirit, to strive together with me in your prayers to God for me (Rom. 15:30).
> And such were some of you; but you were washed, but you were sanctified, but you were justified in the name of the Lord Jesus Christ, and in the Spirit of our God (I Cor. 6:11).
> Now He who establishes us with you in Christ and anointed us is God, who also sealed us and gave us the Spirit in our hearts as a pledge (II Cor. 1:20-21).
> And because you are sons, God has sent forth the Spirit of His Son into our hearts, crying, "Abba! Father!" (Gal. 4:6).
> For through Him [Jesus] we both have our access in one Spirit to the Father (Eph. 2:18).
> For this reason, I bow my knees before the Father, from whom every family in heaven and on earth derives its name, that He would grant you, according to the riches of His glory, to be strengthened with power

through His Spirit in the inner man; so that Christ may dwell in your hearts through faith (Eph. 3:14-17).

And do not get drunk with wine, for that is dissipation, but be filled with the Spirit, speaking to one another in psalms and hymns and spiritual songs, singing and making melody with your heart to the Lord; always giving thanks for all things in the name of our Lord Jesus Christ to God, even the Father (Eph. 5:18-20).

In everything give thanks; for this is God's will for you in Christ Jesus. Do not quench the Spirit (I Thes. 5:18-19).

But we should always give thanks to God for you, brethren beloved by the Lord, because God has chosen you from the beginning for salvation through sanctification by the Spirit and faith in the truth (II Thes. 2:13).

But when the kindness of God our Savior and His love for mankind appeared, He saved us, not on the basis of deeds which we have done in righteousness, but according to His mercy, by the washing of regeneration and renewing by the Holy Spirit, whom He poured out upon us richly through Jesus Christ our Savior (Titus 3:4-6).

When reading Paul's letters we should keep in mind that "God" is his usual way of speaking of God the Father, and "Lord" is his usual designation for Jesus Christ. This is seen clearly in Ephesians 4:4-6, where along with other basics Paul says there are one Spirit and one Lord [Jesus] and one God and Father.

Non-pauline passages with incidental references to the Trinity include I John 4:13-14, "By this we know that we abide in Him and He in us, because He has given us of His Spirit. And we have beheld and bear witness that the Father has sent the Son to be the Savior of the world"; Jude 20-21, "But you, beloved, building yourselves up on your most holy faith; praying in the Holy Spirit; keep yourselves in the love of God, waiting anxiously for the mercy of our Lord Jesus Christ to eternal life"; and Revelation 1:4-5, "Grace to you and peace, from Him who is and who was and who is to come; and from the seven Spirits who are before His throne; and from Jesus Christ." In this last passage the "seven Spirits" are usually thought to be a symbolic reference to the Holy Spirit.[28]

This host of trinitarian passages, added to the abundant testimony to

---

28. We do not include I John 5:7 in our listing because textual criticism raises serious doubt that it was a part of the original text of John's letter.

the deity of Christ and the deity of the Holy Spirit, are the basic Biblical data for the doctrine of the Trinity.

Old Testament Foreshadowings of the Trinity

Although the Old Testament taken by itself would not lead us to conclude that there is a threeness in God, when read in the light of the New Testament it does seem to contain references that foreshadow this doctrine. In fact there are some elements in the Old Testament that are exegetically problematical unless and until they are taken in continuity with the fuller revelation of the Trinity in the New Covenant age. One such element is the fact that the basic Hebrew word for God, i.e., *Elohim*, is plural in form. When it is used for pagan deities it is treated as plural, but when it is used for Yahweh it is treated as singular (e.g., with singular verbs). Why should the plural form be used for the one true God? While other explanations have been offered, it is at least possible that this is a veiled reference to the Trinity. We cannot be dogmatic about this, however.

Another Old Testament phenomenon that has caused difficulty for non-trinitarians is the way God sometimes speaks of himself in plural terms, as in Genesis 1:26, "Let Us make man in Our image, according to Our likeness." After Adam and Eve sinned God said, "Behold, the man has become like one of Us, knowing good and evil" (Gen. 3:22; see 3:5). In connection with the building of the tower of Babel God said, "Come, let Us go down and there confuse their language" (Gen. 11:7). No truly satisfactory explanation of this language was forth-coming until it could be read in the light of New Testament trinitarian teaching.

The phenomenon of the Angel of Yahweh, along with the incident in Genesis 18:1-19:21, is another possible foreshadowing of the Trinity. Genesis 18:2 speaks of "three men" who appeared to Abraham, at least one of whom seems to have been a manifestation of Yahweh (18:13, 22, 33). The other two are called "angels" (19:1; the word *angel* simply means "messenger"; see 19:13), but they seem to operate with divine prerogatives (18:21; 19:22, 24, 29). In passages that deal with the Angel of Yahweh, sometimes the Angel is distinguished from Yahweh (e.g., Ex. 23:20-23) and sometimes identified with him (e.g., Ex. 3:2 and 4:5; Judg. 13:22). At the very least this phenomenon seems to suggest the possibility of a plurality within the divine nature.[29]

One other aspect of Old Testament teaching that corresponds completely with the New Testament revelation of the Trinity is the clear indication that the promised Messiah would be divine. For instance, Psalm 45:6 addresses the coming King as God: "Thy throne, O God, is forever and ever" (see Heb. 1:8). Jesus uses Psalm 110:1 to show that the Messiah's sonship would be divine (Matt. 22:42-45). Isaiah 9:6 declares that the Messiah would be called "Wonderful Counselor, Mighty God, Eternal Father, Prince of Peace." Micah 5:2 says that the one to be born in Bethlehem would already have existed from eternity. These and other passages are fully explained by the explicit New Testament teaching that the Messiah was truly God in the flesh.[30]

Fulton says that some of the efforts to discover the doctrine of the Trinity in the Old Testament (including some of the items mentioned above) are "exegesis of a mischievous, if pious, sort."[31] Perhaps this is so with regard to those who cite passages such as Numbers 6:24-26 (with Yahweh mentioned three times in the benediction) or Isaiah 6:3 ("Holy, Holy, Holy, is the Lord of hosts"—three "Holies"). But this surely is not the case with everything we have mentioned here. We agree rather with Warfield's judgment:[32]

> . . . The upshot of it all is that it is very generally felt that, somehow, in the Old Testament development of the idea of God there is a suggestion that the Deity is not a simple monad, and that thus a preparation is made for the revelation of the Trinity yet to come. . . . After all is said, in the light of the later revelation, the Trinitarian interpretation remains the most natural one of the phenomena which the older writers frankly interpreted as intimations of the Trinity . . . . This is not an illegitimate reading of New Testament ideas back into the text of the Old Testament; it is only reading the text of the Old Testament under the illumination of the New Testament revelation. The Old Testament may be likened to a chamber richly furnished but dimly lighted; the introduction of light brings into it nothing

---

29. See James A. Borland, *Christ in the Old Testament* (Chicago: Moody Press, 1978), for a full discussion of all the relevant passages pertaining to the Angel of Yahweh.

30. For a fuller treatment of this point see B. B. Warfield, "The Divine Messiah in the Old Testament," *Biblical and Theological Studies*, by B. B. Warfield, ed. Samuel G. Craig (Nutley, N.J.: Presbyterian and Reformed, 1952), pp. 79-126.

31. William Fulton, "Trinity," p. 458.

32. B. B. Warfield, "The Biblical Doctrine of the Trinity," pp. 30-31.

which was not in it before; but it brings out into clearer view much of what is in it but was only dimly or even not at all perceived before. The mystery of the Trinity is not revealed in the Old Testament; but the mystery of the Trinity underlies the Old Testament revelation, and here and there almost comes into view. Thus the Old Testament revelation of God is not corrected by the fuller revelation which follows it, but only perfected, extended and enlarged.

Thus taken together, the Old and New Testaments present us with an unmistakable doctrine of the threeness within the divine nature.

THE REALITY OF GOD'S ONENESS

The data surveyed above would not present any difficulty if Biblical religion were polytheistic or at least tritheistic. The Father is God; the Son is God; the Holy Spirit is God. Why not just say we have three Gods and leave it at that? Millions and perhaps billions of people have been content with this kind of theism.

Perhaps this would be easier to accept if it were not for one thing: The Bible from beginning to end teaches that there is but one God. Yahweh—the God of Abraham, the God of our Lord Jesus Christ, the God of the Bible—is the one and only true and living God. The Jews, who follow the Old Testament alone, are fiercely monotheistic. Their golden text is Deuteronomy 6:4-5, "Hear, O Israel! The Lord is our God, the Lord is one! And you shall love the Lord your God with all your heart and with all your soul and with all your might." Muslims, whose concept of God may be traced ultimately to the Old Testament, glory in their monotheism: "There is no God but Allah!" And Christians, too, proclaim their faith in but one God. But Christians also believe that the Father is God, the Son is God, and the Holy Spirit is God. This is the "problem" of the Trinity: how may we reconcile our faith in but one God with our belief that Christ and the Holy Spirit are divine?

One thing Christians are not willing to give up is their full acceptance of the Bible's teaching that God is one.[33] This is simply not negotiable. It is a fact firmly entrenched in Scripture, beginning with the very first of the Ten Commandments: "I am the Lord your God, who brought you

---

33. See the discussion of "The One True God" in Jack Cottrell, *What the Bible Says About God the Creator*, pp. 390-419.

out of the land of Egypt, out of the house of slavery. You shall have no other gods before Me" (Ex. 20:2-3). Deuteronomy 6:4 has already been cited: "Hear, O Israel! The Lord is our God, the Lord is one!" The theme of Isaiah 40-48 is that all other so-called gods are mere pretenders; they have no real existence. "Thus says the Lord, the King of Israel and his Redeemer, the Lord of hosts: 'I am the first and I am the last, and there is no God besides Me'" (Isa. 44:6). Yahweh repeats this exclusive claim again and again: "I am the Lord, and there is no other; besides Me there is no God" (Isa. 45:5). "I am the Lord, and there is none else. . . . Turn to Me, and be saved, all the ends of the earth; for I am God, and there is no other" (Isa. 45:18, 22).

Robert Crossley says, "This tremendous fact that there can be but one God, utterly holy and transcendent, is one of the greatest and most profound truths revealed in the Old Testament." And significantly, the New Testament does not repudiate this monotheistic faith but repeatedly endorses it. As Crossley says, "The unity of God is, in fact, one great pillar on which the whole Christian faith is built. We do not and cannot deny that God is one."[34] When asked which commandment is foremost of all, Jesus replied, "The foremost is, 'Hear, O Israel; the Lord our God is one Lord; and you shall love the Lord your God with all your heart'" (Mark 12:29-30). Here of course he is quoting Deuteronomy 6:4-5. The scribe who asked Jesus the question heartily approved the answer: "Right, Teacher, You have truly stated that He is One; and there is no one else besides Him" (Mark 12:32). Paul affirms God's oneness, also: "Or is God the God of Jews only? Is He not the God of Gentiles also? Yes, of Gentiles also, since indeed God . . . is one" (Rom. 3:29-30). Paul's point is that *of course* God is one; there is not one God for Jews and another for Gentiles. "God is only one," he says (Gal. 3:20), and praises him in a doxology: "Now to the King eternal, immortal, invisible, the only God, be honor and glory forever and ever. Amen" (I Tim. 1:17). James 2:19 makes this well-known point: "You believe that God is one. You do well; the demons also believe, and shudder." James adds, "There is only one Lawgiver and Judge, the One who is able to save and to destroy" (4:12).

The passages most difficult to harmonize with trinitarian belief are

---

34. Robert Crossley, *The Trinity* (Downers Grove: InterVarsity Press, 1977), p. 9.

those that affirm that God the Father is the one true God while at the same time distinguishing him from Jesus Christ. On one occasion, when addressing the Father in prayer, Jesus declared, "And this is eternal life, that they may know Thee, the only true God, and Jesus Christ whom Thou hast sent" (John 17:3). Paul concludes his Roman letter thus: "To the only wise God, through Jesus Christ, be the glory forever. Amen" (Romans 16:27). In I Timothy 2:5 he says, "For there is one God, and one mediator also between God and men, the man Christ Jesus." Jude concludes, "To the only God our Savior, through Jesus Christ our Lord, be glory, majesty, dominion and authority, before all time and now and forever. Amen" (Jude 25). In Ephesians 4:4-6 Paul says there is one Spirit, and one Lord (i.e., Jesus), and "one God and Father of all who is over all and through all and in all." The distinction between Jesus as Lord and the Father as God is also seen in I Corinthians 8:4-6, where the true God is being contrasted with idols. "We know that there is no such thing as an idol in the world, and that there is no God but one," he says. Though there are many false, so-called gods and lords, "yet for us there is but one God, the Father, from whom are all things, and we exist for Him; and one Lord, Jesus Christ, through whom are all things, and we exist through Him."

Such language could easily be seen as endorsing a non-trinitarian belief, one in which the Father alone is divine. But this does not seem consistent with the multitude of references to the full deity of Christ especially, where he is actually called God—even by Paul. And even though Paul prefers to call him Lord while usually reserving the term *theos* ("God") for the Father, we have already seen that the title *kurios* ("Lord") itself has implications of deity. The very fact that Paul brings Jesus into the discussion in I Corinthians 8:4-6 shows that he considers Christ to be in the category of true deity as opposed to idols. There does not seem to be any other reason for even mentioning Christ in this context. If the Father alone were divine, he would have been a sufficient contrast with the idols.

These Biblical emphases on both the threeness and the oneness of God are the source of what is called the "problem" of the Trinity or the question of the Trinity. Many are content, of course, simply to confess faith in both the threeness and the oneness without probing any further into the question. But others are not so content, especially when unbelievers and critics accuse Christians of being irrational and illogical for thinking that three equals one. Thus they feel compelled to address the questions, how can God be both three and one at the same time? How are the threeness and the oneness of God related? If the Father is God, and Jesus is God, and the Spirit is God, how can there be just one God?

HERETICAL APPROACHES TO THE TRINITY

These questions have been answered in a number of ways, many of which have been judged totally unacceptable—even heretical—by the majority of believers down through the centuries. These heretical approaches may be divided into three broad categories: those that deny God's oneness; those that deny his threeness; and those that deny the essential equality of Father, Son and Spirit.[35]

Denials of God's Oneness

Denials of God's oneness are found throughout the world, of course, in the ubiquitous polytheism of paganism. Seldom if ever do pagans retrieve the truth that God is one apart from the impact of special revelation. Within the bounds of Christendom, however, polytheism has but a scant following. In the modern world it seems confined to cults such as Mormonism and Armstrongism. Regarding the former, it seems that at a particular point in his life, while he was in the midst of composing the so-called "Book of Abraham," Joseph Smith made the discovery that the Hebrew word *Elohim* ("God") is plural in form. Thus in chapter 4 of the "Book of Abraham" he switches from speaking of "God" to writing about "the Gods."[36] Mormon theology teaches that the God of the Bible is simply one among many gods, and that faithful Mormons themselves will one day become gods equal to those that already exist. In *Doctrine and Covenants* 132:37 Joseph Smith says that Abraham, Isaac and Jacob have already been exalted "and sit upon thrones, and are not angels but are gods." In 132:19-20 the same is promised to all those who meet all the qualifications: "Then

---

35. See a brief discussion of these views with a good diagram in Roger Nicole, "The Meaning of the Trinity," *One God in Trinity*, ed. Peter Toon and James D. Spiceland (Westchester, Ill.: Cornerstone Books, 1980), pp. 1-4.

36. Joseph Smith, *Doctrine and Covenants* and *The Pearl of Great Price* (Salt Lake City: The Church of Jesus Christ of Latter-day Saints, 1973), *Pearl*, pp. 38ff.

shall they be gods, because they have no end; . . . then shall they be above all, because all things are subject unto them. Then shall they be gods, because they have all power, and the angels are subject unto them."[37]

The teaching of Herbert W. Armstrong is also polytheistic. He deduces from the plural form of *Elohim* that "God" is a class composed of two or more individuals, a "God Kingdom" or "God Family." The problem with trinitarian thinking is that it *limits* the size of the God Family to only three persons. The fact is that all those who are saved will become a part of this God Family and will become every bit as divine as Christ is now.[38]

Christians are often accused of being polytheists or, more specifically, tritheists, because of their belief in the Trinity. While denying this in theory, many Christians do come close to falling into this error on a practical level simply because they forget that God is one or because they do not understand the nature of his threeness in relation to his oneness. Although we need to guard against this kind of excess, this is still not in the same class as those who make the category of deity basically open-ended and say "whosoever will may become gods."

Denials of God's Threeness

A much more serious and widespread heresy within Christendom is the denial of God's threeness and an exclusive emphasis on his oneness. This may appear in one of two major forms. The first of these is unitarianism (as opposed to trinitarianism), which is an outright denial of the Trinity. It says that only the Father is God; neither Jesus nor the Holy Spirit is truly divine. Fourth-century Arianism (along with its modern counterpart, the Jehovah's Witnesses) may be considered as a form of unitarianism. Servetus and Socinus were noted unitarians of the Reformation era. The American unitarian movement stems from the rationalistic background of the Enlightenment. After taking root in New

---

37. Joseph Smith, *Doctrine and Covenants*, pp. 241, 243. For a more complete discussion see Anthony Hoekema, *Mormonism* (Grand Rapids: Eerdmans, 1963), pp. 36-44.
38. Herbert W. Armstrong, ed., *Ambassador College Correspondence Course* (Pasadena: Ambassador College, 1977), Lesson 8, pp. 5, 8, 10. See also Armstrong's booklets, *Why Were You Born?* and *Just What Do You Mean—Born Again?*

England Congregationalism, it became less and less supernaturalistic. Today it is hardly distinguishable from Secular Humanism; a number of the signers of "Humanist Manifesto II" are affiliated with Unitarian churches.

The unitarian heresy is so openly anti-trinitarian that it has always been a clear alternative to trinitarianism rather than simply one form of it. This is not the case with the other view that denies God's threeness, namely, modalism (sometimes called modalistic monarchianism and Sabellianism). From its earliest known forms in the late second century, modalism seems to have been a serious attempt to account for God's threeness while emphasizing his oneness. Thus it may be called a particular view of the Trinity, albeit an heretical one. Brown says that this is "the most common theological error among people who think themselves orthodox," mainly because "it is the simplest way to explain the Trinity while preserving the oneness of God." But, as Brown says, "unfortunately, it is incorrect."[39]

Modalism is basically the view that in his inner nature there are no distinctions within God, threefold or otherwise. However, in his external relationships with his creatures, God assumes different modes in which to make himself known and accomplish his purposes among men. In its original form the contention was that in the Old Testament era God revealed himself as Father; then he became incarnate as the Son; finally, after Jesus' ascension, God relates to his creatures as the Holy Spirit. Thus these modes of relationship are successive, not simultaneous. It should be noted that viewing the Trinity this way allows one to say that Jesus as God the Son was fully divine, and that the Holy Spirit is also divine. The problem is that the Father, Son and Spirit are not really distinguished from one another. In their true being they are one and the same person, a person who assumes different modes in his outward relationships to his creatures. God the Father *is* God the Son, who also *is* God the Holy Spirit.[40]

The first known modalist was Praxeas in the late second century,

---

39. Harold O. J. Brown, *Heresies* (Garden City, N.Y.: Doubleday, 1984), p. 99.
40. This view often merged with another concept considered heretical by many, namely, patripassianism ("the Father suffers"). I.e., if it was the Father who became incarnate in Christ, then it was the Father who suffered and died on the cross. Attempts to avoid this conclusion often led to other problems. (*See* Brown, *Heresies*, p. 101.)

while the best known early modalist was Sabellius in the early third century. In more recent times varying versions of modalism may be found
principally in modernistic religion. Welch says, "Probably the most
widely held concept of the Trinity among contemporary 'liberal'
theologians, especially those who have been influenced by the renewed
emphasis on revelation in Continental theology, may be designated as
'monarchian' or 'modalist.'" These theologians are willing to accept a
Trinity of manifestation or experience, says Welch, but not a "Trinity of
being," a threefold distinction in God's own essential nature.[41] An example is the eminent Liberal, W. N. Clarke. The concept of the Trinity
must be reinterpreted, he says, from "a metaphysical doctrine concerning the interior nature and life of God," to one that is limited to "the field
of divine-human relations."[42] He repudiates an ontologically-based
Trinity with its differentiations in the divine being itself ("an internally
social God") in favor on an "unalterable monotheism," a God who is
one person with a single mind and will who is capable of doing all that
has been accounted for by the doctrine of the Trinity.[43] "For in all works
God suffices. God himself is the Father, God himself is the divine in
Jesus Christ, and God himself is the Holy Spirit. . . . We know the three
relations of God to men, and have the whole God in them all." There is
"one glory thrice revealed." "God is forthshining in the universe, God is
self-revealing in the historical work of holy love, and God is self-
imparting in the inward life of men. In all these God is one, though
variously manifested."[44]

William Fulton likewise repudiates the "Trinity of essence," or "the
essential, immanent, or ontological Trinity," where the threeness is inherent in God's subjective being. He argues for "the Trinity of experience, in which God is self-revealed as the Father or Creator or
Legislator, the Son or Redeemer, and the Spirit or Sanctifier." In other
words, he accepts "the three-fold self-disclosure of God" but not "a
threefold distinction within the divine Nature itself." Modern Christian

---

41. Claude Welch, *In This Name: The Doctrine of the Trinity in Contemporary
Theology* (New York: Charles Scribner's Sons, 1952), pp. 56-57.
42. William Newton Clarke, *The Christian Doctrine of God* (Edinburgh: T. & T.
Clark, 1909), pp. 231, 235.
43. Ibid., pp. 236-239.
44. Ibid., pp. 246-248.

theology, he says, is itself moving back to this original "Trinity of manifestation." Fulton denies that this is Sabellianism since the latter speaks of successive modes or manifestations that are incomplete and temporary, while he himself sees the basis for the three-fold self-manifestation as being eternally rooted in God.[45] Van Dusen, a more recent Liberal, endorses Fulton's view[46] and recites H. E. Fosdick's illustration of how Theodore Roosevelt, though one person, was known through three different modes of self-disclosure: Roosevelt the austere statesman, Roosevelt the robust sportsman, and Roosevelt the gentle family man. Certainly he was "not 'three persons,' but one person in three separate 'modes of operation.'" So it is with God.[47]

Examples such as these could be multiplied from among Liberal writers, but these will suffice. They illustrate the definite tendency toward modalism in modern theology.[48]

We must note, however, that one need not have liberal tendencies to be enticed by the heresy of modalism. Sometimes those who are quite orthodox in other ways will succumb to this view, often having thought of it independently and with an inner satisfaction of having finally "solved the problem of the Trinity." An example is the "Oneness movement" among certain Pentecostal bodies, also known as the "Jesus only" Pentecostals. They are well known for insisting on baptizing people in the name of "Jesus only," but less well known is their modalistic concept of the Trinity that underlies this practice. A trinitarian Pentecostal, Carl Brumback, has written a solid refutation of modalism as expressed in these "Oneness" bodies.[49]

The Restoration Movement has its own examples of modalists. The

---

45. William Fulton, "Trinity," pp. 459, 461.

46. Henry P. Van Dusen, *Spirit, Son and Father* (New York: Charles Scribner's Sons, 1958), p. 151.

47. Ibid., pp. 173-174.

48. Some accuse Karl Barth of having a modalistic doctrine of the Trinity (e.g., James O. Buswell, Jr., *A Systematic Theology*, I:123). Others reject this assessment of Barth, proclaiming him orthodox. For the latter view see Claude Welch, *In This Name*, pp. 167, 183, 203; Edmund Fortman, *The Triune God*, pp. 261-262; and Christopher Kaiser, *The Doctrine of God*, p. 114. Barth does use the term "modes," but he speaks of "modes of existence," not just modes of self-disclosure. See Karl Barth, *Church Dogmatics*, I/1, p. 414.

49. Carl Brumback, *God in Three Persons* (Cleveland, Tenn.: Pathway Press, 1959).

following example is by Elder A. B. Jones, from a book originally published in 1879:[50]

> . . . We conceive the terms "Father, Son and Holy Spirit" to indicate certain manifestations of the "One God," as he reveals himself in different relations to man; these different relations finding the ground of their necessity, possibly in the nature and conditions of man rather than in that of God. This Divine Being, in his relation to us as the author of life and its blessings, is the "Father of all;" in his relation to us as Redeemer, he is the Son, "God manifest in the flesh," the "Word," veiled in the mysteries of the incarnation, the Lord Jesus Christ; and in his relation to us as Sanctifier, as one who aids and energizes our spiritual nature, in its struggle with sin, he is the "Holy Spirit."

This is vintage modalism. A more recent example is a book published in 1977 by Robert Brent Graves entitled *The God of Two Testaments*.[51]

Because of the seriousness of this particular heresy, but more because of its appeal,[52] a few remarks in response to modalism are in order. The first and most obvious point is that this view simply cannot do hermeneutical justice to the many, many passages of Scripture which speak of Father, Son and Spirit together, not only alongside each other but interacting with one another. Sometimes all three persons are described together, and sometimes just two of them, but the implication is the same: the relationship or interaction is real and not just a charade. Luke 1:35 is an example: "And the angel answered and said to her, 'The Holy Spirit will come upon you, and the power of the Most High will overshadow you; and for that reason the holy offspring shall be called the Son of God.'" The most natural explanation is that both the Father (Most High) and the Spirit were involved in the incarnation of the Son. Another example is the baptism of Christ, where Father, Son and

---

50. A. B. Jones, "Consciousness and Its Relation to the Holy Spirit," in *A Symposium on the Holy Spirit*, by A. B. Jones et al. (Joplin, Mo.: College Press, 1966 reprint), p. 3.

51. The first edition has no other publishing information. It is now published by Pentecostal Publishing House of Hazelwood, Mo., a "Oneness" organization.

52. "Modalism often seems like the easiest and most natural way for Christians to digest the mysterious doctrines that the Father is God, the Son God, and the Holy Spirit God, while God is but One. Many attempts, ancient and modern, to explain the Trinity in ordinary language rapidly fall into modalism" (H. O. J. Brown, *Heresies*, p. 127).

Spirit are described as simultaneously being involved in different ways: "And the Holy Spirit descended upon Him in bodily form like a dove, and a voice came out of heaven, 'Thou art My beloved Son, in Thee I am well-pleased'" (Luke 3:22). Here the Father speaks to the Son in direct address. If this is not one person speaking to another, then the narrative or even the act itself is deceptive. The same applies to the many occasions when Jesus addressed the Father in prayer (e.g., Luke 22:42; 23:34; John 11:41-42; 17:1-26). Jesus' teaching concerning the coming of the Holy Spirit in John 14-16 is a welter of double-talk if Father, Son and Spirit are not distinct. For example, Jesus said, "I will ask the Father, and He will give you another Helper" (John 14:16). He speaks of "the Helper, the Holy Spirit, whom the Father will send in My name" (John 14:26). Also, "When the Helper comes, whom I will send to you from the Father, that is the Spirit of truth, who proceeds from the Father, he will bear witness of Me" (John 15:26). The same applies to the record of the fulfillment of this promise in Acts 2; see especially 2:33.

Many other passages are robbed of their natural meaning by modalistic presuppositions. The following examples will suffice: "Therefore when He comes into the world, He says, . . . 'Behold, I have come . . . to do Thy will, O God'" (Heb. 10:5, 7). "I will surely tell of the decree of the Lord: He said to Me, 'Thou art My Son, today I have begotten Thee'" (Ps. 2:7). "The Lord says to my Lord: 'Sit at My right hand, until I make Thine enemies a footstool for Thy feet'" (Ps. 110:1). "But of that day or hour no one knows, not even the angels in heaven, nor the Son, but the Father alone" (Mark 13:32). "And the Word was with God" (John 1:1). "For God so loved the world, that He gave His only begotten Son" (John 3:16). "God has sent forth the Spirit of His Son into our hearts" (Gal. 4:6). "I also overcame and sat down with My Father on His throne" (Rev. 3:21). "Salvation to our God who sits on the throne, and to the Lamb" (Rev. 7:10).

Many other passages could be cited, but these are enough to show that Father, Son and Spirit are distinct persons who exist simultaneously and interact with one another.

H. O. J. Brown points out that modalism not only leaves us with hermeneutical chaos, but also raises serious doubts about the reality of the works of redemption themselves. "Logically," he says, "modalism makes the events of redemptive history a kind of charade. Not being a distinct person, the Son cannot really represent us to the Father."[53] He is thinking of the reality of the substitutionary atonement, where the Father "made Him who knew no sin to be sin on our behalf" (II Cor. 5:21), where God set Jesus Christ forth publicly "as a propitiation" (Rom. 3:24-25). He is thinking of Christ's atoning death, in which "the Lord was pleased to crush Him, putting Him to grief," in which "the Lord has caused the iniquity of us all to fall on Him" (Isa. 53:6, 10). He is thinking of the reality of Christ's role as mediator between us and the Father: "For there is one God, and one mediator also between God and men, the man Christ Jesus, who gave Himself as a ransom for all" (I Tim. 2:5-6). He is thinking of Christ's continuing existence as our Intercessor with the Father: "Hence, also, He is able to save forever those who draw near to God through Him, since He always lives to make intercession for them" (Heb. 7:25). Also, "If anyone sins, we have an Advocate with the Father, Jesus Christ the righteous" (I John 2:1). Brown is surely correct: these vital works of redemption lose all their meaning if the Trinity is understood modalistically.

Other problems also arise in reference to modalism. For example, if outward manifestations or self-disclosures are the key to understanding the Trinity, it seems quite arbitrary to limit God's manifestations to only three. Surely, in terms of outward manifestations, God has represented himself to his creatures in more than three roles. Also arbitrary are the specific aspects of God's nature that are allegedly revealed under the respective guises of Father, Son and Spirit. For example, it is said that God in his role as Father shows us the ultimacy, infinity, eternity, and power of the Divine,[54] or "God in his transcendent being."[55] It is strange that a name so redolent with connotations of intimacy and closeness and tenderness (i.e., "Father") should be forced to bear such abstract and impersonal weight.

It is often noted how some of the common illustrations of the Trinity are really illustrations of modalism and should be avoided. Examples are that of water, which sometimes exists as a solid (ice), sometimes as a liquid, and sometimes as a vapor (steam); and a single human person,

---

53. Ibid., p. 99.
54. Henry P. Van Dusen, *Spirit, Son and Father*, p. 175.
55. Claude Welch, *In This Name*, p. 48.

who can exist simultaneously as a father, a son, and a husband.[56]

The one redeeming feature of modalism is that it acknowledges the full deity of Christ and of the Spirit, unlike classical unitarianism. But in sacrificing the Son's distinctness from the Father, the intelligibility of Scripture and the integrity of Christ's saving work are also lost. This is surely an unacceptable approach to the Trinity.

Denials of the Equality of Father, Son and Spirit

The final heretical approach to the Trinity is one which accepts the distinctness of the trinitarian persons but denies their equality. This is a kind of subordinationism, but this term cannot be used as a general description of this approach because it has other less objectionable connotations. From the second century onward a concept of the Son's subordination to the Father (and the Spirit's subordination to one or both of these) has been combined with a concept of the full equality of essence among the three. Each is seen to be equally, fully and eternally divine, although in their relationships to one another the Father assumes supremacy and the others assume a subordinate role.

This is not the kind of subordination we are talking about in this section, however. The point here is that among the persons of the Trinity, there is a subordination in terms of essence itself. While there may be a sense in which Father, Son and Spirit may all be called "divine," they are not divine in the same sense. Usually the Father's divinity is superior to that of the Son and the Spirit; only the Father is inherently divine. There is a denial of equality on the level of their very being.

The earliest example of this view is adoptionist Christology, also known as dynamic monarchianism. The forerunners of this approach were the Ebionites of the early or mid-second century. They emphasized the human nature of Christ but denied his true divinity. Because of his perfect life, God gave to Jesus a special anointing at his baptism, raising him above ordinary men. Thus "the Christ of the Ebionites may be said to be a religious superman, more glorious . . . than the prophets, perhaps even a kind of angelic being, but no 'metaphysical' eminence in the Biblical sense."[57] Christ may have been superior to other men, but

---

56. Harold O. J. Brown, *Heresies*, p. 127.

57. Bjarne Skard, *The Incarnation: A Study of the Christology of the Ecumenical Creeds*, tr. Herman E. Jorgensen (Minneapolis: Augsburg, 1960), p. 37.

he was inferior to the true God.

Those specifically called adoptionists date from near the end of the second century and reached their peak in Paul of Samosata, who died around A.D. 275. Their basic view was that Jesus began as merely a man, but again because of his exemplary life God honored him by adopting him as his own Son, thus bestowing a special measure of power and "divinity" upon him. Since Jesus' baptism was accompanied by some special acts of God, many adoptionists held that this is where he was promoted to Sonship. Others placed the event at Christ's resurrection. In either case his deity was not his own by nature but was more or less honorary. In such a system there can never be any equality of essence between the Father and the Son; the Son remains inferior in every way to the Father. Brown calls it "a kind of proto-Unitarianism."[58]

Although we have referred to Arianism above as a kind of unitarianism that denies the essential threeness of God, it needs to be mentioned again at this point. In a sense all adoptionists deny the threeness of God even though they may attribute some sort of deity to Christ or even to the Holy Spirit; God the Father remains the only one who is truly God, i.e., who possesses divinity by nature. But they differ from true unitarians in that they do ascribe a kind of deity at least to the Son. This is preeminently the case with Arianism, named after its most famous proponent, Arius, who flourished in the early fourth century. The difference between adoptionism and Arianism is that the former has Jesus beginning on a purely human level, while the latter has him beginning as an exalted heavenly being, usually the first being created by the Father.

According to Arius Jesus is not eternal God equal with the Father but was created out of nothing as the pre-existent Logos in order to become the agent for the rest of creation. Thus he is second only to God in the scale of being, having a truly supernatural nature far above any other creature. Nevertheless he *is a creature*, and his essence can never be the same as that of the Father. In comparing the Father and the Son most Arians used the term *homoiousios*, i.e., having a "similar essence." In this they opposed the orthodox view that Father and Son are *homoousios*, i.e., having the "same essence."

---

58. Harold O. J. Brown, *Heresies*, p. 97.

In addition to his exalted beginning, according to Arianism, the Logos became incarnate as Jesus of Nazareth and lived such a perfect life that he was honored further by being given the title of Son of God. (This is an adoptionist element in the system.) In fact, it is even proper to call him "God," but not in the same sense as the Father is God, of course. In view of the Bible's teaching concerning the full deity of Christ, as noted earlier in this chapter, it is clear that Arianism is an heretical approach both to Christology and to the Trinity. The essential equality of Father and Son is denied. As Skard says, for Arians the Son is merely "an under-god of a lower metaphysical order." The fact is that "this *Logos*-souled super-man of Arianism is neither one thing nor the other. He is not God, nor is He man."[59]

After surveying these heretical approaches to the Trinity we can see that an acceptable view will have to do justice to God's threeness, his oneness, and the equality of essence among Father, Son and Spirit.

THE TRADITIONAL DOCTRINE OF THE TRINITY

Is it possible for finite man to understand the concept of the Trinity? Perhaps the word most commonly associated with it is *mystery*. This doctrine, we are told, "is perhaps the most mysterious and difficult doctrine that is presented to us in the entire range of Scripture."[60] Berkhof asserts, "The Church confesses the Trinity to be a mystery beyond the comprehension of man."[61]

But such a statement may be taken to mean several things. First, it might mean simply that it is impossible for man's unaided reason alone to discover the truth that God is a trinitarian being, and that we are thus totally dependent upon divine revelation for our knowledge of it. But this is something upon which almost everyone agrees, and it is not the point that people usually have in mind when they say the Trinity is a mystery.

In the second place, such a statement as Berkhof's might be taken to mean that the concept of the Trinity is contrary to reason, that it is il-

---

59. Bjarne Skard, *The Incarnation*, pp. 117, 119.

60. Loraine Boettner, *Studies in Theology*, 3 ed. (Grand Rapids: Eerdmans, 1953), p. 79.

61. Louis Berkhof, *Systematic Theology* (London: Banner of Truth Trust, 1939), p. 89.

logical, contradictory or paradoxical. This is a common accusation from Christianity's critics. As Henry notes, they speak of the Trinity as a "self-contradictory doctrine," or "a mathematical monstrosity," or "a futile intellectual effort to resolve inherently contradictory notions of divine unity and divine plurality," or "an illogical formulation that depends for its justification upon the notion that God is a mysterious suprarational reality." The doctrine of the Trinity, they say, "is as fallacious in its claim for the three-in-one God as is the formula $3 x = 1 x$."[62]

But this interpretation of the mysteriousness of the Trinity is rejected by most Christians. Henry disagrees strongly with the critics, contending that when the doctrine is formulated properly it is "both intelligible and noncontradictory." It "does not require belief in rational contradiction." Rather, he says, "New Testament writers nowhere suggest that the Trinity is veiled in incomprehensibility, but associate what they say about the Father, Son and Spirit with intelligible divine self-disclosure."[63] Gordon Clark quite agrees, and objects strongly to the wording of Berkhof's statement. If something is "unintelligible in its essential nature," he says, then it *is* nonsense. But God is not nonsense, and thus is not inherently unintelligible.[64] Neither God nor his thought is qualitatively different from our thought so that he somehow contradicts rationality as we know it. To say that God is incomprehensible simply means that "human beings are ignorant of many divine truths," even some that have been revealed.[65] As Nicole puts it, "It is important to recognise that the doctrine of the Trinity is a mystery. It is not, however, an absurdity."[66]

So what *does* it mean to say that the Trinity is a mystery? It means that this doctrine transcends the limits of our knowledge and perhaps even of our ability to know. It is not contrary to reason, but beyond its capacities. But (and this is very important) it is not *completely* beyond them. This is the main point Clark is trying to make, I think. We *can* understand the concept of the Trinity, at least up to a point. Else why

---

62. Carl F. H. Henry, *God, Revelation and Authority. Volume V: God Who Stands and Stays, Part One* (Waco: Word Books, 1982), p. 165.

63. Ibid., pp. 165-167.

64. Gordon H. Clark, *The Trinity* (Jefferson. Md.: The Trinity Foundation, 1985). p. 48.

65. Ibid., pp. 74-75.

66. Roger Nicole, "The Meaning of the Trinity." p. 4.

would it have been revealed to us at all? Accepting it requires neither a suspension of reason nor a superhuman act of reason. It simply requires care in the way we formulate the doctrine. For example, if we assume that the Trinity means that God is both three and one in the same sense, as in the formula $3\ x = 1\ x$, then we *are* guilty of absurdity. But as Henry comments,[67]

> . . . This description patently distorts the doctrine. Christian theology affirms neither that three gods are one God nor that three isolated persons are one God. Rather, it affirms three eternal personal distinctions in the one God, in short, $3\ x$ in $1\ y$. Such a formulation is both intelligible and noncontradictory.

Clark offers the illustration of the U. S. government, which is one government with three almost independent divisions. "There is nothing self-contradictory about a situation being one in one sense and three in a different respect," he says.[68]

Still, the main point is that there *is* mystery associated with the doctrine of the Trinity. We may have some true understanding of it, but we cannot understand it fully. Brown says, "The doctrine of the Trinity speaks of the inner nature of the transcendent God, a matter that certainly surpasses our human ability to understand and that must be respected as a divine mystery."[69] Consequently, as Boettner says,[70]

> . . . we do not presume to give a full explanation of it. In the nature of the case we can know only as much concerning the inner nature of the Godhead as has been revealed to us in the Scriptures. . . . Its height and depth and length and breadth are immeasurable by reason of the fact that the finite is dealing with the Infinite. As well might we expect to confine the ocean within a tea-cup as to place a full explanation of the nature of God within the limits of our feeble human minds. . . .

Still God has given us enough light on the subject to know that certain formulations of trinitarian doctrine are incorrect, as seen in the last section; and he has given us enough to set forth a basic understanding, which we will now attempt to do in this section.

---

67. Carl F. H. Henry, *God, Revelation and Authority*, V:165.
68. Gordon H. Clark, *The Trinity*, p. 86.
69. Harold O. J. Brown, *Heresies*, p. 128.
70. Loraine Boettner, *Studies in Theology*, p. 79.

The Development of the Doctrine

The early church struggled for three hundred years with questions related to the doctrine of the Trinity before coming to a lasting statement of it at the council of Constantinople in A.D. 381. At first there was no attempt at speculation; the Apostolic Fathers simply accepted the deity of Christ and adopted the New Testament's trinitarian language. Clement asks, "Have we not one God and one Christ and one Spirit of grace that was shed upon us?"[71] He begins an oath with these words: "For as God liveth, and the Lord Jesus Christ liveth, and the Holy Spirit."[72] Ignatius urges the Magnesians to be diligent and prosper "in the Son and Father and in the Spirit."[73] At the same time there is a full acceptance of the oneness of God. This was especially important for Irenaeus as he attempted to refute the multitheistic systems of the Gnostics.[74]

It was the Latin theologian Tertullian who left us the first serious theological treatment of the Trinity, in his treatise "Against Praxeas" at the beginning of the third century. According to Tertullian, this is the "rule of faith" that "has come down to us from the beginning of the gospel" concerning Father, Son and Spirit:[75]

> . . . All are of One, by unity (that is) of substance; while the mystery of the dispensation is still guarded, which distributes the Unity into a Trinity, placing in their order the three *Persons*—the Father, the Son, and the Holy Ghost: three, however, not in condition, but in degree; not in substance, but in form; not in power, but in aspect; yet of one substance, and of one condition, and of one power, inasmuch as He is one God, from whom these degrees and forms and aspects are reckoned, under the name of the Father, and of the Son, and of the Holy Ghost. . . .

In his analysis of the subject it was Tertullian who first began to use the

---

71. Clement of Rome, "To the Corinthians," 46, *The Apostolic Fathers*, ed. J. B. Lightfoot and J. R. Harmer (Grand Rapids: Baker Book House, 1962), p. 33.

72. Ibid., 58; p. 38.

73. Ignatius, "To the Magnesians," 13, *The Apostolic Fathers*, ed. J. B. Lightfoot and J. R. Harmer (Grand Rapids: Baker Book House, 1962), p. 72.

74. See Irenaeus, "Against Heresies," II.i.1, tr. Alexander Roberts. *The Ante-Nicene Fathers*, ed. Alexander Roberts and James Donaldson (New York: Charles Scribner's Sons, 1913), I:359.

75. Tertullian, "Against Praxeas," II, p. 598.

language of one essence or substance (*substantia*) and three persons (*persona*). Though there was considerable confusion when the Greek-speaking theologians tried to find the right comparable terms, in the end the orthodox doctrine of the Trinity was stated in language similar to that introduced by Tertullian.[76]

Another significant step in the development of trinitarian thought was made by Origen when he introduced the idea of the eternal generation of the Son from the Father. This concept arose from a consideration of the question of the relationship between the pre-existent Son or Logos and the Father. Justin Martyr had already given attention to this issue. His solution was that the Logos had existed eternally somehow within the Father (just as our thoughts may exist within us), but at a certain point fhe Father "begat" or brought forth the Logos from his very own essence and gave him his own distinct existence. In this way he explained how he could be begotten (i.e., come into existence) as a Son and still be of the same essence as the Father.[77] But it disturbed Origen that the Logos should be pictured thus as having come into existence at all at some specific point. Thus he proposed that the concept of "begetting" or "generation" describes an eternal relationship between the Father and the Son rather than a single act. He believed that this enhanced the deity of Christ and made him appear less subordinate to the Father.[78] Thus originated the idea of Christ's eternal Sonship in terms of eternal generation.

It may have been Origen himself who introduced the term *homoousios* into the trinitarian discussion.[79] In any case the next step in the development was the Arian controversy, when the church had to decide whether the Son is only similar to the Father in substance (*homoiousios*) or whether he is of the same substance (*homoousios*). The council of Nicaea in A.D. 325 sided with Athanasius and others

---

76. For a good succinct discussion of the complexities of the early trinitarian language, see Harold O. J. Brown, *Heresies*, pp. 129-130.

77. Justin Martyr, "Dialogue of Justin, Philosopher and Martyr, with Trypho, a Jew," LXI, *The Ante-Nicene Fathers*, ed. Alexander Roberts and James Donaldson (New York: Charles Scribner's Sons, 1913), I:227.

78. Origen, "De Principiis," I.ii.1-4, tr. Frederick Crombie, *The Ante-Nicene Fathers*, ed. Alexander Roberts and James Donaldson (New York: Charles Scribner's Sons, 1913), IV:245-247.

79. Harold O. J. Brown, *Heresies*, p. 90.

who favored the latter, declaring the Arian option to be heretical. The statement of faith set forth by the council is a major milestone in trinitarian theology. It says,[80]

> We believe in one God the Father All-sovereign, maker of all things visible and invisible.
>
> And in one Lord Jesus Christ, the Son of God, begotten of the Father, only-begotten, that is, of the substance of the Father, God of God, Light of Light, true God of true God, begotten not made, of one substance [homoousion] with the Father, through whom all things were made, things in heaven and things on the earth; who for us men and for our salvation came down and was made flesh, and became man, suffered, and rose on the third day, ascended into the heavens, is coming to judge living and dead.
>
> And in the Holy Spirit.

It is obvious that this statement focuses mainly on the oneness of essence between the Son and the Father. It does not specifically address the question of distinctness, though it seems to be assumed; nor is the place of the Holy Spirit given any attention whatsoever.

In the next few decades, however, these latter issues did receive a good deal of attention, especially by Athanasius and the Cappadocian fathers (Basil, Gregory of Nazianzus, and Gregory of Nyssa). They argued strongly that the Holy Spirit is also homoousios with the Father and the Son. Then, by focusing on two Biblical words, they explained how the Father, Son and Spirit are distinct from one another as well as related to one another in their interior natures. The two words are beget and proceed. The former had already been used in this connection to explain the distinction between the Father and the Son: the Father begets, and the Son is begotten. The term proceed was simply taken over from John 15:26 to explain how the Holy Spirit is related to the Father. This verse says, "When the Helper comes, whom I will send to you from the Father, that is the Spirit of truth, who proceeds from the Father, He will bear witness of Me." Although in this context Jesus is probably talking about the specific event of Pentecost, the trinitarian theologians adopted the term as a convenient way of describing the

---

80. Documents of the Christian Church, 2 edition, ed. Henry Bettenson (London: Oxford University Press, 1963), p. 35.

eternal relationship between the Father and the Spirit: the Spirit "proceeds" from the Father. Of course, no one claimed to know exactly what *beget* or *proceed* might mean in this context. They all agreed that the terms are not intended to be understood in their ordinary senses, however.

Once these matters had been clarified, or at least formalized, another council was held, this time in Constantinople in A.D. 381. The product of this council, usually called the "Nicene" Creed, essentially repeated what the statement of 325 had already said about God the Son; but it added these affirmations about the Spirit: ["We believe] in the Holy Spirit, the Lord and the Life-giver, that proceedeth from the Father, who with Father and Son is worshipped together and glorified together, who spake through the prophets."[81] (In a council at Toledo in A.D. 589, the Latin term *filioque*, "and from the Son," was added to the creed, though rejected by the Eastern church. It thus came to say that the Spirit "proceedeth from the Father and from the Son.")

With this statement concerning the Holy Spirit, the basic elements of trinitarian theology were in place. The Father, Son and Spirit are all of the same essence and thus one; but they are three persons who are distinguished respectively as the One who is ingenerate or unbegotten (the Father), the One who is begotten (the Son), and the One who proceeds (the Spirit).

The Nature of God's Oneness

The traditional trinitarian view is that God is one in nature/essence/being/substance. What does this mean? In what sense are all three persons *one*? The problem here is the same as that which persists throughout this whole discussion, namely, to avoid modalism on the one hand and tritheism on the other. Two or more items can be one in different ways. Modalism says Father, Son and Spirit are one in the sense that they are absolutely and numerically identical; they are the same individual. "I and the Father are one" (John 10:30) means "I *am* the Father." At the other extreme, tritheism says that Father, Son and Spirit are one in the sense that they belong to a common genus or class. I.e., they are three distinct and separate beings or individuals, all "made

---

81. Ibid., p. 37.

out of" the same *kind* of divine "stuff," but each existing in his own discrete portion of that "stuff."

It is important that we not allow terminology to be a stumbling block in our effort to understand the oneness of God. I have used the term *stuff*, which some may find objectionable in this context. Some object to the Latin word *substantia*, or substance, and to the Greek word *ousia*, or being, as well. There simply is no absolutely satisfactory word to refer to the essence of God's being. Whatever word we use, it will always conjure up in the backs of our minds (if not the fronts) the idea of physical substance. Some think that this is actually what Tertullian had in mind when he spoke of the "one *substantia*" of God, since he seemed to think in Stoic concepts. But we must make every effort to resist this kind of thinking. God is *not* physical substance; he is *spirit* (John 4:24),[82] even *uncreated* spirit. What this is like, we do not know. But whatever it is like, it has being or reality. God is not physical, but he is *something*. Our problem in understanding this is not that we have not yet found the right word (to replace *stuff, substance, essence* or whatever); our problem is in our experience, or lack of it. We simply have not experienced the divine essence, and we probably never will.[83] Thus it requires an effort of will *not* to think in terms of physical substance when we speak of God's essence or being, and to think in the most general terms of his reality. Buswell has the right idea when he says that in this context "'substance' is whatever it is to be the thing we are talking about. The substance of God is whatever it is to be God."[84]

To say that Father, Son and Spirit are one in essence means that the totality of divine "substance," the whole of "whatever it is to be God," belongs to each of them. Trinitarian theology has never said that the three are one in *every* sense, but only that they are one in "substance." The main implication of this is that each is equally divine. In whatever sense God the Father is divine, so also are God the Son and God the Spirit. All the attributes of divinity belong equally to each of the three. It cannot be otherwise, since they share the same being (they are *homoousios*).

---

82. See Jack Cottrell, *What the Bible Says About God the Creator*, pp. 222ff.
83. Ibid., pp. 230-233.
84. James O. Buswell, Jr., *A Systematic Theology*, p. 112.

This means also to some extent that they share in the various divine works. Here we must urge caution, however. Carl Henry says that "the three persons have a common intelligence, will and power since the essence of the Godhead is common to them." This "intimacy of union" means "that the Father is in the Son and the Son in the Father, that where the Father is, there the Son and Spirit are, and that what one person of the Trinity is doing, all are doing."[85] But can we really say that sameness in essence means sameness in works? Is it true that what one is doing, all are doing? To some extent this may be the case; Father, Son and Spirit all seem to be involved in the works of creation, providence, and redemption. But this cannot be true in an absolute sense, else all distinctions among the persons disappear. If they have the same essence and are doing the same works, how is this different from saying they are the same person? Thus sameness in essence does not imply sameness in works. Each person of the Trinity will necessarily to an extent participate in the works of the others, but the work of each individual person may have something about it that is unique to that person. And this is just because God not only is one in essence, but is three persons. This leads to the next section.

The Nature of God's Threeness

God is one, yet he is three. Just what is the nature of this threeness in God, and how is it related to the oneness? As Clark says, whatever term we use, "there must be three somethings" in God. And however we formulate it, the important point is "that there is a difference between what is three and what is one." Thus "it makes no difference what term one uses, provided that he clearly states that they are not synonymous. God is one and three in different senses."[86] We have already discussed the oneness of God in terms of his essence. Now the question remains, how shall we understand his threeness?

Traditionally the word *person* has been used to represent the way in which God is three, ever since Tertullian used the Latin term *persona*. But again, it is important not to think that everything rests upon the use of a specific word. Theologians still argue today about the subtleties of

---

85. Carl F. H. Henry, *God, Revelation and Authority*, V:206.

86. Gordon H. Clark, *The Trinity*, pp. 52-53.

persona versus its Greek counterparts, *prosōpon* and *hupostasis*, and whether these words meant in the fourth century what *person* means to English-speaking people today. Many today urge us especially not to think of a person as a separate center of consciousness. Supposedly this is not what the ancients meant when they used this terminology. "The ancient and medieval conception of person does not correspond to the modern idea of personality: it lacks the mark of consciousness," we are told.[87] Because of this confusion, it is said, the term seems to have outgrown its usefulness.[88]

It is true that when we use this term *person* in the formula, "God in three persons," we must do so cautiously and with self-consciousness, since we are tempted to think of God as personal *in every sense* that human beings are personal. Kaiser urges restraint here, since our usual concept of a person is "an individual who may or may not enter into social relations with others." Persons are totally discrete, and their relationships are arbitrary and external. But such an idea applied to God would be tritheism.[89] Henry says the error here is to "conceive divine personality within the limits of human personality," as if "God were but a more complex image of the human person." When this happens, he says, "then the assertion of tripersonality must in any form involve a numerical plurality of isolated beings and therefore the existence of three gods." The solution is to see that "divine personality is the archetype of human personality, not the reverse."[90] Thus we must be cautious and not press the concept of person too far when applied to God.

But is there anything at all in our concept and experience of persons that applies to God, that warrants our speaking of God as three persons? For quite a long time the idea of a person has included, as Wainwright says, "possession of thought, feeling, and will, and existence as an individual centre of consciousness which is capable of relationships with other persons."[91] There is no doubt that Biblical writers and Chris-

---

87. Robert S. Franks, *The Doctrine of the Trinity* (London: Duckworth, 1953), p. 181.

88. Leslie Dewart, *The Future of Belief: Theism in a World Come of Age* (New York: Herder and Herder, 1966), pp. 146ff.

89. Christopher B. Kaiser, *The Doctrine of God*, p. 65.

90. Carl F. H. Henry, *God, Revelation and Authority*, V:167.

91. Arthur W. Wainwright, *The Trinity in the New Testament*, p. 11.

tians of all ages have thought and spoken of God as being personal in this sense.[92] But the question is, is he *three* persons in this sense? Many do not think so, and do not want to interpret the Trinity as implying so. For example, Karl Rahner says that in God "there are not three consciousnesses; rather the one consciousness subsists in a threefold way. There is only one real consciousness in God, which is shared by Father, Son, and Spirit, by each in his own proper way." He adds, "The 'distinctness' of the persons is not constituted by a distinctness of conscious subjectivities, nor does it include the latter."[93] This seems to be Karl Barth's point also in the following quotation:[94]

> "Person" in the sense of the Church doctrine of the Trinity has nothing directly to do with "personality." Thus the meaning of the doctrine of the Trinity is not that there are three personalities in God. That would be the worst and most pointed expression of tritheism, against which we must here guard. . . .

By "personalities" does he mean "consciousnesses"? Franks thinks so. He summarizes Barth thus: "There are not three consciousnesses in God: that is the worst kind of Tritheism. There is only one consciousness and one God in three moments of His Being. Monotheism is absolute. God is One in all His operations in the world."[95]

We are well aware of the danger of tritheism here, but without the concept of three centers of consciousness, how can we avoid modalism? (Perhaps Barth's critics have some basis, after all, for saying that his view leans toward modalism. See note 48 above.) In my opinion it is possible to retain the idea of a person as an individual center of consciousness and to apply this to God in a threefold sense. There are three persons in God, i.e., three centers of consciousness. Henry is not reluctant to speak of "distinctions of self-consciousness existing side by side in the one Godhead," while at the same time urging caution against projecting this into polytheism.[96] The following summary of B.

---

92. See Jack Cottrell, *What the Bible Says About God the Creator*, pp. 234ff.
93. Karl Rahner, *The Trinity*, tr. Joseph Donceel (London: Burns and Oates, 1970), p. 107.
94. Karl Barth, *Church Dogmatics*, I/1, p. 403.
95. Robert S. Franks, *The Doctrine of the Trinity*, p. 181.
96. Carl F. H. Henry, *God, Revelation and Authority*, V:174.

Lonergan by Fortman seems to be acceptable:[97]

> . . . Lonergan apparently sees no great difficulty in considering the divine persons as "centers of consciousness" in an analogous sense, for he writes that "a divine person is a subject that is distinct and conscious of itself, both as subject and as distinct" and adds that "Father, Son and Holy Spirit through one real consciousness are three subjects conscious of themselves and of the others and of their act," so that "a conscious Father consciously understands, knows, wills; a conscious Son consciously understands, knows, wills; a conscious Spirit consciously understands, knows, wills."

Thus when we say that God is three persons in one essence, we are saying that he is three centers of consciousness sharing one divine essence. Exactly how these three persons share the one essence is where the mystery begins. I simply do not know how to picture this in my mind, and I try to avoid mental images such as one head that has three faces (an image that Van Dusen says is "a very accurate description of the Christian Deity"[98]—but Van Dusen is a modalist!).

The main point is that there is a threeness in God, and this threeness involves different centers of self-consciousness. It seems to me that this is the only way we can account for the separate works of the Father, Son and Spirit, and for the unique aspects of their relationships to one another.

This leads into a discussion of what is sometimes called the distinction between the economic Trinity and the ontological Trinity. The so-called economic Trinity is the various relationships and works of the different persons of the Trinity toward that which is external to God, i.e., the world. The basic point is that there is a kind of division of labor so that not every work is done by all three persons, in the same way at least. This is particularly true of the various works of redemption. The so-called ontological Trinity, on the other hand, has to do with how the three persons are related to one another within their own being, totally apart from any manifestations or works directed outside themselves.

We have already noted Henry's assertion that "what one person of

---

97. Edmund J. Fortman, *The Triune God*, pp. 298-299.
98. Henry P. Van Dusen, *Spirit, Son and Father*, pp. 152-153.

the Trinity is doing, all are doing." A similar statement by Gordon Clark says that "all divine works *ad extra*, i.e. God's external works, his power exercised on and in the universe, are ascribed to all Three Persons."[99] If these statements were literally true, there would be no such thing as the economic Trinity, no "division of labor" among Father, Son and Spirit. But these statements do not seem consistent with the Bible's testimony to the individual works of each person. An example is Peter's trinitarian reference to those "who are chosen according to the foreknowledge of God the Father, by the sanctifying work of the Spirit, that you may obey Jesus Christ and be sprinkled with His blood" (I Peter 1:1-2). God the Father is pictured as foreknowing and choosing (see Rom. 8:29). The Father also sends the Son and the Spirit; he is never the one sent (John 5:37; 14:26; 20:21).

God the Spirit, in turn, is responsible for "sanctifying work," says Peter. This is part of his exclusive work that began on the day of Pentecost when he was offered as a gift to those who would repent and be baptized (Acts 2:38). He is also the agent in inspiration (John 16:13; II Peter 1:21), including speaking in tongues (Acts 2:4). Only blasphemy against the Spirit is unforgivable (Matt. 12:31-32).

The individual works of Jesus, God the Son, receive most of the attention in the New Testament. This is because he is the one who became incarnate and lived among us as a human being. Only the Son thus "became flesh, and dwelt among us" (John 1:14). Only the Son experienced existence as a human being. Only the Son shed his blood on the cross and experienced death in our place. Only the Son was raised from the dead, was taken bodily into heaven, and was seated at the right hand of the Father. Only the Son is High Priest and Mediator between God and man (I Tim. 2:5; Heb. 4:14).

This is not an exhaustive listing of the works performed by the individual members of the Trinity,[100] but it is sufficient for us to see that there are works done by the Father that are not done by the Son or the Spirit, works done by the Son that are not done by the Father or the Spirit, and works done by the Spirit that are not done by the Father or

---

99. Gordon H. Clark, *The Trinity*, p. 110. He seems to be paraphrasing Louis Berkhof, *Systematic Theology*, p. 89.

100. See Carl Brumback, *God in Three Persons*, pp. 87-93, for a fuller listing.

the Son. Most if not all of these exclusive works are related to the glorious plan of redemption, which, as noted earlier, is what makes the trinitarian distinctions known to us in the first place.

It is when we turn to the question of the ontological Trinity that the difficulties begin and the speculations are multiplied. Discerning a threeness in external manifestations and works is not too taxing to our mental powers, but discerning how this threeness is rooted in the divine essence itself is not easy. This is why some opt for modalism, which is in effect granting a threefold external or objective work of God but denying any threefold distinction in God's inner nature. In other words it grants the economic Trinity but denies the ontological Trinity.[101] But this is not traditional trinitarianism, which accepts both, and I believe correctly so.

But whether the traditional approach to the ontological Trinity is satisfying is another question. It is assumed that the basic clue for understanding how the Father and the Son are eternally related lies in these very names themselves, *Father* and *Son*. The natural relationship between a father and a son is that of begetting, i.e., "His only begotten Son" (John 3:16). It has been asserted since Origen that the eternal, intratrinitarian relationship between Father and Son is that of *begetting*. Even though no one understands the content of this term when applied to the Trinity, its use has been considered vital as a way of refuting the Arian contention that the Son was created or made by the Father. If the Son is created, then his essence is inferior to that of the Father. But something that is begotten is of the same essence (*homoousios*) as the begetter. Hence the creed says, specifically in opposition to Arius, "begotten not made." Thus the unique property of the Father, in eternal distinction from the Son and Spirit, is that he is the one who begets or generates but is not himself begotten. And the unique property of the Son, in eternal distinction from the Father and the Spirit, is that he is generate or begotten. As noted above, the term *proceed* is then borrowed from John 15:26 and used to describe the eternal relationship between the Father and Son on the one hand and the Spirit on the other hand. Thus the unique property of the Spirit, in eternal distinction from the Father and the Son, is procession. He proceeds from the Father (and, for the Western church, from the Son).

---

101. William Fulton, "Trinity," p. 461.

Though this has been the accepted way of explaining the ontological Trinity since the fourth century, we must seriously ask whether it is justified by Scripture and whether it is meaningful to use these terms in this context. In my opinion it is altogether doubtful whether the Bible ever intended the concepts of begetting and proceeding to apply to the eternal relationships among the persons of the Trinity. For example, the New Testament applies Psalm 2:7 ("Thou art My Son, today I have begotten Thee") to the resurrection (Acts 13:33), when Jesus became the first-born from the dead (Col. 1:18). The term might well apply to the incarnation (Luke 1:35), as might the term *monogenēs* ("only begotten").[102] It is almost certain that the "proceeding" of John 15:26 refers to Pentecost and not some supposed eternal relationship. Thus I would agree with Buswell, who proposes that we "completely drop the doctrine of the eternal generation of the Son" as well as the idea of the eternal procession of the Spirit.[103] This idea is all the more attractive in view of the fact that these terms were never understood in their ordinary senses; in fact, they were never given any content whatsoever. They have served as empty code words which we do not need to support the concept of the ontological Trinity.

But this raises a much more debatable question, namely, whether the very names of Father, Son and Spirit represent eternal distinctions within the Trinity or whether they are derived from the work of God in the economy of redemption. As applied to the second person of the Trinity especially, is the doctrine of the eternal Sonship of Christ valid? Is the Father-Son relationship ontological and eternal, even if the concept of generation is not? Buswell himself makes it clear that he is *not* denying this aspect of traditional doctrine. "There can be no doubt," he says, "that 'Father, Son, and Holy Spirit' are words intended by the writers of the Scriptures to indicate eternal relationships within the Triune Godhead."[104] This is Warfield's view also,[105] and that of Christendom in general. Not everyone otherwise orthodox in his theism

---

102. See Geerhardus Vos, *The Self-Disclosure of Jesus*, pp. 212-226, for a lengthy discussion of the arguments on both sides of this issue. He opts tentatively for an eternal significance for the term.

103. James O. Buswell, Jr., *A Systematic Theology*, I:110-112, 119-120.

104. Ibid., p. 112.

105. B. B. Warfield, "The Biblical Doctrine of the Trinity," p. 55.

has accepted it, however. Alexander Campbell, for example, taught that Christ was pre-existent as the Logos, but his Sonship began with the incarnation. "While, then, the phrase 'Son of God' denotes a temporal relation, the phrase 'the Word of God' denotes an eternal, unoriginated relation. There was *a word of God* from eternity, but the Son of God began to be in the days of Augustus Caesar." The entire "relation of Father, Son, and Holy Spirit began to be" when the Christian system began.[106]

I personally do not see any issue of orthodoxy at stake here, since nothing seems to be lost by limiting Father, Son and Spirit to the economic Trinity nor gained by extending these relationships into the ontological Trinity. Hence I am not inclined to argue one way or the other, though I tend to agree with Campbell's view. Especially I do not think that the issue of Christ's deity or equality with God depends upon an eternal Sonship relation. Extracting deity from eternal Sonship is an inference anyway, and there are surely enough explicit references to Christ's deity in the Bible to make this truth independent of the question of eternal Sonship.

But if we exclude both the generation-procession relationships *and* the Father-Son-Spirit relationships from the ontological Trinity, what basis remains for speaking of the ontological Trinity? If we cannot explain the eternal, internal trinitarian relationships in these terms, then how can we explain them? Regarding the first of these questions, I think that the various aspects of the economic Trinity (including the above relationships, if they should be limited to this) give us more than sufficient warrant to believe that there definitely is a Trinity of persons in God's eternal, internal being. In other words, the fact of the ontological Trinity is a justified inference from the economic Trinity itself. Regarding the second question, namely, how we may explain this ontological Trinity, I'm not sure that we can, and I'm not sure that it matters. If we know that there are three persons, and if we know that they are each fully and equally divine, then we know that the works of redemption in which they are variously involved are sure and certain; and we can put our complete trust in them. More than this we need not ask.

---

106. Alexander Campbell, *The Christian System* (Cincinnati: Standard Publishing, n.d.), pp. 9-10.

This still leaves one question to be discussed, namely, the subordination of the Son to the Father and the subordination of the Spirit to the Father (and perhaps to the Son). Without doubt the Bible speaks of such subordinationism. "The Father is greater than I," says Jesus (John 14:28). "My food is to do the will of Him who sent Me, and accomplish His work," he says (John 4:34). "God is the head of Christ," says Paul (I Cor. 11:3). The Father and the Son do send the Spirit, and the Spirit does proceed from the Father (John 14:26; 15:26). In his work of inspiration the Spirit does not speak on his own initiative, but speaks what he hears from Christ; his mission is to glorify Christ (John 16:13-14). How shall we explain such passages? The question is whether they imply a subordinationism within the ontological Trinity, or whether the subordination is a function of the economic Trinity only.

Of course Arians and adoptionists see the Father as essentially (ontologically) superior to both Son and Spirit, whose subordination is inherent in the nature of things. But many among the so-called orthodox, those who believe in the essential equality of essence (and thus full divinity) of Father, Son and Spirit, also believe that there are relationships of authority and submission, a kind of chain of command, present within the Trinity by nature. This seems to have been taken for granted from the early centuries (e.g., by Justin Martyr, Tertullian, and Origen) down to the present. Wainwright sees in the New Testament a kind of subordination of the Son to the Father "which is not limited to the earthly life of Christ but which is ultimate and absolute." He does not really like the term *subordinationism*, however; even though Jesus is secondary to the Father, he is still a part of the Godhead. "The Father has priority but both Father and Son are God."[107] Robert Crossley says, "There is a sense in which Jesus is always *sent* by the Father, doing the *will* of the Father, being *loved* by the Father and is in *subjection* to the Father."[108]

Such conclusions regarding an order of authority and submission within the eternal Trinity are drawn not just from the various passages such as are cited above, but from the very titles of Father and Son, and from the terms *generation* and *procession* as imported into the on-

---

107. Arthur W. Wainwright, *The Trinity in the New Testament*, pp. 187-195.
108. Robert Crossley, *The Trinity*, p. 40.

tological Trinity. Both of these latter terms include the connotation of dependence: if the Son is begotten by the Father, then his very existence in some way depends on the Father; if the Spirit proceeds from the Father (and the Son), then his existence likewise is dependent. Honorable sons are always obedient to their fathers. Thus it is easy to see how traditional trinitarianism has usually included this element of subordinationism, even along with a belief in full equality of essence.

But it need not be so, and I do not think that it should be so. We have already seen that the concepts of generation and procession have no firm basis in the ontological Trinity, and that even the Father-Son-Spirit relationships are not necessarily eternal. When these ideas are limited to the economic Trinity, one of the main foundations for subordinationism is removed. But it is important to see that the Father-Son relationship does not *have* to imply subordination. There are those who continue to see this relationship as eternally present in God but deny any kind of ontological subordination as a consequence of it. Buswell is an example. The term "son of" in Jewish usage, he says, "did not generally imply any subordination, but rather equality and identity of nature." This is all we need to read into the Biblical doctrine of Sonship, says Buswell. "The Son is not presented as generated, as a subordinate, or an inferior in any sense. But when Jesus called Himself the Son of God, and claimed that God was His own Father, this was, in the language in which it was understood, 'making himself equal with God' (John 5:18)."[109] All Biblical references to Christ's subordination to the Father "signify a *functional subordination* in the economy of the divine redemptive program." We must always distinguish between economic subordination and essential equality, says Buswell.[110]

This is in essence the same point made by Warfield many years earlier. He says,[111]

It may be very natural to see in the designation "Son" an intimation of subordination and derivation of Being, and it may not be difficult to ascribe a similar connotation to the term "Spirit." But it is quite certain that this was not the denotation of either term in the Semitic consciousness,

109. James O. Buswell, Jr., *A Systematic Theology*, I:105, 112.
110. Ibid., p. 106.
111. B. B. Warfield, "The Biblical Doctrine of the Trinity," p. 52.

which underlies the phraseology of Scripture; and it may even be thought doubtful whether it was included even in their remoter suggestions. What underlies the conception of sonship in Scriptural speech is just "likeness"; whatever the father is that the son is also. The emphatic application of the term "Son" to one of the Trinitarian Persons, accordingly, asserts rather His equality with the Father than His subordination to the Father . . . .

Also, "To be the Son of God in any sense was to be like God in that sense; to be God's *own* Son was to be exactly like God, to be 'equal with God,'" as John 5:18 suggests.[112] Neither does the designation "Spirit of God" convey the idea of derivation or subordination, "but is just the executive name of God—the designation of God from the point of view of His activity—and imports accordingly identity with God." First Corinthians 2:10-11 shows the inner equality of Father and Spirit.[113] Warfield concludes that if "the subordination of the Son and Spirit to the Father in modes of subsistence and their derivation from the Father are not implicates of their designation as Son and Spirit, it will be hard to find in the New Testament compelling evidence of their subordination and derivation," except in reference to their functions in the redemptive process, where the principle of subordination is clearly expressed.[114]

This conclusion deserves acceptance. Even if one projects the Father-Son-Spirit names and relationships into the internal, eternal relationships among the persons of the Trinity, there is no subordination therein. Christ's subordination to the Father was voluntarily assumed as part of his office as Savior; the same would be true of the Spirit.

It is common to find man-made illustrations and analogies, some rather homespun and some quite sophisticated, set forth in an effort to aid our feeble minds to grasp the great truth of the God who is three persons in one essence. Few of these are helpful, and some are even dangerous in that they convey heretical ideas of the Trinity rather than the Biblical one. (We have noted how some are quite modalistic.) Some of the more common illustrations are from human psychology (e.g., man as body, soul and spirit; or the soul itself as intellect, feeling, and will). But such similes bear little resemblance to the Three-in-One God.

---

112. Ibid., p. 53.
113. Ibid., pp. 52-53.
114. Ibid., p. 53.

One can discern triads everywhere, [115] but there is really only one Trinity, for which no illustration is fully adequate.[116]

This section on the traditional doctrine of the Trinity may be summed up in this quote from Warfield: "When we have said these three things, then—that there is but one God, that the Father and the Son and the Spirit is each God, that the Father and the Son and the Spirit is each a distinct person—we have enunciated the doctrine of the Trinity in its completeness."[117]

THE TRINITY IN CHRISTIAN PIETY TODAY

Does the traditional doctrine of the Trinity still have value for twentieth-century Christians? Is it still satisfying intellectually and spiritually? Many, of course, are answering these questions negatively. In keeping with a dominant element in the contemporary mentality, they say that the "three persons in one essence" idea is a product of metaphysical thought-forms borrowed from antiquated Greek philosophy and thus is totally unworkable in our day. As Fortman puts it, they see "a tension between the rigid Hellenic thought patterns of trinitarian theology and the much more elastic thought patterns of modern philosophy and psychology with their extremely (excessively?) heavy stress on function, evolution, process, history, relativity and contingency." They see "a tension between the classical, metaphysical, 'dead' way of presenting the doctrine of the Trinity and the modern tendency to see value only in knowledge that is 'alive' and relevant to the modern way of thinking and living."[118]

This "modern way" follows in the train of the likes of Kant and Ritschl, and accepts the methodological dictum of Adolph Harnack without qualification: "Dogma in its conception and development is a work of the Greek spirit on the soil of the Gospel."[119] An example of

---

115. See Nathan R. Wood's book, *The Secret of the Universe*, 10 ed. (Grand Rapids: Eerdmans, 1955), for an example of creative triadism.

116. See Carl Brumback, *God in Three Persons*, pp. 97-98. He warns against inadequate illustrations but favors one in the form of a triangle used by Raymond Lull, missionary to the Moslems in the fourteenth century.

117. B. B. Warfield, "The Biblical Doctrine of the Trinity," p. 36.

118. Edmund J. Fortman, *The Triune God*, p. 316.

119. Adolph Harnack, *History of Dogma*, tr. Neil Buchanan (New York: Dover Publications, 1961), I:17.

this is the way A. C. McGiffert labels the Nicene distinction of the Son from the Father as a "product of metaphysics" which is no longer necessary for Christian faith.[120] Another example is Leslie Dewart, who calls for a modernizing of the Christian faith through a "comprehensive *dehellenization of dogma*, and specifically that of the Christian doctrine of God."[121] The Trinity itself is an hellenic (Greek) form of thinking, especially the distinction between the concepts of nature and person (as in "three persons in one divine nature"). The imposition of the concept of a Trinity upon Biblical monotheism almost inevitably leads people today, on the level of piety at least, to think in terms of three Gods. "In a word," says Dewart, "we suffer from *crypto-tritheism.*"[122]

Another example is the recent book by Joseph O'Leary, *Questioning Back*, in which he calls for "the overcoming of metaphysics in Christian tradition," as the sub-title indicates. Following the lead of Heidegger, Husserl and others, he maintains that we must convert Christian thinking from the ontological thought-forms of Greek philosophy to contemporary historical categories as exemplified, for example, by today's so-called "narrative theology." The language of Nicea and Chalcedon "is metaphysical through and through," he says, since "it has been fashioned by Greek reason over twenty-five centuries"; and there is no easy way to translate it into modern terms. "Whatever is metaphysical in that language must pass through the crucible of the critique of metaphysics." Also, "the overcoming of metaphysics in theology cannot be adequately achieved except in the form of a full-scale historical hermeneutic: the struggle to purify our language of faith is a struggle with the weight of a complex bimillennial tradition of metaphysical theology."[123] The Nicene theology in particular "testifies to the triumph of metaphysics"; it "launched the greatest period of metaphysical theology."[124] But the New Testament's picture of Christ "can no longer be adequately grasped in the traditional mythical and

---

120. A. C. McGiffert, *A History of Christian Thought* (New York: Charles Scribner's Sons, 1932), I:275.

121. Leslie Dewart, *The Future of Belief*, p. 49.

122. Ibid., pp. 144-147.

123. Joseph S. O'Leary, *Questioning Back: The Overcoming of Metaphysics in Christian Tradition* (Minneapolis: Winston Press, 1985), pp. 3-6.

124. Ibid., p. 154.

metaphysical expression of it, such as those of the Nicene Creed" and elsewhere. Our new "sense of historicity makes mandatory" a "demythologization and dehellenization" of the faith of the Nicene Creed.[125]

These are but a few examples of an approach to theology that is typical of our age.[126] In my opinion it is every bit as culturally condition-ed as was the language of Nicea and does not necessarily involve an ad-vance over that way of thinking and speaking. Dewart subtitles his book "Theism in a World Come of Age," but Bernard Lonergan declares that it "seems to be less 'coming of age' than infantile regression."[127] He also pronounces it as "unhistorical to suppose that Greek philosophy sup-plied all the principal elements in which we have for centuries concep-tualized the basic Christian beliefs of the Trinity and the Incarnation."[128] No one denies that Athanasius and the other Nicene theologians were using Greek terms and concepts (how could they have done otherwise?), but the question is whether these concepts are alien to the Bible or whether they are a fair representation of what the Bible itself teaches. Brown asks this question and answer it thus:[129]

> . . . It is evident that trinitarian theology required the aid of Hellenistic concepts and categories for its development and expression, but they were the tools by means of which the implications of the New Testament were realized; they were not foreign concepts imposed upon an essential-ly simple message.

Henry points out that early Christian thinking did not uncritically adopt just whatever Greek metaphysics had to offer; for example, it rejected the Greek ideas of God, evil, matter and the body. In this connection he rightly says,[130]

---

125. Ibid., p. 212; see pp. 217-220.

126. See my discussion of "the modern aversion to metaphysics" in *What the Bible Says About God the Creator*, pp. 18-34.

127. Bernard J. F. Lonergan, "The Dehellenization of Dogma," *The Future of Belief Debate*, ed. Gregory Baum (New York: Herder and Herder, 1967), p. 88.

128. Ibid., p. 81.

129. Harold O. J. Brown, *Heresies*, pp. 105, 146.

130. Carl F. H. Henry, *God, Revelation and Authority*, V:202. The following com-ment from a *Christianity Today* editorial is relevant: "The Christian doctrine of the Trinity is a true description of what the Bible teaches God is like. The creeds are not

Nonevangelical scholars often scorn the early ecumenical creeds as a translation of Christianity into Greek metaphysics. But the decisive question is whether the creeds affirm what is true. . . . What decided the formulation of the ecumenical creeds was not Greek philosophy or Christian consciousness but rather and only the biblical data. . . .

The conclusion is that neither the Trinity nor traditional trinitarian language is out of date. They are still as relevant to Christian faith and life as when first revealed nearly two thousand years ago and precisely formulated a few centuries later.

In what ways does the doctrine of the Trinity relate to Christian faith and piety? Unfortunately this is not something that often crosses our minds, except perhaps when we sing the "Doxology." It is not a subject often taught and preached about. Gordon Clark remarks that in a thirty-year period of attending worship services from one American coast to the other, he never once heard a sermon on the Trinity.[131] Most preachers would probably have to confess to never preaching one.

What can we say about this doctrine? Why is it important? For one thing, it bears an important relation to the doctrine of creation. It shows us that God did not have to create the world out of some inner need, i.e., because he was lonely or because he needed an object for his boundless love. The interpersonal relationships among Father, Son and Spirit would obviate such needs, making the creation a matter of free choice on God's part.[132] It also helps to answer the ancient question of what God was doing before he created the world. As Buswell says, "The doctrine of the Trinity furnishes the only mode in which we can reasonably conceive of God existing in eternity before the creation of the finite world."[133]

---

philosophical elaborations of biblical truth; they are not philosophical statements at all and were never intended to be. They are statements of what their authors conceived to be certain basic facts. They may occasionally employ philosophical terms, but essentially they are simple confessions of facts the writers wished to state unambiguously and clearly enough that they could be distinguished from other alternative statements which, so the writers of the creeds believed, denied these basic facts" ("I Believe: A 1,600-year-old Confession of Faith," *Christianity Today* [December 11, 1981], 25:11).

131. Gordon H. Clark, *The Trinity*, p. viii.

132. See Jack Cottrell, *What the Bible Says About God the Creator*, pp. 118-119. As Brown says, "He had no inner need to create in order, as it were, to fulfill himself" (*Heresies*, p. 146).

133. James O. Buswell, Jr., *A Systematic Theology*, I:126.

The Trinity also has an important place in our worship. In addition to the occasional references to "Father, Son and Holy Ghost" in our hymns, our prayers are distinctly trinitarian even if we are not specifically conscious of it. Typically, following Jesus' example and teaching (Matt. 6:9), we pray *to* "our Father who art in heaven," and we pray *through* Jesus' name (John 16:23-24). At the same time the Holy Spirit strengthens us and clarifies our thoughts when we are struggling in prayer (Rom. 8:26; Eph. 6:18). Although it has broader applications, Ephesians 2:18 sums up the roles of the Trinity in our prayers: "For through Him [Jesus] we both have our access in one Spirit to the Father."

This helps to answer the question, to whom should our prayers be addressed? Some advocate praying directly to Jesus, citing as precedents the "maranatha" prayer of I Corinthians 16:22 ("Our Lord, come!") and Revelation 22:20 ("Come, Lord Jesus"). Robert Crossley suggests that one might begin his prayer time "by asking the Holy Spirit for his help, that you may be enabled to concentrate and to pray effectively in line with God's will."[134] But the Biblical examples regarding prayer to Christ are scant and specialized to say the least, and non-existent in reference to the Holy Spirit. In my opinion it is best to follow the almost universal Biblical practice of praying to the Father. This in no way demeans the full deity of the Son and the Spirit. It simply respects the reality of the economic Trinity as discussed earlier, i.e., the fact that Father, Son and Spirit have different roles in their redemptive relationships with their creatures. When we pray to Jesus instead of through him, it obscures the uniqueness of his glorious role as high priest and mediator between us and the Father (I Tim. 2:5; Heb. 4:14-16). Also, Crossley's suggestion that we pray directly to the Spirit for strength is contrary to Paul's command that we pray to the *Father* "that He would grant you, according to the riches of His glory, to be strengthened with power through His Spirit in the inner man" (Eph. 3:16; cf. 3:14).

Another important way in which we relate to the Trinity is in our baptism, as Jesus commanded that converts be baptized "in the name of the Father and the Son and the Holy Spirit" (Matt. 28:19). This trinitarian formula is a strong testimony to the deity of the Son and the

---

134. Robert Crossley, *The Trinity*, p. 43.

Spirit and of their equality with the Father, since they are all included within the single "name." Also, the fact that we are baptized "into the name of" (*eis to onoma*) the Father, Son and Spirit indicates that from the very beginning of our Christian lives we are in a saving relationship with all three persons of the Trinity. This helps to explain why baptism has such a prominent place in the New Testament plan of salvation (e.g., Mark 16:16; Acts 2:38; Col. 2:12; I Peter 3:21). With the coming of Christ and the Holy Spirit, and with the consequent revelation of the trinitarian nature of God, even the most basic act of human piety—belief in God—could no longer be the same. Once the work of redemption had been accomplished, not even the Jews were acceptable to God through their old faith in him even though it adhered strictly to the monotheistic tenets of the Old Testament. From this point on, faith in God, while still monotheistic, must be specifically directed toward God as a *Trinity* of Father, Son and Spirit.

This is one reason, I believe, why the concrete act of baptism was added to the basic requirements for acceptance with God (as compared with the Old Testament requirements of faith and repentance alone). It calls attention to the fact that an Old Testament type of faith in God is no longer adequate, and that one must commit himself to faith in the trinitarian God for his salvation. And the requirement is not just baptism as such, but baptism *into the name of the Father and the Son and the Spirit*. Here is where the Son's role in our redemption is indelibly impressed upon our minds, as in baptism we are buried into his death and resurrection for the remission of our sins (Rom. 6:3-5; Acts 2:38). Here is where the Spirit's presence in our lives is made real to us, as baptism is the time God has chosen to give us "the gift of the Holy Spirit" (Acts 2:38). This is why John's baptism cannot be equated with Christian baptism. John's baptism was given and practiced in the age of Old Testament faith, before a trinitarian relationship with God was possible. Christian baptism—baptism into the name of the Father and the Son and the Spirit—was something new, to go with and embody the new faith in the one God who is three persons.

This relation between baptism and the Trinity is important. When we give to baptism a significance anything less than that described in the New Testament, we are weakening the significance of the profound historical transition from the Old Testament pre-trinitarian faith in God to the New Testament trinitarian faith, a transition that Jesus Christ himself has tied to Christian baptism. Also, when we fail to use the trinitarian formula in the baptismal service itself, we are ignoring one of the principal elements of the newness of this new age. I am not saying that such neglect would invalidate a baptism, but it certainly shows little respect for Jesus' command, and it wastes a prime opportunity to testify to our trinitarian faith and to impress upon the convert the fact that he owes his salvation to the work of the Father and the Son and the Spirit.

A final way in which the doctrine of the Trinity is relevant to Christian faith and life is that this is what makes our redemption possible. The very salvation which we have received from God and upon which we rest our hope for eternal life could have been accomplished only by a Triune God. Carl Brumback rightly says,[135]

> That God exists in three Persons, Father, Son, and Holy Spirit, is the only basis on which the Christian doctrine of redemption can be intelligently set forth. Hence, the revelation concerning the plurality of Persons in the Godhead is not given for the mere purpose of presenting something which shall be puzzling and inscrutable to human minds, but as a necessary step in the much fuller revelation concerning the plan of salvation.

The work of Jesus Christ and of the Holy Spirit are the essence of redemption. To understand their work, and to know that it will truly save, we must know how they are related to God. This applies especially to Jesus Christ. If he is not God, and if he is not distinct from the Father, then there is a limit as to what he can do for us. These two elements of divinity and distinctness are emphasized by Brown: "All of the basic Christian convictions about the work of Christ presuppose that he is a distinct Person who can enter into a relationship with the Father. At the same time, Christ must have the attributes of deity with all its power in order to accomplish the gigantic task of reconciliation and redemption."[136] If he is not distinct from the Father, then his role as High Priest and Mediator is a sham, as was pointed out earlier in our discussion of modalism. And if he is not truly divine, how can he accomplish the work of atonement as the Bible describes it to us? As

---

135. Carl Brumback, *God in Three Persons*, p. 99.
136. Harold O. J. Brown, *Heresies*, p. 127.

Brown points out, if he is only *homoiousios* with the father or even less, then it is difficult to see how he has the "divine power and authority he needs to make an atonement on behalf of the whole human race. . . . If Christ is just another created being, even though he is the firstborn and most exalted of all created beings, then it is more natural to think of him as our teacher and example than as our atoning sacrifice." We would then be justified by imitation and not by faith.[137] But if he is God, truly God, then he is able to be that atoning sacrifice, our substitute on Calvary, "the propitiation for our sins; and not for ours only, but also for those of the whole world" (I John 2:2). And he can be God only in terms of the Biblical doctrine of the Trinity.

Thus we see that God the Redeemer is God the Father, God the Son, and God the Holy Spirit—the Trinity. We see also that this is not just some dusty, abstract doctrine that serves as a theologian's pastime, but is vitally related to the very heart of our faith.

---

137. Ibid., p. 119. See also p. 152.

4

THE RIGHTEOUSNESS OF GOD

The key attribute for understanding the nature of God as Redeemer is *righteousness*. The concept of the righteousness or justice of God lies at the very heart of the Biblical idea of redemption. Unless we understand what it means to say that God is righteous or just, it will be difficult for us to understand the nature of the saving work of Jesus Christ, whose cross was a demonstration of this righteousness (Rom. 3:25-26). Other key aspects of Christian faith and life are also directly related to this aspect of God's nature. All in all, as Stephen Mott says, "Justice is a chief attribute of God."[1] It is "one of the major motifs in the witness to God's person," says E. R. Achtemeier.[2] José Miranda agrees with Alfred Jepsen that justice can be spoken of as "the very essence of Yahweh."[3] In Robert Brinsmead's opinion, "Justice (*sadaq*) is arguably

---

1. Stephen Charles Mott, *Biblical Ethics and Social Change* (New York: Oxford University Press, 1982), p. 60.

2. E. R. Achtemeier, "Righteousness in the OT," *The Interpreter's Dictionary of the Bible*, ed. George A. Buttrick (Nashville: Abingdon Press, 1962), IV:82.

3. José Miranda, *Marx and the Bible*. tr. John Eagleson (Maryknoll, N.Y.: Orbis

the most important Old Testament word which describes the character and activity of God."[4] He says correctly that "such questions as the character of God, the meaning of the atonement and the nature of Christian ethics hinge on the biblical concept of justice."[5] Thus, says Brinsmead,[6]

> Justice is the heart of biblical theology. It is central to the message of the Bible. Our understanding of God's justice will therefore affect our view of the atonement, the last things, the church and the nature of Christian existence. If we radically change our concept of justice . . . we must radically change our concept of the atonement, the church and Christian life.

Such estimates of the importance of this subject are reinforced by the fact that recent studies of Biblical righteousness have come to conclusions that differ significantly from traditional views and have thus led to a reinterpretation not only of the nature of God but of the kinds of things Brinsmead mentions above, especially Christian ethics and the nature of the atonement. Such a reinterpretation is important for many today, because it provides them with an ostensible Biblical basis for views that were already being held for philosophical and cultural reasons. Others, especially those who are enamored with contemporary scholarship, are likely to accept this reinterpretation uncritically without having even considered more traditional approaches to the subject of God's righteousness.

In this chapter our purpose is to explain in more detail just what is at stake in this issue, and then to set forth an analysis of the Biblical data concerning the righteousness of God. We will conclude with a brief look at some of the implications thereof.

WHAT IS AT STAKE?

Several things have already been mentioned above as being directly related to the Biblical concept of God's righteousness. Three of these

---

Books, 1974), p. 86.

    4. Robert D. Brinsmead, "The Scandal of God's Justice—Part 1," *The Christian Verdict* (Essay 6, 1983), pp. 3-4.

    5. Ibid., p. 3.

    6. Ibid., p. 4.

will now be explained in more detail, with special attention being given to the modern reinterpretations that are being widely accepted in our day.

The Nature of God

The first thing at stake is, of course, our understanding of the very nature of God. In the most common traditional approach the justice or righteousness of God is usually associated with that side of God's nature having to do with his holiness, according to which he upholds his law and judges people impartially in accordance with their response to it. Since all men are sinners, God's justice thus pours out upon them the wrath and punishment they deserve. All of this is set over against the other side of God's nature, which is his disposition to be loving and merciful and gracious even toward sinners.

An example of this traditional view is A. H. Strong, who uses both terms—righteousness and justice—to designate the two aspects of God's transitive holiness. Righteousness is the mandatory aspect of this holiness, i.e., it demands from all moral beings conformity to the moral perfection of God; and justice is its punitive aspect, i.e., it visits non-conformity to God's perfection with penal loss or suffering. These are not arbitrary but are necessary aspects of God's nature. "As God cannot but demand of his creatures that they be like him in moral character, so he cannot but enforce the law which he imposes upon them. Justice just as much binds God to punish as it binds the sinner to be punished." Neither justice nor righteousness is connected with God's benevolence, nor does it bestow rewards.[7]

Another example of this traditional approach to God's justice is the Wesleyan theologian Miner Raymond. He says, "Justice, considered as an attribute of God, is that in the divine nature which prompts God to exact and to render that which is due."[8] He notes that it is common to distinguish different aspects of justice:[9]

   . . . legislative, that pertaining to the enactment of laws, with their

---

7. Augustus H. Strong, *Systematic Theology*, 3 vols. in 1 (Valley Forge: Judson Press, 1907), pp. 290-293.

8. Miner Raymond, *Systematic Theology* (Cincinnati: Walden and Stowe, 1877), I:363.

9. Ibid., p. 366.

sanctions of reward and punishment; judicial, defining and applying laws, especially in cases of transgression; vindicative, exacting penalty in cases where obligation to punishment has been incurred; but justice is one and the same thing in all cases—it is rendering what is due—the difference is only in the subjects to which it is applied. As all men are sinners, the justice of God, considered in his relations to man and in his administration of human affairs, is revealed chiefly in its relations to sin. Systematic divinity, therefore, mainly considers the divine justice as manifested in the punishment of sin. . . .

Not all traditional views of justice are this one-sided. Some include within God's justice his benevolent bestowal of rewards on the basis of relative merit; but even in such cases the main emphasis is usually on retributive justice or the punishment of sin.[10]

In recent decades, however, a new understanding of the justice of God has arisen, especially but not exclusively in the more modernistic circles. E. R. Achtemeier has this new view in mind when she says, "Righteousness as it is understood in the OT is a thoroughly Hebrew concept, foreign to the Western mind and at variance with the common understanding of the term."[11] The tendency is to interpret God's righteousness basically as his faithfulness to his covenant relationships with his people, the main emphasis being not on the demands of his laws but on the keeping of his promises. Thus the main expression of God's righteousness is his activity that saves and delivers his people from bondage and oppression. It is an almost altogether positive concept, with the ideas of wrath and punishment being practically excluded. It is equated variously with mercy, love or grace; or else it is seen as an expression of one of these. It involves wrath or punishment only to the extent that such might be necessary to express fully the divine grace.

One of the earliest examples of this approach is Albrecht Ritschl, who wrote in the late nineteenth century. H. Berkhof notes that Ritschl was led to eliminate every notion of retribution from the idea of righteousness (except for its eschatological function) and to equate it with grace and forgiveness.[12] Strong quotes Ritschl thus: "The

---

10. For example, see William G. T. Shedd, *Dogmatic Theology* (Grand Rapids: Zondervan, 1969 reprint of 1888 edition), I:364-380. "No one of the Divine attributes is supported by more or stronger evidences, than retributive justice," he says (p. 380).

11. E. R. Achtemeier, "Righteousness in the OT," p. 80.

12. Hendrikus Berkhof, *Christian Faith: An Introduction to the Study of the Faith,*

righteousness of God denotes the manner in which God carries out his loving will in the redemption alike of humanity as a whole and of individual men; hence his righteousness is indistinguishable from his grace."[13]

A more recent and very influential example of the new approach is Norman Snaith's *The Distinctive Ideas of the Old Testament*. Assuming an evolutionary development of Israelite religion, Snaith sees the teaching of the great eighth-century prophets as a definite advance over earlier views of holiness, with the emphasis falling on righteousness as ethical conduct rather than on religious ritual. The standard for such conduct was the nature of God himself. Included within their thinking was the idea that righteousness must be biased in favor of the poor and helpless; that God is righteous means that he takes the side of the oppressed and delivers them from their oppressors. Thus even in the eighth century B.C. righteousness was already connected with the "salvation vocabulary."[14]

But according to Snaith the real advance came with Second Isaiah in the sixth century B.C., who used the terms for righteousness almost exclusively for God's saving work.[15] Summing up the Old Testament development he says that righteousness was "always more than ethical, with a steady bias on behalf of the poor and weak, tending towards Salvation or to a benevolence that is far beyond strict justice, and at last opposed to it."[16] The New Testament builds upon the Old, with righteousness being primarily a salvation-word. God's righteousness is simply his salvation, and the verb form, usually translated "to justify," simply means "to save." It is not something within God's nature that must be satisfied before his mercy can be given, nor is it something he requires from anyone else before he will save. His righteousness is itself his salvation, which he gives to those who believe.[17]

---

tr. Sierd Woudstra (Grand Rapids: Eerdmans, 1979), pp. 128-129. Berkhof says this view is usually considered too one-sided today (p. 129).

13. Augustus H. Strong, *Systematic Theology*, p. 291. He cites the source as *Unterricht*, par. 16.

14. Norman H. Snaith, *The Distinctive Ideas of the Old Testament* (New York: Schocken Books, 1964), ch. III, "The Righteousness of God," especially pp. 51-70.

15. Ibid., pp. 87-93.

16. Ibid., p. 159.

17. Ibid., pp. 161-168.

Another influential statement of the revised concept of God's righteousness is that of Walther Eichrodt, who sees it mainly as an expression of God's covenant love and covenant faithfulness, or as God's "keeping of the law in accordance with the terms of the covenant." It is a relational term and refers to the fulfilling of one's responsibilities that arise out of a particular relationship.[18] Like Snaith, Eichrodt thinks the highest level of development came with Deutero-Isaiah, "who first elevated the concept of God's righteousness to the status of the key to the understanding of the whole divine work of salvation." This writer saw it as the redemptive acts by which God sought to restore his covenant people; thus he connected it with covenant love, loyalty, and succour. Such righteousness might include judgment on the heathen, but the decisive element was God's gift of salvation.[19] Eichrodt sums it up this way:[20]

> From what has been said it will be clear that the essence of the original biblical concept of God's righteousness lies neither in the ethical postulate of a moral world-order nor in an ideal of impartial retribution imposed by some inner necessity nor in the personification of the ethical in God. Instead it exalts over all abstract ethical ideas a *loyalty manifested in the concrete relationships of community.*

Another influential summary of this view is in the twin articles on righteousness in *The Interpreter's Dictionary of the Bible*, which depend heavily on the work of Eichrodt and other Continental researchers. In the Old Testament article E. R. Achtemeier rejects the usual views of righteousness: "It is not behavior in accordance with an ethical, legal, psychological, religious, or spiritual norm. It is not conduct which is dictated by either human or divine nature, no matter how undefiled. . . . It is not equivalent to giving every man his just due." What is it, then? "Righteousness is in the OT the fulfilment of the demands of a relationship, whether that relationship be with men or with God." Each person stands in a number of relationships. "And each of these relationships brings with it specific demands, the fulfillment of which constitutes

---

18. Walther Eichrodt, *Theology of the Old Testament,* tr. J. A. Baker (Philadelphia: Westminster Press, 1961), I:239-241.

19. Ibid., p. 246.

20. Ibid., p. 249.

righteousness. . . . When God or man fulfils the conditions imposed upon him by a relationship, he is, in OT terms, righteous."[21] God's righteousness, then, consists "not in action consonant with his inner nature," nor is it "a distributive justice which rewards the good and punishes the evil." Rather, "Yahweh's righteousness is his fulfilment of the demands of the relationship which exists between him and the people Israel, his fulfilment of the covenant which he has made with his chosen nation." And what does the covenant require? That Yahweh save his people. "His righteousness consists in his intervention for his people, in his deliverance of Zion . . . , in his salvation of his chosen nation." Also, "Yahweh's salvation of Israel is his righteousness, his fulfilment of his covenant with her."[22]

But is there no negative side to God's righteousness? Yes, sometimes the actions that save Israel also destroy her foes. Thus "there are two sides to his righteousness: salvation and condemnation; deliverance and punishment."[23] But the punishment is never separated from the deliverance as an end in itself; it always serves the interests of salvation. Achtemeier says,[24]

> However—and this is an important point—Yahweh's righteousness is never solely an act of condemnation or punishment. There is no verse in the OT in which Yahweh's righteousness is equated with his vengeance on the sinner, and not even Isa. 5:16 or 10:22 should be understood in such a manner. Because his righteousness is his restoration of the right to him from whom it has been taken, it at the same time includes punishment of the evildoer; but the punishment is an integral part of the restoration. Only because Yahweh saves does he condemn. His righteousness is first and foremost saving. He is a righteous God and a Savior.

"Yahweh's righteousness consists in his salvation of his chosen people."[25]

The article on righteousness in the New Testament practically repeats the conclusions of the first article, describing as righteous any act which preserves a covenant relationship. "In the prevailing NT use of this concept, God's righteousness is most clearly demonstrated in his

---

21. E. R. Achtemeier. "Righteousness in the OT." p. 80.
22. Ibid., pp. 82-83.
23. Ibid., p. 83.
24. Ibid.
25. Ibid., p. 84.

saving acts on behalf of man, whereby God, in Christ, upholds, and thus restores, the covenant relationship with sinful man." The few passages that seem to have retributive justice in mind do not really contradict the relational sense. "The retributive punishment of God is against those who harm the covenant people . . . , whereas the just rewards are given to those who act on behalf of their fellow men . . . . Therefore, though not on the surface, the relational understanding of 'righteousness' seems to underlie the retributive sense."[26]

Major theologians seem to concur in merging justice with mercy. Barth asserts that "God's righteousness does not really stand alongside His mercy," but rather "it is itself God's mercy. Just because He is righteous God has mercy."[27] Regin Prenter says, "God's righteousness and God's love are one." Both his wrath and his grace result from the same righteous love, which is related to the covenant. "Righteousness, faithfulness, mercy are one and the same attribute in God." Even the negative, punishing aspect of God's righteousness is based on the positive aspect of steadfast giving mercy. "It is precisely because God wants to give and bless in order to preserve the blessing of the covenant that he is forced to crush all unrighteousness." Thus "even this punishing righteousness is due to God's faithfulness and mercy."[28]

Writers from all across the theological spectrum seem to be accepting this understanding of righteousness. Stephen Mott, an Evangelical, describes justice as an instrument of love[29] and as a manifestation and expression of grace.[30] "It is similar in nature to grace and to grace's expression in love. In Scripture love and justice do not appear as distinct and contrasting principles. Rather there is an overlapping and a continuity."[31] While acknowledging a punitive element in righteousness, Mott sees it mainly as God's gracious saving actions which create and

---

26. P. J. Achtemeier, "Righteousness in the NT," *The Interpreter's Dictionary of the Bible*, ed. George A. Buttrick (Nashville: Abingdon Press, 1962), IV:91, 98.

27. Karl Barth, *Church Dogmatics. Volume II: The Doctrine of God. Part 1*, ed. G. W. Bromiley and T. F. Torrance, tr. T. H. L. Parker et al. (Edinburgh: T. & T. Clark, 1957), p. 387.

28. Regin Prenter, *Creation and Redemption*, tr. Theodor I. Jensen (Philadelphia: Fortress Press, 1967), pp. 417-419.

29. Stephen Mott, *Biblical Ethics and Social Change*, pp. 53, 64.

30. Ibid., pp. 60-61.

31. Ibid., p. 61.

preserve community.[32] At the other end of the spectrum is the liberation theologian José Miranda, who identifies love and justice. "One of the most disastrous errors in the history of Christianity," he says, "is to have tried—under the influence of Greek definitions—to differentiate between love and justice." The only love the Bible knows is "love-justice."[33] There is also a parallel between justice and salvation; "justice is a saving justice." It does have a punitive side, but only against those unjust persons who oppress the weak.[34]

It is evident that this concept of the nature of God is quite different from the traditional one. The righteousness of God is merged with his love and grace, while its negative expressions are seen as somehow necessary to the fulfilment of grace.

The Nature of Ethics

A point that must be kept constantly in mind is that any change in one's view of God will usually have significant consequences in other areas of belief as well. This is eminently true in reference to this question of the righteousness of God. The new way of looking at this aspect of God's nature has resulted in serious changes in the area of Christian ethics. This is true because justice is a key ethical concept and because justice on the human level is rightly patterned after God's justice. "Our justice corresponds to God's justice," as Mott says.[35] So if justice and mercy are distinguished in the nature of God, the tendency is to isolate them on the social level also. Justice is usually identified as the sole responsibility of human government and is defined in terms of the distribution of rewards and punishments (especially the latter) according to what each individual deserves. Meanwhile the church is assigned the responsibility of modeling God's mercy in the world and is told more or less to stay out of the justice business.

But once justice and mercy are merged in the very nature of God, this creates a whole new perspective on the nature of justice in the ethical realm and the respective roles of church and state in the pursuit of justice. The primary difference is that retributive justice (the punish-

---

32. Ibid., pp. 62-63.
33. José Miranda, *Marx and the Bible*, pp. 61-62.
34. Ibid., p. 83.
35. Stephen Mott, *Biblical Ethics and Social Change*, p. 59.

ment of law-breakers) fades into the background or disappears altogether, while the main emphasis falls on distributive justice interpreted (sometimes solely) as doing whatever is necessary to defend the oppressed and meet the needs of the poor. In other words, justice is no longer seen as giving a person what he *deserves* but as giving him what he *needs*.[36] Also, the idea that justice should treat each person impartially is rejected; it is seen as by nature being partial or biased toward the poor. It should be obvious also that the main emphasis is on *economic* justice, which is usually interpreted as equal participation in all the material benefits of this world.

A good example of this approach to ethics is Stephen Mott's book, *Biblical Ethics and Social Change*. All Christian ethics, says Mott, is grounded in and is a response to God's saving grace in Jesus Christ.[37] "The content, the nature of God's grace determines the content and nature of our acts."[38] Both love and justice are simply manifestations of grace.[39] Human justice simply imitates God's justice, which is primarily his saving action on behalf of the poor and the weak.[40] Thus human justice must be primarily distributive, which means that it seeks a loving distribution of the benefits of society to all people, giving special attention to the poor and being partial in their favor. "Justice is primarily spoken of by the biblical writers as activity on behalf of the disadvantaged."[41] The principal subject is material blessings, and the principal consideration is need; distribution is to be made to each according to his need. This is why "Biblical justice is biased in favor of the poor and the weak of the earth."[42]

Within this concept of justice and ethics, the role of human government differs considerably from traditional approaches. First, the concept

---

36. Robert K. Johnston, *Evangelicals at an Impasse: Biblical Authority in Practice* (Atlanta: John Knox Press, 1979), pp. 98-99.

37. Stephen Mott, *Biblical Ethics and Social Change*, pp. 22-29.

38. Ibid., p. 28.

39. Ibid., pp. 39, 61.

40. Ibid., pp. 60-61.

41. Ibid., pp. 62-65.

42. Ibid., pp. 70-71. The idea that justice is biased in favor of the poor is one of the most widespread ideas in contemporary ethical theory. See Norman Snaith, *The Distinctive Ideas of the Old Testament*, pp. 68ff. Referring specifically to one of the Old Testament terms for justice, Miranda agrees that the term "consists in doing justice to the poor, neither more nor less" (*Marx and the Bible*, p. 83).

of retributive punishment is severely truncated or even eliminated. Law-breakers must still be dealt with; but since justice is an expression of love, their "punishment" is interpreted as correction or rehabilitation. For example, Mott offers the term *corrective* as an alternative to *retributive* when describing criminal justice.[43] Second, since justice is seen mainly as distributive, i.e., as guaranteeing significant participation in this world's social and material benefits, the role of government is no longer seen as merely the protection of each person's *rights* to such benefits, but rather as actually *providing* these benefits to those who do not have them. Thus Mott speaks of "institutionalized benevolence" and "the expansion of the role of government to include concerns of social and economic welfare."[44]

The role of the church is likewise amended by this approach to justice. Since the church's main purpose is to proclaim God's love and grace to the world, and since justice is an instrument of love and an expression of grace, it follows that one of the church's main concerns must be justice. The old division of labor which made justice the exclusive prerogative of civil government no longer applies.[45] Justice is also the prerogative, even *responsibility*, of the church. This is why so many denominations and theologians are making issues of social justice one of the main aspects of the church's agenda. The "kingdom of God" announced in the Old Testament and inaugurated by Jesus is understood as including imperatives for social action. While denying that God's kingdom is a social program as such, Mott declares that "faithfulness to its demands for justice necessitates social programs and social struggle."[46]

We must remember that underlying this revision in the understanding of Christian ethics is the new concept of the justice or righteousness of God as discussed in the previous section. This merely demonstrates the fact that one's view of God ultimately determines how he views

---

43. Stephen Mott, *Biblical Ethics and Social Change*, p.71.

44. Ibid., pp. 62, 193.

45. See Carl F. H. Henry, *Aspects of Christian Social Ethics* (Grand Rapids: Eerdmans, 1964), pp. 146-147, for an example of this view. See also Jack Cottrell, *Tough Questions—Biblical Answers, Part Two* (Joplin, Mo.: College Press, 1986 reprint of 1982 edition), chs. 2 and 4.

46. Stephen Mott, *Biblical Ethics and Social Change*, p. 106. See his entire chapter 5, "The Long March of God," which deals with the kingdom of God.

everything else, and it also calls attention to the critical importance of a proper understanding of this particular attribute of God.

The Nature of Redemption

One other significant point at stake in reference to the question of the righteousness of God is the nature of redemption itself, and the atoning work of Jesus Christ in particular. This is true because of the way the New Testament (especially Paul) connects Christ's redemptive work with the righteousness of God, which is said to be revealed in the very gospel itself (Romans 1:16-17). Christ's death on the cross embodied and demonstrated God's righteousness, thus enabling God to be righteous (just) in justifying sinners (Romans 3:25-26). Because of such passages, it cannot be denied that the Bible connects righteousness and redemption. Thus it should be clear that if one changes his thinking about the former, it will definitely affect the way he thinks about the latter. This is especially true when God's righteousness is practically equated with his mercy, love and grace, and when the retributive elements of wrath and punishment are excluded from it. This leads to a rejection of the substitutionary nature of the atonement, i.e., the view that Christ took our place and accepted upon himself the wrath of God and penalty for sins that we deserve. A new understanding of the cross becomes necessary, one that is consistent with the idea that God's righteousness is in itself his gracious saving activity toward those in need.

We have already seen how Snaith equates the righteousness of God in the New Testament with salvation itself, and denies that there is any kind of judicial justice within God's nature that must be satisfied before he can forgive sins. The merciful God forgives as a matter of sovereign decision. One is not saved by righteousness, whether actual or imputed or imparted. Righteousness simply is salvation, and to be justified simply means to be saved. Romans 5:9 would then be translated "saved by his blood."[47] Snaith does not try to explain just how the blood of Christ would be needed for salvation, but clearly it can have nothing to do with satisfying God's just requirement for the punishment of sin.

P. J. Achtemeier, who (as seen above) tries to interpret righteousness in terms of faithfulness to covenant relationships,

---

47. Norman Snaith, *The Distinctive Ideas of the Old Testament*, pp. 164-173.

attempts to explain the cross in these terms. The atonement presupposes the covenant in which God has promised to save his people and in which his people are obligated to obey him. God manifests his righteousness in the cross because by this sacrifice he is enabling man to be saved, thus keeping his covenant promise. The keeping of the promise is itself the essence of this righteousness. Exactly how the cross of Christ enables man to be saved is another question, which has to do more with man's righteousness than God's. Man's problem is that he is supposed to render covenant obedience to God but has disobeyed instead, thus breaking the covenant relationship. Unfortunately man cannot restore this relationship through his own obedience; but Christ's death on the cross, interpreted as an act of obedience to the Father, is accepted in place of our obedience and thus restores our covenant relationship with God.[48] Achtemeier continues,[49]

> . . . It is Christ's act of obedience, in his death on the cross, that nullifies the disobedience of man whereby man broke the covenant relationship with God. This act of obedience restores the relationship of man with God by fulfilling the demand that the relationship had laid upon man: obedience to God. Therefore, by Christ's act of obedience the covenant relationship is restored, and man, by participating in it, may be righteous . . . .

Christ was "fulfilling for man the demand of the relationship, and thus upholding the relationship."[50] Thus whereas Snaith says that only faith and no righteousness of any kind is needed for God to restore the broken relationship with man, Achtemeier says that righteousness is required, but only in terms of the active obedience which the covenant requires of man. Christ is allowed to render such obedience in man's place, thus becoming "our righteousness" and restoring the covenant relationship. The idea that Christ was somehow suffering the penalty for sin is completely excluded.

Brinsmead is quite outspoken in his rejection of the idea that the cross was God's way of satisfying his own wrath upon sin while allowing him to forgive the sinner. Leaning heavily on the work of the

---

48. P. J. Achtemeier, "Righteousness in the NT," pp. 94-95.
49. Ibid., p. 95.
50. Ibid.

Achtemeiers and other modern scholars, Brinsmead distinguishes sharply between the "Latin or Western" concept of justice and the "Biblical or Gospel" concept. The former is defined as conformity to a norm (based on the law); the latter is defined as faithfulness to a relationship (based on grace). Latin justice is giving what is deserved, while Biblical justice is God's carrying out what he has graciously promised. The former is primarily punitive and is in tension with mercy, while the latter is primarily liberating or saving and consists in mercy for all who are oppressed. According to Brinsmead, Western theology has erred mightily in accepting the Latin concept of justice and especially in interpreting the atonement in terms of it. On such a theory the cross becomes an act of "legal manipulation" in which "God becomes a celestial Shylock so passionately committed to the principle of distributive justice that he must have his pound of flesh (this is called 'satisfying God's justice') before he can forgive." The central idea of this Latin theory, says Brinsmead, is "that justice and mercy are in tension and are reconciled only by the act of the cross."[51]

Following the modern line completely, Brinsmead merges God's justice with his mercy and interprets it as God's faithfulness to his promises to save his people. Thus justice is equated with salvation, mercy and deliverance. "Justice is God faithfully carrying out just what divine love had pledged to do."[52] "Therefore it is not justice in tension with mercy, but justice expressed in mercy. It is not justice which is punitive, but justice which brings salvation."[53] In his merciful justice God sides with the oppressed and delivers them from their oppression. This is where the atonement fits into the picture. In the person of Christ God has become one with us in oppression.

> . . . On the cross he not only identified himself *with us* all in our sin and misery, but he went beyond and endured the ultimate consequences of sin *instead of us*. We do not deny that there is substitutionary imagery in the Bible, but we suggest that it is not so much the language of a legal

---

51. Robert Brinsmead, "The Scandal of God's Justice—Part 1," pp. 8-9; also Robert Brinsmead, "The Triumph of God's Justice," *The Christian Verdict* (Essay 8, 1983), pp. 8-9.

52. Robert Brinsmead, "The Scandal of God's Justice—Part 1," pp. 5-7.

53. Robert Brinsmead, "The Scandal of God's Justice—Part 2," *The Christian Verdict* (Essay 7, 1983), p. 9.

transaction as it is the language of love. Love is always for us. It identifies with its object. It bears the other's burden (Gal. 6:2).

Since crucifixion was the ultimate form of degradation in ancient times, Christ's cross was God's ultimate identification with all the oppressed. "He takes the cause of all condemned, wretched, forsaken sinners upon himself and becomes absolutely one with them in all their deprivation and oppression." But this sets the stage for the resurrection, in which God "showed that he was the God who executes justice for all who are oppressed. . . . When God raised this oppressed Man to his own right hand, he thereby justified him—he did him justice and kept his promise that he would deliver the oppressed." The resurrection was thus "the triumph of divine justice over all human oppression summed up in this Oppressed One who was the one for, with, and instead of the many."[54]

There is no denying that this view, like the others summarized above, differs radically from the penal substitution concept of the atonement. In the latter view, rather than identifying himself with the oppressed, God in a sense *is* the oppresser in that he places the curse and penalty due to us upon Christ instead (II Cor. 5:21; Gal. 3:13; Isa. 53:6, 10). But the new view of God's justice includes neither curse nor penalty, thus making it necessary to reconstruct the doctrine of the atonement.

In this section we have attempted to summarize just three of the items that are at stake in connection with this issue of a proper understanding of the righteousness of God, namely, the nature of God, the nature of ethics, and the nature of the atonement. Other issues are also affected, such as universal salvation and the eternal punishment of the lost. But those presented here make it very clear that we are discussing in this chapter a most critical subject.

THE BIBLICAL TERMINOLOGY

Thus far we have been using two English terms, *righteousness* and *justice*, almost interchangeably; and we have made no attempt to define them. At this point we need to examine not only these words but also the Hebrew and Greek words underlying them, in order to arrive at a

---

54. Robert Brinsmead, "The Triumph of God's Justice," pp. 10-11.

basic understanding of this concept of the righteousness of God.

Some choose to make a distinction between the two English words themselves. With regard to God himself, Strong says that *righteousness* is that which demands from all moral beings conformity to the moral perfection of God, while *justice* is that which inflicts penal loss or suffering upon those who do not conform.[55] Erickson also distinguishes them but defines them differently. Righteousness, he says, is that attribute of God which causes him to act in conformity with his own laws or nature; justice is that which requires other moral agents to conform to the same.[56]

When used of man, the two terms tend to represent slightly different connotations in the minds of some, as Carl Henry points out. "The word righteousness tends to fix attention on inner divine-human relationships, whereas the term justice suggests primarily man's conduct toward others," he says. The traditional preference has been for the former term, which emphasizes individual, internal integrity; however, the current preference, says Henry, is for the term *justice*, since it more readily connotes interpersonal relationships and thus better agrees with the present emphasis on social and economic righteousness.[57] In confirmation of this, Brinsmead expresses his own choice of the term *justice*, since *righteousness* is too "churchy" and also "tends to convey a heavenly piety which misses the earthy, robust call for concrete social ethics."[58]

The fact is that there is no basis in the original languages for any kind of distinction between the terms *justice* and *righteousness*. Any distinctions made between these two words will be based on something other than the Biblical terminology and will usually be arbitrary. This accounts for the fact that Strong and Erickson, both of whom distinguish between the terms, do not give them the same definitions. In the final analysis they are expressing personal preferences. The same is true to some extent in the decision to use one or the other of these words as the principal way of translating the original languages. One's choice will depend

---

55. Augustus H. Strong, *Systematic Theology*, p. 290.

56. Millard J. Erickson, *Christian Theology* (Grand Rapids: Baker Book House, 1983), I:286-288.

57. Carl F. H. Henry, *God, Revelation and Authority. Volume VI: God Who Stands and Stays, Part Two* (Waco: Word Books, 1983), p. 404.

58. Robert Brinsmead, "The Scandal of God's Justice—Part 1," p. 3.

to a large extent on his own conclusions concerning the basic meaning of the Greek and Hebrew terms. Those who interpret them to mean conformity to a norm will usually prefer the term *righteousness*; those who think they mean faithfulness to a relationship will probably prefer *justice*.

What are the original terms, and just what do they mean? The main Hebrew words belong to the *ts-d-q* family. The verb *tsādaq* can mean "to be righteous or just" or "to make righteous or just," depending on the form in which it appears. The adjective *tsaddīq* means "righteous or just." The noun occurs 118 times in its masculine form, *tsedeq*, and 156 times in its feminine form, *tsedāqāh*. Either way it means "righteousness or justice"; there is no distinction between the two forms as far as meaning is concerned.[59] In the New Testament the words are *dikaios*, meaning "righteous or just"; *dikaiosunē*, meaning "righteousness or justice"; and *dikaioō*, meaning "to justify."

There is general (though not universal) agreement that the root meaning of the Hebrew term is "to be stiff or straight or firm." *Straightness* seems to capture the idea nicely. The term is used in connection with weights and measures, where it seems to mean "conformity to the proper standards."[60] The Law of Moses specified, "You shall do no wrong in judgment, in measurement of weight, or capacity. You shall have just [*tsedeq*] balances, just weights, a just ephah, and a just hin" (Lev. 19:36). (Literally it says "balances of justice [or righteousness], weights of justice," etc.) See also Deuteronomy 25:15; Ezekiel 45:10. The basic meaning of the terms when applied to human actions seems to be as follows: the adjectives (righteous, just) mean conforming to the proper standard, norm, or law; the nouns (justice, righteousness) mean conformity to the standard, norm, or law.[61] Stigers capsulizes the meaning as "not deviating from the standard"; thus with reference to persons the meaning is "conformity to an ethical

---

59. Norman Snaith, *The Distinctive Ideas of the Old Testament*, p. 72; E. R. Achtemeier, "Righteousness in the OT," p. 80.

60. Colin Brown, "Righteousness, Justification" (part), *The New International Dictionary of New Testament Theology*, ed. Colin Brown (Grand Rapids: Zondervan, 1978), III:356.

61. Louis Berkhof, *Systematic Theology* (London: Banner of Truth Trust, 1939), p. 75; Robert W. Gleason, *Yahweh: The God of the Old Testament* (Englewood Cliffs, N.J.: Prentice-Hall, 1964), p. 36.

or moral standard."[62] In the moral sense, says Hodge, the terms mean "right" or "conformed to what is right"; "that which satisfies the demands of rectitude or law."[63]

At this point we must call attention to one other Hebrew term which does not come from the same root as the terms above but which is often used in conjunction with them, namely, *mishpāt*. This word is used around 400 times and has many shades of meaning, but most generally it signifies "justice" or "judgment" in a legal sense.[64] It means "the due administration of judgment"[65] or strict justice according to law.[66] Sometimes it seems to be used as a synonym for *tsedāqāh*. Miranda counts thirty-one instances where the two terms occur as parallels; in each case, he says, this is a technical expression for social justice or justice for the poor and needy.[67]

One of the more important questions today is whether the etymological background of the Biblical terms really helps us to understand their meaning, or whether we must determine their meaning solely by their use in context. Those who hold to the revisionist concept of God's justice tend to discount etymology and appeal to the contextual usage. Those who do so tend to reject the meaning of "conformity to a norm" and substitute instead the idea of "faithfulness to a relationship." An example is E. R. Achtemeier, who says that etymology is not much help and describes *tsedeq* as "a concept of relationship," namely, "he who is righteous has fulfilled the demands laid upon him by the relationship in which he stands."[68] Those who follow this viewpoint usually specifically reject the idea of justice as conformity to a norm. E. R. Achtemeier is an example, as is P. J. Achtemeier.[69]

In my opinion, however, this is a false choice. We can agree that

62. Harold G. Stigers, "*tsādēq*," *Theological Wordbook of the Old Testament*, ed. R. Laird Harris et al. (Chicago: Moody Press, 1980), II:752-753.

63. Charles Hodge, *Systematic Theology* (Grand Rapids: Eerdmans reprint, n.d.), I:416.

64. Robert D. Culver, "*shāpat*," *Theological Wordbook of the Old Testament*, ed. R. Laird Harris et al. (Chicago: Moody Press, 1980), II:948-949.

65. Robert B. Girdlestone, *Synonyms of the Old Testament* (Grand Rapids: Eerdmans, 1951 reprint of 1897 edition), p. 101.

66. Norman Snaith, *The Distinctive Ideas of the Old Testament*, pp. 70, 74-75.

67. José Miranda, *Marx and the Bible*, p. 93.

68. E. R. Achtemeier, "Righteousness in the OT," p. 80.

69. Ibid.; P. J. Achtemeier, "Righteousness in the NT," p. 91.

fidelity to a relationship is an expression of God's righteousness, but we cannot agree that this is the basic meaning to the exclusion of the conformity definition. In fact, I believe it can be shown that not only the etymology but also the contextual usage confirms the meaning of righteousness as conformity to a norm, both with reference to man and God.

As applied to man, then, we believe that this definition of righteousness is quite adequate: conformity to the proper norm or law. This is how the term *dikaios* was used in the Greek and Hellenistic world. It indicated "one who conforms, who is civilised, who observes custom," or one "who observes legal norms."[70] Colin Brown says, "In the Classical Greek usage of the terms the idea of conformity to a standard was present and the standard was primarily that of social obligation."[71] In Biblical usage, however, the norm or standard is the will of God, and the righteous man is the one whose conduct conforms to the will or law of God. Thus Bavinck says the Biblical terms refer to "the state of a person who adheres to the law," or "the person who is righteous before the law." A righteous or just person is "in harmony with the law."[72] Quell points out that in the Old Testament God is the source of all law, and human righteousness is "constancy in executing and fulfilling the commands of God."[73] The connection of righteousness with law, i.e., the divine law, and thus its forensic (legal) connotation, can hardly be denied. Quell expresses it thus:[74]

> The concept of law exercised so strong an influence on the understanding of all social relationships that even theological reflection on the fellowship established between God and man was decisively affected by it. One may say that law is the basis of the view of God in the OT in so far as it is theologically developed, and that conversely the endowment of legal concepts with religious meaning contributed to an ethicising of law . . . .

---

70. Gottlob Schrenk, "δίχη, δίχαιος, etc." *Theological Dictionary of the New Testament,* ed. Gerhard Kittel, tr. Geoffrey W. Bromiley (Grand Rapids: Eerdmans, 1964), II:182.

71. Colin Brown, "Righteousness, Justification" (part), p. 358.

72. Herman Bavinck, *The Doctrine of God,* ed. and tr. William Hendriksen (Grand Rapids: Eerdmans, 1951), p. 215.

73. Gottfried Quell, "δίχη: The Concept of Law in the OT," *Theological Dictionary of the New Testament,* ed. Gerhard Kittel, tr. Geoffrey W. Bromiley (Grand Rapids: Eerdmans, 1964), II:175.

74. Ibid., p. 174.

"Righteousness is always a forensic concept," says Bavinck.[75] Some deny this, especially with reference to Pauline theology;[76] but Schrenk strongly affirms the forensic character of righteousness in the New Testament. He speaks of "forensic justification" and declares that "righteousness is forensically ascribed to the believer." Regarding the verb *dikaioō* ("to justify"), he says that "in the NT it is seldom that one cannot detect the legal connexion." Especially "in Paul the legal usage is plain and indisputable."[77]

The concept of conformity to a norm or standard does not disappear when the the Biblical terms for righteousness are used with reference to God. In fact, it means exactly this. That God is righteous means that all his actions conform perfectly to the proper standard or norm. This needs to be very carefully explained, however. It does not mean that there is some Eternal Law existing outside of God to which God himself must give allegiance. All law external to God derives from God; he externalizes it not for his own sake but for the sake of his creatures, that they might have access to the perfect standard for righteousness. For God himself, *his own eternally perfect nature* is the law or norm to which all his actions conform. Clarke puts it well when he says that the righteousness of God means that "God is the eternal Right," that "in him all right is grounded." In other words, "what we name his righteousness is the attitude and work of God as the eternal Right, in his relations with other beings."[78] Berkhof makes this comment:[79]

> The fundamental idea of righteousness is that of strict adherence to the law. Among men it presupposes that there is a law to which they must conform. It is sometimes said that we cannot speak of righteousness in God, because there is no law to which He is subject. But though there is no law above God, there is certainly a law in the very nature of God, and this is the highest possible standard, by which all other laws are judged. . . .

---

75. Herman Bavinck, *The Doctrine of God*, p. 219.

76. E.g., Norman Snaith, *The Distinctive Ideas of the Old Testament*, p. 167. He says that "it would be better if we could largely abandon the idea that the Pauline 'justification'-terminology is primarily, or even mainly, 'forensic and judicial'."

77. Gottlob Schrenk, "δίχη, δίχαιος, etc.," pp. 204, 214-215.

78. William Newton Clarke, *The Christian Doctrine of God* (Edinburgh: T. & T. Clark, 1909), p. 187.

79. Louis Berkhof. *Systematic Theology*, p. 74.

This does not mean that whenever God makes a decision or acts, he must pause and examine himself just to make sure that he is acting consistently with his own nature. Anything he does will automatically, as it were, be in accord with his own perfections. Tozer observes, "Justice, when used of God, is a name we give to the way God is, nothing more; and when God acts justly He is not doing so to conform to an independent criterion, but simply acting like Himself in a given situation." In other words, "He simply acts like Himself from within."[80]

Perhaps the key word for understanding the righteousness of God is *consistency*: God's actions are always perfectly consistent with his nature or character. He is always true to himself or in perfect harmony with himself. He is faithful to himself and to his own purposes. He is not fickle in what he wills to do or wills to be done by others, as if somehow his will were detached from his nature. This does not mean that his nature *determines* his willing as if God himself were the victim of an inner determinism. It is simply a matter of consistency. It assures us, to use Brunner's term, of "the constancy of the Divine Will."[81]

An important aspect or implication of the righteousness of God as thus understood is that God is always true to his word. If God is perfectly consistent in his character and actions, if he is always true to himself, then he will always be true to his announced purposes and promises. This is the sense in which righteousness means that God is faithful to his covenant relationship. Those who define righteousness as fulfilling the demands of a relationship are not wrong to include the latter in the former, but they are wrong to limit righteousness to this idea alone. In fact, this is but one aspect of the broader and more precise definition of righteousness as conforming to a norm. God conforms to the eternally perfect norm of his nature when he is true to his covenantal promises—and warnings.

Knowing that God is righteous is thus very important to us creatures who are asked to trust him. Because he is righteous, i.e., because he acts with perfect consistency and constancy, especially in keeping his word, we *can* trust him; we *can* rely on him and put our utter con-

---

80. A. W. Tozer, *The Knowledge of the Holy* (London: James Clarke & Co., 1965), pp. 93-94.

81. Emil Brunner, *The Christian Doctrine of God: Dogmatics. Volume I*, tr. Olive Wyon (Philadelphia: Westminster Press, 1950), p. 275.

fidence in him. We know that whatever he does will be *right*. Speaking specifically of God's relation to Israel, J. A. Ziesler says that God's righteousness means that his treatment of his people "is always informed by an underlying consistency which means that he can be completely relied upon in his government of the world, his judging, his vindication of Israel when oppressed, and his assurance of salvation."[82] This is no less true of Christians today.

Thus in perfect keeping with the basic meaning of the Biblical words and with their meaning as applied to man, the righteousness of God is understood in terms of conformity to a norm. Specifically we can say that his righteousness is the perfect consistency between his nature and his actions.

HUMAN RIGHTEOUSNESS

Before looking at the Biblical data concerning God's righteousness in more detail, we must first survey what Scripture says about human righteousness. This is true for two reasons. First, it will help us to see that the essence of righteousness is conformity to a norm. Second, it will help us to understand better the nature of God's righteousness in his treatment of human beings. This is so because, as we shall see, the Bible distinguishes between *absolute* human righteousness and *relative* human righteousness.

Righteousness as Conformity to God's Law

It is amply clear, from references drawn from the whole range of Biblical writings, that the basic connotation of righteousness in reference to human beings is innocence with regard to the law or conformity to the law. Ultimately the righteous person is the one who respects and keeps God's commandments.

This meaning is clear in a number of passages that depict a righteous person as one who is innocent of wrong-doing. In Genesis 20:4 Abimelech declared to God himself that he and his nation were righteous (*tsaddīq*) with respect to Sarah; in verse 5 he refers to the in-

---

82. J. A. Ziesler, "Righteousness," *The Westminster Dictionary of Christian Theology*, ed. Alan Richardson and John Bowden (Philadelphia: Westminster Press, 1983), p. 507.

tegrity of his heart and the innocence of his hands. The word is used in the same sense in II Kings 10:9, "You are innocent." Several times Job protests that he is righteous, i.e., he has done nothing to deserve the afflictions that have come upon him (Job 9:20; 27:6; 32:1-2; 34:5). Jeremiah declares that Jerusalem was destroyed in part because even her religious leaders "have shed in her midst the blood of the righteous," i.e., of those who had done nothing to deserve it (Lam. 4:13). Both Judas and Pilate's wife testify that Jesus is righteous, i.e., innocent of any crime and not deserving of punishment (Matt. 27:4, 19). Pilate says he is righteous (innocent) of whatever fate befalls Jesus (Matt. 27:24). In several passages the righteous and the innocent are paralleled (Job 17:8-9; 22:19; 27:17; Ps. 94:21).

Of special significance are the passages where the terms for righteousness are used in the context of a court of law or legal judgment, describing those who are innocent before the law or are in the right. Of constant concern is the fact that unscrupulous judges are prone to take bribes from those who have money and thus find in their favor, even if the ones who have no money for bribes are in the right. This is a very real kind of oppression, the essence of which is not being deprived of money as such but rather being deprived of justice before the law. God constantly defends these oppressed ones, not simply because they are poor but because they are righteous, i.e., innocent. He also constantly warns against such unjust treatment and condemns those who take part in it. For example, Exodus 23:6-8 says, "You shall not pervert the justice due to your needy brother in his dispute. Keep far from a false charge, and do not kill the innocent or the righteous, for I will not acquit the guilty. And you shall not take a bribe, for a bribe blinds the clear-sighted and subverts the cause of the just." Leviticus 19:15 makes it clear that the issue is not whether one is rich or poor, but whether one is innocent or guilty: "You shall do no injustice in judgment; you shall not be partial to the poor nor defer to the great, but you are to judge your neighbor fairly." Deuteronomy 16:19-20 tells the judges how to give "righteous judgment" (v. 18): "You shall not distort justice; you shall not be partial, and you shall not take a bribe, for a bribe blinds the eyes of the wise and perverts the words of the righteous. Justice, and only justice, you shall pursue." See Deuteronomy 1:16-17; 25:1. Job declares that he was just such a judge (Job 29:7-17). When deciding cases, he says, "I put on righteousness, and it clothed me; my justice

197

was like a robe and a turban" (Job 29:14). Proverbs echoes this theme: "To show partiality to the wicked is not good, nor to thrust aside the righteous in judgment" (Prov. 18:5). "He who justifies the wicked, and he who condemns the righteous, both of them alike are an abomination to the Lord" (Prov. 17:15). See Proverbs 17:26; 18:17; 29:4; 31:9. Ecclesiastes 5:8 acknowledges the reality of such injustice toward the poor. The prophets constantly condemn it. Isaiah 5:23 denounces those "who justify the wicked for a bribe, and take away the rights of the ones who are in the right" (i.e., the righteous or innocent, tsaddīq). See Isaiah 1:21-23, 26; 29:21; 59:4. Amos 5:12 condemns those "who distress the righteous and accept bribes, and turn aside the poor in the gate." See Ezekiel 45:9-10; Habakkuk 1:4. The long passage in Jeremiah 21:11-22:23 is an exhortation to the king to administer justice and a declaration of condemnation upon the one who refuses.

In all of these cases righteousness is basically innocence before the law, and the righteous person is the one who is in the right, though often victimized by corrupt judges. The righteous judge or king is the one who treats people fairly before the law, judging them only on the basis of guilt or innocence.

This concept extends beyond the official court of judgment and applies to every person in his everyday affairs. The righteous or just person is the one who loves justice and treats others fairly and wants to see fair treatment for everyone. Psalm 15 describes the one "who walks with integrity, and works righteousness" as one who speaks truth, does not slander or ill-treat his neighbor, is honest, and does not take a bribe (Ps. 15:2-5). "The execution of justice is a joy for the righteous" (Prov. 21:15). "The righteous is concerned for the rights of the poor" (Prov. 29:7). Isaiah 1:7 exhorts, "Learn to do good; seek justice, reprove the ruthless; defend the orphan, plead for the widow." The one who "walks righteously" is the one who "rejects unjust gain" and accepts no bribe (Isa. 33:15). Paul warns slaveholders to treat their slaves with "justice and fairness" (Col. 4:1).

A righteous person is concerned not only with seeing the poor person treated fairly before the law and in life in general; he is also willing to go beyond what is deserved and to give freely to those in need simply because they are in need. "The wicked borrows and does not pay back, but the righteous is gracious and gives" (Ps. 37:21). The gracious and righteous person is one "who is gracious and lends," and "the righteous will be remembered forever." Also, "He has given freely to the poor; his righteousness endures forever" (Ps. 112:4-6, 9). "The righteous gives and does not hold back" (Prov. 21:26). In Matthew 25:34-40 Jesus describes "the righteous" as those who have done works of benevolence.

It is not uncommon today for those who equate Christian ethics or Christianity itself with social justice (as in Liberation Theology, for instance) also to equate Biblical righteousness with helping the poor and needy per se. They contend that this is the very definition of justice or righteousness, i.e., a righteous or just person is anyone who gives to the poor or works to improve the lot of the poor. For example, Miranda claims that most Christians systematically ignore the fact that the Bible equates "doing justice" with "almsgiving," as in Psalm 112:9 and Matthew 6:1-2. He calls Psalm 37:21 a *definition* of justice: "The just man has compassion and gives."[83]

It is true, of course, that helping the needy and giving to the poor are *included* in Biblical justice or righteousness, and that a righteous man is one who gives to the poor. It is a serious error, however, to *equate* the two and to *define* righteousness as helping the poor. Righteousness is a much broader term; it means innocence before the law or conformity to the law (especially God's law) in *all* its provisions. Helping the needy or doing justice toward the poor is just one way in which a person is righteous; the whole scope of righteousness involves much more, including the fulfilment of personal religious duties toward God. Passages such as Psalm 37:21; Psalm 112:9; and Matthew 6:1-2 are *descriptions* but not exhaustive *definitions* of a righteous man. The context in each case shows that much more is involved. In Psalm 37:30-31, for example, the righteous man is also described thus: "The mouth of the righteous utters wisdom, and his tongue speaks justice. The law of his God is in his heart; his steps do not slip." Why should we not say that *this* is the essence of righteousness? Those who equate the "righteousness" of Matthew 6:1 with the almsgiving of verse 2 conveniently ignore that it is also identified with prayer (verse 5) and fasting (verse 16). Other passages that describe the nature of righteousness could be treated in the same way, e.g., Ezekiel 18. In this chapter the

---

83. José Miranda, *Marx and the Bible*, pp. 14-15, 85.

righteous man, who practices justice and righteousness" (v. 5), is one who "gives his bread to the hungry, and covers the naked with clothing" (v. 7). But this is not the whole picture. He is also one who avoids idolatry and adultery (v. 6) and who walks in God's statutes and ordinances (v. 9). The new man, recreated in Christ " in righteousness and holiness of the truth" (Eph. 4:24), is one who no longer steals and who shares with the needy (Eph. 4:28). But again this is not the whole picture. His new righteousness means *satisfying the requirements of the law* in all its aspects. Since God's law includes the requirement to be generous in helping the poor, this is included in righteousness; but it is not the definition of it.

There are many, many passages which show that the righteous person is the one who keeps God's commandments, the one who is innocent with respect to God's laws. Some have already been noted above (Ps. 37:30-31; Ezek. 18:9). After rehearsing the heart of God's law to Israel, Moses said, "And it will be righteousness [*tsedāqāh*] for us if we are careful to observe all this commandment before the Lord our God, just as He commanded us" (Deut. 6:25). In Psalm 18:20-24 David declares that God has rewarded him according to his righteousness (*tsedeq*). And of what does this righteousness consist? Verses 21-23 give its content thus: "For I have kept the ways of the Lord, and have not wickedly departed from my God. For all His ordinances were before me, and I did not put away His statutes from me. I was also blameless with Him, and I kept myself from my iniquity." In Isaiah 48:18 God says to Israel, "If only you had paid attention to My commandments! Then your well-being would have been like a river, and your righteousness like the waves of the sea." Those who "pursue righteousness" are those who "seek the Lord" (Isa. 51:1). "Listen to Me, you who know righteousness, a people in whose heart is My law" (Isa. 51:7). "A nation that has done righteousness" is one that "has not forsaken the ordinance of their God" (Isa. 58:2). "The ways of the Lord are right, and the righteous will walk in them" (Hos. 14:9). "Seek the Lord, all you humble of the earth who have carried out His ordinances; seek righteousness, seek humility" (Zeph. 2:3). "The righteous and the wicked" are distinguished as the "one who serves God" and the one who does not (Mal. 3:18). Zacharias and Elizabeth "were both righteous in the sight of God, walking blamelessly in all the commandments and requirements of the Lord" (Luke 1:6). "The doers of the Law" are the ones considered just (Rom. 2:13). The opposite of righteousness is lawlessness (II Cor. 6:14). Scripture in its entirety is profitable for "training in righteousness" that the man of God may be "equipped for every good work" (II Tim. 3:16-17). While "righteous Lot" lived in Sodom, his "righteous soul" was tormented daily by the lawlessness of its inhabitants (II Peter 2:7-8).

What should be clear in all these passages is that human righteousness is equated with conforming to God's laws, with walking in God's ways. It is the same as being upright in heart (Pss. 32:11; 97:11), pure (Job 4:17; 15:14), blameless (Gen. 6:9; Job 12:4; Ps. 18:23-24), and holy (Mark 6:20; Eph. 4:24).

Righteousness: Absolute or Relative?

In reading through the passages of Scripture surveyed above, one might wonder how anyone could be called righteous or blameless with respect to God's law, since all have sinned and have broken at least some of God's commandments. This leads to a very important point, namely, the fact that the Bible speaks of human righteousness in two senses. Sometimes it speaks of it in an *absolute* sense, i.e., righteousness in the sense of perfect obedience to God's law. But most of the time the Bible describes a man as righteous in only a *relative* sense, i.e., as conforming to the requirements of God's law in a general way or in his heart, as compared with the unrighteous or wicked whose hearts are turned against God and his commandments.

Absolute Righteousness

When human righteousness is compared absolutely with the eternally perfect standard of God's will, no one measures up to it; therefore no one is righteous in the absolute sense. The Bible makes this point emphatically and decisively, though not frequently. In Psalm 143:2 David pleads, "Do not enter into judgment with Thy servant, for in Thy sight no man living is righteous." Ecclesiastes 7:20 confirms this: "Indeed, there is not a righteous man on earth who continually does good and who never sins." This is Paul's main point in Romans 1:18-3:20, as summed up in 3:10-12, "As it is written, 'There is none righteous, not even one; there is none who understands, there is none who seeks for God; all have turned aside, together they have become useless; there is none who does good, there is not even one.'" His statement in Romans

2:13 that "the doers of the Law will be justified" is hypothetical only; there are no "doers of the Law" in the absolute sense (cf. Rom. 3:20).

The only exception to this would be Jesus Christ, who is often called righteous (Acts 3:14; 7:52; I John 2:1, 29; 3:7). He is absolutely righteous, since he maintained perfect conformity to God's will and committed no sin whatsoever (II Cor. 5:21; Heb. 4:15). Thus when all are compared with Jesus, he alone is righteous or just, while everyone else is unjust. This is one reason why he is able to be our Redeemer: "For Christ also died for sins once for all, the just for the unjust, in order that He might bring us to God" (I Peter 3:18).

This lack of absolute righteousness must constantly be kept in mind, since this alone keeps us aware of the fact that we do not deserve God's blessings, which are purely a matter of his gracious love. For example, God reminded the Israelites that he was not giving them the land of Canaan because they deserved it: "Know, then, it is not because of your righteousness that the Lord your God is giving you this good land to possess, for you are a stubborn people" (Deut. 9:6). Much later Isaiah 64:6 sounds the same note: "For all of us have become like one who is unclean, and all our righteous deeds are like a filthy garment." Daniel shows us the ultimate basis for our prayers when he includes these words in his own prayer to God: "We do not make requests of you because we are righteous, but because of your great mercy" (Dan. 9:18, NIV).

Our lack of absolute righteousness is the reason why God has provided a perfect righteousness for us through Jesus Christ (Rom. 5:19) as a gift which we may receive through faith (Phil. 3:9). Genesis 15:6, speaking of Abraham, reveals this truth for all subsequent generations: "Then he believed in the Lord; and He reckoned it to him as righteousness." Paul frequently quotes this passage (Rom. 4:3, 9, 22; Gal. 3:6) as confirming the doctrine of justification (being declared righteous) through faith. Habakkuk 2:4 provides another key statement of the same principle: "But the righteous will live by his faith" (cf. Rom. 1:17; Gal. 3:11; Heb. 10:38). Thus even we who are unrighteous or ungodly can be counted righteous (justified), since our "faith is reckoned as righteousness" (Rom. 4:5).

Relative Righteousness

Despite the universal lack of absolute righteousness, the Bible often speaks of "the righteous," and not simply in the sense of their having received the gift of Christ's righteousness through faith. On the contrary, they are called righteous because in a *relative* sense, they *are* righteous. They have a measure of piety and good works, of trust in and dependence upon God, that makes it proper for them to be called righteous—in comparison with the wicked. While such incomplete and relative righteousness is not sufficient to establish any kind of legal or moral claim upon God's blessings, nevertheless God is pleased with such righteousness and chooses to bless those who possess it.

The Bible very clearly demonstrates the reality of this relative righteousness in the way that it compares those who are "more righteous" with those who are less so. In Genesis 38:26 Judah acknowledges that Tamar "is more righteous than I." Saul made the same comparison between himself and David (I Sam. 24:17). Compared with the Canaanites, Israel was righteous (Deut. 9:4-5), though its lack of absolute righteousness showed that it did not *deserve* the land of Canaan any more than the Canaanites (Deut. 9:6). The Lord condemned Joab because he killed "two men more righteous and better than he" (I Kings 2:32). Ezekiel condemns Judah (the southern kingdom) because her deeds were so wicked that she made both Samaria (the northern kingdom) and Sodom "appear righteous" by comparison. "Because of your sins in which you acted more abominably than they, they are more in the right than you. Yes, be also ashamed and bear your disgrace, in that you made your sisters appear righteous" (Ezek. 16:51-52). In Habakkuk 1:13 the prophet notes that the wicked Babylonians swallow up nations "more righteous than they." In all of these comparisons, those called righteous are not so in any absolute sense, but only relatively so when compared with those more wicked than they.

The passages that really establish this concept of relative righteousness, however, are the many, many places where the "righteous" and the "wicked" are contrasted with one another. This way of speaking appears in the Bible almost from cover to cover. Abraham's prayer concerning Sodom was, "Wilt Thou indeed sweep away the righteous with the wicked?" (Gen. 18:23). Deuteronomy 25:1 commands judges to "justify the righteous and condemn the wicked." Solomon prayed for God to condemn the wicked and justify the righteous (I Kings 8:32). Job lamented, "If I am wicked, woe to me!

And if I am righteous, I dare not lift up my head" (Job 10:15). The Psalmists multiply the comparison. "For the Lord knows the way of the righteous, but the way of the wicked will perish" (Ps. 1:6). "O let the evil of the wicked come to an end, but establish the righteous" (Ps. 7:9). "The eyes of the Lord are toward the righteous . . . . The face of the Lord is against evildoers" (Ps. 34:15-16). "For the arms of the wicked will be broken; but the Lord sustains the righteous" (Ps. 37:17). "The wicked borrows and does not pay back, but the righteous is gracious and gives" (Ps. 37:21). "So let the wicked perish before God. But let the righteous be glad; let them exult before God" (Ps. 68:2-3). "And all the horns of the wicked He will cut off, but the horns of the righteous will be lifted up" (Ps. 75:10). The book of Proverbs has so many of these comparisons that we dare not try to list them. Here is just one example from the seven or so that appear in chapter 12 alone: "The thoughts of the righteous are just, but the counsels of the wicked are deceitful" (Prov. 12:5). Ezekiel is told to warn both the wicked and the righteous (Ezek. 3:17-21). Still, "the righteousness of the righteous will be upon himself, and the wickedness of the wicked will be upon himself" (Ezek. 18:20). Malachi 3:18 says, "So you will again distinguish between the righteous and the wicked, between one who serves God and one who does not serve Him." The New Testament continues this kind of comparison. Jesus says God "sends rain on the righteous and the unrighteous" (Matt. 5:45). At the end of the age, he says, the angels shall "take out the wicked from among the righteous" (Matt. 13:49). "I have not come to call the righteous but sinners to repentance," he says (Luke 5:32). "There shall certainly be a resurrection of both the righteous and the wicked," says Paul (Acts 24:15). "Law is not made for a righteous man, but for those who are lawless and rebellious, for the ungodly and sinners," he says (I Tim. 1:9). "And if it is with difficulty that the righteous is saved, what will become of the godless man and the sinner?" asks I Peter 4:18.

In all of this long listing of passages (which is only partial), it should be obvious that those who are called righteous are not perfectly so, yet God deigns to call them such in a relative sense, over against those who do not seek him and his will. It is in this sense that the Bible refers to specific people as righteous: Abel (Matt. 23:35; Heb. 11:4; I John 3:12); Lot (II Peter 2:7-8); Noah, who was "a righteous man, blameless in his time," i.e., as compared with the others of his time (Gen. 6:9;

THE RIGHTEOUSNESS OF GOD

7:1); Zacharias and Elizabeth (Luke 1:6); Joseph (Matt. 1:19); Simeon (Luke 2:25); John the Baptist (Mark 6:20); Joseph of Arimathea (Luke 23:50); and Cornelius (Acts 10:22). At other times Scripture simply speaks of the general category of the righteous or the typical righteous person. For instance, "He who receives a righteous man in the name of a righteous man shall receive a righteous man's reward" (Matt. 10:41). Luke 14:14 speaks of "the resurrection of the righteous." James 5:16 says, "The effective prayer of a righteous man can accomplish much." Hebrews 12:23 refers to "the spirits of righteous men made perfect." This seems to be referring to the saved who have died and are now fully sanctified in their spirits in the presence of Christ. But they were called "righteous" before they were "made perfect." This, like the other examples here, would be in a relative sense only. See also Matthew 13:17; 23:29; Romans 5:7; James 5:6.

We come now to one of the main points that I want to make in this section, namely, that the Bible tells us that God blesses the righteous *just because they are righteous.* This could not be so in the absolute sense, especially with reference to eternal blessings; but for those who are righteous in the relative sense described above, God blesses them *because of* their righteousness, or because in this relative sense they deserve it.

Over and over the Bible describes how God blesses the righteous. "He does not withdraw His eyes from the righteous; but with kings on the throne He has seated them forever, and they are exalted" (Job 36:7). "For it is Thou who dost bless the righteous man, O Lord, Thou dost surround him with favor as with a shield" (Ps. 5:12). "God is with the righteous generation" (Ps. 14:5). "The eyes of the Lord are toward the righteous, and His ears are open to their cry" (Ps. 34:15; cf. I Peter 3:12). "For the arms of the wicked will be broken; but the Lord sustains the righteous" (Ps. 37:17). "I have been young, and now I am old; yet I have not seen the righteous forsaken" (Ps. 37:25). "Cast your burden upon the Lord, and He will sustain you; He will never allow the righteous to be shaken" (Ps. 55:22). "The righteous man will flourish like the palm tree, he will grow like a cedar in Lebanon" (Ps. 92:12). "The righteous will be remembered forever" (Ps. 112:6). "This is the gate of the Lord; the righteous will enter through it" (Ps. 118:20). "The Lord loves the righteous" (Ps. 146:8). "The curse of the Lord is on the house of the wicked, but He blesses the dwelling of the righteous"

(Prov. 3:33). "The Lord will not allow the righteous to hunger, but He will thrust aside the craving of the wicked" (Prov. 10:3). "The righteous is delivered from trouble, but the wicked takes his place" (Prov. 11:8). "Adversity pursues sinners, but the righteous will be rewarded with prosperity" (Prov. 13:21). "The way of the wicked is an abomination to the Lord, but He loves him who pursues righteousness" (Prov. 15:9). "The Lord is far from the wicked, but He hears the prayer of the righteous" (Prov. 15:29). "Open the gates, that the righteous nation may enter, the one that remains faithful" (Isa. 26:2). "The way of the righteous is smooth; O Upright One, make the path of the righteous level" (Isa. 26:7). "You come to the help of those who gladly do right [tsedeq], who remember your ways" (Isa. 64:5, NIV). "And these will go away into eternal punishment, but the righteous into eternal life" (Matt. 25:46). "In every nation the man who fears Him and does what is right, is welcome to Him" (Acts 10:35).

In the passages just surveyed it is stated as a fact that God blesses the righteous, and it is implied that there is no reason for this blessing other than their righteousness. In other places it is more specifically stated that their (relative) righteousness is the reason why they are blessed. In I Samuel 26:23 David says that "the Lord will repay each man for his righteousness and his faithfulness." In II Samuel 22:21 he declares, "The Lord has rewarded me according to my righteousness; according to the cleanness of my hands He has recompensed me" (see Ps. 18:20). Solomon prays a prayer with a similar message: "Then hear Thou in heaven and act and judge Thy servants, condemning the wicked by bringing his way on his own head and justifying the righteous by giving him according to his righteousness" (I Kings 8:32; see II Chron. 6:23). Psalm 7:8 says, "The Lord judges the peoples; vindicate me, O Lord, according to my righteousness and my integrity that is in me." "The wicked earns deceptive wages, but he who sows righteousness gets a true reward. He who is steadfast in righteousness will attain to life" (Prov. 11:18-19). Isaiah 3:10 says, "Say to the righteous that it will go well with them, for they will eat the fruit of their actions."

This leads to the crucial consideration, namely, that one of the very special blessings that God bestows upon the righteous is deliverance from the unjust oppression of the wicked. It seems always to be the case that the wicked, in seeking to satisfy their own greed, take advantage of the righteous. This is true especially if the wicked have money or positions of power, and the righteous are poor and defenseless. But it may be equally true if the righteous one has money; he will be unwilling to use it in unjust ways (such as bribing a judge) and thus may still be the victim of injustice. Thus the righteous are always liable to suffering at the hands of the wicked. Since the poor and helpless are most likely to be victims of such injustice, the law of Moses specifically warns against it (Ex. 23:6-8). It has occurred and continues to occur nonetheless. David laments his own situation: "Let the wicked be put to shame, let them be silent in Sheol. Let the lying lips be dumb, which speak arrogantly against the righteous, with pride and contempt" (Ps. 31:17-18). "The wicked plots against the righteous, and gnashes at him with his teeth. . . . The wicked have drawn the sword and bent their bow, to cast down the afflicted and the needy, to slay those who are upright in conduct. . . . The wicked spies upon the righteous, and seeks to kill him" (Ps. 37:12, 14, 32). "They band themselves together against the life of the righteous, and condemn the innocent to death" (Ps. 94:21). Proverbs 24:15 warns, "Do not lie in wait, O wicked man, against the dwelling of the righteous." Ecclesiastes 5:8 cynically advises, "If you see oppression of the poor and denial of justice and righteousness in the province, do not be shocked at the sight, for one official watches over another official, and there are higher officials over them." These are the kind "who justify the wicked for a bribe, and take away the rights of the ones who are in the right" (Isa. 5:23). They "cause a person to be indicted by a word, and ensnare him who adjudicates at the gate, and defraud the one in the right with meaningless arguments" (Isa. 29:21). This is one of the very things that led to God's punishment of his own people. Amos 2:6 says, "Thus says the Lord, 'For three transgressions of Israel and for four I will not revoke its punishment, because they sell the righteous for money and the needy for a pair of sandals.'" Amos 5:12 continues, "For I know your transgressions are many and your sins are great, you who distress the righteous and accept bribes, and turn aside the poor in the gate." Habakkuk 1:4 describes these conditions in Judah as a prelude to the Babylonian captivity: "Therefore, the law is ignored and justice is never upheld. For the wicked surround the righteous; therefore, justice comes out perverted." The same was still the case in New Testament times, as James condemns the rich who cheat their hired help and who "have condemned and put to death the righteous man; he does not resist you" (James 5:4-6).

The point is that God sees this oppression and delivers the righteous from the hands of the wicked, *because they are righteous and are suffering unjustly*. This is the criterion for God's righteous intervention on their behalf. It is not their poverty *per se* that causes God to intercede for them and deliver them; it is the fact that *they are in the right*. Because they are thus righteous (relatively speaking), their vindication is *deserved* (relatively speaking). The fact is that the poor will most often be the ones victimized by the wicked, thus the poor and needy and helpless are often singled out as the objects of God's righteous aid. But I repeat: God helps them because they are righteous, not because they are poor as such. God is partial to the righteous, and thus to the righteous poor, but not to the poor *as poor*. It must be remembered, of course, that no one—poor or rich—is righteous in an absolute sense and thus has an absolute claim upon God's assistance. But God chooses to honor the relative righteousness of those who seek his face and to intervene on their behalf, while punishing the wicked who oppress them. The essence of this point can be seen quite clearly in Psalm 34:15-22,

> The eyes of the Lord are toward the righteous, and His ears are open to their cry. The face of the Lord is against evildoers, to cut off the memory of them from the earth. The righteous cry and the Lord hears, and delivers them out of all their troubles. The Lord is near to the brokenhearted, and saves those who are crushed in spirit. Many are the afflictions of the righteous; but the Lord delivers him out of them all. He keeps all his bones; not one of them is broken. Evil shall slay the wicked; and those who hate the righteous will be condemned. The Lord redeems the soul of His servants; and none of those who take refuge in Him will be condemned.

Psalm 37:39-40 says this: "The salvation of the righteous is from the Lord; He is their strength in time of trouble. And the Lord helps them, and delivers them; He delivers them from the wicked, and saves them, because they take refuge in Him." Psalm 58:10-11 graphically depicts both the negative and the positive side of God's righteous intervention: "The righteous will rejoice when he sees the vengeance; he will wash his feet in the blood of the wicked. And men will say, 'Surely there is a reward for the righteous; surely there is a God who judges on earth!'" The Psalmist prays in accord with these truths, "I have done justice and righteousness; do not leave me to my oppressors" (Ps. 119:121). The destruction of the wicked oppressors is a part of the divine intervention not just because it is a means of setting the oppressed free, but because the wicked *deserve* to be destroyed. The wicked are destroyed because they are wicked, just as the righteous are delivered because they are righteous. Two statements from Psalm 34 (quoted above) speak to this point: "The face of the Lord is against evildoers, to cut off the memory of them from the earth. . . . Evil shall slay the wicked; and those who hate the righteous will be condemned" (vv. 16, 21). Psalm 37:12-15 says, "The wicked plots against the righteous, and gnashes at him with his teeth. The Lord laughs at him; for He sees his day is coming. . . . Their sword will enter their own heart, and their bows will be broken." The prophets declare that the injustices of the rulers and the mighty are among the reasons for Israel's destruction:

> . . . You have plowed wickedness, you have reaped injustice, you have eaten the fruit of lies. Because you have trusted in your way, in your numerous warriors, therefore, a tumult will arise among your people and all your fortresses will be destroyed . . . . Thus it will be done to you at Bethel because of your great wickedness. At dawn the king of Israel will be completely cut off (Hosea 10:13-15).

Amos 5:6-7 pleads, "Seek the Lord that you may live, lest He break forth like a fire, O house of Joseph, and it consume with none to quench it for Bethel, for those who turn justice into wormwood and cast righteousness down to the earth." When Habakkuk complained that in Judah "the law is ignored and justice is never upheld," and "the wicked surround the righteous; therefore justice comes out perverted" (Hab. 1:4), God replied by saying that he was sending the Babylonian armies to destroy the nation for just that reason (Hab. 1:5-11). Isaiah 3:10-11 sums up the principle thus: "Say to the righteous that it will go well with them, for they will eat the fruit of their actions. Woe to the wicked! It will go badly with him, for what he deserves will be done to him."

This perception that there is a relative human righteousness, as opposed to absolute righteousness, and that this relative righteousness is the basis for the oppressed person's cry for deliverance, is a key point for a proper understanding of the righteousness of God, to be discussed in the next section. Those who focus on poverty *per se* or upon oppression *per se*, rather than this relative righteousness, are guilty of distorting the nature of God's righteousness.

DIVINE RIGHTEOUSNESS

We come now to the heart of this chapter, namely, a detailed look at the nature of God's righteousness according to the Biblical meaning and usage of the various terms. We should remember that the terms *righteousness* and *justice* are often used interchangeably, and we should note that all of the Hebrew and Greek terms surveyed earlier are used in abundance with regard to God and his works.

Affirmations of Divine Righteousness

Unequivocal affirmations of the righteousness or justice of God appear throughout Scripture, from Genesis to Revelation. This classic confession is included in Abraham's plea for God to spare Sodom: "Far be it from Thee to do such a thing, to slay the righteous with the wicked, so that the righteous and the wicked are treated alike. Far be it from Thee! Shall not the Judge of all the earth deal justly?" (Gen. 18:25). I.e., shall he not do right, or do justice (*mishpāt*)? The final book of Scripture includes these words of heavenly praise: "Great and marvelous are Thy works, O Lord God, the Almighty; righteous and true are Thy ways, Thou King of the nations. . . . For all the nations will come and worship before Thee, for Thy righteous acts have been revealed" (Rev. 15:3-4).

This theme is ubiquitous in Scripture. "The Lord is righteous" (Ps. 129:4); "the Lord is righteous in all His ways" (Ps. 145:17; cf. Dan. 9:14). "The Rock! His work is perfect, for all His ways are just; a God of faithfulness and without injustice, righteous and upright is He" (Deut. 32:4). "For the Lord is righteous; He loves righteousness" (Ps. 11:7). "He loves righteousness and justice" (Ps. 33:5; cf. Pss. 37:28; 45:7; Heb. 1:9). "For I, the Lord, love justice," he says (Isa. 61:8). His "right hand is full of righteousness" (Ps. 48:10), and "righteousness and justice are the foundation of [His] throne" (Ps. 89:14). His righteousness is infinite: it reaches to the heavens (Ps. 71:19), and it is everlasting (Pss. 111:3; 119:142). "Righteous art Thou, O Lord," confesses the Psalmist (Ps. 119:137). Even "the heavens declare His righteousness" (Pss. 50:6; 97:6), as do the children of men. Pharaoh: "The Lord is the righteous one, and I and my people are the wicked ones" (Ex. 9:27). The leaders of Israel: "The Lord is righteous" (II Chron. 12:6). Ezra: "O Lord God of Israel, Thou art righteous" (Ezra

9:15). The Levites: "Thou art righteous" (Neh. 9:8). David: "O my righteous God" (Ps. 4:1, NIV). And Jesus himself: "O righteous Father" (John 17:25).

The Messiah, God the Son, is often called righteous. It is a common theme of Messianic prophecy. "With righteousness He will judge the poor . . . . Also righteousness will be the belt about His loins" (Isa. 11:4-5). His kingdom will be established in justice and righteousness (Isa. 9:7). As "the Righteous One" he will justify the many (Isa. 53:11). "He is just" (Zech. 9:9); he is "a righteous Branch" who will "do justice and righteousness in the land" (Jer. 23:5; cf. 33:15). "And this is His name by which He will be called, 'The Lord our righteousness'" (Jer. 23:6). The New Testament calls him "the Righteous One" (Acts 3:14; 7:52; 22:14; I Peter 3:18 (NIV); I John 2:1, 29; 3:7).

The Meaning of Divine Righteousness

What does it mean to say that God is righteous? In the general word study earlier in this chapter we concluded that righteousness as such means conformity to a norm or standard, or satisfying the requirements of the law. We have seen that this conclusion is borne out by the way the terms are used in Scripture regarding human righteousness. We have suggested that there is no reason to think the terms mean something different when applied to God, and that divine righteousness is thus also conformity to a norm, that norm being his own nature. In this section we will be examining the actual Biblical usage of the terms as applied to God, and we shall see that the above conclusion is correct. Biblical usage confirms that God is righteous in the sense that everything he says and does conforms to the perfection of his own nature. His actions are always consistent with or true to his eternally perfect being; God is always true to himself, to his purposes, and to his word. As Henry puts it, "He in himself consistently affirms his nature and is unswervingly faithful to his own promises and his covenant."[84] This is the meaning of the righteousness of God. Any other proposed meaning (e.g., faithfulness to a relationship, saving activity on behalf of the oppressed) must be included within this as only a possible aspect of it.

Perhaps the Biblical term that does most closely express the concept

---

84. Carl F. H. Henry, *God, Revelation and Authority*, VI:425.

of righteousness is *faithfulness*, with the primary emphasis being on God's faithfulness to himself and to his word (as law and promise) rather than to others. This concept is seen most clearly in Deuteronomy 32:4, "The Rock! His work is perfect, for all His ways are just; a God of faithfulness and without injustice, righteous and upright is He." The connection of faithfulness with justice is unmistakable, and the reference to God as a Rock emphasizes this concept of dependability even further. The same close connection is seen in Psalm 143:1, "Hear my prayer, O Lord, give ear to my supplications! Answer me in Thy faithfulness, in Thy righteousness!" And likewise in the Levitical prayer in Nehemiah 9:33, "Thou art just in all that hast come upon us; for Thou hast dealt faithfully, but we have acted wickedly." The same parallel appears in Psalm 119:75, "I know, O Lord, that Thy judgments are righteous, and that in faithfulness Thou hast afflicted me." Of the Messiah it is said, "Also righteousness will be the belt about His loins, and faithfulness the belt about His waist" (Isa. 11:5). See Psalms 33:5; 36:5-6; 98:2-3.

That God's righteousness means faithfulness to himself as the standard is seen in the way his own actions are called righteous as opposed to all wickedness. Pharaoh's confession states this contrast: "I have sinned this time; the Lord is the righteous one, and I and my people are the wicked ones" (Ex. 9:27). I.e., it was Pharaoh who deviated from the norm, not the righteous God. See also the Levites' confession: "Thou art just . . . but we have acted wickedly" (Neh. 9:33). "Surely, God will not act wickedly, and the Almighty will not pervert justice," says Elihu (Job 34:12). In Psalm 69:27 God's righteousness is contrasted with human iniquity. Psalm 45:7 says of God the Son, "Thou hast loved righteousness, and hated wickedness." This is quoted in Hebrews 1:9 thus: "Thou hast loved righteousness and hated lawlessness," a choice of words that clearly shows the nature of righteousness as respect for law and conformity to law.

Because God is true to himself (i.e, righteous), he is also true to his word. When God speaks, he speaks righteously, which means that he will always carry out what he has spoken. "I, the Lord, speak righteousness declaring things that are upright," he says in Isaiah 45:19. "I have sworn by Myself, the word has gone forth from My mouth in righteousness and will not turn back" (Isa. 45:23). This applies to his covenant promises as well as to his covenant judgments. That God is righteous means that he is faithful in keeping his promises. Referring to the Abrahamic covenant regarding the land (Gen. 17:8), Nehemiah 9:8 says, "And Thou hast fulfilled Thy promise, for Thou art righteous." Psalm 119:123 (NIV) says, "My eyes fail, looking for your salvation, looking for your righteous promise." If God pronounces judgment upon a sinner in accord with his stated warnings, that too is righteous: "Against Thee, Thee only, I have sinned, and done what is evil in Thy sight, so that Thou art justified [tsādaq] when Thou dost speak, and blameless when Thou dost judge" (Ps. 51:4). The fact that God's word always comes to pass is a basis for saying, "He is righteous!" (Cf. Isaiah 41:26; the word is tsaddīq.)

Perhaps the most significant confirmation of the fact that God's righteousness is the consistency of his actions with his nature is the fact that his own laws, which are the very expression of his nature, are called righteous. God's laws or commandments are themselves true to his nature and thus are righteous or just. Also, the fact that God's judgments are made in accordance with his laws and in accordance with how we respond to them, is what makes his judgments just. In other words, God's law is the very symbol of his righteousness, i.e., his acting faithfully according to law. Scripture says, "The Lord was pleased for His righteousness' sake to make the law great and glorious" (Isa. 42:21). His law is equated with his justice (Isa. 51:4). Moses emphasized the righteous character of God's law to the Israelites: "Or what great nation is there that has statutes and judgments as righteous as this whole law which I am setting before you today?" (Deut. 4:8).

Psalm 119:142 shows the connection between God's righteousness and God's law: "Thy righteousness is an everlasting righteousness, and Thy law is truth." The entire psalm extols the righteousness of God's commandments, using a number of terms to represent the latter. "Thou has commanded Thy testimonies in righteousness and exceeding faithfulness," says verse 138. "Thy testimonies are righteous forever" (v. 144). In verse 40 God's precepts are paralleled with his righteousness. There are several references to God's righteous judgments or ordinances (mishpāt), literally, his "judgments of righteousness" (vv. 7, 62, 106, 164; cf. Ps. 19:9, "The judgments of the Lord are true; they are righteous altogether"). Finally, in verse 172 the Psalmist says, "Let my tongue sing of Thy word, for all Thy commandments are righteousness." Paul echoes this in Romans 7:12, "So

213

then, the Law is holy, and the commandment holy and righteous and good."

God's laws, God's commandments are true to his own nature and therefore are righteous. They represent God's nature to us and therefore constitute an objectification of the eternal norm for the conduct of all moral beings. They do not command anything contrary to his own perfection. We can obey them and know that we are in the right; they will not lead us astray. Indeed, they show us the way God is and the way God acts. But mostly they are given to show us how *we* should act, so that *we* can be the way *God* is and act as he acts. The norm is righteous because it is God's norm, and we are righteous insofar as we conform to that norm. (Our righteousness is not so much the content of our actions as it is the *way* we act, i.e., with a view to fulfilling all the requirements of God's law. Righteousness describes the *form* of our obedient actions rather than their content, which is better described by the term *holiness*. The same would be true of God. His righteousness is not the sum of the various moral virtues that constitute his holiness, but rather the way all his actions conform to those virtues.)

God's righteousness comes into expression in his actions toward and relationships with his creatures. To say that the way he acts toward his creatures is righteous is to say that his actions are in accord with the perfect norm. This means first of all that his deeds are consistent with his own perfections, or that "his treatment of his creatures conforms to the purity of his nature,"[85] which includes being true to his covenant promises and warnings. But it also means that God's actions toward his creatures are in accord with *his creatures'* correspondence to that perfect norm as they know it in the form of God's laws. In other words, God's actions are righteous because he takes account of the righteousness and wickedness of men and treats them accordingly, blessing the righteous and condemning the wicked. It is because he is righteous that he responds to human righteousness with blessing and to human wickedness with wrath.

In other words, the perfect norm to which God's righteous deeds conform has two foci, one within God himself (his own nature) and one external to God (his own nature as objectified in his law). God's treat-

---

85. Augustus H. Strong, *Systematic Theology*, p. 290.

ment of his creatures is consistent with his own nature, and it is consistent with how his creatures have related to the norm. This is true in both the absolute and the relative senses. In the absolute sense, *no* man or woman has related perfectly to that norm; thus *all* are judged to be wicked and are under God's wrath and condemnation. This is the circumstance that calls for the redeeming work of Jesus Christ. But in the relative sense, some are righteous and some are wicked; and thus they merit different treatment. It is extremely important that we recognize that most of the Biblical data regarding God's righteous actions toward men are from the perspective of the latter's *relative* righteousness or wickedness, not the absolute.[86] This is true because most of the data are from the Old Testament, where God is dealing with mankind not on the basic universal level of Creator to creature, but within the unique context of his covenant relationship with just one nation, the people of Israel. Though this relationship with Israel is very special, it is only a relative context and not the ultimate context for the expression of God's righteousness. Thus it is quite appropriate for God to respond to them and to those with whom they interact according to their relative righteousness or wickedness.

The Impartiality of Divine Righteousness

Whether in the relative or absolute context, the essence of God's righteousness is always the same. It means that he applies the same standard to all people impartially, in accord with their own righteousness or wickedness. In making this application he must act as a Judge. He must examine the character and actions of men and determine what kind of treatment is merited by each. In his capacity as

---

86. This key concept of the distinction between the absolute and relative righteousness of men needs further exploration. W. G. T. Shedd gives a brief discussion of the difference between "relative merit" and "absolute merit," as he puts it (*Dogmatic Theology*, I:366ff.). Herman Bavinck touches on the point when he notes that Israel is very sinful and merits heavy punishment; "nevertheless, over against the heathen nations Israel is in the right; in spite of all its transgressions, it favors a righteous cause; it is on the side of right" (*The Doctrine of God*, p. 218). The distinction between eternal and temporal punishment is relevant. In relating divine justice with the purpose of civil government, Stephen A. James distinguishes "absolute retribution" from "partial, or limited, retribution" ("Divine Justice and the Retributive Duty of Civil Government," *Trinity Journal* [Autumn 1985; new series], 6:201).

Judge, he is righteous. "The heavens declare His righteousness, for God Himself is judge" (Ps. 50:6). He is called a "righteous judge" (Ps. 7:11; II Tim. 4:8). "For Thou hast maintained my just cause; Thou dost sit on the throne judging righteously" (Ps. 9:4).

God the righteous Judge will sit in absolute judgment in the Last Day, "and He will judge the world in righteousness" (Ps. 9:8). "He is coming to judge the earth. He will judge the world in righteousness, and the peoples in His faithfulness" (Ps. 96:13). Acts 17:31 says that on that day God will judge the world in righteousness through the risen Christ.

But God judges not just in the Final Judgment, but also with temporal judgments in the limited contexts of this world. In his righteous judgments he determines how he will treat and respond to the sons of men here and now. For example, Job pleaded with God to judge him righteously: "Let Him weigh me with accurate scales, and let God know my integrity" (Job 31:6). Here he is asking God to take account of his (Job's) relative righteousness, and thus to realize that he does not deserve the sufferings that have come upon him. On the other hand, appealing to the other focus of divine justice, David asks God to act in accord with his own (God's) perfect righteousness: "Judge me, O Lord my God, according to Thy righteousness; and do not let them rejoice over me" (Ps. 35:24).

It was said above that the essence of God's justice is that he applies the same standard to all people impartially, in accord with their own righteousness or wickedness. The idea that righteousness means impartial judgment and impartial treatment is denied by many today, especially within the context of the new social gospel and Liberation Theology. The concept of impartiality, it is said, is a part of the pagan Latin or Western theory of justice and has been read into the Bible, which does not teach it. Instead, we are told, Biblical justice is quite partial—to the poor, the oppressed, the needy, the weak, the helpless, the afflicted.[87] Mott says, "A justice which includes partiality to those who are afflicted in their social relations extends the meaning of the creative power of grace and love." He says, "Justice is primarily spoken of by the biblical writers as activity on behalf of the disadvantaged."[88]

---

87. Stephen Mott, *Biblical Ethics and Social Change*, pp. 61-64.
88. Ibid., pp. 63-65.

Brinsmead affirms, "The Old Testament is full of evidence that divine justice is biased in favor of the oppressed."[89]

Such language is very common today, but is it warranted by Scripture? Is it true that God is partial in his judgments and treatment of his creatures, or is he impartial? If impartiality means treating everyone in absolutely the same manner, then of course God is partial, because he does *not* treat everyone in exactly the same way. But if impartiality means announcing in advance that people in different categories will receive different treatment, and then treating all those who fall into a particular category in the same pre-announced way, regardless of who they may be, then God *is* impartial, for this is what impartiality means.

But there is another consideration, namely, whether there is a fitting or relevant connection between the specified treatment and the specified group. If a company president decided that his own relatives would always be promoted first, regardless of merit, that would be partiality. If a teacher announced that only those who could dunk a basketball would be allowed to pass math class, that would be partiality. If a government announced that only those with a certain skin color could live in a certain area, that would be partiality. If God decreed that all those with red hair and blue eyes would be saved, while all others would not, that would be partiality. In all of these cases there is no obvious connection between the treatment and the group, so they would seem to be examples of partiality.

But what if a government announced that all its poor, i.e., those whose assets were below a certain level and who had no way of earning more than a certain amount, would be allowed to live without cost in a particular housing development? Surely there is a reasonable congruity between the group and the treatment, so this would seem to be an impartial condition. But what if all the inmates in the jails or prisons within that government's jurisdiction suddenly applied to live in that development? Most would probably qualify in terms of assets and earning power, but it is unlikely that they would be allowed to move! In such a case poverty alone would not be a sufficient condition to qualify one for government aid; the government must obviously distinguish between its "righteous" poor and its "unrighteous" poor. True impartiality must take

89. Robert Brinsmead, "The Triumph of God's Justice," p. 10.

righteousness into account.

This is a somewhat crude analogy of the nature of God's treatment of people. Yes, God does promise to give special blessings to a particular group. Whoever belongs to that group will be blessed and assisted, no matter who he may be; and there is a relationship of congruity between the assistance offered and the group specified. It is true that God promises to help the poor and that he condemns the rich, but it is also true that poverty and wealth *alone* are *not* the final criteria for determining whom God will bless and whom he will curse. He has blessed some who were wealthy (Gen. 13:2) and cursed some in their poverty (Prov. 6:6-11). Rather, the final criterion for determining how God will treat his people is their own (relative) righteousness or wickedness. Generally speaking, the poor in Israel were poor because of unjust treatment or were victims of unjust treatment just because they were poor and thus helpless before the unscrupulous rich. God's ultimate concern as a righteous God is neither poverty nor wealth *per se*, but justice and injustice. He is for those who are victims of injustice, whether they be poor or rich (but usually they are poor); and he is against those who perpetrate injustice, whether they are poor or rich (but usually they are rich). This is not partiality, because those whom he promises to help are the *righteous*, i.e., those who are in the right, and thus (in a relative sense) *deserve* to be helped; and those whom he promises to condemn are the *wicked* who *deserve* to be condemned.

The Biblical witness to God's impartiality is abundant. "For the Lord your God is the God of gods and the Lord of lords, the great, the mighty, and the awesome God who does not show partiality, nor take a bribe" (Deut. 10:17). "The Lord our God will have no part in unrighteousness, or partiality, or the taking of a bribe" (II Chron. 19:7). Peter declared, "I most certainly understand now that God is not one to show partiality, but in every nation the man who fears Him and does what is right, is welcome to Him" (Acts 10:34-35). Romans 2:11 flatly states, "For there is no partiality with God." He "impartially judges according to each man's work," says I Peter 1:17. (The KJV uses the expression "no respect of persons" or "without respect of persons.")

Certain provisions in the Mosaic Law show that impartiality before the law is of the very essence of justice or righteousness. "You shall not pervert the justice due to your needy brother in his dispute," it says;

"nor shall you be partial to a poor man in his dispute" (Ex. 23:3, 6).
"You shall do no injustice in judgment; you shall not be partial to the
poor nor defer to the great, but you are to judge your neighbor fairly"
(Lev. 19:15). "You shall not show partiality in judgment; you shall hear
the small and the great alike" (Deut. 1:17). Judges are told to give
"righteous judgment," i.e., "You shall not distort justice; you shall not
be partial, and you shall not take a bribe" (Deut. 16:18-19).

Likewise, this is the nature of God's justice or righteousness. *Just
because* he is a righteous God, he is impartial; impartiality is of the very
essence of his righteousness. He measures all by the same standard;
and those who measure up to the standard (the righteous) are blessed,
while those who do not (the wicked) are condemned. This is why
Abraham could not believe that God would treat the righteous and the
wicked in Sodom in the same way: "Wilt Thou indeed sweep away the
righteous with the wicked?" (Gen. 18:23). Then he expresses his confidence in God's justice: "Far be it from Thee to do such a thing, to slay
the righteous with the wicked, so that the righteous and the wicked are
treated alike. Far be it from Thee! Shall not the Judge of all the earth
deal justly?" (Gen. 18:25; see Eccl. 9:2-3). This is also why it seems so
improper for the righteous to suffer and the wicked to prosper: it is the
very opposite of justice; it should be the other way around. This is why
Habakkuk could not understand why God permitted the injustice
among his people to continue (Hab. 1:2-4), and this is why Jeremiah
asked these pointed questions: "Righteous art Thou, O Lord, that I
would plead my case with Thee; indeed I would discuss matters of
justice with Thee: Why has the way of the wicked prospered? Why are
all those who deal in treachery at ease?" (Jer. 12:1). The Psalmist com-
plains, "How long will you judge unjustly, and show partiality to the
wicked?" He then states how this injustice should be corrected: "Vindicate the weak and fatherless; do justice to the afflicted and destitute.
Rescue the weak and needy; deliver them out of the hand of the wicked" (Ps. 82:2-4). Job's great problem was his perception that he was
suffering even though he was righteous and therefore did not *deserve* to
suffer. (He was erroneously assuming that all suffering is caused by God
as retribution for evil.) Elihu's answer to Job included his assurance that
God does not act unjustly: "Far be it from God to do wickedness, and
from the Almighty to do wrong. For He pays a man according to his
work, and makes him find it according to his way. Surely, God will not

act wickedly, and the Almighty will not pervert justice" (Job 34:10-12).
He continues,

> Can he who hates justice govern? Will you condemn the just and
> mighty One? Is he not the One who says to kings, "You are worthless,"
> and to nobles, "You are wicked," who shows no partiality to princes and
> does not favor the rich over the poor, for they are all the work of his
> hands? (Job 34:17-19, NIV).

"The Almighty . . . will not do violence to justice and abundant
righteousness" (Job 37:23). Recognizing this impartial justice of God,
David pleaded to be delivered from his enemies (Ps. 7:1-2); but he was
willing to be beaten by these enemies if he had done something to
deserve it (Ps. 7:3-5). But since he did not think this was the case, he
cried out, "Vindicate me, O Lord, according to my righteousness and
my integrity that is in me. O let the evil of the wicked come to an end,
but establish the righteous" (Ps. 7:8-9).

What is being acknowledged in such passages as these is the truth
that is reiterated throughout God's word, that the righteous God judges
and rewards men according to their works. This principle is stated as
early as II Chronicles 6:30, "Then hear Thou from heaven Thy dwelling
place, and forgive, and render to each according to all his ways." It is
stated in Job 34:11, cited above: "For He pays a man according to his
work." Isaiah 59:18 declares, "According to their deeds, so He will
repay, wrath to His adversaries, recompense to His enemies." In
Jeremiah 17:10 the Lord says, "I, the Lord, search the heart, I test the
mind, even to give to each man according to his ways, according to the
results of his deeds." See Psalm 62:12; Proverbs 24:12; Jeremiah
32:19; and Ezekiel 33:20. The New Testament repeats the same principle many times. See Matthew 16:27; 25:31ff.; Acts 10:34-35; Romans
2:6; Colossians 3:25; Revelation 2:23; 20:12-13; 22:12. This last
passage is Jesus' promise, "Behold, I am coming quickly, and My
reward is with Me, to render to every man according to what he has
done." This is what we would expect from a righteous God. Erickson
says, "The justice of God means that he is fair in the administration of
his law. He does not show favoritism or partiality. Who a person is is not
significant. What he has done or not done is the only consideration in
the assigning of consequences or rewards."[90]

---

90. Millard Erickson, *Christian Theology*, 1:288.

This means that they are being too hasty who reject the idea that Biblical justice means "giving what is due." An example is E. R. Achtemeier, who asserts that righteousness "is not equivalent to giving every man his just due."[91] Brinsmead simply echoes Achtemeier.[92] It may well be that this particular terminology ("giving what is due") is Aristotelian,[93] but the concept is not foreign to Scripture. The righteousness or justice of God means exactly this, that he gives the righteous their due and he gives the wicked their due.

The Scope of Righteousness

What shall we say, then, of the current trend almost to equate righteousness with salvation? We noted several examples of this at the beginning of this chapter. E. R. Achtemeier asserts, "Yahweh's righteous judgments are *saving* judgments"; his "righteousness consists in his salvation of his chosen people."[94] Brinsmead remarks on the "surprisingly kind face of God's justice" and on the Bible's "remarkable repetitiveness" by which "God's justice is associated with his acts of salvation and deliverance, and with his deeds of mercy and forgiveness."[95] God's justice "is a saving justice," says Miranda.[96] What shall we say of this? Flatly and simply, that it is incorrect. Those who take this approach either underestimate the significance of the many passages that connect God's righteousness with his wrath and punitive judgments, or they ignore them altogether. It is a prime example of selective exegesis. For example, in his imitative efforts to revise the concept of righteousness, Brinsmead quotes thirteen Old Testament passages that relate it to salvation, mercy, forgiveness, and deliverance of the oppressed.[97] He mentions not one of the approximately forty passages that connect it with wrath and punishment.

At the same time, this recent emphasis on righteousness as salvation is a corrective to some traditional approaches that have tended to ignore *this* aspect of it and have over-emphasized the negative aspects of wrath

---

91. E. R. Achtemeier, "Righteousness in the OT," p. 80.
92. Robert Brinsmead, "The Scandal of God's Justice—Part 1," p. 8.
93. See Herman Bavinck, *The Doctrine of God*, pp. 220-221.
94. E. R. Achtemeier, "Righteousness in the OT," pp. 83, 84.
95. Robert Brinsmead, "The Scandal of God's Justice—Part 1," pp. 2, 5.
96. José Miranda, *Marx and the Bible*, p. 83.
97. Robert Brinsmead, "The Scandal of God's Justice—Part 1," pp. 5-6.

and retribution. Mott and others who complain about the unbiblical separation of justice from love and mercy do have a point[98] (though they are just as wrong when they try to merge them into one another). The many Biblical references to justice as salvation cannot be ignored.

What emerges from a study of the way the Bible uses the terms for justice or righteousness is that this is a concept that is broad enough to include both wrath and mercy, both condemnation and blessing. It is that attribute of God which leads him to test every man's works according to the revealed norm and to reward him accordingly, *either* with blessing and mercy and deliverance if his works are righteous, *or* with condemnation and wrath and punishment is they are wicked. This principle is clearly stated in Romans 2:9-11, "There will be tribulation and distress for every soul of man who does evil, of the Jew first and also of the Greek, but glory and honor and peace to every man who does good, to the Jew first and also to the Greek. For there is no partiality with God." This is the essence of God's righteousness, and it includes both wrath and mercy. E. R. Achtemeier has said, "Yahweh's righteousness consists, not in action consonant with his inner nature . . . . Nor is Yahweh's righteousness, as it is commonly thought, a distributive justice which rewards the good and punishes the evil, as good and evil are defined in the law."[99] In my opinion, this statement is the exact opposite of truth, because I believe this is exactly what God's righteousness is.

References to Righteousness as Both Salvation and Retribution

What follows here is a survey of the Biblical evidence for this understanding of divine justice or righteousness. The passages that will be cited below all involve the use of one or more of the terms for this concept and thus help us to discern its meaning. We begin with a number of passages that speak of God's justice and include within its purview *both* salvation for the righteous *and* punishment for the wicked. The first is Psalm 5:8-12. Verse 8 says, "O Lord, lead me in Thy righteousness [*tsedāqāh*] because of my foes; make Thy way straight before me." The next two verses (9-10) then speak of judgment upon

---

98. Stephen Mott, *Biblical Ethics and Social Change*, p. 62.
99. E. R. Achtemeier, "Righteousness in the OT," p. 82.

these foes: "Hold them guilty, O God; by their own devices let them fall! In the multitude of their transgressions thrust them out, for they are rebellious against Thee" (v. 10). Then the last two verses (11-12) speak of deliverance: "But let all who take refuge in Thee be glad . . . . For it is Thou who dost bless the righteous man, O Lord, Thou dost surround him with favor as with a shield."

Psalm 7:6-11 is a similar plea for the righteous God to deliver David from his enemies. First he pleads for wrath upon the wicked: "Arise, O Lord, in Thine anger; lift up Thyself against the rage of my adversaries . . . . O let the evil of the wicked come to an end" (vv. 6, 9). At the same time he asks for deliverance because he is in the right: "Awake, my God; decree justice [mishpāt]. . . . Judge me, O Lord, according to my righteousness, according to my integrity, O Most High. O righteous God, who searches minds and hearts, bring to an end the violence of the wicked and make the righteous secure" (vv. 6-9, NIV). He ends the section with this affirmation: "God is a righteous [tsaddīq] judge, a God who expresses his wrath every day" (v. 11, NIV). The connection between divine righteousness on the one hand and both wrath and salvation on the other hand is impossible to deny.

In back-to-back passages in Psalm 9 the same expression, "judging in righteousness [tsedeq]," is used first for the destruction of the wicked and then for the deliverance of the oppressed. First,

> When my enemies turn back, they stumble and perish before Thee. For Thou has maintained my just cause; Thou dost sit on the throne judging righteously. Thou hast rebuked the nations, Thou hast destroyed the wicked; Thou hast blotted out their name forever and ever. The enemy has come to an end in perpetual ruins, and Thou hast uprooted the cities; the very memory of them has perished (vv. 3-6).

And then,

> But the Lord abides forever; He has established His throne for judgment [mishpāt], and He will judge the world in righteousness; He will execute judgment for the peoples with equity. The Lord also will be a stronghold for the oppressed, a stronghold in times of trouble, and those who know Thy name will put their trust in Thee; for Thou, O Lord, hast not forsaken those who seek Thee (vv. 7-10).

The same expression (vv. 4, 8) thus has the dual content. It can refer both to wrath and to mercy.

Another such passage is Psalm 11:4-7, which reads thus:

> The Lord is in His holy temple, the Lord's throne is in heaven; His eyes behold, His eyelids test the sons of men. The Lord tests the righteous and the wicked, and the one who loves violence His soul hates. Upon the wicked He will rain snares; fire and brimstone and burning wind will be the portion of their cup. For the Lord is righteous [*tsaddīq*]; He loves righteousness [*tsedāqāh*]; the upright will behold His face.

The main emphasis of the passage is on the destruction of the wicked, who are not pictured simply as oppressors of the righteous but as people who fail God's test of goodness. These he punishes *just because he is righteous and loves righteousness*. The passage concludes with the affirmation of blessing upon the upright.

Psalm 72:1-4 reverses the emphasis but still includes both aspects within the scope of divine righteousness as carried out by the King (perhaps the Messiah):

> Give the king Thy judgments, O God, and Thy righteousness [*tsedāqāh*] to the king's son. May he judge Thy people with righteousness [*tsedeq*], and Thine afflicted with justice [*mishpāt*]. Let the mountains bring peace to the people, and the hills in righteousness. May he vindicate the afflicted of the people, save the children of the needy, and crush the oppressor.

Psalm 143:11-12 is similar: "For the sake of Thy name, O Lord, revive me. In Thy righteousness [*tsedāqāh*] bring my soul out of trouble. And in Thy lovingkindness cut off my enemies, and destroy all those who afflict my soul; for I am Thy servant." The same dual emphasis within God's righteousness can be seen in Psalm 145:17-20,

> The Lord is righteous [*tsaddīq*] in all His ways, and kind in all his deeds. The Lord is near to all who call upon Him, to all who call upon Him in truth. He will fulfill the desire of those who fear Him; He will also hear their cry and will save them. The Lord keeps all who love Him; but all the wicked He will destroy.

In Isaiah 11:4-5 the Messiah's righteousness includes both helping the poor and afflicted as well as slaying the wicked with the breath of his mouth.

Isaiah 59:1-20 describes Israel's state of oppression resulting from the lack of justice, and God's righteous response to this state. Verses 1-8 enumerate the sins of the wicked, concluding thus: "They do not know the way of peace, and there is no justice [mishpāt] in their tracks." Then verses 9-15 describe the resulting oppression that engulfed the whole nation, probably a reference to the Babylonian captivity. In such a state they still suffered from a lack of justice and righteousness (vv. 9, 14), but the prophet acknowledges that they deserved their fate because they had been so sinful (vv. 12-13). Then verses 15-20 describe how Yahweh, being touched by their oppression and their confession of sin, determines to deliver them, probably a reference to the restoration from exile. The heart of this last segment is verse 17, "And He put on righteousness [tsedāqāh] like a breastplate, and a helmet of salvation on His head; and He put on garments of vengeance for clothing, and wrapped Himself with zeal as a mantle." Here righteousness is obviously equated with the salvation of his people (vv. 16-17), and less obviously but probably equated with the vengeance and wrath upon his enemies (vv. 17-18).

Isaiah 63:1-6 also shows the close connection between righteousness, salvation, and wrath. Verse 1 asks the Lord to identify himself, and he replies, "It is I who speak in righteousness [tsedāqāh], mighty to save." But this righteous salvation, as seen in verses 2-6, is accomplished through a terrible execution of wrath upon the wicked peoples. Redemption comes through vengeance (v. 4), and salvation through wrath (v.5). But both the salvation and the wrath are the result of God's righteousness.

A final passage that speaks of punishment and salvation together as God's righteous deeds is Daniel 9:14-16. Verse 14 refers to the Babylonian captivity as a calamity which the Lord had brought upon Jerusalem in accordance with his warnings in the Law of Moses (vv. 11-13; cf. Deut. 28:15-68). But because of their sins the people deserved it, therefore "the Lord our God is righteous with respect to all His deeds which He has done," i.e., he is righteous in bringing this calamity upon us. But then in verse 16 Daniel appeals to the same righteousness of God as the basis of hope for deliverance from captivity: "O Lord, in accordance with all Thy righteous acts, let now Thine anger and Thy wrath turn away from Thy city Jerusalem."

225

In these passages we have seen how God's righteousness is not limited either to his salvation or to his wrath, but includes both. A multitude of other passages speak singly either of salvation as the work of divine righteousness or of wrath as a work of the same. Those in each category will now be listed.

References to Righteousness as Salvation

Some may be surprised to see how often God's righteousness is connected with and even paralleled with his work of deliverance and salvation. Some may even be forced to revise their understanding of this attribute if they have tended to associate it mainly with holy retribution. But if we remember that divine righteousness or justice is simply God's being true to his own nature, we should expect there to be a positive element as well as a negative element in it, since God's nature includes both his benevolent love and mercy as well as his holy wrath and retribution. When God acts in lovingkindness to save his people, especially when he has made a covenant commitment to them and especially when their hearts are turned toward him (in relative righteousness), he is acting righteously simply because he is acting in accord with his nature.

This use of the terms and this aspect of God's righteousness are perfectly illustrated in I Samuel 12:7, where Samuel speaks to Israel of the many acts of deliverance God had already performed on their behalf, namely, "all the righteous acts [*tsedāqāh*] of the Lord which He did for you and your fathers."

The Psalms are a veritable storehouse of such references. David says that the righteous person, "he who has clean hands and a pure heart" and has lived in truth, "shall receive a blessing from the Lord and righteousness [*tsedāqāh*] from the God of his salvation" (Ps. 24:3-5). In Psalm 31:1 he says, "In Thee, O Lord, I have taken refuge; let me never be ashamed; in Thy righteousness [*tsedāqāh*] deliver me." He believed that God would do this for his own name's sake (v. 3) and because he, David, feared the Lord and was faithful: "How great is Thy goodness, which Thou hast stored up for those who fear Thee" (v. 19); "O love the Lord, all you His godly ones! The Lord preserves the faithful" (v. 23). In Psalm 35 David calls Yahweh to his defense: "Judge me, O Lord my God, according to Thy righteousness [*tsedeq*]," and "let them shout for joy and rejoice, who favor my vindication [tsedeq]; and let them say continually, 'The Lord be magnified, who delights in the prosperity of His servant.' And my tongue shall declare Thy righteousness [tsedeq] and Thy praise all day long" (vv. 24, 27-28). "O continue Thy lovingkindness to those who know Thee, and Thy righteousness [tsedāqāh] to the upright in heart" (Ps. 36:10).

The identification with faithfulness and salvation continues: "I have proclaimed glad tidings of righteousness [tsedeq] in the great congregation. . . . I have not hidden Thy righteousness [tsedāqāh] within my heart; I have spoken of Thy faithfulness and Thy salvation; I have not concealed Thy lovingkindness and Thy truth" (Ps. 40:9-10). "Deliver me from bloodguiltiness, O God, Thou God of my salvation; then my tongue will joyfully sing of Thy righteousness [tsedāqāh]" (Ps. 51:14). "By awesome deeds Thou dost answer us in righteousness [tsedeq], O God of our salvation" (Ps. 65:5). In Psalm 71 tsedāqāh is used four times in this sense: "In Thy righteousness deliver me, and rescue me" (v. 2). "My mouth shall tell of Thy righteousness, and of Thy salvation all day long," and "I will make mention of Thy righteousness, Thine alone" (vv. 15-16). "For Thy righteousness, O God, reaches to the heavens, Thou who hast done great things" (v. 19). See Psalm 85:9-13, where tsedeq is used three times with the same meaning (vv. 10, 11, 13). See also Psalm 98:2-3.

In Psalm 82 the verb form is used: "Vindicate the weak and fatherless; do justice [tsādaq] to the afflicted and destitute. Rescue the weak and needy; deliver them out of the hand of the wicked" (vv. 3-4). This passage, like many others, speaks of righteousness as the deliverance of the afflicted and needy "out of the hand of the wicked." God's justice is concerned not just with their distress but also with the injustice lying behind it. Psalm 103:6 says, "The Lord performs righteous deeds [tsedāqāh], and judgments [mishpāt] for all who are oppressed," but verses 17-18 remind us that our own relative righteousness is a consideration: "But the lovingkindness of the Lord is from everlasting to everlasting on those who fear Him, and His righteousness [tsedāqāh] to children's children, to those who keep His covenant, and who remember His precepts to do them." This same point is seen in Psalm 146:7-8, which says that God is one who "executes justice [mishpāt] for the oppressed; who gives food to the hungry. The Lord sets the prisoners free. The Lord opens the eyes of the blind; the Lord raises up those who are bowed down; *the Lord loves the righteous"* (emphasis added). See also Psalms 89:14-16; 94:14-15; 116:5-6; 129:1-4.

The prophets continue the emphasis on God's righteousness as salvation and deliverance. This is especially true of Isaiah, the latter part of which (called "Second Isaiah" by some critics) receives a great deal of attention from the new social gospel advocates in their efforts to identify righteousness almost exclusively with salvation. The attention is somewhat unwarranted, however, since the book of Psalms has an even greater witness to this fact and since the main subject matter of Isaiah 40-66 (deliverance from Babylon as a type of salvation) in itself calls for such an emphasis. Also, as we shall see, the prophets, including Isaiah, are equally emphatic about the identification of God's righteousness with wrath and punishment.

In any case the former emphasis is there. Isaiah 1:27 says, "Zion will be redeemed with justice [*mishpāt*], and her repentant ones with righteousness [*tsedāqāh*]." The reference to repentance (a necessary element in relative righteousness) is significant. Also, Isaiah 30:18 says, "Therefore the Lord longs to be gracious to you, and therefore He waits on high to have compassion on you. For the Lord is a God of justice [*mishpāt*]."

The rest of the Isaiah references are from the latter portion of the book. "Do not fear, for I am with you; do not anxiously look about you, for I am your God. I will strengthen you, surely I will help you, surely I will uphold you with My righteous [*tsedeq*] right hand" (Isa. 41:10). Isaiah 42:1-4 says three times that the Messiah will bring justice (*mishpāt*) to the peoples. In Isaiah 45:8 the Lord exclaims, "Drip down, O heavens, from above, and let the clouds pour down righteousness [*tsedeq*]; let the earth open up and salvation bear fruit, and righteousness [*tsedāqāh*] spring up with it." In the last part of this chapter (verses 21-25) a classic example of the connection between righteousness and salvation appears:

> . . . Declare and set forth your case; indeed, let them consult together. Who has announced this from of old? Who has long since declared it? Is it not I, the Lord? And there is no other God besides Me, a righteous [*tsaddīq*] God and a Savior; there is none except Me. Turn to Me, and be saved, all the ends of the earth; for I am God, and there is no other. I have sworn by Myself, the word had gone forth from My mouth in righteousness [*tsedāqāh*] and will not turn back, that to Me every knee will bow, every tongue will swear allegiance. They will say of Me, "Only in the

Lord are righteousness [*tsedāqāh*] and strength." Men will come to Him, and all who were angry at Him shall be put to shame. In the Lord all the offspring of Israel will be justified, and will glory.

This is indeed an impressive example of the point that we are making, but we should not be deceived into thinking that the expression "a righteous God and a Savior" is meant to limit divine righteousness *exclusively* to salvation.

Still the emphasis continues. "I bring near My righteousness [*tsedāqāh*], it is not far off; and My salvation will not delay. And I will grant salvation in Zion, and My glory for Israel," says the Lord (Isa. 46:13). "My righteousness [*tsedeq*] is near, My salvation has gone forth, and My arms will judge the peoples . . . . My salvation shall be forever, and My righteousness [*tsedāqāh*] shall not wane" (Isa. 51:5-6; cf. v. 8). In this passage the promises are directed to those "who know righteousness [*tsedeq*], a people in whose heart is My law" (Isa. 51:7). Again, "Preserve justice, and do righteousness, for My salvation is about to come and My righteousness [*tsedāqāh*] to be revealed" (Isa. 56:1). See Isaiah 54:11-17; 61:10-11.

Jeremiah declares that the coming Savior will "do justice and righteousness [*mishpāt* and *tsedāqāh*]," and his name will be "The Lord our righteousness [*tsedeq*]" (Jer. 23:5-6; cf. 33:16). In Hosea 2:19 God tells his erring people that he will receive them back, and "I will betroth you to Me in righteousness and in justice [*tsedeq* and *mishpāt*]." In Hosea 10:12 the people are told "to seek the Lord until He comes to rain righteousness [*tsedeq*] on you." Micah declares, "I will bear the indignation of the Lord because I have sinned against Him, until He pleads my case and executes justice [*mishpāt*] for me. He will bring me out to the light, and I will see His righteousness [*tsedāqāh*]" (Micah 7:9). See Zechariah 8:8; 9:9.

Two New Testament references complete the listing of passages connecting God's righteousness with salvation. John tells us that "if we confess our sins, He is faithful and righteous [*dikaios*] to forgive us our sins and to cleanse us from all unrighteousness" (I John 1:9). Paul says that in the Last Day "the Lord, the righteous [*dikaios*] Judge" will award a crown of righteousness to the faithful (II Tim. 4:8).

References to Righteousness as Retribution

From this lengthy list of passages it should be clear that God bestows *salvation* because he is righteous; his righteousness or justice underlies his work of redemption. But what must be recognized is that there is just as lengthy a list of passages showing that God bestows *wrath and retribution* because he is righteous; his righteousness or justice underlies his punitive judgments also. Those who want to emphasize only the former try to define righteousness as faithfulness to a relationship or faithfulness to one's covenant obligations and promises. For example, Brinsmead says, "God is faithful to his covenant promise. . . . Justice is God faithfully carrying out just what divine love had pledged to do."[100] What is overlooked is that God's covenant with Israel included not only promises of blessing but also fearsome warnings of curses and destruction if they proved to be unfaithful (Deut. 28:15-68). Thus even if defined as covenant faithfulness, divine righteousness includes wrath and punishment.

The new social prophets' usual approach to this element of divine righteousness, if it is acknowledged at all, is that it is only incidental to deliverance from oppression. E. R. Achtemeier, for example, grants that there are two sides of God's righteousness: salvation and condemnation, deliverance and punishment. Yet, she says, "we need not dwell too long on the point that throughout the OT Yahweh condemns evil." Why not? Because "Yahweh's righteousness is never solely an act of condemnation or punishment." It is "never equated with his vengeance on the sinner." It is just a necessary part of delivering people from oppression: the same act that delivers the afflicted results in suffering for the oppressors. "The punishment is an integral part of the restoration. Only because Yahweh saves does he condemn. His righteousness is first and foremost saving."[101] As Brinsmead parrots this view, "Deliverance of the oppressed implies destruction of the oppressor."[102] Mott grudgingly recognizes that Biblical justice is sometimes punitive, but this admission is almost completely lost in his one-sided presentation of justice as gift, abundance, generosity, relief, release, deliverance, victory, vindication, and creation of community. The punitive side is in-

---

100. Robert Brinsmead, "The Scandal of God's Justice—Part 1," p. 7.

101. E. R. Achtemeier, "Righteousness in the OT," p. 83. See the same view in P. J. Achtemeier, "Righteousness in the NT," p. 98.

102. Robert Brinsmead, "The Scandal of God's Justice—Part 1," p. 9.

cidental to deliverance. In the prophets justice represents "God's victory for the innocent or the oppressed, the negative side of which is the defeat of the wicked or the oppressors, often described with terms other than those of justice."[103]

It is true that the condemnation of the wicked often occurs in conjunction with the deliverance of the oppressed, but this is not always the case. And even when it does so occur, it is a complete misrepresentation to picture it as only incidental to God's "real purpose," namely, salvation. This error can be traced in part to the tendency to interpret sin as mainly one's mistreatment of his fellow human beings rather than as rebellion against God. As Miranda says, for example, "it is not worthy of God" to avenge and punish such sins as "irreligiosity," i.e., sins relating to one's religious relationship with God. Rather, "the sin against which God intervenes . . . is specific: It is injustice and the oppression of the weak by the powerful."[104] We must conclude that this writer has been totally blinded by his ideology, for the Bible most definitely pictures God as condemning *all* sin, including injustice toward other people, because it is a rebellion against his own sovereign authority. This is seen, for example, in David's appeal to the righteous God to deliver him from his foes, "for they are rebellious against Thee" (Ps. 5:10).

In their zeal to exclude retribution from righteousness, the writers that have been cited here have made a number of blatantly and patently false statements regarding the Biblical use of the terms for justice. E. R. Achtemeier says, "There is no verse in the OT in which Yahweh's righteousness is equated with his vengeance on the sinner."[105] "It is highly significant," says Mott, that *tsedāqāh* "is never used in Scripture to speak of God's punishment for sin. It deals with God's *positive actions*."[106] (Even if this statement were correct, which it is not, it would be irrelevant since *tsedāqāh* and *tsedeq* are completely interchangeable.) Mott also claims that the New Testament word for righteousness, *dikaiosunē*, is similarly positive. "Paul follows the Old Testament pattern in that the power of judgment is never the righteousness of God but is rather the wrath (*orgē*) of God."[107] (Mott

---

103. Stephen Mott, *Biblical Ethics and Social Change*, pp. 62-63.
104. José Miranda, *Marx and the Bible*, p. 83.
105. E. R. Achtemeier, "Righteousness in the OT," p. 83.
106. Stephen Mott, *Biblical Ethics and Social Change*, p. 63.
107. Ibid.

forgets Paul's statement in Acts 17:31 and ignores the negative occurrence of the adjective *dikaios* in II Thes. 1:6.) Brinsmead's false claim is probably the most extravagant. He says, "Unlike *sadaq, mishpat* is also used to refer to punishment and wrath."[108] The implication that *sādaq* (or *tsādaq*), presumably in all its forms, is never used for punishment and wrath is absolutely incredible, as is Mott's implication above that the "Old Testament pattern" separates God's righteousness from the power of judgment.

These and other efforts to detach divine righteousness from wrath and retribution crumble in the face of even a cursory survey of the Biblical usage of the terms. We have already discussed the places where the various words seem to include references both to salvation and to wrath; these alone are sufficient to disprove the implications of Brinsmead and Mott mentioned in the last sentence of the last paragraph above. One should review especially Psalms 7:11; 9:4; 11:7; Isaiah 63:1; and Daniel 7:14. Particularly important are Psalm 11:7 and Isaiah 63:1, where *tsedāqāh* is used as the basis for punitive judgment (contrary to Mott's claim given at footnote 106 above).

In addition to these dual references already dealt with, there are a host of passages that relate God's righteousness or justice to his wrath and retribution alone. We may begin a survey of these with a look at Deuteronomy 32:1-43, which deals almost entirely with divine vengeance upon sinners, and attributes it to divine righteousness. Moses sets the stage with words of praise to God, concluding with a great paean to his justice: "The Rock! His work is perfect, for all His ways are just [*mishpāt*]; a God of faithfulness and without injustice, righteous [*tsaddīq*] and upright is He" (v.4). Then Moses predicts how the children of Israel will abuse God's fatherly care for them and will forsake the true God and worship idols (vv. 5-18). There is no mention of injustice or oppression; the problem is rebellion against God. "They have acted corruptly toward Him" (v. 5); "you neglected the Rock who begot you, and forgot the God who gave you birth" (v. 18). Then in verses 19-33 Moses speaks of the righteous anger that God will pour out on his people, foreshadowing their coming captivity. But for his

---

108. Robert Brinsmead, "The Scandal of God's Justice—Part 2," p. 5. He always uses the transliterated verb form even when the adjective or noun forms are called for.

own sake God does not destroy them completely (vv. 26-27), but has compassion on them instead (v. 36). Implying but not specifically mentioning their future deliverance, Moses devotes the last part of the song (vv. 34-43) to God's bloody vengeance to be wreaked upon his enemies and the enemies of his people, presumably the nations that took Israel into captivity. "If I sharpen My flashing sword, and My hand takes hold on justice [mishpāt], I will render vengeance on my adversaries, and I will repay those who hate Me" (v. 41). This reference to mishpāt here in verse 41 connects this whole section on vengeance and retribution to the description of God in verse 4 as a righteous God whose ways are mishpāt. And there is no hint that the retribution on either Israel or her enemies is somehow done for the sake of salvation or is somehow incidental to deliverance. In both cases the righteous God renders mishpāt for his own sake.

Several times, after being punished for their sins, the people of God confess that he has been righteous (tsaddīq) in punishing them. When Rehoboam was unfaithful, God allowed Shishak's Egyptian army to devastate the land. But "the princes of Israel and the king humbled themelves and said, 'The Lord is righteous'" (II Chron. 12:6). After the great city of Jerusalem was reduced to rubble by the Babylonian army, Jeremiah puts this confession into the mouth of unfaithful Israel: "The Lord is righteous; for I have rebelled against His command" (Lam. 1:18). Ezra recalls the sins that led to Israel's Babylonian captivity and confesses that God has been righteous in reducing the once-proud nation down to a remnant (Ezra 9:15).[109] The Levites likewise reflect on the captivity and make the same kind of confession in Nehemiah 9:33, "Thou art just in all that hast come upon us; for Thou has dealt faithfully, but we have acted wickedly." In each of these cases that which is attributed to God's righteousness is punishment and retribution, totally unconnected with a concurrent deliverance.

Two passages from the Psalms may be noted. After David's sins

---

109. Some interpret this passage as a reference to God's mercy for permitting at least a remnant to escape, but the context better supports the view that God has been righteous in a punitive sense. Keil and Delitzsch say, "God has shown Himself to be just by sorely punishing this once numerous nation, that only a small remnant which has escaped destruction now exists" (C. F. Keil and F. Delitzsch, *Biblical Commentary on the Old Testament: The Books of Ezra, Nehemiah, and Esther*, tr. Sophia Taylor [Grand Rapids: Eerdmans, 1950 reprint], p. 125).

with Bathsheba and against Uriah, the prophet Nathan pronounced severe punishments from God upon him (II Sam. 12:10-14). David responds in these words: "Against Thee, Thee only, I have sinned, and done what is evil in Thy sight, so that Thou art justified [tsādaq] when Thou dost speak, and blameless when Thou dost judge" (Ps. 51:4). Psalm 97:1-9 declares God's general retribution on his enemies, especially on idolaters, and bases it all upon his righteousness and justice.

> The Lord reigns; let the earth rejoice; let the many islands be glad. Clouds and thick darkness surround Him; righteousness and justice [tsedeq and mishpāt] are the foundation of His throne. Fire goes before Him, and burns up His adversaries round about. His lightnings lit up the world; the earth saw and trembled. The mountains melted like wax at the presence of the Lord, at the presence of the Lord of the whole earth. The heavens declare His righteousness [tsedeq], and all the peoples have seen His glory (vv. 1-6).

(It is significant to compare this with Psalm 89:14-16, which also says that "righteousness and justice are the foundation of Thy throne," but makes this the source of blessing instead of wrath.)

Several passages from Isaiah picture God's justice as punitive. Two of them speak of God's mishpāt upon wicked Israel (Isa. 3:14; 4:4), and one of God's mishpāt upon Edom: "For My sword is satiated in heaven, behold it shall descend for judgment upon Edom, and upon the people whom I have devoted to destruction" (Isa. 34:5). Most significant are those passages which speak of God's tsedāqāh as the source of retribution, and retribution alone, contrary to the protestations of E. R. Achtemeier and others as given above. Isaiah 5:13-17, speaking of the coming conquest and exile, says ominously,

> Therefore My people go into exile for their lack of knowledge; and their honorable men are famished, and their multitude is parched with thirst. Therefore Sheol has enlarged its throat and opened its mouth without measure; and Jerusalem's splendor, her multitude, her din of revelry, and the jubilant within her, descend into it. So the common man will be humbled, and the man of importance abased, the eyes of the proud also will be abased. But the Lord of hosts will be exalted in judgment [mishpāt], and the holy God will show Himself holy in righteousness [tsedāqāh]. Then the lambs will graze as in their pasture, and strangers will eat in the waste places of the wealthy.

The destruction of the nation will be so complete that only a remnant will remain, and that destruction stems from God's righteousness:

> A remnant will return, the remnant of Jacob, to the mighty God. For though your people, O Israel, may be like the sand of the sea, only a remnant within them will return; a destruction is determined, overflowing with righteousness [tsedāqāh]. For a complete destruction, one that is decreed, the Lord God of hosts will execute in the midst of the whole land (Isa. 10:21-23).

We recall E. R. Achtemeier's contention, "There is no verse in the OT in which Yahweh's righteousness is equated with his vengeance on the sinner, and not even Isa. 5:16 or 10:22 should be understood in such a manner."[110] Such an idea must be flatly repudiated, for there is no other reasonable way to understand these two passages, among the many others also being noted here. This includes Isaiah 41:1-2, which says, "Let us come together for judgment [mishpāt]. Who has aroused one from the east whom He calls in righteousness [tsedeq] to His feet? He delivers up nations before him, and subdues kings. He makes them like dust with his sword, as the wind-driven chaff with his bow." This seems to be a reference to Babylon, God's instrument for righteous judgment upon the wicked.

Jeremiah likewise connects God's righteousness with punishment. "And I will pronounce My judgments [mishpāt] on them concerning all their wickedness, whereby they have forsaken Me and have offered sacrifices to other gods" (Jer. 1:16). A strong wind "will come at My command; now I will also pronounce judgments [mishpāt] against them" (Jer. 4:12). See also Jeremiah 48:21, 47. Concerning the wicked inhabitants of Jerusalem and Judah who had forsaken God and were plotting against his own life, Jeremiah says, "O Lord of hosts, who judges righteously [tsedeq], who tries the feelings and the heart, let me see Thy vengeance on them, for to Thee have I committed my cause" (Jer. 11:20).

Other Old Testament references to God's punitive justice, all using the word mishpāt, are Ezekiel 5:8; 34:16; 39:21; Hosea 5:1, 11; Micah 3:1, 8; Habakkuk 1:12; Zephaniah 3:15; and Malachi 2:17.

---

110. E. R. Achtemeier, "Righteousness in the OT," p. 83.

Finally, in the New Testament, Paul says of those who persecute the church, "For after all it is only just [dikaios] for God to repay with affliction those who afflict you" (II Thes. 1:6). Speaking of retributive judgments, Revelation 16:5-7 says,

> And I heard the angel of the waters saying, "Righteous [dikaios] art Thou, who art and who wast, O Holy One, because Thou didst judge these things; for they poured out the blood of saints and prophets, and Thou has given them blood to drink. They deserve it." And I heard the altar saying, "Yes, O Lord God, the Almighty, true and righteous [dikaios] are Thy judgments."

In a similar context Revelation 19:2 declares, "His judgments are true and righteous [dikaios]." A fitting climax to this whole series of passages depicting righteousness as a source of retribution is Revelation 19:11, "And I saw heaven opened; and behold, a white horse, and He who sat upon it is called Faithful and True; and in righteousness [dikaiosunē] He judges and wages war." Then follows one of the most graphic depictions of unadulterated wrath and vengeance that one could imagine (vv. 12-21)—all stemming from the righteousness of the righteous God.

Our basic conclusion in this section is that divine righteousness is that consistency or constancy in God by which all his actions are faithful to the eternally perfect norm or standard of his own nature. This means that his treatment of his creatures must be not only consistent with his own inner self (as norm), but also consistent with the creatures' positive or negative relation to the same norm as objectified in his law. That is, because he is righteous he treats his creatures impartially according to their own works, according to whether they are righteous or wicked. The righteous he blesses; the wicked he curses. This is true in both a relative and an absolute sense. Absolutely speaking, no one is righteous; thus God is consistent with himself when he condemns all to eternal punishment. Relatively speaking, some are righteous and some are wicked; so in the various limited contexts of this world some are righteously blessed and others righteously punished. Divine righteousness properly includes both the positive and the negative aspects, and all one-sided views must be rejected.

RIGHTEOUSNESS AND OTHER DIVINE ATTRIBUTES

There is considerable confusion as to the way God's justice or righteousness relates to his other moral or communicable attributes.[111] Part of the reason for this may be the fact that so many distinctions are made within divine justice, and so many different labels are used to describe these distinctions—with no semblance of uniformity or agreement. One may read of justice as distributive, retributive, remunerative, rectoral, legislative, evangelical, punitive, vindicative, or vindictive. On top of this, some distinguish between justice and righteousness.

But in addition to the confusion of terminology, there is a genuine disagreement concerning the interrelationships between the various attributes. A basic question that evokes different answers is whether there is a single attribute of God under which all the rest may be subsumed and of which they are just varying expressions. Some do not like to speak of two or more "equally ultimate" aspects of God's being, as if somehow this would lead to a schizophrenic deity.[112] Thus they posit some all-encompassing attribute into which all the rest may ultimately be resolved, such as holiness or love. Others have no qualms, however, about speaking of "equally ultimate" attributes.

In any case the disagreement continues. For example, some make God's righteousness an aspect of his holiness.[113] Brunner says, "Righteousness, therefore, is simply the Holiness of God, as it is expressed when confronted with the created world . . . . The Nature of God which is Holy, manifests itself over against His creature as the divine quality of Righteousness."[114] Justice, says Shedd, is "a mode of holiness."[115] Dale Moody agrees, declaring righteousness to be a property of God's holiness.[116] On the other side are those who make justice an expression of God's love or grace. Mott's view on this has already been cited: love is the basis of justice; justice is an instrument of

---

111. On the classification of attributes see Jack Cottrell, *What the Bible Says About God the Creator* (Joplin, Mo.: College Press, 1983), pp. 40-43.

112. "God is not subject to fits of schizophrenia during which two contrary impulses conflict in him, one to love and one to be angry" (R. P. C. Hanson, *The Attractiveness of God* [Richmond: John Knox Press, 1973], p. 148).

113. Whether they mean ontological holiness or ethical holiness is not always clear, though the latter is more likely. On the distinction see Cottrell, *What the Bible Says About God the Creator*. pp. 213-214.

114. Emil Brunner, *The Christian Doctrine of God: Dogmatics, Volume I*, tr. Olive Wyon (Philadelphia: Westminster Press, 1950), p. 278.

115. William G. T. Shedd, *Dogmatic Theology*, I:364.

116. Dale Moody, *The Word of Truth* (Grand Rapids: Eerdmans, 1981), p. 98.

love and a manifestation of grace.[117] R. T. France says that *tsedāqāh* is the consequence of *chesed*, or faithful covenant love.[118] Erickson says that "love is not fully understood unless we see it as including justice," agreeing with Joseph Fletcher that "justice is simply love distributed."[119] (We should remember that Erickson is one who makes a distinction between righteousness and justice.) Edward Farley says, "All God's acts are acts of grace, even his judgment, for in judgment God is God in relation to us and is not ignoring us."[120] Prenter equates God's righteousness with his love and says, "Both his wrath and his grace result from the same righteous love."[121] Shuffling these same factors into another arrangement, Bavinck says that punishment is derived from God's wrath while salvation is the result of God's righteousness.[122] For Carl Henry, love and righteousness are "equally ultimate,"[123] with wrath and punishment being the result of righteousness.

Thus, with the realization that I am adding one more arrangement to an already-chaotic situation, I would offer the following analysis of the relationship among the moral attributes of God. First, it seems to me that the attempt to elevate a single attribute above all the others, from which all the others derive at least part of their content, is not warranted by Scripture. I agree with Carl Henry, that the Bible gives us the picture of a God in whose nature at least two attributes are equally ultimate, though I would not agree that justice is one of them. In view of the way the Bible uses justice terminology, I conclude that it simply cannot be paired with love in this manner. The two attributes that I see as equally fundamental in God's nature are *love* and *holiness*.[124] In the latter at-

---

117. Stephen Mott, *Biblical Ethics and Social Change*, pp. 48, 53, 61.

118. R.T. France, *The Living God* (Downers Grove: InterVarsity Press, 1970), p. 94.

119. Millard Erickson, *Christian Theology*, I: 298.

120. Edward Farley, *The Transcendence of God: A Study in Contemporary Philosophical Theology* (Philadelphia: Westminster Press, 1960), p. 217.

121. Regin Prenter, *Creation and Redemption*, p. 417.

122. Herman Bavinck, *The Doctrine of God*, p. 216.

123. Carl F.H. Henry, *Aspects of Christian Social Ethics*, p. 146.

124. H. Orton Wiley says, "All the perfections of God as manifested in His moral government may be resolved into two – His holiness and His love" *(Christian Theology* [Kansas City, Mo.: Beacon Hill Press, 1940], p. 366). Donald Bloesch says, "God in his essence is both love and holiness . . . . God is love, but his love exists in tension with his holiness" *(Essentials of Evangelical Theology, Volume One: God, Authority, and Salvation* [San Francisco: Harper & Row, 1978], p. 32).

tribute I believe that I am including most of what Henry means by "justice," so the disagreement is more a matter of terminology than content. In this context I am using the term *holiness* to mean God's perfect moral character, i.e., his ethical holiness as distinct from his ontological holiness. The term *love* refers to his basic good-will toward other moral beings.

These attributes are equally ultimate in God's nature, which means that neither one is over the other nor cancels the other nor dictates the contents of the other. God's love is not just a function of his holiness, nor is his holiness just a way his love expresses itself. This does not mean that they are totally separate from one another, however, as if there were a duality within God. We may say that each qualifies the other to the extent that God's love is *holy* love, and his holiness is *loving* holiness.

The next two chapters will be a detailed examination of God's holiness and God's love, as we try to understand how each side of his nature is manifested in relation to mankind. We will see how each is related to man simply as creature, and how each is related to man as sinner. First of all, we will explain how man as creature relates to holiness in terms of God's *law*, with its commandments and penalties; but then how he as sinner relates to it in terms of *wrath, vengeance*, and *condemnation*. God's law is the positive expression of his holiness, and his wrath is its negative expression. The latter includes what many would call retributive justice. Then moving to the other aspect of God's nature, we will see how man as creature is the recipient of God's love in terms of *blessing, kindness, benevolence* and *good-will*; then how man as sinner relates to God's love in the forms of *mercy, patience*, and *grace*.

The difficult part in all of this is to see how God relates to man as sinner. Here is where the righteousness of God comes into the picture. That God is righteous means that he is always true to himself, his nature and his word. But how can he be true to both sides of his nature in his relation to man as sinner? How can he fulfill both his holiness and his love toward the sinner at the same time? The distinction between absolute and relative righteousness in man will be of some help here, but from our finite perspective it still seems that the righteousness of God places him in a kind of dilemma insofar as man as sinner is concerned. As we shall see, it is this dilemma posed by the righteousness of God that leads to the work of redemption in Jesus Christ.

In giving this overview of my understanding of the attributes of God in terms of the two sides of his nature, I still have not stated how righteousness relates to it all. I have not placed it on one side or the other, nor have I posited it as the one ultimate attribute from which all the others spring (as if love were one half of righteousness and holiness the other half). So how does it relate? It seems to me that the righteousness of God in the Biblical sense of the term is something set apart by itself, as a kind of formal attribute that does not add content to the nature of God as such but is a qualifier of the other attributes. As an illustration, someone may describe his automobile engine as having so many cylinders, so much horsepower, a certain level of fuel economy, a certain kind of carburetion, and so on; and then he may say, "And it is a very *sound* engine." But the attribute of "soundness" is not the same kind of attribute as the others. It is not a part of the engine's make-up as such, but is a way of describing how the various parts of the engine function. I.e., it is a way of saying that they function as they are intend-ed to function, or that the engine in its operation is being true to itself as designed and manufactured. God's righteousness is something like the "soundness" of this engine. That he is righteous means that his actions are always true to all his attributes. They are always in perfect accord with his holiness and with his love.

IMPLICATIONS OF THIS VIEW

At the beginning this chapter we pointed out that a number of things are at stake in relation to one's view of the righteousness of God, especially certain crucial issues regarding ethics and the nature of redemption itself.

Implications for Ethics

With reference to ethics, if my analysis of divine righteousness is cor-rect, then those are wrong who trace all ethics to the single attribute of love or grace. This is, of course, the common procedure for those who merge justice into love and make love or grace the single over-arching attribute in terms of which all of God's relationships with man are con-ducted. Mott's book on ethics is a perfect example of this. He actually makes grace the ultimate category, but relates it very closely to love, which he describes as "the fullest expression of God's grace."[125] He describes Christian ethics as being "grounded in God's acts of grace" and as being "grounded in love."[126] "All Christian conduct," he says, "is grounded in the grace of Jesus Christ. . . . Christian social action builds on everything that the Scriptures say about the grace of God in salvation." Grace is the foundation of ethics in the Old Testament also. Grace is prior to ethics "in the sense that the root is prior to the stem."[127] "The content, the nature of God's grace determines the content and nature of our acts."[128] As already noted, Mott makes justice—a key concept for ethics (e.g., "social justice")—a sub-category of love and grace.[129] He specifically rejects attempts to relate them to different sides of God's nature.[130]

Such a view of ethics, in my opinion, is erroneous not only because it is based on the Christological fallacy[131] but also because it stems from a faulty view of the attributes of God. I believe that those who have approached Christian ethics from the assumption that there *are* two equally ultimate sides in God's nature are basically correct, and that they are basically correct also in relating the work of civil government to one side and the work of the church to the other. This is the view of Carl Henry, for example, who says that the idea that justice and love are equally ultimate in the divine nature is "the historic evangelical emphasis." He continues,[132]

> . . . In accord with biblical theology, evangelical Christianity affirms that justice is an immutable divine quality, not reducible to a mere mode of divine benevolence on the fallacious theory that love is the exclusive center and core of God's being. . . . This equal ultimacy of justice and benevolence in the nature of God has fundamental consequences for man in society. In the sphere of social ethics it is reflected in the biblical emphasis that the role of government in the world is to preserve justice,

---

125. Stephen Mott, *Biblical Ethics and Social Change*, p. 39.

126. Ibid., pp. 23, 40.

127. Ibid., pp. 22, 25.

128. Ibid., p. 28.

129. Ibid., p. 48, "Love [is] the basis of justice"; p. 53, "Justice is a necessary instrument of love"; p. 61, "Human justice is a manifestation of grace."

130. Ibid., pp. 61-62.

131. See Jack Cottrell, *What the Bible Says About God the Creator*, pp. 166ff.

132. Carl F. H. Henry, *Aspects of Christian Social Ethics*, pp. 146-147.

with an eye on human rights and duties as sanctioned and stipulated and supported by the will of God. The Church's role in the world, on the other hand, is essentially redemptive and benevolent, alert to man's spiritual needs.

My only quarrel with this, as noted earlier, is that I would speak of the equal ultimacy of *holiness* and love, rather than justice and love. I would follow through with the same implications for the distinctions between the roles of government and church, however.

With regard to justice itself, here is one way in which the understanding of the righteousness of God set forth in this chapter may be relevant for ethics, especially for delineating the specific roles of government and church. On the one hand, it would seem that governments are supposed to imitate the way in which God's justice applies to the *relative* righteousness and wickedness of man. I.e., civil governments must distinguish between the righteous and the wicked, and must apply temporal punishments to the wicked. On the other hand, the church must champion and imitate the way God distinguishes between the *absolute* righteousness and sinfulness of man. I.e., it must treat *all* people as sinners, warning them of God's eternal wrath to be visited upon them in the end and offering them the free gift of God's grace as their only hope.

Implications for Redemption

The most important implications of the present analysis of divine righteousness have to do with the nature of redemption itself, particularly the meaning of the death of Jesus Christ. As indicated near the beginning of this chapter, those who eliminate or explain away the retributive aspect of God's justice usually abandon the historic view of the substitutionary atonement, where Jesus' death is seen as a propitiation of the wrath of God.[133] They then create new interpretations of the atonement without reference to the satisfaction of God's holy wrath upon sin. The only "righteousness" that must be satisfied is God's covenant promise and loving desire to save us. The most difficult part of such a

---

133. I suspect – though I cannot document it—that in some cases an *a priori* rejection of propitiation has probably preceded the acceptance of the one-sided, non-retributive concept of justice. the latter being formulated as a way of justifying the former.

reconstruction is explaining why the death of Christ is needed in the first place.

But if the analysis of justice as presented here is correct, then the traditional understanding of the atonement as a propitiation of the divine wrath cannot be so easily dismissed. True, there is a side of God's nature which produces a "loving desire to save us," and the righteous God must be true to that aspect of himself. But there is also a side of God's nature that reacts in wrath against sin and must pour out holy retribution upon it, and the righteous God must be true to that aspect of himself as well. Hence any acceptable view of the atonement must take both sides of God's nature into account.

We conclude this chapter on the righteousness of God with another reflection on the vital importance of this subject for many areas of Christian thought. These words are from Carl Henry:[134]

> Christian doctrine is a harmonious unity whose main axis is the nature of God. For this reason a correct understanding of the whole range of Christian faith and duty turns on a proper comprehension of divine attributes. How the theologian defines and relates God's sovereignty, righteousness, and love actually predetermines his exposition of basic positions in many areas—in social ethics no less than in soteriology and eschatology. Even the smallest deviation from the biblical view of divine justice and divine benevolence eventually implies far-reaching consequences for the entire realm of Christian truth and life.

---

134. Carl F.H. Henry, *Aspects of Christian Social Ethics*, p. 146.

5

THE HOLINESS OF GOD

The holiness of God seems to be an especially important attribute, according to the Bible's own witness. In both the Old and New Testaments angelic creatures are pictured as worshiping God by exalting his holiness with triple emphasis: "Holy, Holy, Holy, is the Lord of hosts, the whole earth is full of His glory" (Isa. 6:3); "Holy, Holy, Holy, is the Lord God, the Almighty, who was and who is and who is to come" (Rev. 4:8). In Hebrew idiom repeating something even once gave it special emphasis; a threefold formula "expresses an extraordinary superlative of unheard-of intensity."[1] As Charnock pointed out long ago, we find no other attribute trebled in this manner.[2] We never read, "Eternal, eternal, eternal"; or "Love, love, love"; or even

---

1. Petro B. T. Bilaniuk, "The Holiness of God in Eastern Orthodoxy," *God: The Contemporary Discussion*, ed. Frederick Sontag and M. Darrol Bryant (New York: Rose of Sharon Press, 1982), p.46. See also R.C. Sproul, *The Holiness of God* (Wheaton: Tyndale House, 1985), pp. 38-40.

2. Stephen Charnock, *The Existence and Attributes of God* (Grand Rapids: Kregel reprint, 1958), pp. 449-450.

"Almighty, almighty, almighty." In the revelation given to us, holiness alone is emphasized in this way.

This chapter attempts to explain the meaning and implications of God's holiness in all its forms and expressions. First holiness itself will be discussed, then its extensions in the forms of law and wrath will be explained. All of these elements together form one major aspect of God's moral nature, especially as he relates to his creatures.

HOLINESS

As explained in the first volume in this series, the best understanding of the Old Testament word for *holy* is that it means "to cut, to separate" in its verb form. Thus to say that something is holy means that it is separated or set off from other things. It was also explained how the term *holy* has two basic connotations in Biblical usage when applied to God, namely, the ontological and the ethical or moral.[3] The main focus of this section is the latter.

Ontological Holiness and Ethical Holiness

God's ontological holiness is equivalent to his transcendence and may well be the most significant of all the divine attributes. It is grounded in the fact of *ex nihilo* creation, and it asserts that the being of God the Creator is qualitatively different from all created being. It emphasizes his uniqueness as God and stands for his very deity or divinity itself.[4] This aspect of God's holiness is in the forefront in such passages as the following: "Who is like Thee among the gods, O Lord? Who is like Thee, majestic in holiness?" (Ex. 15:11). "There is no one holy like the Lord, indeed, there is no one besides Thee" (I Sam. 2:2). "Let them praise Thy great and awesome name; holy is He. . . . Exalt the Lord our God, and worship at His footstool; holy is He. . . . Exalt the Lord our God, and worship at His holy hill; for holy is the Lord our God" (Ps. 99:3, 5, 9).

While ontological holiness signifies God's separateness from creatures as such, ethical holiness refers to his separateness from *sin*

---

3. Jack Cottrell, *What the Bible Says About God the Creator* (Joplin, Mo.: College Press, 1983), pp. 212-214.
4. Ibid., pp. 214-216.

and from *sinners*. In this sense holiness is "a general term for the moral excellence of God."[5] It means that his essence is pure moral goodness and is the very opposite of all evil. It is "a glorious, radiant and searching purity, a positive goodness incomparable, which is to all sin and wrong what the sun is to the night."[6] This is the aspect of holiness that seems to be most prominent in the following verses: "Then Joshua said to the people, 'You will not be able to serve the Lord, for He is a holy God. He is a jealous God; He will not forgive your transgression or your sins. If you forsake the Lord and serve foreign gods, then He will turn and do you harm and consume you'" (Joshua 24:19-20). "But like the Holy One who called you, be holy yourselves also in all your behavior; because it is written, 'You shall be holy, for I am holy'" (I Peter 1:15-16).

Those who approach the Bible from an evolutionary perspective usually interpret the former of these aspects (ontological holiness) as being the earlier or more primitive concept, sometimes even relating it to the pagan notion of "taboo."[7] The idea of ethical holiness is said to have developed later under the influence of the prophetic movement; thus it is the "higher" concept. Clarke says, "As knowledge of God became truer, his holiness was more and more identified with his moral excellence, offered to men as standard and inspiration of goodness."[8] While the former is never eliminated altogether, the idea of holiness as "moral purity and blamelessness" becomes dominant from this time forward.[9]

We reject the idea that the notion of God underwent such an evolutionary development among the Hebrews and deny, along with Robert Gleason, that the prophets "altered the concept [of holiness] from a magical one to an ethical one."[10] Although the concept of ontological

---

5. Charles Hodge, *Systematic Theology* (Grand Rapids: Eerdmans reprint, n.d.), I:413.

6. William Newton Clarke, *The Christian Doctrine of God* (Edinburgh: T. & T. Clark, 1909), p. 94.

7. W. R. Matthews, *God in Christian Experience* (New York: Harper & Brothers, 1930), pp. 73-74.

8. William Newton Clarke, *The Christian Doctrine of God*, p. 96.

9. See the full discussion of the alleged development in Walther Eichrodt, *Theology of the Old Testament*, tr. J. A. Baker (Philadelphia: Westminster Press, 1961), I:270ff. See especially pp. 277-278.

10. Robert W. Gleason, *Yahweh: The God of the Old Testament* (Englewood Cliffs, N.J.: Prentice-Hall, 1964), p. 27.

holiness is the fundamental one and the terminology for holiness is used predominantly for this concept throughout the Bible, nevertheless the idea of ethical holiness is also present from beginning to end, even though the terms are not used as often in this sense. It is because God is holy that sinful Adam and Eve hid from him (Gen. 3:8). It is because he is holy that God punished Cain for his sin against Abel (Gen. 4:10-13). It is because he is holy that he destroyed the sinful population through the Great Flood.

It is very important that we make this distinction between the two aspects of holiness. If the distinction is not observed, then there will be some confusion concerning the relation between holiness and the other attributes. For example, Strong rightly distinguishes holiness and love; but because he tends to see holiness as a single concept (moral excellence), he elevates it to a higher level than love and leans toward including love within holiness.[11] Such a move would be more justifiable if he were thinking in terms of ontological holiness, but holiness as moral excellence alone cannot be the general category of which love is a part. Rather, as I have indicated earlier, ethical holiness and love are parallel and equally ultimate attributes of the divine nature. Neither includes the other; neither is derived from the other.

Though ontological holiness and ethical holiness are distinct, they are similar in that they both are grounded in God's work of creation. The former is grounded in the fact of *ex nihilo* creation as such, while the latter has to do with the creation of a certain type of creature, namely, *moral* beings such as angels and human beings. These are called moral beings because they were made with free will or freedom of choice, i.e., the freedom to choose to do right or to do wrong. Apart from the creation of these moral beings, the whole concept of "right or wrong" would have been irrelevant. When God exists totally by himself, he simply is who he is. There is no right or wrong, as if something God may choose could be wrong. This does not mean that God is beyond right and wrong in the sense that no standards apply to his actions; it simply means that in a context of divine isolation such a concept would be superfluous. The same would be true even after creation, if the creation

---

11. Augustus H. Strong, *Systematic Theology*, 3 vols. in 1 (Valley Forge: Judson Press, 1907), pp. 271-272.

included no moral beings. If there were only rocks and trees and animals, "right and wrong" would still not be applicable. But with the creation of angels and men, who have the unique capacity consciously to choose to act either within or against the will of God, right and wrong suddenly become meaningful concepts, since there now exists the *potential* for the reality of moral evil or sin. This is true even before the actual choice of sin is made. The mere possibility of wrong choice by a free-will creature is enough to give meaning to "right and wrong."

This is where the ethical holiness of God first becomes "operative," as it were, since his ethical holiness is that aspect of God's nature from which the distinction between right and wrong springs. Clarke points out that "such holiness in God sets the distinction of right and wrong on eternal foundations."[12] This is true not just of the distinction between them but also of the very *concepts* of right and wrong. These concepts may first become *meaningful* with the creation of free-will beings, but this is not their *origin*. They are grounded in the very nature of God. Because God is who he is, the very words *right* and *wrong* make sense to us. Because God is who he is, going against either his nature or his will is *wrong*, while staying within his will is *right*. Because God is who he is, certain specific things are right and certain specific things are wrong, even if these wrong things could never be actualized without the free-will choices of created moral beings. And because God is who he is, it is infinitely important to him whether his moral creatures choose right or wrong.

Thus, like ontological holiness, the ethical holiness of God is understood in view of his creation. The former means that he is separate from all created being *per se*, while the latter means that he is separate from all sin, which is given potentiality only through the creation of free-will beings. In this sense Pope is right when he says, "The holiness of God is displayed always on the dark background of sin,"[13] even if that sin is only potential. And perhaps we can even say, with Louis Berkhof, that the idea of ethical holiness "developed out of" that of the "majesty-holiness," as he calls it.[14] This would be true not in any

---

12. William Newton Clarke, *The Christian Doctrine of God*, pp. 106-107.

13. William Burt Pope, *A Compendium of Christian Theology*, 3 ed. (Cleveland: Thomas and Mattell, n.d.), I:333.

14. Louis Berkhof, *Systematic Theology* (London: Banner of Truth Trust, 1939), p. 73.

evolutionary sense, but simply in the sense that the concept of creation in general (and thus the concept of ontological holiness) would be "prior to" the concept of the creation of moral beings (and thus the concept of ethical holiness).[15]

In the remainder of this discussion, the term *holiness* will be used in the sense of ethical holiness unless otherwise specified. We now turn to a fuller discussion of this concept.

Aspects of Ethical Holiness

God's ethical holiness is usually seen as having both a positive and a negative aspect. The positive aspect is what God *is* and what he is *for*; the negative aspect is what God is *not* and what he is *against*.

To say that God is holy means, positively, that he is absolute ethical perfection and purity, that he is unconditionally upright in his essence and in his actions. He is the ultimate standard of rectitude and integrity. His holiness is his total moral excellence, or what Strong calls simply "moral rightness."[16] The Biblical emphasis on God's holiness can be seen in the giving of the law, especially in the section of Leviticus known as the "holiness code." Here, in the midst of a long list of ceremonial and moral laws, God several times reiterates this basic fact: "For I am the Lord, who brought you up from the land of Egypt, to be your God; thus you shall be holy for I am holy" (Lev. 11:45; see v. 44). "Thus you are to be holy to Me, for I the Lord am holy" (Lev. 20:26). See Leviticus 19:2; 20:7; 21:6-8. This is the background of Peter's exhortation, "But like the Holy One who called you, be holy yourselves also in all your behavior; because it is written, 'You shall be holy, for I am holy'" (I Peter 1:15-16). The Psalmist says, "With the blameless Thou dost show Thyself blameless; with the pure Thou dost show Thyself pure" (Ps. 18:25-26; cf. II Sam. 22:26-27). Speaking of the risen Christ, John says that "He is pure" (I John 3:3). Psalm 25:8 says, "Good and upright is the Lord; therefore He instructs sinners in the way." The righteous should "declare that the Lord is upright . . . and there is no unrighteousness in Him" (Ps. 92:15). In Isaiah 26:7 Yahweh

---

15. See Jack Cottrell, *What the Bible Says About God the Creator*, pp. 179-183, for a discussion of the concept of priority in relation to creation.
16. Augustus H. Strong, *Systematic Theology*, p. 273.

is called the "Upright One." God the Son incarnate as Jesus of Nazareth is often called holy. He is the "holy offspring" (Luke 1:35); "the Holy One of God" (Mark 1:24; Luke 4:34; John 6:69); the "Holy One" (Acts 2:27); "the Holy and Righteous One" (Acts 3:14); "Thy holy servant Jesus" (Acts 4:27, 30); and the one "who is holy" (Rev. 3:7).

To the fact that God's nature *is* holy in this sense, we must add the idea that God has a very strong positive *attitude* toward his holiness, both as it exists in himself and as it is imitated by his moral creatures. His holiness is not just his moral uprightness, but his *zeal* for moral uprightness. This leads him both to *demand* holiness in his moral creatures and to *delight* in it. As Charnock says, "He values purity in his creatures," and "he hath a delight and complacency in everything agreeable to his will."[17] "He loves righteousness and justice" (Ps. 33:5), which would certainly include holiness. "Who may ascend into the hill of the Lord? And who may stand in His holy place? He who has clean hands and a pure heart" (Ps. 24:3-4; cf. Ps. 15:1-5).

Holiness includes a negative side also, which is God's perfect freedom from all sin, his absolute opposition to it, his total hatred of it. Considering the root meaning of holiness as separation, Bloesch says simply that "holiness connotes separation from all that is unclean," and "this applies to God par excellence."[18] As far as God is concerned, there is nothing more unclean than sin; thus he is totally separate from it in the sense that there is no hint of it in his nature, will, or actions. As Charnock says, "He cannot positively will or encourage sin in any. . . . Light may sooner be the cause of darkness, than holiness itself be the cause of unholiness."[19]

The Bible is clear on this point. "Far be it from God to do wickedness, and from the Almighty to do wrong. . . . Surely, God will not act wickedly, and the Almighty will not pervert justice" (Job 34:10-12). "For Thou art not a God who takes pleasure in wickedness; no evil dwells with Thee" (Ps. 5:4). The Psalmist cries out, "My God, my God, why hast Thou forsaken me? . . . O my God, I cry by day, but Thou dost not answer" (Ps. 22:1-2). Then he humbly confesses, "Yet

---

17. Stephen Charnock, *The Existence and Attributes of God*, p. 452.
18. Donald G. Bloesch, *Essentials of Evangelical Theology, Volume One: God, Authority, and Salvation* (San Francisco: Harper & Row, 1978), 1:33.
19. Stephen Charnock, *The Existence and Attributes of God*, p. 458.

Thou art holy, O Thou who art enthroned upon the praises of Israel" (Ps. 22:3). By this he seems to mean, "You are holy; you would never do wrong." Many feel that Isaiah's vision of the holy God must have impressed him with the divine aversion to sin. When the seraphim cried out, "Holy, Holy, Holy, is the Lord of hosts," Isaiah's immediate response was, "Woe is me, for I am ruined! Because I am a man of unclean lips, and I live among a people of unclean lips." That it was his sinfulness and not just his creatureliness that bothered him is seen in the action of one of the seraphim, who touched his lips with a coal from the heavenly altar and said, "Behold, this has touched your lips; and your iniquity is taken away, and your sin is forgiven" (Isa. 6:3-7).[20] Isaiah later puts this truth into these words: "Your iniquities have made a separation between you and your God, and your sins have hid His face from you, so that He does not hear" (Isa. 59:2). Habakkuk expresses his faith in God's holiness despite what seemed like evidence to the contrary: "Thine eyes are too pure to approve evil, and Thou canst not look on wickedness with favor" (Hab. 1:13). Even in his human existence the incarnate Logos was "without sin" (Heb. 4:15). No doubt sinful Peter was aware of the stark contrast between himself and the Sinless One when "he fell down at Jesus' feet, saying, 'Depart from me, for I am a sinful man, O Lord!'" (Luke 5:8). James adds this warning: "Let no one say when he is tempted, 'I am being tempted by God'; for God cannot be tempted by evil, and He Himself does not tempt any one" (James 1:13). God's eternal city will be completely cleansed from all vestiges of evil: "And nothing unclean and no one who practices abomination and lying, shall ever come into it" (Rev. 21:27).

But now it must be added here, just as with positive holiness, that God's negative holiness is not just the *absence* of sin from his nature, but his strong *attitude* against it, an attitude of abhorrence and hatred. Just as he has a zeal for the right, he is zealous in his opposition to all sin. Trench rightly observes that God "would not love good, unless He hated evil, the two being so inseparable, that either He must do both or neither."[21] Lightner says, "God is said to hate. All sin is hated by him

---

20. See Walther Eichrodt, *Theology of the Old Testament*, I:279.
21. Richard C. Trench, *Synonyms of the New Testament* (Grand Rapids: Eerdmans, 1958 reprint of 1880 ed.), p. 134.

because he is absolutely holy and altogether apart from it in his person. . . .
The hatred of God speaks of his total opposition and aversion to sin."[22]
He hates it *necessarily*, says Charnock. "A love of holiness cannot be
without a hatred of everything that is contrary to it." Since he is infinitely
good, God "cannot but abhor unrighteousness, as being most distant
from him, and contrary to him." Thus "he doth not hate it out of choice,
but from the immutable propension of his nature."[23] "Thou hast loved
righteousness, and hated wickedness," says the Psalmist to the divine
Messiah (Ps. 45:7; cf. Heb. 1:9). The Canaanites were destroyed
because "every abominable act which the Lord hates they have done
for their gods" (Deut. 12:31). Specific sins hated and detested by God
are idolatry (Deut. 7:25; 16:22; Jer. 44:4); occultism (Deut. 18:9-14);
haughty eyes, a lying tongue, hands that shed innocent blood, hearts
that devise wicked plans, feet that run to do evil (Prov. 6:16-18; cf.
Prov. 12:22; 15:26); false weights (Prov. 11:1); hypocritical
ceremonialism in worship (Amos 5:21; Isa. 1:14); arrogance and false
trust (Amos 6:8); lying and injustice (Zech. 8:17); divorce (Mal. 2:16);
and "the deeds of the Nicolaitans" (Rev. 2:6). Charnock emphasizes
God's hatred of sin in a most effective way:[24]

> . . . He cannot look on sin without loathing it, he cannot look on sin
> but his heart riseth against it. It must needs be most odious to him, as that
> which is against the glory of his nature, and directly opposite to that which
> is the lustre and varnish of all his other perfections. It is the "abominable
> thing which his soul hates," Jer. xliv.4; the vilest terms imaginable are us-
> ed to signify it. Do you understand the loathsomeness of a miry swine, or
> the nauseousness of the vomit of a dog? These are emblems of sin, 2
> Peter ii.22. Can you endure the steams of putrefied carcasses from an
> open sepulchre? Rom. iii.23. Is the smell of the stinking sweat or ex-
> crements of a body delightful? the word [filthiness] in James i.21 signifies
> as much. Or is the sight of a body overgrown with scabs and leprosy
> grateful to you? [See Isa. 1:5-6.] So vile, so odious is sin in the sight of
> God. It is no light thing, then, to fly in the face of God, to break his eternal
> law, to dash both the tables in pieces, to trample the transcript of God's
> own nature under our feet, to cherish that which is inconsistent with his
> honour, to lift up our heels against the glory of his nature, to join issue

---

22. Robert P. Lightner, "Hate," *Evangelical Dictionary of Theology*, ed. Walter A.
Elwell (Grand Rapids: Baker Book House, 1984), p. 495.
23. Stephen Charnock, *The Existence and Attributes of God*, pp. 455, 510.
24. Ibid., p. 509.

with the devil in stabbing his heart and depriving him of his life. Sin, in every part of it, is an opposition to the holiness of God . . . .

Perhaps in this light we can understand the stern assertion of Procksch, "In the holiness of God there is the deathdealing element which must destroy . . . uncleanness." Also, commenting on Isaiah 10:16, he says, "To all the unholy, the light of Israel will be a fire and the Holy One a flame . . . by which it will be consumed and destroyed."[25] Eichrodt is probably following Procksch when he speaks of "the annihilating power of holiness."[26] It is in this light that Bavinck speaks of holiness as "the principle of punishment and chastisement," and the "principle of destruction and object of fear."[27] We can see this in Amos 4:2, where, when God swears by his holiness, it is unto destruction. The surviving but contrite Beth-shemites, in the aftermath of God's punitive destruction among them, declared, "Who is able to stand before the Lord, this holy God?" (I Sam. 6:20). The martyred saints under the heavenly altar seemed to grasp this "annihilating power of holiness" when they called upon their holy Lord to judge and avenge their blood on their persecutors (Rev. 6:10).

In conclusion to this section, we may note one of Leon Morris' descriptions of wrath, and apply it more appropriately to holiness itself, that it is God's "burning zeal for the right coupled with a perfect hatred for everything that is evil."[28] That the God of the Bible is such a God is why he stands in such sharp contrast with pagan deities, most of which may be included in Kleinknecht's description of the Greek gods, namely, that in them "we find no trace of moral seriousness or of what is for us the characteristic trait of holiness."[29] This is also why, as Charnock notes, that the sinner hates nothing as much as he hates the holiness of

---

25. Otto Procksch, "ἄγιος etc.." *Theological Dictionary of the New Testament.* ed. Gerhard Kittel, tr. Geoffrey W. Bromiley (Grand Rapids: Eerdmans, 1964), I:93-94.

26. Walther Eichrodt, *Theology of the Old Testament.* I:281.

27. Herman Bavinck, *The Doctrine of God,* ed. and tr. William Hendriksen (Grand Rapids: Eerdmans, 1951), p. 214.

28. Leon Morris, *The Apostolic Preaching of the Cross,* 2 ed. (Grand Rapids: Eerdmans, 1960), p. 181.

29. Hermann Kleinknecht, "Θεός etc." (part), *Theological Dictionary of the New Testament.* ed. Gerhard Kittel, tr. Geoffrey W. Bromiley (Grand Rapids: Eerdmans, 1965), III:70.

God.[30] It judges him and threatens him, and often drives him to atheism because he would rather believe in no God at all than in a holy God.[31]

Holiness and Love

As has been noted, the relation between God's holiness and God's love is a perennial issue in theology. On the one hand, there are those who would make love the primary and inclusive attribute. For example, Gustaf Aulén says, [32]

> . . . The inmost character of the conception of God is love. Consequently, every affirmation about God becomes an affirmation about divine love. Nothing can be said about God, his power, his opposition to evil, or anything else, which is not in the last analysis a statement about his love. The Johannine statement, "God is agape," summarizes . . . everything that can be said about the character of the Christian idea of God. No other divine "attributes" can be co-ordinated with love . . . .

Another example is Nels Ferré, who says that "love and holiness are one in God" in the sense that love is always holy. But love must be primary, since love is a characteristic of God while holiness is a characteristic or rather a function of love. Holiness must always be defined in terms of love, i.e., as the negative side of love, as God's negative work in relation to sin. Even when holiness judges and convicts, it does so in the interests of love and for our own good. "God as love is the source, standard and performer of this function of holiness."[33]

We have noted how Strong takes the opposite position. He specifically denies the view given above, stating that "holiness is not identical with, or a manifestation of, love." Holiness cannot be love, he says, "because love is irrational and capricious except as it has a standard by which it is regulated, and this standard cannot be itself love, but must be holiness." Nor is holiness simply a means to love, which would make love the superior attribute. Rather, since holiness provides the

---

30. Stephen Charnock, *The Existence and Attributes of God*, p. 500.
31. Ibid., p. 501.
32. Gustaf Aulén, *The Faith of the Christian Church*, tr. Eric H. Wahlstrom and G. E. Arden (Philadelphia: Muhlenberg Press, 1948), p. 131.
33. Nels F.S. Ferré, *The Christian Understanding of God* (New York: Harper & Brothers, 1951), pp. 115-116.

norm or standard for love, it "must be the superior of love." Using a quaint illustration he says that "holiness is the track on which the engine of love must run. The track cannot be the engine. If either includes the other, then it is holiness that includes love . . . . God is not holy because he loves, but he loves because he is holy."[34] Finally he says unequivocally that "holiness is the fundamental attribute in God."[35]

I cannot agree with either of the above views. In the final analysis both of them are due largely to a one-sided understanding of the righteousness of God, with the former wrongly identifying the divine righteousness with love and the latter identifying it with a retributive type of justice. When righteousness is properly understood as a distinct attribute in its own right, we are able to get a better perspective on love and holiness as equally fundamental sides of the nature of the God "who is able to save and to destroy" (James 4:12). Paul reflects both aspects of God in Romans 11:22, "Behold then the kindness and severity of God." While each is tempered by the other, each may be expressed independently of the other. W. B. Pope takes this approach when he says, correctly I think, that all the moral perfections of God "hang upon two, Holiness and Love." These are the two fundamental attributes of God in reference to his moral government.[36] Unfortunately Pope fails to distinguish between the ontological holiness and the ethical holiness of God, which leads to some unnecessary problems of another kind;[37] but his general alignment of the attributes is correct.

If one feels compelled to single out one attribute as fundamental, the least violence would be done to Biblical teaching in general by accepting Strong's view that holiness is more basic in God's nature than love. Matthews makes a good point when he says that "it is only safe to approach the doctrine of the divine Love through the doctrine of the divine Holiness."[38] The latter must not be eliminated nor shoved into the

---

34. Augustus H. Strong, *Systematic Theology*, pp. 271-272.
35. Ibid., p. 296.
36. William Burt Pope, *A Compendium of Christian Theology*, I:326, 329.
37. See ibid., pp. 332-334, where he says that since God's holiness must be unique, all creatures must be in some measure impure. This could lead to a kind of metaphysical dualism, and it does lead him to think of I Peter 1:15-16 as a paradox. This confusion would be eliminated if he understood ontological holiness as the absolutely unique and incommunicable attribute, and ethical holiness as a communicable attribute rightly shared by God's moral creatures.
38. W. R. Matthews, *God in Christian Experience*, p. 80.

background. Nor must it be construed as merely a relationship or as a function of the "real" attribute of love. The fact that God swears by his holiness (Ps. 89:35; Amos 4:2) places this attribute within his very essence. (Cf. Gen. 22:16, "By Myself I have sworn.")

But I personally see no reason why a single attribute must underlie all the others. Even Strong himself recognizes that "upon occasion of man's sin, holiness and love in God become opposite poles or forces."[39] Perhaps the word *opposite* is too strong, but this acknowledgement of two poles or forces is in the right direction.

The holiness of God is indeed one of his most glorious attributes. As Bates says, "Of all the perfections of the Deity, none is more worthy of his nature, and so peculiarly admirable, as his infinite purity."[40] Charnock declares that "the nature of God cannot rationally be conceived without it. . . . The notion of a God cannot be entertained without separating from him whatsoever is impure and bespotting, both in his essence and actions." No matter what other attributes we ascribe to this deity, without holiness they will all be less than perfect; and he will be more of a monster or a devil than a god. Thus "it is a less injury to him to deny his being, than to deny the purity of it; the one makes him no God, the other a deformed, unlovely, and a detestable God."[41]

Divine Holiness and Human Holiness

As much and perhaps more than any other attribute of God, the divine holiness has many important implications and applications for human beings. We will now touch upon a few of the more important ones.

God's Holiness and Our Creation in God's Image

First we should note that the holiness of God is a key to understanding the nature of our being created in God's image (Gen. 1:26). What it means to be so created can be seen primarily in the New Testament passages that speak about being re-created in God's image as an aspect of our salvation. Referring to the process of renewal, Paul says that the

---

39. Augustus H. Strong, *Systematic Theology*, p. 272.
40. William Bates, *The Harmony of the Divine Attributes* (Philadelphia: Presbyterian Board of Publication, n.d.), p. 249.
41. Stephen Charnock, *The Existence and Attributes of God*, p. 449.

new self has been "created to be like God in true righteousness and holiness" (Eph. 4:24, NIV). In Colossians 3:10 he says that the new self "is being renewed in knowledge in the image of its Creator" (NIV). We assume that whatever the image of God is being renewed into is what it was in the beginning and what it is supposed to be now. We note that its content is described here as righteousness, holiness and knowledge. Holiness is thus at the very heart of our nature as created in God's image; our holiness is intended to mirror God's holiness.

This is true in at least three ways. The first is the fact of *conscience*. As noted above, the most basic element in the divine holiness is the reality of the very concepts of right and wrong. These concepts are grounded in God's holiness; the fact that God is holy is what makes them meaningful. But if we are in God's image and thus are holy, then there is something in us that by nature acknowledges the reality of rightness and wrongness. This is what we call the conscience. It functions because our Creator is holy, and because he has made us in his image.

The second way that we mirror God's holiness in our very nature is in our *knowledge* of what is right and what is wrong. God's holiness is his perfect moral character, and he has a perfect self-knowledge of the content of his character. When he made us in his image, he implanted within us a finite knowledge of the content of holiness, or a knowledge of what is called the moral law. (This I take to be the meaning of the "knowledge" in Colossians 3:10.) This implanted knowledge is reflected in Romans 2:14-15, which says that even those who have no knowledge of God's specially-revealed Law (i.e., the Bible) nevertheless "are a law to themselves, in that they show the work of the Law written in their hearts." (The same passage also says that the conscience, using this innate law as a reference point, judges particular works to be good or bad.) Of course this knowledge has been obscured by sin and thus must be renewed through redemption (Eph. 4:24; Col. 3:10), but it is an integral aspect of the image of God.

The third way that genuine human nature mirrors God's nature is by the actual *imitation* of his holiness. Before sin entered the world, this was a more or less natural thing for those human beings blessed to have experienced this state. But now that sin has entered and has marred the image within us, the imitation of God's holiness lies beyond the reach of our best efforts and requires divine help. This help is provided in the aspect of salvation known as sanctification.

God's Holiness and Our Sanctification

Our renewal in God's image is called sanctification because the image of God is one of holiness, and sanctification is just another word for holiness. To be more precise, to be sanctified is to be made holy (or, to coin a word, to be "holified"). This happens in a formal way at the beginning of the Christian life when we are "set apart" or separated from the old life and given a whole new set of relationships (I Cor. 6:11). But sanctification in the sense of learning to imitate God's perfect moral character is a process that continues and intensifies over the whole course of the Christian life, as God constantly sets before us the challenge of I Peter 1:15-16, "But like the Holy One who called you, be holy yourselves also in all your behavior; because it is written, 'You shall be holy, for I am holy.'" As Jesus says it, "Therefore you are to be perfect, as your heavenly Father is perfect" (Matt. 5:48). Our goal is to "share His holiness" (Heb. 12:10), or to "become partakers of the divine nature" (II Peter 1:4) in this moral sense. We are to purify ourselves, even as he is pure (I John 3:3). See also Luke 1:75; Romans 6:19, 22; II Corinthians 6:14-7:1; I Thessalonians 3:13; 4:7.

Two main factors in the sanctification process are God's law and God's Spirit. One purpose of God's law, whether in its Old Testament or New Testament form, is to show God's people the content of holiness so that they will know *how* to be holy as God is holy. This will be discussed further in the next section. The purpose of the gift of the Holy Spirit (Acts 2:38), on the other hand, is to provide us with an indwelling source of moral power by which we are enabled to conform our lives to the pattern set forth in his revealed law (Rom. 8:13; Eph. 3:16; Phil. 2:13). This is probably one reason why he is called the *Holy* Spirit, namely, because his principal work in the economy of redemption is to help us to be holy, i.e., to sanctify us.

God's Holiness and Our Repentance

Another aspect of our holiness directly affected by divine holiness is repentance, which is not only a principal element in our sanctification but a prerequisite to the very reception of salvation (Acts 2:38). How can we develop a truly repentant heart? Basically, by learning to imitate the negative aspect of God's holiness, especially his hatred of sin. This is the essence of repentance, namely, the hatred of sin in our own lives. When we come to understand and appreciate God's attitude toward sin in terms of hatred and disgust, as noted earlier, we begin to see what our own attitude should be. We know then that we must have a hatred for all sin, but especially a hatred and disgust and grief for our own sins in particular. "The fear of the Lord is to hate evil," says Proverbs 8:13. Only the ungodly "does not despise evil" (Ps. 36:4).

True repentance can arise in our hearts only when we have perceived God as the "Holy, Holy, Holy" one. Then we will fling ourselves down before him and mourn with Isaiah, "Woe is me, for I am ruined!" (Isa. 6:3-5). True repentance will remain in our hearts only when we maintain our awareness of a divine holiness that is a "consuming fire" against sin (Heb. 12:29).

God's Holiness and Ethics

Love gives; holiness demands. This is one of the most basic distinctions between these two sides of God's nature. Because he is love, he offers himself and his blessing to us; but because he is holy, he makes demands of us. Clarke rightly speaks of "the reasonable demand of the divine perfection," and of the "claim" and the "call of divine holiness."[42] In this sense the holiness of God is fundamental to the whole enterprise of human ethics.

The basic ethical question is "What ought I to do?" In this question the "what" is the problem of ethical *knowledge*, and the "ought" is the problem of ethical *obligation*. Divine holiness is the starting point for the solution to both problems. In the first place, God's ontological holiness is the foundation of oughtness. The fact that God is our transcendent creator is the reason—and the *only* reason—why we "ought" to do *anything*.[43] God's holiness, not his love, is the "divine imperative." It obligates us to do whatever he commands us to do, and the obligation is absolute and true. Apart from the supreme holiness of God, any other obligation is only relative and hypothetical ("*If* you want . . ., *then* you ought . . . .").

In the second place, God's ethical holiness is the starting point for

---

42. William Newton Clarke, *The Christian Doctrine of God*, pp. 103-104.
43. See Jack Cottrell, *What the Bible Says About God the Creator*, pp. 163-164.

discerning ethical knowledge, for learning *what* we ought to do. "Therefore you are to be perfect, as your heavenly Father is perfect" (Matt. 5:48). "But like the Holy One who called you, be holy yourselves also in all your behavior" (I Peter 1:15). The holy character of God is the model and pattern for right human conduct and is the basis of the moral law, and we have sufficient knowledge of its content through the word revelation he has given us in the Bible. His holy law, rightly divided according to his covenantal intentions, is the fundamental framework for ethics.

Finally we should remember that the whole concept of "right and wrong," which is a fundamental ethical assumption, derives its meaning from the holiness of God.

God's Holiness and Our Worship

Certainly God is worthy of our worship just because he is God, and every one of his attributes is worthy of praise. But there is something about the holiness of God that makes it a special focus of worship, as indicated by the adoring proclamations of the heavenly beings, "Holy, Holy, Holy!" (Isa. 6:3; Rev. 4:8). As Hodge observes, "Infinite purity, even more than infinite knowledge or infinite power, is the object of reverence."[44]

Conclusion

This concludes our discussion of the nature of holiness as such. What remains now is to see the specific forms that God's holiness takes as it touches our lives. First we will see that in reference to human beings simply as creatures, God's holiness is known to us mainly in and through his *law*. Then we will see that in reference to human beings as sinners, God's holiness expresses itself primarily in *wrath*.

HOLINESS AS LAW

The holy God is the source of all law. Scripture says, "The Lord is our judge, the Lord is our lawgiver, the Lord is our king" (Isa. 33:22). James 4:12 says, "There is only one Lawgiver and Judge, the One who is able to save and to destroy." Bavinck comments, "God is, indeed, the

---

44. Charles Hodge. *Systematic Theology*. I:413.

supreme Lawgiver, and the entire judicial order with respect to every sphere is rooted in him."[45]

Many different terms are used to describe the law that he reveals to us, most of them being used many times throughout Psalm 119. In addition to the term *law*, we find such expressions as *commandments, statutes, testimonies, word, judgments, precepts,* and *ordinances.* God's law has also been revealed in different forms. Scripture speaks of the Law written in the heart (Rom. 2:15), "the Law of Moses" (Heb. 10:28), and "the law of Christ" (Gal. 6:2). It uses the term in a number of other senses as well.[46] We must be careful to discern whether a certain specific form of law is the subject in any given reference, so as to avoid false generalizations with reference to the nature and purpose of law as such.

In its most general sense ("law as such"), the term *law* refers to the preceptive will of God,[47] or "the will of God which requires and regulates human action."[48] It might be called "the transcript of an eternal norm,"[49] that norm being the nature and will of God. David equates God's law and God's will in Psalm 40:8, "I delight to do Thy will, O my God; Thy Law is within my heart."

God's Law and God's Holiness

God gives us law basically because he is a holy God who has an infinite zeal for right and wrong. This is why there is such a thing as law in the first place. "The whole moral code follows from his holiness," as Erickson says.[50] This accounts for the fact that law includes two distinct elements, namely, commandments and penalties. The former are derived mostly from the positive aspect of divine holiness (i.e., the

---

45. Herman Bavinck, *The Doctrine of God,* p. 222.

46. See James M. Boice, *Foundations of the Christian Faith, Volume II: God the Redeemer* (Downers Grove: InterVarsity Press, 1978), pp. 56-57.

47. See Jack Cottrell, *What the Bible Says About God the Ruler* (Joplin, Mo.: College Press, 1984), p. 311.

48. W. Gutbrod, "νόμος etc.," *Theological Dictionary of the New Testament,* ed. Gerhard Kittel, tr. Geoffrey W. Bromiley (Grand Rapids: Eerdmans, 1967), IV:1078.

49. Hans-Helmut Esser, "Law, Custom, Elements," *The New International Dictionary of New Testament Theology,* ed. Colin Brown (Grand Rapids: Zondervan, 1976), II:440.

50. Millard J. Erickson, *Christian Theology* (Grand Rapids: Baker Book House, 1983), I:285.

character of God), while the latter are derived from the negative aspect of his holiness (i.e., his opposition to sin).

The Commandments of the Law

Usually when we think about law we are thinking of its content or its commands. Here we see God's holiness, his perfect moral character, put into verbal form. Thus we may say that the moral law is the mirror[51] or the transcript[52] of divine holiness. For this reason the moral law is the primary source of our knowledge of the nature of his holiness. (This assumes, of course, that the commands are given to us by divine revelation and are not just the product of advanced human wisdom.[53]) If we desire to imitate God's holiness, we look to his law and obey his law.

This is not to neglect the example of Jesus Christ as a model for holiness. From a purely human perspective Christ is sinless (Heb. 4:15), and thus even as a human being he is a perfect representation of God's purity. But since he is also God in the flesh, he is a first-hand demonstration of divine holiness. It is a mistake, however, to think that he somehow makes law obsolete or even secondary as a pattern for holiness. Insofar as his life is meant to be imitated, it simply parallels the moral law and in a sense becomes another form of it. But most importantly we must remember that Christ's main purpose for living among us in human form was not to set an ethical example but to be the redemptive sacrifice for our sins. This means that some aspects of his life had to do with his own unique mission and were not meant to be imitated by us (e.g., his non-resisting death on the cross).[54] In other words Christ's example is an important form of the moral law, but it is not the only one.

We said above that the commandments of the law are derived *mostly* from the holy nature of God, i.e., they are God's holiness in a verbalized imperative form. Such commandments are usually called the

---

51. R. C. Sproul, *The Holiness of God* (Wheaton: Tyndale House, 1985), p. 121.

52. Stephen Charnock, *The Existence and Attributes of God*, p. 525.

53. An example of the opposite view is W. N. Clarke, who asks, "How then shall we tell what his holiness includes?" There is only one way to know, he says, namely, "the way of our own worthiest conceptions of what is good." We begin with "our best conceptions" of what is good, and project them in an infinite degree into the divine nature. See *The Christian Doctrine of God*, pp. 99-100.

54. See the discussion of the Christological fallacy in Jack Cottrell, *What the Bible Says About God the Creator*, pp. 166ff.

"moral law" and are universally and eternally applicable. But this is not the whole picture as far as the content of the commandments is concerned. Some commands, while always consistent with his holiness, are not necessary and inevitable projections of it. In other words, some commands are based on the *works* of God, and some may be based simply on his *will*. These have traditionally been called "positive laws" and may be limited in their application and may even be subject to change. An example is the Old Testament Sabbath commandment, which was based upon God's work in the original creation (Ex. 20:11) and his work in redeeming Israel from Egypt (Deut. 5:15). Since both of these works have been superseded by a new creation and a new and more complete work of redemption through Jesus Christ, the Sabbath commandment has also been superseded by the precedent for Lord's Day observance. Another example of such positive laws would be baptism and the Lord's supper, which are also grounded in the redemptive work of God in Christ.

Recognizing this distinction helps us to answer the ancient puzzle, "Is the good *good* because God wills it, or does God will it *because* it is good?" The answer is that both are true, the first possibility applying to the positive laws and the second one to the moral law. That God wills some things because they are good does not require some higher law outside and above God himself; it simply acknowledges that God's own nature is a necessary standard for basic morality. God could not give us laws that go against his own holiness.

Whether we are speaking of the moral law or of positive laws, the holiness of God is their ultimate foundation because it is the reason why God gives us laws of any sort. His holy zeal concerning right and wrong makes it impossible for moral creatures to exist without divine commandments in some form.

The Penalties of the Law

Law consists not only of commandments but also of penalties. Throughout Scripture, punishments and curses are either explicitly or implicitly attached to the commands. This is seen in one of the very first laws given to mankind: "From the tree of the knowledge of good and evil you shall not eat, for in the day that you eat from it you shall surely die" (Gen. 2:17). Many of the individual laws of Moses had specific penalties attached (e.g., Ex. 21:12-27), and the law as a whole was ac-

companied by the most severe curses. "Cursed is he who does not confirm the words of this law by doing them" (Deut. 27:26). "But it shall
come about, if you will not obey the Lord your God, to observe to do all
His commandments and His statutes which I charge you today, that all
these curses shall come upon you and overtake you" (Deut. 28:15; cf.
vv. 16-68). Paul refers to this general curse in Galatians 3:10, "Cursed
is every one who does not abide by all things written in the book of the
law, to perform them." The universal penalty for all sin is pronounced
by Ezekiel: "The soul who sins will die" (Ezek. 18:4). This is reiterated
by Paul: "The wages of sin is death" (Rom. 6:23). This is the meaning
of I Corinthians 15:56, "The power of sin is the law." Sin has power
over us through the *penalty* of the law; it is the law of God that sinners
shall die. This seems to be the point of Romans 4:15 also, "The Law
brings about wrath." It is not the commandments of the law that bring
wrath, but its penalties.

Here we see not the positive aspect of divine holiness at work, but its
negative side, the dark side of God's unconditional opposition to sin
and his hatred of it. We have said that law is the form of God's holiness
made known to his creatures simply as creatures, even apart from their
sin. Even before sin entered there was law, both the positive laws given
to Adam and Eve (Gen. 1:28; 2:15-17) and the moral law written in
their hearts (Rom. 2:15). But even in this pristine state, before their
souls were stained by sin, the penalty of the law was already known to
them (Gen. 2:17; Rom. 1:32). In these penalties they could perceive
the shadow of God's holy wrath, even though unexpressed as yet.

Here we see the full meaning of Paul's pronouncement in Romans
7:12, "So then, the Law is holy, and the commandment is holy and
righteous and good" (cf. vv. 14, 16). God's law in its totality, including
both its commands and its penalties, is a mirror of God's holiness in *its*
totality, including both its positive and its negative aspects.

Some would say that God's law is derived basically from his love
rather than from his holiness as such. This will always be the case, of
course, with those who dissolve all of God's attributes in the universal
solvent of love. Stählin speaks for many when he says, "Like the
Gospel, the Law is a gift of the love of God." Thus "if God is angry
because of transgression of the Law, this is the reaction of spurned love,
which sought to benefit man through the Law."[55] We cannot deny that
the law is a benefit to us, nor can we deny that God's love desires us to

obey the law so that we may receive its benefit and avoid its penalty. But it is an outrageous distortion and an affront to the holiness of God to say that law is a product of love and that the wrath evoked by disobedience to the law is simply spurned love. (This will be discussed later in this chapter.) The law is a product of and an expression of the *holiness* of God, a holiness that has an independent integrity within the nature of God and is not just a handmaiden of his love.

The Purpose of Law

In view of the above discussion we are now prepared to ask about the purpose of law. What purpose does it serve with respect to man as creature? In answering this question we must again be careful not to generalize from statements made about specific forms of law, particularly the Law of Moses. For example, in Romans 5:20 Paul says that "the Law came in that the transgression might increase," and in Galatians 3:19 he says that the Law "was added because of transgressions." But it seems that in these passages he is speaking specifically of the Law of Moses and not of law as such. The purpose of law as such must be stated in slightly different terms.

Law Defines Right and Wrong

The Bible has many general exhortations such as this one from Isaiah 1:16-17, "Cease to do evil, learn to do good." We are exhorted to "cleanse ourselves from all defilement of flesh and spirit, perfecting holiness in the fear of God" (II Cor. 7:1). But the question often is this: just what constitutes good and evil? Or we might ask, what is the difference between defilement and holiness? How can we tell which acts go into which category? The answers to such questions are found in God's law, which has been given for the explicit purpose of defining good and evil, right and wrong. "'Come, let us go up to the mountain of the Lord, to the house of the God of Jacob; that He may teach us concerning His ways, and that we may walk in His paths.' For the law will go forth from Zion, and the word of the Lord from Jerusalem" (Isa. 2:3; cf. Micah 4:2). "His ways" and "his paths" are learned from "his laws."

---

55. Gustav Stählin, "ὀργή etc." (part), *Theological Dictionary of the New Testament*, ed. Gerhard Friedrich, tr. Geoffrey W. Bromiley (Grand Rapids: Eerdmans, 1967), V:433.

The background of this verse from Isaiah is the giving of the Mosaic Law from another "mountain of the Lord," Mount Sinai. This law was given in order to instruct Israel in God's ways: "Now the Lord said to Moses, 'Come up to Me on the mountain and remain there, and I will give you the stone tablets with the law and the commandment which I have written for their instruction'" (Ex. 24:12). The Psalmist could thus speak of God's law as "a lamp to my feet, and a light to my path" (Ps. 119:105). Paul describes its purpose thus: "All Scripture is inspired by God and profitable for teaching, for reproof, for correction, for training in righteousness; that the man of God may be adequate, equipped for every good work" (II Tim. 3:16-17). This includes New Testament Scripture as well, which is the specific reference in the Messianic prophecy of Isaiah 2:3, i.e., the law that will go forth from Zion or Jerusalem. The New Testament revelation continues to define right and wrong for those who live on this side of Pentecost.[56] James 1:25 refers to it as "the perfect law, the law of liberty," and compares it with a mirror into which one may look to see the kind of person he *ought* to be.

The Bible especially stresses the fact that the law gives us the knowledge of sin (Rom. 3:20). Paul says, "I would not have come to know sin except through the Law; for I would not have known about coveting if the Law had not said, 'You shall not covet'" (Rom. 7:7). Boice says, "The primary means by which God reveals sin to be sin . . . is the law of God contained in the Scriptures."[57]

Once we learn from God's law what is right and what is wrong, then ideally we will follow the right and shun the wrong. As the result of this knowledge we are able to live holy lives. "We conform to his holiness when we regulate ourselves by his law," as Charnock says.[58] We can be like King Hezekiah, who did "what was good and right and faithful before the Lord," because he did everything "in obedience to the law and the commands" (II Chron. 31:20-21, NIV). If one could do this absolutely, always without exception obeying whatever commands applied to him, he would have eternal life. "Do this, and you will live"

---

56. This is not to say that the Old Testament is irrelevant for this purpose today, but the proper end of its civil laws for Israel as a nation (Ephesians 2:11-18) and of its ceremonial laws for Israel as a religious body (Hebrews, *passim*) must be observed.

57. James M. Boice, *Foundations of the Christian Faith*, II:55.

58. Stephen Charnock, *The Existence and Attributes of God*, p. 525.

(Luke 10:28) is the rule of law. In the final analysis, the law's purpose of defining right and wrong was originally intended to serve a more basic purpose, namely, to enable God's moral creatures to be perfect and to live forever in his uninterrupted good will. As Paul says, the commandment "was intended to bring life" (Rom. 7:10, NIV).

The well-known and intensely-regretted fact is that no one has taken advantage of the law's good purpose of defining good and evil in order to accomplish this positive end, for "all have sinned and fall short of the glory of God" (Rom. 3:23). Thus while the law is still eminently useful for defining right and wrong, it is impossible for it to serve the transcendent and noble purpose of bringing life.

Law Encourages Right and Discourages Wrong

The second purpose of law is connected with its penalties. In view of the penalty attached to doing wrong, the law as given to God's creatures is intended to encourage them to do right and to discourage them from doing wrong. This is true of law as such, even before human sinfulness is taken into consideration, as is evident from Genesis 2:17. Certainly the threat of death was intended to deter Adam and Eve from breaking this specific commandment. But once sin has entered and human hearts have become diseased and inclined toward sin (Jer. 17:9), the law with its penalties is needed all the more. This seems to be Paul's point in I Timothy 1:8-9, "But we know that the Law is good, if one uses it lawfully, realizing the fact that law is not made for a righteous man, but for those who are lawless and rebellious." Here he is of course using the terms *righteous* and *lawless* in their relative sense, and he is saying that the law is like a bridle. Relatively speaking, the docile and well-trained horse does not need the bridle in order to be restrained, but only to be guided. On the other hand, the unruly and unbroken horse needs the bridle as a restraining instrument, to keep him from harming or killing himself and others.

The unholy irony of the situation is that in the rebellious heart, the law often does just the opposite. Instead of restraining sin as intended, it incites the "mind set on the flesh" (Rom. 8:6) to indulge in it instead. Thus Paul says that "while we were in the flesh, the sinful passions, which were aroused by the Law," followed after sin (Rom. 7:5). Faced with the commandment not to covet, "sin, taking opportunity through the commandment, produced in me coveting of every kind" (Rom.

7:8). Since the very essence of sin is lawlessness (I John 3:4), the sinful heart delights to know the law just so it can flout it.

The legitimate purposes of law remain, however, even if limited and perverted by sinners. Its true purposes are to define right and wrong by verbalizing the positive holiness of God, and to encourage the right and discourage the wrong by magnifying the negative side of God's holiness in its penalties.

Law and Sin

"The Lord was pleased for His righteousness' sake to make the law great and glorious" (Isa. 42:21). In spite of this fact, and in spite of its noble purposes as outlined above, the whole race of mankind has fallen into sin. "For all have sinned and fall short of the glory of God" (Rom. 3:23). Charnock thinks that the "glory" of which this passage speaks is none other than the holiness of God, as he interprets it in relation to II Corinthians 3:18.[59] This makes sense when we understand that God's holiness is known to us in his law, which he has made "great and glorious." All have sinned and fallen short of the ideal of God's holiness as portrayed in his law, which is his glory.

The sin which pervades the heart of every man is truly the very opposite of God's law and thus of God's holiness. "Every one who practices sin also practices lawlessness; and sin is lawlessness" (I John 3:4). The word here is *anomia*, which means not merely transgression of the law but more basically opposition to the law. It is a rebellion against law, a rebellion against authority, a demonic zeal for autonomy and for a false freedom from law of all kinds. It is a desire to live without law, a desire notably expressed in the Marxist-Leninist blueprint for the ideal society of the future[60] and read into the Bible by some Marxist-leaning Liberation Theologians.[61]

The sinful heart is hostile toward law; but even many Christians, as the result of a misunderstanding of the relation between law and grace, are quite indifferent toward law (i.e., God's commands as they apply to-

---

59. Ibid., p. 508.

60. Francis Nigel Lee, *Communist Eschatology* (Nutley, N.J.: Craig Press, 1974), pp. 392-394.

61. See Jose Miranda, *Marx and the Bible*, tr. John Eagleson (Maryknoll, N.Y.: Orbis Books, 1974), pp. 187-192. "Paul wants a world without law," he says (p. 187). "God destroys sin and law forever" (p. 191).

day) and do not consider it to be binding upon them. They disdain the so-called "letter of the law" and embrace a false freedom in which the only "imperative" is a nebulous subjectivity euphemistically known as "love." Such an approach may begin as an honest misunderstanding, but it is always secretly fed by the heart's sinful tendency toward lawlessness. What *must* be understood is this: since God's law is the outward expression of his own holy nature, any rebellion against *law* is also a *rebellion against God personally*. Charnock has well said,[62]

> It is a contemning the holiness of God when we charge the law of God with rigidness. We cast dirt upon the holiness of God when we blame the law of God, because it shackles us, and prohibits our desired pleasures; and hate the law of God, as they did the prophets, because they did not "prophesy smooth things." . . . We are contrary to the law when we wish it were not so exact, and therefore contrary to the holiness [of] God, which set the stamp of exactness and righteousness upon it. . . .

We may pause to note that sin is not just a defilement of the holiness of God, but is an outrage against all his attributes. Bates says,[63]

> . . . It is the violation of his majesty, who is the universal Sovereign of heaven and earth; a contrariety to his holiness, which shines forth in his law; a despising of his goodness, the attractive to obedience; the contempt of his omniscience, which sees every sin when it is committed; the slighting of his terrible justice and power, as if the sinner could secure himself from his indignation; a denial of his truth, as if the threatening were a vain terror to scare men from sin . . . .

Throughout Scripture sin is seen as a personal affront against God. "Against Thee, Thee only, I have sinned," cries David (Ps. 51:4). "Thy word I have treasured in my heart, that I may not sin against Thee" (Ps. 119:11). The Old Testament prophets taught that "violation of the Law is apostasy from Yahweh."[64] Likewise for Paul, "the Law forbids sin, and also intensifies it to the level of actual rebellion against God."[65] Paul says forcefully in Romans 8:7 that not subjecting oneself to the law of

---

62. Stephen Charnock, *The Existence and Attributes of God*, p. 507.
63. William Bates, *The Harmony of the Divine Attributes*, pp. 235-236.
64. W. Gutbrod, "νόμος," p. 1039.
65. Ibid., p. 1074.

God is hostility toward God. According to Gutbrod, the "inner force" of the term *anomia* (lawlessness) in I John 3:4 is "rebellion or revolt against God, or alienation from Him." The verse thus says in effect that "he who commits sin is thereby in revolt against God; indeed, sin is nothing but rebellion against God."[66] This is why James says, "For whoever keeps the whole law and yet stumbles in one point, he has become guilty of all" (James 2:10). There is a sense in which all laws are one, in that they are all identified with the will or nature of the Lawgiver. No matter which arrows of sin we launch, and whether it be one or many, they all ultimately come to rest in the heart of God. "For He who said, 'Do not commit adultery,' also said, 'Do not commit murder.' Now if you do not commit adultery, but do commit murder, you have become a transgressor of the law" (James 2:11)—and thus a despiser of God's own pure and holy nature. These words from Sproul sum it up well:[67]

> Sin is cosmic treason. Sin is treason against a perfectly pure Sovereign. It is an act of supreme ingratitude toward One to whom we owe everything, to the One who has given us life itself. Have you ever considered the deeper implications of the slightest sin, of the most minute peccadillo? What are we saying to our Creator when we disobey Him at the slightest point? We are saying no to the righteousness of God. We are saying, "God, Your law is not good. My judgment is better than Yours. Your authority does not apply to me. I am above and beyond Your jurisdiction. I have the right to do what I want to do, not what You command me to do."
>
> The slightest sin is an act of defiance against cosmic authority. It is a revolutionary act, a rebellious act where we are setting ourselves in opposition to the One to whom we owe everything. It is an insult to His holiness. . . .

The Uses of the Law

Discussions of God's law in Protestant theology usually include a section on the *uses* of the law. This is slightly different from the question of the *purpose* of the law. The latter has to do with God's original intentions concerning his law as given to man as a moral creature. The former question asks what uses may be made and should be made of

---

66. Ibid., p. 1086.
67. R. C. Sproul, *The Holiness of God*, pp. 151-152.

the law now that man is a sinner.

The first and most important point, now that man is a sinner, is that the law does not and cannot have a *soteric* use. It cannot be used to save a person from his sins. Once a person is a sinner, no amount of law-keeping can make him right with God. Even if originally the law "was to result in life" (Rom. 7:10) through perfect obedience, it is no longer able to do so (Gal. 3:21). Hence any attempt to be justified by works of law is futile (Rom. 3:28), whether it be the Mosaic Law or any other form of law.

But now that sin has entered, the law does serve a very important function not included in God's original intention for it. This is called the *didactic* use, a term based on Galatians 3:24, where the law is called a tutor or schoolmaster to bring us to Christ. This has been understood to mean that the law not only defines sin for us but convinces us that we personally are sinners and thus that we need a Savior.[68] It reveals to us not only the holiness of God but also our own unholiness, and thus drives us to Christ as the only available remedy for our sinful condition.

The other two uses of the law roughly correspond to its original purposes. One is called the *governmental* use, which means that it still functions as a restraint upon evil. It helps God to maintain his moral government of the universe. It is also the main tool used by civil governments to maintain order in society. Without the restraints of law, including both its commands and its penalties, sin or lawlessness would abound, as is suggested by Romans 1:24-32 and II Thessalonians 2:7. See also Romans 5:20; Galatians 3:19; I Timothy 1:8-9.

The final use of the law is its *normative* function, which brings us back to the original purpose of the law as a way of defining right and wrong. This is how the Mosaic Law functioned for Israel. Just before their entrance into the promised land, Moses rehearsed for them all the statutes and laws that God had given through him. "You shall not add to the word which I am commanding you, nor take away from it, that you may keep the commandments of the Lord your God which I command you" (Deut. 4:2). He reminded them of the glory of the law:

----

68. See James M. Boice, *Foundations of the Christian Faith*, II:55. I do not agree with his statement that this is the "main purpose" of the law, since I would distinguish purpose and use; nor am I convinced that this use is the "main" one. But it is certainly *one* of the main uses of the law.

See, I have taught you statutes and judgments just as the Lord my God commanded me, that you should do thus in the land where you are entering to possess it. So keep and do them, for that is your wisdom and your understanding in the sight of the peoples who will hear all these statutes and say, "Surely this great nation is a wise and understanding people." For what great nation is there that has a god so near to it as is the Lord our God whenever we call on Him? Or what great nation is there that has statutes and judgments as righteous as this whole law which I am setting before you today? (Deut. 4:5-8)

After Moses' death the Lord reiterated this exhortation to Joshua (Josh. 1:7-8).

Though we do not follow the Mosaic Law today, the New Covenant still contains laws and commandments that define the norm by which we are to live. Salvation by grace abolishes law as a means of salvation, but not as a norm for living. We are not saved by law-keeping, but we keep it nonetheless because that is what we are supposed to do. This is how we "practice righteousness" (I John 2:29; 3:7), namely, by conforming to the norm of God's law. Being holy and obeying commandments are the same thing. Leviticus 20:7-8 says, "You shall consecrate yourselves therefore and be holy, for I am the Lord your God. And you shall keep My statutes and practice them." This is the section in Leviticus from which Peter draws his exhortation to us, "But like the Holy One who called you, be holy yourselves also in all your behavior; because it is written 'You shall be holy, for I am holy'" (I Peter 1:15-16). Being holy and blameless still means following the law of God. Psalm 119:1 equates them: "How blessed are those whose way is blameless, who walk in the law of the Lord." Verse 9 adds, "How can a young man keep his way pure? By keeping it according to Thy word."

Christians should not despise this normative use of the law, but should glory in it. For just as sin is committed not just against law but against the Lawgiver, so also is obedience to law not just to the commandments as such but to the Lawgiver himself. We obey not just in blind commitment to some impersonal and abstract norm, but "we do it with respect to the purity of the Lawgiver beaming in it."[69] We cannot separate obedience to the law from love for the God who gave it. In the midst of the Ten Commandments God speaks of "those who love Me

---

69. Stephen Charnock, *The Existence and Attributes of God*, p. 525.

and keep My commandments" (Ex. 20:6). He always connects obedience to his law with a personal relationship to him.

> And now, Israel, what does the Lord your God require from you, but to fear the Lord your God, to walk in all His ways and love Him, and to serve the Lord your God with all your heart and with all your soul, and to keep the Lord's commandments and His statutes which I am commanding you today for your good? (Deut. 10:12-13; cf. Deut. 11:13; Josh. 22:5)

"I command you today to love the Lord your God, to walk in His ways and to keep His commandments" (Deut 30:16; cf. Deut. 11:1). God wants his law to be in the hearts of his people (Isa. 51:7; Jer. 31:33). And lest we think this is just some obsolete Old Testament principle, we need only to recall the simple reminder of our Lord, "If you love Me, you will keep My commandments" (John 14:15). First John 5:3 reminds us gently, "For this is the love of God, that we keep His commandments; and His commandments are not burdensome."

Because we cannot separate the law from the Lawgiver, if we love the Lawgiver we will not only obey his law but will also love it. The Psalmist speaks thus of the righteous man: "His delight is in the law of the Lord, and in His law he meditates day and night" (Ps. 1:2). How can the Christian do less than the Psalmist himself, who declares, "I shall delight in Thy commandments, which I love. . . . O how I love Thy law! It is my meditation all the day" (Ps. 119:47, 97). The more we love God, the more we will love his law; and the more we love it, the more we will prize obedience to it and hate disobedience—both in ourselves and in others. The more others mock and scorn God's law, the more we should value it and defend it. As the Psalmist says, "It is time for the Lord to act, for they have broken Thy law. Therefore I love Thy commandments above gold, yes, above fine gold" (Ps. 119:126-127). Commenting on the lawbreakers mentioned in this passage, Charnock says, "By their scorn of [the law] my love to it shall be the warmer, and my hatred of iniquity shall be the sharper. The disdain of others should inflame us with a zeal and fortitude to appear in the behalf of his despised honour."[70]

---

70. Ibid., p. 524.

Conclusion

In this main section our point has been to explain how God's holiness is related to his law. It is mainly the reflection of the positive aspect of his holiness, namely, his perfect moral character, as this is expressed in the form of commands. But it also contains an intimation of the negative side of holiness in that it includes penalties, showing us God's deep hatred of sin. In the next main section we will see a further unfolding of this negative side when we discuss not just God's attitude toward potential sin but his reaction to actual sin.

HOLINESS AS WRATH

The wrath of God is not a pleasant subject to contemplate, and most of us would rather just pass it by. But this cannot be done, for as Stählin says, "Wrath is an essential and inalienable trait in the biblical and NT view of God."[71] Thus we must give attention to it. It is especially crucial in our study of God as Redeemer. Without it we cannot properly appreciate the doctrines of redemption, as Boice notes.[72] Not only this, but we cannot even properly *understand* the doctrines of redemption without a right understanding of divine wrath.

We have maintained that there are two sides to God's moral nature, one most generally described as love and the other as holiness. His holiness expresses itself further in the forms of law and wrath, the former being directed to man in his status as creature and the latter to man as sinner. Thus we must think of the wrath of God as not essentially different from his holiness, but as holiness itself in its confrontation with actual sin.

The Terminology of Wrath

Morris notes that in the Old Testament alone there are more than twenty words that express the concept of God's wrath in over 580 occurrences.[73] Neither the variety nor the frequency is as great in the New Testament; but its testimony to the concept is still formidable, with Jesus himself having more to say about it than any other New Testament

---

71. Gustav Stählin, "ὀργή," p.423.
72. James M. Boice, *Foundations of the Christian Faith*, II:93.
73. Leon Morris, *The Apostolic Preaching*, p. 131.

witness.

In the Old Testament,[74] two of the main terms for wrath come from verbs that mean "to be hot, to burn, to kindle." One of these words is *chēmāh*, which means "hot displeasure, indignation, wrath, rage, fury." It is used for God's wrath about ninety times, including Deuteronomy 9:19, "For I was afraid of the anger and hot displeasure *[chēmāh]* with which the Lord was wrathful against you in order to destroy you." The other word, *chārōn*, means "heat, inward burning of anger." The verb form means "to be kindled," as in Numbers 11:1, "And when the Lord heard it, His anger was kindled, and the fire of the Lord burned among them and consumed some." These words, says Eichrodt, refer to "the inward fire of the emotion of anger" in God.[75]

The most common Old Testament word for divine wrath (170 times) is *'ap*, which basically refers to the nose or nostrils. It comes from the verb *'ānap*, which means "to snort, to be angry." Some have observed that in the Old Testament the nose is less the organ of smell than of wrath.[76] For instance, Psalm 18:8 says that when God was angry, "smoke rose from his nostrils [*'ap*]; consuming fire came from his mouth, burning coals blazed out of it" (NIV). Usually the word is used in a less picturesque way, as in Psalm 2:5, "Then He will speak to them in His anger [*'ap*] and terrify them in His fury." Another common word is *ka'as*, which along with its verb form is used around fifty times for divine wrath. For example, Judges 2:12 says that the Israelites through their idolatry "provoked the Lord to anger."

Three other words have the connotation of "foaming" or "boiling over," says Eichrodt.[77] One is *'ebrāh*, which some think comes from a verb meaning "to be full, to overflow." Thus it means "to be angry, to be full of wrath, to be overflowing with fury." For example, "He sent upon them His burning anger, fury [*'ebrāh*], and indignation, and trouble, a

74. For concise discussions of the various terms, see the article on *orgē* in *Theological Dictionary of the New Testament*, V:392-394; and the various articles on individual words in the *Theological Wordbook of the Old Testament*, 2 vols. (Chicago: Moody Press, 1980).

75. Walther Eichrodt, *Theology of the Old Testament*, I:258.

76. Oskar Grether and Johannes Fichtner, "ὀργή etc." (part), *Theological Dictionary of the New Testament*, ed. Gerhard Friedrich, tr. Geoffrey W. Bromiley (Grand Rapids: Eerdmans, 1967), V:392.

77. Walther Eichrodt, *Theology of the Old Testament*, I:258-259.

band of destroying angels" (Ps. 78:49). The other two words with this connotation are zā'ap and zā'am. The former is used (for example) in Micah 7:9, "I will bear the indignation of the Lord"; and the latter in Nahum 1:6, "Who can stand before His indignation?" Both carry the connotation of intense anger, the former being related to words that mean "to storm, to rage."

A final Old Testament word is qetsep, which Eichrodt relates to "the breaking forth of something under pressure."[78] The noun and the verb together are used nearly fifty times for God's anger. For example, "At His wrath [qetsep] the earth quakes, and the nations cannot endure His indignation" (Jer. 10:10).

In the New Testament only two main words represent the concept of God's wrath, thumos and orgē. Of these, the former is used only in the book of Revelation (14:10, 19; 15:1, 7; 16:1, 19; 19:15), except for Romans 2:8, where both words appear. Bavinck's distinction, that the New Testament uses "thumos for inward wrath, and orgē for wrath which manifests itself,"[79] does not seem sound. The more commonly accepted view is stated by Trench, namely, that thumos represents "more of the turbulent commotion, the boiling agitation of the feelings," and orgē "is more of an abiding and settled habit of mind."[80] The former is more commonly associated with intermittent, passionate outbursts of wrath or a sudden up-flowing of rage, which makes it quite appropriate to be used in the apocalyptic scenes of Revelation. On the other hand, the term orgē represents a constant and settled state of controlled indignation, more like an attitude than a sudden emotion. As an illustration, one may consider how the sun is a constantly seething and boiling mass of burning gases, from which occasionally a sunspot will flare up with consuming intensity. This is not unlike the way in which God's wrath is a constantly burning indignation against all sin, but on specific occasions bursts forth in acts of consuming judgment. "For our God is a consuming fire" (Heb. 12:29).

From these terms and the way they are used we are able to discern the nature of God's wrath in a fairly conclusive way. First of all it is clear

---

78. Ibid., p. 259.
79. Herman Bavinck, The Doctrine of God, p. 216.
80. Richard C. Trench, Synonyms of the New Testament, p. 131.

that it is not to be equated with an uncontrolled fit of temper such as is common among human beings. As Packer says, "God's wrath in the Bible is never the capricious, self-indulgent, irritable, morally ignoble thing that human anger so often is."[81] It is not just a sudden flaring up of passion which is soon over, as Morris says, but is "a strong and settled opposition to all that is evil arising out of God's very nature."[82] It is the natural and inevitable and eternal recoil of the all-holy God against all that is unholy.[83] It is "the absolute implacable hostility of the Divine Holiness to every form of moral evil," and "the implacable antagonism of holiness for evil, an antagonism that burns eternally."[84]

It is appropriate that the image of fire occurs so often in connection with the concept of God's wrath, for this well illustrates how his wrath is not just an occasional and uncharacteristic action performed by God but is a constant and abiding aspect of his very essence, namely, his holiness itself. The holiness of God always burns against the very thought of sin, but this is not obvious and not observed until sin actually comes into existence. At that point the holiness of God is unveiled as a "consuming fire" that must by nature engulf and destroy the offending evil, just as a hot stove instantly vaporizes drops of water that fall upon it. It is like an oven that is constantly maintained at 451 degrees Fahrenheit, and sins are like bits of paper that spontaneously burst into flame when cast into that oven.

Wrath and Sin

It is already obvious that there is a close connection between wrath and sin, but there are some issues that call for a more detailed inspection. Thus in this section we will affirm that according to Scripture God's wrath is always evoked by sin as disobedience to law, and that God's wrath takes the form of deserved vengeance and retribution upon sin.

Wrath Is Evoked by Sin

We have seen that God in his holiness manifests an infinite zeal for right and against wrong, as these are defined by his law. He issues his

---

81. J. I. Packer, *Knowing God* (Downers Grove: InterVarsity Press, 1973), p. 136.
82. Leon Morris, *The Apostolic Preaching*, pp. 162-163.
83. See ibid., p. 130, especially the citation from Maldwyn Hughes.
84. G. O. Griffith, *St. Paul's Gospel to the Romans* (Oxford, 1949), pp. 20, 85ff.; cited in Leon Morris, *The Apostolic Preaching*, p. 159, fn. 1.

sovereign commands, and demands that they be obeyed; and he threatens dire penalties for those who disobey. Thus we should not be surprised when God in his holiness responds to disobedience with a fierce and burning wrath, i.e., with an infinite inner displeasure against both the law-breaker and his sin, and with terrible outward penalties and curses and retribution. We should not be surprised, simply because *God is holy*, and wrath is the natural response of holiness toward sin. In Pink's words, "The wrath of God is His eternal detestation of all unrighteousness. It is the displeasure and indignation of Divine equity against evil. It is the holiness of God stirred into activity against sin."[85] We can put it in the form of a question: if God is truly holy, how could he possibly *not* be angry toward sin?[86] Would we not be surprised if God did *not* become angry when his law is broken? Would we not consider such indifference toward sin to be a moral blemish?[87] Morris says, "Because He is a moral Being, His anger is directed towards wrongdoing in any shape or form." Wrath is but "the stern reaction of the divine nature to evil in man. It is aroused only and inevitably by sin."[88] William Evans says,[89]

> The Divine wrath is to be regarded as the natural expression of the Divine nature, which is absolute holiness, manifesting itself against the wilful, high-handed, deliberate, inexcusable sin and iniquity of mankind. God's wrath is always regarded in the Scripture as the just, proper, and natural expression of His holiness and righteousness which must always, under all circumstances, and at all costs be maintained.

Bloesch agrees that "the wrath of God must properly be understood as the necessary reaction of his holiness to sin."[90] This is why God's wrath cannot be called capricious or fickle or arbitrary. It is totally consistent, being directed only against sin and always against sin.[91]

---

85. Arthur W. Pink, *The Attributes of God* (Swengel, Pa.: Reiner Publications, 1968), p. 76.

86. R. C. Sproul, *The Holiness of God*, p. 224.

87. Arthur W. Pink, *The Attributes of God*, p. 75.

88. Leon Morris, *The Apostolic Preaching*, p. 131.

89. William Evans, "Wrath," *International Standard Bible Encyclopedia*, ed. James Orr (Chicago: Howard-Severance, 1915), V:3113.

90. Donald G. Bloesch, *Essentials of Evangelical Theology*, I:34.

91. Leon Morris, *The Apostolic Preaching*, p. 131; James M. Boice, *Foundations of the Christian Faith*, II:96.

It is difficult to deny that divine wrath is evoked by sin, but there is a serious disagreement as to just what there is about sin that causes God to react in this way. *Why* is God angry with sin? A common view today is that God becomes angry when we sin because sin is a rejection of his *love* toward us, a rejection of the covenant-love that he wants us to have. Thus it is not the sin as such that draws forth his wrath, but the spurning of his love. For example, Stählin agrees that "a profound reason for the wrath of God" is "the human hubris which basically despises God and seeks to live without Him." But alongside and above it all stands "His love, whose violation is an ever new occasion of His wrath." Thus "God's wrath is that of wounded love"; it is a "holy wrath of despised mercy and wounded love."[92] Another writer says the same thing: "God does not reject his people for failing to measure up to standards of achievement . . . . Instead he rejects them for failure to respond to his grace."[93] Another agrees; wrath is "a reaction of God to the rejection of his grace."[94] Conservative sources are echoing this same thought: "Thus it is the wounding of his gracious love, the rejection of his proffered mercy, which evokes his holy wrath."[95] "When either people from without, or the covenant people themselves, profane, thwart or reject this love of the covenant God, God expresses his vexation, agitation, displeasure, anger and/or hatred: he pours out his wrath."[96]

Alleged Scriptural support for this idea is scant, but it comes from such passages as Deuteronomy 32:15, which says that God condemned Israel because "he forsook God who made him, and scorned the Rock of his salvation." Psalm 78:21-22 would also be cited: "Therefore the Lord heard and was full of wrath, and a fire was kindled against Jacob, and anger also mounted against Israel; because they did not believe in God, and did not trust in His salvation" (cf. vv. 31-32). In Jesus' parable, the unforgiving servant was handed over to the torturers

---

92. Gustav Stählin, "ὀργή," pp. 420, 423, 428.

93. Ronald M. Hals, *Grace and Faith in the Old Testament* (Minneapolis: Augsburg, 1980), p. 72.

94. Adrio König, *Here Am I! A Christian Reflection on God* (Grand Rapids: Eerdmans, 1982), p. 44.

95. William Childs Robinson, "Wrath of God," *Evangelical Dictionary of Theology*, ed. Walter A. Elwell (Grand Rapids: Baker Book House, 1984), p. 1196.

96. Gerard Van Groningen, "qātsap," *Theological Wordbook of the Old Testament*, ed. R. Laird Harris et al. (Chicago: Moody Press, 1980), II:808.

because he mocked the abundant mercy he had just received by refusing to forgive his fellow servant (Matt. 18:23-35). Jesus became angry
with the Jewish leaders when they opposed his act of mercy, i.e., healing on the Sabbath (Mark 3:1-6). Paul says the unbelieving Jews "are
storing up wrath for yourself in the day of wrath," thus despising the
"kindness and forbearance and patience" of God (Romans 2:4-5).

In response to this, we find it necessary to repudiate vigorously this
view that God pours out his wrath upon sin mainly because sin is a rejection of his love. We do not doubt that there is an element of the
despising of God's love in all sin, but it involves an even greater despising of God's *holiness*, and it is the latter that produces the reaction of
wrath against sin. Wounded love has its own response to sin, but it does
not include wrath. Instead of speaking of "the wrath of wounded love,"
we should speak of "the wrath of injured holiness and transgressed
justice," to cite Barclay.[97]

The idea that spurned love is the element in sin that displeases God
is to be expected from those who make love the one supreme and all-
embracing attribute of God, but it finds no real support in Scripture. To
be sure, Israel's rejection of God was the rejection of a loving Savior
(Deut. 32:15; Ps. 78:22), but it took the form of idolatry, to which God
refers as "this abominable thing which I hate" (Jer. 44:4), and the form
of commandment-breaking in general (cf. Ps. 78:10). In Psalm
78:21-22, 31-32 the specific reason for God's wrath is said to be Israel's
unbelief. These are all affronts to his holiness. The spurning of kindness
and patience and offered mercy (cf. Rom. 2:4-5) is not the fundamental
object of wrath; it is simply an added affront that compounds an
already-detestable despite.

Regarding Jesus' anger, Scripture describes a number of things that
evoked his righteous indignation,[98] but spurned love is never mentioned as one of them. In the instances mentioned above, i.e., the parable
and the Sabbath-healing, the obvious object of wrath is a lack of love for
the needy and afflicted, which is a violation of the second greatest commandment of the law of God (Matt. 22:39). In Mark 3:5 Jesus was also

---

97. William Barclay, *New Testament Words* (Philadelphia: Westminster Press,
1974), p. 275.

98. See Carl F.H. Henry, *God, Revelation and Authority, Volume VI: God Who
Stands and Stays, Part Two* (Waco: Word Books, 1983), p. 332.

angry at how the Pharisees had perverted God's law, adding their own traditions to it and giving them as much authority as the very word of God (cf. Mark 7:6-13).

We should note, too, that God's wrath is directed also and even more fervently toward those nations that were outside the sphere of God's covenant-love in Old Testament times and toward those who are outside the scope of the special revelation of love and grace in any time (cf. Rom. 1:18-32). It is very difficult to see how their wrath-evoking sins can be interpreted as a rejection of covenant-love.

The over-whelming testimony of Scripture is against the view just discussed and in favor of the idea that sin evokes God's wrath because it is a rebellion against the law and therefore against his own holiness. Gleason well says, "It is the rebellion of man against His holy will that calls out the divine wrath."[99] Hahn says, "For it is man's transgression of the Law . . . that is the ground of the righteous anger of God."[100] This pervasive Biblical theme is summed up in Isaiah 5:24-25,

> Therefore, as a tongue of fire consumes stubble, and dry grass collapses into the flame, so their root will become like rot and their blossom blow away as dust; for they have rejected the law of the Lord of hosts, and despised the word of the Holy One of Israel. On this account the anger of the Lord has burned against His people, and He has stretched out His hand against them and struck them down . . . .

Other examples of this theme are as follows. In Deuteronomy 8:19 God warns Israel that they will perish "if you ever forget the Lord your God, and go after other gods and serve them and worship them." In verse 11 he has explained what it means to "forget the Lord your God," thus: "Beware lest you forget the Lord your God by not keeping His commandments and His ordinances and His statutes which I am commanding you today" (Deut. 8:11). In Deuteronomy 28:1 Moses explains that "if you will diligently obey the Lord your God, being careful to do all His commandments which I command you today," then you will be blessed. But verse 15 says, "But it shall come about, if you will not obey the Lord your God, to observe to do all His commandments

---

99. R. W. Gleason, *Yahweh: The God of the Old Testament*, p. 80.

100. H. C. Hahn, "Anger, Wrath" (part), *The New International Dictionary of New Testament Theology*, ed. Colin Brown (Grand Rapids: Zondervan, 1975), I:112.

and His statutes which I charge you today, that all these curses shall come upon you" (Deut. 28:15; cf. v. 45).

After describing the great destruction that will befall the land as the result of disobedience, Moses says in Deuteronomy 29:24-28,

> And all the nations shall say, "Why has the Lord done thus to this land? Why this great outburst of anger?" Then men shall say, "Because they forsook the covenant of the Lord, the God of their fathers, which He made with them when He brought them out of the land of Egypt. And they went and served other gods and worshiped them, gods whom they have not known and whom He had not allotted to them. Therefore, the anger of the Lord burned against that land, to bring upon it every curse which is written in this book; and the Lord uprooted them from their land in anger and in fury and in great wrath, and cast them into another land, as it is this day."

The cause of God's anger, he says, is idolatry and forsaking God's covenant. What does he mean by "forsaking God's covenant"? It is a mistake to interpret this as meaning the rejection of God's covenant-love. Rather, it is clear that it refers to all the laws and commands and conditions which God gave the people through Moses and to which they bound themselves under penalty of destruction. The first verse of Deuteronomy 29 says, "These are the words of the covenant which the Lord commanded Moses to make with the sons of Israel in the land of Moab, besides the covenant which He had made with them at Horeb" (Deut. 29:1). The expression "words of the covenant" refer back to the commandments in the preceding chapters and especially to the exposition of the curses that would befall Israel for disobedience. Forsaking God's covenant simply means breaking God's commandments. This is the reason why God poured out his wrath upon Israel: they broke his commandments, contrary to their own covenant commitment (Ex. 19:8; Deut. 26:17).

This point is confirmed in many other places. Second Kings 17:13ff. tells how the Lord warned Israel and Judah through the prophets, "Turn from your evil ways and keep My commandments, My statutes according to all the law which I commanded your fathers." But they would not believe and would not obey. "They rejected His statutes and His covenant which He made with their fathers, and His warnings with which He warned them" (v. 15). They turned to idolatry. "So the Lord was very angry with Israel, and removed them from His sight" (v. 18). It is clear from this passage that God's anger was due to Israel's covenant breaking, which was equivalent to commandment breaking. Psalm 78:10 equates them also: "They did not keep the covenant of God, and refused to walk in His law." We find the same in Isaiah 24:5, "The earth is also polluted by its inhabitants, for they transgressed laws, violated statutes, broke the everlasting covenant." In Jeremiah 11:1-11 God speaks of "all the words of this covenant, which I commanded them to do" (v. 8). Because the people did not listen to God's voice (v. 7), hear the words of the covenant (v. 6), nor do all which was commanded (v. 4), God brought disaster on them (v. 11). Spurned commandments, not spurned love, evoked God's wrath.

This is confirmed in many other places. "If you will not listen to the voice of the Lord, but rebel against the command of the Lord, then the hand of the Lord will be against you" (I Sam. 12:15). "Why do you transgress the commandments of the Lord and do not prosper? Because you have forsaken the Lord, He has also forsaken you" (II Chron. 24:20). "Thou has rejected all those who wander from Thy statutes" (Ps. 119:118). The Levites confessed that God's punishment of the nation was just, "for our kings, our leaders, our priests, and our fathers have not kept Thy law or paid attention to Thy commandments and Thy admonitions with which Thou hast admonished them" (Neh. 9:33-34). "Who gave Jacob up for spoil, and Israel to plunderers? Was it not the Lord, against whom we have sinned, and in whose ways they were not willing to walk, and whose law they did not obey? So He poured out on him the heat of His anger" (Isa. 42:24-25). When the people ask, "For what reason has the Lord declared all this great calamity against us? And what is our iniquity, or what is our sin which we have committed against the Lord our God?", this is what Jeremiah is told to answer: "It is because your forefathers have forsaken Me . . . and have followed other gods and served them and bowed down to them; but Me they have forsaken and have not kept My law. You too have done evil, even more than your forefathers." You have walked in your own stubborn ways, says the Lord, "without listening to Me" (Jer. 16:10-12). "Listening to Me" is the same as "walking in My law" (Jer. 26:4-5).

God says in many ways that the calamity that befell his people was due to their failure to walk in his law. "Hear, O earth: behold, I am bringing disaster on this people, the fruit of their plans, because they have not listened to My words, and as for My law, they have rejected it" (Jer. 6:19). "Because they have forsaken My law which I set before them, and have not obeyed My voice nor walked according to it . . . , I will feed them, this people, with wormwood and give them poisoned water to drink" (Jer. 9:13-15). See Jeremiah 32:23; 44:10-23. Through Jeremiah Israel confesses that she deserves the punishment: "The Lord is righteous; for I have rebelled against His command" (Lam. 1:18). "Indeed all Israel has transgressed Thy law and turned aside, not obeying Thy voice; so the curse has been poured out on us" (Dan. 9:11). "My people are destroyed for lack of knowledge," says the Lord. Knowledge of what? "You have forgotten the law of your God" (Hosea 4:6). "For three transgressions of Judah and for four I will not revoke its punishment, because they rejected the law of the Lord and have not kept His statutes . . . . So I will send fire upon Judah, and it will consume the citadels of Jerusalem" (Amos 2:4-5). "He who does not obey the Son shall not see life, but the wrath of God abides on him" (John 3:36). "For the wrath of God is revealed from heaven against all ungodliness and unrighteousness of men" (Rom. 1:18). Paul says that it is the law that brings about wrath (Rom. 4:15), i.e., by putting us in the position of being able to defy God's own holiness through our defiance of the law, thus bringing his wrath upon us.

This would appear to be sufficient testimony to establish the basic point that God's wrath is directed against sin because sin violates his law, not because it violates his love. Stählin attempts to neutralize this point by asserting that love is the origin of the law; thus violation of law *is* violation of love. "If God is angry because of transgression of the Law, this is the reaction of spurned love, which sought to benefit man through the Law."[101] But we have already seen that this argument will not work, because law is not the gift of love but the demand of holiness. In the end there is only one reason why sin evokes wrath; and that is because by violating the law, sin is a direct challenge to the holiness of God. Wrath is the reaction of holiness defied.

Wrath Inflicts Retribution for Sin

God's wrath is not just his intense inner displeasure against sin, but also his active, outward punitive response to sin. Sometimes no im-

---

101. Gustav Stählin, "ὀργή," p. 433.

mediate outward response is recorded (e.g., Ex. 4:14; II Chron. 28:25), but it usually comes in time: "In due time their foot will slip; for the day of their calamity is near" (Deut. 32:35).

God's wrathful response upon sin is described in Scripture in the most violent and ferocious—even brutal—terms. It is pictured as a horrifying, terrifying experience: "It is a terrifying thing to fall into the hands of the living God" (Heb. 10:31). Those under God's wrath are called his enemies (Rom. 5:10; Col. 1:21; James 4:4). "Behold, I am against you," God says to the objects of his wrath (Jer. 50:31; cf. Jer. 21:13; 23:31-32). Concerning Israel he says, "Behold, I am against you; and I shall draw My sword out of its sheath and cut off from you the righteous and the wicked" (Ezek. 21:3; cf. Ezek. 13:8; 15:7; 26:3). "The face of the Lord is against those who do evil" (I Peter 3:12). "God is opposed to the proud" (I Peter 5:5). Could anything be more terrifying than to hear God say, "I am against you"?

Sometimes we hear that God hates the sin but loves the sinner. This is not true, as Strong observes.[102] God hates the sin, *and he also hates the sinner.* "Thou dost hate all who do iniquity. Thou dost destroy those who speak falsehood; the Lord abhors the man of bloodshed and deceit" (Ps. 5:5-6). This and many other passages show that God's hatred is directed against the *person* who sins and not just the sin itself. Sometimes just a general category is mentioned. "Everyone who acts unjustly is an abomination to the Lord your God," says Deuteronomy 25:16. "The Lord tests the righteous and the wicked, and the one who loves violence His soul hates" (Ps. 11:5). The seven things that God hates in Proverbs 6:16-19 include "a false witness who utters lies, and one who spreads strife among brothers." He also hates "the perverse in heart" (Prov. 11:20), "everyone who is proud in heart" (Prov. 16:5), and whoever justifies the wicked or condemns the righteous (Prov. 17:15). Other passages describe God's hatred for specific persons. Leviticus 20:23 speaks of God as abhorring or loathing the Canaanites. Sometimes his hatred is directed against Israel. When the Lord saw their idolatry, "He was filled with wrath, and greatly abhorred Israel" (Ps.

---

102. Augustus H. Strong, *Systematic Theology*, p. 290. Strong also observes that God both hates *and loves* the sinner at the same time: "hates him as he is a living and wilful antagonist of truth and holiness, loves him as he is a creature capable of good and ruined by his transgression."

78:59). "I have come to hate her," he says (Jer. 12:8; cf. Hosea 9:15).
He also hated Esau (Edom), says Malachi 1:3 (cf. Rom. 9:13).

We must not take these passages lightly. To be hated by the holy
God is a terrible, terrifying thing. The Old Testament word translated
"to hate" has the following meaning:[103]

> . . . It expresses an emotional attitude toward persons and things
> which are opposed, detested, despised and with which one wishes to
> have no contact or relationship. It is therefore the opposite of love.
> Whereas love draws and unites, hate separates and keeps distant. The
> hated and hating persons are considered foes or enemies and are con-
> sidered odious, utterly unappealing.

Could anything be more terrifying than to hear God say, "I hate you"?

The "vocabulary of dread"[104] intensifies as we learn that sinners are
under God's curse. The first sin brought the first curses (Gen. 3:14ff.).
The Mosaic Law includes a catalogue of curses (Deut. 27:15ff.;
28:15ff.). Whoever is not under grace is under a curse: "For as many as
are of the works of the Law are under a curse; for it is written, 'Cursed is
every one who does not abide by all things written in the book of the
law, to perform them'" (Gal. 3:10). To the wicked on the day of judgment Christ will say, "Depart from Me, accursed ones, into the eternal
fire which has been prepared for the devil and his angels" (Matt. 25:41).
Henry says that God's curse is "a judicial action that brings direct
punishment by his supernatural power; the very act of cursing implies its
fulfillment."[105]

Could anything be more terrifying than to hear the Lord say, "Accursed ones!"?

But this is what it means to be under God's wrath. It means to be
God's enemy, to be hated by God, to be under his curse. It means, in
short, to be marked for punishment of the most dreaded sort. Packer
takes up the question of whether this amounts to cruelty, as some often
charge. Two things show that it does not, he says. In the first place,
God's wrath is always *judicial*, that is, "it is the wrath of the Judge, ad-

---

103. Gerard Van Groningen, "sānē'," *Theological Wordbook of the Old Testament*,
ed. R. Laird Harris et al. (Chicago: Moody Press, 1980), II:880.
104. Carl F. H. Henry, *God, Revelation and Authority*, VI:327.
105. Ibid.

ministering justice." The wrath he bestows is the wrath he owes; we get only what we deserve. In the second place, God's wrath is something we choose for ourselves in the sense that we know sinners will be cursed but we choose to sin anyway. It is really our own works that condemn us.[106]

These points by Packer are well taken, and they lead us to the main point of this section, namely, that the wrath of God inflicted upon sinners is *divine retribution*. It is punishment poured out upon the sinner because—and *simply* because—he deserves it. The person who freely chooses to break the commandments of the Lord of the universe, thereby dishonoring and defiling his infinite holiness, deserves and merits the wrath that engulfs him. This is why sin is called a *debt* (Matt. 6:12); when we sin, God *owes* us punishment. "The wages of sin is death" (Rom. 6:23); we have *earned* it.

Another way of saying this is that divine wrath is a penalty inflicted upon us by God the righteous Judge. What the sinner experiences as the result of God's wrath is not merely suffering, but *deserved* suffering, namely, punishment or penalty as established by law. We will remember that God's law includes not only commandments but also penalties, and God metes out these penalties as the omniscient Judge. "He will remember their iniquity, He will punish their sins" (Hosea 9:9; cf. 8:13). There will be a "day of judgment and destruction of ungodly men" (II Peter 3:7), who must exist with "a certain terrifying expectation of judgment, and the fury of a fire which will consume the adversaries" (Heb. 10:27). The most significant point, however, is that God is a *righteous* Judge (II Tim. 4:8); the only penalties he inflicts are those that are deserved. Isaiah 5:16 says, "But the Lord of hosts will be exalted in judgment, and the holy God will show Himself holy in righteousness." The context is speaking of punishment upon the wicked; and this verse says that when God judges them, he will be true to his holy nature. He is the "Lord of hosts, who judges righteously, who tries the feelings and the heart" (Jer. 11:20). "He has fixed a day in which He will judge the world in righteousness" (Acts 17:31). He is to be praised "because His judgments are true and righteous" (Rev. 19:1-2).

Penalty inflicted and suffered because it is deserved is nothing less

---

106. J. I. Packer, *Knowing God*, pp. 137-139.

than retribution. It is the product of retributive justice in the popular sense of the term. Of course, many today have excluded this element from the righteousness of God, as we saw in the last chapter. Thus they interpret wrath and punishment as something other than retribution. König, for example, says that God's wrath does have a purpose. In fact, he names two of them. First, God at times expresses his anger in order to teach us what is right and what is wrong, and to show his utter revulsion toward the wrong. This goal, however, as we saw earlier in this chapter, is fulfilled by the law itself; wrath does not have to be expressed in order to accomplish this purpose. But second, says König, God's wrath often has the purpose of bringing people to repentance, i.e., it is an act of love that seeks the rehabilitation of its object.[107] Ronald Hals agrees with this second point, that wrath is not punitive (oriented toward the past) but that it is corrective (oriented toward the future) with the goal of bringing about a change.[108]

This view, however, confuses wrath with chastisement and simply refuses to look objectively at the Biblical data, which testify conclusively to the retributive character of God's wrath. Shedd remarks that "no one of the Divine attributes is supported by more or stronger evidences, than retributive justice."[109] He points out that retribution is indeed "retrospective in its primary aim. It looks back to what has been done in the past. Its first object is requital." The one sufficient reason for punishing the law-breaker is "the fact that the law has been violated, and demands the punishment of the offender for this reason simply."[110] Those who think that such a view of divine punishment is not found in Scripture have missed the whole point of its teaching on the subject. Packer says that we could even call the Bible "the book of God's wrath, for it is full of portrayals of divine retribution," from the cursing and banishment of Adam and Eve in Genesis 3 to the great judgment of Revelation 20.[111]

For our purposes here, however, we will cite only two lines of

---

107. Adrio König, *Here Am I!*, p. 94.
108. Ronald M. Hals, *Grace and Faith in the Old Testament*, p. 72.
109. William G. T. Shedd, *Dogmatic Theology* (Grand Rapids: Zondervan, 1969 reprint of 1888 edition), I:380.
110. Ibid., p. 381.
111. J. I. Packer, *Knowing God*, p. 135.

evidence that the expressions of God's wrath are punitive or retributive in the fullest sense of the word. The first of these is the strong Biblical teaching that the infliction of God's wrath upon the sinner is an act of divine *vengeance*. He acts "to stir up wrath and take revenge" (Ezek. 24:8, NIV). While this concept must not be distorted into something like the petty, spiteful and often unjust revenge we see among human beings, neither must its content be softened into something like the impersonal natural consequences of one's sins. Vengeance is an intensely personal act, coming from the heart and will of one who has experienced wrongdoing against himself. Thus God's vengeance is something he deliberately and personally inflicts. As he said to sinful Israel, "And My eye will show no pity, nor will I spare. I will repay you according to your ways, while your abominations are in your midst; then you will know that I, the Lord, do the smiting" (Ezek. 7:9). As this verse shows, however, the purpose of vengeance is not just to vent personal feelings, but to repay the wrongdoer the just wages of his sin. "For the Lord is a God of recompense, He will fully repay" (Jer. 51:56). Sin against God is not just a personal insult to him, but is also an attack upon the whole moral system that he has established in his creation. White thus speaks of God's vengeance as "the reaction of positive holiness, of active righteousness, asserting the moral order of the world, vindicating truth, right, and goodness against all that is corrupt, false, and evil."[112]

The classic Old Testament passage affirming the reality of divine vengeance and retribution (the passage upon which Jonathan Edwards based his famous sermon, "Sinners in the Hands of an Angry God") is Deuteronomy 32:35, "It is mine to avenge; I will repay. In due time their foot will slip; their day of disaster is near and their doom rushes upon them" (NIV). This verse is quoted twice in the New Testament, first in Romans 12:19, "Never take your own revenge, beloved, but leave room for the wrath of God, for it is written, 'Vengeance is Mine, I will repay, says the Lord.'" This is true of God in both a relative and an absolute sense, but in this passage it is applied to the relative context of civil government. The reason we should not take personal revenge is that God has appointed civil authorities to avenge wrongdoing against

---

112. R. E. O. White, "Vengeance," *Evangelical Dictionary of Theology*, ed. Walter A. Elwell (Grand Rapids: Baker Book House, 1984), p. 1138.

us in this life (Rom. 13:1-4; I Peter 2:14) Thus one who enforces civil laws is specifically called "a minister of God, an avenger who brings wrath upon the one who practices evil" (Rom. 13:4). The other New Testament verse that quotes the Deuteronomy passage applies it in the absolute sense of eternal punishment. This is in Hebrews 10:30, in the midst of a passage dealing with those who do in fact spurn God's love and mercy in Jesus Christ. In this passage, however, the Lord is not telling us how his *love* responds to its own rejection, but rather how his *holiness* responds, namely, with fury and vengeance and retribution. Nor does his holiness respond thus because someone has rejected his love as such, but because this one has willfully sinned against God's holy will (Heb. 10:26). The full force of this passage must be allowed to penetrate our minds and hearts:

> For if we go on sinning willfully after receiving the knowledge of the truth, there no longer remains a sacrifice for sins, but a certain terrifying expectation of judgment, and the fury of a fire which will consume the adversaries. Anyone who has set aside the Law of Moses dies without mercy on the testimony of two or three witnesses. How much severer punishment do you think he will deserve who has trampled under foot the Son of God, and has regarded as unclean the blood of the covenant by which he was sanctified, and has insulted the Spirit of grace? For we know Him who said, "Vengeance is Mine, I will repay." And again, "The Lord will judge His people." It is a terrifying thing to fall into the hands of the living God. (Hebrews 10:26-31)

This is the nature of God's avenging wrath. Such a picture of "fury of a fire," "without mercy," "severer punishment," and "terrifying" vengeance should make us all the more glad that there is *another* side to God's nature than the one shown here.[113]

Other Biblical testimony to God's vengeance is just as sobering. "If I sharpen My flashing sword, and My hand takes hold on justice, I will render vengeance on My adversaries, and I will repay those who hate Me" (Deut 32:41; cf. v. 43). Psalm 94:1-3 says, "O Lord, God of vengeance; God of vengeance, shine forth! Rise up, O Judge of the earth; render recompense to the proud. How long shall the wicked, O

---

113. Attributing such an arsenal of retribution to God's love rather than his holiness is a travesty. "With friends like these, who needs enemies?"

Lord, how long shall the wicked exult?" This reminds us of the cry of the slain martyrs in Revelation 6:10, "How long, O Lord, holy and true, wilt Thou refrain from judging and avenging our blood on those whc dwell on the earth?" In answer to both questions Jesus has assured us, "Shall not God bring about justice for His elect, who cry to Him day and night, and will He delay long over them? I tell you that He will bring about justice for them speedily" (Luke 18:7-8). The Psalmist knew that God is such a God, "the God who executes vengeance for me" (Ps. 18:47). "He will recompense the evil to my foes; destroy them in Thy faithfulness" (Ps. 54:5; cf. Pss. 58:10; 79:10).

In the prophets the theme of divine vengeance is frequent. God says in Isaiah 1:24, "I will be relieved of My adversaries, and avenge Myself on My foes." "For the Lord has a day of vengeance, a year of recompense for the cause of Zion" (Isa. 34:8; cf. Is. 61:2; 63:4). "Behold, your God will come with vengeance; the recompense of God will come" (Isa. 35:4). He comes wearing "garments of vengeance for clothing," and "according to their deeds, so He will repay, wrath to His adversaries, recompense to His enemies" (Isa. 59:17-18). "For that day belongs to the Lord God of hosts, a day of vengeance, so as to avenge Himself on His foes; and the sword will devour and be satiated and drink its fill of their blood" (Jer. 46:10; cf. Joel 3:21; Micah 5:15). "So I will punish them for their ways and repay them for their deeds" (Hosea 4:9; cf. 12:2).

Specific nations or cities are mentioned as objects of divine vengeance, e.g., Midian (Num. 31:3); Babylon (Isa. 47:3; Jer. 50:15, 28; 51:6, 11, 36); Edom (Ezek. 25:14, 17); and Nineveh, of whom Nahum 1:2 says, "A jealous and avenging God is the Lord; the Lord is avenging and wrathful. The Lord takes vengeance on His adversaries, and He reserves wrath for His enemies." See II Timothy 4:14.

The many Biblical references to God's wrath as vengeance leave little doubt that it is a form of holy retribution upon those who deserve it.

The second line of evidence that God's wrath is retributive is the fact of hell. Many of the above references to vengeance are dealing with temporal or relative retribution, i.e., judgments and punishments within the scope of history; and they deal with man in his relative wickedness. The penalty of hell, however, is absolute or eternal retribution; and it considers man's wickedness from the absolute perspective. It is unmitigated and irreversible recompense upon those who have sinned against the holy will of the holy God. It will be inaugurated "when the Lord Jesus shall be revealed from heaven with His mighty angels in flaming fire, dealing out retribution to those who do not know God and to those who do not obey the gospel of our Lord Jesus. And these will pay the penalty of eternal destruction" (II Thes. 1:7-9). It will be "the punishment of eternal fire" (Jude 7).

Many are offended at the concept of hell and thus deny it altogether. Such is Nels Ferré, who says, "The very conception of an eternal hell is monstrous and an insult to . . . the Christian doctrine of God's sovereign love."[114] Others do not feel this free to deny a reality so plainly taught in the Bible, but they seek to soften its severity by removing it from the context of wrath and retribution and placing it instead within the context of God's fatherly love, a love whose only choice is to give up on those who will not accept him. Explaining how he thinks God's love manifests itself as wrath against those who reject him, even into the eternal state of hell, one writer offers this as an illustration:[115]

> Imagine a young lady to whom a newly-born colt has been given. It becomes the object of her constant care, her every affection. She feeds it, trains it, rescues it from danger; nurses it in disease; rejoices in its victories and suffers when it suffers. But let tragedy strike in the form of incurable, painful affliction. The horse is in perpetual pain with no possibility of relief. It is love that takes the rifle and kills, thus putting the animal out of its misery.

It is difficult to imagine how anyone who has read the Biblical teaching on God's wrath, God's vengeance, and the nature of hell could even begin to think that this illustration bears any resemblance whatsoever to the motivation behind God's wrath against sin. One needs only to compare it with the passage discussed above, Hebrews 10:26-31, to see that any alleged relationship between this illustration and God's eternal retribution upon sinners is pure fantasy. It is also difficult to see how any of the suggested alternatives to the concept of retribution (e.g., chastisement, correction, rehabilitation) can be thought to fit into the notion of

---

114. Nels F.S. Ferré, *The Christian Understanding of God*, p. 228.
115. Owen L. Crouch, "The Wrath of God!", *Christian Standard* (Sept. 7, 1975), 110:13.

eternal hell.

Those who have difficulty accepting the notion of hell altogether or even the idea of hell as eternal retribution need to reconsider their very concept of the nature of God. R. C. Sproul makes these thoughtful comments about those who are skeptical of the wrathful God as depicted by Jonathan Edwards' sermon:[116]

> . . . Do we consider the wrath of God as a primitive or obscene concept? Is the very notion of hell an insult to us? If so, it is clear that the God we worship is not a holy God: indeed, He is not a God at all. If we despise the justice of God we are not Christians. . . . If we hate the wrath of God, it is because we hate God Himself. We may protest vehemently against these charges but our vehemence only confirms our hostility toward God. We may say emphatically, "No, it is not God I hate, it is Edwards that I hate. God is altogether sweet to me. My God is a God of love." But a God of love who has no wrath is no God. He is an idol of our own making as much as if we carved Him out of stone.

Those who continue to plead that God is a loving and forgiving God as a basis for denying retributive wrath need to consider the fact that unless God's wrath and hell itself are something we really *deserve*, then forgiveness has little meaning. This is a point well made by Leon Morris:[117]

> Then, too, unless we give a real content to the wrath of God, unless we hold that men really deserve to have God visit upon them the painful consequences of their wrongdoing, we empty God's forgiveness of its meaning. For if there is no ill desert, God *ought* to overlook sin. We can think of forgiveness as something real only when we hold that sin has betrayed us into a situation where we deserve to have God inflict upon us the most serious consequences, and that it is upon such a situation that God's grace supervenes. When the logic of the situation demands that He should take action *against* the sinner, and He yet takes action *for* him, then and then alone can we speak of grace. But there is no room for grace if there is no suggestion of dire consequences merited by sin.

When we read about the horrors of hell and think about the severity of God's retributive wrath, instead of worrying about how this reflects

---

116. R. C. Sproul, *The Holiness of God*, p. 228.

117. Leon Morris, *The Apostolic Preaching*, p. 185. (Emphasis supplied.)

upon his love, we should rather reflect that it shows us how much he *hates sin*. It shows us that he hates it so much that, as Bates says, "although God is infinitely good to us, yet he doth not prefer the happiness of man before his own blessedness."[118]

Conclusion

Our purpose in this section has been to discuss how God's wrath is related to sin. We have seen that his wrath is evoked by sin and by sin alone, since sin is rebellion against his holy will as expressed in his law. We have also seen that his wrath is poured out in retribution upon sin, the retributive aspect being well established by the nature of wrath as vengeance and by the reality of hell. The next section seeks to give an even more vivid impression of the severity of divine wrath by looking at the various groups or individuals upon whom it is inflicted.

The Objects of God's Wrath

Ever since sin entered the world with Adam and Eve, the whole world has been under the wrath of God in some sense. Paul speaks of those who are outside of God's grace as being "by nature children of wrath" (Eph. 2:3). Even if this means no more than being under the penalty of physical death (Rom. 5:12; I Cor. 15:22), the whole world is nevertheless considered to be a sphere of wrath as the result of sin. A near-universal act of wrath came upon the whole world at the time of the flood, bringing to pass the fruition of the Adamic curse for everyone at the same time, with the exception of Noah and his family.

Most of the Bible's teaching about God's wrath is found in connection with specific events and specific people or groups of people. Most but by no means all of its teaching has to do with temporal punishments rather than eternal punishment. Most of the former is in the Old Testament context of God's dealings with Israel.

Wrath on Individuals

The Mosaic Law specified that any individual guilty of injustice toward widows and orphans or of idolatry would become the object of God's wrath (Ex. 22:22-24; Deut. 29:18-21). The latter is particularly

---

118. William Bates, *The Harmony of the Divine Attributes*, p. 291.

cursed: "The Lord shall never be willing to forgive him, but rather the anger of the Lord and His jealousy will burn against that man, and every curse which is written in this book will rest on him, and the Lord will blot out his name from under heaven" (Deut. 29:20).

Other references to wrath on individuals name specific people, beginning with none other than Moses (Ex. 4:14; Deut 1:37). His brother Aaron likewise comes under divine wrath, for his complicity in the people's idolatry (Deut. 9:20) and for complaining against Moses, along with his sister Miriam (Num. 12:9). Nadab and Abihu were singled out for wrath after they offered strange fire on the altar of God (Lev. 10:1-2, 6). Uzzah was stricken for touching the ark of the covenant: "And the anger of the Lord burned against Uzzah, and God struck him down there for his irreverence" (II Sam. 6:7). Others who are named are all members of the monarchy: Solomon (I Kings 11:9), Jereboam (I Kings 14:9), Baasha (I Kings 16:2), Ahab (I Kings 16:33; 21:22), Ahaziah (I Kings 22:53), Amaziah (II Chron. 25:15), Ahaz (II Chron. 28:25), and Manasseh (II Chron. 33:6).

Although the term *wrath* is not mentioned specifically, the execution of Ananias and Sapphira (Acts 5:1-11) would certainly be another instance of God's angry retribution upon individuals.

All the instances mentioned here, at least those involving named individuals, are cases of temporal punishment only; there is no specific reflection upon their eternal state. Also, the punishments (where specified) all seem to be retribution rather than chastisement.

Wrath Against Israel

By far the most prevalent teaching concerning God's wrath is in connection with his own chosen people, the nation of Israel. From very early in their wilderness wandering, as a result of their complaining and their idolatry, God's wrath was kindled against them and many died from fire and plague (Num. 11:1, 33; 16:46; 25:3). "The Lord's anger burned" so much against them for their unbelief that he did not allow any males who were twenty or older at the exodus to enter the promised land (Num. 32:10-11). Even before the younger generation had crossed over into their new land, God warned them that their idolatry would lead to their future destruction: "They have made Me jealous with what is not God; they have provoked Me to anger with their idols. So I will make them jealous with those who are not a people; I will provoke them to anger with a foolish nation, for a fire is kindled in My anger, and burns to the lowest part of Sheol" (Deut. 32:21-22; cf. 29:22-28).

The historical books record the continuing rebellion and idolatry of the people after they come into the land, and after the monarchy begins and divides. The northern kingdom provoked God so much that he eradicated it through the Assyrians. "So the Lord was very angry with Israel, and removed them from His sight" (II Kings 17:18). The southern kingdom likewise provoked God; so he ordained destruction and exile for it. "Because they have forsaken Me and have burned incense to other gods that they might provoke Me to anger with all the work of their hands, therefore My wrath burns against this place, and it shall not be quenched" (II Kings 22:17). When he was about to bring the Babylonians upon them, God sent prophets to plead with them to repent; "but they continually . . . despised His words and scoffed at His prophets, until the wrath of the Lord rose against His people, until there was no remedy" (II Chron. 36:16).

The message borne by the prophets was heavily laced with threats of divine wrath of the most intense kind. Most of them cannot be cited here, and a few have already been quoted in other connections above. We repeat this one from Isaiah 5:24-25,

> Therefore, as a tongue of fire consumes stubble, and dry grass collapses into the flame, so their root will become like rot and their blossom blow away as dust; for they have rejected the law of the Lord of hosts, and despised the word of the Holy One of Israel. On this account the anger of the Lord has burned against His people, and He has stretched out His hand against them and struck them down, and the mountains quaked; and their corpses lay like refuse in the middle of the streets. For all this His anger is not spent, but His hand is still stretched out.

Because Israel did not obey God's laws, "He poured out on him the heat of His anger and the fierceness of battle" (Isa. 42:24-25). "Rouse yourself! Rouse yourself! Arise, O Jerusalem, you who have drunk from the Lord's hand the cup of His anger; the chalice of reeling you have drained to the dregs" (Isa. 51:17; cf. vv. 20, 22).

Jeremiah brought this message from the Lord: "Behold, My anger and my wrath will be poured out on this place, on man and on beast and on the trees of the field and on the fruit of the ground; and it will burn and not be quenched" (Jer. 7:20). "And I will make you serve your enemies in the land which you do not know; for you have kindled a fire in My anger which will burn forever" (Jer. 17:4). "And I myself shall war against you with an outstretched hand and a mighty arm, even in anger and wrath and great indignation" (Jer. 21:5). "Behold, the storm of the Lord has gone forth in wrath, even a whirling tempest; it will swirl down on the head of the wicked. The anger of the Lord will not turn back until He has performed and carried out the purposes of His heart" (Jer. 23:19-20). In Lamentations 4:11 Jeremiah notes that God has kept his word: "The Lord has accomplished His wrath, He has poured out His fierce anger; and He has kindled a fire in Zion which has consumed its foundations." God's message through Ezekiel was the same:

> Thus My anger will be spent, and I will satisfy My wrath on them, and I shall be appeased; then they will know that I, the Lord, have spoken in My zeal when I have spent My wrath upon them. . . . So it will be a reproach, a reviling, a warning and an object of horror to the nations who surround you, when I execute judgments against you in anger, wrath, and raging rebukes. I, the Lord, have spoken. (Ezek. 5:13, 15)

"Now the end is upon you, and I shall send My anger against you; I shall judge you according to your ways, and I shall bring all your abominations upon you" (Ezek. 7:3; cf. vv. 8-9). "And I shall pour out My indignation on you; I shall blow on you with the fire of My wrath, and I shall give you into the hand of brutal men, skilled in destruction. You will be fuel for the fire; your blood will be in the midst of the land" (Ezek. 21:31-32). One of the strongest emphases on God's wrath against his people is in Zephaniah:

> Near is the great day of the Lord, near and coming very quickly; listen, the day of the Lord! In it the warrior cries out bitterly. A day of wrath is that day, a day of trouble and distress, a day of destruction and desolation, a day of darkness and gloom, a day of clouds and thick darkness . . . . Neither their silver nor their gold will be able to deliver them on the day of the Lord's wrath; and all the earth will be devoured in the fire of His jealousy, for He will make a complete end, indeed a terrifying one, of all the inhabitants of the earth. Gather yourselves together, yes, gather, O nation without shame, before the decree takes effect – the day passes like the chaff – before the burning anger of the Lord comes

upon you, before the day of the Lord's anger comes upon you. (Zeph. 1:14-2:2).

These and other passages that speak of divine wrath upon Israel are referring again to temporal judgments, or punishment administered within the sphere of history. Though God's anger was directed against the nation as a whole, not every individual within Israel suffered the same consequences. For example, during the wilderness wandering, on one occasion of rebellion only 14,700 were destroyed by a plague (Num. 16:46-49), and on another occasion 24,000 (Num. 25:3-9). But in other instances the whole nation suffered the flame of God's wrath, as in the Assyrian conquest of the northern kingdom and the Babylonian conquest of the southern kingdom.

In connection with these punishments upon the nation(s) as a whole, the question of wrath versus chastisement must be addressed. It is sometimes suggested that the wrath poured out on Israel was not retributive but corrective, since it came to an end and the nation was rescued and restored to its own land. The idea is that even in their darkest moments God was just teaching them a lesson in love. Now, even if it were true of the southern kingdom, this could not be the case with the ten northern tribes, since they were not restored. The wrath upon them even as a nation was final. But what of the southern kingdom itself? Was their restoration from Babylon in 536 B.C. an indication that their suffering was not retributive wrath but only chastisement? No, this idea must be rejected for three reasons. First, the overwhelming emphasis on vengeance and retribution in the prophets is not consistent with loving chastisement. Second, we must distinguish on the one hand between God's concern for preserving the nation as such, and on the other hand his destroying vengeance upon the idolatrous individuals within the nation. Yes, God did love the nation and he was determined to preserve at least a remnant of it, for the sake of his promise to the patriarchs and for the sake of his own redemptive purpose to be carried out through this nation. For these reasons the nation as such was preserved, though chastised, while the rebellious individuals within it perished in true retribution and wrath. Third, once God's purpose for the nation was completed with the first coming of Christ, he gave it up once more for destruction and dissolution (in A.D. 70), after enduring "with much patience vessels of wrath prepared for destruction" (Rom.

9:22). See I Thessalonians 2:16.

Wrath Against the Nations

A large measure of divine wrath was reserved for the unbelieving nations, particularly those that came into contact with the chosen people. Since Israel's glory was her worship of the one true God, her name was inseparable from the name of Yahweh. Thus whoever opposed Israel opposed her God as well. The enemies of God's chosen people are God's enemies as well. Even David assumed that his own enemies were God's enemies, too; and he called upon the Lord to fling his wrath against them. "Arise, O Lord, in Thine anger; lift up Thyself against the rage of my adversaries, and arouse Thyself for me" (Ps. 7:6). Except for Israel's (and David's) chosen status, such a plea would be quite presumptuous. But these were God's own people, and it was his will to defend them and vindicate them.

This began with God's wrath against Egypt: "And in the greatness of Thine excellence Thou dost overthrow those who rise up against Thee; Thou dost send forth Thy burning anger, and it consumes them as chaff" (Ex. 15:7). "He sent upon them His burning anger, fury, and indignation, and trouble, a band of destroying angels. He leveled a path for His anger; He did not spare their soul from death, but gave over their life to the plague" (Ps. 78:49-50). Against Babylon Isaiah 13:9 declares, "Behold, the day of the Lord is coming, cruel, with fury and burning anger, to make the land a desolation; and He will exterminate its sinners from it." The following tribulation is pronounced against the nations in general: "For the Lord's indignation is against all the nations, and His wrath against all their armies; He has utterly destroyed them, He has given them over to slaughter. So their slain will be thrown out, and their corpses will give off their stench, and the mountains will be drenched with their blood" (Isa. 34:2-3). "According to their deeds, so He will repay, wrath to His adversaries, recompense to His enemies" (Isa. 59:18). This final example pictures Yahweh returning from Edom, covered with the blood he had shed in wreaking vengeance upon this unbelieving nation:

Who is this who comes from Edom, with garments of glowing colors from Bozrah, this One who is majestic in His apparel, marching in the greatness of His strength? "It is I who speak in righteousness, mighty to save." Why is Your apparel red, and Your garments like the one who treads in the wine press? "I have trodden the wine trough alone, and from the peoples there was no man with Me. I also trod them in My anger, and trampled them in My wrath; and their life blood is sprinkled on My garments, and I stained all My raiment. For the day of vengeance was in My heart, and My year of redemption has come. And I looked, and there was no one to help, and I was astonished and there was no one to uphold; so My own arm brought salvation to Me; and My wrath upheld Me. And I trod down the peoples in My anger, and made them drunk in My wrath, and I poured out their lifeblood on the earth." (Isa. 63:1-6)

Wrath upon the Enemies of God

In this last section dealing with the objects of divine wrath, we will consider those who are God's enemies in general. As is definitely the case with the other three categories above, including the nations just discussed, it may be that some of the references here are speaking of temporal judgments only, especially some of those from the Old Testament. But unlike the other categories, many of the passages dealing with God's wrath upon his enemies in a general sense are speaking of the eternal retribution of the Last Judgment.

First we will cite some Old Testament passages, in which we may not always be able to tell whether the perspective is historical or eternal. The reality of God's wrath is the same in either case, however. We note first the Lord's reaction to the rebellious kings in Psalm 2:5, "Then He will speak to them in His anger and terrify them in His fury." David draws this poetic picture in Psalm 18:7-8, "Then the earth shook and quaked; and the foundations of the mountains were trembling and were shaken, because He was angry. Smoke went up out of His nostrils, and fire from His mouth devoured; coals were kindled by it." Again, "Your hand will find out all your enemies; your right hand will find out those who hate you. You will make them as a fiery oven in the time of your anger; the Lord will swallow them up in His wrath, and fire will devour them" (Ps. 21:8-9). David calls upon the Lord to "destroy them in wrath, destroy them, that they may be no more; that men may know that God rules in Jacob, to the ends of the earth" (Ps. 59:13). Isaiah 30:27 adds, "Behold, the name of the Lord comes from a remote place; burning is His anger, and dense is His smoke; His lips are filled with indignation, and His tongue is like a consuming fire." Isaiah 66:14-16 says,

301

> . . . He shall be indignant toward His enemies. For behold, the Lord will come in fire and His chariots like the whirlwind, to render His anger with fury, and His rebuke with flames of fire. For the Lord will execute judgment by fire and by His sword on all flesh, and those slain by the Lord will be many.

As a prelude to his oracle against Nineveh, Nahum gives this stern description of the Lord's wrath in general:

> A jealous and avenging God is the Lord; the Lord is avenging and wrathful. The Lord takes vengeance on His adversaries, and He reserves wrath for His enemies. The Lord is slow to anger and great in power, and the Lord will by no means leave the guilty unpunished. In whirlwind and storm is His way, and clouds are the dust beneath His feet. . . . Who can stand before His indignation? Who can endure the burning of His anger? His wrath is poured out like fire, and the rocks are broken up by Him. (Nahum 1:2-3, 6)

In the New Testament the passages that speak of God's wrath against his enemies in general are almost certainly speaking of his enemies as sinners in the absolute sense and of his wrath as that which leads to eternal retribution. Those who are presently under his wrath, if they remain so, will suffer the eternal consequences on the great day of his wrath when through the "unrestrained display of His wrath His absolute justice will be completely vindicated."[119] This is the wrath of which John the Baptist speaks in condemning the Jewish leaders: "You brood of vipers, who warned you to flee from the wrath to come?" (Matt. 3:7; cf. Luke 3:7). Jesus warned that "he who does not obey the Son shall not see life, but the wrath of God abides on him" (John 3:36). Paul says, "The wrath of God is revealed from heaven against all ungodliness and unrighteousness of men, who suppress the truth in unrighteousness" (Rom. 1:18). The stubborn and unrepentant "are storing up wrath for yourself in the day of wrath and revelation of the righteous judgment of God" (Rom. 2:5; cf. vv. 8-9). By Jesus' blood we are "saved from the wrath" (Rom. 5:9). "Let no one deceive you with empty words," says Paul, "for because of these [sins] the wrath of God comes upon the sons of disobedience" (Eph. 5:6; cf. Col. 3:6). We have cited II Thessalo-

---

119. R. V. G. Tasker, *The Biblical Doctrine of the Wrath of God* (London: The Tyndale Press, 1951), p. 45.

nians 1:7-9 and Hebrews 10:26-31 in other connections, but they should be noted here.

Finally we have the testimony of the book of Revelation to the fierceness of God's final retributive wrath upon his enemies, who themselves will cry out to the rocks and the mountains when they see him on that day, "Fall on us and hide us from the presence of Him who sits on the throne, and from the wrath of the Lamb; for the great day of their wrath has come; and who is able to stand?" (Rev. 6:16-17). Revelation 14:19 speaks of eternal punishment as "the great wine press of the wrath of God." This awesome image (from Isaiah 63:1-6) is also used in Revelation 19:15, which describes the conquering Christ as he rides forth in victory over his enemies: "And from His mouth comes a sharp sword, so that with it He may smite the nations; and He will rule them with a rod of iron; and He treads the wine press of the fierce wrath of God, the Almighty."

Conclusion

In this section we have looked at the objects of God's wrath, considering them in several categories. But I will confess at this point that my main purpose in this section was not just to divide the recipients of wrath into these groups, however meaningful that may be. Rather, I have just been using this four-fold division as an orderly way of setting forth some of the more impressive Biblical references to the wrath of God itself. Whether it be directed against individuals, against Israel, against her enemies, or against God's enemies in general, God's wrath is one. It is his absolute and implacable and all-consuming passion to destroy everything that insults and violates his own holiness. We need to understand the reality of this wrath, as well as the fury of it. And we need to see just how prevalent the subject is in God's holy word. To this end I have quoted these many passages, some at length.

God's Wrath and God's Love

The question of the relation between wrath and love is the final variation on a theme that has appeared in several forms already. First of all, it goes back to the question of how love and *holiness* are related. Are they separate and distinct aspects of God's nature, or does one include the other? As we have seen, a fairly common view is that his love is his supreme and all-inclusive attribute; all other moral attributes are just the different ways that love manifests itself. The position taken here is that love and holiness are distinct. The second form of this question is whether God's *law* is a product of his holiness or of his love. I have argued for the former, but those who make love supreme argue that this is where law originates in the nature of God. The third variation of this question is whether *sin* is abhorrent to God primarily because it violates his love or because it violates his holiness. I have defended the latter view.

Now, at the first level of these questions, it may not be too difficult for one to convince himself that love is primary and that holiness is somehow included within it. After all, the concept of "holy love" sounds very neat and quite acceptable (which it is, when properly understood). Even at the second and third levels, where law and sin have to be reconciled with the primacy of love, it is still possible to make it sound plausible. But once one has committed himself to this way of thinking, he cannot stop here. He must face this final question of the relation between wrath and love, where the task of maintaining the primacy of love would seem to be much more formidable.

Wrath as the Sinner's Perennial Problem

Coming to terms with the reality of God's wrath has always been a problem for mankind. It is quite understandable that sinners would have great difficulty with the idea and would seek ways to deny it or at least neutralize it. Such an enterprise is a form of self-defense and self-deception, as those who know they are guilty before God try to escape their just punishment by altering their conception of God. The common cry is that retributive wrath is "unworthy of God." Sometimes this complaint is due to a misunderstanding of the nature of wrath or of the seriousness of sin,[120] but underneath the confusion lies the all-to-clear knowledge of personal guilt and the need to defend oneself against "the wrath to come." (I.e., it is a matter of anthropodicy as much as theodicy.)

One form of defense is simply to deny that there is such a thing as wrath in the nature of God in any shape or form. Such was the ap-

---

120. See J. I. Packer, *Knowing God*, pp. 136-139, for a good discussion of this.

proach of the second-century heretic Marcion, who distinguished the Old Testament God of wrath (Yahweh) from the true and higher God of love made known to us through Jesus Christ.[121] Modern Liberal theology approximates this view by imposing evolutionary theory upon the Bible and tracing the alleged development of the concept of God from the primitive early Old Testament idea of a wrathful God to the idea of a loving God in the later prophets and especially Jesus. For example, a few decades ago one denominational official made the headlines by referring to the God of the Old Testament as a "dirty bully." Morris cites a modern philosopher, Nicholas Berdyaev, as saying, "The wrath of God described in the Bible is only an exoteric expression of the Divine Countenance as it appeared to the Hebrew mind." In reality, "anger in every shape and form is foreign to God, Whose mercy is infinite."[122]

Another form of self-defense against the wrath of God is to redefine it, changing it from the personal vengeance of an offended holy God into an impersonal cause-and-effect principle that is just built into the universe. If one sins, he will suffer in the end; that's just the way the world is put together. (This is similar to the Eastern concept of *karma*.) For example, Clarke says this is the only kind of universe a holy God could make, namely, one in which sin could not prosper. Thus "the retributive element in life is a part of the very fact of life"; "life is so ordered that in holiness is welfare and in sin is doom." It is only right and fair "that corresponding consequences to the doer should follow the doing of right and wrong."[123] The most familiar example of this view is C. H. Dodd, who argues (on very weak grounds)[124] that wrath is not a personal attitude in God but is simply "the effect of human sin,"

---

121. Harold O. J. Brown, *Heresies* (Garden City, N.Y.: Doubleday, 1984), p. 61.
122. Nicholas Berdyaev, *Freedom and the Spirit* (London, 1944), p. 92; cited by Leon Morris, *The Apostolic Preaching*, p. 180.
123. William Newton Clarke, *The Christian Doctrine of God*, pp. 105, 188. "Punishment is disciplinary," he says (p. 190). H. F. Rall agrees completely with this view (*Religion as Salvation* [Nashville: Abingdon-Cokesbury Press, 1953], pp. 80-83).
124. That wrath is not a personal attitude in God follows, he says, from the fact that Paul never uses the verb form of wrath with God as its subject, and from the fact that Paul speaks only three times of the "wrath *of* God," at other times speaking simply of "the wrath" in an impersonal way. (C. H. Dodd, *The Epistle of Paul to the Romans* [New York: Harper & Brothers, 1932], p. 21)

305

a way of describing "an inevitable process of cause and effect in a moral universe." "Sin is the cause, disaster the effect." Wrath is "deserved disaster." The idea of personalized wrath is a primitive concept that "breaks down as the rational element in religion advances."[125] In other words he denies that sin brings wrath which brings disaster, and says instead that sin brings disaster (which some call wrath).

Morris shows how such a view as this is contrary to the Old Testament representation of the wrath of God, which is extremely personal. He cites Amos 3:6, "If a calamity occurs in a city has not the Lord done it?" He also refers to Ezekiel 7:8-9, where the Lord announces in multiple terms the imminence of his wrath and concludes, "Then you will know that I, the Lord, do the smiting." Morris comments, "It is difficult to imagine how the prophets and psalmists could possibly have expressed more strongly the personal aspect of the wrath of God." He agrees that disaster *is* the inevitable result of sin, but only "because a holy God wills to pour out the vials of His wrath upon those who commit sin."[126] Eichrodt states, "The transformation of God's reaction to sin into the action of an impersonal order of things, an objectively necessary universal law such as is implied by philosophical thought, is an idea quite foreign to the Israelite outlook."[127] Addressing the same point, Tasker believes that Dodd's view is quite unsatisfactory in light of Paul's statements in Romans 1:24ff., that "God gave them over" to the "due penalty of their error."[128]

Wrath Neutralized as a Form of Love

Probably the most common way of escaping the full force of the Biblical teaching on the wrath of God is to interpret it as a form of love. This is the conclusion that we would expect to be reached by those who follow the line of thought mentioned at the beginning of this section, namely, those who merge holiness with love and give love the primacy. And this is exactly what we find. After establishing the pattern by arranging holiness, law and sin under the umbrella of love, they bravely attempt to find a place for wrath under it, too. Wrath is thus neutralized

125. Ibid., pp. 22-24.
126. Leon Morris, *The Apostolic Preaching*, pp. 133-134.
127. Walther Eichrodt, *Theology of the Old Testament*, I:265.
128. R. V. G. Tasker, *The Biblical Doctrine of the Wrath of God*, p. 16.

by calling it an expression of the love of God.

I must confess that I was quite surprised—almost shocked—to see how prevalent this view is in the theological world today, even among conservative theologians. It appears in almost epidemic proportions. In order to show the seriousness of this problem, I will cite quite a few examples. The large number appears to be all the more serious in view of the fact that I did not deliberately seek out these examples but simply noted them in the course of general research on the subject.

An older example is H. Martensen from the mid-nineteenth century, who says that "the expression, the *wrath of God*, simply embodies this truth, that the relations of God's love to the world are unsatisfied, unfulfilled" because of man's sins. "For this wrath is holy love itself, feeling itself so far hindered because they have turned away from its blessed influence whom it would have received into its fellowship. This restrained manifestation of love" from one perspective is wrath, but from another perspective it is simply divine grief and compassion.[129] Albert Knudson apparently agrees with Martensen, that wrath is "included within the divine love as a modified form of it." He says that "thwarted love" contains "a militant element and this on the moral plane finds vent in indignation." Thus we may speak of wrath as "an instrument of love or an altered form of it."[130]

Perhaps the most influential source for this view in modern times is the article on *orgē* in the Kittel-Friedrich *Theological Wordbook of the New Testament*. In his section on the Old Testament view of wrath Fichtner declares that the "central motive for God's wrath against Israel" was that the people had "forgotten its God, turned from Him, and despised His love. This is the deepest root of the concept of wrath . . . . It is Yahweh's wounded love which awakens His wrath." Again, "the wrath of Yahweh has a very profound basis in the fact that it is proclaimed as an expression of the wounded holy love of Yahweh, as a reaction against the ingratitude and unfaithfulness of Israel towards His gracious turning to it." In other words, "the wrath of God against Israel is the reverse side of His love." This same motivation also applies to a large

129. H. Martensen, *Christian Dogmatics*, tr. William Urwick (Edinburgh: T. & T. Clark, 1898), p. 303.

130. Albert C. Knudson, *The Doctrine of God* (Nashville: Abingdon-Cokesbury Press, 1930), p. 347.

portion of God's wrath against the nations, says Fichtner.[131] In his section on the New Testament Stählin says the same thing: "God's wrath is that of wounded love." He says plainly that "the wrath of God arises from His love and mercy." Also, "where mercy meets with the ungodly will of man rather than faith and gratitude, with goodwill and the response of love, love becomes wrath."[132]

This view has been accepted by many in Neo-orthodox circles. Emil Brunner, for example, asks about the relation between the "contradictory ideas" of the wrath and the love of God. Claiming to be following the view of Martin Luther, Brunner says, "Because God takes Himself, His Love, infinitely seriously, and in so doing also takes man infinitely seriously, He cannot do otherwise than be angry, although 'really' He is only Love. His wrath is simply the result of the infinitely serious love of God." Through the natural world we know him only as a wrathful God, but through Christ and his cross "the inmost being of God is disclosed as the abyss of Love."[133] Gustaf Aulén agrees, saying that divine wrath is actually "merged with love." It is "love's radical opposition to evil" whereby love maintains its purity. "In the last anaysis love and wrath stand in intimate relation. . . . Love shines behind the dark cloud of wrath; yea, even more, it is active even in wrath."[134] Regin Prenter says that what are apparently two wills in God, i.e., "a hardening creative will of wrath and a redemptive will of grace," are really just a single will. "Both his wrath and his grace result from the same righteous love." Wrath is just the way "in which his holy mercy expresses itself"; it is "the reaction of the holy mercy itself against the hardening of sin." Also, "the fire of God's wrath is precisely the fire of his mercy."[135] Another example is Hendrikus Berkhof, who says that God's justice and wrath are "the expressions of his holy love. God meets us here as injured love, by which he tries to make us aware of our estrangement in order to induce

131. Johannes Fichtner, "ὀργή etc." (part), *Theological Dictionary of the New Testament*, ed. Gerhard Friedrich, tr. Geoffrey W. Bromiley (Grand Rapids: Eerdmans, 1967), V:403-404, 407-408.

132. Gustav Stählin, "ὀργή" (part), pp. 420, 425.

183. Emil Brunner, *The Christian Doctrine of God: Dogmatics, Volume I*, tr. Olive Wyon (Philadelphia: Westminster Press, 1950), pp. 168, 170, 173.

134. Gustaf Aulén, *The Faith of the Christian Church*, pp. 136-139.

135. Regin Prenter, *Creation and Redemption*, tr. Theodor I. Jensen (Philadelphia: Fortress Press, 1967), pp. 220, 222, 417.

us to surrender to his love." God's final word and deepest nature are love, and it is this love that is operative in his judgment and wrath. "Wrath may not be confused with hatred; it speaks of a violation of the covenant, and it is an expression of the injured love of God."[136]

Other writers that share this same general position include R. P. C. Hanson, who begins his spirited diatribe against retributive wrath with the words, "The other side of God's love is God's wrath."[137] He says the idea that there are two sides to God's nature is "a horrible caricature" that subjects God "to fits of schizophrenia." It is irrational to think that God could be angry with sinners and love them at the same time. He punishes us, of course, but "God's punishment is not retributory; it is reformatory and remedial and deterrant. He does not punish in anger. God is never angry with anyone. We should exorcize from our thinking this nightmare of an angry God." Wrath is really the obverse of love, the other side of the coin. "Wrath is what happens when you reject God's love. We cannot remain unaffected by God's love. It must either redeem us or ruin us."[138] A similar view is that of Ronald Hals, who declares that the root of wrath is frustrated and jealous love. "Because his gracious love is frustrated, he moves to judgment—but it is a purposeful judgment, a gracious one."[139] Another such example is Adrio König, who says there is definitely a relationship between love and wrath: "Had God not been loving, he would never have been angry. . . . His wrath is injured love." The Bible says that God is love, but it never says that God is wrath.[140] "Wrath does not belong to his being in the way that love does. . . . He *became* angry; but he *is* love." The two are so closely related, however, "that his wrath is actually something for which we may be glad. Without wrath—as injured love—there could be no love."[141]

Moving more toward the conservative end of the theological spec-

---

136. Hendrikus Berkhof, *Christian Faith: An Introduction to the Study of the Faith*, tr. Sierd Woudstra (Grand Rapids: Eerdmans, 1979), pp. 125-127.

137. R. P. C. Hanson, *The Attractiveness of God: Essays in Christian Doctrine* (Richmond: John Knox Press, 1973), p. 146.

138. Ibid., pp. 148-151.

139. Ronald M. Hals, *Grace and Faith in the Old Testament*, pp. 71-73.

140. But it says, "Our God is a consuming fire." This is the same as saying "God is wrath."

141. Adrio König, *Here Am I!*, pp. 93-95.

trum, we find the same kind of thinking. In his popular-level book on hell, Harold Bryson combines this view with the cause-and-effect view discussed in the previous section. Wrath does not contradict love, he says, because *wrath* is simply an expression implying God's creation of an orderly, moral world. It is a moral law, just as gravity is a physical law. Out of love, for our highest good, God structured the world on moral maxims. "Therefore, when the Bible speaks of the 'wrath of God,' it means that man has violated the principles by which God ordered the universe." In love God seeks for people to live according to his will. "Yet, when love is rejected, judgment follows. It is not another side of God. It is love acting in judgment." And what about hell itself? "Hell represents the rejection of love."[142] Gerard Van Groningen, who wrote most of the articles on the words for wrath in the conservative *Theological Wordbook of the Old Testament*, follows this same line of thought. He speaks of God's destructive judgment on the objects of his wrath. "This judgment, in keeping with God's justice is not contrary to divine love. Rather, it is an expression of divine love which has been offended, rejected and deeply grieved. Divine love suffers long; it also defends itself and removes the objects of its vexation and sorrow."[143] According to Donald Bloesch, God's wrath "is one form of his holy love."[144] In the original ISBE article on wrath, William Evans says that it is always closely related to love and compassion. "If we rightly estimate the Divine anger we must unhesitatingly pronounce it to be but the expression and measure of that love."[145] H. O. Wiley says, "The Christian position generally, is that wrath is but the obverse side of love and necessary to the perfection of the Divine Personality, or even to love itself." Divine wrath "is in some proper sense the same emotion which exercised towards righteousness is known as divine love."[146] We may be surprised to hear Tasker say that anger is "an essential element of

---

142. Harold T. Bryson, *Yes, Virginia, There Is a Hell* (Nashville: Broadman, 1975), pp. 112-113.

143. Gerard Van Groningen, *"ka'as,"* Theological Wordbook of the Old Testament, ed. R. Laird Harris et al. (Chicago: Moody Press, 1980), I:451.

144. Donald G. Bloesch, *Essentials of Evangelical Theology*, I:34.

145. William Evans, "Wrath," p. 3113.

146. H. Orton Wiley, *Christian Theology* (Kansas City, Mo.: Beacon Hill Press, 1940), I:385-386.

divine love."[147] And even Leon Morris says that God's wrath is "but the other side" of love, "the expression of his love." Also, "sin must be punished because God is loving."[148] We should see Biblical wrath as "a wrath which is the reverse side of a holy love, a flame which sears but purifies."[149]

Two examples from Restoration Movement writers will conclude this survey. One is Curtis Dickinson, who says that "Judgment is the product of love." Also, "God's wrath against sin is predicated upon His love for the good. It is His love that will bring about the judgment." This includes the final judgment.[150] The last example is Owen Crouch, who says that God's wrath "in fact is His love manifesting itself under the circumstances of sin's making." The essence of God's nature is love, and wrath "is love reacting in the presence of sin. Love cannot tolerate sin." This is why "God's love arrives on us as though He were angry"; "it appears that God is angry with us." In fact, he is angry, but not in a punitive sense. His anger "is the penetration of God's love into the corruption of our souls to push out the poison of sin that destroys us."[151]

Wrath is Not a Form of Love

The twenty writers quoted above certainly do not represent the same theological viewpoint, nor do they all approach the subject of the wrath of God in the same way. Some would be much more consistent than others in making it an instrument or expression of love. It may be that some simply find the concept of "injured love" clever and appealing, but have not really thought the issue through very carefully. Nevertheless it is being said by so many people from so many different backgrounds that it becomes necessary to make this point very emphatically: wrath is not a form of love. We may not want to respond as sharply as Robert Gleason, who says, "It is the worst stupidity to believe that Yahweh cannot be angered,"[152] because those who take the posi-

---

147. R. V. G. Tasker, The Biblical Doctrine of the Wrath of God, p. vii.
148. Leon Morris, Testaments of Love (Grand Rapids: Eerdmans, 1981), pp. 82-83.
149. Leon Morris, The Apostolic Preaching, p. 159.
150. Curtis Dickinson, "Love and Judgment," The Witness (January 1983), 23:1-2.
151. Owen L. Crouch, "The Wrath of God!", pp. 13-14.
152. Robert W. Gleason, Yahweh: The God of the Old Testament, p. 79.

tion surveyed above are not necessarily denying that God can be angered. They are simply saying that whatever this thing called wrath may be, it springs from God's love and thus must have a loving purpose. This is not as serious as denying the reality of divine wrath, but it surely takes the sting out of it and leaves us with a one-sided picture of God. I reject it very strongly, and thus appropriately side with A. H. Strong when he says, "To be told that God is only benevolence, and that he punishes only when the happiness of the universe requires it, destroys our whole allegiance to God and does violence to the constitution of our nature." He notes that in Scripture "punishment is many times traced to God's holiness, but never to God's love."[153]

In view of everything Scripture says about the wrath of God as involving hatred (of sin *and* the sinner), vengeance, and retribution, I find it simply incredible—no, outrageous—that it should be called an expression of his love. It is rather a form of his holiness. Of course God's love is injured and wounded and thwarted by sin, but it does not therefore mutate into wrath. Love has its own way of responding to sin, which includes grief, compassion, and grace; but none of these can be equated with wrath. Also, it is quite the case that wrath is tempered by love. God is "slow to anger," as Scripture says repeatedly (e.g., Neh. 9:17; Ps. 103:8; 145:8). His wrath is restrained by his love (Hos. 11:9; 14:4; Micah 7:18). But this does not mean that his wrath is swallowed up by his love; it is still real and distinct from love. Nor is it incompatible with love, as if it were not possible for God to exist with both or to carry out his purposes without violating one or the other.

There are no doubt many different reasons why people feel that it is necessary to merge wrath into love. Some are based on an *a priori* commitment to evolutionary rationalism (e.g., Dodd's idea that personalized wrath is a primitive concept "which breaks down as the rational element in religion advances"[154]), but others arise within the context of strong Biblical faith. Here the problem is usually a key hermeneutical or theological error. One such error is the tendency to generalize from Israel's unique status in the history of redemption. For example, the idea of "wounded love" is much more appropriate when speaking of

---

153. Augustus H. Strong, *Systematic Theology*, I:272.
154. C. H. Dodd, *The Epistle of Paul to the Romans*, p. 24.

God's relationship with Israel than his relationship with Babylon or Assyria. Another example of this is Fichtner's statement, "The consistent linking of nouns for wrath with Yahweh, the covenant God, is of supreme theological significance. It shows that the idea of wrath is closely bound up with belief in the covenant."[155] But this is very doubtful when we are thinking of God's wrath upon the heathen, who had no covenant with him unless creation itself be considered a kind of covenant.

Another error leading to a confusion between wrath and love is the failure to distinguish properly between retributive punishment and chastisement. There may be a measure of anger in chastisement (cf. Ps. 38:1; Jer. 10:24), but it must be considered primarily as an act of love (Heb. 12:5-6). However, it is difficult to see anything but wrath in God's retributive punishment. As Strong says, love chastens, but only holiness punishes.[156] The Biblical teaching concerning God's wrath lends itself very well to retributive punishment, but very poorly to chastisement.

Another error that may be the source of the confusion being discussed here is an exaggerated idea of the simplicity of God, or the idea that God's nature must be totally undifferentiated if he is truly perfect. This is the notion that God must be ONE in every sense of the word, and thus that there are no real distinctions among the various attributes within God's nature. This leads to a tendency to see just one of the divine attributes as the "real" essence of God, and often this is love, on the strength of I John 4:8, "God is love." But this concept of the divine simplicity is too extreme. True, there are no *divisions* within the divine nature, but there are *distinctions*.[157] Terms such as holiness and love represent truly distinct aspects of God. There *are* two sides to his nature, which Paul calls his "kindness and severity" (Rom. 11:22). "God is love" (I John 4:8), but "God is a consuming fire" also (Heb. 12:29). Why should any Bible believer balk at this idea? Indeed, the fact that there are two sides in God's nature that have been placed in a rela-

---

155. Johannes Fichtner, "ὀργή," p. 396.
156. Augustus H. Strong, *Systematic Theology*, p. 272.
157. See the discussion of this point in Jack Cottrell, *What the Bible Says About God the Creator*, pp. 37-40.

tionship of tension by the occasion of man's sin[158] *is the very root of both the necessity and the genius of the divine work of redemption.*

The Necessity of God's Wrath

Another question that needs to be addressed is whether the wrath of God is something that must *necessarily* be expressed, or whether God is free to choose whether he will express it or not. A different but related question is whether the divine wrath is a part of the divine essence, or whether it is simply an external relationship between God and his creatures. It would seem that how one answers the second question should determine how he answers the first one. If wrath is part of the divine essence, then it is something that *must* be poured out against sin. But if it is not a part of God's nature, but is only a relationship, then it should be a matter of God's choice whether he will express it or not. If this relationship between the questions is valid, and I believe it is, then Donald Bloesch seems to contradict himself when he says on the one hand that wrath is a "necessary reaction" of God's nature to sin, and on the other hand that "wrath is not what God is in himself, but it signifies what he can be in relation to the world of the creature."[159] If it is not what God is in himself, then why is it a "necessary reaction"? It would seem to be necessary only if it is within God's nature in some way.

The idea that wrath is not a part of God's nature is widely accepted, however. "Wrath is not part of the divine essence," says Stählin bluntly.[160] Eichrodt says it never forms one of the permanent attributes of God but is like "a footnote to the will to fellowship of the covenant God." It is transient, not permanent; it operates only in individual acts of punishment.[161] "God's wrath does not belong to his essence, or at least not in the same way as his love," says König. "He *became* angry, but he *is* love."[162] Morris says that "God is by nature merciful rather than wrathful." The "holy God *wills* to pour out the vials of His wrath upon

---

158. See Augustus H. Strong, *Systematic Theology*, p. 272: "So, upon occasion of man's sin, holiness and love in God become opposite poles or forces. The first and most serious effect of sin is not its effect upon man, but its effect upon God."

159. Donald G. Bloesch, *Essentials of Evangelical Theology*, I:34.

160. Gustav Stählin, "ὀργή," p. 438.

161. Walther Eichrodt, *Theology of the Old Testament*, I:262, 266.

162. Adrio König, *Here Am I!*, pp. 44, 95

those who commit sin."[163] "The Bible never speaks of God's wrath as a divine attribute," says Prenter. "Wrath is not *in* God, but it is kindled on earth against his enemies."[164]

If this point of view is correct, then it would seem that wrath is not really necessary. Some see this as a question of preserving the sovereignty of God. If wrath is necessary, then God is not sovereign; he is being forced to do something without having any choice in the matter. Thus Hanson says, "We limit God's sovereignty if we envisage him as complying, even complying reluctantly, with the demands of justice, or of law."[165] Then let us assume for a moment that this view is correct, that wrath is not in God but only on earth, that it is not really necessary. What difference would this make? What is really at stake here? No less than the nature of our redemption. For if wrath is not really necessary, why cannot God simply forgive us without the necessity of the cross? Indeed, why cannot he simply forgive us without even the necessity of our own trusting response to him? Bavinck recognizes this point and even seems to accept it. He says, "It would seem that there is nothing in God's nature that would make it necessary for him to deal out punishment; why would it be impossible for him, the Almighty One, to forgive without demanding satisfaction or exacting punishment?"[166] Also, this is the very context in which Hanson insists upon maintaining the sovereignty of God over against a necessary expression of wrath: he is vehemently rejecting the substitutionary atonement of Jesus Christ. That Christ died "to meet the demands of God's wrath or justice" is what he calls "a horrible caricature." That the innocent Christ voluntarily endured God's anger against us is "nothing less than disgusting"; it is "a despicable theology."[167]

What shall we say to this? Is God's wrath necessary, or is it not? To be sure, denying its necessity does not of itself lead one into the dangerous negations expressed by Hanson. But it does raise the question of why God then chooses to punish sinners if in fact his nature does not demand it. One answer often given is that God's veracity or

---

163. Leon Morris, *The Apostolic Preaching*, pp. 134-135. (Emphasis supplied.)
164. Regin Prenter, *Creation and Redemption*, p. 220.
165. R. P. C. Hanson, *The Attractiveness of God*, p. 148.
166. Herman Bavinck, *The Doctrine of God*, p. 221.
167. R. P. C. Hanson, *The Attractiveness of God*, pp. 148, 150.

truthfulness is at stake. God gave his law and attached a penalty to it. Now if he does not punish sinners, he will have gone against his own word. Shedd says, "God cannot lay down a law, affix a penalty, and threaten its infliction, and proceed no further, in case of disobedience. The divine veracity forbids this."[168] As God says in Exodus 34:7, "Yet He will by no means leave the guilty unpunished." So he must keep his word. Bavinck carries it back a step further and grounds the necessity of God's punitive wrath in the type of universe he created. Not "that it would be wholly impossible as far as the creature is concerned to receive forgiveness apart from punishment," but "because of the order of justice which he himself has established once for all, and because of his name and honor, God is obliged . . . to punish the wicked."[169]

But it seems to me that there is more to it than this. If God was free to attach penalties to his laws or not, why did he choose to attach penalties involving such terrible wrath? If he was free to make some other kind of world and still have moral creatures, why did he not do that instead of making one that could end in hell for so many of them? It seems more reasonable and more Biblical to me to say that God's wrath is inherent in his very nature and therefore it must necessarily be expressed, once there are moral creatures who have sinned. Nahum 1:2 seems to be describing God's nature when it says, "A jealous and avenging God is the Lord; the Lord is avenging and wrathful." In a context of wrath Deuteronomy 4:24 says, "For the Lord your God is a consuming fire, a jealous God." In a context of warning Hebrews 12:29 repeats this truth: "For our God is a consuming fire." He is a consuming fire. *This is his wrath, and it is what he IS.* It is an aspect of his very nature. It is really no different from his holiness; it is his holiness in relation to sin. "It is because of his holiness, that God is a consuming fire," says Hodge.[170]

Because wrath is inherent in his very nature, it must necessarily be expressed against sin. "Divine justice is originally and necessarily obliged to punish evil," says Louis Berkhof.[171] Wrath is "a right and

---

168. William G. T. Shedd, *Dogmatic Theology*, I:373.

169. Herman Bavinck, *The Doctrine of God*, p. 223.

170. Charles Hodge, *Systematic Theology*, I:413.

171. Louis Berkhof, *Systematic Theology*, p. 75.

necessary reaction to objective moral evil," says Packer.[172] God is free
to make moral creatures or not, and allow them to sin or not, says Charnock,[173]

> . . . but if he sees good to suffer it, it is impossible but that he should
> detest that creature that goes cross to his righteous nature. His holiness is
> not solely an act of his will, for then he might be unholy as well as holy, he
> might love iniquity and hate righteousness, he might then command that
> which is good, and afterwards command that which is bad and unworthy;
> for what is only an act of his will, and not belonging to his nature, is indif-
> ferent to him. . . .

Charnock affirms that "sin cannot escape a due punishment. A hatred
of unrighteousness, and consequently a will to punish it, is as essential
to God as a love of righteousness." Indeed, "his detestation of sin must
be manifested," for "he doth not hate it out of choice, but from the immutable propension of his nature." Then Charnock touches the nerve
of this whole issue: "If God could have hated sin without punishing it,
his Son had never felt the smart of his wrath."[174]

We must point out that there is no violation of the sovereignty of
God in this. In the first place, divine sovereignty does not mean total arbitrary freedom to make any decision whatsoever; God's own rational
and moral nature rule out certain choices (e.g., those involving rational
contradictions or moral evil).[175] That God's holy nature would require
him to punish sin no more violates his sovereignty than his holy nature
prevents him from committing sin. In the second place, God's freedom
is preserved at the point of creation itself. That is to say, God did not
have to create, nor did he have to create moral beings who might sin.
That he did so was his own free choice.[176] But once he freely chose to
create moral beings, his nature was bound to act in a certain way if those
creatures sinned. In the third place, God *does* have a choice with
respect to the punishment of sinners. He is free either to punish the sinner himself, or to punish the sin in the person of a substitute. Shedd

---

172. J. I. Packer, *Knowing God*, p. 136.
173. Stephen Charnock, *The Existence and Attributes of God*, p. 453.
174. Ibid., pp. 509-510.
175. See Jack Cottrell, *What the Bible Says About God the Ruler*, p. 272.
176. Jack Cottrell, *What the Bible Says About God the Creator*, pp. 117ff.

says, "The sovereignty and freedom of God in respect to justice, therefore, relates not to the *abolition*, nor to the *relaxation*, but to the *substitution* of punishment."[177] This is exactly what God has sovereignly and freely chosen; that is why he is God our Redeemer.

This is the point. It is the wrath of God, indeed, the *necessity* of the wrath of God, that leads to the cross. Without a proper understanding of God's wrath, we will never understand the meaning of Christ's death on Calvary. Of course, the necessity of God's wrath *alone* does not account for the cross, for God could simply have consigned us all to hell. That would have satisfied his wrath. But there is another side to God's nature to which he must also be true, namely, his love. It was his love that led him to choose the substitute, his only-begotten Son. But the point here is this: if wrath did not *have* to be satisfied, then this choice was not necessary. But God's wrath *is* real, and it *must* be poured out as punishment for sin. God's nature makes it so. And this is what was happening on the cross. The cup which Jesus drank (Matt. 26:42; John 18:11) was the cup of God's wrath (Isa. 51:17).

God's Wrath and Christian Piety

Speaking of God's wrath, France reminds us that "there is a fierceness about the holiness of God which is foreign to much of our thinking," and a destructive power that can be quite terrifying.[178] It is certainly not one of the most pleasant topics to think about. Why then would Pink say, "The wrath of God is a perfection of the Divine character upon which we need to frequently meditate"?[179] Several reasons may be given. First, as Morris says, it will help us to understand the seriousness of sin.[180] This is Pink's point, that we should meditate on it in order that our hearts may be impressed by God's own detestation of sin. "We are ever prone to regard sin lightly, to gloss over its hideousness, to make excuses for it. But the more we study and ponder God's abhorrence of sin and His frightful vengeance upon it, the more likely are we to realize its heinousness,"[181] and thus to hate it and want

---

177. William G. T. Shedd, *Dogmatic Theology*, I:377.
178. R. T. France, *The Living God* (Downers Grove: InterVarsity Press, 1970), p. 65.
179. Arthur W. Pink, *The Attributes of God*, p. 77.
180. Leon Morris, *The Apostolic Preaching*, pp. 156-157.
181. Arthur W. Pink, *The Attributes of God*, p. 77.

to avoid it.

The second benefit of meditating on the wrath of God is that it should increase our love and our gratitude toward him when we realize the magnitude of the penalty from which we have been saved. This is true only for the Christian, of course. Anyone not under the blood of Christ should be filled only with terror at the thought of God's wrath. But this should not be the Christian's reaction. Instead we should be all the more grateful for our redemption, and especially all the more thankful to Christ our Redeemer when we realize that he has suffered this wrath in our place.

Finally, meditating on the wrath of God should instill within us a greater desire for evangelism, a greater desire to see others accept God's free offer of pardon and deliverance from the wrath to come. It should cause us to want to "save others, snatching them out of the fire" (Jude 23).

CONCLUSION

In this chapter we have sought to expound the nature of God's holiness. We have seen that it has a positive side and a negative side. Positively, it is his own pure moral character; negatively, it is his utter hatred of all sin. We have also seen how God's holiness is expressed first in relation to man as creature then in relation to man as sinner. Regarding the former, God's holiness takes the form of his law, which includes both commands and penalties. Regarding the latter, it takes the form of wrath, which is deserved punishment.

The holiness of God is indeed something for which we can praise him, singing with the angels, "Holy, Holy, Holy!" But in truth, if this were the only side to God's moral nature, our situation as sinners would be desperate indeed. This is why we praise him even more for his love, which is the subject of the next chapter.

6

THE LOVE OF GOD

Having discussed the holiness of God, we now turn to the subject of his love. I believe Matthews is right, that "it is only safe to approach the doctrine of the divine Love through the doctrine of the divine Holiness."[1] This keeps us from making statements that are too extravagant,[2] and it helps us to appreciate all the more what the Bible says about his marvelous love.

In this chapter we will touch briefly on the broad category of the goodness of God,[3] then discuss the love of God as such. Then we will deal with the specific forms in which God's love expresses itself toward human beings as sinners: his mercy or compassion, his patience or

---

1. W. R. Matthews, *God in Christian Experience* (New York: Harper & Brothers, 1930), p. 80.

2. E.g., "All His perfections are the perfections of His love" (Karl Barth, *Church Dogmatics, Volume II: The Doctrine of God, Part 1,* ed. G. W. Bromiley and T. F. Torrance, tr. T. H. L. Parker et al. [Edinburgh: T. & T. Clark, 1957], p. 351).

3. For a more detailed discussion see Jack Cottrell, *What the Bible Says About God the Ruler* (Joplin, Mo.: College Press, 1984), pp. 289-295.

long-suffering, and his grace. Regarding the last of these we will be particularly interested in whether his grace is universal and conditional or whether it is particular and unconditional.

THE GOODNESS OF GOD

We have said that there are two sides to the nature of God as far as his moral attributes are concerned, namely, his holiness and his love. In its most general sense, however, the latter side of God's nature might be called his *goodness*. This is quite a broad concept and might be taken in several ways, even when applied to God.[4] Barth says, "We understand by goodness the sum of all that is right and friendly and wholesome."[5] The connotation that is most relevant here is the second of these, that God is *friendly* toward his creation. It is his attitude of benevolence, kindness, and good will toward the creatures made by him. It is his will and desire to bless his creatures and to do good for them.

Goodness is the very nature of God. When Moses asked to see the very glory of God, he received this reply: "I Myself will make all My goodness pass before you, and will proclaim the name of the Lord before you" (Ex. 33:19). This certainly roots this attribute in the divine essence itself. Jesus says, "No one is good except God alone" (Mark 10:18), i.e., in any absolute and essential meaning of the word. God is called "the good Lord" (II Chron. 30:18). "The Lord is good" is a frequently-occurring refrain in the Psalms (Pss. 100:5; 106:1; 107:1; 118:1, 29; 135:3; 136:1; cf. Jer. 33:11). "O taste and see that the Lord is good" (Ps. 34:8)! This is summed up in Psalm 119:68, "Thou art good and doest good."

God is good (benevolent, kind) not only toward human beings but toward his whole creation. Louis Berkhof defines the concept to include this breadth. Divine goodness, he says, is "that perfection of God which prompts Him to deal bountifully and kindly with all His creatures."[6] He

---

4. See ibid., pp. 290-291; see Andrew Bowling, "*tōb*," *Theological Wordbook of the Old Testament*, ed. R. Laird Harris et al. (Chicago: Moody Press, 1980), I:345, for five general meanings of the Hebrew word, all of which have some application to God, he says (p. 346).

5. Karl Barth, *Church Dogmatics, Volume II: The Doctrine of God, Part 2*, ed. G. W. Bromiley and T. F. Torrance, tr. G. W. Bromiley et al. (Edinburgh: T. & T. Clark, 1957), p. 708.

6. Louis Berkhof, *Systematic Theology* (London: Banner of Truth Trust, 1939), p.

conveyed his goodness toward the physical universe in the very creation of it (Gen. 1:4, 10, 12, 18, 21, 25). He continues to manifest his goodness in general providence: "The Lord is good to all, and His mercies are over all His works. . . . The eyes of all look to Thee, and Thou dost give them their food in due time. Thou dost open Thy hand, and dost satisfy the desire of every living thing" (Ps. 145:9, 15-16). The Lord was pleased to spare Nineveh not only because of the innocent people there but also because of its "many animals" (Jonah 4:11). He cares for birds and flowers, says Jesus (Matt. 6:26, 28); and not one sparrow "will fall to the ground apart from your Father" (Matt. 10:29).

Our concern in this chapter, however, is with God's goodness as it is expressed toward human beings. In this more specific form it is also and more frequently called love. It is his loving desire to bless the creatures he has made in his own image. This aspect of goodness is surely summed up in the Aaronic blessing in Numbers 6:24-26, "The Lord bless you, and keep you; the Lord make His face shine on you, and be gracious to you; the Lord lift up His countenance on you, and give you peace."

THE LOVE OF GOD

When understood in its true Biblical sense, love as a divine attribute is unique to the Judaeo-Christian concept of God. Clarke calls it "the Christian specialty."[7] Brunner notes how hollow the affirmation "God is love" sounds when one tries to apply it to other so-called deities of the world. Not even the greatest philosophers in their highest conceptions of God would ever have come to this conclusion, he says.[8]

"God Is Love"

The New Testament specifically declares what the whole Bible implicitly proclaims: "God is love" (1 John 4:8, 16). Brunner calls this "the most daring statement that has ever been made in human language."[9]

---

70. Italics omitted.

7. William Newton Clarke, *The Christian Doctrine of God* (New York: Charles Scribner's Sons, 1909), p. 84.

8. Emil Brunner, *The Christian Doctrine of God: Dogmatics, Volume I,* tr. Olive Wyon (Philadelphia: Westminster Press, 1950), p. 183.

9. Ibid., p. 185.

He continues, "The fact that God is love is the quintessence, the central word of the whole Bible."[10] Most would agree that this is a statement about the very essence of God. His very nature is love, and it is natural for him to act lovingly. "God's being is His loving," says Barth.[11] "Love is of the essence of his being," says Morris.[12] Nygren speaks of the "metaphysic of Agape," by which he means that the statement "God is love" is a statement about the very metaphysical essence of God. "Love is one with the substance of God; God is love . . . eternally in Himself."[13] This is why Brunner thinks it is misleading to distinguish between the "metaphysical" attributes of God and his "ethical" or moral attributes, and then to assign love to the latter category. In fact, he says, the love of God is not an attribute at all, but "the fundamental Nature of God."[14]

There is important truth here in the assertion that love is of the very essence of God. But to equate it completely with God's nature rather than to think of it as an attribute is a distortion; it implies that God's nature is love only and that everything else that one says about God is also a statement about love. Many hold to this view, as we have seen; but we have rejected it as a one-sided view of God that does not do justice to the totality of Biblical teaching. John's assertion that "God is love" must not be taken to imply that he is love *only*. Clarke's claim that "nowhere else does the simple copula bind a noun to the divine name"[15] is false and misleading. It is false because I John 1:5 says "God is light," using the very same word structure as I John 4:8. It is misleading because it implies that the copula ("is," *estin*) must be present for a clause to have affirmative force, which in Greek is not the case. Two other statements without a copula make simple assertions as to the nature of God: "God is spirit" (John 4:24) and "God is a consuming fire" (Heb. 12:29).[16] All of these statements are statements concerning

---

10. Ibid., p. 199.

11. Karl Barth, *Church Dogmatics*, II/1, p. 351.

12. Leon Morris, *Testaments of Love: A Study of Love in the Bible* (Grand Rapids: Eerdmans, 1981), p. 136.

13. Anders Nygren, *Agape and Eros*, tr. Philip Watson (Philadelphia: Westminster Press, 1953), p. 151.

14. Emil Brunner, *The Christian Doctrine of God*, p. 192.

15. W. N. Clarke, *The Christian Doctrine of God*, p. 86.

16. I am always amazed at the frequency with which writers state or imply that God is exclusively love. Almost as amazing is the fact that those who recognize that this is not

the very essence of God.

Scripture describes the divine love with attributes that do describe the inmost nature of God. His love is great (Eph. 2:4), infinite (Eph. 3:18-19), eternal (Jer. 31:3; Eph. 1:4-5), and dependable (Rom. 8:35).

The Terminology of Love

Much can be learned about the love of God just from a study of the various words used in Scripture to represent the concept. We should remember that etymology or word study as such is seldom decisive in theological matters; context and usage are often more important. Also, as Morris says, "the idea of God's love is much more pervasive than the specific use of the terminology of love."[17] Still, a survey of these words will give us an important perspective on the whole subject. Also, certain key aspects of the doctrine of love are directly related to the specific meanings of two of the main words, namely, *chesed* and *agapē*.

The undisputed Old Testament word for love is *'ahab*, along with its cognates or words within the same family. It is a general term and is used for both human and divine love. It is the one most commonly used in the Hebrew text where the English versions use "love."[18] Another word, used only once for God's love, is *chābab* (Deut. 33:3).

The other major Old Testament word is *chesed*, whose meaning has been the subject of considerable discussion and dispute. The King James Version usually translates it "mercy," e.g., "for his mercy endureth forever" (Ps. 136, throughout). The NASB ordinarily uses "lovingkindness" ("for His lovingkindness is everlasting"), while many recent versions simply use "love" ("His love endures forever," NIV; "his love is eternal," Today's English Version). In 1927 Nelson Glueck wrote a doctoral dissertation on the meaning of the Hebrew word, and it has

---

consistent with the Biblical affirmations just listed usually cite only the first three and omit any reference to the last one, "God is a consuming fire." An example is Arthur W. Pink, who says flatly that "there are three things told us in Scripture concerning the *nature* of God," and then quotes the first three passages given here, that God is love, light, and spirit (*The Attributes of God* [Swengel, Pa.: Reiner Publications, 1968], p. 70).

17. Leon Morris, *Testaments of Love*, p. 78.

18. See ibid., p. 9, for details. Morris' book gives basic data on all the terms relating to love, mercy and grace. The discussions of the individual words in the *Theological Wordbook of the Old Testament* are in most cases helpful.

been the major point of reference ever since.[19] Glueck's conclusion is that the word is used only in the context of a relationship of mutual duty and obligation, particularly a covenant relationship. It is a kind of covenantal loyalty; within such a relationship each person is bound to show *chesed* to one another. It does not necessarily involve affectionate feelings or grace or mercy.[20] All of this applies to God as well as to man. At times it may include connotations of divine mercy or love or favor, but its main point is still the faithfulness and loyalty with which God lives up to his covenant obligations. It may be translated in various ways according to the context, including "loyalty," "mutual aid," and "faithful love."[21] Many have followed Glueck's thinking rather closely, especially those who make the covenant motif primary in Scripture. For example, Mont Smith says that Glueck is "the leading authority on *hesed* (having done exhaustive study of that one word for his doctoral dissertation)." Thus Smith accepts the idea that "follow-thru on obligation is the root idea" of the term. He adds to this the concept of mercy, on the strength of the fact that the Septuagint translators used the Greek term *eleos* ("mercy") to represent the Hebrew word; but he redefines mercy by giving it a limited covenantal connotation: "follow-through on commitments so the other partner may not suffer because of my unfaithfulness." Thus *chesed* is a relational obligation to act in the other's best interest; it is "promoting the best interest of the other, according to the covenant."[22] The trend today, however, is away from Glueck's rather narrow conception of *chesed* and toward the view that it refers to a genuine affection of lovingkindness that is freely given without the necessitating bonds of a covenant (though it is quite appropriately used within a covenant context). For example, Morris likes the connotation of loyalty within a relationship, such as a covenant relationship, but suggests that both the relationship and the loyalty are grounded in a prior attitude of love or goodwill or "deep, lasting affection." He approves such translations as "loyal affection," "steadfast love," or · "love

---

19. Nelson Glueck, *Hesed in the Bible*, tr. Alfred Gottschalk (Cincinnati: Hebrew Union College Press, 1967).

20. Ibid., pp. 49, 54-55, 69.

21. Ibid., pp. 73, 81-82, 88, 102.

22. Mont W. Smith, *What the Bible Says About Covenant* (Joplin, Mo.: College Press, 1981), pp. 22-29, 345-346.

strengthened by loyalty."[23] For another example, R. Laird Harris sees an even weaker connection between *chesed* and covenant, except insofar as *chesed* is the "eternal divine kindness" within God that led him to make the covenant in the first place. He says it means simply love or merciful love, and that the King James Version's archaic "lovingkindness" is "not far from the fulness of meaning of the word."[24] The better case can be made, I think, for either Morris' or Harris' view and against Glueck's, in which case the word *chesed* is an important Old Testament word for love.

Other Old Testament words that are close to the connotation of love are *chāshaq*, which means "to desire, to love, to set love on, to be attached to"; *chāpēts*, meaning "to favor, to have delight in"; and *rātsāh*, meaning "to delight in, to be pleased with, to accept favorably."[25]

The main New Testament word for love is *agapaō*, whose noun form is *agapē*. This is but one of several Greek terms representing different types of love.[26] The term *storgē* (noun form) means "family love, family affection"; it is the kind of love that a mother should naturally have for her child or that siblings should have for one another. It is not used in the New Testament as such, though its negative form is condemned as a sin in Romans 1:31 and II Timothy 3:3 ("without natural affection," KJV), and a compound form is commanded in Romans 12:10 ("kindly affectioned," KJV; "devoted," NASB). Another Greek word is *philia*, which is the affectionate love between friends, or just friendship. Its verb form is used twice to refer to God's love: "The Father loves the Son" (John 5:20), and "The Father Himself loves you [apostles]" (John 16:27). A compound form appears in Titus 3:4 and is translated as God's "love for mankind." A fourth Greek word is *erōs*, which means romantic or sexual love, the strong attraction between the sexes. It includes the recognition of something desirable in its object, and the desire of the lover to possess its object. It is not used at all in the

---

23. Leon Morris, *Testaments of Love*, pp. 67-72. See his good summary of the data concerning the use of the term on pp. 65-67.

24. R. Laird Harris, "*chesed*," *Theological Wordbook of the Old Testament*, ed. R. Laird Harris et al. (Chicago: Moody Press, 1980), I:306-307.

25. These are the verb forms; cognates should also be noted. See Morris' discussion of these in *Testaments of Love*, pp. 89-95.

26. See Morris' discussion on "Greek Words for Love," *Testaments of Love*, ch. 6; and C. S. Lewis, *The Four Loves* (London: Geoffrey Bles, 1960).

New Testament, not even for human love. This is not because the Bible considers *erōs* or sexual love wrong as such, but because the term had become current for so many perversions of such love that it was expedient to avoid it.

The verb *agapaō* was the general Greek term for love, though the noun *agapē* was virtually unknown in the Greek world. It occurs in the Septuagint twenty times and in a few Jewish writings prior to the New Testament, but no undisputed secular occurrences from this period have been found.[27] Some feel that its general nature and its lack of a widely-used substantive are the very reasons why this term was selected for use in the New Testament. Henry says, "Because of its very colorlessness as a nonbiblical term the biblical writers could impart to *agapaō* a highly selective intention and a distinctive connotation."[28] This was desirable because, as Morris says, the New Testament writers "had a new idea about the essential meaning of love"; so it was only appropriate that they should use the relatively neutral word and (in the case of *agapē*) a practically new word for love.[29] Their new idea was that Christian love is just the opposite of *erōs* in certain crucial respects. Instead of its being a love for the worthy, it is a love given irrespective of merit; and instead of desiring to possess, it seeks to give.[30] This contrast will be explored in more detail below.

The Objects of God's Love

We have said that goodness is a general term that embraces God's benevolent attitude not only toward mankind but toward the whole creation. Love, however, is an attitude of affection that one personal being can have only toward another personal being. Thus the objects of God's love are the personal or moral beings within his creation.

Love Within the Trinity

There is an exception to this that must be mentioned first, however. It is a love even more basic than God's love for mankind, a love that is

---

27. See Leon Morris, *Testaments of Love*, p. 124, for a succinct summary of the data.
28. Carl F. H. Henry, *God, Revelation and Authority. Volume VI: God Who Stands and Stays, Part Two* (Waco: Word Books, 1983), p. 346.
29. Leon Morris, *Testaments of Love*, p. 125.
30. Ibid., p. 128.

eternal and is the prototype for all other forms of love. It is the eternal love that exists among the three persons of the Trinity. As Wiley says, "Love has its origin in the triunity of God."[31] Numerous times the Bible describes the Son as being loved by the Father. "Thou didst love Me before the foundation of the world," says Jesus to his Father (John 17:24). The Father called him "My beloved Son" (Matt. 3:17; 17:5; cf. Col. 1:13). See also John 10:17; 15:9; 17:23, 26; Eph. 1:6; II Peter 1:17. On one occasion Jesus refers to his love for the Father (John 14:31). There is no specific reference to their love for the Spirit or the Spirit's love for them, but Romans 15:30 refers generally to "the love of the Spirit" (cf. II Cor. 13:14).

God Loves All Human Beings

The intratrinitarian love is eternal (John 17:24); and in a sense God's love for his creatures is eternal (Jer. 31:3; Eph. 1:4-5), in view of his "predetermined plan and foreknowledge" with reference to the creation of man. (Since there is no reference to God's love for angels, we will omit any speculation about this.) Here we will remain within the practical limits set by Genesis 1, however, and declare that ever since the creation of the first human beings, the objects of God's love have been the entire human race. God's love in the sense of his benevolent kindness and good will is directed toward every member of the human race, simply in view of their status as his creatures made in his own image. Nothing else is required to make us the objects of his love; and nothing, not even sin, can negate this status and nullify the love given to those who enjoy it. He loves us as his own image-bearing creatures, whether we be sinful or righteous, and whether this be taken in a relative or an absolute sense. *God loves all human beings.* "He loves those he has made, and his love leads to action to meet their needs."[32] Though he hates sinners *as sinners* (as we saw in the preceding chapter), he loves them as his creatures.

Scriptural testimony to the universal love of God begins in the Old Testament. Psalm 33:5 says, "The earth is full of the lovingkindness [*chesed*] of the Lord" (cf. Ps. 119:64). The verses that immediately

---

31. H. Orton Wiley, *Christian Theology* (Kansas City, Mo.: Beacon Hill Press, 1940), I:378.
32. Leon Morris, *Testaments of Love*, p. 5.

follow (vv. 6-9) summarize God's work of creation. If there is a covenant concept in *chesed*, then God's original and basic covenant was with all mankind at the creation itself. Hosea 6:7 suggests as much when it says that "like Adam ['ādām] they have transgressed the covenant." If *chesed* is only lovingkindness, then it is nevertheless universal. God's fatherhood is grounded in creation in Malachi 2:10, "Do we not all have one father? Has not one God created us?" In either case the goodness of God has abounded toward his creatures from the very beginning, and the earth is still full of his *chesed*.

As noted above, at several stages God acknowledged the impartation of his own goodness to the creation ("and God saw that it was good"); but only after his own image-bearers had been created did he say, "It was very good" (Gen. 1:31). As soon as he created them, he blessed them (Gen. 1:28; 5:2). He prepared a bountiful garden for them (Gen. 2:8ff.). He continues to bless, even though sin has complicated the original arrangement. "The earth has yielded its produce; God, our God, blesses us" (Ps. 67:6; cf. Pss. 65:9-13; 85:12).

The New Testament is more specific concerning God's love for all mankind, righteous or wicked. When Jesus admonishes us to love not only our neighbors but also our enemies, he says that in so doing we will be imitating our heavenly Father, "for He causes His sun to rise on the evil and the good, and sends rain on the righteous and the unrighteous" (Matt. 5:43-48). How could the Lord command *us* to have a love that is universal if God himself did not love all men? A parallel command is in Luke 6:35-36, "But love your enemies, and do good, and lend, expecting nothing in return; and your reward will be great, and you will be sons of the Most High; for He Himself is kind to ungrateful and evil men. Be merciful, just as your Father is merciful." On several occasions Jesus argues from the lesser to the greater in showing us that God loves us as human beings. If he thinks enough of birds and flowers to care for them, will he not care for us, who are so much more important to him than they (Matt. 6:26, 30; 10:31)? If evil men do good for their children, will not the heavenly Father "give what is good to those who ask Him" (Matt. 7:11)?

This loving care for all, even the pagans, is noted in Acts 14:17, where Paul says to the idol-worshipers at Lystra that God had been bearing witness to them all along "in that He did good and gave you rains from heaven and fruitful seasons, satisfying your hearts with food and gladness." James 1:17 says, "Every good thing bestowed and every perfect gift is from above, coming down from the Father of lights." God "richly supplies us with all things to enjoy," says Paul (I Tim. 6:17; cf. 4:4).

The most powerful and most moving testimony to God's universal love comes in the context where all men are regarded as sinners and in need of redemption. The most familiar passage is John 3:16, "For God so loved the world, that He gave His only begotten Son, that whoever believes in Him should not perish, but have eternal life." Some try to avoid the universal reference of God's love in this passage (thus limiting it to "the elect") by saying that "the world" means something other than all the *people* of the world,[33] but this expression coupled with "whoever" makes the reference to all mankind undeniable. That this is the case is seen when we compare two passages from John's first epistle, 2:2 and 4:10. In the latter John says the very epitome of love is "not that we loved God, but that He loved us and sent His Son to be the propitiation for our sins." That his love was directed toward all people is obvious from the former passage, "He Himself is the propitiation for our sins; and not for ours only, but also for those of the whole world." Three facts emerge from these verses: (1) "the world" means "all people"; (2) God *loves* the world, i.e., all people; and (3) his love for all people is demonstrated in the giving or sending of his own Son to be the propitiation for them all.

In the New Testament many affirmations of God's love appear to be limited only to believers within the church, e.g., "God demonstrates His own love toward us, in that while we were yet sinners, Christ died for us" (Rom. 5:8). Some think the "us" and "we" are intended to exclude "them" from God's love and Christ's atonement, but this is not the case. It is just the normal way of speaking when one is addressing an audience directly and intimately; he uses first person plural. That this is so in seen in John's first epistle itself, where God's love for the whole world is seen in his giving his Son as a propitiation for them all (I John 2:2; 4:10). In 2:2 John says Christ "is the propitiation for our sins," which is quite appropriate for an intimate letter; but then he immediately adds, "and not for ours only, but also for those of the whole world,"

---

33. C. Samuel Storms, *The Grandeur of God* (Grand Rapids: Baker Book House, 1984), pp. 142ff.

as if anticipating that someone would try to exclude those outside his audience from God's love and Christ's atonement. I believe we can conclude from this that other New Testament references (such as Romans 5:8) which say that "God loves *us*" also have an implicit universal reference. Some examples are Ephesians 5:2, "Christ loved us and gave himself up for us" (NIV); I John 3:16, "We know love by this, that He laid down His life for us"; I John 4:19, "We love, because He first loved us;" and Revelation 1:5, "to Him who loves us, and released us from our sins by His blood."

God Loves Israel

Practically all of the Old Testament deals with God's special relationship with the people of Israel. Thus most of its teaching about the love of God occurs within this context and has to do with God's special covenant love toward Israel in particular. The basic reason why God chose this nation and loved this nation was that he was using it as a means of bringing the Redeemer of *all* mankind into the world. The climactic promise to Abraham was this, "And in you all the families of the earth shall be blessed" (Gen. 12:3). In view of this redemptive purpose, in which the eternal destiny of the whole creation was at stake, it is no wonder that God had a special love for the people through whom he was going to accomplish it. In this connection it should be noted that God's special love for Israel was primarily directed toward the nation as such, and not necessarily toward all the individuals within it.[34]

Once God had led Israel out of Egypt and established them as his own people and nation (Ex. 19:5-6), he made it clear that he loved them dearly, but that his love and choice of them really went back to his original love and choice of "the fathers" (Abraham, Isaac and Jacob) for the ultimate accomplishment of his redemptive purpose. "Because He loved your fathers, therefore He chose their descendants after them" (Deut. 4:37). "The Lord did not set His love on you nor choose you

---

34. Gottfried Quell notes "how seldom the OT says that God loves a specific person," and that "basically the love of Yahweh is not usually related to individuals." "For the most part only collective objects of the love of God are mentioned," and the OT testimony to the love of God "moves for the most part in national trains of thought" ("ἀγαπάω, etc." [part], *Theological Dictionary of the New Testament*, ed. Gerhard Kittel, tr. Geoffrey W. Bromiley [Grand Rapids: Eerdmans, 1964], I:30-31). There are very few exceptions to this.

because you were more in number than any of the peoples, for you were the fewest of all peoples, but because the Lord loved you and kept the oath which He swore to your forefathers" (Deut 7:7-8; cf. v. 13). "Yet on your fathers did the Lord set His affection to love them, and He chose their descendants after them, even you above all peoples" (Deut. 10:15). Nevertheless the love is real. The Lord turned Balaam's "curse into a blessing for you because the Lord your God loves you" (Deut. 23:5). "Indeed, He loves the people" (Deut. 33:3).

The great pronouncements on love in the prophets are directed toward Israel (or Judah), the nation. "Since you are precious in My sight, since you are honored and I love you, I will give other men in your place and other peoples in exchange for your life" (Isa. 43:4). Speaking of God's "great goodness toward the house of Israel," Isaiah says, "In His love and in His mercy He redeemed them; and He lifted them and carried them all the days of old" (Isaiah 63:7-9). "I have loved you with an everlasting love; therefore I have drawn you with lovingkindness," says God to the nation (Jer. 31:3). "When Israel was a youth I loved him, and out of Egypt I called My son" (Hosea 11:1). "I will heal their apostasy, I will love them freely" (Hosea 14:4). All the passages just cited use the general term *'ahab*, but the following uses *chesed*. It is one of the greatest passages on love in the Bible, but its specific reference is to Israel, and even more specifically, to Abraham.

> Who is a God like Thee, who pardons iniquity and passes over the rebellious act of the remnant of His possession? He does not retain His anger forever, because He delights in unchanging love. He will again have compassion on us; He will tread our iniquities under foot. Yes, Thou wilt cast all their sins into the depths of the sea. Thou wilt give truth to Jacob and unchanging love to Abraham, which Thou didst swear to our forefathers from the days of old. (Micah 7:18-20)

(In this translation the entire expression, "unchanging love," represents the single word *chesed* in the original.)

The New Testament refers to this love for the nation of Israel in Romans 9:13 (quoting Malachi 1:2), and in Romans 11:28. The latter passage clearly shows how God's love for the nation throughout Old Testament history was grounded in the purpose for which the patriarchs were originally called: "From the standpoint of the gospel they are enemies for your sake, but from the standpoint of God's choice they are beloved for the sake of the fathers." (Jeremiah 11:15 and 12:7 also refer to Israel as God's "beloved.")

A few specific individuals within Israel are named as objects of God's love, such as David (II Sam. 22:20; I Chron. 28:4) and Solomon (II Sam. 12:24). Isaiah 42:1 probably refers to the Messiah, and some think Isaiah 48:14 may refer to Cyrus. References to Jacob (Ps. 47:4; Mal. 1:2) refer to the whole nation.

Most of the other Old Testament references which do not refer specifically to God's love for Israel or an individual fall into three categories: The first is numerous prayers for God to bestow his love on his people or simply upon the individual praying, e.g., "Wondrously show Thy lovingkindness, O Savior of those who take refuge at Thy right hand" (Ps. 17:7). Next are statements of general praise to God for his love or especially his *chesed*. "How precious is Thy lovingkindness, O God!" (Ps. 36:7). "Because Thy lovingkindness is better than life, my lips will praise Thee" (Ps. 63:3). "The Lord's lovingkindnesses indeed never cease" (Lam. 3:22). These are just a very few examples of many such statements of praise. (It should be noted that in most of these the implicit reference is to God's love or lovingkindness *toward Israel*.)

The third category includes those statements referring to the *types* of individuals whom God loves. This is very significant in relation to God's love for Israel in general, which seemed to exist and persist no matter what evil the people did (although this point itself needs clarification and will be discussed later). But within the nation as such, God makes it very clear that any special love toward individuals is conditioned upon their relative righteousness. Psalm 11:7 says, "For the Lord is righteous; He loves righteousness; the upright will behold His face." Psalm 37:28 adds, "For the Lord loves justice, and does not forsake His godly ones" (cf. Isa. 61:8). Psalm 146:8 simply states, "The Lord loves the righteous." In Proverbs 8:17 Wisdom says, "I love those who love me." Proverbs 15:9 says that God "loves him who pursues righteousness." In Exodus 20:6 God says that he shows *chesed* "to those who love Me and keep My commandments."[35] He shows *chesed* to those "who walk before Thee with all their heart" (I Kings 8:23; cf. II Chron. 6:14).

---

35. This same statement occurs a number of times: Deut. 5:10; 7:9; Neh. 1:5; Dan. 9:4.

Chesed will surround him "who trusts in the Lord" (Ps. 32:10). "Let Thy lovingkindness, O Lord, be upon us, according as we have hoped in Thee" (Ps. 33:22). "Great is His lovingkindness toward those who fear Him" (Ps. 103:11). "The Lord favors those who fear Him" (Ps. 147:11).

Thus in the Old Testament we see that God had a special collective love for his chosen nation, and a special conditional love for any individual within that nation who opened his heart toward God and made it receptive to what God was ready to bestow: "For Thou, Lord, art good, and ready to forgive, and abundant in lovingkindness to all who call upon Thee" (Ps. 86:5).

God Loves the Church

A similar pattern appears in the New Testament in reference to the church, which is now the chosen people of God, having replaced Israel in that position by the eternal purpose of God (Eph. 2:11-3:11). Just as Israel was chosen as a nation in the beloved Abraham (II Chron. 20:7; Isa. 41:8; Micah 7:20),[36] so the church is chosen as a people in the beloved Christ (Eph. 1:4-6). Just as Israel became the beloved nation (Jer. 11:15; 12:7), so now the church is the beloved people. Paul refers to Christians as "those who have been chosen of God, holy and beloved" (Col. 3:12). We hear in this passage an echo of Exodus 19:4-6. See also I Thessalonians 1:4; II Thessalonians 2:13; Jude 1. Thus we can say that just as God loved Israel as a nation, so also does he love his church as a people. As Ephesians 5:25-27 says, "Christ also loved the church and gave Himself up for her, . . . that He might present to Himself the church in all her glory, having no spot or wrinkle or any such thing; but that she should be holy and blameless." He "nourishes and cherishes" the church as his very own body (Eph. 5:29-30).

At the same time there is a conditionality with respect to relative righteousness that governs the individual reception and enjoyment of God's love even within the New Testament church. This element is not emphasized as much as in the Old Testament, because the perspective now is almost entirely from the point of view of our lack of absolute

---

36. The term *friend* in II Chron. 20:7 and Isa. 41:8 is a form of the basic word for love, *'ahab*.

righteousness and therefore our need for the righteousness of Christ; but it is present nonetheless. This is by no means saying that God's love for the Christian (any more than for the true Israelite of old) is dependent on man's prior love toward God. That would be totally erroneous and even blasphemous to think. God's love is always prior to ours, both in eternity and in the cross. Our love is *always* a response to God's love: "We love, because He first loved us" (I John 4:19). But we cannot ignore the teaching that once we have responded to that love, our hearts are then opened to receive it and enjoy it in a special way. Jesus says, "He who has My commandments and keeps them, he it is who loves Me; and he who loves Me shall be loved by My Father, and I will love him" (John 14:21). There is a conditionality here that cannot be ignored, and a new dimension of love upon the one who loves Christ that goes beyond the love that sent the Son to be a propitiation for all men in general. We are now loved, not just as sinners in need of redemption, but as children adopted into God's own family. And what a great love this is: "See how great a love the Father has bestowed upon us, that we should be called children of God" (I John 3:1)!

The Definition of God's Love

Having surveyed the terminology of love and the Biblical teaching concerning the objects of God's love, we are now in a position to attempt to define the concept of love as it applies to God. What do we mean when we say that God is love? What is the meaning of this attribute or aspect of his nature? I will offer this definition: God's love is his self-giving affection for his image-bearing creatures and his unselfish concern for their well-being that lead him to act on their behalf and for their happiness and welfare. The individual aspects of this definition will now be discussed.

Concern

The first aspect of God's love is his concern for the well-being and happiness of his creatures. This is what Erickson specifically labels benevolence, defined as "the concern of God for the welfare of those whom he loves." He is unselfishly interested in us for our own sake; he *cares* whether we are truly happy and self-fulfilled.[37] Others would call

---

37. Millard J. Erickson, *Christian Theology* (Grand Rapids: Baker Book House, 1983), I:292.

this God's kindness or philanthropy.[38] In truth this element of unselfish concern is what lies at the very heart of the idea of *agapē*. When one says *agapē*, he says concern.

God is concerned about us simply because we are his creatures. He would not have made us only to ignore us or treat us with indifference. He is then doubly concerned about us now that we are sinners. He is concerned not only to give us the positive blessings of his good creation, but to remove the negative consequences of sin. Thus in terms of concern, God does not love us less now that we are sinners; he loves us even more.

Self-giving

The second aspect of divine love is his desire to give of himself in whatever way necessary to achieve his creatures' happiness. This is an element that is found in most definitions of God's love. Louis Berkhof makes it the whole definition, as he says love is "that perfection of God by which He is eternally moved to self-communication."[39] Erickson says, "In general, God's love may be thought of as his eternal giving or sharing of himself."[40] Storms says, "Love is simply the communication by God *of Himself* to His creatures."[41] According to Quell, "Love in the OT is basically a spontaneous feeling which impels to self-giving."[42] Brunner agrees: "Love is the self-giving of God," the desire and will to impart himself.[43] Clarke expands this slightly by saying it is the "desire to impart himself and all good to other beings";[44] but this would probably be considered redundant since the imparting of himself would include "all good."

This element of self-giving is inherent in the very act of creation, as God pours out the bounty of his power and wisdom and goodness by

---

38. H. Orton Wiley, *Christian Theology*, I:391.

39. Louis Berkhof, *Systematic Theology*, p. 71. Italics omitted. Here Berkhof seems to be repeating Strong's view, as the latter says, "By love we mean that attribute of the divine nature in virtue of which God is eternally moved to self-communication" (Augustus H. Strong, *Systematic Theology*, 3 vols. in 1 [Valley Forge: Judson Press, 1907], p. 263).

40. Millard J. Erickson, *Christian Theology*, I:292.

41. C. Samuel Storms, *The Grandeur of God*, p. 129.

42. Gottfried Quell, "ἀγαπάω, etc.," p. 22.

43. Emil Brunner, *The Christian Doctrine of God*, pp. 185, 188, 192.

44. W. N. Clarke, *The Christian Doctrine of God*, p. 85.

just bringing this world into existence. The self-giving is intensified in the making of a creature in his own image who not only could consciously receive and appreciate this bounty but also could thank and praise the Creator and love him in return.[45] In this sense Barth refers to divine love as "the Creator's will for fellowship with His creature."[46]

The ultimate act of self-giving, of course, and thus the ultimate act of love, was God's giving of himself in the person of his only-begotten son as a propitiation for our sins. This leads to the next point.

Action

God's love is more than a *concern* for his creatures' well-being and a *desire* to impart himself in order to secure that well-being. Both concern and desire are internal. But God's love does not remain internal; he externalizes it in the form of *action* on behalf of those whom he loves. As Erickson puts it, "God inherently not only feels in a particular positive way toward the objects of his love, but he acts for their welfare. Love is an active matter."[47] H. Berkhof says that it is correct to characterize love as self-giving, and then adds:[48]

> . . . But that is still too pale when we realize what we have here. It is a love that stops for nothing, that is resolutely devoted to the other, however far away and hostile that other may be; it is a love which is unmotivated and for which no sacrifice is too great to enrich people who did not ask for it or [who] even oppose it. . . .

This statement reminds us that the people who are the objects of God's active concern are sinners, and that he is still willing to act on their behalf in spite of their sin. Indeed, he is willing to do even more for them now, since more is required in order to restore them to happiness and well-being. This is what makes divine love such a "strange and amazing attitude," as H. Berkhof puts it.[49] This is well illustrated in God's love for

---

45. See Jack Cottrell, *What the Bible Says About God the Creator* (Joplin, Mo.: College Press, 1983), pp. 120-124.

46. Karl Barth, *Church Dogmatics*, II/1, p. 369.

47. Millard J. Erickson, *Christian Theology*, I:294.

48. Hendrikus Berkhof, *Christian Faith: An Introduction to the Study of the Faith*, tr. Sierd Woudstra (Grand Rapids: Eerdmans, 1979), p. 119.

49. Ibid.

his chosen nation in the Old Testament. Hosea describes idolatrous Israel as a wife who has abandoned her husband for a life of wanton adultery and harlotry (Hos. 2:1-13), and God as a husband who continues to love her and does everything he can to win her back. "Therefore, behold, I will allure her, bring her into the wilderness, and speak kindly to her," says the Lord (Hos. 2:14); he would not stop until she became his faithful wife once more (Hos. 2:19-20). In a later period God addresses his people thus in Jeremiah 31:3, "I have loved you with an everlasting love." His people's idolatry and rebellion against him had not abated. But, as Morris says regarding this remarkable statement, "in the face of all this God still loves Judah. He does not simply tolerate the people—he loves them with all the fervor of his holy nature . . . . When everything else leads us to expect that God will abhor these sinful people, we find that instead he loves them . . . with an everlasting love."[50] Even though he sent them into captivity for punishment and chastisement, he brought them back to their own land and actively blessed them. This active love is well summed up in this statement about his beloved people: "And I will rejoice over them to do them good, and I will faithfully plant them in this land with all My heart and with all My soul" (Jer. 32:41).

From God's experience with Israel and from other places we learn that love sometimes must act with apparent harshness, since there are times when the only way that sinners can be helped is through chastisement. But when the welfare of the beloved is at stake, active love does not hesitate to chastise. "My son, do not reject the discipline of the Lord, or loathe His reproof, for whom the Lord loves He reproves, even as a father, the son in whom he delights" (Prov. 3:11-12; cf. Heb. 12:5-6). "He disciplines us for our good" (Heb. 12:10). God's treatment of Israel as a nation is an example of this. He says in Hosea 10:10, "When it is My desire, I will chastise them." "'O Jacob My servant, do not fear,' declares the Lord, 'for I am with you. For I shall make a full end of all the nations where I have driven you, yet I shall not make a full end of you; but I shall correct you properly and by no means leave you unpunished'" (Jer. 46:28; cf. 30:11; 31:18).

The supreme example of God's loving action on behalf of sinners is,

---

50. Leon Morris, *Testaments of Love*, p. 11.

of course, the cross. This is where God's love is shown to be the greatest possible love, because it is the ultimate form of self-giving action. "Greater love has no one than this, that one lay down his life for his friends," says Jesus (John 15:13). Then he proceeded to do just this, when he gave himself for us on Calvary. Boice notes, "Only at the cross does God show his love fully and without ambiguity." He then points out how difficult it is to find a verse in the New Testament that speaks of God's love without also speaking of Christ's death of the cross.[51] That Christ "loved me, and delivered Himself up for me" (Gal. 2:20) just seem to go together naturally. See John 3:16; Romans 5:8; Ephesians 5:2, 25; I John 3:16; 4:9-10; Revelation 1:5. This is what Leon Morris is talking about when he says that the New Testament writers "had a new idea about the essential meaning of love." This new understanding was brought about by the cross; all existing ideas of love were "revolutionized by what the cross meant." Truly, "it is the cross that teaches us what love is."[52]

We must be careful here to avoid extreme claims regarding the connection between God's love and Christ's cross. While it would seem to be impossible to exaggerate this connection, I am a bit uneasy about Morris' statement that "we would not know what *agapē* is were it not that Christ died for sinners," or his statement that "without the cross we would never have known what *agapē* is, let alone have experienced it."[53] This is similar to Brunner's claim that Christ's redeeming work "and this alone—shows us what the love of God means." But Brunner goes even further and says, "To reveal this love, that is the Mission of Jesus, that is the content of the New Covenant."[54] But surely God's love (even as *agapē*) is known to us in ways other than through the cross. If this were not the case, then God's attitude toward Israel, for example, would have no teaching power for us. It is better to say that we could never know the *full extent* of God's love for us without the cross, which is definitely true. And it is much better to amend Brunner's latter state-

---

51. James M. Boice, *Foundations of the Christian Faith. Volume II: God the Redeemer* (Downers Grove: InterVarsity Press, 1978), p. 210.

52. Leon Morris, *Testaments of Love*, pp. 125, 129-131, 144.

53. Ibid., p. 143.

54. Emil Brunner, *The Christian Doctrine of God*, p. 184. The latter statement is an example of the Christological fallacy. See Jack Cottrell, *What the Bible Says About God the Creator*, pp. 371ff.

ment to read, "To *do that* which reveals this love, that is the Mission of Jesus, that is the content of the New Covenant."

Affection

Divine love has been defined above (in summary) as self-giving affection and concern that lead to action. We have discussed the self-givingness, the concern and the action. What remains is affection. In some ways this should have been first, since it is this genuine affection for his image-bearing creatures that gives rise to the concern for their well-being and the desire to achieve that well-being through self-giving action. But we have saved it until last because there is some question as to whether this should even be included within the concept of God's love. When we speak of affection we are approaching or even invading the realm of feelings and emotions. Is it proper to say that God has tender and affectionate feelings for his creatures who are now sinners? Is he in any sense *drawn* to us? Is it proper to say that he has feelings or emotions of *any* kind?

Some would answer these questions negatively. Based on philosophical concepts of immutability (cf. chapter eight below), some would argue that it is impossible for the divine nature to be moved in any sense with feelings of any kind, such as sorrow or joy or affection. Based on preconceived concepts of sovereignty, others would argue that it is impossible for the divine nature to be conditioned in any sense by anything outside of itself. Strong may not be going quite this far, but nonetheless he speaks of God's love as "a rational and voluntary affection, grounded in perfect reason and deliberate choice." Also, "it involves a subordination of the emotional element to a higher law than itself, namely, that of truth and holiness."[55] We will remember, too, that Glueck's idea of *chesed* emphasizes objective duty and obligation rather than feeling. (This does not mean that he necessarily excludes feeling from the connotation of other words for love.) Finally, affection is often taken to be part of the natural content of the other Greek words for love, but not of *agapē*.

On the other hand, there are those who do not hesitate to speak of God's love as a kind of feeling or emotion that comes from his very

---

55. Augustus H. Strong, *Systematic Theology*, pp. 264-265.

heart (as it were). Erickson says that God's love is "a disposition of affection toward us."[56] Eichrodt says it "belongs to those spontaneous emotional forces which are their own justification," and says that 'ahab "always retains the passionate overtones of complete engagement of the will accompanied by strong emotion."[57] Tozer comments, "It is a strange and beautiful eccentricity of the free God that He has allowed His heart to be emotionally identified with men."[58] Barth declares, "The personal God has a heart. He can feel, and be affected. He is not impassible."[59]

It seems to me that the latter view is correct, and that the Bible does picture God's love as involving true affection for mankind. As noted earlier, agapē is not the only Greek word used for divine love. The verb form of philia is used twice (John 5:20; 16:27) and a compound form once (Titus 3:4), and most agree that this word includes affection. Several of the Old Testament words mentioned above (i.e., rātsāh, chāshaq, and chāpēts), have connotations such as "be attached to, take delight in." Wood says that the last of these, chāpēts, definitely includes emotional involvement and means "to experience emotional delight."[60] "Delight" may not always apply (cf. Isa. 53:10), but it probably does in Isaiah 62:4, where the prophet says that the restored Israel will be called, "My delight is in her." We have already pointed out that many feel Glueck's interpretation of chesed as covenantal loyalty or obligation is too emotionally barren. Morris says the word "indicates a deep, lasting affection."[61]

The great Biblical analogies which picture God's relationship with his people surely embody the concept of tender affection. The father-child analogy is most prevalent. In the Old Testament God is portrayed as a father to his chosen nation. Israel is described as an abandoned baby squirming in its own birth-blood when God found him and gave him life

---

56. Millard J. Erickson, *Christian Theology*, 1:294.

57. Walther Eichrodt, *Theology of the Old Testament*, tr. J. A. Baker (Philadelphia: Westminster Press, 1961), 1:250.

58. A. W. Tozer, *The Knowledge of the Holy* (London: James Clarke & Co., 1965), p. 107.

59. Karl Barth, *Church Dogmatics*, II/1, p. 370.

60. Leon J. Wood, "chāpēts," *Theological Wordbook of the Old Testament*, ed. R. Laird Harris et al. (Chicago: Moody Press, 1980), 1:310.

61. Leon Morris, *Testaments of Love*, p. 68.

(Ezek. 16:3-6). "He found him in a desert land, and in the howling waste of a wilderness; He encircled him, He cared for him, He guarded him as the pupil of His eye" (Deut. 32:10). "When Israel was a youth I loved him, and out of Egypt I called My son" (Hos. 11:1; cf. v. 4). God's general attitude is that of a father: "Just as a father has compassion on his children, so the Lord has compassion on those who fear Him" (Ps. 103:13). In the New Testament the analogy is continued as "Father" becomes almost a personal name for the first person of the Trinity. He is "our Father who art in heaven" (Matt. 6:9). We are his adopted children who call him not only "Father" but even "Abba" (Rom. 8:15), a name which "to Israelite ears . . . had the ring of an unusual intimacy."[62]

God also compares his love for his people with the love of a mother for her infant, and says that his is even stronger. "Can a woman forget her nursing child, and have no compassion on the son of her womb? Even these may forget, but I will not forget you," says the Lord (Isa. 49:15). "As one whom his mother comforts, so I will comfort you; and you shall be comforted in Jerusalem" (Isa. 66:13).

The husband-wife analogy is also a very prevalent way of describing God's love for his people. Eichrodt calls it "the supreme demonstration of God's attitude to Israel."[63] Thinking specifically of Hosea, Eichrodt speaks of "the strong emphasis on the inexplicable and paradoxical character of God's love, which is portrayed in terms of the wooing of a wanton."[64] Though Israel was to him as a shameless adulterous wife is to her cuckolded husband, God loved her still and made every attempt to allure her back (Hos. 2:1-20). As Hosea acted out the drama in his own marriage, God told him, "Go again, love a woman who is loved by her husband, yet an adulteress, even as the Lord loves the sons of Israel, though they turn to other gods" (Hos. 3:1). This same husband-wife analogy is carried over into the New Testament, again as a way of describing how much God loves his people. As a husband should love his wife, so "Christ also loved the church and gave Himself up for her" (Eph. 5:25; cf. II Cor. 11:2).

---

62. Hendrikus Berkhof, *Christian Faith*, p. 120. See Joachim Jeremias, *The Central Message of the New Testament* (London: SCM Press, 1965), pp. 9-30.
63. Walther Eichrodt, *Theology of the Old Testament*, I:251.
64. Ibid., p. 252.

One last analogy depicting God's love of tender affection is that of a shepherd and his flock. "The Lord is my shepherd, I shall not want," says David; then he elaborates on the solicitous care with which the shepherd watches over him (Ps. 23:1-4). God is called the "Shepherd of Israel, Thou who dost lead Joseph like a flock" (Ps. 80:1). He led them like a flock out of Egypt (Ps. 78:52), and he brought them again like a flock out of Babylon (Jer. 31:10; Ezek. 34:11-24). In the latter passage the Lord shows his shepherd's heart when he says, "Behold, I Myself will search for My sheep and seek them out. . . . I will feed My flock and I will lead them to rest . . . . I will seek the lost, bring back the scattered, bind up the broken, and strengthen the sick . . . . I will deliver My flock, and they will no longer be a prey" (Ezek. 34:11, 15-16, 22). Isaiah 40:11 describes him thus: "Like a shepherd He will tend His flock, in His arm He will gather the lambs, and carry them in His bosom; He will gently lead the nursing ewes." Every single characteristic of affection, care, and effort that belongs to a loving shepherd was embodied in Jesus our Redeemer, who says, "I am the good shepherd; the good shepherd lays down His life for the sheep" (John 10:11).

How can we say that God has no affection for his creatures whom he made to be in fellowship with himself? Does a father have no feeling for his son? Does a mother have no emotional attachment to her infant daughter? Does a husband have no deep attachment to his wife? Does a shepherd have no affection for his sheep? Surely these analogies teach us that God's love is warm and tender and deeply personal. They help us to feel the depth of his passion when he contemplates his rebellious people and (as Isaiah says) "longs to be gracious to you, and therefore He waits on high to have compassion on you" (Isa. 30:18). We hear the pathos when he says, "Is Ephraim My dear son? Is he a delightful child? Indeed, as often as I have spoken against him, I certainly still remember him; therefore My heart yearns for him" (Jer. 31:20). We feel with him when he cries, "How can I give you up, O Ephraim? How can I surrender You, O Israel? . . . My heart is turned over within Me, all my compassions are kindled" (Hos. 11:8). We can picture Jesus' tears of love when he said, "O Jerusalem, Jerusalem, who kills the prophets and stones those who are sent to her! How often I wanted to gather your children together, the way a hen gathers her chicks under her wings, and you were unwilling" (Matt. 23:37; cf. Luke 19:41).

With such affection as this, no wonder our loving God is concerned

344

for our well-being; no wonder he desires to give completely of himself to accomplish it; no wonder he has already actively accomplished our redemption even though it meant an infinite cost to himself.

Agapē or Erōs: A False Choice?

Before we leave the subject of the love of God, one last question must be addressed, namely, are *agapē* and *erōs* mutually exclusive types of love? Or to put the question theologically, is God then not *erōs* in any sense? The question requires some clarification. It is not just a matter of terminology, for as we have already seen, the fact that God is *agapē* does not preclude the use of words in the *philia* family to describe God's love. Even the absence of words in the *erōs* family from the New Testament does not in itself rule out the presence of the concept, or at least certain aspects of the concept, as that is presently defined. Also, this is not a matter of whether *erōs* in its sexual or romantic sense applies to God; that is totally out of the question. The issue is whether *erōs* as philosophically defined (e.g., by Nygren) in no sense characterizes the nature of God's love.

The Traditional Contrast

In his book *Agape and Eros* Nygren has, among other things, very specifically defined and sharply contrasted these two types of love in their very essence. Of course he is concerned to show that the *agapē* motif, as he understands it, applies to God in every way, while the *erōs* motif is totally absent from the nature of God. He summarizes the main features of *agapē* thus: (1) It is spontaneous and unmotivated, i.e., there is nothing outside of God that causes him to love. The only ground for his love is within himself. God's love is not drawn to us by anything within us. (2) This leads to the second feature, namely, *agapē* is "indifferent to value." God does not love us because there is anything worth loving within us. He loves us because he is loving, not because we are lovely. *Agapē* does not consider either the worthiness or the unworthiness of its object. (3) *Agapē* is creative. This means that it does not find value in its object, but *imparts* value to it. The Liberal concept of "the infinite value of the human soul" is actually destructive to *agapē*, since such an inherent value would be a motive for God to love us, thus destroying its spontaneous and unmotivated character. (4) Finally, *agapē* takes the initiative in establishing fellowship. God comes to us;

we do not come to God.[65]

By way of contrast, Nygren summarizes the concept of *erōs* thus: (1) It is *acquisitive* love. It is characterized by desire and longing. Its object is seen as something desirable to fill a need within the one who loves. Thus only that which is deemed valuable can be the object of such love. It can never be spontaneous and unmotivated, since it is motivated by the value of its object. It desires to acquire or possess that which it values. (2) *Erōs* is descriptive of all human attempts to find a way to God. In non-Christian systems, where *agapē* is unknown, the deity does not come seeking for man; so man must seek for God. His upward longings are the essence of *erōs*. (3) Finally, *erōs* is an egocentric type of love. The *erōs*-lover loves for his own sake not for the sake of his object. He desires to possess the object so that it may fill his own needs.[66]

In reference to the love of God, Nygren dismisses the *erōs* motif completely. "Eros is yearning desire; but with God there is no want or need, and therefore no desire nor striving." God is *agapē*, and *agapē* only.[67]

Of course, Nygren is not alone in his view. In fact, it is quite generally accepted and already was to some extent before Nygren's influential work was published in 1930. For example, Strong had already said that when God is described as *agapē*, "it is already implied that God loves, not for what he can get, but for what he can give."[68] Later writers say the same thing, but with details supplied mostly by Nygren. For example, after summarizing Nygren's explanation of *erōs*, Brunner says, "The Love of God, the *Agape* of the New Testament, is quite different. It does not seek value, but it creates value or gives value; it does not desire to get but to give; it is not 'attracted' by some lovable quality, but it is poured out on those who are worthless and degraded."[69] König says it is apparent "that God's love is not desire, and that the object of his love is *not* in fact desirable. Even in his created universe as such

---

65. Anders Nygren, *Agape and Eros*, pp. 75-81.
66. Ibid., pp. 175-181. See p. 210 for a convenient chart with the main points of contrast between the two motifs.
67. Ibid., pp. 211-212.
68. Augustus H. Strong, *Systematic Theology*, p. 264.
69. Emil Brunner, *The Christian Doctrine of God*, p. 186.

there was nothing desirable in the sense that it met a need or lack in him." God's love *gives*. It "goes out to a worthless object, giving it value."[70] Erickson describes God's love as "an unselfish interest in us for our sake." God "is concerned with our good for our own sake, not for what he can get out of us. God does not need us. . . . Thus, his love for us and for his other creatures is completely disinterested."[71] Leon Morris sums it up thus:[72]

> . . . *Erōs* has two principal characteristics: it is a love of the worthy and it is a love that desires to possess. *Agapē* is in contrast at both points: it is not a love of the worthy, and it is not a love that desires to possess. On the contrary, it is a love given quite irrespective of merit, and it is a love that seeks to give.

A False Choice

What shall we say about this? First of all, we acknowledge that the general thrust of the distinction is quite appropriate, and that many of the details are acceptable and quite commendable. *Agapē* certainly is a creative love, and it surely does take the initiative in the God-man relationship. Nygren's analysis of the upward and downward motifs is a beautiful contribution to Christian thought. Also, it is quite true that God does not love in order to fulfill a *need* in himself. He has no needs, and he does not need us. This must be emphasized, over against the *erōs* concept.

I believe, however, that the contrast between *agapē* and *erōs* has been carried too far, and that something of the love of God has been lost in the process. In a sense, a false choice between the two types of love has been created. Why, for example, is it not possible for God to love us for our sakes *and* for his own sake? Or why cannot God's love be truly rooted in his own divine nature, and at the same time be drawn to something within us? These are the two issues I will address specifically, and I will insist that it is unnecessary, even unbiblical, to set up an either-or choice on both issues. There is no compromise of the essential nature of *agapē* when we recognize that there *is* something in

---

70. Adrio König, *Here Am I! A Christian Reflection on God* (Grand Rapids: Eerdmans, 1982), p. 37.

71. Millard J. Erickson, *Christian Theology*, pp. 292-293.

72. Leon Morris, *Testaments of Love*, p. 128.

human beings that is worthy of God's love, and when we see that God does desire to possess us for his own sake.

God's Love Finds Value in Us

First, it is said that God's *agapē* is not at all attracted by anything out-side himself, that it is uninfluenced by the worthiness of its object (or lack thereof), that it is disinterested and indifferent. I question this whole idea. If this is true, why does God not love stones and flies in the same way that he loves men? Morris himself has pointed out that there is nothing in the word *agapē* itself that excludes value in its object. Indeed, this is the very love the Father has for the Son, and the Son has for the Father.[73] Also, it is the kind of love we are to have for God (Matt. 22:37) and for Christ (John 14:15). Once we begin to direct our *agapē* toward God, a lot of the Nygrenian contrast goes out the window. But what about God's love for us? Is there anything within us that attracts God's love to us? Here is where an important distinction must be made. On the one hand, we must see ourselves as the creatures God made in his own image, made "a little lower than God," crowned with glory and majesty, made to rule over other created things (Ps. 8:3-8). On the other hand, we must see ourselves as we have been corrupted by our own sin and rebellion, as we have sullied the image, made ourselves slaves to other created things, and lost our crowns in the miry clay of sin. Thus in the total present makeup of every sinful creature, there are both what God has contributed and what the sinner has contributed. Nygren and others are correct to stress that there is nothing worthy of God's love in us from the latter perspective. I.e., when we consider what we have made (or unmade) of ourselves, there is nothing of value that God should be attracted to us. But from the former perspective, from the point of view of what God has placed within us from the very beginning (Gen. 1:27), there is value—indeed, tremendous value—in every single human being. This value has not been forfeited or com-promised by sin. It is there, like a jewel in a garbage pail. And why should God not recognize the value he has placed within his own creatures and love them for what he himself has made them to be? This in no way compromises the remarkable nature of the fact that he *still*

---

73. Ibid., pp. 137-138.

loves us *in spite of* what we have done to ourselves by our own sin. Another way of saying this is that he loves us not for what we have done (our works) but for what we are (his works).

Thus I believe it is a false choice to say, as Morris does, that God "loves not because of what we are, but because of what he is," or that *agapē* "is not a love drawn from God by attractiveness in men; it is the expression of his own innermost nature."[74] Though the latter is certainly dominant, the former cannot be totally dismissed. It is simply not true to say that "*nothing* in men can account for God's love."[75] There is nothing in man that can wholly account for it or even mostly account for it, but the fact that man is God's own image-bearing creature counts for *something*. God cannot be indifferent toward or disinterested in such works of his own hands.

Louis Berkhof recognizes this point but does not elaborate on it when he says that God does not "withdraw His love completely from the sinner in his present sinful state, though the latter's sin is an abomination to Him, since He recognizes even in the sinner His image-bearer."[76] Erickson has stated this idea in more detail and approaches the view that I have given above. He says, "God loves us on the basis of that likeness of himself which he has placed within us, or in which he has created us." But he then dilutes the whole idea by saying this means simply that "he loves himself in us."[77] It also seems to be inconsistent with his characterization of God's love as "completely disinterested."[78]

God Loves Us for His Own Sake

This leads to the second false choice in the *agapē-erōs* contrast, i.e., the idea that God loves us for our sakes alone and not at all for his own sake. Another way of stating this is that God loves us for what he can give us and not for what he can get from us. Now, this is true if we are thinking only in terms of a possible *need* or *lack* within God which can be filled only by means of his loving us. But I think we must distinguish between what God needs, and what he *wants* or *desires* from a relation-

---

74. Ibid., pp. 142-143.
75. Ibid., p. 271. Emphasis supplied.
76. Louis Berkhof, *Systematic Theology*, p. 71.
77. Millard J. Erickson, *Christian Theology*, I:294.
78. Ibid., p. 293.

ship with his image-bearers. It is a fundamental fact that everything God does, he does for his own glory, beginning with the initial creation itself.[79] Thus the constantly underlying goal even of his love, and even in its supreme manifestation in the redemptive work of Christ, is his own glory. This is seen quite clearly in the grand summary of redemption in Philippians 2:5-11, where the entire saving history of Jesus Christ is said to climax in "the glory of God the Father." This is in no way unworthy of God, nor does it diminish the genuineness of his self-giving for our sakes.

But this is not the whole point to be made here. It is my opinion that in his fellowship with his creatures, God desires more than his own transcendent glory, namely, he desires the *fellowship itself*. He finds delight and even joy in such fellowship. Otherwise why did he even create beings in his own image who are capable of such a relationship? All this is seen, I believe, in the fact that love includes the aspect of affection, as noted above. In a sense what we are saying is that God not only loves us, but he also *likes* us, and likes being in fellowship with us. Jesus says that when a single sinner repents, "there is joy in the presence of the angels of God" (Luke 15:10). *In the presence of* the angels? Is this not, then, God's own joy? In the three parables in this chapter, the three figures representing God all rejoice when the lost is found. The extravagant reaction of the prodigal's father can hardly be called "disinterested." Packer has made the interesting comment that once God has freely decided to make image-bearers with which to fellowship, "he has in effect resolved that henceforth for all eternity His happiness shall be conditional upon ours."[80]

For these reasons I do not find it at all objectionable to say that God's love is a love that desires to possess us for his own sake, for the joy of the fellowship for which he created us in the first place. It is simply false to think that this somehow dilutes his infinite concern for our welfare for our own sakes, or that he has no selfless motives for his self-giving. Clarke's methodology is faulty in that he begins with human love and draws his conclusions about God's love on that basis, but his conclusions are not too far from the Bible's own representation of the love

---

79. See Jack Cottrell, *What the Bible Says About God the Creator*, pp. 124-128.
80. J. I. Packer, *Knowing God* (Downers Grove: InterVarsity, 1973), p. 113. For one thing, I find it interesting that a Calvinist would make a statement like this!

of God. He says, "God, then, is moved by the well-known desire to impart himself and all good to other beings, and to possess them as his own in spiritual fellowship. This is his love."[81] Wiley agrees with Clarke that divine love includes the desire to possess the object loved, alongside the desire for self-giving.[82]

As important as it is to distinguish between the *erōs* and the *agapē* motifs, we must not press the contrast so completely that we lose sight of these important aspects of Biblical love and of God's love in particular.

Conclusion

This concludes the discussion of the love of God as such. What remains is to see how this love takes certain specific forms as it encounters human beings as sinners. Specifically, we shall now discuss God's love in its forms of mercy, patience, and grace.

LOVE AS MERCY

We have seen how God's goodness and love encompass all human beings simply as his creatures. But we do not exist any longer simply as creatures. We are sinners. His goodness and love continue, to be sure; but because of sin and its consequences, his love takes on certain specialized forms. The first of these is *mercy*. God is "rich in mercy, because of His great love with which He loved us" (Eph. 2:4). It might be possible to think of mercy apart from sin (cf. Ps. 145:9), but its essence is really understood only in this light.

The key point is that sin has produced suffering and misery for mankind in general and for individuals in specific ways. Mercy is the love of God as it is directed toward man in his pain, suffering, need, misery and distress as caused by sin. It is a sympathetic concern and a deep compassion, leading to a desire to relieve the distress. Thus Louis Berkhof defines it as "the goodness or love of God shown to those who are in misery or distress, irrespective of their deserts."[83] Barth says,

---

81. W. N. Clarke, *The Christian Doctrine of God*, p. 85. See his whole thought-provoking discussion of this, pp. 84-86.

82. H. Orton Wiley, *Christian Theology*, I:379-380. See also A. W. Tozer, *The Knowledge of the Holy*, p. 107: "Self-sufficient as He is, He wants our love and will not be satisfied till He gets it."

83. Louis Berkhof, *Systematic Theology*, p. 72.

"The mercy of God lies in His readiness to share in sympathy the distress of another, a readiness which springs from His inmost nature and stamps all His being and doing." It refers to God's "compassion at the sight of the suffering which man brings upon himself, His concern to remove it, His will to console man in this pain and to help him to overcome it."[84] It is demonstrated in Christ's feelings toward the multitudes: "And seeing the multitudes, He felt compassion for them, because they were distressed and downcast like sheep without a shepherd" (Matt. 9:36; cf. 14:14).

The fact that man has brought this suffering upon himself through his sin is in the final analysis irrelevant as far as mercy and compassion are concerned. This is what Berkhof means by "irrespective of their deserts." Sometimes a person brings his misery upon himself through his own irresponsible and sinful living, but more often than not it is the cumulative result of other people's sins. Much of it can be traced to the first sin in Eden and the consequent cursing of nature (Gen. 3:16-19). But regardless of its cause, God is moved with compassion when he sees his creatures suffering.[85]

The Terminology of Mercy

Brief attention may be given to the various Biblical terms related to the concept of mercy. There is but one relevant Old Testament word, *rācham* and its cognates. It means "to yearn, to have compassion, to have mercy, to pity." Its noun form in the singular means "womb," and in the plural means "tender mercy, compassion." Morris says, "When this term is used, the meaning 'love' is never far from the surface, though characteristically it is love for those in distress or in need."[86]

The New Testament has several comparable words, chief among which is *eleos* (the noun and its cognates). It is generally equivalent to the Old Testament concept of compassion, mercy and pity. Its verb form "marks that breaking in of the divine mercy into the reality of

---

84. Karl Barth, *Church Dogmatics*, II/1, pp. 369, 371-372.

85. This is what makes mercy different from grace. Mercy is blind to the question of what is or is not deserved; grace is specifically aware of the fact that sinners deserve wrath but is willing to give them the very opposite of what they deserve.

86. Leon Morris, *Testaments of Love*, p. 86.

human misery."[87] It is also used in connection with God's selecting someone for a particular role or office in his service, e.g., Paul (I Cor. 7:25; II Cor. 4:1) and Israel (Rom. 9:15, 18).[88] Another word used less frequently is *oiktirmos*; cf. Romans 12:1, "the mercies of God." Another is *splangchna*, which literally refers to the entrails ("bowels" in the KJV; cf. Phil. 2:1) and figuratively means pity, mercy or compassion. It is the term used most frequently in the gospels to refer to Christ's compassion, and it is the word translated "tender" in the reference to "the tender mercy of our God" in Luke 1:78.

God Is Merciful

Since mercy is a form of love, and love is the very nature of God, we must also say that mercy is the very nature of God. I.e., the nature of God shows itself as merciful in the face of human misery and distress. God does not *choose* to be merciful; he *is* merciful. Other considerations may affect whether or not he chooses to give concrete expression to his mercy, but he always *wants* to show mercy because he is merciful. "Forever His mercy stands, a boundless, overwhelming immensity of divine pity and compassion."[89] He is ready to hear those who will call upon him in their distress: "The eyes of the Lord are toward the righteous, and His ears are open to their cry" (Ps. 34:15). He is ready to relieve this distress: "The eternal God is a dwelling place, and underneath are the everlasting arms" (Deut. 33:27). He is ready even to share in their misery, as witnessed by the incarnation.

In God's revelation of his basic nature to Moses in Exodus 34:6, he describes himself as "compassionate and gracious, slow to anger, and abounding in lovingkindness and truth." Of all these marvelous attributes, the first to be mentioned is compassion. This same formula is repeated numerous times in the Old Testament; cf. Nehemiah 9:17; Psalms 86:15; 103:8; 145:8; Joel 2:13; Jonah 4:2. Moses assures the people, "For the Lord your God is a compassionate God; He will not fail you nor destroy you" (Deut. 4:31). "His mercies are great," says

---

87. Hans-Helmut Esser, "Mercy, Compassion," *The New International Dictionary of New Testament Theology*, ed. Colin Brown (Grand Rapids: Zondervan, 1976), II:595.

88. See Jack Cottrell, *What the Bible Says About God the Ruler*, pp. 205-206.

89. A. W. Tozer, *The Knowledge of the Holy*, p. 97.

David (II Sam. 24:14; cf. Ps. 119:156). "His compassions never fail. They are new every morning" (Lam. 3:22-23). "Yes, our God is compassionate" (Ps. 116:5). Romans 12:1 speaks of "the mercies of God"; he is called "the Father of mercies and God of all comfort" (II Cor. 1:3). The tenderness of Jesus is beautifully described thus: "A battered reed He will not break off, and a smoldering wick He will not put out" (Matt. 12:20).

The Objects of God's Mercy

We may understand the richness of divine mercy better through a survey of those to whom it is directed in Scripture. First, it is directed toward numerous *individuals* who suffer from various kinds of pain and distress. David often found himself threatened by his enemies and cried out for God's compassion: "According to the greatness of Thy compassion, turn to me, and do not hide Thy face from Thy servant, for I am in distress" (Ps. 69:16-17; cf. 40:11). Daniel prayed for God to have compassion and intervene to save him from death (Dan. 2:18). Sick and afflicted people came to Jesus with the plea, "Have mercy on us" (Matt. 9:27; 15:22; 17:15; 20:31; Luke 17:13). And he responded in mercy: "He saw a great multitude, and felt compassion for them, and healed their sick" (Matt. 14:14). When two blind men asked for mercy, he was "moved with compassion" and healed them (Matt. 20:34). "Moved with compassion," he also healed a leper (Mark 1:41). "God had mercy on" Epaphroditus and made him well (Phil. 2:27). Compassion likewise moved Jesus to give deliverance to demoniacs (Mark 5:19), to comfort the bereaved (Luke 7:13; John 11:35), and feed the hungry (Matt. 15:32). "He will have compassion on the poor and needy" (Ps. 72:13); in him "the orphan finds mercy" (Hosea 14:3).

A major object of God's mercy in Scripture is the nation of Israel. "Thou wilt arise and have compassion on Zion," the Psalmist confidently exults (Ps. 102:13). The Lord heard their cries while they were in Egyptian bondage: "I have surely seen the affliction of My people who are in Egypt, and have given heed to their cry because of their taskmasters, for I am aware of their sufferings" (Ex. 3:7). After he delivered them, even as they complained and rebelled in the wilderness, his compassion did not fail: "Thou, in Thy great compassion, didst not forsake them in the wilderness" (Neh. 9:19; cf. v. 17). During numerous oppressions by various enemies as they occupied their promised land, God continued to have mercy on them. He gave them judges to deliver them, "for the Lord was moved to pity by their groaning because of those who oppressed and afflicted them" (Judg. 2:18). See II Kings 13:23; Nehemiah 9:27-28; Psalm 106:44-46.

The most numerous expressions of mercy on Israel are related to the Babylonian captivity. Over and over God promises the people, even before they enter their exile, that he will have compassion on them and deliver them. "For the Lord will vindicate His people, and will have compassion on His servants; when He sees that their strength is gone" (Deut. 32:36). "Shout for joy, O heavens! And rejoice, O earth! . . . For the Lord has comforted His people, and will have compassion on His afflicted" (Isa. 49:13). "Now I shall restore the fortunes of Jacob, and have mercy on the whole house of Israel" (Ezek. 39:25). "For a brief moment I forsook you, but with great compassion I will gather you" (Isa. 54:7). Daniel's plea for his nation's deliverance is based solely on God's "great compassion" (Dan. 9:18). See Isaiah 14:1; Jeremiah 12:15; 30:18; 31:20; 33:26; Hosea 1:7; Zechariah 1:12; 10:6. This grateful acknowledgement followed their restoration: "In Thy great compassion Thou didst not make an end of them or forsake them, for Thou art a gracious and compassionate God" (Neh. 9:31).

We cannot overlook the fact that several passages show that the outpouring of mercy is conditioned on the people's returning to a repentant state of mind. Moses told the people in advance that the nation would be exiled, but it would be restored when "you return to the Lord your God and obey Him with all your heart and soul according to all that I command you today" (Deut. 30:1-3; cf. 4:30-31). "The Lord has compassion on those who fear Him" (Ps. 103:13; cf. Luke 1:50). "For the Lord your God is gracious and compassionate, and will not turn His face away from you if you return to Him" (II Chron. 30:9). Jonah knew that God is "a gracious and compassionate God, slow to anger and abundant in lovingkindness, and one who relents concerning calamity" (Jonah 4:2); but he also knew that Nineveh would have to repent before this gracious compassion would actually be bestowed on them. That is why he tried to avoid warning them; it is also why God went to so much trouble to get him to fulfill his commission. Even though his heart is compassionate, he requires repentance before his mercy is applied.

This leads to the final category of the objects of God's mercy, namely, sinners as such. When God looks upon us, he sees us as sinners whose principal need is grace and forgiveness and salvation. This is why so many of the passages that speak of God's compassion also speak of his grace and his forgiveness. Eleven times the expressions "gracious and compassionate" or "compassionate and gracious" appear in the Old Testament.[90] Glueck characterizes God's mercy as "forgiving love."[91] "To the Lord our God belong compassion and forgiveness," says Daniel 9:9. "Let the wicked forsake his way, and the unrighteous man his thoughts; and let him return to the Lord, and He will have compassion on him; and to our God, for He will abundantly pardon" (Isa. 55:7). David's great prayer of repentance begins, "Be gracious to me, O God, according to Thy lovingkindness; according to the greatness of Thy compassion blot out my transgressions" (Ps. 51:1). And "He, being compassionate, forgave" (Ps. 78:38). "In wrath remember mercy," is Habakkuk's humble and confident plea (Hab. 3:2). God's reply is seen in Isaiah 54:8, "In an outburst of anger I hid My face from you for a moment; but with everlasting lovingkindness I will have compassion on you."

In the Old Testament most of the acts of compassion and even forgiveness are related to temporal blessings, but in the New Testament we find the same connection between mercy and forgiveness in relation to eternal salvation. "Because of the tender mercy of our God," he has given "the Sunrise from on high . . . to shine upon those who sit in darkness and the shadow of death," and "to give to His people the knowledge of salvation by the forgiveness of their sins" (Luke 1:77-79). In the midst of his enormous sin, Saul of Tarsus "was shown mercy" (I Tim. 1:13). God has saved us not by our works "but according to His mercy" (Titus 3:5). "According to His great mercy" he "caused us to be born again to a living hope" (I Peter 1:3). "Mercy triumphs over judgment" for those who are in Christ (James 2:13).[92]

---

90. Ex. 34:6; II Chron. 30:9; Neh. 9:17, 31; Pss. 86:15; 103:8; 111:4; 112:4; 145:8; Joel 2:13; Jonah 4:2. Sometimes the term *merciful* is used instead of *compassionate*, but the Hebrew word is the same.

91. Nelson Glueck, *Hesed in the Bible*, p. 84.

92. This is quoted out of context, but it is nevertheless a true and beautiful way of relating God's mercy to our salvation, as is well illustrated in the parable of the unmerciful servant (Matt. 18:23-35).

LOVE AS PATIENCE

Another specialized form which love takes in the face of sin is *patience* or *longsuffering*. The Old Testament expression for this means literally "long of nose (*'ap*)." We will remember that *'ap*, whose basic meaning is "nose, nostrils," is one of the Hebrew words for wrath. Thus the expression means "long of wrath," or "slow to wrath." One of the main Greek words, *makrothumia*, is similar in meaning. In adjectival form it means "long of passion, longsuffering, patient." Another Greek term is *anochē*, which means "endurance, forbearance, restraint."

Like mercy, patience is of the very inmost nature of God. The expression "slow to anger" is used about ten times for God in the Old Testament, most of them in repetitions of the formula given by God to Moses in Exodus 34:6, "The Lord, the Lord God, compassionate and gracious, slow to anger, and abounding in lovingkindness and truth." "The Lord is slow to anger and great in power," says Nahum 1:3.

The Essence of Patience

In considering the patience of God we are brought face to face with the apparent tension within God between his love and his wrath. This is so because the main element in divine patience is *delay and restraint in the execution of wrath*. God's wrath is real and deserved, but out of his great love ("Love is patient," I Cor. 13:4) he withholds it for a time or reduces its intensity or even sets it aside altogether.[93] "For the sake of My name I delay My wrath, and for My praise I restrain it for you, in order not to cut you off," says God of his chosen people (Isa. 48:9). Wiley thus gives this definition: "Forbearance is love in the deferring or abating of punishment."[94] Louis Berkhof says it is "that aspect of the goodness or love of God in virtue of which He bears with the froward and evil in spite of their long continued disobedience. . . . It reveals itself in the postponement of the merited judgment."[95] It means that "He does not give free rein to His anger but restrains Himself and waits."[96] If

---

93. This can be done only because of the cross, as will be seen later.
94. H. Orton Wiley, *Christian Theology*, I:391.
95. Louis Berkhof, *Systematic Theology*, pp. 72-73.
96. Johannes Fichtner, "ὀργή, etc." (part), *Theological Dictionary of the New Testament*, ed. Gerhard Friedrich, tr. Geoffrey W. Bromiley (Grand Rapids: Eerdmans, 1967), p. 405.

God determined to give us what we deserve as soon as we deserve it, we would all have perished long ago. It is his loving patience that puts the punishment "on hold" until it is either set aside (with regard to the one who deserves it) or ultimately applied.

This element of divine patience is seen in the contexts of many Old Testament occurrences of the expression "slow to anger." For example, in Numbers 14:18 Moses is praying for God to forgive his rebellious people: "The Lord is slow to anger and abundant in lovingkindness, forgiving iniquity and transgression." When this incident is recalled in Nehemiah 9:17, the same language is used. Jeremiah makes this plea to God in the face of his impending judgment on Israel: "You understand, O Lord; remember me and care for me. Avenge me on my persecutors. You are long-suffering – do not take me away; think of how I suffer reproach for your sake" (Jer. 15:15, NIV). In Joel 2:13 it is the basis of the prophet's plea for the people to repent. Jonah knew that it could result in forgiveness for Nineveh (Jonah 4:2).

In the New Testament, Paul explains how God "endured with much patience" the idolatrous nation of Israel, though they really deserved his wrath, just so salvation for all nations could be brought about through them (Rom. 9:22-23). He used himself as a good example of God's patience (I Tim. 1:16). The parable of the unmerciful servant illustrates the nature of patience as delay of wrath. Each debtor asked for patience (Matt. 18:26, 29), or postponement of the time when the debt must be paid. In reference to our debt of eternal punishment, postponement is no solution; so the lord in the parable (representing God) had compassion on the first servant and forgave the debt altogether.

This is exactly what God has done for us in the redemption that is in Christ Jesus. He does not simply postpone the time of payment, but remits the debt completely. He was already doing this in Old Testament times. While many temporal punishments were carried out, many others—even of this temporal kind—were abated or rescinded completely. And certainly, the eternal punishment for all Oid Testament saints was set aside. Now surely (someone will say), this shows that the love of God is stronger and deeper and more fundamental in his nature than his holiness and wrath! The wrath was deserved, but he delayed it, and even cancelled it at times! Where, then, is the vaunted holiness of God, and the punitive wrath that is supposed to be of his very essence? Have they not withered away under the blazing radiance of the love of God?

But wait. Here is where we come to the most significant New Testament passage on the patience of God, one that relates specifically to God's lenience with Israel of old, and one that shows us that patience is truly the *delay* of divine wrath and never the complete cancellation of it. In Romans 3:25 Paul says that God, because of his very patience or forbearance, "passed over the sins previously committed" until a very specific time. He did not cancel his wrath, but rather delayed the outpouring of it *until that time*. And when was that time? It was the day when he set Jesus forth "as a propitiation in His blood through faith."

This is the *reason* why God in his patience could delay his wrath or even cancel it for Israel or David or Nineveh. He was not ignoring it or just letting it evaporate; he was looking ahead to the time when this wrath would be poured out on Jesus Christ in his atoning death, the time when Jesus would suffer this wrath in our place. *This is the basis of the patience of God*, whether it be patience with Old Testament sinners or New Testament sinners. God can delay the execution of his wrath, and even rescind it altogether for the individual as in the parable of the unmerciful servant, because that wrath has been borne by Christ on the cross. But (someone will say) is not the *love* of God the basis of his patience? Why cannot the *love* of God in and of itself just sovereignly say, "I will not execute My fierce anger" (Hosea 11:9). But this is the very point. It *is* love that permits the patient delay of punishment, because it is God's love that sent his son to be the propitiation for sin (1 John 4:10). When God said to Israel, "I will not execute My fierce anger," it was his infinite love that caused him to say in his heart, "I will not execute it *on you*, because I will execute it *on myself* when I, the Logos, become Jesus of Nazareth and die on Calvary." This is the essence of God's patience, whether it be with Israel of old or with John D. Christian in the twentieth century.

The Purpose of Patience

What is the purpose for God's patience? Why does he delay the execution of his wrath? The main reason is to provide the guilty party time to repent and be forgiven and avoid the wrath altogether. As Fichtner says, God's longsuffering gives "space for repentance and conversion," whether it be Israel or Nineveh or anyone else.[97] Barth says, "Patience

---

97. Ibid.

exists where space and time are given with a definite intention, where freedom is allowed in expectation of a response. God acts in this way. He makes this purposeful concession of space and time."[98]

That it is God's nature to want to give this time is clear from the teaching of the Bible. "The patience of God kept waiting in the days of Noah," though none responded to Noah's preaching (1 Peter 3:20). The people of Israel generally ignored God's attempts to lead them to repentance: "However, Thou didst bear with them for many years, and admonished them by Thy Spirit through Thy prophets, yet they would not give ear" (Neh. 9:30). This stubbornness persisted into apostolic times. In Romans 2:4-5 Paul reminds the Jews specifically that God in his kindness, forbearance and patience has been trying to lead them to repentance; but by refusing to repent "you are storing up wrath for yourself in the day of wrath and revelation of the righteous judgment of God." God's patience, i.e., the delay of his wrath, is of no benefit to the individual unless the opportunity to repent is acted upon.

The apostle Peter sums up this point in II Peter 3:9, "The Lord is not slow about His promise, as some count slowness, but is patient toward you, not wishing for any to perish but for all to come to repentance." Thus we must "regard the patience of our Lord to be salvation" (II Peter 3:15). The lesson of God's patience, then, is this: "Seek the Lord while He may be found; call upon Him while He is near" (Isa. 55:6).

God is patient; he does delay the execution of his wrath in order to give time for repentance. But the somber note is this: he will not delay it forever. There comes a time when his patience runs out, and the opportunity for repentance is withdrawn. "If a man does not repent, He [God] will sharpen His sword; He has bent His bow and made it ready. He has also prepared for Himself deadly weapons; He makes His arrows fiery shafts" (Ps. 7:12-13). The time came when God gave up on Israel, the northern kingdom. He said through Hosea that this people might just as well be called "Lō-ruchāmāh" ("no mercy"), "for I will no longer have compassion on the house of Israel, that I should ever forgive them" (Hosea 1:6). The southern kingdom, Judah, would be forgiven (Hosea 1:7), but as for the other, "I will have no compassion on her children, because they are children of harlotry" (Hosea 2:4). Even Judah could

---

98. Karl Barth, *Church Dogmatics*, II/1, p. 408.

not escape destruction and temporary captivity, for God's patience ran out with her also: "So the Lord was no longer able to endure it, because of the evil of your deeds, because of the abominations which you have committed; thus your land has become a ruin, an object of horror and a curse, without an inhabitant" (Jer. 44:22). God told Jeremiah not even to pray for them; their doom was sure (Jer. 14:11-12). Not even Moses or Samuel could cause him to relent (Jer. 15:1). There is no use to mourn, "'for I have withdrawn My peace from this people,' declares the Lord, 'My lovingkindness and compassion'" (Jer. 16:5).

The time of the second coming of Christ will mark the end of God's patience forever. The time allotted for repentance will be over. The final outpouring of God's wrath will no longer be delayed. Cries like that of the rich man in Hades – "Have mercy on me!" (Luke 16:24) – will be too late.

LOVE AS GRACE

When we say grace, we are also saying goodness and love. Where we find grace, usually we find mercy and patience also. But when we say grace, we have carried goodness and love beyond mercy and even beyond patience. For grace is the absolute extremity of love. Grace in its full New Testament sense, i.e., in its soteriological sense, is *God's willingness and desire to accept us in spite of our sin.* To understand this, and to get the full impact of it, we must remember what sin means to the holy God—how it goes against everything that he is, how it violates his good and righteous will, how he hates it with a holy hatred, and how it is his very nature to consume it in wrath. Yet despite all of this, in his infinite love he is still willing to receive rebellious sinners back unto himself. He is not just *willing* to receive them, but lovingly *desires* to receive them. This is grace.

The Terminology of Grace

Since grace is a specific form of love, we must remember all that has already been said about love itself as the basic content of grace. But to go beyond this and find the unique essence of grace, we must look first of all at the Biblical terms that are closest to this concept.

Old Testament Terms

In the Old Testament the main terms for grace come from the same stem. They are *chēn*, the noun meaning "grace"; *chānan*, the verb "to be gracious"; and *channūn*, the adjective "gracious." Unfortunately these terms are not especially useful for helping us to see the precise meaning of grace as taught in the New Testament. Sometimes they mean no more than an attitude of general benevolence.[99]

The noun *chēn* is least helpful. Sometimes it can be translated "grace," but its most common connotation is "favor," usually in the sense of someone's "finding favor" in another person's eyes. It suggests that the former is worthy of the approval of the latter. There are many examples of this on the human level alone. For instance, Jacob sought to "find favor in the sight of" Esau (Gen. 33:8, 10). David "found favor in" Saul's sight (I Sam. 16:22). "Esther found favor in the eyes of all who saw her" (Est. 2:15). More important is the way the term is used of God's approval of certain human beings. For example, "Noah found favor in the eyes of the Lord" (Gen. 6:8). God told Moses, "You have found favor in My sight" (Ex. 33:17). This expression was often used when one person "asked a favor" of another, or when individuals prayed to God: "If I have found favor in your sight," then grant my request. This is how Moses approached God with the request to see his glory (Ex. 33:13). This is how Gideon prefaced his request to the Angel of Yahweh (Judg. 6:17). This suggests a connotation of worthiness, i.e., "If you deem me worthy," then grant my request. Such a use of the basic term for grace causes discomfort for some, because it seems to suggest the very opposite of the New Testament understanding of grace, i.e., favor shown to the *unworthy*. But it simply means that this word is not very helpful in establishing the doctrine of grace. Only a couple of times does it refer to something God gives to us: "The Lord gives grace and glory" (Ps. 84:11); "He gives grace to the afflicted" (Prov. 3:34).

The verb *chānan* is somewhat closer to the fully-revealed concept of grace, but it is still fairly general. It means "to be favorable or act favorably toward, to bless, to come to one's aid." Zimmerli says it "denotes the kind turning of one person to another as expressed in an act of assistance."[100] It does not necessarily include the idea of the wor-

---

99. For data on the numerical occurrence of each term and their general meanings, see Leon Morris, *Testaments of Love*, pp. 95-97.

100. Walther Zimmerli, "χάρις, etc." (part), *Theological Dictionary of the New Testa-*

thiness of the one assisted; it implies only a favorable attitude or disposition and a decision to help or bless. For example, Jacob urged Esau to accept a large gift from him "because God has dealt graciously [*chānan*] with me" (Gen. 33:11). When Joseph said to Benjamin, "May God be gracious to you, my son" (Gen 43:29), he was simply invoking God's blessings on him. When Israel was being oppressed by the king of Aram, "the Lord was gracious to them and had compassion on them" and came to their aid (II Kings 13:23). A prayer for such aid is Psalm 102:13, "Thou wilt arise and have compassion on Zion; for it is time to be gracious to her." At the same time, the Psalmist asks God *not* to be gracious to his enemies: "And Thou, O Lord God of hosts, the God of Israel, awake to punish all the nations; do not be gracious to any who are treacherous in iniquity" (Ps. 59:5). Isaiah 26:10 notes, "Though the wicked is shown favor [*chānan*], he does not learn righteousness . . . and does not perceive the majesty of the Lord." It is obvious that "being gracious" in such contexts as these refers to temporal blessing and not spiritual salvation.

Thus in the Old Testament when a man of God prayed "Be gracious unto me," he was simply asking God to hear and answer the prayer that was about to follow. He was saying, in effect, "God, I pray that you think well enough of me to answer this prayer"; and then he stated the content of his prayer. David said concerning his prayers about his and Bathsheba's child, "Who knows, the Lord may be gracious to me, that the child may live" (II Sam. 12:22). This way of introducing a prayer occurs about twenty times in the Psalms, e.g., "Be gracious to me and hear my prayer" (Ps. 4:1). The contents of the prayers differ, including pleas for healing, deliverance from afflictions and distress, redemption, forgiveness, rescue from enemies, protection, and other such forms of assistance.[101] The essence of this kind of prayer is Psalm 67:1, "God be gracious to us and bless us." See Isaiah 33:2, "O Lord, be gracious to us; we have waited for Thee." Isaiah tells the people that God is waiting to hear their prayers and answer them: "Therefore the Lord longs to be gracious to you . . . . He will surely be gracious to you at the sound of

---

ment, ed. Gerhard Friedrich, tr. Geoffrey W. Bromiley (Grand Rapids: Eerdmans, 1974), IX:377.

101. See Pss. 6:2; 9:13; 25:16; 26:11; 27:7; 30:10; 31:9; 41:4, 10; 51:1; 56:1; 57:1; 86:3, 16; 119:29, 58, 132; 123:3.

your cry; when He hears it, He will answer you" (Isa. 30:18-19).

Thus the basic connotation of *chānan* seems to be God's favorable attitude that moves him to bless and to answer prayer. This helps us to understand certain familiar passages and not to read into them more than is warranted by this term. For example, when the Psalmist asks, "Has God forgotten to be gracious? Or has He in anger withdrawn His compassion?" (Ps. 77:9), he is probably complaining about God's non-intervention in Israel's physical afflictions rather than reflecting on the theological tension between wrath and grace. The great Aaronic blessing in Numbers 6:24-26 says, "The Lord bless you and keep you; the Lord make His face shine on you, and be gracious to you; the Lord lift up His countenance on you, and give you peace." To Christian ears, "The Lord be gracious to you" is parallel to "The Lord forgive your sins though you don't deserve it." But to Aaron it probably meant "The Lord be favorable to you and bless you." Finally, when Moses prayed to see God's glory (Ex. 33:18), God replied, "I Myself will make all My goodness pass before you, and will proclaim the name of the Lord before you; and I will be gracious to whom I will be gracious, and will show compassion on whom I will show compassion" (Ex. 33:19). Much heavy theological ore has been mined from this verse, including the doctrine of unconditional election. But a proper understanding of the word *chānan* shows that God is not speaking of soteriological grace here, but of his sovereignty in deciding whom he will bless and whom he will not bless. Moses had been putting strong pressure on God to grant his request (Ex. 33:12-18). God replies, in effect, "All right, I will do what you ask, though it is highly unusual. And I want you to know that I am not doing this just because you have won an argument with me or have backed me into a corner. I am granting your request because I want to. I still decide what prayers I will answer and whom I will bless." In Romans 9:15 Paul quotes Exodus 33:19 to prove that God has a sovereign right to choose whomever he desires to fill certain roles in the historical accomplishment of redemption. He also has the right to reject whomever he desires. His point is that just as God had a right to bless Israel by choosing her for the unmatched privilege of producing the Messiah, so he has a right to revoke her privileged status now that her task has been completed. Neither in Exodus nor in Romans is personal salvation in view.

The point is that we must be careful not to read the fullness of the

New Testament connotation of grace back into these Old Testament terms, especially the noun and the verb. It is thought, however, that the adjective *channūn* for some reason is closer to the New Testament concept. The main reason for thinking this is that this adjective occurs in the great archetypal description of God's nature in Exodus 34:6, "The Lord, the Lord God, compassionate and gracious [*channūn*], slow to anger, and abounding in lovingkindness and truth." The word occurs about a dozen more times, most of them in the almost ritual repetition of Exodus 34:6 and all but one in combination with other terms representing God's loving and gracious nature.[102] It is likely that the word in itself has no stronger meaning than its noun and verb forms, but it only seems so because of the cumulative effect of all the terms together (in Exodus 34:6 and elsewhere).

The important thing to remember is that doctrines are not based merely on the meaning of words as such. The fact that these Old Testament terms do not contain the full content of grace is not a problem of any kind. Also, it does not mean that the doctrine of grace is absent from the Old Testament. Its essence is there, as we will see shortly.

New Testament Terms

The New Testament terminology is more significant and does help us to understand the meaning of God's saving grace. The basic word is the noun *charis*, which is often translated "grace." But even this word has a number of non-soteriological shades of meaning that must be noted. The most basic connotation of the word seems to be something like "a gift that makes glad." In its non-biblical use, according to Esser, this term with its cognates referred to "things which produce well-being"; and thus the noun came to have such meanings as grace, favor, beauty, thankfulness, gratitude, delight, and kindness.[103] As Conzelmann says, *charis* is what delights; it is "an act that causes pleasure." for Paul's own use of the term, "the linguistic starting-point is the sense of 'making glad by gifts,' of showing free unmerited

---

102. The one exception is Ex. 22:27. Its other occurrences are the same as in footnote 90 above, with the addition of Ps. 116:5.

103. Hans-Helmut Esser, "Grace, Spiritual Gifts," *The New International Dictionary of New Testament Theology.* ed. Colin Brown (Grand Rapids: Zondervan, 1976), II:115.

grace."[104]

This is the meaning of *charis* in which we are most interested, namely, the saving (soteriological) grace that includes especially the gift of the forgiveness of sins on the basis of the redemptive work of Jesus Christ. We will discuss this in more detail in the next section. Here we will call attention to the other connotations of the term as it is used in the New Testament. Sometimes it means "favor," in a sense similar to *chēn* in the Old Testament. For example, Stephen notes that Joseph was granted favor (*charis*) in the eyes of Pharaoh (Acts 7:10). Luke says of the boy Jesus that he "kept increasing in . . . favor with God and men" (Luke 2:52). See Luke 1:30; 2:40. At other times the word *charis* means simply "a gift." Paul refers to the Corinthians' offering for the poor as "your gift to Jerusalem" (I Cor. 16:3; cf. II Cor. 1:15; Eph. 4:29). Still another meaning is "thanks," or the gratitude given to someone for a gift received. Paul says, "But thanks [*charis*] be to God, who gives us the victory through our Lord Jesus Christ" (I Cor. 15:57). The word occurs numerous times in this sense.

Two other uses of *charis* are of special significance. First, it is used of the various spiritual gifts with which the Holy Spirit equips Christians or special offices to which he calls them. (In this sense it is similar to *charisma*, which will be mentioned below.) This is the connotation in I Peter 4:10, when Peter refers to "the manifold grace of God"; and in Romans 12:6, when Paul says "we have gifts that differ according to the grace given to us" (cf. Eph. 4:7). Paul uses the term regularly to refer to his own calling as an apostle (Rom. 1:5; 12:3; 15:15; I Cor. 3:10; 15:10; Gal. 1:15; 2:9; Eph. 3:7-8). The other significant use of *charis* is for divine aid in general. For example, II Corinthians 9:8 says, "God is able to make all grace abound to you, that always having all sufficiency in everything, you may have an abundance for every good deed." This seems to refer to material blessings. On the other hand, Christ's promise to Paul, "My grace is sufficient for you" (II Cor. 12:9), is definitely spiritual strength. Paul says to Timothy, "Be strong in the grace that is in Christ Jesus" (II Tim. 2:1). Hebrews 4:16 says that at the "throne of

---

104. Hans Conzelmann, "χάρις, etc." (part), *Theological Dictionary of the New Testament*, ed. Gerhard Friedrich, tr. Geoffrey W. Bromiley (Grand Rapids: Eerdmans, 1974), IX:373, 394.

grace" we may find "grace to help in time of need." See Hebrews 13:9;
Acts 13:43; 14:26; 15:40.

The point is that we must be aware of other meanings of the term
and not try to read the "unmerited favor" concept into each occurrence.

Other forms of this same Greek root must also be noted. The verb
form is *charizomai*, which means "to give, to grant, to forgive." Esser
notes that even in secular use it had such meanings as "to do something
pleasant for someone, to be kind, gracious, or obliging," and in certain
contexts "to grant, remit, forgive, or pardon."[105] In the New Testament
it means both "give" and "forgive." Another noun form is *charisma*,
which means "gift." It is used in this basic sense in Romans 6:23, "The
free gift of God is eternal life in Christ Jesus our Lord" (cf. Rom.
5:15-16). More often it is used to refer to the gifts of the Holy Spirit, or
"spiritual gifts."

Two other words of similar meaning should also be noted, namely,
dōrea and *dōrean*. The former means "gift," and is used in such
passages as John 4:10; Acts 2:38; and Romans 5:15, 17. The latter
means "freely," as in Matthew 10:8, "Freely you received, freely give";
and in Romans 3:24, which says we are "justified freely by his grace
through the redemption that came by Christ Jesus" (NIV).

The Essence of Saving Grace

We turn now to a systematic examination of the concept of saving
grace. The first thing to note is that when we speak of grace in this
sense, we are speaking of the very nature of God. Just as God's nature
is love, so his nature is grace, since grace is a form of love. We can
agree with Barth that "grace is an inner mode of being in God Himself."
It is "the very essence of the being of God," he says. When God acts
graciously toward us, especially in the forgiveness of sins, "He reveals
His very essence in this streaming forth of grace."[106]

The very heart of grace, and its existence in the very heart of God,
may be seen in a few key passages of Scripture which will now be
quoted in their entirety before we proceed to analyze the concept. First
is the passage already cited many times in part, Exodus 34:6-7,

---

105. Hans-Helmut Esser, "Grace, Spiritual Gifts," p. 116.
106. Karl Barth, *Church Dogmatics*, II/1, pp. 353, 356.

> Then the Lord passed by in front of him and proclaimed, "The Lord,
> the Lord God, compassionate and gracious, slow to anger, and aboun-
> ding in lovingkindness and truth; who keeps lovingkindness for
> thousands, who forgives iniquity, transgression and sin; yet He will by no
> means leave the guilty unpunished . . . ."

This is the first such revelation of the gracious nature of God. It is important to see that it was given in the context of grievous sin on Israel's part
and their need for forgiveness (Ex. 32:30ff.). The revelation itself emphasizes forgiveness. Psalm 99:8 refers back to this time in Israel's
history: "O Lord our God, Thou didst answer them; Thou wast a forgiving God to them, and yet an avenger of their evil deeds." The immediate consequence of this wilderness revelation was that God spared
the people and continued with them in their wanderings (blessings that
were primarily temporal).

The next passage is Numbers 14:17-20. This is in the context of
another rebellion on the part of the people of Israel. God tells Moses
that they deserve to be destroyed (Num. 14:11-12). But Moses prays
for God to spare them, and he appeals to the truth God revealed about
himself in Exodus 34:6-7 as the basis for his plea:

> . . . "But now, I pray, let the power of the Lord be great, just as Thou
> hast declared, 'The Lord is slow to anger and abundant in lovingkindness,
> forgiving iniquity and transgression; but He will by no means clear the
> guilty . . . .' Pardon, I pray, the iniquity of this people according to the
> greatness of Thy lovingkindness, just as Thou also hast forgiven this peo-
> ple, from Egypt even until now." So the Lord said, "I have pardoned
> them according to your word . . . ."

When Nehemiah 9:17 recalls these times of rebellion, it exalts the
gracious nature of God as the reason for Israel's continuing existence:
"But Thou art a God of forgiveness, gracious and compassionate, slow
to anger, and abounding in lovingkindness; and Thou didst not forsake
them." The essence of grace could not be more succinctly put: God is
"a God of forgiveness."

Another passage is Psalm 103:8-14, which is not speaking of any
particular historical event but is simply rejoicing in the fact that God's
eternal nature is one of grace:

> The Lord is compassionate and gracious, slow to anger and aboun-

ding in lovingkindness. He will not always strive with us; nor will he keep His anger forever. He has not dealt with us according to our sins, nor rewarded us according to our iniquities. For as high as the heavens are above the earth, so great is His lovingkindness toward those who fear Him. As far as the east is from the west, so far has He removed our transgressions from us. Just as a father has compassion on his children, so the Lord has compassion on those who fear Him. For He Himself knows our frame; He is mindful that we are but dust.

Only one other Old Testament passage that gives us this same insight into the gracious nature of God will be cited here, Micah 7:18-20,

> Who is a God like Thee, who pardons iniquity and passes over the rebellious act of the remnant of His possession? He does not retain His anger forever, because He delights in unchanging love. He will again have compassion on us; He will tread our iniquities under foot. Yes, Thou wilt cast all their sins into the depths of the sea. Thou wilt give truth to Jacob and unchanging love to Abraham, which Thou didst swear to our forefathers from the days of old.

The context here is deliverance for the nation of Israel, but what he does for them reveals his unparalleled inmost nature as one "who pardons iniquity."

The New Testament does not focus as much on eloquent descriptions of God's gracious nature as it does on the grand historical event that embodied and portrayed that grace before the whole world, namely, the cross of Jesus Christ. A passage that summarizes the essence of grace both as God's inner essence and as his gracious action on our behalf is Romans 3:24-26,

> . . . being justified as a gift by His grace through the redemption which is in Christ Jesus; whom God displayed publicly as a propitiation in His blood through faith. This was to demonstrate His righteousness, because in the forbearance of God He passed over the sins previously committed; for the demonstration, I say, of His righteousness at the present time, that He might be just and the justifier of the one who has faith in Jesus.

In this as in the other passages, the giving and forgiving nature of God is clearly seen. This is the essence of grace.

Grace Means Giving

To say that God is gracious means that it is his nature to *give* of

369

himself and of his bounty to his creatures. We have already seen that love itself includes the element of self-giving. And we have seen how the New Testament words for grace emphasize this point above all else. This is illustrated in the use of *charizomai* in Romans 8:32, "He who did not spare His own Son, but delivered Him up for us all, how will He not also with Him freely give us all things?" The point is made in Romans 6:23 also, "For the wages of sin is death, but the free gift of God is eternal life in Christ Jesus our Lord." Barth says, "His inclination, good will and favour . . . is a sheer gift."[107]

That grace means giving serves to highlight the difference between this side of God's nature and his holiness. As we remarked earlier, love gives and holiness demands. When love in the form of grace reaches down to us even in the depths of our sin, the gift it gives is salvation itself, *redemption* from sin and its consequences. And just because it comes to us by grace, it *must* be a *gift*, for this is the only way that grace operates. If we were being saved by God's holiness or (in Biblical terms) by God's law, then it would be proper for God to demand something from us to make us in some sense deserving of salvation. But then it would not be a gift, and it would not be grace. According to Scripture, God saves sinners out of his nature as a gracious God. Since grace means giving, salvation must be a gift.

Grace Means Forgiving

Being forgiven by one whom you have offended is the greatest gift that person can give you. When the one offended is the Holy God, and when the offense is sin against his holy law, then his forgiveness is the greatest imaginable gift. And this is exactly what the God of grace is willing and *desires* to give to every sinner. Desiring to forgive those who have sinned against him lies at the heart of God and the heart of grace. It is the ultimate expression of God's benevolent nature: "For Thou, Lord, art good, and ready to forgive" (Ps. 86:5). "To say grace is to say the forgiveness of sins," as Barth well says.[108] We will remember how

---

107. Ibid., p. 355. Barth's characterization of grace as "the free inclination of an unconditionally superior towards one who is unconditionally subordinate" (pp. 369, 407) I believe introduces an element that is not of the essence of grace itself. This relationship does exist between God and man, but not as the result of grace *per se*.
108. Ibid., p. 360.

the passages of Scripture that develop the essence of grace, as quoted at the beginning of this section, focus on the forgiveness of sins. The verb form of *charis* can specifically mean "to forgive," and is used in this sense several times in the New Testament. See Luke 7:42-43; II Corinthians 2:7, 10; 12:13; Ephesians 4:32; Colossians 2:13; 3:13. In Colossians 2:13 Paul says, "And when you were dead in your transgressions and the uncircumcision of your flesh, He made you alive together with Him, having forgiven us all our transgressions." Moffatt says that Paul used this verb because of "his consciousness of the divine grace in pardon. When he thought, 'God gives,' he instinctively thought, 'God forgives.'"[109]

The passages that speak of God's forgiveness as the gift of his gracious nature are much too many to be cited here, but in addition to those at the beginning of this section on the essence of grace, we may note the following. In Psalm 25:6-7 David prays, "Remember, O Lord, Thy compassion and Thy lovingkindnesses, for they have been from of old. Do not remember the sins of my youth or my transgressions." In Psalm 25:11 he pleads, "For Thy name's sake, O Lord, pardon my iniquity, for it is great." In Psalm 32:1-5 he rejoices in forgiveness received:

> How blessed is he whose transgression is forgiven, whose sin is covered! How blessed is the man to whom the Lord does not impute iniquity, and in whose spirit there is no deceit! . . . . I acknowledged my sin to Thee, and my iniquity I did not hide; I said, "I will confess my transgressions to the Lord"; and Thou didst forgive the guilt of my sin.

This is significant because the first two verses are quoted by Paul in Romans 4:7-8 as the essence of justification apart from works (i.e., apart from a consideration of our *sinful* works). Another Psalm emphasizing the grace of forgiveness is Psalm 51. It begins, "Be gracious to me, O God, according to Thy lovingkindness; according to the greatness of Thy compassion blot out my transgressions. Wash me thoroughly from my iniquity, and cleanse me from my sin" (vv. 1-2; cf. vv. 7, 9-10, 14). Psalm 130:3-4 sums it up: "If Thou, Lord, shouldst

---

109. James Moffatt, *Grace in the New Testament* (New York: Ray Long & Richard R. Smith, 1932), p. 103.

371

mark iniquities, O Lord, who could stand? But there is forgiveness with Thee, that Thou mayest be feared." In Isaiah 1:18 God promises, "Though your sins are as scarlet, they will be as white as snow." And in Isaiah 43:25, "I, even I, am the one who wipes out your transgressions for My own sake; and I will not remember your sins." The main New Testament word for forgiveness is *justification*, and this is pictured as the very heart of grace: "Being justified as a gift by His grace through the redemption which is in Christ Jesus" (Rom. 3:24).

What makes forgiveness such a marvelous gift and such an infinite act of grace is the twofold nature of God's response to human sin. On the one side, our sin evokes the wrath of God and the necessity to vindicate his holy nature and his holy law against this violation and transgression. But at the same time, on the other side, our sin evokes the mercy and compassion of God and the desire to remedy this situation not only for his own sake but for the sake of the sinner also. There is no way that this tension within the nature of God can be denied, and there is no way that we can really understand it or appreciate its magnitude. We have already touched on it in the discussion of divine patience as the delay of the execution of wrath, but now it must be emphasized even further.

Several passages of Scripture, mostly in the Old Testament, picture God's love as rising up in the face of his own wrath and as overcoming it. The image is that of a kind of struggle within God's nature, with love winning out over wrath. Divine wrath is not denied, but it is overcome and set aside by the seemingly superior strength of divine love. "Love conquers all." The Psalmist pictures this struggle and an apparent victory for wrath in Psalm 77:7-9, "Will the Lord reject forever? And will He never be favorable again? Has His lovingkindness ceased forever? Has His promise come to an end forever? Has God forgotten to be gracious? Or has He in anger withdrawn His compassion?" The answer is given in Psalm 103:8-10, "The Lord is compassionate and gracious, slow to anger, abounding in love. He will not always accuse, nor will he harbor his anger forever; he does not treat us as our sins deserve or repay us according to our iniquities" (NIV). While staring at the ruins that were once his beloved Jerusalem, at the beginning of the Babylonian captivity, Jeremiah says, "For the Lord will not reject forever, for if He causes grief, then He will have compassion according to His abundant lovingkindness. For He does not afflict willingly, or grieve the sons of men" (Lam. 3:31-33). Two such passages are in Hosea, where God declares his intention to forget his wrath and the punishment deserved by his people, and to let his love prevail. The first is Hosea 11:8-9,

> How can I give you up, O Ephraim? How can I surrender you, O Israel? How can I make you like Admah? How can I treat you like Zeboiim? My heart is turned over within Me, all my compassions are kindled. I will not execute My fierce anger; I will not destroy Ephraim again. For I am God and not man, the Holy One in your midst, and I will not come in wrath.

This is followed by Hosea 14:4, "I will heal their apostasy, I will love them freely, for My anger has turned away from them." Micah 7:18 says, "Who is a God like Thee, who pardons iniquity and passes over the rebellious act of the remnant of His possession? He does not retain His anger forever, because He delights in unchanging love." Some might also mention the principle in James 2:13, "Mercy triumphs over judgment." It is in light of these passages that Isaiah 28:21 is usually cited, which refers to God's acts of wrath as "his strange work" and "his alien task" (NIV).

There is no question that every saved person will be eternally grateful (literally) for this triumph of grace over wrath. But how may we explain it? Some would appeal to the last verse cited (Isaiah 28:21) and conclude that since wrath and judgment are "strange" and "alien" works for God, they are not really rooted in his essence. These are not his nature, but love is; therefore there is no real struggle within God, and it is a relatively simple matter for him to set aside his wrath in love. I do not agree with this, since I believe that holy wrath is just as much a part of God's nature as is his loving grace. But if this is so, how do we explain the passages above?

Perhaps in the final analysis we do not *have* to explain it, just accept it. But there are some relevant considerations that make it less of a mystery than it seems. First, regarding the two sides of God's nature, I believe it proper to characterize them thus: holiness requires; love desires. Holiness means that there is something God *must* do; love means that there is something God *wants* to do. This distinction is of course not exclusive, since God certainly wills to do what his holy nature requires, and his loving desires are grounded in his very nature. Nevertheless there is still a sense in which holiness is better characterized by "require" and love by "desire." And here is the tension: sometimes God's holiness requires him to do the very opposite of what his love desires. To put it another way, when God is acting in wrath, he is doing what he does not really *want* to do from his heart. Thus Lamentations 3:33 says, "He does not afflict willingly"; and the word rendered "willingly" means literally "from his heart." Here is what God's heart desires: he "desires all men to be saved and to come to the knowledge of the truth" (I Tim. 2:4). "He is patient with you, not wanting anyone to perish, but everyone to come to repentance" (II Peter 3:9). But because his nature is holy, he *does* afflict, and some *will* perish. But this is not what God desires with his loving heart; in this sense it is his strange or alien work.

So what we see in the above Scriptures that speak of God's love "triumphing" over his wrath is the fact that it is God's *desire* to treat men according to his love and not according to his wrath. He is "ready to forgive," as Psalm 86:5 says. And in fact he *does* forgive, which means that with regard to those who are forgiven, his grace in a sense *does* "win out" over his wrath. But does this mean that God goes against one side of his own nature (i.e., his holiness) in order to fulfill the desires of the other side of his nature? Is this what we mean by the "triumph of grace"? Does God sacrifice his holiness on the altar of his love? In a word, NO! The grace of God makes forgiveness freely available, but not at the expense of his holiness. Here are two reasons why this is so.

First and most important, the gift of forgiveness which God freely offers is made possible *only* by the atoning death of Jesus on the cross, wherein God was satisfying the requirement of his own holy wrath to punish sin by placing it upon Jesus instead of the sinner. In whatever age and in whatever form, the grace of forgiveness is the result of the cross. Tozer says, "Grace takes its rise far back in the heart of God, in the awful and incomprehensible abyss of His holy being; but the channel through which it flows out to men is Jesus Christ, crucified and risen."[110] When God said to Israel, "I will not execute My fierce anger" (Hosea 11:9), he was not casting his anger aside but was regarding it as satisfied in the cross that was sure to come. When he said "I will not execute My fierce anger . . . for I am God and not man, the Holy One in

---

110. A. W. Tozer, *The Knowledge of the Holy*, p. 100.

your midst" (Hosea 11:9), he was not declaring that anger has no true place in the divine nature, but that he as God in his infinite love and wisdom has a way of being true both to his holiness and to his love at the same time. It is called "the way of the cross." Zimmerli's idea that divine grace is "incomparably stronger than the burning wrath of the jealous God"[111] is simply not true. God's wrath and God's grace meet in the cross, where each prevails in its own way.

We have said that grace makes forgiveness freely available, but that there are two reasons why this is not at the expense of holiness. The first reason is the cross, and now the second reason is the fact that forgiveness is actually given only to those who are willing to receive it in repentance. God is *ready* to forgive, but he guards his holiness by bestowing the gift only on those whose attitude toward sin is the same as his own, i.e., when they have come to hate it and despise it and want to be rid of it. Those who quote Hosea 14:4, "I will heal their apostasy, I will love them freely, for My anger has turned away from them," sometimes forget the verses that precede it, which make repentance a condition for Israel's restoration: "Return, O Israel, to the Lord your God, for you have stumbled because of your iniquity. Take words with you and return to the Lord. Say to Him, 'Take away all iniquity, and receive us graciously'" (Hosea 14:1-2). God "is not wishing for any to perish but for all to come to repentance" (II Peter 3:9). Only those who do come to repentance will not perish; the others will experience his wrath. Leon Morris repeats a common idea that for God "the last word . . . is not a wrathful one, but a loving one."[112] The fact is that this depends on our response to God's free offer of the grace of forgiveness. For those who respond in repentance, God's last word *is* a loving one; but for those who persist in unrepentance, his last word is one of wrath.

Grace Means "Favor Bestowed When Wrath Is Owed"[113]

Sometimes we try to catch the wonder of God's grace by defining it as "unmerited favor," or his gracious gift to those who are "unworthy" of it. Tozer says it is "the good pleasure of God that inclines Him to

---

111. Walther Zimmerli, "χάρις, etc.," p. 383.
112. Leon Morris, *Testaments of Love*, p. 75.
113. I think this formula was provided by Ranny Grady, one of my theology students, in a class session on grace some years ago.

bestow benefits upon the undeserving."[114] Erickson says that grace "means that God supplies us with undeserved favors."[115] Such words as *unmerited, unworthy,* and *undeserved* do apply to the concept of grace, but they are not really strong enough to reveal the full extremity of grace. The fact is that grace is not merely undeserved or unmerited; it is the very opposite of what is deserved or merited. We are not just unworthy of God's forgiveness; we are actually worthy of its opposite. One could walk up to a perfect stranger and give him a thousand dollars for no reason at all. That gift would certainly be unmerited. But if the thousand dollars were given to a thief who had just stolen the giver's car, the gift would be the very opposite of the punishment deserved. The latter is more like God's grace. Thus instead of speaking of grace as "unmerited favor," we should think of it as "favor bestowed when wrath is owed." This idea does surface a bit in Tozer's description of grace as God's "goodness directed toward human debt and demerit."[116] It may be so that grace in its general, non-soteriological sense means "the free bestowal of kindness on one who has no claim on it"; but in the context of salvation we must be more specific, as Louis Berkhof is when he says grace is "the unmerited goodness or love of God to those who have forfeited it, and are by nature under a sentence of condemnation."[117] As Packer puts it, "The grace of God is love freely shown towards guilty sinners, contrary to their merit and indeed in defiance of their demerit."[118] Sometimes the term *undeserving* is replaced by *ill-deserving,* as in Pink's description of grace as "the favour of God shown to those who not only have no positive deserts of their own, but who are thoroughly ill-deserving and hell-deserving."[119] If God were to give us what we deserve, i.e., if he were to pay us what we have earned, we would receive "the wages of sin," namely, death. But grace gives us the opposite of what we have earned: "the free gift of God is eternal life in Christ Jesus our Lord" (Rom. 6:23). This makes the gift element of grace all the more amazing.

---

114. A. W. Tozer, *The Knowledge of the Holy,* p. 100.
115. Millard J. Erickson, *Christian Theology,* I:294.
116. A. W. Tozer, *The Knowledge of the Holy,* p. 100.
117. Louis Berkhof, *Systematic Theology,* p. 71. Italics omitted.
118. J. I. Packer, *Knowing God,* p. 120.
119. Arthur W. Pink, *The Attributes of God,* p. 60.

To conclude this section we may summarize the essence of God's grace thus: it is his infinite willingness and desire to give us the gift of forgiveness, even though we deserve his wrath, and even though it costs him the cross.

Is Grace Universal or Particular?

We have seen that God is a God of grace, a God of forgiveness. We must now ask the question, *to whom* is God gracious? To whom is his grace directed? To all people, or only to some? Is his grace universal, or is it particular? The answer, I believe, is that God's grace is universal in some senses and particular in another. When grace is considered as an attitude within God, i.e., his attitude of graciousness and willingness to forgive those who sin against him, it must be considered universal. He has the same desire to forgive all people (I Tim. 2:4; II Peter 3:9). Also, when grace is thought of in the sense of the atoning death of Christ that makes such forgiveness possible, it must be considered universal. Christ died for all men (John 3:16; I John 2:2). But when grace is being considered as the actual application of Christ's redeeming work to individuals, it must be considered particular.

But not all agree with this. There are several differing views besides the one affirmed above, all of which I would consider to be unacceptable. Some have a false concept of the universality of grace, and others have a false concept of its particularity. We will examine these views here briefly.

False or Misleading Views of Universal Grace

The idea that God's grace includes all men is a blessed thought and is Biblical when rightly understood. But when falsely understood it can be misleading if not dangerous. The most serious of such views is that grace is not only universal with regard to God's attitude and God's action for us in Christ, but is also universal in its *application* to all men. This is the error of universalism, or universal salvation. The idea is that in some way the grace of God made available in Jesus Christ finds its way into the hearts of all people sooner or later, so that all are saved by his grace. We saw above in chapter two that this is a tendency in Liberation Theology. Roman Catholic theologian Karl Rahner has done much to establish this view through his notion of "anonymous Christianity." He says that belief in God through Jesus Christ is not limited to Christianity, but also "embraces those forms of faith which existed before and exist along with it as unconscious participations in the pardoning and divinizing grace of Christ."[120] This view is argued by Richard Cote in a little book called *Universal Grace: Myth or Reality?* Following Rahner's "new thinking on universal grace," he says it is a reality.[121] "Today there is a growing Christian awareness of the anonymous presence and workings of grace in the lives of all people, and with this heightened awareness the difference between Christians and non-Christians . . . is no longer being regarded in absolute terms," Cote says. "As members of the saved race, non-Christians or non-believers are not simply people; they are redeemed people, germinally baptized in Christ and personally in touch with divine grace."[122] This new form of universalism is gaining more and more popularity, but it must be rejected as a false concept of the universality of grace. We must continue to think of grace as being universal with regard to God's attitude and Christ's work, but not with regard to its actual experience in the lives of individuals. Here it is particular.

Another unacceptable view of universal grace is one that applies the term *grace* in the broadest possible sense, making it include not only God's work of redemption but also his works of creation and providence. This may or may not include a doctrine of universal salvation. The main point is that the term itself is simply broadened in scope to include everything God does. Much of this thinking stems from Barth's concept of the covenant of grace as preceding and embracing all works of God, including creation.[123] Mikolaski has popularized this view for Evangelicals, stating that "grace is the key feature of God's relation to the world and to Man."[124] He says that grace is the rationale and central feature of the work of creation, and is "the mode of God's relation to His creation." He continues, "Grace is prevenient in the actual world order to the interests of God's purpose generally, as well as to the work

---

120. Karl Rahner, *Do You Believe in God?* (New York: Paulist Press, 1969), p. 86.

121. Richard G. Cote, *Universal Grace: Myth or Reality?* (Maryknoll, N.Y.: Orbis Books, 1977), p. 2.

122. Ibid., pp. 85-87.

123. Karl Barth, *Church Dogmatics, Volume III: The Doctrine of Creation, Part One*, tr. J. W. Edwards et al. (Edinburgh: T. & T. Clark, 1958), pp. 42ff.

124. Samuel J. Mikolaski, *The Grace of God* (Grand Rapids: Eerdmans, 1966), p. 10.

of redemption specifically."[125] Another writer says, "Everything in creation, providence and redemption, accomplished by the triune God,
through His good Will, is a manifestation of Grace."[126] Ditmanson says,
"There is a marked disposition today to reconsider the scope of grace
and to discern the gracious presence of God in areas often thought to be
merely natural, sinful, or worldly." He asserts that "every work of God
is the expression of one grace," including "the grace of creation and
preservation." It is "the single and all-embracing work of God. There is
no part of the divine activity in calling the universe into being and in sustaining and restoring finite existence" which falls outside its scope. "Or,
to put it another way, *nature is included in grace*. Grace is the *ultimate
context* within which all created objects, persons, and events have their
being."[127]

Now, the only way that such a view could be justified is if the word
grace is used in its broadest possible sense of "gift" or "divine
assistance." But when the term is used this way, the significance of the
saving work of Jesus Christ and the significance of grace as forgiveness
are seriously obscured. The grace that saves sinners is unique when
compared with the other works of God, and it is gravely misleading to
include all God's works together under this one term. As MacDonald
well says, we "flatten out the majesty of that most central salvific word in
the New Testament" when we include within it the gifts of creation and
providence.[128] John 1:17 says that "grace . . . came through Jesus
Christ"—not the pre-existent Creator-Logos (John 1:3), but the Logos
incarnate as Jesus of Nazareth who died on the cross. The words
benevolence and *goodness* are the general terms that should be used to
embrace all of the divine works (that come "through His good Will," as
one of the statements above puts it). We should reserve the term *grace*
to refer to that loving work of God that responds to sin. Grace presupposes sin and would not have been openly expressed (any more than

---

125. Ibid., pp. 63-64, 73.
126. *The Doctrine of Grace*. ed. W.T. Whitley (London: SCM Press. 1932). p. 6.
This statement is in the introduction.
127. Harold H. Ditmanson, *Grace in Experience and Theology* (Minneapolis:
Augsburg, 1977), pp. 62, 65, 66, 73.
128. William G. MacDonald. "'. . . The Spirit of Grace' (Heb. 10:29)," *Grace
Unlimited*, ed. Clark H. Pinnock (Minneapolis: Bethany Fellowship. 1975), p. 78.

wrath) if man had not sinned. Moffatt recognizes that the term itself has a broad range of meanings. But still, he says,[129]

> . . . much as one appreciates this, it is fair to insist that later extensions of its usage must not be taken to represent the authentic core of that truth which in the dawn of Christianity man often found they could not otherwise express than by calling it "grace," namely, the love of God in power and beauty, shining against the dark background of human demerit.

This is not simply a question of terminology, for there are a few doctrinal errors that are just a half-step away from universalizing the scope of grace in this way. In addition to the weakening of the uniqueness of the redemptive work of Christ, there is also a danger that the integrity of the doctrine of creation will be lost. Also, if every work of God is considered a work of grace, the integrity of the holiness of God and the reality of his wrath are brought into question; we are brought back to the view that God's love is the one all-inclusive attribute. Finally, the doctrine of universal salvation is difficult to resist when one interprets all God's works as works of grace.

One other less dangerous but still questionable way of universalizing grace is to divide it into two categories and to specify that one kind of grace is soteric and the other is not. For example, Roman Catholic theology distinguishes between natural grace (creation and providence) and supernatural grace (salvation).[130] Also, Reformed theology sometimes makes the same distinction but uses the expressions "common grace" and "special grace."[131] The clear distinction between the two kinds of grace will help to avoid some of the difficulties mentioned in the previous paragraph; but it is still questionable whether those things in the categories of creation and providence are properly called grace, however carefully they may be distinguished from the grace that comes through Jesus Christ.

---

129. James Moffatt, *Grace in the New Testament,* p. 5.

130. Joseph Pohle, *Grace Actual and Habitual,* ed. Arthur Preuss (St. Louis: B. Herder, 1912), pp. 7ff.

131. See Cornelius Van Til, *Common Grace* (Philadelphia: Presbyterian and Reformed, 1947); and C. Samuel Storms, *The Grandeur of God,* pp. 118ff. Storms justifies using the term *grace* for such non-saving gifts as rain and sunshine because they are "undeserved" (p. 122). This simply illustrates a point made earlier, that such terms as *undeserved* are too weak as definitions of grace.

The False View of Particular Grace

The other unacceptable answer to the question of whether grace is universal or particular is that it is particular in *every* way. (We are thinking now only of God's grace as it has to do with salvation.) This view says that grace is limited not only in its application to a certain number of human beings, but also in its very existence in God's nature and in its accomplishment on the cross. This is the view most commonly known as Calvinism or Reformed theology. It says that from the very beginning God's grace has not included everyone, that God's ultimate desire to save and forgive sinners does not apply to all people but only to a certain portion of them selected by him and known as the elect. This is the Reformed distinction between common grace and special grace. The former is called "common" because it is directed to all people in common. It is a measure of "good will," but it is non-saving. On the other hand, special grace is reserved only for the elect; it alone is saving grace. It in no way applies to the non-elect. Some would include love itself within this particularity and say that God does not even *love* the non-elect.[132]

Whether it be called love or grace, this view says that God's desire to save is restricted to particular people whom God chooses. It is called a "choosing love,"[133] a "distinguishing grace."[134] Stauffer calls *agapē* "a love which makes distinctions, choosing and keeping to its object." It is "preferential love which includes separation and special calling." As an "electing love," the love of God "implies election."[135] Pink says, "The distinguishing grace of God is seen in saving that people whom He has sovereignly singled out to be His high favourites. By 'distinguishing' we

---

132. The best example of this view is Herman Hoeksema, whose view is summarized by James Daane thus: "God loves the elect because they are righteous in Christ; he hates the reprobate because they are sinners. The elect alone are the object of grace; for them alone the gospel is good news. For the reprobate God has no blessing at all, but only an eternal hatred. Rain and sunshine . . . are curses heaped on the reprobate" (James Daane, *The Freedom of God* [Grand Rapids: Eerdmans, 1973], p. 24). Hoeksema "denies that there is a divine love for sinners" (ibid., p. 92).

133. James M. Boice, *Foundations of the Christian Faith*, II:216.

134. Arthur W. Pink, *The Attributes of God*, p. 62.

135. Ethelbert Stauffer, "ἀγαπάω, etc." (part), *Theological Dictionary* of the New Testament, ed. Gerhard Kittel, tr. Geoffrey W. Bromiley (Grand Rapids: Eerdmans, 1964), I:37, 48, 49.

mean that grace discriminates, makes differences, chooses some and passes by others."[136] "The love of God is a love which chooses," says France.[137] Storms says,[138]

> Thus, to say that love is sovereign is to say it is distinguishing. It is, by definition as *saving* love, bestowed upon and experienced by those only who are in fact *saved* (i.e., the elect). Although there is surely a sense in which God loves the non-elect, He does *not* love them redemptively. If He did, they would certainly be redeemed. God loves them, but *not* savingly, else they would certainly be saved. All this is but to say that God's eternal, *electing* love is not universal but particular. . . .

Examples cited as proof of this view are usually Noah (Gen. 6:8), Abraham (Deut. 10:15), Jacob (Mal. 1:2-3), and Israel as a nation (Deut. 4:31; 7:6-8; 9:4-5). A major proof text is Exodus 33:19, "I will be gracious to whom I will be gracious, and will show compassion on whom I will show compassion."

This view which particularizes saving grace in every way, and even love itself, must be vigorously rejected. It simply cannot do justice to passages which state that it is God's desire that all men should be saved, and it goes against the basic Biblical teaching that God is no respecter of persons, or "God is not one to show partiality" (Acts 10:34). Exodus 33:19 has been explained earlier as not relating contextually to the question of salvation at all but to God's free decision to answer Moses' prayer.

We must continue to insist that God's grace as it appears within his own nature in the form of a desire to give forgiveness to sinners is universal in scope. It is true that this gift is actually given only to particular individuals, but the limitation is the result of man's choice and not God's. It was God's choice to create man with a relative independence and a relatively free will.[139] He does not force his own desires upon man, but respects the integrity of the free will with which he endowed his image-bearers at the time of creation. The reason why some receive grace and some do not is because some freely reject it and some freely

---

136. Arthur W. Pink, *The Attributes of God*, p. 62.
137. R. T. France, *The Living God* (Downers Grove: InterVarsity, 1970), p. 87.
138. C. Samuel Storms, *The Grandeur of God*, p. 133.
139. Jack Cottrell, *What the Bible Says About God the Ruler*, pp. 191ff.

accept it. This is to say that the actual reception of grace is conditional, i.e., it is conditioned upon a man's willingness to accept it. The question of conditionality is very important and will be discussed in more detail in the last main section of this chapter. We will see there that God's choosing of Noah, Abraham, Jacob and Israel as a nation was not totally uncaused but was quite in keeping with the way he usually distributes his grace, namely, conditionally.

The Freedom of Grace

The preceding discussion leads directly into a consideration of the question of the freedom of grace. The principal basis of the view that grace is particular or selective is the idea that grace is free, i.e., that God is free to choose whether to show grace or not, and thus he is free to choose the objects of his grace. A part of the reasoning here is the very essence of grace as a *gift*. If it is a gift, then it must be free; God must be under no obligation to give it. Another consideration is the sovereignty of God. Since God is sovereign, his grace must be sovereign. That is, God and God alone will decide to whom he will show grace and from whom he will withhold it.

Several examples will illustrate and explain this view further. Bates says, "The freeness of God's mercy is evident by considering there was no tie upon him to dispense it." In certain contexts love may be a duty, but not from God to man. "The love of God to man is a pure, free, and liberal affection, no way due."[140] Grace is free and absolutely sovereign, says Pink, "because God exercises it toward and bestows it upon whom he pleases." "Just because grace is unmerited favour, it must be exercised in a sovereign manner. . . . The great God is under no obligation to any of His creatures, least of all to those who are rebels against Him."[141] Regarding God's love he says, "The love of God is free, spontaneous, uncaused. The only reason why God loves any is found in His own sovereign will." Love must be sovereign because "God Himself is sovereign, under obligations to none, a law unto Himself, acting always according to His own imperial pleasure. . . .

---

140. William Bates, *The Harmony of the Divine Attributes* (Philadelphia: Presbyterian Board of Publication, n.d.), pp. 127-128.
141. Arthur W. Pink, *The Attributes of God*, p. 61.

Because God is God, He does as He pleases; because God is love, He loves whom He pleases."[142] Packer agrees: "The love of God is free, spontaneous, unevoked, uncaused. God loves men because He has chosen to love them . . . . No reason for His love can be given save His own sovereign good pleasure."[143] Grace itself presupposes the truth of the sovereign freedom of God, says Packer. God is not "obliged to love and help us," nor "is He bound to show us favour." The only thing we have a claim on is God's justice, and "God does not owe it to anyone to stop justice taking its course. He is not obliged to pity and pardon; if He does so it is an act done, as we say, 'of His own free will', and nobody forces His hand." Grace is free in the sense "of proceeding from One who was free not to be gracious."[144] This final statement, from Storms, clearly illustrates this view and shows the connection between it and the concept of the particularity of grace:[145]

> Grace is also sovereign. That is to say, it is optional in its exercise and extent. Although God *is* gracious in His eternal being, He need not *be* gracious or shower His grace upon anyone. If grace were at any time an *obligation* of God, it would cease to be grace. God's grace, therefore, is distinguishing. He graciously saves some but not all, not based on anything present in the creature either possible or actual, foreseen or foreordained, but wholly according to His sovereign good pleasure.

What shall we say of this understanding of the freedom of grace? Basically, that it is a combination of truth and error. It is definitely true that grace is free from the standpoint of the sinner. This means two things. First, it is free in the sense that the sinner has no claim on it. By his sin he has forfeited his friendly relationship with God, and it is true that the only thing God owes him is wrath. There is nothing in the sinner himself that obligates God to be gracious to him, as if it were a debt owed. If salvation were by works, then eternal life would be wages due (Rom. 4:4); but this is the opposite of grace. Grace is a gift. We cannot

---

142. Ibid., pp. 70, 72.
143. J. I. Packer, *Knowing God*, p. 112.
144. Ibid., p. 119.
145. C. Samuel Storms, *The Grandeur of God*, p. 126.

demand that a gift be given, nor is God under obligation to give it. Second, grace is free in the sense that God does not require us to pay for it. He does not require us to purchase it with our works. He demands no compensation; it is a gift. We do not "pay him back" with our good deeds. So in these two senses, grace is free. It is not something God owes us for our works, nor are our works something we owe God for his grace.

However, from the standpoint of God himself, the idea that grace is free in the sense described in the quotations above is a serious error. To say that God's sovereignty in the matter of grace means that he is free to be gracious or not, that he is free to show grace to some and not to others, that grace is something *optional* with God—to say these things reflects an inconsistent and unbiblical view of God, as well as an unbiblical view of man. I will make two main points here, one regarding grace as an attitude within God and the other regarding the application of grace to the individual.

First, the view of sovereign grace described above is false because it completely severs God's *will* from his *nature*. It assumes, at least for this particular issue, that God's nature in no way has any effect on his attitudes or choices. It is one thing to say that God's grace is free and spontaneous in the sense that it is uninfluenced or uncaused by anything in the *creature*, but it is quite another to say that it is arbitrary and optional and thus uninfluenced even by God's own nature. It makes his will a kind of free-floating entity within the divine being that is open to any and all possible choices.[146] It usually is put in the form of a false choice: either God must be influenced by something in the creature (a view rejected with horror), or else he must be free to love or not and to love whom he pleases.[147] But I say this is a false choice because there is a third possibility, namely, that his love and grace are influenced *by his own nature*. There are very few who would deny that

---

146. I do not believe that this concept would be endorsed by the writers quoted above nor by most Reformed theologians. They would probably be repelled by it. But my point is that this is the only view consistent with the idea of a grace that is optional. The fact that they are implicitly willing to embrace such a notion in reference to grace but not in other matters is a serious inconsistency.

147. An example is Arthur W. Pink, *The Attributes of God*, p. 72.

love is the very *nature* of God.[148] First John 4:8 is difficult to ignore: "God is love." My question is this: how is it possible to say that love is the very *nature* of God, but at the same time to say that its exercise is completely a matter of his *will*, that it is completely free and optional? I believe that Storms must have winced a bit at his own statement that "although God *is* gracious in His eternal being, He need not *be* gracious or shower His grace upon anyone."[149] If God *is* gracious by nature, how could he possibly choose *not* to be gracious? How can it possibly be *optional*? We may recall the discussion of God's righteousness in chapter four above, and the definition of God's righteousness as his being true to his own nature. The righteous God must be true to his own nature as *love*. Divine sovereignty does not mean that God is free to do anything he wants without even being influenced by his own nature.

At this point we are speaking only of grace as an attitude within God, and we are saying that because love and mercy and grace are of the very *essence* of God, he is *not* free either to love or not to love, either to be gracious or not to be gracious. The very meaning of grace is the willingness and desire to forgive sinners and to receive them back into fellowship. Thus it is God's very nature to want to forgive sinners and to accept them back to himself. This is not "optional" with God. And if it is not optional as such, then it is not optional with regard to its objects. If it is God's nature to be gracious in his attitude toward sinners, then it is his nature to be gracious in his attitude toward *all* sinners. Particularism at this level is completely unbiblical.

But now the question will be asked, if God *must* because of his very nature be gracious to *all* sinners, does this not require him actually to save them all? No, the universality of God's gracious attitude does not imply a universal application of saving grace to *every* individual. This is true because of the nature of man as a moral or free-will being. Again, it

---

148. See H. Orton Wiley, *Christian Theology*, p. 383. He discusses the view of A. H. Strong that holiness and not love is the basic nature of God, thus severing the love of God from his nature and thus making love voluntary and optional. This, he says, is the basis of the Calvinistic view that God's grace can be selective. I believe, however, that most Calvinists would disagree with the view that love is not at least part of the basic nature of God. The problem as a rule is not that they deny that love is the nature of God, but that they are unwilling to follow through on the implications of this for the concept of grace.

149. C. Samuel Storms, *The Grandeur of God*, p. 126. The italics are his own.

was God's sovereign choice to create man with a relative independence and a relatively free will. In so doing, God freely chose to limit himself with respect to man by allowing man to make his own moral choices. God does not go against his own plan by forcing choices upon the creatures that he himself has made to be free.[150] Thus with respect to the application of grace to particular individuals, *God is not free,* and this by his own choice. It is not an inherent limitation upon God, but one that he freely chose to place upon himself by the very creation of free-will beings. Thus it is no contradiction to his inherent sovereignty.

Thus *by nature* God is not free to choose whether to be gracious or not, i.e., to desire the salvation of all or not. Such a desire is grounded in his very nature. Also, *by choice* God is not free to apply his saving grace to just anyone. By his own design he has made us with the freedom to accept his gift of grace or to reject it. In this indirect sense the particularizing of grace may be said to be the result of God's choice, but the choices that actually divide men into saved and unsaved are men's own choices, not God's.

This is the only view that makes sense of the passages that declare God's desire that all should be saved (I Tim. 2:4; II Peter 3:9) and passages that picture God as inviting and pleading with all, only to be rejected by many. Isaiah 30:18 says, "Therefore the Lord longs to be gracious to you, and therefore He waits on high to have compassion on you." In Isaiah 65:1-2 God pictures himself as begging his rebellious people to repent and return to him: "I permitted Myself to be sought by those who did not ask for Me; I permitted Myself to be found by those who did not seek Me. I said, 'Here am I, here am I,' to a nation which did not call on My name. I have spread out My hands all day long to a rebellious people." Then he says that he will have to destroy them (though not completely, v. 8) "because I called, but you did not answer; I spoke, but you did not hear" (v. 12). Jesus' lament over Jerusalem surely comes from a heart that desires to see all men saved: "O Jerusalem, Jerusalem, who kills the prophets and stones those who are sent to her! How often I wanted to gather your children together, the way a hen gathers her chicks under her wings, and you were unwilling" (Matt. 23:37).

---

150. See Jack Cottrell, *What the Bible Says About God the Ruler,* pp. 187ff.

The conclusion is that grace is free in reference to man in that it is not something God owes us nor do we have to pay for it, but it is not free in reference to God in that his own nature constrains him to be gracious toward sinners though he will not violate their own freedom in order to force grace upon them.

A question that remains unanswered is whether the work of redemption as such was necessary or whether it was something God could freely choose either to do or not do. In other words, was the cross necessary or optional? The question is not whether the cross was necessary as over against other potential ways of saving man. The issue is whether it was necessary for God to do *anything at all* to bring about man's salvation. If God by his very nature as loving grace *desires* to save all men, does his nature also dictate that he do everything (or the only thing) possible in order to make salvation available to us? And if the cross is the only thing that can make forgiveness possible, does this make the cross a necessary act on God's part? And if God did it out of necessity and not freely, how can we praise him and glorify him and thank him for it?

At this time I am not ready to say that the cross was necessary or that God had (has) to do everything possible in order to save us, even though it is his nature to be gracious. I will leave the question open. But even if it should turn out to be a necessary act, this in no way would lead us into determinism, nor would it diminish the praiseworthiness of this act. This is so for two reasons. One is that anything God does with reference to men that is called necessary is only relatively necessary, its necessity being ultimately preceded by the free and contingent act of creation itself. God's choice to create anything at all, and his choice to create free-will beings, was a free and sovereign choice. But God knew that if this choice were made, then certain things would become necessary because of his own nature. For example, he knew that if man sinned, his holiness would require him to punish that sin. If he were not willing to punish sin, he would simply have chosen not to create in the first place. We could think of the work of redemption in the same way. We could say that God knew that if man sinned, his grace would require him to provide a way of redemption, even though the only way to do this would be via incarnation and the cross. If he were not willing to go through with the work of redemption, he would simply have chosen not to create in the first place. Thus, knowing what would be necessary *if* man sinned, God's choice to create was *at the same time* a free choice to give himself in the person of the Logos to be a propitiation for the sins of the world.

Another reason why a necessary work of redemption would still be praiseworthy is that its necessity would be the necessity of *love* and not just some abstract force. From our own experience we know the compulsion of love to be a unique kind of compulsion. We have either seen or been involved in situations where an act of heroism or sacrifice has been described as flowing from the necessity of love: "It was the only thing I could do. I really had no choice." In such a case we praise not only the act itself, but also the love that necessitated the act. The same would be true of God in an infinitely greater sense. If it should be that the cross was necessary because God's nature is to love and be gracious to sinners, then we should praise God not only for the act of the cross but also for the love from which it springs.

Is Grace Conditional or Unconditional?

A final question concerning the grace of God is whether it is conditional or unconditional. This is interrelated with the previous question and has already been addressed to some degree. Those who say grace is particular in every way usually say that it is unconditional, with God choosing to whom he will apply it and from whom he will withhold it without being influenced in any way by anything in the creatures themselves. Most of those who say grace is universal (unless they believe in universal salvation) usually say that it is conditional, with God applying it only to those who meet certain conditions. Not everything related to this issue can be discussed here,[151] but we will touch on certain aspects of it that have been raised in relation to our discussion thus far.

Alleged Examples of Unconditional Grace

Much if not most of the alleged evidence for unconditional grace is in the Old Testament. For example, Noah is said to demonstrate the unconditional electing love of God. Genesis 6:8 says, "But Noah found favor in the eyes of the Lord." According to Zimmerli, "Undoubtedly

---

151. See ibid., chapter nine, "Predestination."

there is implied here the mystery of the free divine decision whereby Noah came to have this attractiveness for God."[152] While discussing the word *chēn*, Esser makes the remarkably presumptuous statement that with reference to God "it is used mostly in the sense of his undeserved gift of election," and cites Noah as a prime example.[153] A second example is God's choice of Abraham and the other fathers of the chosen nation. While addressing Israel Moses tells them, "Yet on your fathers did the Lord set His affection to love them, and He chose their descendants after them, even you above all peoples" (Deut. 10:15). "It was distinguishing grace which selected Abraham," says Pink.[154] God's choice of Jacob and rejection of Esau are also noted: "Yet I have loved Jacob; but I have hated Esau" (Mal. 1:2-3). Henry says, "Yahweh's sovereign love explains his choice of Jacob; had he wished, he might have chosen Esau instead."[155] Morris notes that the Bible says Israel was chosen as a nation because God loved the patriarchs, "but no reason is provided for God's love for the patriarchs." God did love the patriarchs, but he "seems to have no reason that men can discern for loving them." Indeed, "we might reason that God loved the fathers because they were upright and honorable men, but that would be our reasoning—Deuteronomy does not say this. No reason is given for God's love."[156]

The most commonly-cited example of unconditional grace is God's choice of Israel itself. The following passages are common stock in the discussion: "Because He loved your fathers, therefore He chose their descendants after them" (Deut. 4:37). "The Lord did not set His love on you nor choose you because you were more in number than any of the peoples, for you were the fewest of all peoples, but because the Lord loved you and kept the oath which He swore to your forefathers,

---

152. Walther Zimmerli, "χάρις, etc.," p. 380.

153. Hans-Helmut Esser, "Grace," p. 117. Leonard Coppes also tries to read "God's unconditioned choice" into another Old Testament word, *rācham*. He cites Ex. 33:19 as his proof, a passage we have already shown to be taken out of context when used in this way. (Leonard J. Coppes, "*rācham*," *Theological Wordbook of the Old Testament*, ed. R. Laird Harris et al. [Chicago: Moody Press, 1980], II:842.)

154. Arthur W. Pink, *The Attributes of God*, p. 62.

155. Carl F. H. Henry, *God, Revelation and Authority, Volume VI: God Who Stands and Stays, Part Two* (Waco: Word Books, 1983), p. 347.

156. Leon Morris, *Testaments of Love*, pp. 27-28, 90.

the Lord brought you out by a mighty hand" (Deut. 7:7-8). God says that he expelled the Canaanites and gave Israel the land not because of the latter's righteousness but because of the former's wickedness. "It is not for your righteousness or for the uprightness of your heart that you are going to possess their land, but it is because of the wickedness of these nations that the Lord your God is driving them out before you, in order to confirm the oath which the Lord swore to your fathers" (Deut. 9:5; cf. 10:15, quoted above). After citing these passages France says the only reason why God could have chosen Israel "is sheer undeserved, unconditioned, free love."[157] Morris uses them as proof that God's love is "unmotivated." He says, "It seems that God delights in this people simply because he chooses to do so."[158] Throughout their later history of idolatry and rebellion, God remained faithful to his covenant with them, and "the only ground for this is to be found in his electing grace and love." At least in the prophets, "Yahweh's love is the sole and incredible basis for his future actions in saving his lost people."[159]

Is Israel a Proper Paradigm for Grace?

It is interesting that the first place to which many turn for an answer to the question whether grace is conditional or unconditional is to the Old Testament and to the example of Israel in particular. Perhaps chronology has something to do with this, but nevertheless an inordinate amount of space is usually given to God's choice of Israel, which is then used as a paradigm for unconditional grace in general.[160] My contention, however, is that this is improper methodology mainly because of the unique position which Israel had in the economy of redemption. God's choice of and dealings with Israel are not a proper paradigm for God's gracious dealings with individuals in reference to their eternal salvation. We cannot generalize from God's relationship

---

157. R. T. France, *The Living God*, p. 87.

158. Leon Morris, *Testaments of Love*, pp. 89-90, 93.

159. Walther Günther and Hans-Georg Link, "Love (part), *The New International Dictionary of New Testament Theology*, ed. Colin Brown (Grand Rapids: Zondervan, 1976), II:540-541.

160. For example, Brunner begins his discussion of God's love with a reference to Hosea, who shows that the love of God is a "love that is not based upon any quality in Israel, but solely in the election which is rooted in the will of God." (Emil Brunner, *The Christian Doctrine of God*, p. 184)

with Israel to his relationship with individuals on the matter of conditional or unconditional grace. Several reasons for this will now be given.

The main reason why Israel is not a proper paradigm is that this nation was chosen for a unique role in God's plan of redemption. God chose them for his own purposes and used them as an instrument in carrying out those purposes. This applies to the choice of Abraham and of Jacob as well as the choice of the nation. God did not choose them for their own sakes but for *his* sake and for the sake of the whole world (Gen. 12:3; 28:14). He chose them for the privilege of preparing for the coming of the Messiah into the world. In order to provide a context of expectation and piety, God decided to choose a nation and develop a relationship with them and make them the custodians of his revelation. Perhaps in the final analysis it did not matter which nation he chose; but he made a choice, committed himself to it via a covenant, and stuck to it. The important point is that he did not do any of this for *Israel's* sake as such, but for his *own* sake and for the sake of the whole world. This does not mean that God really did not love Israel or care for them; he did. "The Lord will not abandon His people, nor will He forsake His inheritance" (Ps. 94:14). But what was at stake here was God's eternal plan of redemption. *This* in the final analysis is the only thing that made God's choice of Israel unconditional. He was unconditionally committed to keeping this nation intact, even if only in remnant form, until its Messianic purpose was fulfilled.

This is the purpose that lay behind God's covenants with Abraham, Israel and David. On the many occasions when God renewed his love to Israel for the sake of the covenants, the purpose of these covenants themselves must be understood as the basic reason for his patience with this faithless nation. "But the Lord was gracious to them and had compassion on them and turned to them because of His covenant with Abraham, Isaac, and Jacob, and would not destroy them or cast them from His presence" (II Kings 13:23). "He has remembered His covenant forever, the word which He commanded to a thousand generations, the covenant which He made with Abraham, and His oath to Isaac. Then He confirmed it to Jacob for a statute, to Israel as an everlasting covenant" (Ps. 105:8-10; cf. vv. 42-44). See Deuteronomy 7:8; 9:5; Psalm 106:45; Micah 7:20. Concerning the Davidic covenant, see II Samuel 7:16; Psalm 89:3-4, 28-29, 33-37.

This is also why on many occasions God told Israel that he was saving them only for his own name's sake. The immediate reference was usually that his reputation among the nations would suffer if he completely abandoned Israel, thus he determined to stick with them or rescue them to prevent his name from being further profaned. "Nevertheless He saved them for the sake of His name, that He might make His power known" (Ps. 106:8). God tells Israel, "For My own sake, for My own sake, I will act; for how can My name be profaned? And My glory I will not give to another" (Isa. 48:11). Regarding his bringing them back from Babylon he says, "It is not for your sake, O house of Israel, that I am about to act, but for My holy name, which you have profaned among the nations where you went. And I will vindicate the holiness of My great name which has been profaned among the nations" (Ezek. 36:22-23). See Exodus 32:12-13; Numbers 14:13-17; Deuteronomy 32:26-27; Isaiah 43:25; Ezekiel 20:9; Daniel 9:17-19. The point is that God had made a covenant with this people and he was going to keep it for his own sake, whether they liked it or not. It was not just his immediate reputation that was at stake, but his ultimate redemptive plan.

A second reason why God's dealings with Israel are not a proper paradigm is that his main relationship was with Israel as a *nation* and not with the individuals making up the nation. Any unconditional element in his love for Israel applied to the nation, not to individuals. As Quell says, "What the OT has to say about the love of God moves for the most part in national trains of thought."[161] Henry acknowledges that "the covenant-relationship is collective and not primarily individual."[162] That God's underlying concern was the conservation of the nation as a nation and not the preservation of the individuals in it is clearly seen in his offer to Moses in Exodus 32:10, "Now then let Me alone, that My anger may burn against them, and that I may destroy them; and I will make of you a great nation" (cf. Num. 14:12). Though God entered a covenant with Israel to make them a great nation, none of the men who were twenty years old or older at the time the covenant was made (except Joshua and Caleb) lived to enter the promised land (Num. 14:22ff.). After they entered their land, uncounted plagues and military

---

161. Gottfried Quell, "ἀγαπάω, etc.," p. 31.
162. Carl F. H. Henry, *God, Revelation and Authority*, VI:347.

conquests decimated the population, including all of the ten northern tribes; but the nation continued to exist in the form of the southern kingdom. The final great chastening even of this shrunken empire—the Babylonian captivity—produced horrible suffering and death for most of the individuals, but the nation *as a nation* was chastised and continued its remnant existence. See Jeremiah 30:11; 31:18; 46:28. And this point cannot be ignored, either: the great prophetic announcements concerning God's everlasting love are directed principally toward Israel *as a nation*. This includes the celebrated statements in Jeremiah 31:3; Hosea 11:1-9; 14:4; and Micah 7:18-20. This does not imply that they tell us nothing of God's love for individuals, of course. I have used them myself for this purpose. The point is that God's love for Israel as a nation, especially in view of its unique status, may not be the same in every respect as his love for individuals.

The third reason why Israel is not a proper paradigm for God's grace toward individuals is that his choice of Israel was for the purpose of service, not salvation. Even if God's choice of Abraham, Isaac, Jacob, and the nation *were* unconditional—and this has not yet been established, this would not necessarily tell us anything about how God gives saving grace to individuals. Christ chose twelve apostles for service, but one was a devil (John 6:70). Being chosen for service does not guarantee anything with respect to salvation. This should especially be noted in connection with Romans 9-11, a passage in the New Testament often used as a proof of unconditional grace. But this passage is not dealing with election to salvation, but election to service in God's plan of redemption. The main question has to do with God's choice of Israel as a nation, beginning with the choice of the patriarchs. We must not think that we can use this material to show how God elects individuals for salvation.[163]

A final reason why Israel is not a proper paradigm for our understanding of saving grace is that most of the blessings and curses connected with the apparently unconditional relationship between God and Israel were temporal or historical in nature and did not necessarily imply eternal blessings or curses on their recipients. One needs only to read Deuteronomy 28 to get the point of this. Even the great passages

---

163. See Jack Cottrell, *What the Bible Says About God the Ruler*, pp. 204-207.

that speak of God's wrath as temporary and his favor as eternal are talking about the temporal punishment of Babylonian captivity or some other national oppression, and physical deliverance therefrom.[164] Again this does not mean that we can learn nothing from them about how God's wrath and grace apply to individuals, but we must be true to the original historical context and be cautious about generalizing from it.

Grace Is Conditional

Now that we have placed God's choice of Israel in its proper perspective, it is time to establish the premise that God's grace is indeed conditional with respect to its application to individuals for the purpose of salvation. This is true in the Old Testament as well as the New. In the Old Testament, except for God's unconditional commitment to keep the *nation* alive until the coming of the Messiah, everything else with respect to the bestowal of grace was conditional. This applies even to the nation itself with regard to whether it would avoid punishment or not, and it applies to individuals with regard to whether they were in God's favor or not. To use a term introduced earlier in connection with the righteousness of God, we may say that God's favor toward individuals and even toward the nation itself in most respects was conditioned upon their *relative righteousness*, with this sometimes being understood in the most general sense of turning one's heart toward God in faith and repentance.

This is true even of those examples usually cited as evidence of unconditional grace. To quote Genesis 6:8, that "Noah found favor in the eyes of the Lord," and to omit verse 9 is inexcusable: "Noah was a righteous man, blameless in his time; Noah walked with God." In Genesis 7:1 the Lord says to Noah, "Go into the ark, you and your whole family, because I have found you righteous in this generation" (NIV). In view of this latter statement, it is difficult to see how anyone could say God's choice of Noah was unconditional.

The same applies to God's choice of Abraham. Those who say this choice was completely unconditional have concentrated too much on the passages in Deuteronomy and have overlooked Nehemiah 9:7-8.

---

164. See Ps. 30:5; Isa. 10:25; 12:1; 54:7-8; 60:10; Jer. 3:12-13; Lam. 3:31-33; Ezek. 16:42; Hosea 11:8ff.; Micah 7:18-20.

Verse 7 says, "Thou art the Lord God, who chose Abram and brought him out from Ur of the Chaldees, and gave him the name Abraham." But this much is already known from the Pentateuch. The significant addition is in verse 8: "And Thou didst find his heart faithful before Thee, and didst make a covenant with him." As to the choice of Jacob over Esau, no such positive statement is made of Jacob, but Esau is described as an "immoral [and] godless person" (Heb. 12:16), something that God in his foreknowledge would know even before the twins were born.

Was the choice of Israel then unconditional or conditional? We know that Israel was chosen because of God's love for and promises to the fathers (Deut. 4:37; 7:7-8), but we have just seen that God's choice of Abraham was related to the latter's "faithful heart." Thus it is a significant overstatement to say that the choice of Israel (and of their fathers before them) was completely unconditional. But even at the time when God called Israel out of Egypt and made them his people, his covenant with them was conditional. The condition is clearly stated in Exodus 19:5, "Now then, if you will indeed obey My voice and keep My covenant, then you shall be My own possession among all the peoples." The people were reminded of this condition just before their entrance into the promised land: "The Lord will establish you as a holy people to Himself, as He swore to you, if you will keep the commandments of the Lord your God, and walk in His ways" (Deut. 28:9). How long shall we continue to pretend that these verses are not in the Bible?

God also made it very clear to his people that they would continue in his favor and avoid curses and destruction *if* they continued to walk in his ways. In the midst of oppression and captivity, they were told (usually prophetically) that they would be delivered *if* they repented and returned to the Lord. All such conditional statements are too numerous to cite here, but here are a few examples, beginning with warnings spoken by Moses at the threshold of Canaan: "And it shall come about if you ever forget the Lord your God, and go after other gods and serve them and worship them, I testify against you today that you shall surely perish" (Deut. 8:19). "See, I am setting before you today a blessing and a curse: the blessing, if you listen to the commandments of the Lord your God, which I am commanding you today; and the curse, if you do not listen to the commandments of the Lord your God" (Deut. 11:26-28). Joshua repeated these warnings near the end of his life

(Josh. 23:11-16; 24:20).

The promises concerning deliverance from captivity are almost always stated in conditional form. A typical statement is II Chronicles 30:9, where the promise of grace is surrounded by conditions: "For if you return to the Lord, your brothers and your sons will find compassion before those who led them captive, and will return to this land. For the Lord your God is gracious and compassionate, and will not turn His face away from you if you return to Him." God says in Psalm 81:13-14, "Oh that My people would listen to Me, that Israel would walk in My ways! I would quickly subdue their enemies, and turn My hand against their adversaries." In Isaiah 55:6-7 God promises pardon, but only to those who forsake wickedness and return to him: "Seek the Lord while He may be found; call upon Him while He is near. Let the wicked forsake his way, and the unrighteous man his thoughts; and let him return to the Lord, and He will have compassion on him; and to our God, for He will abundantly pardon." "Therefore, thus says the Lord, 'If you return, then I will restore you'" (Jer. 15:19). For other such conditional promises see Isaiah 1:18-20; 26:2; 33:15-16; Jeremiah 3:10-13; 12:15-17; Hosea 5:15; 14:1-2; Joel 2:12-14; Amos 5:15; and Zephaniah 2:3. See Solomon's prayer in I Kings 8:46-51.

The list of passages that make relative righteousness on the part of individuals a condition for acceptance with God seems almost endless. Only a few examples will be given. Exodus 20:6 says God shows lovingkindness "to those who love Me and keep My commandments." "The Lord is good to those who wait for Him, to the person who seeks Him" (Lam. 3:25). "Thou, O Lord, hast not forsaken those who seek Thee" (Ps. 9:10). "The eyes of the Lord are toward the righteous, and His ears are open to their cry" (Ps. 34:15). "Do preserve my soul, for I am a godly man; O Thou my God, save Thy servant who trusts in Thee" (Ps. 86:2). Here is God's promise: "Because he has loved Me, therefore I will deliver him; I will set him securely on high, because he has known My name. He will call upon Me, and I will answer him" (Ps. 91:14-15). "Do good, O Lord, to those who are good, and to those who are upright in their hearts" (Ps. 125:4). "The Lord is near to all who call upon Him, to all who call upon Him in truth. He will fulfill the desire of those who fear Him; He will also hear their cry and will save them. The Lord keeps all who love Him; but all the wicked, He will destroy" (Ps. 145:18-20).

In all of these cases the condition for acceptance is only a relative righteousness, else no one would receive grace. But that such relative righteousness *is* a condition could not be clearer from the passages cited. This contrast makes it even clearer: "Thou dost hate all who do iniquity" (Ps. 5:5); "the Lord loves the righteous" (Ps. 146:8). Morris' statement thus seems quite extreme: "Nothing in men can account for God's love."[165] At the very least one must acknowledge Yahweh as God (and in New Testament times, Christ as Lord and Savior), and turn his heart toward God in true repentance, in order to receive the gift of grace. God offers his favor to man, but the condition for actually giving it is that man must respond with an open and contrite heart. Of course God is not nonchalant about his offer, and he is not indifferent as to whether man responds. As we have seen, he pleads with men to respond. He does not wait for men to seek him, but places himself in front of them and calls out to them, "Here I am! Here I am!" But they must call back, else they are rejected: "I called, but you did not answer" (Isa. 65:1, 12).[166] Those who refuse to respond to God's call and are thus rejected are still loved by God (Jer. 11:15; 12:7), but they are rejected just the same.

In the New Testament the context changes radically, but the gracious gift of forgiveness is still conditional. The context is different because the revelation is no longer dealing mainly with a nation chosen for service, where the favor or disfavor of God is related mostly to temporal results. In the New Testament, grace is being offered to individuals for the purpose of eternal salvation. (This is not absent from the Old Testament, of course, but there the national and temporal context dominates.) Also, in the New Testament the emphasis falls not so much on the *need* for *relative* righteousness as on the *lack* of *absolute* righteousness, for which the only solution is the free gift of the righteousness of Christ. Nevertheless even here it is clear that God gives this gift only to those who turn their hearts toward him in a believing,

---

165. Leon Morris, *Testaments of Love*, p. 271.

166. Brunner cites Isaiah 65:1ff. as proof that "the fulfilment of the Covenant with God is based upon this divine love alone, not upon the fact of Israel's repentance" (Emil Brunner, *The Christian Doctrine of God*, p. 184). Unfortunately he did not read far enough into the chapter, because the whole point of this passage is that repentance *is* required.

repentant response. Such passages as the following cannot be lightly dismissed: "Unless you repent, you will all likewise perish" (Luke 13:3). "Whoever believes in Him should not perish, but have eternal life" (John 3:16). "He who believes in the Son has eternal life; but he who does not obey the Son shall not see life, but the wrath of God abides on him" (John 3:36). "Repent, and let each of you be baptized in the name of Jesus Christ for the forgiveness of your sins" (Acts 2:38). "Believe in the Lord Jesus, and you shall be saved" (Acts 16:31). "Everyone who calls on the name of the Lord shall be saved" (Acts 2:21). "Arise, and be baptized, and wash away your sins, calling on His name" (Acts 22:16). "If you confess with your mouth Jesus as Lord, and believe in your heart that God raised Him from the dead, you shall be saved" (Rom. 10:9). Those already in possession of the gift will keep it, "if indeed you continue in the faith firmly established and steadfast" (Col. 1:23).

Some find it difficult to accept the conditionality of grace because they equate *unmerited* with *unconditional*. These are not the same at all. The conditions for receiving grace are not works, for they are not responses to law or commandments but rather responses to promises and the necessary preparation of the heart for receiving what is promised. The conditions for receiving God's gift of forgiveness are not equivalent to holding out a payment to God in order to purchase it, they are equivalent only to holding out one's empty hand to grasp the gift. But one *must* open his hand and hold it out.

CONCLUSION

In this lengthy chapter we have attempted to set forth the Biblical teaching concerning the benevolent side of God's nature. We have seen that God's good will toward mankind considered simply as his creatures is known as love. But we have seen how this love takes on different forms when it confronts man as sinner. In response to man's sin-caused misery and suffering, love takes the form of mercy. In response to man's persistence in sin, it shows itself as patience. And in response to the sinner's condemnation and lostness, it becomes forgiving grace.

We have also indicated that sin has resulted in a kind of tension within God between his nature as holiness and his nature as love. We have also seen how God has dealt with this tension so that he can be completely righteous (i.e., true to both sides of his nature) by sending Jesus to be the propitiation for our sins. This is the essence of redemption, which will be examined in detail in the next chapter.

7

THE WORK OF REDEMPTION

If we define redemption very loosely as including everything done by God to reverse the effects of sin, then most of the historical works of God recorded in Scripture would be redemptive in nature. The series of redemptive events would begin at least as early as the call of Abraham in Genesis 12, and then would include all of God's dealings with Abraham's family through Isaac and Jacob and with the nation of Israel. It would also include, of course, the life and work of Jesus Christ, as well as the sending of the Holy Spirit and his work in the church.

But not all the works of redemption are equal in intensity and in effect. Some are preparatory; some are primary; some are derivative. Part of the work is direct, while most of it is indirect. In this chapter we are focusing mainly on the only primary and direct work of redemption, namely, the death and resurrection of Jesus Christ. All other works of redemption are secondary to and dependent upon this work of Christ. Some lead up to it and others grow out of it, but Christ's work is the focal point of all redemption. Everything before it looks ahead to it, and everything after it looks back to it.

The Old Testament is basically the record of God's *preparation* for the main work of redemption. This preparatory work includes everything that has to do with Israel, from the call of Abraham through the work of John the Baptist in the Gospels. Israel's very existence as a nation, its covenant with Yahweh, its system of civil and ceremonial laws, the prophetic revelation entrusted to this people, their geographical and religious isolation in a land of their own, much of their political and military interaction with other nations—all of this is part of the preparation for the coming of the Redeemer and thus has a second-dary redemptive significance of its own. Much attention is given in the Old Testament to the land promised to Abraham and possessed by Israel, but this must not be regarded as primary. The possession of the land, along with everything else related to Israel, is a means to an end, namely, the first coming of Jesus into the world. In order to prepare for the Messiah's coming it was important to have a nation of people with unity and continuity, one to whom revelation could be given and by whom it could be guarded and cherished. This revelation would include the knowledge of the true God and his law in order to provide a context of godliness and piety; it would also include predictive prophecy of the Messiah in order to generate hope and expectation. This could best be done with a single nation confined to a concentrated geographical location. Such was the purpose of Israel, and in this general sense her whole history is a preparatory work of redemption.

But within this general history of Israel, there are certain specific elements that directly foreshadow the redemptive work of Christ. The clearest and most specific are the Messianic prophecies, including the great predictions of the death of Jesus in Psalm 22 and Isaiah 53. Less clear at the time but clear enough from the perspective of the New Testament is the sacrificial system included in the Law of Moses. Especially significant are the sin offerings (Lev. 4:1-35), the trespass or guilt offerings (Lev. 5:6-6:7), and the sacrifices on the Day of Atonement (Lev. 16:1-28). In these offerings the sins of the people were symbolically transferred from the sinners themselves to the innocent substitutes, who were then put to death in the place of the guilty ones. This transfer was graphically enacted in the case of the scapegoat on the Day of Atonement, as described in Leviticus 16:21-22,

Then Aaron shall lay both of his hands on the head of the live goat, and confess over it all the iniquities of the sons of Israel, and all their transgressions in regard to all their sins; and he shall lay them on the head of the goat and send it away into the wilderness by the hand of a man who stands in readiness. And the goat shall bear on itself all their iniquities to a solitary land . . . .

Concerning this ceremony Motyer says, "The laying on of hands . . . expresses the transference of sin from the guilty to the innocent, so that the latter actually becomes a 'sin-bearer.'"[1]

All these sacrifices taught the people of Israel the basic principle of redemption, namely, that the debt or price for their sins could be paid by a substitute. There can be little doubt that their ultimate purpose was to be a prophetic type of the sacrifice offered by Jesus on Calvary. The specific word for the guilt or trespass offering is used for the Suffering Servant (the coming Messiah) in Isaiah 53:10, "But the Lord was pleased to crush Him, putting Him to grief; if He would render Himself as a guilt offering, He will see His offspring, He will prolong His days." In the New Testament Jesus is specifically called "an offering and a sacrifice to God" (Eph. 5:2). The Book of Hebrews makes it clear that the Old Testament system was a deliberate foreshadowing of the reality of Christ's sacrifice of himself; it was "a symbol for the present time" (Heb. 9:9). All of chapters 9 and 10 are relevant, especially these words from 9:12-14,

> . . . Not through the blood of goats and calves, but through His own blood, He entered the holy place once for all, having obtained eternal redemption. For if the blood of goats and bulls and the ashes of a heifer sprinkling those who have been defiled, sanctify for the cleansing of the flesh, how much more will the blood of Christ, who through the eternal Spirit offered Himself without blemish to God, cleanse your conscience from dead works to serve the living God?

Concerning all these Old Covenant sacrifices Packer asserts, "These rituals are the immediate background of Paul's teaching on propitiation: it is the fulfilment of the Old Testament sacrificial pattern that he proclaims."[2]

---

1. J. A. Motyer, "Atonement, Day of," *Evangelical Dictionary of Theology*, ed. Walter A. Elwell (Grand Rapids: Baker Book House, 1984), p. 98.
2. J. I. Packer, *Knowing God* (Downers Grove: InterVarsity Press, 1973), p. 169.

The Messianic prophecies and the sacrificial system are a very important part of the Old Testament preparation for the coming Redeemer, but just as significant are the two great redemptive acts of God that are the keystones of Israel's history, namely, the exodus from Egypt and the restoration from Babylon. These parallel events demonstrate the nature of God as Redeemer even before the coming of the Messiah himself. It is mainly in connection with these two acts of deliverance that God is called Redeemer and Savior in the Old Testament; the language of salvation and redemption is applied most liberally to them, as we saw in chapter one above. Just prior to the great exodus God made this promise: "I am the Lord, and I will bring you out from under the burdens of the Egyptians, and I will deliver you from their bondage. I will also redeem you with an outstretched arm and with great judgments" (Ex. 6:6). Henceforward he was known to them as "the Redeemer of Israel" (Isa. 49:7).

The parallel between the the exodus and the restoration on the one hand and the redemptive work of Christ on the other hand is so remarkable that the former must have been designed as historical types of the latter. Each is an act of deliverance from a kind of bondage, the former being physical (slavery in Egypt, exile in Babylon) and the latter being spiritual ("slaves of sin," Rom. 6:17). Each involves a kind of restoration to a saved state, the former again being physical (life in the "promised land" or homeland) and the latter spiritual (fellowship with God). Finally—and this cannot be just a coincidence—in each case the restoration was led or accomplished by a man named *Joshua* (Hebrew)[3] or *Jesus* (Greek), identical names meaning "Yahweh is salvation." These were Joshua, the successor of Moses (Josh. 3:7ff.); Joshua, the high priest who helped lead the restoration (Ezra 3:8; Hag. 1:1); and of course Jesus of Nazareth, "the Savior of the world" (I John 4:14).

While these great Old Testament works of redemption have only a temporal result and do not contribute directly to our redemption from sin, they help prepare for the work of "eternal redemption" (Heb. 9:12) by preserving Israel and by dramatically portraying on the stage of history what the Almighty God is willing and able to do to save his people. Ronald Hals believes that the exodus in particular is a perfect model

---

3. This name was sometimes written *Jeshua*, but the meaning is the same.

of redemption by God's grace, since it very clearly pictures God and God alone as performing the works that save: "But Moses said to the people, 'Do not fear! Stand by and see the salvation of the Lord which He will accomplish for you today . . . . The Lord will fight for you while you keep silent'" (Ex. 14:13-14). It also pictures Israel as being "saved by faith," as suggested by Exodus 14:30-31, "Thus the Lord saved Israel that day from the hand of the Egyptians . . . . And when Israel saw the great power which the Lord had used against the Egyptians, the people feared the Lord, and they believed in the Lord and in His servant Moses."[4]

Thus when we come to the New Testament, we have already been prepared to think of God as the Redeemer who works great works of redemption to save his people, and who is willing to provide a substitute to bear the guilt of their sins in their place. The rest of this chapter will focus on that single primary work of redemption to which all of this Old Testament background points, namely, the death and resurrection of Jesus.[5]

MAN'S NEED

The nature of the work of redemption will be determined in part by the nature of the predicament from which man must be redeemed. When we discussed the alternatives to Biblical redemption in chapter two above, we saw just how crucial is the question, "*From what* is man redeemed?" We saw there that in most non-biblical approaches to the subject, man is seen as having two basic problems (or a combination thereof), namely, ignorance and weakness. For example, we saw that Hinduism understands man's suffering to be the result of his ignorance of his own true self, and that Existentialism traces man's inauthentic existence to his weak-willed failure to assert himself as an individual in the face of cultural and societal pressures.

When man's problem is defined in terms of ignorance and weakness, his salvation will then be accomplished by some form of knowledge, some form of power, or a combination of both. In many

---

4. Ronald M. Hals, *Grace and Faith in the Old Testament* (Minneapolis: Augsburg, 1980), pp. 27ff.

5. Though they are two discrete steps, the death and resurrection of Jesus should be regarded as a single unified work of redemption.

cases the salvation is wrought by man himself without divine intervention. In classical Hinduism and Buddhism, the key is knowledge or enlightenment achieved through one's own efforts or with the help of a teacher. The same is true in Hellenistic philosophy. In secular philosophies such as Existentialism or Humanism, the basic solution to the human problem is for individuals to assert themselves through acts of will to do what they know ought to be done.

In some cases the solution comes through divine intervention, with the deity providing the needed knowledge and/or power. Gnosticism is an example of a salvation system which includes a divine savior, whose role is to reveal the knowledge necessary for escape from this world. Other examples are the Liberal and Secular forms of Christianity, which interpret man's problem as a combination of ignorance and weakness resulting from his evolutionary origin, and which interpret Jesus as "revealing" the needed knowledge and strengthening our will and motivation through his own inspiring example and especially through his death on the cross.

In almost all non-biblical forms of salvation, the one thing that seems to be missing is the concept of *sin against a personal God.* This is especially true in the non-Christian religions and philosophies, but sadly it is also true for some schools of so-called Christian thought. Where the view of sin is weak or non-existent, the concept of salvation will also be weak. Even where a Savior is posited, such as in *bhakti* Hinduism or True Pure Land Buddhism or even Liberal Christianity, he is not seen as dealing with man's true problem; he is not interpreted as a *sin-bearer* who is healing a breach between God and man caused by that sin. In the few cases where sin against a personal God is acknowledged as the basic problem, i.e., traditional Judaism and Islam, there is no sin-bearer at all.

If we are to have a proper understanding of and appreciation for the work of redemption, then we must go beyond all these inadequate views to a right understanding of man's basic need. It is certainly true that part of our problem is ignorance and weakness, but these are not basic or primary. As serious as these may be, ignorance and weakness as such would not make *redemption* necessary in any real sense of the word. Insofar as they are truly problems, they are the result of the single underlying problem that gives rise to all of man's other difficulties, namely, *sin.* And this sin must not be understood in any weak or distorted fashion, such as the residue of our alleged animal nature, or sin against oneself or one's fellow man and no more. No, the underlying problem is that man is a sinner in the sense that he has violated the will of the holy God. This is the Biblical teaching. Sin is sin against God and against his law.

What makes sin so problematic is not just the sin itself, but its consequences for the sinner himself and for the world as a whole. That the entire world has been affected can be seen from the curse in Genesis 3:14-19 and from Paul's reflection on this in Romans 8:19-22. The individual sinner suffers from an inner spiritual death (Eph. 2:1, 5) and from the curse of physical death (Rom. 8:10). These problems are serious enough, but the worst consequence of sin is the individual's *guilt* before the holy Lawgiver and Judge. I am not referring to subjective guilt feelings, but to the objective state of being a law-breaker and thus of being in a wrong relationship to the law of God and being under its penalty. Thus it is a legal or judicial concept similar to a person's being found guilty in a human court of law, only infinitely worse since it is God's law that has been violated and the penalty of eternal hell that has been incurred.

Scripture clearly teaches the concept of guilt. James 2:10 says, "For whoever keeps the whole law and yet stumbles in one point, he has become guilty of all." The word used here is *enochos*, which is a technical legal term meaning "guilty, subject to or liable to penalty." Romans 3:19 says that the whole world is "guilty before God" (KJV). The word here is *hupodikos*, which means "liable to judgment, worthy of punishment, accountable." The term *accountable* is really too weak to capture the full meaning of the Greek term, since some connotations of this English word do not specify whether a person is guilty or not, but simply imply that he must give an account for his actions, good or bad. But the term *hupodikos* is much more specific and connotes actual guilt. In classical usage it referred to anyone liable to penal justice who "must be subjected to a trial, to judicial examination, prosecution and punishment: 'guilty' in the sense of having offended against the law."[6] Another term denoting the sinner's guilt is *opheilō*, meaning "to owe, to be in

---

6. Christian Maurer, "ὑπόδικος," *Theological Dictionary of the New Testament*, ed. Gerhard Friedrich, tr. Geoffrey W. Bromiley (Grand Rapids: Eerdmans, 1972), VIII:557.

debt, to be under obligation." One noun form of this word, *opheilēma*, is used in Matthew 6:12 as a synonym for sin: "Forgive us our debts." Another noun form, *opheiletēs* ("debtor") is used in Luke 13:4 as a synonym for sinner (cf. v. 2); the NIV translates it as "guilty." The significance of this is that the sinner owes a debt of punishment to the law, or more precisely to the Lawgiver who stands behind the law.

The reality of guilt brings us face to face with the wrath of God. The guilty sinner does not merely stand under some abstract penalty of an impersonal law; rather, he is the deliberate object of the personal vengeance and wrath of the holy God. The punishment of eternal hell is not just the regrettable but natural result of the sinner's rejection of God; it is God's own decreed rejection of the sinner who presumes to violate his holy law. It is sheer wrath.

But here is a fact that must not be forgotten: although the sinner as sinner is the object of God's deserved wrath, *at the same time*, as creature, he is the object of God's love and compassion and grace. God justly condemns the sinner for his sin, but at the same time is willing to save him and actually desires to save him from his sins in spite of his sins. Here is the source of tension between the two sides of God's nature, a tension rooted in the divine righteousness. As we have seen, righteousness means conformity to a law or satisfying the requirements of a law. The "law" to which the righteous God conforms is his own nature: he must be true to himself; he must always act in accord with his own character and being. The tension or dilemma with reference to sin is simply this: how can God be true to both sides of his nature at the same time? How can he satisfy both his wrath *and* his love? If he were to condemn the sinner to hell as his holy nature demands, then his righteousness would be upheld with reference to his holiness but not his love. If he were simply to save the sinner from eternal punishment as his loving nature desires, then his righteousness would be upheld with reference to his love but not his holiness. Either way he would not be acting in full accord with his total nature.

Let us be sure we understand one thing at this point. Of the two possibilities just mentioned, even if the dilemma could be resolved with regard to both, God is not really interested in the first one but only in the second. He does not really want to condemn the sinner just to satisfy his wrath if only he could find a way of being true to his love at the same time. As we saw in the last chapter, God's grace in a sense "triumphs over" his wrath in this regard. *What he desires to do is to save the sinner while finding a way to be true to his holiness at the same time.* In other words, he desires to *justify* the sinner while remaining *just* or righteous with respect to his holiness and wrath (Rom. 3:26). This is the essence of the enterprise of redemption, and it is the key to understanding the meaning of the cross.

THE ATONEMENT

The main point of the preceding section is that one must have a proper understanding of man's predicament in order to have a correct view of the nature of redemption. Our predicament is that we have sinned against the holy law of the personal Creator-God, and we stand guilty before him and are the deserving objects of his wrath. Thus given the three types of salvation categorized in chapter two above, Biblical redemption falls into the third category, i.e., the healing of a broken relationship between God and man. The other two types of redemption—inner personal healing and the healing of interpersonal relationships—are not the primary focus of Christianity but are the welcome results of the reconciliation of God and man to one another.

Reconciling God and man, or bringing them to a relationship of at-one-ment, is the task that Jesus came to accomplish. His work is *the* redemption. There are other redemptive acts, but what Christ has done is fundamental. Without his work, all the rest is irrelevant, and even impossible.

We will discuss the work of Jesus in two sections, dealing first with the cross and then with the resurrection. Regarding the cross, we would note that it is practically synonymous with atonement. Though in an indirect sense the whole of Jesus' life and work could be called atonement, in the most direct and specific sense the atonement was the result of the cross. Just how this is so has been a point of strong disagreement down through the Christian centuries. Many of the so-called "theories of atonement" are not really true to Scripture, usually because of a faulty view of God, or because of a faulty view of man's predicament, or both. Such false views of the cross need to be identified and rejected because they dishonor God and rob him of his glory by distorting the true nature of redemption. Thus in this section, before we look at the Biblical teaching regarding the cross, we will examine some major false or incomplete views of atonement.

Inadequate or Incomplete Concepts of Atonement

What was the work of Christ, especially his death, meant to accomplish? What difference was his death designed to make in the God-man relationship? In trying to classify the variety of answers that have been given to this kind of question, some have distinguished between objective and subjective theories of atonement. In objective theories the specific goal of the atonement, the purpose that made the cross necessary in the first place, is attained on the cross itself in the very act of Christ's dying for us. It happens outside ourselves and is an accomplished fact before we ever hear of it and even if we never hear of it. In subjective theories, on the other hand, the specific goal of the cross is to bring about some inner change within the hearts and lives of those who come to know about it.

Another way of distinguishing and relating the various views of atonement is to arrange them, as Warfield says, "according to the conception each entertains of the person or persons on whom the work of Christ terminates."[7] That is to say, who is the specific object of Christ's work? The cross is intended to do something very specific, but to whom? for whom? Within whom lies the problem that only the cross can solve? Within whom lies the obstacle to salvation that can be removed only by the cross? Though some combinations may be found, there are really just three main answers to this kind of question. The work of the cross will terminate either on Satan, or on man, or on God.

Satan as the Object of the Cross

A rather unlikely view of the cross is that it was directed primarily toward the Devil.[8] This view was held by a number of the early church fathers into the fifth century (including Augustine), and appears even

---

7. B. B. Warfield, "The Chief Theories of the Atonement," *The Person and Work of Christ*, by B. B. Warfield, ed. Samuel G. Craig (Nutley, N.J.: Presbyterian and Reformed, 1950), p. 356.
   8. Ibid., pp. 356-357; Gustaf Aulén. *Christus Victor: An Historical Study of the Three Main Types of the Idea of Atonement*, tr. A. G. Hebert (New York: Macmillan, 1951), pp. 47-55.

later in modified form in such men as Bernard and Luther.[9] The basic idea seems to be based on Christ's statement that he came "to give His life a ransom for many" (Mark 10:45). The reasoning was that a ransom must be paid to somebody, and the most likely such person is Satan. Sinful man is seen as being in Satan's control, with some even acknowledging the control to be legal and just since man has sold himself into Satan's grip by his sin. In any case man can be saved only by being rescued from this bondage to the Devil. According to this view, this was the main purpose of the cross (though not necessarily its only purpose). In one way or another the cross was an integral part of a plot to wrest man away from Satan. For some it was a simple power play; for others it was the payment of a demanded ransom; for still others it was part of a plot by which God deceived or outwitted the Devil.

An example of the ransom concept is found in the following quotation from Origen (third century A.D.):[10]

> . . . If, therefore, we were bought with a price, as Paul also bears witness, without doubt we were bought from some one whose servants we were, and who demanded the price which he wished in order to discharge those whom he held. Now, the devil was the one who held us, to whom we had been delivered by our sins. He demanded, therefore, as our price, the blood of Christ. . . .

The deception theory was not uncommon, the idea being that the miracle-working Christ would be regarded as such a prize that the Devil would be willing to accept him in trade for everyone else. What the Devil did not realize was that through the incarnation the divine Logos was concealed within the human nature of Jesus of Nazareth and would implement his own escape from Satan via resurrection once the captives had been released. A good example of this is found in the following explanation by Gregory of Nyssa (fourth century A.D.):[11]

---

9. On Luther's occasional use of the imagery, see Aulén. *Christus Victor*, pp. 103ff.

10. Origen, *On the Epistle to the Romans*, II.ii; cited in Hugo Grotius, *A Defence of the Catholic Faith Concerning the Satisfaction of Christ*, tr. Frank Hugh Foster (Andover: Warren F. Draper, 1889), pp. 226-227.

11. Gregory of Nyssa, "An Address on Religious Instruction," 22-26, *Christology of the Later Fathers*, ed. Edward R. Hardy; "Library of Christian Classics," Vol. III (Philadelphia: Westminster Press, n.d.), pp. 299-303.

. . . In the same way, when once we had voluntarily sold ourselves, he who undertook out of goodness to restore our freedom had to contrive a just and not a dictatorial method to do so. And some such method is this: to give the master the chance to take whatever he wants to as the price of the slave.

But how can we recount in detail each of the gospel miracles? When the enemy saw such power, he recognized in Christ a bargain which offered him more than he held. For this reason he chose him as the ransom for those he had shut up in death's prison. Since, however, he could not look upon the direct vision of God, he had to see him clothed in some part of that flesh which he already held captive through sin. Consequently the Deity was veiled in flesh, so that the enemy, by seeing something familiar and natural to him, might not be terrified at the approach of transcendent power. So when he saw this power softly reflected more and more through the miracles, he reckoned that what he saw was to be desired rather than feared.

. . . Hence it was that God, in order to make himself easily accessible to him who sought the ransom for us, veiled himself in our nature. In that way, as it is with greedy fish, he might swallow the Godhead like a fishhook along with the flesh, which was the bait. Thus, when life came to dwell with death and light shone upon darkness, their contraries might vanish away. For it is nót in the nature of darkness to endure the presence of light, nor can death exist where life is active.

. . . By the principle of justice the deceiver reaps the harvest of the seeds he sowed with his own free will. For he who first deceived man by the bait of pleasure is himself deceived by the camouflage of human nature. But the purpose of the action changes it into something good. For the one practiced deceit to ruin our nature; but the other, being at once just and good and wise, made use of a deceitful device to save the one who had been ruined. . . .

The idea of deceiving the Devil occurs quite frequently. Augustine used the simile of baiting a mouse trap, and Luther repeats the analogy of baiting a fishing hook.[12] It seems quite out of character for the holy God, however. As is obvious, Gregory's attempt to defend it in the last paragraph quoted from him above is an "end justifies the means" ethic. There is certainly an element of truth in the idea that Christ's work was

---

12. Gustaf Aulén. *Christus Victor.* pp. 53, 103-104.

in part directed against Satan (Heb. 2:14-15; I John 3:8), but it is a matter of overcoming him through sheer power and not by deception nor by ransom. Also, it is accomplished more directly by the resurrection than the cross. The main object of the cross is not Satan, but someone else.

Man as the Object of the Cross

This leads to the second way of interpreting the atonement, namely, that its object was man and not Satan. The idea here is that the only real obstacle to salvation is in man himself; thus the main purpose of the cross is to have some kind of effect upon the heart and life of man. Most if not all of the variations of this view are thus subjective in nature. That is, whatever is accomplished by the cross does not lie outside of man but within him.

Several general comments may be made on the views that are grouped together here. First, most but not necessarily all of them assume that man's basic problem is something less than sin against a holy God. Ignorance and weakness are the main problems, at least insofar as the cross is concerned. Thus in order to address these problems, the cross provides knowledge and/or power. It is God's way of *revealing* something to us, and this in turn *influences* us to act in a certain way. Second, most of the views that make man the direct object of the cross do not make a material distinction between the cross as such and the whole of Jesus' life and work. Whatever is accomplished by the cross was already being accomplished just by his being here and by his general ministry and teaching. The cross is but an intensification and a focusing of his overall purpose. In the minds of some, the cross is not inherently necessary for the accomplishing of this purpose. Given more time and a different response from the Jews, Christ could have achieved his goal without it. Third, most but not necessarily all of those who hold a man-directed view of the cross do so because they have adopted other doctrinal positions that virtually limit them to some version of this theory. Those who have a weak view of sin, a weak view of divine wrath, or a weak view of the deity of Christ will almost of necessity present some such view of the cross. Those who reject the miraculous, the supernatural, or even the forensic will do the same. The same is true of those who redefine righteousness to exclude retributive justice and to

413

mean salvation only, and of those who deny the reality of the imputation of either sin or righteousness.

The Moral Influence Theory. Among those who see the atoning work of Christ as terminating on man, there are two main approaches: the moral influence theory and the governmental theory. The essence of the classical moral influence theory is that God himself is ready, willing and able to forgive man; the only thing man must do to receive the gift of forgiveness is to accept it in repentance and faith. Nothing else is needed: no cross, no resurrection, no incarnation. The problem, however, is that man in his stubbornness refuses to accept the gift. Therefore as a demonstration of his infinite love God goes to the extreme of sending his Son into the world, even to die on the cross if necessary, in order to break down man's resistance and convince him to believe and repent. This is the "moral influence," i.e., the power to persuade and to motivate the will of man to do what is necessary for him to receive salvation. When we thus perceive just how much we are loved, this "breaks down our opposition to God, melts our hearts, and brings us as prodigals home to the Father's arms."[13]

The first major example of this view is Peter Abelard (1079-1142), who was quite a free-thinking liberal for his day. He taught that God's giving up his Son to suffering and death reveals his amazing love for us, and thereby enkindles in us a responsive love and repentance, on the basis of which God forgives our sins. Christ's great example of love evokes a similar love in us.

A more recent and more influential example is Horace Bushnell (1802-1876), who presented his view in two volumes entitled *The Vicarious Sacrifice* (1865) and *Forgiveness and Law* (1874). According to Bushnell man's sin offends God deeply, but he is willing to forgive even though it costs him much inner suffering and pain. The real problem with forgiveness is in man, who feels the burden of his sin and guilt so much that he considers himself unworthy to return to God, even though God offers him free forgiveness. God's greatest problem, then, is "how to put confidence in the bosom of guilt."[14] As Strong describes

---

13. B. B. Warfield, "The Chief Theories of the Atonement," p. 362.
14. Horace Bushnell, *Forgiveness and Law* (New York: Scribner, Armstrong & Co., 1874), p. 206.

this view, the problem is not how to satisfy divine justice, but how to soften human hearts and lead them to repentance; it is not how to remove an obstacle to the pardon of sinners that exists in God, but how to convince sinners that there is no such obstacle.[15] This is what Christ is doing through the cross. He is revealing or demonstrating in a moment of time God's eternal suffering love and his eternal readiness to forgive.[16] Such a demonstration has the power to transform the character of the sinner. It is able to "pierce, and press, and draw, and sway, and, as it were, new crystallize the soul." This is "the Moral Power of God." It is a "moral power which masters the soul's inward disorder, and renews it in holiness of life."[17]

This view is standard in modern Liberal Theology. For example, W. A. Brown says of Christ's atonement that "its saving efficacy consists in its moral influence in arousing repentance and faith."[18] By observing the way Christ bore his suffering, "men have seen a new revelation of the possibilities of humanity, and of the victorious power of love," and thus have been moved to turn to God in penitence and faith in order to receive the strength to love as Christ loved.[19] Another example is L. H. DeWolf, who says that the cross reconciles us to God by revealing the awfulness of sin and the love of God, which in turn move us to repent and return to God.[20]

One other example of the moral influence theory comes from Roger Haight's book, *An Alternative Vision: An Interpretation of Liberation Theology* (1985). It is typical of that perspective. According to Haight, the key concepts for understanding the work of Jesus are revelation and

---

15. Augustus H. Strong, *Systematic Theology*, 3 vols. in 1 (Valley Forge: Judson Press, 1907), p. 733.

16. Horace Bushnell, *Forgiveness and Law*, pp. 60, 71-75.

17. Ibid., pp. 169-174, 180.

18. William Adams Brown, *Christian Theology in Outline* (New York: Charles Scribner's Sons, 1906), p. 365.

19. Ibid., p. 368.

20. L. Harold DeWolf, *A Theology of the Living Church* (New York: Harper & Brothers, 1953), pp. 264-268. For a description of similar views by other Liberals, see Kenneth Cauthen, *The Impact of American Religious Liberalism* (New York: Harper & Row, 1962), pp. 77ff. (H. E. Fosdick), pp. 124-125 (A. C. Knudson), and p. 164 (Shailer Mathews). Cauthen observes, "In the background of this moral influence theory is a doctrine of God in which the element of wrath or holiness has been absorbed into divine love. This continuity between holiness and love makes an objective atonement unnecessary" (p. 125).

example. His whole life, including his death, is a revelation of the nature of God, the importance of the Kingdom of God, and the heinousness of sin. Thus this is "an exemplary theory of redemption: Jesus Christ is the teacher and model of salvation as the first saved and in the sense of being the paradigm of salvation itself." The resurrection was God's "final and absolute yes" to Jesus' message and life. His work goes beyond mere revelation by inaugurating a way of life that is intended to be "generalized or extended out into the social sphere of public history," thus creating the possibility for a just and meaningful human history.[21]

These are only a few examples of a view of the cross that is very widespread today. Some version of it will almost invariably be found in non-traditional and Liberal theologies, and occasionally it appears in a theology that is fairly conservative.[22] And of course, there is truth contained in this view. Jesus' death *is* a revelation or demonstration of God's infinite love and of the terrible nature of sin. It certainly is a power that softens and moves the hardened wills of sinners (John 12:32; Rom. 1:16). The serious error of this view, however, is to say that this is the only purpose of the cross, or even its main purpose. That which gives the cross its revelatory and influencing power is the deeper and more significant fact that it is a propitiation for man's sins. Unless it is primarily this, its inner logic is lost; and explaining just *how* the cross is a revelation of God's love and just *why* it should move the soul will always be a challenge and an opportunity for the enterprising theologian.

The Governmental Theory. Under the general heading of views that see the atonement as terminating on man as such, we also include what is called the governmental theory. With regard to its form it is practically identical with the moral influence theory. It sees no obstacle to forgiveness within the nature of God, who is ready, willing and able to forgive as far as he himself is concerned. The only problem is a particular attitude in man which can be corrected by the cross. Thus God gave his Son to be crucified in order to demonstrate something to man, and to persuade man to engage in a certain course of action. As a result God is able to dispense his forgiveness freely.

---

21. Roger Haight, *An Alternative Vision: An Interpretation of Liberation Theology* (New York: Paulist Press, 1985), pp. 127-134.
22. See, for example, C. S. Lewis' chapter on "The Perfect Penitent" in *Mere Christianity* (New York: Macmillan, 1960), pp. 56-61.

Though similar in form, the governmental theory is quite the opposite of the moral influence theory. Basically it sees the cross as a demonstration of God's *wrath* against sin, the purpose of which is to instill *fear* into the hearts of men in order to deter them from the wholesale sinning that would probably break out once forgiveness is known to be freely available.

This view was formulated first by Hugo Grotius (1583-1645), a Dutch lawyer and theologian. Grotius denied that there is anything in the nature of God that requires sin to be punished. As far as God is personally concerned, he could simply forgive without punishment. But there is more to it than this. As moral ruler of the universe, God is bound to uphold his law, lest his government fall into ruin and disorder. In other words, punishment of sin is a governmental expedient.[23] If God goes around forgiving sins right and left, respect for his law will decline and his moral government of the universe will collapse.[24] Thus God must punish sin in order to demonstrate what a serious matter it is. But how can he punish sin and save the sinner at the same time? This is where the cross comes in. God sends his Son, not to bear the punishment that he must necessarily pour out upon us, but to be a kind of example or object lesson to show us the kind of punishment sin actually deserves. Thus the cross is not a *satisfaction* of God's wrath, but a *demonstration* of it. The cross sets forth the high estimate God places on his law, and the heinous guilt incurred by violating it, and the wrath deserved by lawbreakers. It acts as a deterrant to sin, allowing God to forgive sin while maintaining order and respect for his moral government. Its object is to instill fear in men's hearts, lest God's forgiveness should lead them to scoff at the law and abandon themselves to sin.[25] Thus Christ's cross becomes an object lesson for us; God "makes an example of" his Son before the eyes of the world.

Grotius' explanation of the atonement was influential in some circles, notably New England Puritanism and Wesleyan Arminianism. A major theologian from the latter group is Richard Watson, whose teaching on this subject in his *Theological Institutes* is excerpted by

---

23. Hugo Grotius, *A Defence of the Catholic Faith Concerning the Satisfaction of Christ*, pp. xvi, 54, 64.
24. Ibid., p. 106.
25. Ibid., pp. 107-109, 137.

Alexander Campbell in a lengthy quotation in *The Christian System*.[26]

We may mention just two problems with the governmental theory. One is the idea that the holy God is free either to punish sin or not to punish sin, as he chooses. This does not seem to be consistent with the Bible's teaching concerning the holiness and wrath of God. The other problem is that this view is almost totally speculative and has practically no Biblical basis. The texts that describe the death of Christ present a different picture altogether.

God as the Object of the Cross

We have examined the classical views of the atonement that picture Satan and man as being the primary objects of Christ's atoning death. In my opinion neither of these approaches gets to the heart of the Bible's teaching on the work of redemption. Only the third option can be defended Biblically, namely, that the primary object of the cross is God himself. The cross is necessary not because of something in Satan or something in man, but because of something in God. The only obstacle to forgiveness that requires the cross is God's own holy wrath. This is the view that will be presented in the section below on the Biblical view of the atonement.

Some of the views that see God as the object of the cross are not adequate, however. One of these will be noted briefly here, namely, the view of Anselm (1033-1109), whose work *Cur Deus Homo* attempts to answer the question of why God became man. As Anselm understood it, when man sins he robs God of the honor due him and incurs a debt to him. It is not enough simply to repay the debt of withheld obedience. Because God's honor has been injured, additional satisfaction or recompense must be rendered. Thus sinful man is left with two alternatives. He can either repay his debt plus the additional satisfaction, or he can be eternally punished. The former is impossible, though, since everything we can now do for God we already owe him; thus no present or future obedience can make up for past sins. Eternal punishment is all that remains for sinners.[27] There is no other alternative, since God's justice requires either the satisfaction or the punishment. "It is

---

26. Alexander Campbell, *The Christian System* (Cincinnati: Standard Publishing, n.d.), pp. 27-30.

27. Anselm, *Cur Deus Homo* (Edinburgh: John Grant, 1909), pp. 23-24, 49-50.

therefore necessary that either the honour abstracted shall be restored, or punishment shall follow; otherwise, God were either unjust to Himself, or were powerless for either, which it is a shame even to imagine."[28] Here is why God became man. Christ came to take man's place and to do for him what he cannot do for himself. But we must remember that man has two choices: either repay his debt with added satisfaction, or suffer eternal punishment. Either way, God's honor will be satisfied. Christ as our Savior chose to do the former, not the latter. He did not suffer our punishment in our place, but repaid our debt and made satisfaction for us. He did this through his death. How does the cross accomplish this? Because Jesus himself lived a perfect life, he was under no obligation to die. Therefore when he did die, his life was so good and great and lovable that when yielded up in death it outweighed all the sins of men. Thus his death was a kind of excess merit that he can apply to our accounts, paying off our debts and recompensing God for his injured honor.[29] In this way the death of Christ provides for our forgiveness.

Anselm's view is certainly going in the right direction in that he sees the obstacle to forgiveness within God's own nature. But it does fall short of a proper Biblical understanding and should not be equated with the Bible's own teaching on the atonement. For one thing, the concept of injured honor is not the same as violated holiness; it has a connotation of pettiness unworthy of God. Also, the distinction between satisfying God's honor and suffering eternal punishment is unwarranted and misleading. The *only* way that God's violated "honor" or holiness can be satisfied *is* through eternal punishment. Thus Christ's vicarious death must be understood in terms of eternal punishment; there is no alternative.

Other Recent Views of the Cross

Not all views of the atonement fall neatly into one of the three categories discussed above. Thus before we turn to our examination of the Biblical view of atonement, we will give brief attention to two recent views that may or may not come under one of the above headings but

---

28. Ibid., p. 28.
29. Ibid., pp. 79, 84, 100-101, 104-106.

which are quite unacceptable nonetheless.

The Covenantal Theory. Interpreting the death of Jesus purely in terms of God's covenant relationship with man seems to be becoming increasingly popular. A common version of this is to begin with God's covenant with Israel as God's definitive relationship with mankind as a whole. The terms of this covenant relationship are that God will bless and save Israel (mankind) if Israel (mankind) will obey God's commands. As the history of Israel shows, God remains faithful to his side of the covenant, but the human partner constantly fails and thus threatens the whole relationship. What is needed, then, is a representative covenant-keeper who can take the place of sinful man and render acceptable obedience to God and thus preserve the covenant. This is how the work of Jesus is understood.

An example of this view is Hendrikus Berkhof. As he presents it, the covenant that God established with Israel is the general framework within which all salvation occurs. Jesus was just continuing what had been begun with Israel; "Israel's way and the way of Jesus Christ are together the *one* way of the *one* God."[30] "Christ was God's next and decisive step as a continuation of the way he had gone with Israel before."[31] God's part in the covenant is expressed in the words "I will be your God"; he promises to save and deliver and protect his people. "But the covenant cannot function without man who responds to it"; the human covenant partner must trust and obey.[32] But while God was always faithful to his covenant promise, Israel repeatedly rebelled. God's problem, then, is to preserve the covenant while maintaining its integrity from the human side. "The one-sided faithfulness of the great covenant partner triumphs over the unfaithfulness of his partner."[33]

God does this by sending Jesus Christ as one who symbolizes the remnant of Israel and "who vicariously and on behalf of guilty Israel will realize the covenant." This is God's ultimate act of covenant faithfulness. Jesus "came to complete God's way with Israel through a supreme gesture of love and reconciliation from the side of the cove-

---

30. Hendrikus Berkhof, *Christian Faith: An Introduction to the Study of the Faith,* tr. Sierd Woudstra (Grand Rapids: Eerdmans, 1979), p. 222.

31. Ibid., pp. 225-226.

32. Ibid., pp. 230-231.

33. Ibid., p. 239.

nant partner who had always remained faithful—a gesture consisting in the sending of a human partner who vicariously confirms the covenant for the people." In this connection "Jesus saw himself as Israel's representative, as the obedient man in whom the covenant would be made firm, as the faithful remnant expected by the prophets."[34] Jesus' role, then, is that of "the faithful covenant partner" representing man before God; but since he is provided by God himself, he also represents God's loving faithfulness before the people.[35] Within this covenant framework the death of Jesus has no special purpose separate from the purpose of his life as a whole. "In his person and ministry Jesus came to fulfill the covenant." But it was inevitable that if he lived it and fulfilled it as one truly should, "he could not but perish." This is the same price anyone would pay if he lived the kind of life that Jesus did. "But the price of the radical surrender of our life to God and our neighbor, which we refuse to pay for our redemption and renewal, is here substitutionarily paid by the new man." Christ as our "representative has gone the limit in his obedience to the Father," and thus in his death has overcome the fact of "covenant estrangement."[36] This is confirmed in the resurrection, which shows that "God's faithfulness overcomes the unfaithfulness of his people."[37] Thus, all in all, Jesus is "the savior of the covenant."[38]

This view is presented also by P. J. Achtemeier. Like Berkhof, his starting point is the covenant relationship God inaugurated with man in the Old Testament but which man nullified by his disobedience. Thus Christ comes as the representative covenant-keeper, satisfying the demands of the covenant from man's perspective through his own obedience. Achtemeier says,[39]

It is Christ's act of obedience, in his death on the cross, that nullifies the disobedience of man whereby man broke the covenant relationship with God. This act of obedience restores the relationship of man with God

---

34. Ibid., pp. 252-253.

35. Ibid., p. 283. Jesus is "the true human covenant partner" (p. 294).

36. Ibid., pp. 299-303.

37. Ibid., p. 255.

38. Ibid., p. 307.

39. P.J. Achtemeier, "Righteousness in the NT," *The Interpreter's Dictionary of the Bible*, ed. George A. Buttrick (Nashville: Abingdon Press, 1962), IV:95.

> by fulfilling the demand that the relationship had laid upon man: obe-
> dience to God. Therefore, by Christ's act of obedience the covenant rela-
> tionship is restored, and man, by participating in it, may be righteous . . . .

Christ was "fulfilling for man the demand of the relationship, and thus upholding the relationship."[40]

Brinsmead's view is similar. It will be remembered that he, like Achtemeier, has joined the popular rush to redefine the concept of God's righteousness or justice to exclude retributive justice and include saving activity only. As he sums it up, "The justice revealed in the gospel event is a justice based on grace, and it consists in God's faithfulness to his covenant promise."[41] From this starting point he goes on to reject the so-called "Latin theory of the atonement," or the one that sees Christ's death as satisfying God's wrath or retributive justice.[42] The cross does reveal God's righteousness or justice (Romans 1:17; 3:21, 25-26), but it is the justice of promise-keeping "biased in favor of the oppressed."[43] Herein lies the meaning of Jesus' life and death. God is so fully on the side of the deprived and the oppressed that he became such himself. "In the person of his Son he has become one with us in oppression." In Christ "he takes the cause of all condemned, wretched, forsaken sinners upon himself and becomes absolutely one with them in all their deprivation and oppression." "Jesus so fully identified himself with the suppressed, the depressed and the oppressed that he bore their curse and experienced their rejection," even unto death.[44] But then comes the "triumph of God's justice"—when he raised Jesus from the dead. "When God raised Jesus from the dead, he showed that he was the God who executes justice for all who are oppressed. . . . When God raised this oppressed Man to his own right hand," he "kept his promise that he would deliver the oppressed." "The resurrection, therefore, was the triumph of divine justice over all human oppression summed up in this Oppressed One who was the one for, with, and instead of the

---

40. Ibid.

41. Robert Brinsmead, "The Triumph of God's Justice," *The Christian Verdict* (Essay 8, 1983), p. 7.

42. Ibid., pp. 8-9.

43. Ibid., p. 10.

44. Ibid.; also Robert Brinsmead, "The Scandal of God's Justice—Part 2," *The Christian Verdict* (Essay 7, 1983), p. 9.

many. He was one with us in all our oppression in order that we might become one with him in his resurrection and justification."[45]

The covenantal interpretation of the atonement is interesting but quite erroneous. For one thing, as the last two examples show, it is undergirded by a faulty view of God's righteousness and thus an unwarranted exclusion of the penal or propitiatory aspect of the cross. Also, there is little or no Biblical warrant for imposing the covenant framework on the meaning of the work of Jesus, as Berkhof and Achtemeier have so explicitly done. Christ's death is the means of establishing the new covenant, to be sure (Luke 22:20; Heb. 9:16; 10:29);[46] but the idea of Christ's death as the culmination of a life of representative covenant-keeping is completely speculative and ignores the teaching of the passages that do speak about the meaning of the cross. More seriously, it reverses the Biblical relationship between the covenant with Israel and the death of Christ. In Scripture the covenant is a means and Christ's death is its purpose or goal (Rom. 9:3-5). But in the covenantal view the cross (along with Jesus' life as a whole) is just a means to preserving the covenant relationship established at Sinai. This is simply poor hermeneutics. A final error, found in Brinsmead's creative but unbiblical reconstruction, is the idea that in his life Jesus is identifying himself so much with the poor and oppressed that he suffers the ultimate human injustice of death. The idea that Jesus is the "Oppressed One" who suffers from "human oppression" but is liberated by God's raising him from the dead goes completely counter to the clear Biblical teaching that it was God who "oppressed" Jesus by placing our sins and guilt and deserved punishment upon him. He was "smitten of God"! "The Lord has caused the iniquity of us all to fall on Him," and "the Lord was pleased to crush Him, putting Him to grief" (Isa. 53:4, 6, 10). God is the one who set him forth as a propitiation (Rom. 3:25) and "made Him who knew no sin to be sin on our behalf" (II Cor. 5:21).

The covenantal theory of the atonement is thus seriously flawed and

---

45. Robert Brinsmead, "The Triumph of God's Justice." pp. 10-11.

46. It is a mistake, though, to say that this is the *only* purpose of the cross, as Dallas Roark does in his book, *The Christian Faith: An Introduction to Christian Thought* (Grand Rapids: Baker Book House, 1977 reprint of 1969 edition), pp. 157-168, 172. His distorted interpretations result in an impoverished view of Christ's death.

fails to do justice to the Scriptural teaching on the work of redemption through Christ. It must be soundly rejected.

The Interpersonal Theory. Another recently expounded and seriously inadequate view of the atonement is that set forth by Virgil Warren in his book, *What the Bible Says About Salvation.* Warren's basic (and arbitrary) presupposition is that salvation must be understood only in *interpersonal* terms such as love, friendship, forgiveness, repentance, and reconciliation. He says, "From the nature of the case what constitutes personhood and personal relationship constitutes the governing principles for salvation."[47] This stands opposed to "the legal imagery based on the Old Testament," which "should not be read as ultimately definitive for understanding the ministry, death, and resurrection of the Savior."[48] Such language is only figurative; these images are models rather than realities.[49] "We take this position despite several legal imageries used for the atonement in the Bible," says Warren.[50] What would be included in these non-definitive legal images? The language of ransom, sacrifice, substitution, bearing sin, and especially imputation.[51] Despite the prevalence and intensity of such language, Warren says this: "We infer that scripture describes atonement under legal terms as an approximate way of saying what is really an interpersonal occurrence."[52]

The concept of imputation is especially denied as a matter of principle. It is impossible for guilt, penalty, or righteousness to be transferred from one person to another. "The implications for the atonement are all too obvious: strictly speaking, the atonement does not involve transfer of sins to Christ nor transfer of righteousness to sinners." Indeed, "it seems contrived to suppose punishment was transferred at Calvary."[53] "The reality set forth under the imagery of transfer is that God has offered to treat us according to our intents, aspirations, motives, com-

---

47. Virgil Warren. *What the Bible Says About Salvation* (Joplin, Mo.: College Press, 1982), p. 5.
48. Ibid., p. 69.
49. Ibid., p. 68.
50. Ibid., p. 79.
51. Ibid., pp. 79-80.
52. Ibid., p. 80.
53. Ibid., pp. 63-64. "Transferring our guilt or his righteousness does not, and indeed cannot, happen strictly speaking" (p. 80).

mitments, and goals to be like Messiah rather than according to our achievements. Such an approach is an interpersonal one." The New Testament writers used the legal imagery because their Jewish readership would be familiar with it; thus it was "a psychological point of contact" and was not meant to be literal.[54]

What, then, is the meaning of the atonement, according to Warren? "The atonement is to be understood within the framework of interpersonal relationship."[55] It presupposes broken fellowship and the need for reconciliation. It is the process of removing the guilt and the sense of guilt in both the offender and the one offended. This involves eradicating the effects of the past on the present. "Removing the sense of guilt calls for removing the displeasure of the offended one who keeps the past relevant to the present through memory and alienation." This requires three things. The first thing required is repentance, or the repudiation of past sins. This removes our past from us as far as we are concerned. The second thing needed is apology or confession, "which helps bridge the gulf between offender and offended by expressing repentance from the past." Finally, forgiveness is needed, for it "removes our past as far as the other person is concerned, too." Reconciliation thus occurs "when the past no longer affects the present subjectively because of repentance or objectively because of forgiveness."[56] These elements are the basic dynamics of reconciliation, but as Warren says, "a moment's reflection reveals that they include no necessary role for Jesus of Nazareth." Thus "our task consists in verbalizing the need for that additional something Messiah supplied."[57]

Technically all that are needed for forgiveness are repentance and confession, but man must be *motivated* to do these things. This is one need supplied by the atoning work of Christ; "it provides a unique source of motivation to repent." It does so in that it "demonstrates six truths that move us to repentance," namely, God's love, sin's sinfulness, God's holiness, man's worth, death's demise, and sin's forgiveness. As a result "repentance comes more easily," and "hopeful-

---

54. Ibid., p. 80.
55. Ibid., p. 59.
56. Ibid., pp. 56-58. Italics omitted.
57. Ibid., p. 58.

ly we will be motivated to 'clean up' our lives."[58] This point is summed up in the following paragraphs:[59]

> The motivational value of Christ's atoning death lies in the extent of its identification with humanity. Adopting the full degree of the human situation demonstrates that God himself is willing to do what he calls upon men to do so that they are without any rational or emotional excuse for continued estrangement from the Father. It is not just Messiah's death, but his whole life that figures into the foundation of the atonement; death resulted from his consummate devotion to the Father.
>
> His *incarnation* unto death serves as a divine (a) word about God's love, our sinfulness, our worth, and our eternal hope. His *obedience* unto death serves as (b) an example for our emulation. As (c) moral influence it elicits the high resolve to go and do likewise (Phil. 2:1-8). He is more than a symbol of total commitment; he is an example of it. In Christ God took his strongest initiative to bring us to the repentance and apology conditional for forgiveness. If we were to wonder why God could not simply forgive because of repentance, we could say that in some respects perhaps he could have, but the atonement supplies antecedent motivation to repent unto that forgiveness.

Repentance and confession cleanse away all past obstacles to the forgiveness of sins, but another prerequisite to forgiveness is a commitment to future righteousness. Here is the second aspect of Christ's atoning work. Through his sinless life and perfect example, he is "the divinely appointed object of identification unto perfection." He gives us a living model we can imitate. But here is where God's grace enters. He does not require us actually to imitate Jesus's perfect righteousness as a condition for forgiveness; he requires only that we desire to imitate him and that we identify ourselves with him and commit ourselves to live according to his perfect example. "In Christ he offers to accept aspiration for achievement and commitment to the Perfect One in place of personal perfection."[60] This identification with Christ is what the New Testament calls *faith*. "Men 'trust' that being 'identified' with Jesus Messiah will have the effect of being acceptable to God."[61] Even those

---

58. Ibid., pp. 70-73. Italics omitted.
59. Ibid., p. 74. Warren objects to calling his view a "moral influence" theory, but it will be noted that in this quotation he uses this very terminology. See also p. 75.
60. Ibid., p. 75. Italics omitted.
61. Ibid., p. 78.

heathen who commit themselves to "obey conscience" (i.e., the "unevangelized elect") "have classified themselves with Second Adam unto salvation."[62]

These two aspects of the atoning work of Christ are summarized in the following statement:[63]

> The general proposal is that since atonement operates in the medium of interpersonal relationship, it occurs in the mind—the mind of God and in the mind of men. On the positive side the actual perfection of Jesus is connected with us by God, who identifies Jesus' righteousness with us after we identify our ideals with him completely, permanently, and exclusively. On the negative side, our sins are separated from us by our repentance and apology plus his forgiveness. . . .

Limitations of time and space prohibit a full critique of the interpersonal theory of the atonement, but a few pertinent comments must be made here. First, the setting aside of legal concepts and the exclusive focus on interpersonal concepts (as far as what *really* happened is concerned) is completely arbitrary and has no basis in Scripture. It is acknowledged that the New Testament uses such legal terminology extensively. It should also be noted that there is no suggestion in Scripture itself that such language should be taken as merely figurative. The fact is that the very distinction between personal and legal is quite arbitrary, since the legal and the personal are not necessarily exclusive. This is especially true in the Bible, where the law of God cannot be separated from God himself, and where our relation to his law is the same as our relation to him.

Second, we must strongly object to Warren's outright rejection of imputation (the transfer of guilt and righteousness from one person to another). This error seems to stem from a false application of the principle stated in Ezekiel 18:4, 20 to the atoning work of Christ.[64] Ezekiel's principle ("The person who sins will die") may well apply when one is working within the sphere of law alone, but the atoning work of Christ transcends law and operates also within the sphere of grace, which as a principle is quite the opposite of law. We may capsulize the concept of

---

62. Ibid., p. 77.
63. Ibid., p. 78.
64. See ibid., pp. 55, 63.

law thus: "Keep the commandments and escape the penalty; break the commandments and suffer the penalty." This is just what Ezekiel is saying. But the system of grace is quite different. It can be summarized thus: "Keep the commandments but suffer the penalty; break the commandments but escape the penalty." As one can see, this is in many ways the very opposite of law and of Ezekiel's principle. But this is exactly the meaning of the cross, as II Corinthians 5:21 shows: "He made Him who knew no sin to be sin on our behalf, that we might become the righteousness of God in Him."[65] Our sin is imputed to Christ, and his righteousness is imputed to us. Such is possible because of grace, not law. This distinction between law and grace is probably the most important distinction to be made with reference to our salvation. When one fails to make the distinction properly, his whole system of salvation will be distorted, as is the case with the interpersonal theory of atonement.

A third serious problem with this view is that it shifts the real atoning power of Christ from his death to his sinless life and example. The attributing of the actual atonement to Christ's sinlessness is another example of reversing the end and the means. Warren sees the death of Christ as contributing to his sinlessness,[66] with the sinlessness itself being the actual atoning factor and the object of faith. Scripture on the contrary sees the sinlessness of Jesus as a means to his being the perfect sacrifice for sin (I Peter 1:19), the sacrifice itself being the basis of atonement and the object of faith (Rom. 3:24, NIV).

This leads to the final and most important problem, namely, that according to the interpersonal theory the death of Christ is not really necessary and has no inherent connection with the forgiveness of sins. Warren realizes that he must establish "the need for that additional something Messiah supplied,"[67] but he does not really succeed in doing so as far as the Messiah's death is concerned. He attempts to establish a relative necessity for the *life* of Christ, on the basis that he alone was *sinless*. "No one else possessed the qualifications appropriate to the atonement," since all others are sinners. But even this relative necessity is compromised by the next statement, that "as to theory someone else

---

65. See Jack Cottrell, *His Truth* (Cincinnati: Standard Publishing, 1980), pp. 52-55.

66. Virgil Warren, *What the Bible Says About Salvation*, pp. 83-84.

67. Ibid., p. 58.

that possessed [the qualifications] could have been designated."[68] It is also compromised by the idea that the heathen may be saved by their intent to obey their consciences and the limited revelation they do have.[69] But the *death* of Christ seems to be left without any unique rationale or purpose at all. Basically it is pictured as the climax of Jesus' life of sinless obedience, as the "last measure of devotion" to the Father.[70] "His refusal to compromise his calling led to the death that climaxed his sinlessness."[71] In fact it is not his death as such that is significant even here, but rather the violent nature of it. "That incarnate obedience unto violent death qualified him in the Father's mind for appointment as the Sinless One with whom men are called to identify as a condition for forgiveness. Atonement derives from Christ's obedience to the extent of bloodshed, not from the blood shed."[72] Thus "the death of Christ is not the whole basis of atonement, but epitomizes it as the highest expression of Messiah's sinlessness. It is then sinlessness unto bloodshed that establishes the basis of atonement."[73] The following comments show that according to this theory, in the final analysis the death of Christ is superfluous for reconciliation and atonement:[74]

> . . . It is at least conceivable that Jesus of Nazareth would not have had to die even though it is *most* appropriate that his obedience be demonstrated to this extent in order to become a complete opposite of what it antithesized and in order to demonstrate in the basis for atonement the extent of obedience his followers are called upon to perform. . . . The reason for the Father's will that he die came, we infer, from the added appropriateness of appointing Jesus as Messiah; it also set the stage for resurrection in proof of his claims.

> . . . His death would certainly happen, but it did not have to happen of necessity. Had the Jews accepted him, the program of world-wide reconciliation to God could have gone forward without his death. Had the Jews accepted their Messiah, the preceding prophecy would have been worded otherwise and the system of animal sacrifice would not have been divinely instituted in anticipation of his death.

---

68. Ibid., p. 61.
69. Ibid., p. 77.
70. Ibid., p. 81.
71. Ibid., p. 83.
72. Ibid., pp. 83-84.
73. Ibid., p. 84.
74. Ibid., pp. 84-85.

It seems to me that the New Testament from beginning to end cries out against such a view as this, which makes the death of Christ of such little import. Paul's summary of the gospel in I Corinthians 15:3-4 says nothing of Christ's sinless life but includes "as of first importance . . . that Christ died for our sins according to the Scriptures, and that He was buried, and that He was raised on the third day according to the Scriptures."

For all the reasons given here, the interpersonal theory of the atonement must be vigorously repudiated. It is grounded in faulty premises; it does violence to clear Biblical teaching; it robs the gospel of its very heart.

The Biblical Concept of Atonement

We have examined many views of the atonement and have found them all to be either erroneous or inadequate as an explanation of God's work of redemption through the cross of Christ. In this section we will turn to an examination of the Biblical teaching on the atonement. We will limit the discussion to two of the main terms used in the New Testament to describe the meaning of Christ's death, namely, propitiation and redemption.

Propitiation

In my judgment the concept that best summarizes and explains the meaning of Christ's death and the nature of our redemption is *propitiation*, the basic meaning of which is "an offering that turns away wrath." It comes from a family of Greek words, three of which are used in the New Testament: *hilaskomai*, "to propitiate, to turn away wrath by an offering" (Luke 18:13; Heb. 2:17); *hilasmos*, "a propitiation, a propitiatory offering" (I John 2:2; 4:10); and *hilastērion*, "a propitiation, a propitiatory offering, that which propitiates God" (Rom. 3:25), and sometimes "mercy-seat" (Heb. 9:5). The terms were widely used in pagan circles, where they had the connotation of appeasing or placating angry deities. The crude pagan connotation must not be carried over into the Biblical usage, however, not because the terms mean something different in the Bible but because the God of the Bible is different from the false heathen deities. He is not merely a God of wrath but is also a God of love and grace who takes the initiative in providing the offering that turns away his own wrath. He does not wait in an angry pout until the anxious sinner brings him an offering that he deems suitable, nor does the kind-hearted Son "win over" the hard-hearted, angry Father through his death on the cross. We must not think that the term *propitiation* carries only such primitive connotations. The terms are used often in the Septuagint, where they do not have "the usual pagan sense of a crude propitiation of an angry deity," something which "is not possible with the God of Israel."[75] But neither can we say that the terms were meant to have an entirely different meaning when used there. The translators of the Septuagint used these words because they wanted to convey the concept of propitiation.[76]

It is true that one of these words, *hilastērion*, is used in the Septuagint to represent the mercy-seat (the lid that covered the ark of the covenant), and that it seems to have that meaning in Hebrews 9:5. This is a unique connotation, however; and it would be a mistake to think that the term must have this specialized meaning rather than its general connotation in its other New Testament use in Romans 3:25. As Morris points out, the passage in Romans "does not move in the sphere of Levitical symbolism," and the context requires the general meaning of "a propitiatory offering."[77]

The key element in the concept of propitiation is the wrath of God. It is "an offering that turns away *wrath*." If God were not a God of wrath, then the concept of propitiation would not apply at all. As we saw in chapter five above, there are many who deny God's wrath or who compromise the integrity of it by making it an aspect of his love. This is why many prefer the translation *expiation* in such passages as Romans 3:25, since it does not necessarily include the connotation of wrath. But as we saw also in chapter five, the reality of God's wrath is a theme that pervades the Bible. Also, in the context leading up to Romans 3:25 especially, Paul's main point is that sinners are under the wrath of God. The main section preceding this begins with the words, "For the wrath of God is revealed from heaven against all ungodliness and unrighteousness of men" (Rom. 1:18). Paul then proceeds to show

---

75. Leon Morris, *The Apostolic Preaching of the Cross*, 2 ed. (Grand Rapids: Eerdmans, 1960), p. 155.

76. Ibid.

77. Ibid., pp. 171-172.

how this applies to all people, Jews and Gentiles alike (cf. Rom. 2:5-9). His main point in this section, in agreement with the Bible as a whole, is that no one can be saved by law-keeping because everyone has broken whatever law applies to him and thus is under the condemnation of the law and the wrath of God. This is man's basic problem. Thus when this section of Romans ends at 3:20, we would expect the next section (3:21ff.), which deals with the solution to this problem, to say something about how we may escape God's wrath. Thus as Morris says, the context not only makes the reference to propitiation in 3:25 natural, but even demands such a reference. "Wrath has occupied such an important place in the argument leading up to this section that we are justified in looking for some expression indicative of its cancellation in the process which brings about salvation. More than expiation is required."[78]

Since man's basic problem is that his sin has made him the object of divine wrath, we would expect God's work of redemption to be designed to solve this problem. That is, we would expect the solution to the problem of wrath to be at the very heart of Christ's redemptive work. Thus when we speak of the purpose of the incarnation or the mission of Christ, we must bring to mind above all else the words of I John 4:10, that God loved us and "sent His Son to be the propitiation for our sins." And exactly what is there about the mission of Christ that accomplishes propitiation? It is not his life as such, including his ministry, his sinlessness, or his example. It is not his prophetic work of teaching and of revealing the Father. Rather, it is his death on the cross. On Calvary he offered himself up as an offering to turn God's wrath away from us. There can be no mistake about this. I John 2:2 says Christ "is the propitiation for our sins." John has just made the remark in I John 1:7 that "the blood of Jesus His Son cleanses us from all sin." It is his blood poured out in death that is the propitiation; Christ on the cross is the propitiation for our sins. This is made explicit in Romans 3:25, which says God displayed Jesus publicly as a propitiation. How was he displayed? On the cross. This is clear from the reference to "in His blood." Though I prefer the translation "a propitiation through faith in His blood" (KJV), some translations reverse the latter two phrases and

---

78. Ibid., p. 169.

make it "a propitiation in His blood through faith" (NASB). But either way, the propitiation is accomplished only through his blood.

This brings us to the crucial question, exactly how is the death of Jesus a propitiation, or how does it turn the wrath of God away from us? In the most simple terms, Jesus turns God's wrath away from us by taking it on himself. Our sin makes us guilty and places us under the penalty of wrath. When we say that Jesus "died for our sins" or "bore our sins upon Calvary," we mean that he put himself in our place and let our sins be counted as his own. Thus he also bore the *guilt* of our sins and the consequent *penalty* which they deserve; he bore the wrath of God in our place. Herein lies the concept of *imputation*: our sins, along with their guilt and penalty, are imputed to Christ. This means that they are reckoned or charged to his account so that they are treated as his own. Herein also is the idea of *satisfaction*: Jesus satisfied the requirements of God's law for us; he satisfied the retributive justice and the wrath of God in our place. As Packer says, "Jesus Christ has shielded us from the nightmare prospect of retributive justice by becoming our representative substitute, in obedience to His Father's will, and receiving the wages of sin in our place."[79] And herein also is *substitution*: Jesus not only did all these things for us or on our behalf; he actually did them in our place and instead of us.[80]

This is the consistent and uncontradicted testimony of Scripture. The great prophecy of Isaiah 53 stresses the Messiah's role as sin-bearer: "Surely our griefs He Himself bore, and our sorrows He carried . . . . He was pierced through for our transgressions, He was crushed for our iniquities; the chastening for our well-being fell upon Him, and by His scourging we are healed" (vv. 4-5). "The Lord has caused the iniquity of us all to fall on Him" (v. 6). "For the transgression of my people he was stricken. . . . By his knowledge my righteous servant will justify many, and he will bear their iniquities. . . . For he bore the sin of many, and made intercession for the transgressors" (vv. 8, 11-12; NIV). Alluding to this prophecy I Peter 2:24 says, "He Himself bore our sins in His body on the cross, that we might die to sin and live to righteousness;

---

79. J. I. Packer, *Knowing God*, p. 170.
80. See Millard Erickson, *Christian Theology* (Grand Rapids: Baker Book House, 1984), II:812-814.

for by His wounds you were healed." Galatians 3:13 shows that his death was both substitutionary and forensic: "Christ redeemed us from the curse of the Law, having become a curse for us—for it is written, 'Cursed is everyone who hangs on a tree.'" Both substitution and imputation are found in II Corinthians 5:21, "He made Him who knew no sin to be sin on our behalf, that we might become the righteousness of God in Him." Christ's work as sin-bearer made it natural for him to be compared with the Old Testament sacrificial lamb: "Behold, the Lamb of God who takes away the sin of the world!" (John 1:29). "For Christ our Passover also has been sacrificed" (I Cor. 5:7); as a lamb he was slain so that his blood could deflect the wrath of God from us. To these passages should be added those which specifically call Christ our propitiation (Rom. 3:25; I John 2:2; 4:10).

If Christ actually took our place in bearing the wrath of God, this means that he bore the full force of God's wrath; he suffered the equivalent of eternity in hell for every sinner. Some do not understand how this can be possible because they do not understand the nature of Christ's suffering. It included not just the moment of death, but all the torture and anguish he began to suffer at least as early as the Garden of Gethsemane. Also, it included both physical and spiritual dimensions. The physical agony of scourging and crucifixion has been well documented, so we have some idea of the bodily pain Jesus suffered in the hours before his death.[81] But even as intense as this was, if this were all that Jesus suffered, we still might wonder how that could be the equivalent of the eternal punishment of the whole human race. After all, there were others who went through this kind of torture both before and after Christ, and many Christian martyrs endured untold cruelties at the hands of sadistic pagans and "Christians" alike. So what was different about Jesus' suffering? The difference lies mainly in the spiritual agony he bore.

Spiritual (mental, emotional, psychological) suffering is quite common, and many have testified that it is by far worse than its physical counterpart. As someone put it, "Soul suffering is more grievous than

---

81. See Don Clark, "A Custom of Cruelty," *Christian Standard* (March 22, 1969), 104:3-4; Jim Bishop, *The Day Christ Died* (New York: Pocket Books, 1959), pp. 302-303, 320-326.

physical pain." When applied to Jesus Christ, this spiritual agony takes on infinite, unimaginable proportions. This is so for two reasons. First, he was *sinless*, yet he was facing the penalty for sin. His soul was not toughened and scarred by numerous trespasses; thus the searing, piercing wrath of God must have penetrated to its infinite depths with unbelievable intensity. Second, he was *God*, the living God, yet he was facing the very antithesis of both life and deity—death itself. What kind of feelings must have crowded his consciousness as he came face to face with that enemy and that curse that God himself had imposed upon mankind as the penalty for sin? How can we measure the agony permeating his whole being as the divine nature itself experienced what it was like to die?

We must keep in mind that both the physical and the spiritual suffering of Christ was experienced by one who was by nature divine and thus infinite in his being. Thus, even though he suffered for only a finite period of time, the suffering itself was infinite; it cannot be quantified. This helps to answer two questions. First, how can the suffering of Christ, which lasted only a few hours, be the equivalent of eternity in hell for the whole human race? *Because he was God.* The finite suffering of an infinite being would seem to be equivalent to the infinite suffering of finite beings. This is one of the main reasons why the atonement could be accomplished only by God himself and not by any creature, man or angel. Second, did Christ suffer only for the "elect" or those who will be ultimately saved? No, his suffering was infinite and has no limit. Thus it is improper to try to quantify the atonement in any sense or to think that it could be limited to a certain number of people. His suffering was infinite and thus satisfied the wrath of God for every human being.[82]

The death of Jesus as a propitiation of the wrath of God is the basis of the justification of those who put their trust in Christ and what he has done for them. Because of the cross God is able to forgive sins without violating his own holy nature. It makes forgiveness possible. This is how we are "justified by His blood" (Rom. 5:9). It should be noted that although the wrath of God has been satisfied with reference to "the sin of the world" (John 1:29), this does not mean that everyone is actually

---

82. See Millard Erickson, *Christian Theology*, II:804.

forgiven; it does not lead to universal salvation. ~~Justification is not only~~ ~~"by His blood," but also "by faith" (Rom. 3:28; 5:1)~~ The pardon purchased by Christ on Calvary is offered to all, but it is actually given only to those who accept it through a faith-commitment to Christ as Savior and Lord. ~~Some of those bought by his blood will be lost (II Peter 2:1)~~.

The modern attack on propitiation, while expected, is unjustified. Much of it comes from those who deny divine wrath in the first place,[83] but we have seen that such denials are inconsistent with clear Biblical teaching. Others argue that propitiation is a concept unworthy of God, but they usually present only a caricature of the Biblical teaching patterned after pagan ideas of appeasement. God is pictured as an angry deity who is persuaded to love and forgive man only after Christ offers himself on Calvary. As noted above, this ignores the Bible's own teaching that it was God's prior love that provided the propitiation in the first place (I John 4:10). Others take the position that propitiation is an immoral concept; it is immoral for one person to suffer the punishment for another's sins. The problem here, says H. E. Guillebaud, is trying to understand the atonement in terms of human analogies, especially the analogy of human justice. Perhaps it would be wrong for a human judge to punish an innocent third party for a crime someone else has committed against the law of the land. But this does not apply to God, because he himself is not only the Judge but also the Law sinned against as well as the innocent Substitute. Guillebaud says,[84]

> . . . God was not administering someone else's law, but His Own, and the sin was not committed against someone else but against Him: and above all He did not take someone else and accept him as substitute for the condemned sinner . . . , but He came Himself, took upon Him the nature of the guilty ones, and bore the penalty of His own Law. . . .

This is another reason why only God himself could make atonement for our sins, and thus why Jesus the Redeemer must be divine. "We may freely admit that the Bible doctrine of vicarious punishment is not defen-

---

83. See Leon Morris, *The Apostolic Preaching of the Cross*, pp. 180ff.

84. H. E. Guillebaud, *Why the Cross?*, 2 ed. (London: InterVarsity Fellowship, 1946), p. 147.

sible apart from a full recognition of the Bible teaching of the Divinity of Christ."[85]

Still others attack propitiation by trying to show that the Greek words do not actually mean propitiation but rather mean only a covering or a cancelling of sin. C. H. Dodd takes this position, arguing from the way the words are used in the Septuagint.[86] Packer responds to Dodd by claiming that at best he has shown only that the word-group does not always *have* to mean propitiation, "but he has not shown that the word-group cannot mean 'propitiation' in contexts where this meaning is called for."[87] And the context of Romans 3:25 especially *does* call for this meaning.[88]

Those who reject the concept of propitiation usually prefer expiation instead. Whereas propitiation is aimed toward God and denotes the removal of his wrath, expiation is aimed toward the sin itself and denotes its removal or covering. Since this latter concept is included within propitiation also, Packer keenly notes that "expiation only means half of what propitiation means."[89] Propitiation not only speaks of the covering of sin, but shows *how* it is covered, i.e., through the blood of Christ which absorbs the wrath that would otherwise be poured out upon it. Expiation speaks of the covering of sin, but there is no coherent explanation of how the blood of Christ accomplishes this.

In conclusion to this section on propitiation, we must emphasize how crucial this teaching is for the whole concept of redemption and for the doctrine of God as Redeemer. I must agree with Packer that it is "the heart of the gospel."[90] He says, "A gospel without propitiation at its heart is another gospel than that which Paul preached. The implications of this must not be evaded."[91]

---

85. Ibid., p. 148.

86. C. H. Dodd, *The Bible and the Greeks* (London: Hodder & Stoughton, 1935), pp. 82-95.

87. J. I. Packer, *Knowing God*, p. 164.

88. For more specific points of refutation of Dodd's thesis, see George E. Ladd, *A Theology of the New Testament* (Grand Rapids: Eerdmans, 1974), pp. 429-430. See also Roger Nicole, "C. H. Dodd and the Doctrine of Propitiation," *Westminster Theological Journal* (1955), 17:117-157.

89. J. I. Packer, *Knowing God*, p. 163.

90. Ibid., pp. 161ff.

91. Ibid., p. 163.

Redemption

The other key concept for understanding the atonement is redemption itself. The basic words for this idea have already been introduced in chapter one. The New Testament words are derived from *luō*, which means "to loose, to set free, to ransom"; and from *agora*, which means "a marketplace." The simple noun form derived from *luō* is *lutron*, which has the unambiguous meaning of "a ransom, a ransom price." It is used by Jesus to describe his mission (Matt. 20:28; Mark 10:45). The word *antilutron* is similar in meaning and is used of Christ in I Timothy 2:6. The verb *lutroō* is derived directly from *lutron* and thus has the specific connotation of ransoming. In the active voice it means "to hold for ransom"; in the middle voice it means "to pay a ransom." The latter form occurs in key New Testament passages (Luke 24:21; Titus 2:14; I Peter 1:18). Another noun form is *apolutrōsis*, which means "redemption" (Rom. 3:24; 8:23; Heb. 9:15).[92] Two other key words are derived from *agora*. They are *agorazō*, "to buy, to purchase" (1 Cor. 6:20; 7:23; II Peter 2:1; Rev. 5:9); and *exagorazō*, "to buy, to purchase" (Gal. 3:13; 4:5). The former has the connotation of a simple purchase: "to buy in the marketplace," while the addition of the preposition *ek* in the latter word gives it the connotation "to buy *out of* the marketplace."

The fundamental idea in all these words is the same, namely, the payment of a price in order to release someone or set him free. This is the essence of redemption. The Old Testament practice providing the sharpest background for understanding Christ's redeeming work is the redemption of first-born males from their status of special consecration to God (cf. Ex. 13:11ff.; Num. 18:15ff.). God decreed that *every* first-born male, man or beast, belonged to him. From those animals classified as clean, the first-born was to be sacrificed as an offering to God. With unclean animals such as a donkey, there was a choice. One could either break its neck, thus destroying it; or he could redeem it — buy it back — by paying the price of a lamb to be sacrificed in its place

---

92. For a meticulously detailed study of this word group, see B. B. Warfield, "The New Testament Terminology of 'Redemption,'" *The Person and Work of Christ*, by B. B. Warfield, ed. Samuel G. Craig (Nutley, N.J.: Presbyterian and Reformed, 1950), pp. 429ff.

(Ex. 13:13).[93] It was expected that everyone would choose the second option (Num. 18:15). With regard to human beings there was no choice. Every first-born male had to be redeemed—bought back from God—by paying the "money of the redemption," five shekels of silver (about two and one-half ounces). See Numbers 18:16.

This practice demonstrates the basic meaning of redemption, i.e., the payment of a price to set someone or something free. The term *lutron* is literally a ransom, "the price paid as a ransom in order to secure release,"[94] "the price paid to effect someone's deliverance."[95] Thus when this concept is used with reference to the atonement, there can be no mistake: when Jesus died on the cross, he was giving his life or his blood to set us free from the consequences of our sins. He declared that he came "to give His life a ransom for many" (Matt. 20:28). His own life was the price paid. This does not mean his life simply as he *lived* it, but his life as he gave it up unto *death*. This is clear from the references to his blood as the price of our redemption: "You were not redeemed with perishable things like silver or gold . . . but with precious blood, as of a lamb unblemished and spotless, the blood of Christ" (I Peter 1:18-19). "In Him we have redemption through His blood" (Eph. 1:7). The church was "purchased with His own blood" (Acts 20:28; cf. Rev. 5:9). For other references to Christ as the ransom price, see I Timothy 2:6 and Titus 2:14. See also Hebrews 9:15.

Exactly how is Christ's death a ransom price? From what does he set us free? The terms for redemption were commonly used with reference to slavery. Someone could be redeemed from slavery through the payment of the proper price (cf. Ex. 21:8; Lev. 25:47ff.). This would certainly apply to our redemption in Christ: we are redeemed from slavery to Satan and to sin (Rom. 6:16-18; II Tim. 2:26). The main point of redemption, however, seems to lie elsewhere. Precisely speaking, through his death on the cross Jesus redeemed us from the *penalty* of sin. We have seen how sin involves us in debt to God; as a result of it we owe to God the debt of eternal punishment. No greater debt could be imagined. In New Testament times the debtor's prison must have been

---

93. This presents an interesting image of the atoning work of Christ: "a Lamb for a donkey."

94. B. B. Warfield, "The New Testament Terminology of 'Redemption,'" p. 434.

95. William Barclay, *New Testament Words* (Philadelphia: Westminster Press, 1974), p. 189.

a reality; in his parable of the unforgiving servant Jesus pictures him as having his fellow servant cast into prison until he paid what was owed (Matt. 18:30). Because of his own debt, his lord "handed him over to the torturers until he should repay all that was owed him" (Matt. 18:34). This well describes our own condition and our prospect for eternity, and it is exactly that from which Christ has redeemed us. He redeemed us from the debt of eternal punishment by paying the debt for us in his own infinite suffering on the cross. "Christ redeemed us from the curse of the Law, having become a curse for us" (Gal. 3:13). Barclay describes a *lutron* or ransom as "a payment which releases a man from an obligation which otherwise he was bound to fulfil."[96] We are no longer obligated to pay the penalty for sin, because Christ has paid it for us. This answers the question of *to whom* Christ gave himself as a ransom (Matt. 20:28): the ransom was paid to God himself. "What has been said leaves us in no doubt but that God is the recipient of the ransom," says Buchsel.[97] God is the one who demands the penalty be paid; Jesus pays it for us. In this way redemption is seen to be practically identical with propitiation, as we would expect from the way they are paralleled in Romans 3:24-25. Likewise, since it is the removal of the penalty of sin, redemption is equated with pardon or forgiveness when it is applied to the sinner (Eph. 1:7; Col. 1:14). Its full and precise meaning is summed up in the chorus of a well-known gospel song:

> Sing, O sing of my Redeemer;
> With His blood He purchased me!
> On the cross he sealed my pardon,
> Paid the debt, and made me free!

Sin-Bearer

The nature of atonement as summed up in the words *propitiation* and *redemption* makes Christianity's doctrine of salvation absolutely unique. Of all the religious systems of the world, Christianity alone provides the only thing that can save man from his lost state, namely, a sin-

---

96. Ibid., p. 190.
97. Friedrich Büchsel, "λύω, etc." (part), *Theological Dictionary of the New Testament,* ed. Gerhard Kittel, tr. Geoffrey W. Bromiley (Grand Rapids: Eerdmans, 1967), IV:344.

bearer. Of all the alleged redeemers in the world, Jesus alone can and does bear the sins of mankind in such a way that their consequences may be escaped. Bhakti Hinduism speaks of grace, but it does not even have a proper view of sin, much less a sin-bearer. True Pure Land Buddhists call Amida a savior because he shares his merits with others, but Amida has done nothing to solve the problem even of his own guilt, much less the guilt of the human race. No matter how many good works he may be credited with or how many merits he may have accumulated, he has not borne the penalty for sin nor resolved the problem of the wrath of God. Osiris does not qualify for the title of redeemer, nor does the Gnostic deliverer. Neither attempts to deal with the sin problem. Although Judaism and Islam understand the true nature of man's problem as sin against God, neither can offer the only real solution to it, namely, a sin-bearer. At best, Muhammad is only a prophet and a teacher. But even many versions of Christianity fare no better when they reduce Christ down to the level of Muhammad by making him no more than a revealer of God and an example for man. Such a Christ and such a Christianity are as impotent to save as are the other false religious systems of the world.

Without a sin-bearer there is no redemption, and other than Christ there is no sin-bearer. He alone "bore our sins in His body on the cross" (I Peter 2:24). He alone was able to do so, because he alone was God incarnate in the person of a sinless man. This shows the supreme importance of a right doctrine of both the person and the work of Christ. Those who compromise the deity of Christ and the propitiatory nature of his death are not simply arguing abstract theology; they are removing the very foundation of the doctrine of salvation itself.

THE RESURRECTION

In the broader sense of the term, the work of redemption was not completed when Jesus died on the cross. When he cried, "It is finished!" (John 19:30), he was not referring to his work as such but only to that aspect of his work that involved humiliation and suffering. The triumphant phase of his work was yet to come, and was begun just three days later when he arose from the dead. Thus the resurrection of Jesus is a vital and integral part of the redemptive process. How this is so is the subject of this section.

To understand the significance of the resurrection of Jesus, we must

441

understand the nature of the penalty imposed upon sinners and upon the sinful world by God's holy judgment. It can be summarized in the word *death*: "the wages of sin is death" (Rom. 6:23). This judgment includes physical death; all human beings die physically as the result of Adam's sin (Rom. 5:12; 8:10). It also includes spiritual death; all sinners are spiritually dead before God even while they live in this world (Eph. 2:1, 5; I Tim. 5:6). Finally the judgment culminates in eternal death in the lake of fire (Rev. 20:14-15). Now, the penal aspect of death in all its forms is removed for the redeemed by the blood of Jesus Christ; but death as a condition still remains. Here is where "the power of His resurrection" (Phil. 3:10) does its redemptive work. Through his resurrection from the dead Jesus makes available to us a power that is able to reverse the condition of death and restore us to life once more.

Concerning the nature of Christ's resurrection, two things must be stressed. One is that the resurrection was a literal, historical, bodily event. By no means can it be equated with the subjective "rise of faith" in the hearts of his disciples, nor can it be explained as a parapsychological contact between Jesus and the disciples that did not involve his actual body. What happened in the resurrection happened to the dead body of Jesus; it was brought back to life so that Jesus was able to walk about and meet people face to face in his body just as he did before his death. The change or transformation that we call "resurrection" occurred in the physical aspect of his human nature. It is crucial to maintain this truth because the consequences of his resurrection are to be felt ultimately by the whole of God's physical creation, including the bodies of the redeemed. Attempts to redefine the resurrection of Jesus as anything less than the resuscitation and transformation of his original body have the effect of diluting the fullness of our redemption.

A second point to be stressed is that the event we call the resurrection of Jesus really includes two separate but related events, namely, his actual rising from the dead *and* the later transformation of his body into the glorified human nature that it now is. Contrary to the common assumption, Jesus' body was not glorified in the tomb at the moment of his resurrection. When he came out of the tomb, he had the same recognizable, wound-bearing body that he had when he was buried. We cannot relegate the resurrection to some special level of history or reality outside the sphere of our everyday experiences. The unusual events related to his resurrection appearances are easily explainable by "or-

dinary" miracle and have parallels in other miraculous events unconnected with the resurrection.[98] The Apostle John, who certainly saw
Jesus after he arose from the dead, testifies that the present glorified
nature of our Lord is not known to us: "It has not appeared as yet what
we shall be. We know that, when He appears, we shall be like Him,
because we shall see Him just as He is" (I John 3:2). It may be that the
Apostle Paul saw the glorified Christ (Acts 9:1-9; I Cor. 9:1; 15:8), but
what he saw was surely more than the other apostles had seen prior to
the ascension.

It seems best to conclude that Jesus arose in his not-yet-glorified
body so that there could be no mistake on the part of those who knew
him that he was the same Jesus who had died on the cross and that he
was now truly alive again. Also, the best inference is that he received his
transformed and glorified body at the time of his ascension. Thus what
is often called "the resurrection body of Jesus" was not actually received
at the resurrection but upon his re-entry into the spiritual or heavenly
dimension when he ascended into "the glory of the Lord" (Ex.
40:34-38). He was "taken up in glory" (I Tim. 3:16). However, for
theological purposes it is proper to think of these two events (the rising
from the dead and the ascension) as simply two stages of a single event
which may appropriately be called "the resurrection."[99] Thus our conclusions concerning the nature and theological meaning of the resurrection of Jesus must *not* be based on the phenomena of his resurrection
appearances, but on the apostolic teaching. The meaning and implications of the resurrection are known only by revelation; they are not
perceivable from the post-resurrection (i.e., post-resuscitation) appearances or actions of Jesus.

The Resurrection as New Creation

We are now ready to ask the question, what *is* the theological meaning of the resurrection of Jesus? What is its significance as a part of
God's work of redemption? This may best be answered in terms of the

---

98. E.g., walking on water (Matt. 14:22-33); the multiplication of the loaves and
fishes (John 6:1-13); the dematerializing and rematerializing of Philip (Acts 8:39-40).

99. For a more complete presentation of this view, see Jack Cottrell, "Faith,
History, and the Resurrection Body of Jesus," *The Seminary Review* (December 1982),
28:143-160.

Biblical motif of *new creation*. The first or "old" creation in its entirety has suffered the effects of sin, particularly in the presence of disease, decay and death. But the promise of salvation is the promise of a new creation: "Behold, I am making all things new" (Rev. 21:5). This promise and this reality are grounded in the resurrection of Jesus unto glory.

The Beginning of the New Creation

The resurrection of Jesus (including especially his ascension in his glorified nature) was the actual beginning of God's new creation. Colossians 1:18 calls Jesus "the first-born from the dead," which in this case means not only pre-eminence but also first in time. His resurrection was the first event of its kind, ever. It was something entirely new, unlike any previous miracle or even any previous resurrection. Jesus alone was "raised from the dead . . . never to die again" (Rom. 6:9; cf. Acts 13:34). By virtue of the glorification of his body he was raised into a new kind of existence, a new dimension of physical creation.[100] This was a stupendous event comparable only to the original creation of Genesis 1:1 (cf. the paralleling of creation and resurrection in Romans 4:17). Karl Heim has said,[101]

> . . . The Resurrection of Christ is in no way an event belonging to the present order of time as a link in the chain of events. Neither is it one of those miraculous events which do happen from time to time in our order of time, like the miracles of healing or the raising of dead as we find them in the apostolic age. The Resurrection of Christ is something fundamentally distinguished from all events which take place on the level of the present time. It is the beginning of the perfecting of the world . . . . The Resurrection of Christ therefore is the beginning of the new creation of the world which has been interrupted for a certain time by the "creative interval" in which we are still living at the moment, before it is entirely completed.

---

100. This is probably the meaning of Rev. 3:14. Jesus was the beginning of the *new* creation of God. Cf. Rev. 1:5.

101. Karl Heim, *Jesus the World's Perfecter*, tr. D. H. van Daalen (Edinburgh: Oliver and Boyd, 1959), p. 166. Heim accepts the common view that Jesus received his new body as soon as he was revived from the dead. His comments are quite pertinent, however, when taken as referring to the ascended, glorified Christ.

Thus we may think of Jesus' resurrection as inaugurating a whole new order of existence, the "new heavens and a new earth" of the eschaton itself (II Peter 3:13). It is the prelude to the eschatological age, the most significant feature of which is that it will be cleansed of all the effects of sin and death, and will never again be touched by their alien power. "There shall no longer be any death," nor any of the things related to it: no "mourning, or crying, or pain" (Rev. 21:4). The resurrection of Jesus was a defeat for Satan, the one who "had the power of death" up to that time (Heb. 2:14). When Jesus rose from the dead he crushed the serpent's head (Gen. 3:15) and broke the power of death forever; "death no longer is master over Him" (Rom. 6:9) or over those who are in him. When he emerged from death's demolished fortress he gave the victory cry: "Do not be afraid; I am the first and the last, and the living One; and I was dead, and behold, I am alive forevermore, and I have the keys of death and of Hades" (Rev. 1:17-18). His glorified body was the first instance of the new order from which death is forever excluded. This is why Jesus' resurrection is often called an "eschatological event." The new and eternal eschatological age has actually already begun; it began with his resurrection!

The Foundation of the New Creation

Jesus' resurrection is not only the beginning point of the new creation; it is also the very foundation of it. I.e., there is a cause-and-effect relationship between what happened to Jesus and what will happen to the rest of creation. We may compare the original creation with a magnificent building that has fallen into ruins. When it first came from the hand of its builder, it was beautiful indeed. But now it lies in collapse, its once-glorious wood and stone reduced to a pile of splinters and chips. Then in the fullness of time the original builder comes to the very site of the ruins in order to begin anew. When his work is finished, there appears amidst the heap of rubble a new and firm foundation laid upon solid rock. This unshakable foundation is our risen Lord himself.

As the foundation of the new creation, Jesus' resurrection is the event upon which all eschatological resurrections rest; his is the life upon which all life now depends. It is "the power of [his] indestructible life" (Heb. 7:16) that infuses new life into our souls and bodies, sustains the living church in the midst of a dying world, and offers hope for the new creation to come. This is what Paul calls "the power of His resurrection" (Phil. 3:10).

Paul's designation of Jesus as the second and last Adam (I Cor. 15:45, 47) emphasizes the foundational nature of his resurrection. The image is introduced into the midst of the description of the nature of the resurrection body. Because of his resurrection Jesus has established a new family that will be like him rather than the first Adam. When we are raised we will bear his likeness, "that He might be the first-born among many brethren" (Rom. 8:29).

The Guarantee of the New Creation

Finally, the resurrection of Jesus is not only the beginning and the foundation of the new creation, but it is also the *guarantee* that such a new creation will occur and will continue. The risen Christ is described as the "first fruits" (I Cor. 15:20, 23). The "first fruits" are a kind of promise of further harvest. If Jesus is the *first*, this in itself implies a second, and a third, and so on. The same is implied in his description as the "first-born" (Rom. 8:29; Col. 1:18; Rev. 1:5). Heim makes this comment on the concept of first fruits:[102]

> . . . According to Paul the Risen One is the first fruits . . . of the approaching harvest of the world. "For as by one man came death, by one man has come also the resurrection of the dead. For as in Adam all die, so also in Christ shall all be made alive" [I Cor. 15:21-22]. That is to say, as the process of death, once the stone has started rolling, can no longer be stopped but changes the whole of world history into one great dance of death, so also can the resurrection of the world once it has started no longer be stopped. It is like the awakening of the spring of the world. The movement cannot cease until the whole creation has become new. . . .

As the guarantee of the new creation, the resurrection of Jesus is the basis of our faith in the promises of salvation, which require us to believe in God's power to raise the dead to life again. Why should we believe the promises of spiritual and bodily resurrection? Why should we believe that it will happen to us? Because God raised *Jesus* from the dead, thereby demonstrating his sovereignty over death and the validity of the facts and promises revealed in his name. This is an aspect of the

---

102. Ibid.

apologetical value of the resurrection of Christ. It is the very reason for our hope (I Peter 3:15); we are "born again to a living hope through the resurrection of Jesus Christ from the dead" (I Peter 1:3).

By way of contrast, we should also note that the resurrection of Jesus is the guarantee of judgment upon those who reject him, for God "has fixed a day in which He will judge the world in righteousness through a Man whom He has appointed, having furnished proof to all men by raising Him from the dead" (Acts 17:31).

The Redemptive Results of the Resurrection

What exactly is the work of new creation that presupposes and builds upon the resurrection of Jesus? We have seen how the atoning work of Jesus results mainly in the removal of the penal aspects of sin, which in reference to believers results in justification (remission, forgiveness, pardon). Now we will summarize the results of the work of resurrection, which brings changes to our actual condition.

The Regeneration of Believers' Spirits

The first phase of the new creation following the resurrection of Jesus began on the day of Pentecost when the risen Christ poured forth the Holy Spirit upon his waiting disciples (Acts 2:24-33). The purpose of this out-pouring was to bestow a new gift upon the people of God, one not experienced in Old Testament times (John 7:37-39). This was the gift of the indwelling of the Holy Spirit in the very life and body of believers (Acts 2:38; I Cor. 6:19). Certain Old Testament saints were given the Holy Spirit as an equipping power, but the Spirit's indwelling, life-giving presence was a gift from the risen Christ.

The immediate result of the Spirit's presence goes by many names in the New Testament, such as new birth (John 3:5), "regeneration and renewing" (Titus 3:5), and new creation itself (II Cor. 5:17; Eph. 2:10). But the most significant description of the result of the Spirit's redemptive presence within us is *resurrection* or *making alive*. Through "the power of His resurrection" (Phil. 3:10) brought into our souls in the person of the life-giving Spirit (John 6:63), our condition of inner spiritual death is replaced by spiritual life: "Even when we were dead in our transgressions, [God] made us alive together with Christ (by grace you have been saved), and raised us up with Him" (Eph. 2:5-6). We have "passed out of death into life" (John 5:24; I John 3:14). Romans 6:3-4 says that

447

when a sinner is buried in the waters of baptism he encounters the saving power of Jesus' death; and when he arises from the waters of baptism he has within him the power of Jesus' resurrection, enabling him to "walk in newness of life."

This connection between baptism, Christ's resurrection, and our own spiritual resurrection is seen also in Colossians 2:12-13,

> . . . having been buried with Him in baptism, in which you were also raised up with Him through faith in the working of God, who raised Him from the dead. And when you were dead in your transgressions and the uncircumcision of your flesh, He made you alive together with Him, having forgiven us all our transgressions.

This passage tells us what in part is going on during the act of baptism: nothing less than a resurrection from the dead, a work of new creation. This redemptive work of God takes place "through faith in the working of God," i.e., through faith that God is doing something here to save us from our sins as he has promised (Mark 16:16; Acts 2:38). We do not trust the water or the one baptizing us; our trust is completely in the power of God. We believe that just as surely as we are being buried into and raised up out of the water, so also is God raising our soul up out of that grave of spiritual death. Why should we believe that God can and will do this for us? Because he is the same God "who raised Him from the dead." The resurrection of Christ is thus the foundation of our faith that God can give life to our dead souls. The power which he displayed in raising Christ is the measure of the power he exerts upon us (Eph. 1:19-20). This is why Peter can say that "baptism now saves you . . . through the resurrection of Jesus Christ" (I Peter 3:21).

Those who have experienced this spiritual resurrection constitute the collective body called the church, which is built only from "living stones" (I Peter 2:5). The church itself is the form in which the new creation exists in this present age. It has already begun to overcome the reign of death (Rom. 5:14) and thus forms an island of life in the midst of a sea of death. Because it is built upon the risen Christ, the "gates of Hades," i.e., the "forces of death" (NEB) will never overpower it (Matt. 16:18).

The Redemption of Believers' Bodies

The second phase of the new creation will be the day of the second

448

coming of Jesus, when all the redeemed will receive new, glorified bodies.[103] Most will receive them at the moment of resurrection itself, but living believers will receive them in an instantaneous change: "In a moment, in the twinkling of an eye, at the last trumpet . . . the dead will be raised imperishable, and we shall be changed" (I Cor. 15:52). This event is called "the redemption of our body," and Paul says this is what we are "waiting eagerly for" (Rom. 8:23). See II Corinthians 5:1-5.

The glorified resurrection body of Jesus is the prototype or model after which our own glorified bodies will be patterned. Jesus "will transform the body of our humble state into conformity with the body of His glory, by the exertion of the power that He has even to subject all things to Himself" (Phil. 3:21). This is what Paul means when he says that foreknown believers are "predestined to become conformed to the image of His Son" (Rom. 8:29). That is, our own new bodies will be of the same nature as the glorified human body of Jesus. "We shall be like Him, because we shall see Him just as He is" (I John 3:2). (I.e., we shall be like him in his human bodily nature, not in his divine nature.)

Again, the guarantee of the redemption of our bodies is the resurrection of Jesus from the dead. We know that we will be raised from the dead because Jesus himself has already been raised. "We know that the one who raised the Lord Jesus from the dead will also raise us with Jesus and present us with you in his presence" (II Cor. 4:14; NIV). Our bodily resurrection is just as certain as that of Jesus (I Cor. 15:12ff.). This again shows why it is so important that we maintain a firm faith in the literal, historical, bodily resurrection of Christ, and why Paul says that believing "that God raised Him from the dead" is a condition of salvation (Rom. 10:9). Salvation in a very large measure *is* resurrection, and it flows from the redemptive fountain of the resurrection of Jesus Christ.

The Renewal of the Universe

The final phase of the new creation is the making of a new heavens

---

103. Only the redeemed will receive glorified bodies. The nature of the eschatological bodies of the lost is not described in the Bible, but we can safely conclude that it will not be the same as that of the bodies of the saved. The lost do experience a resurrection (Dan. 12:2; John 5:29), but it is not redemptive in nature. In no sense do the lost share in the results of the redemptive work of God.

and a new earth (II Peter 3:13; Rev. 21:1). In this expression the term *heavens* refers to the "starry heavens" above, or the farthest reaches of space. The expression as a whole thus refers to the totality of this physical universe, or "the creation." The renewal of the whole of creation is the ultimate result of the work of Jesus' resurrection.

When God first created this universe, it was "very good" (Gen. 1:31); but the entrance of sin brought the whole creation under the pall of corruption and death (Rom. 8:20). Exactly how this has affected the nature of matter itself is not spelled out; we only know that it now exists in a kind of "slavery to corruption" (Rom. 8:21) that makes it unfit or unsuitable for eternal existence. For this reason the whole material universe is included within the scope of redemption. Paul promises "that the creation itself also will be set free from its slavery to corruption into the freedom of the glory of the children of God" (Rom. 8:21). How this will be done is described in II Peter 3:10-13, where the apostle pictures a great conflagration "in which the heavens will pass away with a roar and the elements will be destroyed with intense heat, and the earth and its works will be burned up." This will happen in the final day, "the day of God." Out of this cosmic holocaust will come "new heavens and a new earth, in which righteousness dwells." Whether we take the judgment on the old creation to be annihilation or just purification, the result is the same: a new creation that includes a new earth that will be a suitable eternal home for creatures with glorified bodies (Rom. 8:22-23). See Revelation 21:1-22:5.

THE WORK OF REDEMPTION AND THE NATURE OF GOD

It is our contention that the view of the work of redemption as described in this chapter is the one that is most consistent with the nature of God as it is taught in Scripture. This applies particularly to the nature of the atonement as a propitiation. Only when the death of Jesus is understood in this sense is it consistent with the justice or *righteousness* of God. In this section we will first examine this point; then we will see how the work of redemption exhibits the *power* of God.

Redemption and Righteousness

In chapter four above we saw that the basic meaning of righteousness is conformity to a norm or standard. When used of human beings it refers to conformity to the law of God or satisfying the requirements of God's law. With reference to divine righteousness the meaning is the same, except the law or norm to which God's actions always conform is not something outside or above himself but is his own nature. God is just or righteous in the sense that everything he does is consistent with the perfection of is own nature. It is his perfect integrity, the absolute self-consistency of his nature and actions. It is his faithfulness to himself, to his word, and to his law.

In chapters five and six above we saw that there are two basic and distinct aspects of God's moral nature, his holiness and his love. Understanding these as distinct and different is no problem until sin enters the picture. But once sin enters God's universe of free-will creatures, God must respond to it according to his nature. Here is where the problem arises, since in his holiness God responds to sin with wrath, and in his love he responds with grace. The question of the ages is this: how can he do both at the same time? This is actually a question of the righteousness of God, since we are asking how he can be true both to his holiness and to his love at the same time. How can he maintain the perfect consistency between his nature and his actions? If he acts in accordance with his wrath and destroys all sinners, then he is not honoring the desires of his love. But if he acts in accordance with his grace and saves all sinners, then he is not being true to his holiness. In the face of sin, how can God be righteous?

Herein lies the heart of the gospel, namely, that the cross of Jesus Christ enables God to save sinners while maintaining his righteousness with reference to his holiness and wrath. This is why Paul can say that the gospel is "the power of God for salvation," because it reveals "the righteousness of God" (Rom. 1:16-17). That is, the cross itself, as a propitiation, demonstrates how God can be righteous even though he forgives sins (Rom. 3:25). It shows how he can be both righteous or just, and at the same time "the justifier of the one who has faith in Jesus" (Rom. 3:26).

True to His Holiness

We may ask specifically, how does the cross enable God to be true to his holiness (and thus be righteous)? Since God's holiness is summed up and expressed in his law, God is true to his holiness when he upholds his law, or when he sees to it that the requirements of his law are satisfied. But a key question is this: *how* can the requirements of the law be satisfied? And the key answer is this: the requirements of the law can be satisfied in two different ways. First, the requirements of its *commandments* can be satisfied through perfect holiness or obedience. But second, if there is disobedience, the requirements of its *penalties* can be satisfied through eternal punishment. It is this second way, and it alone, that explains the cross.

The problem is that man has sinned and broken God's law. Thus the only way that God can uphold his law and be true to his holiness is to inflict the required penalty of eternal punishment. But in his love he desires to save his creatures, even though they are law-breakers and deserve this penalty. It is the redemptive work of Jesus that enables God to do this. Jesus came for the specific purpose of upholding God's holiness (and thus his righteousness) by upholding the integrity of his law even though law-breakers are saved. The only possible way that he could do this was to suffer the penalty of the law (eternal punishment) in the place of the law-breakers. This he did on the cross. Thus he satisfied the requirements of God's law, and he did it by suffering its penalty. This unfathomable work of redemption thus allows God to be both just (true to his holiness) and to save sinners at the same time.

This helps us to understand the unique way Paul uses the expression "the righteousness of God" in such passages as Romans 1:17; 3:21-22; 10:3; II Corinthians 5:21; and Philippians 3:9. Since the days of Martin Luther it has been understood that "the righteousness of God" in these passages is referring not to that aspect of God's nature by which he is righteous in himself, but rather to the gift of righteousness that God gives to the believing sinner or imputes to his account. This imputed righteousness of God is the essence of justification. It is substituted for our own righteousness (which is but filthy rags—Isa. 64:6) and becomes the basis of our acceptance with God (Phil. 3:9).

What exactly is this "righteousness of God" that is imputed to us? Many have assumed that it includes both Jesus' satisfaction of the commandments of the law through his perfect obedience (his "active righteousness") *and* his satisfaction of the penalty of the law through his propitiatory death (his "passive righteousness"). They assume that Christ's "doing and dying" are imputed to us. But this is not correct. Only the latter constitutes "the righteousness of God" that is imputed to sinners for their justification. Jesus certainly did satisfy the commands of the law, but not so that his obedience could be imputed to our account. The fact is that his obedience was necessary for *himself*. If Jesus of Nazareth kept *every* commandment of God's law—and he did—it was only because that is what he *should* have done. There are no "extra merits" in the "active righteousness" of Christ which may be shared with anyone else. His perfect obedience or sinlessness is related to his redemptive work, however, in that it enabled him to be the spotless and unblemished sacrifice that could suffer sin's penalty in our place. If he had sinned just once, then even *his* suffering would have been for himself. But since he "knew no sin" (II Cor. 5:21), his infinite suffering could be for others and not for himself. This is what is imputed to us: his "one act of righteousness" (Rom. 5:18), his satisfying of the *penalty* of the law in our place on the cross. Because of this imputation, we are considered righteous before God not in the sense that we are counted as having perfectly obeyed but in the sense that we are counted as having *already paid our penalty*. Yes, we are sinners; but God "justifies the ungodly" (Rom. 4:5) anyway, because our penalty has been paid. This is why "there is therefore now no condemnation for those who are in Christ Jesus" (Rom. 8:1), namely, the condemnation has already been suffered by him.[104]

True to His Love

It should not be difficult to see how the cross enables God to be righteous with respect to his love. In his love and grace he desires to save sinners in spite of their sin; the cross removes the obstacle of his own wrath or retributive justice and thus allows him to do what his love desires.

Sometimes it is thought that the interpretation of the cross as a propitiation somehow detracts from the love of God as the primary motive for Christ's redemptive work. The idea is that if the cross is necessary

---

104. Every view that locates the essence of Christ's redeeming work in his "active obedience" must be rejected. This includes the idea that Jesus saves us by being a substitute "covenant-keeper," thus upholding the covenant in our place. It also includes any view that sees Christ's life—and death—as merely an example for us to follow. We must understand that Christ's obedience involved his own unique mission to be the sin-bearer for mankind. His obedience cannot simply be substituted for ours, since the will of God for Jesus in many ways was not the same as the will of God for us.

only to satisfy the wrath of God, then somehow God's wrath takes precedence over his love and becomes the dominant attribute in the divine nature. Such an objection, however, is not very well thought out. If wrath were the dominant attribute of God, then all sinners could just be sent to hell; there need not be any thought about their redemption. But such is not the case. Though his wrath is real, his love is just as real and is willing to do whatever is necessary to save sinners while honoring the requirements of his wrath. In view of the fact that the only way to do this is for God himself to become incarnate in human nature and suffer the pangs of hell in man's place, it should be obvious that the love of God is infinitely strong for him to be willing to do even this in order to save sinners. God loves sinful man so much that he is willing to go to this unthinkable extreme in order to make salvation possible. How can anyone say that this diminishes God's love? It only enhances it! The more we understand about the propitiatory nature of the cross, the further we delve into the depths of the love of God. In fact, I John 4:10 sets this forth as the very essence of love: "In this is love, not that we loved God, but that He loved us and sent His Son to be the propitiation for our sins."

The fact is that *only* the concept of propitiation enables us to think of the cross itself as the supreme expression of God's love. Anything less than this weakens the relation between divine love and the cross and makes it difficult to see just exactly *how* Jesus' dying on the cross should demonstrate how much God loves us. For example, if you were to see a non-swimmer fall off a pier into water just over his head, it might be considered an act of love if you, also a non-swimmer, were to jump into the water and lie on the bottom so that he could stand on your body and thus be saved. The rationale of such a sacrifice is clearly seen, and the act is clearly understood as one of love. But if instead you see the non-swimmer fall into the water and, while crying out "Let me show you how much I love you!", you jump in alongside him and drown with him, observers would probably be puzzled as to how such an act was a demonstration of love.[105] The same applies to the cross if it is anything less than Jesus suffering the wrath of God in our place.

We conclude that the cross as a propitiation sets forth the

---

105. See Millard Erickson, *Christian Theology*, II:819-820, for similar examples.

righteousness of God in two ways. It is the means by which God is true to his nature as a holy God whose wrath must consume sin (Heb. 12:29), and it is the means by which he is true to his nature as a loving God whose grace desires to receive even sinners unto himself (I John 4:8-10). Thus Packer can say, "Redeeming love and retributive justice joined hands, so to speak, at Calvary."[106] Morris says, "The concept of propitiation witnesses to two great realities, the one, the reality and the seriousness of the divine reaction against sin, and the other, the reality and the greatness of the divine love which provided the gift which should avert the wrath from men."[107]

Redemption and Power

One other aspect of the nature of God that is manifested in the work of redemption is *power*. It is necessary to emphasize this because it has become fashionable in some theological circles to emphasize the weakness of God, particularly in relation to Christ and his cross. Dietrich Bonhoeffer felt that too much dependence on the constant intervention of an omnipotent God hinders mankind's quest for maturity, so he emphasized the practical absence and weakness of God. "God lets himself be pushed out of the world on to the cross. He is weak and powerless in the world."[108] The Bible is unique in that it "directs man to God's powerlessness and suffering; only the suffering God can help."[109] Christ sets the example for weakness and suffering, and we are summoned to share in this suffering and to participate in the powerlessness of God in the world.[110] Hendrikus Berkhof speaks of God's "defenselessness," especially as it is manifested in Jesus in his role as victim. "This defenselessness reaches its nadir on the cross where he is unable to save himself, where God is silent, and where free and rebellious man triumphs over God."[111] Moltmann says that the true God is recognized "through his helplessness and his death on the scan-

---

106. J. I. Packer, *Knowing God*, p. 170.

107. Leon Morris, *The Apostolic Preaching of the Cross*, p. 183.

108. Dietrich Bonhoeffer, *Letters and Papers from Prison*, enlarged edition, ed. Eberhard Bethge, tr. Reginald Fuller et al. (New York: Macmillan, 1972), p. 360.

109. Ibid., p. 361.

110. Ibid., pp. 361-362.

111. Hendrikus Berkhof, *Christian Faith*, p. 135.

dal of the cross of Jesus."[112]

Such statements as these are seriously misleading. It is true that the Apostle Paul speaks of the "foolishness" and "weakness" of God (I Cor. 1:25), and he does so in reference to "Christ crucified" (I Cor. 1:23). But his point is that this is not true foolishness or weakness, but only appears to be such from the perverted standpoint of sinful man. What men consider to be weakness in God is stronger than man's greatest strength: "Because the foolishness of God is wiser than men, and the weakness of God is stronger than men" (I Cor. 1:25). To the Christians who know the facts, Christ crucified is both "the power of God and the wisdom of God" (I Cor. 1:24). The reply will come back, "Yes, but it is a different kind of power. Rather than the power of 'sheer almightiness,' it is 'the power of suffering love.'"[113] But this is a false choice, because the redemptive work of Christ includes both. Even the cross has an element of "almightiness" or omnipotence in that it is a crushing defeat of Satan himself, though not even Satan may have thought so at the time. Still, Hebrews 2:14 says that through his death the Son of God rendered Satan powerless. Also, what except sheer omnipotence could enable Jesus to experience and yet to withstand the wrath of God poured out upon him for the sins of the world?

The notion of the helplessness and weakness of God in relation to the death of Christ is the result of the rejection of the Biblical understanding of the cross as a propitiation and the reinterpretation of it as the culmination of Jesus' identification with the helpless and oppressed of the world. Migliore speaks of the power in Christ's forgiveness of sinners, and "in his solidarity with the poor."[114] In line with Jesus' example, "in the early church the interests of the weak, the powerless, and the poor were central."[115] We may remember how Brinsmead emphasizes Jesus' identification with the oppressed. "He takes the cause of all condemned, wretched, forsaken sinners upon himself and becomes absolutely one with them in all their deprivation and oppression," says

---

112. Jürgen Moltmann, *The Crucified God*, tr. R. A. Wilson and John Bowden (New York: Harper & Row, 1974), p. 195.
113. Daniel Migliore, *The Power of God* (Philadelphia: Westminster Press, 1983), pp. 60, 73.
114. Ibid., p. 60.
115. Ibid., p. 66.

Brinsmead. "All human oppression [is] summed up in this Oppressed One."[116] "Jesus so fully identified himself with the suppressed, the depressed and the oppressed that he bore their curse and experienced their rejection."[117] This whole way of thinking contains a fundamental error, however. It pictures Jesus identifying himself with the righteous but powerless oppressed who are suffering at the hands of wicked and powerful oppressors. But the fact is that Jesus is identifying himself more with the wicked and powerful oppressors as he is allowing himself to accept the divine punishment deserved by their wickedness. He is taking the place of sinners *as sinners*, not as weak and helpless victims. And the one who is "oppressing" him with the suffering of the cross is none other than God the Father, who is pouring out upon him the horrors of eternal wrath. Whatever "defenselessness" we may discern in Christ as he faces and endures the cross is due not to any decision to champion the weak but to his firm and solid resolve to carry out the will of the Father by drinking the cup of wrath to its dregs (Matt. 26:42; John 18:11).

Having said this, we now reaffirm the point that God's work of redemption was indeed a demonstration of his power. We may speak boldly of the power of God exhibited in the cross. This includes, as mentioned above, sheer almighty strength in confronting Satan and bearing divine wrath. But there is another kind of power at work in the cross of Jesus Christ. It is the power of love itself, which is the kind of power that can move wills and hearts. It is indeed the power of moral influence. Those who hold to a moral influence theory of the atonement are not wrong in their claim that the cross has such power; their error is in saying that this is the primary purpose and function of Christ's death. Its primary purpose was propitiation, which reveals the love of God as nothing else can. And when this act of love is properly understood and received by sinners, it is indeed, as Paul says, "the power of God for salvation" (Rom. 1:16). Jesus himself speaks of the drawing power of the cross in John 12:32, "And I, if I be lifted up from the earth, will draw all men to Myself." This, according to Brunner, is the true test of om-

---

116. Robert Brinsmead, "The Triumph of God's Justice," *The Christian Verdict* (Essay 8, 1983), pp. 10-11.

117. Robert Brinsmead, "The Scandal of God's Justice—Part 2," *The Christian Verdict* (Essay 7, 1983), p. 9.

nipotence and its highest expression, i.e., the ability to draw forth a responsive love from free-will creatures. He says,[118]

> . . . God so wills to be "almighty" over us, that He wins our hearts through His condescenion in His Son, in the Cross of the Son. No other Almighty Power of God could thus conquer and win our hearts. . . . The love of the Crucified—which [is] the only power that can do so—subdues our pride, conquers our fears, and thus wins our hearts. The turning of the rebellious despairing heart of man to God as the result of His turning to man, man being dethroned from his position of likeness to God by the stooping down of God from His Throne—that is the supreme proof of the divine Omnipotence, because it is His most difficult work. . . .

When we turn to consider "the power of His resurrection" (Phil. 3:10), we are once more speaking of "sheer almightiness." Though Jesus was crucified because of human weakness, "yet He lives because of the power of God" (II Cor. 13:4). In the Bible, resurrection from the dead is compared only with creation from nothing as a display of power (Rom. 4:17); these are the two master-works in the repertoire of omnipotence. The power flowing from Jesus' resurrection in the person of the Holy Spirit is that which works regeneration and sanctification within us (Eph. 3:16), and it is also the power that will raise us up in the last day (Rom. 8:11). "Now God has not only raised the Lord, but will also raise us up through His power" (I Cor. 6:14).

THE WORK OF REDEMPTION AND THE WAY OF SALVATION

One final point must be made in this chapter, namely, that the nature of the work of redemption determines the way in which we receive its benefits. In the final analysis there are only two possible ways to be saved or to be in fellowship with God. Ephesians 2:8-9 sums them up: one is saved either "by grace . . . through faith," or "as a result of works." In all world religions, either because they lack a redeemer altogether or because the "redeemer's" work is inadequate, the emphasis is on salvation by works.[119] If the alleged redeemer's work is

---

118. Emil Brunner, *The Christian Doctrine of God: Dogmatics*, Vol. I, tr. Olive Wyon (Philadelphia: Westminster Press, 1950), p. 254.

119. The only exception I know to this rule is in True Pure Land Buddhism, where salvation is offered solely by faith. The problem, however, is that Amida Buddha did not (and could not) work the work of redemption that would make such an offer legitimate.

merely to give us knowledge, it is up to us to use that knowledge to save ourselves. This is salvation by works. If the redeemer's work is to provide us with divine aid of some kind, it is still our works that save us, even if we had some help with them. Those versions of Christianity that interpret Christ as no more than an ideal ethical example, a great teacher, a revealer of God, or a moral influence likewise of necessity are restricted to salvation by works. Every one of them is a counterfeit gospel and a purveyor of false hope, for no one can be saved "as a result of works" (Eph. 2:9).

Paul's main point in the first five chapters of Romans is that the only possible way for a sinner to be saved is by grace. He also makes the related point that the only thing that makes the way of grace possible is the propitiatory death of Christ (Rom. 3:24-26). Without Christ as our sin-bearer, there is no saving grace. Paul also stresses the point that salvation by grace is through faith and not works (Rom. 3:28; 4:16). This also is true because of the very nature of the work of redemption. If it is true, as we affirm in the gospel song, that "Jesus paid it all," then there is nothing left for us to pay with our works. Every attempt to earn or secure our salvation by our own efforts is an implicit denial of the sufficiency of Christ's work as our sin-bearer. Salvation "by grace, through faith, not as a result of works" is the only way of salvation compatible with the work of redemption done on our behalf by our Lord.

So here are the only two options from which a sinner may choose: 1) true Christianity, in which Christ the sin-bearer offers salvation "by grace . . . through faith; or 2) anything else, in which one must futilely try to save himself "as a result of works." All religion, all philosophy, all of life itself comes down to this choice; and the glory of the gospel is that there is such a choice in the first place. All praise to God the Redeemer, whose infinite grace and infinite suffering have provided us ill-deserving sinners with this choice!

8

THE IMMUTABILITY OF GOD

This final chapter in our study of the doctrine of God deals with the subject of divine immutability. To say that God is immutable is to say that he does not change or cannot change. This is a characteristic generally attributed to God by Christians and non-Christians alike, though it is interpreted in a variety of ways.

If this doctrine were merely a matter of saying that the essence of God does not change in the sense of undergoing growth or decay, it could have been dealt with quite appropriately in our discussion of God as Creator, for it would follow quite naturally from such attributes as aseity and eternity. It would be a purely ontological or metaphysical attribute, describing the nature of God's being. Immutability is much more than this, however. It has to do not only with God's essence but also—and perhaps even primarily—with his purposes and his works, especially his work of redemption. Its central core is *faithfulness*. That God is immutable means that he is faithful and true to his word; he does not waver in the carrying out of his promises. The redeeming work accomplished by Jesus Christ is the ultimate fulfilment of promise (cf. Acts

461

13:32-35) and thus the ultimate expression of God's faithfulness and immutability. Thus it is appropriate to discuss this attribute following our discussion of the work of redemption.

THE BIBLICAL DATA

The basic fact that God is unchanging is concluded from several passages of Scripture, beginning with Exodus 3:14. Here, in reply to Moses' request for his name, God makes this most notable declaration: "I AM WHO I AM." This seems to assert that God's identity remains eternally the same despite the passage of time. It is often noted that the verbal form translated "I am" is basically tense-neutral, allowing such other translations as "I will be that I will be"[1] and "I shall be what I was."[2] Dr. E. J. Young once stated in the classroom at Westminster Seminary that all nine of the possible combinations are implicit in the declaration: "I was who I was"; "I was who I am"; "I was who I will be"; "I am who I was"; etc. He is always the same.

This fact is explicitly stated in Psalm 102:25-27, where God's eternal sameness is contrasted with the mutability of the physical universe:

> Of old Thou didst found the earth; and the heavens are the work of Thy hands. Even they will perish, but Thou dost endure; and all of them will wear out like a garment; like clothing Thou wilt change them, and they will be changed. But Thou art the same, and Thy years will not come to an end.

This passage teaches not only the eternity of God ("Thou dost endure") but also his unchanging nature ("Thou art the same"). Charnock begins his lengthy discourse on divine immutability with an exposition of this passage. He makes this comment: "The essence of God, with all the perfections of his nature, are pronounced the same, without any variation from eternity to eternity. So that the text doth not only assert the eternal duration of God, but his immutability in that duration."[3]

---

1. E. L. Mascall, *He Who Is: A Study in Traditional Theism* (London: Darton, Longman & Todd Libra edition, 1966), p. 5.

2. Adrio König, *Here Am I! A Christian Reflection on God* (Grand Rapids: Eerdmans, 1982), p. 68.

3. Stephen Charnock, *The Existence and Attributes of God* (Grand Rapids: Kregel reprint, 1958), p. 103.

The classic proof text for this doctrine is Malachi 3:6, "For I, the Lord, do not change; therefore you, O sons of Jacob, are not consumed." Here the point seems to be that God's unchanging love (Micah 7:18-20) is the only thing that keeps him from destroying his unfaithful people. This passage highlights the idea that the central point of God's immutability is his faithfulness to his purpose and to his word. Such faithfulness is set in stark contrast with the unfaithfulness of Israel.

Two other Old Testament passages should be noted. In I Samuel 15:29 the prophet declares, "The Glory of Israel will not lie or change His mind; for He is not a man that He should change His mind." The verb for "change His mind" is *nācham*, which is often translated "repent," as it is in the NASB version of Numbers 23:19, "God is not a man, that He should lie, nor a son of man, that He should repent." The NIV consistently translates it "change his mind" in the latter passage as well as in the former. In both cases the reference is to the certainty of God's word. When God declares his intention to do a thing, we can consider it done.[4] Numbers 23:19 adds these words to show that this is indeed the idea: "Has He said, and will He not do it? Or has He spoken, and will He not make it good?" Thus the emphasis once more is on God's faithfulness and truthfulness.

The New Testament continues this theme in Hebrews 6:18, which speaks of "two unchangeable things, in which it is impossible for God to lie." The context here deals with God's promise to Abraham in Genesis 22:17, "Indeed I will greatly bless you, and I will greatly multiply your seed" (cf. Heb. 6:14). According to the writer to the Hebrews, for the sake of increasing Abraham's confidence God did more than make a simple promise; he also added his oath, "By Myself I have sworn" (Gen. 22:16; cf. Heb. 6:13, 17). These are the "two unchangeable things, in which it is impossible for God to lie," namely, his promise and his oath. His word is sure and certain, and we can depend on it.

This is not to say that in Scripture the immutability of God is reduced completely to his faithfulness to his promises. Underlying this faithfulness and forming the basis for it is the unchangeableness of his

---

4. At the same time we must take account of the fact that God's declarations of intended courses of action are sometimes conditional, i.e., he will do a particular thing (e.g., destroy Nineveh) *unless* a desired response (e.g., repentance) is forthcoming from his audience (cf. Jonah 3:4, 10). This point will be discussed later in this chapter.

nature and character. We have already seen this affirmed in Exodus 3:14 and Psalm 102:25-27. In the New Testament the latter passage is quoted in Hebrews 1:10-12. James 1:17 adds this testimony: "Every good thing bestowed and every perfect gift is from above, coming down from the Father of lights, with whom there is no variation, or shifting shadow." The NIV translates this to read that God "does not change like shifting shadows." The contextual point is that God can always be counted on to be a source of good and not evil. His nature does not change.

Finally, this same point is made in Hebrews 13:8 concerning Jesus Christ, who is "the same yesterday and today, yes and forever." Carl Henry argues that this affirmation goes beyond the idea of "unfailing reliability" and includes the notion of ontological immutability. Jesus is "the same" (*ho autos*) throughout eternity. This, says Henry, "refers not simply to faithfulness but also to changelessness." This is of fundamental importance for our redemption. "Because Christ is ontologically changeless his salvation is permanently reliable; a changing Christ is no sure ground of hope."[5]

The Bible thus appears to present the picture of a God who is unchanging in his nature and character and thus is completely reliable and faithful in his dealings with man. The exact interpretation of this picture is a matter of considerable dispute, however. This is true because there are certain teachings in the Bible that do not seem consistent with a view of absolute divine immutability, such as the references to God's "repentance" and the reality of the incarnation. Thus in the following sections we will attempt to survey the contemporary discussion of the doctrine of immutability and to arrive at an understanding of it that is consistent with Biblical teaching as a whole.

THE CONTEMPORARY DISCUSSION

Among Christian philosophers and theologians today, immutability is one of the most discussed attributes of God. There is considerable criticism of what is called classical theism, along with a close examination of the option offered by modern process philosophy and theology.

---

5. Carl F. H. Henry, *God, Revelation and Authority, Volume V: God Who Stands and Stays, Part One* (Waco: Word Books, 1982), p. 294.

There appears to be a significant movement away from the former and in the direction of the latter, even among some conservative Protestant theologians. Of course, the degree of movement varies from person to person. The conservative theologians are especially cautious and want to make sure that any revised notion of immutability does not violate Biblical teaching as properly understood. There is widespread agreement, though, that some of the classical notions of immutability must be considered as extreme, and thus at least some revision or clarification is required.

Two Extreme Views of Immutability

Actually, from the conservative point of view there are two extreme views of immutability, with the correct or Biblical view falling somewhere between them. These two extremes are well described by Ronald Nash in his book, *The Concept of God*.[6] One is the view of classical theism as represented by Thomistic theology, which appears to some degree at least to be patterned after the view of the classical Greek philosophers. The other is the view of process philosophy and theology, as represented by the philosophers Alfred North Whitehead and Charles Hartshorne. The former view seems to think of God as absolutely unchanging in every possible way, while the latter pictures God as in the process of development and growth along with the world.

Absolute Immutability

That God is absolutely beyond all change in any sense whatever was taught by the great Greek philosophers such as Plato and Aristotle. As Küng notes, Plato's desire was to do away with the extremely anthropomorphic and capricious gods of Homer and the popular mind of his day, and to replace them with the idea of "the divine primordial principle as absolutely unmoving and unchanging."[7] Plato's basic argument is summarized thus: God is eternally perfect; any change in a perfect being is a change for the worse; therefore God does not change.[8]

---

6. Ronald H. Nash, *The Concept of God* (Grand Rapids: Zondervan, 1983), pp. 99-105.

7. Hans Küng, *Does God Exist? An Answer for Today*. tr. Edward Quinn (Garden City, N.Y.: Doubleday, 1980), p. 186.

8. Stephen T. Davis, *Logic and the Nature of God* (Grand Rapids: Eerdmans, 1983), p. 41.

Aristotle agreed with this, viewing God as "so rigidly unchangeable and so radically exclusive of any movement" that he could think only the one perfect thought of his own perfect being "and could sustain no action or deed in regard to anything else. Any movement would mean change, and any change would imply a not-yet, an unactualized potentiality, a defect, which would contradict the absolute perfection of the Deity."[9] All change is from the potential to the actual, as an acorn (the potential) becomes an oak tree (its actualized state). If God is changing or ever did change, this means that he must at some point have been in a state of potentiality and thus a state less than perfection, which is impossible. Davis summarizes the argument thus: God's potentialities are completely actualized; a being changes only if it has unactualized potentialities; therefore God does not change.[10] He is absolutely static or immobile (unmoved, unmoving) and has no relationships with the world or involvement in our history. His influence on the world is entirely passive as creatures are drawn toward him in something like magnetic attraction.[11] Thus Aristotle's God is called "the unmoved mover."

One aspect the Greeks particularly excluded from God was feeling or emotion of any kind, such as anger or grief or suffering or joy. They called this characteristic *apatheia* ("apathy"), which was "a total inability to feel any emotion whatever."[12] Moltmann describes it more fully as meaning "incapable of being affected by outside influences, incapable of feeling, as is the case with dead things," also unchangeableness and insensitivity. "Since Plato and Aristotle," he says, "the metaphysical and ethical perfection of God has been described as *apatheia*. . . . As the perfect being, he is without emotions. Anger, hate and envy are alien to him. Equally alien to him are love, compassion and mercy."[13]

As unbiblical as this concept of God sounds, it was adopted in large measure by classical Christian theology. "Christian Theology was in

---

9. Hans Küng, *Does God Exist?*, p. 186.
10. Stephen T. Davis, *Logic and the Nature of God*, p. 41.
11. See Adrio König, *Here Am I!*, pp. 62-63.
12. James M. Boice, *Foundations of the Christian Faith, Volume I: The Sovereign God* (Downers Grove: InterVarsity Press, 1978), p. 185.
13. Jürgen Moltmann, *The Crucified God*, tr. R. A. Wilson and John Bowden (New York: Harper & Row, 1974), pp. 267-268.

thorough agreement with this view," says Bavinck approvingly.[14] According to Küng the agreement was not complete, since Christian thinkers "corrected the Greek idea of unchangeability up to a point," for God is always seen as "the living God." However, their theology was often compromised in that it remained "tied to the Greek idea of unchangeability: here, too, a real change would seem to imply a defect in God."[15] It emphasized God's absolute immutability, his impassibility (equivalent to *apatheia*), his immobility. All Biblical references to change with reference to God were written off as anthropomorphisms. The early church fathers were especially insistent on the impassibility of God.[16] Augustine formulated his doctrine of immutability in Platonic terms, while Thomas Aquinas used Aristotle's distinction between potentiality and act. "God, being self-existent, is pure act; he actualises all his potentialities simultaneously; hence there is no form or degree of being that he can either acquire or lose."[17]

Protestant theology has had its share of participants in this extreme view. From the period of scholasticism we may cite this statement from the Lutheran Quenstedt: "*Immutability* is the perpetual identity of the divine essence and all its perfections, with the absolute negation of all motion, either physical or ethical."[18] Lester Kuyper cites the Reformed theologians Turretin and Charnock as representatives of this extreme. He calls the latter's work on the subject "definitive" for Protestant scholasticism.[19] Charnock describes God as immutable in wisdom, power, knowledge, will, essence, nature, and perfections. He is always "entirely the same. He wants nothing, he loses nothing, but doth uniformly exist by himself, without any new nature, new thought, new will, new purpose, or new place."[20] Bavinck comes very close to this

---

14. Herman Bavinck, *The Doctrine of God*, ed. and tr. William Hendriksen (Grand Rapids: Eerdmans, 1951), p. 147.

15. Hans Küng, *Does God Exist?, p. 187.*

16. See Robert M. Grant, *The Early Christian Doctrine of God* (Charlottesville: University Press of Virginia, 1966), pp. 111-114.

17. H. P. Owen, *Concepts of Deity* (New York: Herder and Herder, 1971), p. 23.

18. In Heinrich Schmid, *The Doctrinal Theology of the Evangelical Lutheran Church*, 3 ed., tr. Charles A. Hay and Henry E. Jacobs (Minneapolis: Augsburg, 1961 reprint of 1899 edition), p. 119.

19. Lester J. Kuyper, "The Suffering and the Repentance of God," *Scottish Journal of Theology* (September 1969), 22:266-267.

20. Stephen Charnock, *The Existence and Attributes of God*, p. 104.

when he says, "He who predicates of God any change whatsoever, whether with respect to essence, knowledge, or will, belittles every one of his attributes" and "robs God of his divine nature."[21] Even this statement by Packer seems to echo this extreme: "God does not change in the least particular."[22]

The elements of classical theism that contribute most to this extreme view of immutability are impassibility, timelessness, and the eternal decree. Though all of these are not found in the same degree in all representatives of this perspective, each in its own way has helped to foster this view. Regarding impassibility, it has been argued that the idea that God suffers any kind of anguish or grief is incompatible with the idea of his perfect blessedness. Not only is God the Father beyond all suffering; so also is the divine nature of Jesus. Thus only the human nature of Jesus suffered when Jesus died for our sins. Regarding timelessness, it has been argued that God transcends the flow of time in every way so that there is no succession of moments for God; everything is a kind of "frozen present" to him. Thus not only his being but also his knowledge and even his actions are in some way eternally the same. Regarding the eternal decree, it is argued that it is not only eternal but also unconditional, all-inclusive, efficacious, and immutable.[23] As such God may be regarded as acting but never as being acted upon and thus as never reacting, e.g., in true grief or sorrow or joy.

When we inquire concerning the origin of this particular view of immutability, it should be acknowledged that it is not taught in exactly this way in Scripture but is a chosen interpretation of the passages discussed in the previous section. Some would argue that the interpretation is not truly warranted by Scripture itself but is imported from the Greek philosophical view discussed above. This is no doubt true in many instances, but seldom would it be done consciously. Though there is probably an indirect and unconscious influence from the Greeks, the most common procedure for arriving at this interpretation of immutability is to infer it from other attributes. This is especially true of the concept of

---

21. Herman Bavinck, *The Doctrine of God*, p. 151.
22. J. I. Packer, *Knowing God* (Downers Grove: InterVarsity Press, 1973), p. 68.
23. Louis Berkhof, *Systematic Theology* (London: Banner of Truth Trust, 1939), pp. 104-105.

perfection. Nash summarizes the argument thus:[24]

> . . . A perfect being must be incapable of change. After all, change must either be for the better or the worse. God cannot change for the better because it is impossible to improve on perfection. And obviously God cannot change for the worse since this would result in His becoming less than perfect. Therefore God cannot change. . . .

This is one of Charnock's arguments: "If God were changeable, he could not be the most perfect being." If he were to change "to the better, he was not perfect, and so was not God; if to the worse, he will not be perfect, and so be no longer God after that change."[25] (It will be remembered that Plato and Aristotle argued in this very same way.)

Similar arguments are made from other attributes. Divine simplicity necessarily implies total immutability, since change takes place only in beings composed of parts.[26] Also, "God's aseity implies his immutability."[27] Similarly Charnock argues that God is immutable because he is a necessary being. "He is necessarily what he is, and therefore is unchangeably what he is. Mutability belongs to contingency."[28] Finally, God's eternity interpreted as absolute timelessness also implies immutability. "Any being that is timelessly eternal is also immutable," says Davis.[29] "True eternity is true immutability," says Charnock. "Whatsoever is eternal is immutable."[30] Henry agrees: "Timelessness logically entails changelessness and unchangeableness, or immutability. . . . Change is predicable only of subjects existing in time. If we affirm that God is timeless we must also affirm that he is unchanging."[31]

However arrived at, the view of God as an impassible, timeless, unmoving, totally unchanging being is regarded by many today as an ex-

---

24. Ronald Nash, *The Concept of God*, pp. 99-100.

25. Stephen Charnock, *The Existence and Attributes of God*, p. 116.

26. Ibid., p. 117. See also A. W. Tozer, *The Knowledge of the Holy* (London: James Clarke & Co., 1965), p. 56.

27. Herman Bavinck, *The Doctrine of God*, p. 145.

28. Stephen Charnock, *The Existence and Attributes of God*, p. 105.

29. Stephen Davis, *Logic and the Nature of God*, p. 44. Owen says, "The immutability, or changelessness, of God is entailed by his eternity (in the sense of timelessness)" (*Concepts of Deity*, pp. 22-23).

30. Stephen Charnock, *The Existence and Attributes of God*, pp. 104. 112.

31. Carl F. H. Henry, *God, Revelation and Authority*, V:288.

treme interpretation of the Biblical data and one that must be carefully reexamined, along with the other extreme, to which we now turn.

God in Process

At the other extreme is the view that God is in a constant process of growth and development along with the world, even in his very being. Henry identifies three examples of this view: pantheists who identify God with the natural universe; philosophers of the personal idealist school who hold that nature is a part of God; and process philosophy and theology.[32] This last view, also known as panentheism, is the one to be briefly explained here.

The process view begins by rejecting traditional theism as completely unsatisfactory. Hartshorne summarizes this dissatisfaction in a book called *Omnipotence and Other Theological Mistakes*. Singled out as especially serious "mistakes" are not only omnipotence but also the classical ideas of God's perfection, omniscience, love, and of course immutability.[33] The process view argues against God's immutability except perhaps for his righteousness, and posits a God who is changeable and alterable in many other ways including in his very being.[34]

Process thought makes a fundamental metaphysical distinction within the nature of God.[35] On the one hand there is his *primordial* nature, which is an unchanging unity but is also completely abstract and devoid of consciousness. This side of God functions not as the creator but as the underlying ground of the world. It is bursting with unrealized potentialities in conceptual form.[36] On the other hand there is God's *consequent* nature, which is multiple and concrete but thus also changing and relative. These two aspects together form the totality of God and explain the term *panentheism*. This word means that all the relativities of the universe are contained within God and are a necessary part of him via his consequent nature, yet God transcends the world

---

32. Ibid., p. 290.

33. Charles Hartshorne, *Omnipotence and Other Theological Mistakes* (Albany: State University of New York, 1984), pp. 1-32.

34. Ibid., p. 2.

35. See Charles Hartshorne, *The Divine Relativity: A Social Conception of God* (New Haven: Yale University Press, 1948), pp. 79ff.

36. See Hans Küng, *Does God Exist?*, p. 178.

and is independent of it by virtue of his primordial nature.[37]

It is obviously through his consequent nature that God is most intimately related to the world. In this aspect he is eternally and completely interdependent with the world, interacting with it in complete reciprocity. As Hartshorne puts it, God is the "supreme cause of all effects" and the "supreme effect of all causes."[38] This interaction with the evolving universe is the source of all concreteness and consciousness in God. His nature grows and develops along with the world as the result of his relationships with it. The content of his knowledge increases as the events of this world unfold (he has no foreknowledge). Thus God and the universe together are involved in an endless process of evolution toward no particular goal. Meaning is derived merely from the "creativity" of the process, or the way it produces newness and novelty. God's own life and consciousness are enriched through his experience of this newness, as the conceptual potentialities of his primordial nature become realized or objectivized.[39] The infinite richness of God (call it perfection if you like) is still open to increase and thus to change.[40]

It is argued that the greatest advantage of this view is that it sees God as totally involved with this world and its history. It enables us to speak of God's love for us without qualifying it or defining it away. God actually participates in the events of the world; he experiences everything that happens, including all the joy and sorrow that we experience. In complete sympathy he feels everything that we feel.[41]

Here, then, are the two views that are generally regarded as extremes occupying opposite ends of the spectrum, the static view of God allegedly influenced by Greek philosophy and the process view which seems to take its cues from the modern Hegelian philosophy of flux. Although some Christian theologians are content with one or the other of the extremes, most are looking for a view somewhere in between. Hendrikus Berkhof expresses the essence of this search: "One needs to

---

37. Charles Hartshorne, *The Divine Relativity*, pp. 89-90. See also Joseph F. Donceel, *The Searching Mind: An Introduction to a Philosophy of God* (Notre Dame: University of Notre Dame Press, 1979), p. 168.

38. Charles Hartshorne, *The Divine Relativity*, p. 80.

39. Hans Küng, *Does God Exist?*, pp. 177-178.

40. Charles Hartshorne, *Omnipotence*, p. 7.

41. Ibid., pp. 29, 39, 120.

be very precise here lest he fall into the Scylla of the Hegelian God concept (the absolute Mind realizing itself in the world), even as theology
has for centuries succumbed to the Charybdis of the Aristotelian God-
concept."[42]

The Search for Balance

As we try to analyze the contemporary search for balance on this
matter of the immutability of God, first we shall summarize the main
criticisms of the two options discussed above and then we shall see what
alternatives are being suggested.

Criticisms of the Extremes

Many today feel that neither of the options just presented is without
serious weaknesses when examined in the full light of Scripture.
Classical theism is thought to be especially vulnerable in a number of
ways. First, the Greek model of perfection as excluding all change is
said to be faulty. For example, Stephen Davis argues that perfection
need not exclude change because "some properties of perfect beings
seem quite unrelated to their perfection." Thus it is incorrect to say that
any change in a perfect being would have to be for the worse.[43] Second, the notion of divine impassibility is widely rejected as an idea alien
to Scripture. Pinnock argues that it "is emphatically Greek and not
biblical in origin." For anyone "to say that God cannot experience sorrow, sadness, or pain sounds incredible to the reader of the Bible."[44]
Pinnock and others likewise reject the notion of a deity who is completely timeless and thus unable to experience the succession of moments in
common with the changing universe. Augustine is credited with the
dubious honor of introducing this Platonic notion into Christian
theology.[45] A fourth problem is with the notion of absolute simplicity,
which, says W. Norris Clarke, "has in fact remained too rigid and 'sim-

---

42. Hendrikus Berkhof, *Christian Faith: An Introduction to the Study of the Faith*,
tr. Sierd Woudstra (Grand Rapids: Eerdmans, 1979), p. 146.

43. Stephen Davis, *Logic and the Nature of God*, p. 50.

44. Clark Pinnock, "The Need for a Scriptural, and Therefore a Neo-Classical
Theism," *Perspectives on Evangelical Theology*, ed. Kenneth Kantzer and Stanley Gundry (Grand Rapids: Baker Book House, 1979), pp. 39, 41.

45. Ibid., pp. 39-40.

ple' in St. Thomas and his tradition." Why, some ask, "should simplicity be put on a higher ontological level than a rich multiplicity?"[46]

It is then argued that these false understandings of perfection and simplicity, along with the false notions of timelessness and impassibility, lead to a concept of a God who is static, immobile, rigid, impassive and apathetic. According to some, they turn "the divine infinity into a motionless, impassive block indifferent to all outside itself."[47] Barth comments, "The pure *immobile* is—death. If, then, the pure *immobile* is God, death is God. . . . And if death is God, then God is dead."[48] The problem is to understand how such a God can have any real relationships with or involvement in the world. Understood consistently, he would be totally unaffected by anything that happens in the world. There would be no reciprocity between God and the world, no action upon God and reaction by God. He thus would have to be indifferent to good and evil. The creation and the incarnation would also seem to be inconsistent with such a view of God.[49] Explaining the Biblical references to God's involvement as figures of speech or anthropomorphisms just creates an uncrossable gulf between God as he reveals himself to us and God as he really is, thus isolating God even further from our own history.

All of this, however, seems to run contrary to the Biblical view of a God who is living and loving, who is not indifferent to the world and who enters into its history to act and to react in mercy and judgment. Thus an alternative to the classical view of God's immutability would seem to be necessary.

At the same time, although the process view of God seems to offer many correctives to the classical view, it too is open to serious criticism. First, insofar as it is a reaction to the objectionable elements of the classical view, it is an *over*-reaction with unacceptable extremes of its own. Second, in rejecting the paganizing influence of Plato and Aristotle, process thought has simply replaced it with the paganizing influence

---

46. W. Norris Clarke, *The Philosophical Approach to God: A Neo-Thomist Perspective* (Winston-Salem: Wake Forest University, 1979), pp. 100-101.

47. Ibid., p. 100.

48. Karl Barth, *Church Dogmatics, Volume II: The Doctrine of God, Part One*, ed. G. W. Bromiley and T. F. Torrance, tr. T. H. L. Parker et al. (Edinburgh: T. & T. Clark, 1957), p. 494.

49. Joseph F. Donceel, *The Searching Mind*, pp. 164-165, 173.

of Hegel.[50]

A third criticism is that process thought has elevated the concept of change itself to the highest place, making it a principle to which God himself is subject. Donceel says, "Whitehead's God is finite, unconscious, and he stands at the service of some higher creativity."[51] Henry concurs: "Whitehead's basic metaphysical principle is not God but creativity."[52] Hartshorne himself has stated this point thus: "It more and more appears that creative becoming is no secondary, deficient form of reality compared to being, but is . . . 'reality itself.'"[53] Over against this view it is argued that the idea of a God whose inner essence is *becoming* rather than *being* is quite inconsistent with Scripture. "The contrast between being and becoming marks the difference between the Creator and the creature," says Bavinck.[54] The idea of a "God who becomes," so dear to modern man, is a mythological and unreal idea, says Brunner. "A God who is constantly changing is not a God whom we can worship."[55]

A fourth criticism is that process thought makes God necessarily dependent upon the world, an idea that "compromises quite seriously the absolute or unqualified dimensions of God."[56] It is not enough to reserve a primordial aspect that is absolute; Scripture presents God as free and independent in his relationships to the world as well. "God is not bound to our time and space by necessity, as process metaphysics insists," says Gruenler; "rather his experience of our world and his participation in our suffering as Redeemer is of his own sovereign and gracious choosing."[57]

---

50. Hendrikus Berkhof, "The (Un)changeability of God," *Grace Upon Grace: Essays in Honor of Lester J. Kuyper*, ed. James I. Cook (Grand Rapids: Eerdmans, 1975), p. 25.

51. Joseph F. Donceel, *The Searching Mind*, p. 167.

52. Carl F. H. Henry, *God, Revelation and Authority*, V:290.

53. Charles Hartshorne, *Omnipotence*, p. 8.

54. Herman Bavinck, *The Doctrine of God*, p. 149.

55. Emil Brunner, *The Christian Doctrine of God: Dogmatics, Vol. I*, tr. Olive Wyon (Philadelphia: Westminster Press, 1950), p. 269.

56. Millard Erickson, *Christian Theology* (Grand Rapids: Baker Book House, 1983), I:280.

57. Royce Gordon Gruenler, *The Inexhaustible God: Biblical Faith and the Challenge of Process Theism* (Grand Rapids: Baker Book House, 1983), p. 76. Gruenler offers other penetrating criticisms of process thought which cannot be explored here.

Thus it seems that both classical theism and process thought have some serious problems requiring us to seek a reformulation of the concept of immutability that will fall somewhere between them. The following section is an analysis of some recent attempts to do this.

An Emerging Consensus?

The term *immutable* ("unchangeable"), when taken at face value, seems to rule out *every* conceivable kind of change in God. But the question is now being asked, does this term apply to God in an absolute and unqualified way? Or, is there any sense at all in which we may say that God does change? A consensus seems to be emerging that we should say that God changes in some ways but not in others. In the words of Nash, "Attributing immutability to God should not be taken to mean that God cannot change in *any* way." Thus "the Christian theist can recognize senses in which even an immutable and perfect God can change."[58] Pinnock agrees. "The idea that God must be unchangeable in *every* conceivable sense is completely foreign to the Bible," he says. "Changing is something God can do, and more wonderfully it is something God wills to do for the sake of our salvation. We have to say that the Greek idea of utter unchangeableness in God is false and misleading when measured by the Scripture."[59]

One problem is to determine what is meant by the term *change*. Bavinck seems to equate change with *becoming*, as opposed to *being*.[60] But the connotation of becoming is too narrow for this simple identification; it conjures up thoughts of ontological process and development. Not all change is of this nature, however. For example, a computer may be programed to perform different functions. On a given day it may be called upon to perform several of them. In so doing its activity varies greatly, and its inner circuitry experiences an immense number of successive states; but the computer does not *become* something other than it already was. If one insisted on equating change with becoming, he would have to agree with Wolterstorff that "not every variation among

---

58. Ronald Nash, *The Concept of God*, pp. 101, 105.
59. Clark Pinnock, "The Need for a Scriptural, and Therefore a Neo-Classical Theism," pp. 38, 40. Italics omitted.
60. Herman Bavinck, *The Doctrine of God*, pp. 147-149.

the aspects of an entity constitutes change therein."[61] But is we understand that change is not equivalent to becoming, we do not need to make this distinction.

What, then, do we mean by change? Davis distinguishes four types: change in relationships; change in position or location; change in age, or growing older; and alteration, or "change entailed by having a (certain type of) property at one point in time and not at another." Only the fourth one is crucial for the present discussion.[62] This seems to be what Charnock has in mind when he says, "A thing is said to be changed, when it is otherwise now in regard of nature, state, will, or any quality than it was before," either by addition or subtraction or alteration.[63] Applying this to the illustration of the computer, we would have to say that it did indeed change in the sense that its inner states and outward activities altered or varied from moment to moment, although the computer remained itself throughout all these alterations.

How does this apply to God? Are we willing to say that God undergoes change in the sense of experiencing alterations or variations of any kind? Many today are saying yes. Then how are we to distinguish the ways in which he changes from the ways in which he remains immutable? A common distinction is to say that God changes in his relationships to his creatures, but not in his being or character. Usually this is said in an attempt to exclude any real change within God himself. But this is being recognized as unrealistic, since, as Davis says, relational changes are real changes.[64] That is, they have an effect on both parties in the relationship. Thus there seems to be a need for another kind of distinction.

It appears to me that at least a limited consensus is emerging that we should say that God is unchanging in his essence and character, but changes in his states of consciousness and in his activities. The former part of this statement would be disputed by few, since it is definitely in agreement with classical theism. "God is unchangeable in his essence,"

---

61. Nicholas Wolterstorff, "God Everlasting," *God and the Good: Essays in Honor of Henry Stob*, ed. Clifton Orlebeke and Lewis Smedes (Grand Rapids: Eerdmans, 1975), p. 187.

62. Stephen Davis, *Logic and the Nature of God*, pp. 42-44.

63. Stephen Charnock, *The Existence and Attributes of God*, p. 104.

64. Ibid., p. 44.

says Charnock. "He is unalterably fixed in his being, that not a particle of it can be lost from it, nor a mite added to it."[65] This is what some mean when they say God's *life* does not change; he is eternally enduring (Ps. 102:25-27), incorruptible (Rom. 1:23), and immortal (I Tim. 6:16). As Packer sums it up, "He exists for ever; and He is always the same. He does not grow older. His life does not wax or wane. He does not gain new powers, nor lose those that He once had. He does not mature or develop. He does not get stronger, or weaker, or wiser, as time goes by."[66] This applies to his character as well, since his character or moral attributes are no less a part of his essence than are his power and wisdom. It means "that God has always been and will always be the holy, righteous and gracious God, who is absolutely worthy of all confidence and love."[67]

The point that God is unchanging in his essence is made in agreement with classical theism and over against the process view that God's nature grows and develops along with the universe. But the idea that God does change in the sense that his states of consciousness and his outward activities may vary from time to time is the point where the emerging consensus departs from the classical view. On the one hand, it is said that changes occur in God's *consciousness*. This means different things to different people, however. To some it means simply that God is fully aware of the succession of moments taking place in our own history and experiences them with us. To others it means that the content of God's knowledge increases with the passage of time. To others it means that God experiences different states of feeling or emotion in response to events in our history. Some might even accept all of these ideas. On the other hand, to say that God's *activities* vary simply means that God's actions upon our world are real and that he is not doing all of them at the same time. For example, for a period of time God was engaged in the work of creation, but at a particular point he ceased this activity (Gen. 2:3) and began something else. His revealing work with Moses began and ended long before he began and ended the same work with Jeremiah. There are works which God has not even begun

---

65. Stephen Charnock, *The Existence and Attributes of God*, p. 106.
66. J. I. Packer, *Knowing God*, p. 69.
67. William Newton Clarke, *The Christian Doctrine of God* (New York: Charles Scribner's Sons, 1909), p. 311.

yet (e.g., the final judgment). Hence we may say that God varies his works according to his purposes and according to the "fullness of time."

We may cite some examples of this way of thinking from both inside and outside conservative circles. First of all, Ronald Nash, in his book *The Concept of God*, tries to steer a safe course between the two extremes by affirming with the classical theists that "God cannot change with respect to His nature or character," and by tending to agree with the revisionists that "the contents of God's consciousness can be contingent, varied, and many" and that the relations between God and his creatures are real. "Human beings can make a difference to God."[68] The one with whom Nash agrees most is W. Norris Clarke, a Jesuit theologian who has shifted away from his classical Thomistic stance in the direction of process thought (though not all the way by any means). Clarke would thus be another example of the emerging consensus. He says that while God's intrinsic inner being and perfection are unchanging, he is so truly related to the world in the order of his personal consciousness that "His consciousness is contingently and qualitatively *different* because of what we do." Thus change actually occurs in "the relational dimension of God's consciousness."[69]

Another who takes basically the same position is Stephen Davis, who says, "There are important senses in which God is immutable and there are also senses in which he changes." He remains the same in his "basic nature and faithfulness to his promises," though he changes in the content of his knowledge.[70] A similar view is held by Nicholas Wolterstorff, who says God's involvement in the world of temporality involves him in change, "not a change in his 'essence,' but nonetheless a change on his time-strand."[71] Richard Rice likewise agrees that while God's existence and character remain changeless, he is "open in His experience of the world." God experiences the events of the world as they happen, thus the contents of his experience and knowledge are "constantly increasing."[72] One of the most precise statements of the view I

---

68. Ronald Nash, *The Concept of God*, pp. 101-105.
69. W. Norris Clarke, *The Philosophical Approach to God*, pp. 91-92, 95.
70. Stephen Davis, *Logic and the Nature of God*, pp. 47, 51.
71. Nicholas Wolterstorff, "God Everlasting," p. 193.
72. Richard Rice, *God's Foreknowledge and Man's Free Will* (Minneapolis: Bethany House, 1985 reprint of 1980 edition entitled *The Openness of God*), pp. 30, 39.

have called the "emerging consensus" is that of Clark Pinnock, who says, "While God is unchangeable in essence and character, he is changeable in his knowledge and actions."[73]

A final example is Karl Barth, who speaks of God's immutability but prefers the term *constancy*, which he believes is more consistent with the Biblical picture of a living God who acts and interacts but who maintains the continuity of his being throughout.[74] God has "the capacity to alter His attitudes and actions," says Barth, but "He Himself does not alter" as he does so.[75] Though he is the living God, "He is not Himself subject to or capable of any alteration, and does not cease to be Himself."[76] The affirmation of the immutability of the divine essence is quite specific and emphatic:[77]

> . . . There neither is nor can be, nor is to be expected or even thought possible in Him, the One and omnipresent being, any deviation, diminution or addition, nor any degeneration or rejuvenation, any alteration or non-identity or discontinuity. The one, omnipresent God remains the One He is. This is His constancy. . . .

Using Aristotelian terms, Barth says God "is in eternal actuality. He never is it only potentially (not even in part). . . . But always at every place He is what He is continually and self-consistently."[78] At the same time, "there is such a thing as a holy mutability of God." There is a sense in which he partakes of the alteration of the ages, "so that there is something corresponding to that alteration in His own essence. His constancy consists in the fact that He is always the same in every change." Also, "in Biblical thinking God is certainly the immutable, but as the im-

---

73. Clark Pinnock, "God Limits His Knowledge," *Predestination and Free Will*, ed. David Basinger and Randall Basinger (Downers Grove: InterVarsity Press, 1986), p. 155.

74. Karl Barth, *Church Dogmatics*, II/1, p. 495.

75. Ibid., p. 498.

76. Ibid., p. 491.

77. Ibid. In another place he says, "The divine being does not suffer any change, any diminution, any transformation into something else, any admixture with something else, let alone any cessation" (*Church Dogmatics, Volume IV: The Doctrine of Reconciliation, Part 1*, ed. G. W. Bromiley and T. F. Torrance, tr. G. W. Bromiley [Edinburgh: T. & T. Clark, 1956], p. 179).

78. Karl Barth, *Church Dogmatics*, II/1, 494.

mutable He is the living God and He possesses a mobility and elasticity which is no less divine than His perseverance."[79]

The main concern motivating these and other theologians to find a view of immutability between the two extremes is the desire to take full account of the Bible's teaching concerning God's involvement in the history of our world, especially in the work of redemption. It is felt that the classical view, consistently maintained, does not permit genuine involvement. The distinction between unchanging being and changing relationships in and of itself is inadequate; it leaves God in himself still isolated from the world.[80] In Pinnock's view, "Scripture on the one hand presents a God who is a personal agent relating dynamically to history, whereas Greek philosophy bequeaths an image of deity which is strictly changeless, locked into a timeless present, and incapable of sharing the sufferings of his creatures."[81] Over against the immobility and sterility of an inactive God, Erickson speaks of a God who is stable but active. "He is active and dynamic, but in a way which is stable and consistent with his nature."[82] Though we speak truly of God as unchangeable, says Brunner, we must also say that in a certain sense he is not unchangeable if he is going to have any part in our temporal world, if his wrath and mercy mean anything, if he truly hears our prayers, if he is to enter at all into the activity of man and react accordingly.[83]

An important element of the emerging consensus is that the main point of the Bible's teaching concerning divine immutability is the faithfulness of God. Even the classic doctrine "was designed to preserve the view that God is faithful in keeping his promises, that his basic benevolent nature remains the same; that he is not fickle and capricious and can be relied upon," says Davis; and this is still the focal point of the modified doctrine of immutability.[84] What we are dealing with, says Erickson, is God's dependability.[85] At stake is God's "unshakeable

---

79. Ibid., p. 496.

80. See Hendrikus Berkhof, "The (Un)changeability of God," pp. 22-28.

81. Clark Pinnock, "The Need for a Scriptural, and Therefore a Neo-Classical Theism," p. 41.

82. Millard Erickson, *Christian Theology*, I:279.

83. Emil Brunner, *The Christian Doctrine of God*, pp. 268-269. See also Hans Küng, *Does God Exist?*, pp. 187-188.

84. Stephen Davis, *Logic and the Nature of God*, pp. 47-48, 51.

85. Millard Erickson, *Christian Theology*, I:279.

trustworthiness," says Muller.[86] Hendrikus Berkhof describes the essence of immutability as "the unchangeableness of God's faithfulness. God is not unreliable or capricious. He adheres to his purpose and does not forsake the work of his hands."[87] The point of Malachi 3:6, says Wolterstorff, "is that God is faithful to his people Israel—that he is unchanging in his fidelity to the covenant he has made with them."[88] As summed up by König, "It is the word 'faithful' that provides the key to unlock the biblical meaning of the unchangeableness of God."[89]

Although I have referred to this view as a kind of consensus, it must be acknowledged that not all of the participants in the modern discussion are in favor of it. Some would feel that it does not go far enough since it still maintains that God is immutable in his essence or nature. This seems to be König's view, as he suggests the concept of faithfulness not just as the focal point of immutability but as an alternative to it. This allows for real change in God's nature, as in the incarnation, in which "God became man, and therefore changed, becoming what he was not previously": "Jesus is God emptied."[90] Other writers make statements that at first glance seem to allow for change in God's essence. For example, Wolterstorff argues strongly against what he calls "ontological immutability."[91] Barth says that when God partakes of the changes of our history, "there is something corresponding to that alteration in His own essence."[92] Pinnock says that "although the Scriptures plainly teach God's constancy and reliability in the moral and religious sphere, nowhere do they teach or imply immutability in the strong metaphysical sense which was adopted in the classical tradition."[93] Whether such

---

86. Richard A. Muller, "Incarnation, Immutability, and the Case for Classical Theism," *Westminster Theological Journal* (Spring 1983), 45:39.

87. Hendrikus Berkhof, *Christian Faith*, p. 140.

88. Nicholas Wolterstorff, "God Everlasting," p. 201. Kuyper likewise identifies unchangeability with covenant faithfulness ("The Suffering and Repentance of God," p. 269).

89. Adrio König, *Here Am I!*, p. 68.

90. Ibid., pp. 88-89.

91. Nicholas Wolterstorff, "God Everlasting," pp. 201-202.

92. Karl Barth, *Church Dogmatics*, II/1, p. 496. For a similar statement see Hendrikus Berkhof, "The (Un)changeability of God," p. 25.

93. Clark Pinnock, "The Need for a Scriptural, and Therefore a Neo-Classical Theism," p. 38.

statements are to be taken at face value I cannot say with certainty, although I tend to doubt it. They are more likely affirming that although God's essence cannot be altered into something different from what it is, nevertheless it can be *affected* by events of this world to the extent that alterations occur in God's consciousness and experience. If this is what is meant, however, the use of words such as *ontological* and *metaphysical* are misleading.[94]

On the other side of the coin, some participants in the modern discussion feel that the revisionists go too far in saying that God may undergo changes as the result of his being acted upon by creatures, e.g., that his states of consciousness may be altered by the things we do. For example, Berkouwer apparently defends the impassibility of God as he argues against theopaschitism ("God-suffering").[95] Also, Carl Henry argues for God's timelessness as the basis for his immutability, and argues against a view that "leaves open the door to God's response to others, and to divine knowledge that changes as the objects of God's knowledge change."[96] Sometimes it is objected that classical theism is unjustly caricatured when it is portrayed as precluding any interaction of God with the world. Even Thomas Aquinas never said that God is *sheer* immutability, says Gruenler.[97] Richard Muller presents his "case for classical theism" against Pinnock and Barth. He describes God as "eternally active, eternally and without alteration begetting and proceeding in the divine essence itself. Since the divine activity is constant and continuous it implies no change in God: it is an immutable activity."[98] All of these men argue strongly that the God of classical theism, though immutable, is fully involved in the events of history.[99] Others would say

---

94. We may remember that Pinnock has said God is unchangeable in his essence (see page 479 above), and that Barth goes to great lengths to affirm that God's essence is unchanging (see pp. 479-480 above).

95. G. C. Berkouwer, *The Triumph of Grace in the Theology of Karl Barth*, tr. Harry R. Boer (Grand Rapids: Eerdmans, 1956), pp. 303ff.; also *The Work of Christ*, tr. Cornelius Lambregtse (Grand Rapids: Eerdmans, 1965), pp. 264ff.

96. Carl F. H. Henry, *God, Revelation and Authority*, V:288-289.

97. Royce Gruenler, *The Inexhaustible God*, p. 123.

98. Richard A. Muller, "Incarnation, Immutability, and the Case for Classical Theism," p. 29.

99. Ibid., p. 37; Carl Henry, *God, Revelation and Authority*, V:287, 289, 292-293.

that they are just being inconsistent or that their God is still not as fully involved as the Biblical teaching requires. Indeed, the God of the Bible not only acts but interacts with human beings, responding to their prayers and their sins and their misery. Consistent Calvinism cannot accept such responsive interaction on the part of God, however. Its doctrine of the eternal, unconditional decree and its doctrine of sovereignty as unconditionality simply rule it out.[100] Thus it is not surprising that a number of Calvinists are among those who are critical of the suggested changes in the doctrine of immutability.

As a final point under this heading of the emerging consensus, it should be noted that not all those who share this general approach agree on all details. Indeed, although I agree with the consensus, there are a number of ideas held by some of the writers quoted above that I cannot personally accept and which I believe are not essential to the point we are trying to make. For example, both Rice and Pinnock interpret God's eternity and omniscience in such a way that divine foreknowledge is precluded.[101] I strongly disagree and have argued that timeless knowledge does not preclude God's experiential involvement in the temporal flow of history.[102] For another example, some argue that God's changeableness is a matter of his freedom or his will, i.e., he is free to change himself or not. As Hendrikus Berkhof says, "In his sovereign love God has made himself changeable."[103] Stressing God's freedom and love, Barth makes the enigmatic statement that "He alone could assail, alter, abolish or destroy Himself," although he cannot and will not do such a thing.[104] Moltmann (not quoted in this immediate context) says that God is not "intrinsically unchangeable" but is "free to change himself, or even free to allow himself to be changed by others of his own free will."[105] In my opinion such statements as these are

---

100. See Jack Cottrell, *What the Bible Says About God the Ruler* (Joplin, Mo.: College Press, 1984), pp. 217ff.

101. Richard Rice, *God's Foreknowledge*, pp. 25ff., 53ff.; Clark Pinnock, "God Limits His Knowledge," pp. 156-157.

102. Jack Cottrell, *What the Bible Says About God the Creator* (Joplin, Mo.: College Press, 1983), pp. 181ff., 250ff., 279ff.

103. Hendrikus Berkhof, *Christian Faith*, p. 146.

104. Karl Barth, *Church Dogmatics*, II/1, pp. 494-495.

105. Jürgen Moltmann, *The Crucified God*, p. 229.

misleading if not erroneous. Whether God is changeable or un-changeable is not a matter of his will but of his nature. If God is by nature unchangeable in his essence, then no act of will can bring about a change in it. And if God is changeable in his states of consciousness and experience, he is such by nature and not because he decided to be so. What we should say is that in those areas where God is by nature changeable, any *specific* changes are directly or indirectly the result of his own free choice.

The point is that despite objections from some and despite excesses in certain details, a modest consensus seems to be developing that God remains unchangeable in his essence and character but is able to ex-perience change or alteration in his consciousness and in his activity. How this relates to specific Biblical teaching will be discussed in the final sections of this chapter.

IMMUTABILITY, CREATION AND PROVIDENCE

In this section our concern is to ask how the immutable God relates to the world in the works of creation and providence. Since the work of providence embraces a large part of God's redemptive activity as well, what is said here will be relevant for our understanding of the nature of God as Redeemer. It will be mostly of a general nature, however, with the exception of a discussion of the specific problem of God's repent-tance.

Is God Timeless or Temporal?

A basic issue is whether God is timelessly eternal or temporally eter-nal.[106] A God who is completely *timeless*, i.e., existing totally outside the flow of time and being unaffected by that flow, is the legacy of the Greek philosophers and the classically immutable God.[107] Such a God experiences no succession of moments. All his thoughts and actions are eternally simultaneous; there can be no temporal relationships among them (e.g., before or after). On the other hand, a God whose eternality is understood *temporally* is an everlasting God whose existence has no

---

106. See Stephen Davis' discussion of this point in *Logic and the Nature of God*, pp. 8ff. He argues that God is temporally eternal.

107. Ibid., p. 44; Emil Brunner, *The Christian Doctrine of God*, pp. 266ff.

beginning or end but endures forever along a real time-line. Such a God experiences the succession of moments as well as changes in the contents of his consciousness.

The latter option is the one being adopted by many who are joining the new consensus on immutability, e.g., Davis, Pinnock, Rice, Wolterstorff, and Brunner. Why? Because they understand that only such a God can truly act within our history, and only such a God can truly interact with and respond to man's own actions. Because of this, only such a God can be a Redeemer. Wolterstorff says, "God the Redeemer cannot be a God eternal. This is so because God the Redeemer is a God who *changes*. And any being which changes is a being among whose states there is temporal succession."[108] Thus he prefers to speak of God as "everlasting" rather than "eternal."

Although I have sympathy with the latter view and believe that its basic premise is correct, nevertheless I must reject both positions as too one-sided in their exclusiveness. We do not have to choose between timeless eternality and temporal eternality. This is a false choice, because to a certain degree God is both. He is timeless in that he is not limited to the flow of time in his consciousness but at all times has a complete knowledge of its eternal scope: infallible "memory" of the past, infinite awareness of the present, and a total foreknowledge of the future. At the same time he is temporal in that he everlastingly and consciously exists along a time-line where before, now and after are real in his consciousness and experience. In other words, he experiences a succession of moments without being bound thereby.[109] Speaking of our history specifically, Barth well says that God can enter time and "be temporal in it, yet without ceasing to be eternal, able rather to be the Eternal in time."[110]

It is important to see that God's temporality does not rule out his timelessness or transcendence of time as far as his knowledge is concerned, for this enables us to have a God who both is temporally involved in our history and has true foreknowledge of future contingent events,

---

108. Nicholas Wolterstorff, "God Everlasting," p. 182.

109. See the fuller discussion of this in *What the Bible Says About God the Creator*, pp. 255ff.

110. Karl Barth, *Church Dogmatics*, IV/1, pp. 187-188.

including our free-will choices. Contrary to much popular thought, such foreknowledge does not itself render the future certain and thus eliminate free will, as I have shown in the discussion of God as Creator.[111] Likewise, it does not entail an absolutely immutable knowledge in the Greek sense, where the contents of God's consciousness are frozen in eternal simultaneity. God's foreknowledge of free-will decisions is genuinely dependent upon those decisions, as I have also suggested in the volume on God as Creator.[112] Also, God's foreknowledge of an event does not preclude the genuineness of his experience of that event when it actually happens, nor does his predetermination to act and react in certain ways destroy the integrity of such action when it does take place. In other words, foreknowledge does not throw us back into an "Augustinian timelessness" where all change in God's consciousness and activity is ruled out. Not only is it quite compatible with the emerging consensus on immutability, but it is also required by a sound exegesis of certain Biblical passages, especially in Isaiah 40-48.[113] Likewise, it is required to account for at least certain predictive prophecies. Rice, who along with Pinnock denies foreknowledge, tries to explain predictive prophecy as the result of God's ability to calculate the future from his infinite knowledge of the past and present, as the result of God's intentions to do specific things, or as the result of a combination of these.[114] This is an extremely weak chapter in Rice's book and a very vulnerable aspect of this whole position. Too many prophecies involve the knowledge of free choices of individuals too long before those choices are actually made to account for them in any way except true foreknowledge. Examples are Psalm 22:18; Psalm 41:9; Isaiah 44:28; and Zechariah 11:12-13.

Relatedness to the World

The point of the previous section is to show how the nature of God's

---

111. Jack Cottrell, *What the Bible Says About God the Creator*, pp. 279ff.

112. Ibid., pp. 179-183. In this discussion I may have been too cautious when I labeled the sequence in the pre-creation counsels of God as logical rather than chronological. If God's eternal existence is on a time-line, then his decision to create could have been at a specific point on that line, prior to which there would not have been any foreknowledge of the creation. Cf. ibid., pp. 262-263.

113. See ibid., p. 280.

114. Richard Rice, *God's Foreknowledge and Man's Free Will*, pp. 75ff.

eternality does not prevent him from entering into real relationships with his creatures. This is important, because one of the most criticized aspects of classical theism is that it does not permit true involvement if held consistently. Now, those who hold to this view usually do affirm that God is active in the world. Bavinck says, "Immutability should not be confused with monotonous inactivity or immobility. Scripture itself describes God to us in his manifold relations to his creatures. Though unchangeable in himself, God lives the life of his creatures, and is not indifferent to their changing activities."[115] What is denied is that such involvement necessitates any kind of change in God: "There is change round about him; there is change in the relations of men to God; but there is no change in God."[116]

This is the very point that recent thinking has tended to deny. The idea is that it is not enough to speak of change in relationships, since a change of relationship must involve at least *some* kind of change in God himself, at least in his consciousness and experience. This is what Clarke calls "relational mutability."[117] God actually experiences the flow of history with his creatures; he acts, is acted upon, and reacts. This is inevitable in view of the reality of creation and of the historical process. Hendrikus Berkhof asks this question: "Do the creation of our world and the course of human history create a history in God himself and thus affect his very nature?"[118] Whereas the traditional answer is no, Berkhof and others are saying yes: "There is no other God behind the God who passes through a history with mankind. . . . It would be blasphemous to say that this history leaves God himself unaffected and unmoved."[119] Barth says, "God has a real history in and with the world created by Him. . . . In this history God does not become nor is He other than He is in Himself from eternity and in eternity. But again, His constancy does not hinder Him from being the real subject of this real history."[120] Küng says, "In the light of this *historicity* of God, the *biblical message* of a God who by no means persists unmoving and unchanging

---

115. Herman Bavinck, *The Doctrine of God*, p. 151.
116. Ibid. Cf. also p. 146.
117. W. Norris Clarke, *The Philosophical Approach to God*, p. 108.
118. Hendrikus Berkhof, "The (Un)changeability of God," p. 22.
119. Ibid., p. 27.
120. Karl Barth, *Church Dogmatics*, II/1, p. 502.

in an unhistorical or suprahistorical sphere, but is alive and active in history, can be understood better than in the light of classical Greek or medieval metaphysics."[121]

God is thus involved in the history he has created, but he is not limited thereto (hence the reality of foreknowledge). "There is no question that God is engaged in process," says Gruenler; "but the limitation of God to time and space has to be considered a modern idolatry."[122] Relationships do not entail relativity.

Only an interactive involvement in history does justice to the idea of a God who is both personal and loving. As Clarke says,[123] God

> . . . enters into deep personal relations of love with His creatures. And an authentic interpersonal relation of love necessarily involves not merely purely creative or one-way love, but genuine mutuality and reciprocity of love, including not only the giving of love but the joyful acceptance of it and response to it. . . .

Buswell declares that "the love of God as represented throughout the Scriptures is totally denied if it does not imply specific chronological relationships between God and His creatures."[124]

God Acts Upon the World

That God is related to the world means first of all that he acts upon the world, as is well attested by his works of creation and providence. It is sometimes said that all change is activity, but not all activity is change. The point usually is that God does act but his actions do not involve him in change.[125] But if this were the case, we would be limited to the Greeks' timeless God whose actions are eternally and immutably the same, i.e., who is always doing everything is one simultaneous now. This is indeed the picture of God drawn by Muller. He uses as examples

---

121. Hans Küng, *Does God Exist?*, p. 188.

122. Royce Gruenler, *The Inexhaustible God*, p. 105.

123. W. Norris Clarke, "A New Look at the Immutability of God," *God, Knowable and Unknowable*, ed. Robert Roth (New York: Fordham University Press, 1973), p. 44.

124. James Oliver Buswell, Jr., *A Systematic Theology of the Christian Religion* (Grand Rapids: Zondervan, 1962), I:55.

125. Richard Muller, "Incarnation, Immutability, and the Case for Classical Theism," pp. 28-29.

of such immutable activity the eternal begetting of the Son by the Father, the Spirit's eternal proceeding from the Father and the Son, and the constant sustaining of the universe by God's power.[126] It is significant that he cites nothing else, since the bulk of God's activity toward the world simply cannot be understood according to these paradigms. All of his actions upon the world—even sustaining it in existence (unless we are willing to say the world is eternal)—have temporal boundaries. They begin and they end at points on the time-line. Insofar as this is the case, God changes in his experience and activity from not-doing-X to doing-X to not-doing-X. This is in agreement with Davis' contention that "there are at least some sorts of causality which imply change in the cause."[127]

How does this apply to the work of creation? According to Charnock, there was no change in God when he began to create the world; the only change was in the creature. "Nor is there any new relation acquired by God by the creation of the world."[128] Now, we can agree with Charnock and with Henry that creation "does not alter God ontologically,"[129] or bring about any change in his essence. "The constancy of the divine essence is repugnant to all conceptions of this kind," says Barth.[130] But given this qualification, we have to agree with Hendrikus Berkhof that the act of creation involved God in enormous change. Berkhof says,[131]

> . . . The creation of a world outside himself is the greatest change which God has made. But by making this change God also experienced it himself. From the time of creation God was changed. He had now become a creator and sustainer. He had received an "opposite": a finite existence beside his eternal existence. And when he created man he changed again. He created a center of freedom and initiative over against himself. . . .

---

126. Ibid., p. 29.

127. Stephen Davis, *Logic and the Nature of God*, p. 49.

128. Stephen Charnock, *The Existence and Attributes of God*, pp. 121, 123.

129. Carl F. H. Henry, *God, Revelation and Authority*, V:292.

130. Karl Barth, *Church Dogmatics*, II/1, p. 499. He continues, "This means that when God becomes the Creator and Lord of the world He does not become anything that He was not before. . . . Creation cannot bring Him any increase, decrease or alteration of His divine being and essence" (ibid.).

131. Hendrikus Berkhof, *Christian Faith*, p. 141.

Contrary to Charnock, once the creation was brought into existence, God himself existed in new relationships. And the act of creation itself was a new act; otherwise we would have to say that this world has existed eternally.

As far as providence is concerned, the various events of history are occasions for new actions on the part of God and new relationships with his creatures. The single historical event introducing the most changes of this nature is the first sin, recorded in Genesis 3:1ff. From this point on, completely new aspects are present in the God-man relationship, including the expression of such now-familiar divine attributes as wrath, mercy, patience, and grace. Completely new acts are now called for as the result of the entrance of sin. (Because of his foreknowledge God already knew that the sin would happen and that these new relationships would result and these new actions would be necessary, so that God's knowledge and plan were not changed at the time when the sin occurred. Still, this pre-creation knowledge and plan were in a sense contingent upon the event itself as foreknown. Also, such foreknowledge does not mean that the changes in relationships and actions resulting from the first sin were not real changes in God's own experience.)

What is true of the event of the Fall is true of all historical events at least in some small degree. Other significant events could be discussed in more detail, such as God's entrance into the covenant relationship with Abraham and later with Israel at Mount Sinai, but space does not permit any more discussion at this point. Further details will emerge in subsequent sections in other connections.

The World Acts Upon God

That God acts upon the world is denied by very few; that the world acts upon God is not as widely accepted. Both are necessary, however, for a complete view of God's relationship with the world.

The presupposition of the fact that the world acts upon God is the reality of the *relative independence* of both nature and human beings.[132] This means that God by his own sovereign choice has built into the

---

132. For a discussion of relative independence see Jack Cottrell, *What the Bible Says About God the Ruler*, pp. 105ff., 191ff.

created world various forces and laws that cause nature to progress "from within," though constantly sustained by God's power and subject to intervention "from without" if God's special purposes should require it. It also means that God by his own sovereign choice has made creatures who have the free will to make decisions "from within," and who at the same time are subject to God's sovereign control without having their decisions caused by God. Thus it is not of necessity but of his own free choice (i.e., the choice to create this world) that God has placed himself in the position of being acted upon by the world. Gruenler states this point well in his criticism of process thought's view that "God will be influenced by all events that follow me." Concerning this idea Gruenler says,[133]

> . . . This statement is acceptable only if one qualifies it by saying that the sovereign God freely gives his creatures limited freedom by sheer grace and makes himself available to their needs through his gracious love. Thus he graciously allows finite creatures to participate in the making of this world and in the choosing of their own destinies. As such he is the God who cares and who responds to our needs. . . .

Process thought is faulty because it pictures God as being "of necessity limited by the independent power, however small, that I and other creatures hold over against him." In Biblical perspective "creaturely freedom is not a metaphysical right, but a bestowed gift of God."[134]

As noted earlier, such a view as this is not possible in consistent Calvinism, for which the sovereignty of God is maintained only if God's knowledge and actions are completely unconditioned by creatures. This concept of unconditionality rules out all actions by God that are true responses or reactions to creaturely acts.

But once this arbitrary definition of sovereignty is set aside, there is no reason to deny that the world acts upon God within the framework of relative independence. What happens in the world makes a difference to God. As Clarke affirms, "In some real and genuine way God is affected positively by what we do."[135] Also, "Our God is a God who

---

133. Royce Gruenler, *The Inexhaustible God*, pp. 130-131.
134. Ibid., p. 31.
135. W. Norris Clarke, *The Philosophical Approach to God*, p. 92.

really cares, is really concerned with our lives and happiness, who enters into truly reciprocal personal relations with us, who responds to our prayers—to whom, in a word, our contingent world and its history somehow make a genuine difference."[136] We can agree with Boice's statement that God "is affected by the obedience, plight or sin of his creatures."[137]

In these quotations several specific things to which God responds are mentioned, such as obedience, to which he responds with pleasure or joy (Heb. 13:16); plight, to which he responds with mercy or compassion (Hosea 14:3; James 5:11); sin, to which he responds with wrath and grace (Ex. 22:24; Eph. 2:8); and prayer, to which he responds with blessing (Ex. 3:7-9). In these various responses we see that God experiences changes in his actions (as when he answers prayer) and in his states of consciousness.

Special attention must be given to how events in our history alter God's states of consciousness. Clarke rightly affirms that "God is really and truly related to the world in the order of His personal consciousness," and that "His consciousness is contingently and qualitatively *different* because of what we do."[138] How is this so? First of all, God's *knowledge* is changed by the events of the created world. This is one of the main points of disagreement with classical theism, which affirms that the content of God's knowledge is eternally and immutably the same; nothing is ever added to it or subtracted from it.[139] Those who argue on the other hand that God is temporally eternal affirm that God's knowledge increases as the result of events in the world. This is Davis' view,[140] as well as that of Pinnock ("New information flows in, and God takes account of it").[141] Rice likewise affirms of God that "His knowledge of the world is constantly increasing."[142] Nash notes "that

---

136. W. Norris Clarke, "A New Look," p. 44. Nash agrees with Clarke: "Human beings can make a difference to God" (Ronald Nash, *The Concept of God*, p. 105).

137. James M. Boice, *Foundations of the Christian Faith*, I:185.

138. W. Norris Clarke, *The Philosophical Approach to God*, pp. 91-92.

139. Stephen Charnock, *The Existence and Attributes of God*, pp. 108-111; Herman Bavinck, *The Doctrine of God*, p. 149; Carl F. H. Henry, *God, Revelation and Authority*, p. 289.

140. Stephen Davis, *Logic and the Nature of God*, pp. 45ff.

141. Clark Pinnock, "God Limits His Knowledge," p. 147.

142. Richard Rice, *God's Foreknowledge and Man's Free Will*, p. 39.

such a view implies that God's knowledge of what His creatures do is determined by or causally dependent on their actions."[143] Pinnock acknowledges that such is the case:[144]

> . . . He is, therefore, dependent on [the world], at least in the sense of knowing about it. God takes account of what is happening in the world and responds appropriately. Thus, in a sense, God is dependent on the world for information about the world. But God's nature is not changed because of this. Only the content of his experience of the world changes. Such cognitive dependency is something God accepted when he made a significant universe outside of himself. . . .

For reasons such as these Clarke is willing to speak of God's relational consciousness as finite.[145]

I must agree with these latter writers on the basic point that the content of God's knowledge is affected by and increased by what happens in the world, and in that sense his knowledge is dependent upon the world. This is the state of affairs that God has freely chosen for himself, as I have indicated above. But again I must note my strong disagreement with Rice and Pinnock and others who deny foreknowledge and believe that the contents of God's knowledge increase moment by moment as the history of the world unfolds. In my view, once God in his pre-creation counsels had determined to create this particular world, he immediately foreknew its entire history in one act of cognition. God is thus dependent upon the foreknown events of this world for this increase in his knowledge. This view, I believe, preserves everything Pinnock and others want to preserve without requiring us to compromise crucial Biblical teachings and to adopt a view very close to process philosophy. Rice admits that his view is really the same as process theism in this respect,[146] and his explanations in chapter two of his book are hardly distinguishable from those of Hartshorne. Gruenler refers to Rice's position as "the halfway house of conservative process theism."[147] He strongly disagrees with both it and the original full-fledged version,

---

143. Ronald Nash, *The Concept of God*, p. 103.
144. Clark Pinnock, "God Limits His Knowledge," pp. 146-147.
145. W. Norris Clarke, *The Philosophical Approach to God*, p. 97.
146. Richard Rice, *God's Foreknowledge and Man's Free Will*, p. 33.
147. Royce Gruenler, *The Inexhaustible God*, p. 44.

and rightly says that "biblical faith would not agree that God is 'influenced' by cosmic events as though he were processing in time and were surprised at the unfolding of possibilities as actualities." Then Gruenler makes this keen observation: "God does participate in time because he has a privileged access to the time that he has created and that he continually sustains."[148] This "privileged access" to time, even before its beginning, is what I have been arguing for.[149]

Our point is that even though God is immutable in his essence and character, his consciousness is changed with respect to its knowledge content by the things that happen in this world. A second point is that God's *attitudes* toward individual creatures change in response to their various actions. Brunner says, "If it be true that there really is such a fact as the Mercy of God and the Wrath of God, then God, too, is 'affected' by what happens to His creatures. . . . He alters . . . in accordance with the changes in men. God 'reacts' to the acts of men, and in that He 'reacts', He changes."[150] We often hear it said that God himself never changes; his attitudes toward sin and misery and faith remain eternally the same. *We* are the ones who change, thus shifting about in our relationships to the immutable God.[151] This is true to an extent, but it does not take account of the fact that God's attitude toward a particular individual *does change* when that individual's relationship to God changes. "Draw near to God, *and He will draw near to you*," says James 4:8.

A third point is that (for want of a better term) what may be called God's "*feelings*" change relative to changes in men and circumstances. Referring to Old Testament passages particularly in Hosea, König points out how God finds joy and pleasure in his relationship with Israel when

---

148. Ibid., p. 131.

149. W. Norris Clarke also makes this relevant observation: "I have the impression that process thinkers tend to move too quickly here and take for granted without sufficient exploration of other hypotheses that the only way to register in consciousness differences deriving from a changing world is by being immersed in the same kind of time-flow. I do not see how they have ruled out the possibility that the divine consciousness is present to the contingent changing world in a mode of presence that transcends our time-succession" (*The Philosophical Approach to God*, p. 93).

150. Emil Brunner, *The Christian Doctrine of God*, p. 268.

151. See A. W. Tozer, *The Knowledge of the Holy*, p. 59.

they respond to him in love.[152] He also points out how God is pained and hurt and deeply disturbed at Israel's rebellion, how it gives him inward conflict, distress and bitter disappointment.[153] How could it be otherwise, in view of the fact that God is *agape?* Could a God who truly loves his people be unaffected by their actions, especially when (as we saw in chapter six) his love includes genuine affection? How could he not be joyful when they love him? How could he not be hurt when they reject him? This is even more evident when we remember the point (also made in chapter six) that God's love really includes two elements usually associated with *erōs,* namely, he loves us because he finds value in us, and he loves us for his own sake. I.e., he desires the joy of the fellowship for which he created us in the beginning. How then can we deny the reality of his joy in such fellowship, and of his pain in our rejection of him? (A specific discussion of the impassibility of God will follow.)

Although this is language borrowed from process thought, it is not improper to say that God is "enriched" through his relationships with his creatures. Hendrikus Berkhof says,[154]

> . . . We believe that not only we, but also God, will in the end be enriched by the covenant process. . . . The father of the prodigal son was not the same after his son returned. God is enriched by renewed sons and daughters. That is his eternal goal. That is why he is so passionately interested in human affairs. . . .

This is true because of the nature of God's relatedness to his creation. Not only does he act upon the world, but it acts upon him and makes a real difference in his own activities and consciousness.

---

152. Adrio König, *Here Am I!*, pp. 72-75. "In short," he says, "we learn to know God as One who changes in his inward attitude" (p. 75). Clarke agrees "that He receives love from us and experiences joy *precisely because* of our responses" (*The Philosophical Approach to God,* p. 92).

153. Adrio König, *Here Am I!*, pp. 74-77. Kazoh Kitamori bases his view of "the pain of God" mainly on two Old Testament passages, Isaiah 63:15 and Jeremiah 31:20 (*Theology of the Pain of God* [Richmond: John Knox Press, 1965], pp. 151ff.).

154. Hendrikus Berkhof, "The (Un)changeability of God," p. 28. *See* also W. Norris Clarke, *The Philosophical Approach to God,* pp. 89, 97-98.

The Meaning of God's Repentance

One of the more troublesome aspects of Biblical teaching is the group of passages that speak of God's "repentance,"[155] a term that is itself no longer crucial to the discussion. Though it was used in the relevant passages in the King James Version and thus has become the standard way of referring to the problem, recent translations mostly use other terms instead of this one. One reason is that repentance usually is associated with sorrow for sin, something no one has seriously attributed to God as the intended meaning of these passages.

At stake is thé meaning of a single Hebrew word, *nācham*, which is used in all of the passages being considered here. In other places it has such meanings as "to comfort" (mainly in its piel forms) and "to have compassion" (cf. Deut. 32:36; Judg. 2:18; Ps. 135:14). In the present passages it is translated in a variety of ways by the NASB and the NIV, including "relent," "regret," "change his mind," "reconsider," "think better of," "be sorry," and "be grieved." The problem is how to reconcile such concepts with the fact of God's immutability. If God is unchanging in his knowledge and his will, how can he "change his mind"? Such an idea would seem to imply ignorance or lack of foreknowledge on God's part, or else an error in judgment or an impotence to carry out an intended plan.[156] Those who see God as immersed in the flow of time and who thus deny the reality of his foreknowledge seem to have no difficulty with these passages.[157] But those of us who are committed not only to God's immutability but also to his foreknowledge must make an effort to show how these passages are consistent with this view.

God's Announced Plans Are Often Conditional

Sometimes the Bible pictures God as announcing his intention to do a certain thing, then "relenting" or "changing his mind" and deciding not to do it after all. An example is Jonah's message to Nineveh: "Yet forty days and Nineveh will be overthrown" (Jonah 3:4). But the king of

---

155. The passages are Gen. 6:6; Ex. 32:14; I Sam. 15:11, 35; II Sam. 24:16; I Chron. 21:15; Ps. 106:45; Jer. 15:6; 18:8-10; 26:3, 13, 19; 42:10; Joel 2:13; Amos 7:3, 6; Jonah 3:9-10; 4:2.
156. Stephen Charnock, *The Existence and Attributes of God*, pp. 124-125.
157. E.g., see Adrio König, *Here Am I!*, p. 66.

Nineveh called on his people to repent, saying, "Who knows, God may turn and relent [nācham], and withdraw His burning anger so that we shall not perish?" (Jonah 3:9). And sure enough, "When God saw their deeds, that they turned from their wicked way, then God relented concerning the calamity which He had declared He would bring upon them. And He did not do it" (Jonah 3:10). Later Jonah describes God as "one who relents concerning calamity" (Jonah 4:2).

How may this be explained? The most obvious answer is that quite often an announced course of action is *conditional*, depending on the human response to the announcement. This may be true even if the condition is not specifically stated. Thus in the case of Nineveh, the complete message would be, "Yet forty days and Nineveh will be overthrown, unless you repent in the meantime." But what warrant do we have for assuming this was the intent of the message? We have the unassailable warrant of God's own explanation of how he operates in such cases. In Jeremiah 18:7-10 he says,

> . . . At one moment I might speak concerning a nation or concerning a kingdom to uproot, to pull down, or to destroy it; if that nation against which I have spoken turns from its evil, I will relent [nācham] concerning the calamity I planned to bring on it. Or at another moment I might speak concerning a nation or concerning a kingdom to build up or to plant it; if it does evil in My sight by not obeying My voice, then I will think better of [nācham] the good with which I had promised to bless it.

Thus we may say of most judgments concerning temporal things that there is "a tacit condition in the simple intimation," as Calvin puts it.[158]

This is the obvious explanation of several of the relevant passages, including Jeremiah 26:3, "Perhaps they will listen and everyone will turn from his evil way, that I may repent of the calamity which I am planning to do to them because of the evil of their deeds." The same applies to Jeremiah 26:13; 42:10. From other passages it seems that the implied conditions that may influence God to change his announced course of action include fervent intercessory prayer by a third party. This is the case in Amos 7:1-6, when God twice "changed His mind"

---

158. John Calvin, *Institutes of the Christian Religion*, I.xvii.14, ed. John T. McNeill, tr. Ford Lewis Battles (Philadelphia: Westminster Press, 1960), 1:228).

about an impending curse as the result of Amos' prayers. The same is true of the announcement of Hezekiah's death (Jer. 26:19), though the fervent prayer this time was by Hezekiah himself (Isa. 38:1-5). The intercessory prayer of Moses (Ex. 32:11-13) caused God to decide against destroying Israel as he declared he wanted to do (Ex. 32:9-10). "So the Lord changed His mind about the harm which He said He would do to His people" (Ex. 32:13).

In such cases as these, we believe that God foreknew that the prayers would be made and the conditions met, so that he did not literally have to change his mind in the midst of the situation. This is no different from any answered prayer. God foreknows the prayer itself and thus is able to predetermine how he will respond.[159] There is no literal change in God's plan or God's mind. A better translation of *nācham* in these passages is "relented" or "decided against."

In some cases, however, God makes an irrevocable decision with no conditions attached. These are things about which there will be no relenting; the judgment is final. For example, "The Lord has sworn and will not change His mind [*nācham*], 'Thou art a priest forever according to the order of Melchizedek'" (Ps. 110:4). Such finality is expressed in the same way in Jeremiah 4:28; 20:16; Ezekiel 24:14; Zechariah 8:14. This is no doubt the meaning of Numbers 23:19, "God is not a man, that He should lie, nor a son of man, that He should repent [*nācham*]; has He said, and will He not do it? Or has He spoken, and will He not make it good?" This and the similar statement in I Samuel 15:29 are referring to specific irrevocable decisions where neither intercession nor repentance would avail.

The Significant Change Is in Others, Not in God

It follows from the preceding point that the significant change in the conditional cases is in others, not in God. God's own heart is ready to bless or to curse, depending on the relative righteousness or unrighteousness of people (or in some cases on the fervency of prayer). When the people themselves change from one relative state to the other, they come into a different relationship to God, whose own attitudes toward sin and righteousness do not change. As Charnock says,

---

159. Jack Cottrell, *What the Bible Says About God the Ruler*, pp. 367ff.

"The change in these cases is in the creature; according to the alteration in the creature, it stands in a various relation to God."[160] As Haley says, "If man changes, the very immutability of God's character requires that his feelings should change toward the changed man."[161]

Most will admit that although the significant change occurs in man, at least God's outward actions change in that there is a reversal in his announced intention and sometimes a reversal in the course of action itself. This would be the case in the passages quoted in the last section. It would also apply to II Samuel 24:16 and I Chronicles 21:15, where the Lord "relented" in the midst of a punitive pestilence and stopped it before it could destroy Jerusalem. See also Psalm 106:45 for a similar reference. In Jeremiah 15:6 God says to his fickle people, "I am tired of relenting!", indicating that he was tired of giving in and backing off from previously-announced judgments.

Again we may note that such outward changes would be taken into account in God's foreknowledge and would already be worked into his overall plan. The following statement by Calvin cannot be lightly dismissed: "Neither God's plan nor his will is reversed, nor his volition altered; but what he had from eternity foreseen, approved, and decreed, he pursues in uninterrupted tenor, however sudden the variation may appear in men's eyes."[162]

Nācham as the Intrusion of Strong Feelings

God's "repentance" is not just a matter of changes in outward relationships and actions, however. It also includes inward changes in God's consciousness in the form of the intrusion of strong feelings within God brought about by the actions of men. The origin of the root for nācham, says Wilson, "seems to reflect the idea of 'breathing deeply,' hence the physical display of one's feelings, usually sorrow, compassion, or comfort."[163] Thus the feeling could take the form of grief or

---

160. Stephen Charnock, *The Existence and Attributes of God*, p. 128. See Millard Erickson, *Christian Theology*, I:279.

161. John W. Haley, *An Examination of the Alleged Discrepancies of the Bible* (Nashville: Gospel Advocate, 1951 reprint of 1874 edition), p. 66. Italics omitted.

162. John Calvin, *Institutes of the Christian Religion*, I.xvii.13; (I:227).

163. Marvin R. Wilson, "nācham," *Theological Wordbook of the Old Testament*, ed. R. Laird Harris et al. (Chicago: Moody Press, 1980), p. 570.

relief, depending upon the character of the human action to which it is a response. Most often stated or implied is the feeling of grief. Thus in Genesis 6:6 the idea that God "repented" because he made man simply means that he was filled with great sorrow and grief as the result of his creatures' utter wickedness: "The Lord was grieved [nācham] that he had made man on the earth, and his heart was filled with pain" (Gen. 6:6; NIV). This is also the best translation of I Samuel 15:11, 35. Here we read that "the Lord was grieved that he had made Saul king over Israel" (NIV). This meaning appears in II Samuel 24:16 and I Chronicles 21:15 as well (NIV).

Anthropomorphic Language

A final consideration in explaining the so-called "repentance" of God is the possibility that such language is meant to be figurative or anthropomorphic. The idea would be that there is nothing in human experience that truly corresponds with the divine reaction described by the word nācham, but this term is used because it comes closer than any other. Still, one should not attempt to press it for its literal meaning when applied to God. In the midst of a lengthy defense of this point, Carl Henry says, "When all due allowance is made for the literal and objective truth conveyed by figurative statements, divine repentance is itself an anthropomorphic representation."[164] Calvin says that such language is used because of our weakness; it "must be accommodated to our capacity so that we may understand it."[165]

Though this has been a traditionally common way of explaining the nācham passages, it is often criticized today as an easy way out of a supposed difficulty and as unnecessary if we are willing to accept a more limited concept of God than classical theism has bequeathed to us. Pinnock says that the appeal to anthropomorphism in this connection is just a case of "trying to avoid what the Bible says."[166]

I can agree with this up to a point, since the concept of anthropomorphism is often carried to an extreme and used to negate the reality of any true feelings in God. This is the case with Charnock, who

---

164. Carl F. H. Henry, *God, Revelation and Authority*, V:304.

165. John Calvin, *Institutes of the Christian Religion*, I.xvii.13 (I:227).

166. Clark Pinnock, "God Limits His Knowledge," p. 155. See "The Need for a Scriptural, and Therefore a Neo-Classical Theism," p. 40.

declares that "no proper grief can be imagined to be in God," and "we must not conclude him to have passions like us."[167] But I do not think we can rule out anthropomorphic elements altogether, especially when the idea of "changing his mind" seems to be implied in a text. Given the acceptability of anthropomorphic language as such, as in the references to God's bodily parts, there is no inherent impropriety in suggesting that it applies in this case as well.

Thus we conclude that the references to God's "repentance" are consistent with the general view of divine immutability being defended here, that God is unchangeable in his essence and character but subject to variation in his states of consciousness.

IMMUTABILITY AND REDEMPTION

The final section of our study of God is the relation between immutability and redemption. Wolterstorff declares that the only way God can be our Redeemer is if he is a God who changes: "God cannot be a redeeming God without there being changeful variation among his states."[168] Is this true? Yes, we must grant that in the work of redemption God is involved in some significant changes. At the same time we must assert that the only way God can be our Redeemer is if he remains unchanging in certain ways. Now we must ask, in what ways does God change and in what ways does he remain the same in connection with our redemption?

God's Eternal Purpose Does Not Change

The section on God's "repentance" raised the question whether God's will or plan changes; the answer was no. It has been pointed out that only two things could ever force God to change his plan or purpose: either lack of foreknowledge to anticipate all possible contingencies, or lack of power to carry out what has been planned.[169] But God is lacking in neither. Because of his foreknowledge and his omnipotence, the plans he has made from eternity past will stand; they will be carried

---

167. Stephen Charnock, *The Existence and Attributes of God*, p. 125.

168. Nicholas Wolterstorff, "God Everlasting," p. 182.

169. C. Samuel Storms, *The Grandeur of God* (Grand Rapids: Baker Book House, 1984), p. 111.

out.[170]

That God's purpose and plan are unchanging does not mean that he cannot work in a variety of ways and implement changes in his methods and strategies. As one writer says,[171]

> . . . [Immutability] suggests no singleness in mode of working, but rather has in it all the breadth and fulness of infinity. It is entirely consistent with endless variety in operation. It does not prevent God from working differently in different conditions, or employing whatever method may suit his purpose best. The greatness of God is an infinite versatility, rendering natural to him an infinite variety of action, adapted to the infinite variety of needs and occasions. . . .

But because of God's foreknowledge, all changes in strategy and action are themselves built into the eternal purpose; they do not represent some kind of on-the-spot revision of the plan. This applies to those occasions that called for God's "repentance" as discussed above. It also applies to the more comprehensive shifts of strategy such as the institution of the plan of redemption following the entrance of sin (Gen. 3:15), and the transition from the Old Covenant to the New Covenant (Jer. 31:31-34).

The Bible specifically teaches the immutability of God's purpose or counsel. "The Lord nullifies the counsel of the nations; He frustrates the plans of the peoples. The counsel of the Lord stands forever, the plans of His heart from generation to generation" (Ps. 33:10-11). "Many are the plans in a man's heart, but the counsel of the Lord, it will stand" (Prov. 19:21). "The Lord of hosts has sworn saying, 'Surely, just as I have intended so it has happened, and just as I have planned so it will stand'" (Isa. 14:24; cf. 46:10; 54:10). The New Testament specifically says that God has had an eternal purpose since before the foundation of the world, and that this purpose includes our redemption through the blood of Christ. Christ the Redeemer and his redeeming work were "foreknown before the foundation of the world" (I Peter 1:20). Paul

---

170. Richard Rice, denying the foreknowledge of God, also denies the reality of an unchanging plan. God has an unchanging general purpose, but the way he carries it out in this world must be "constantly modified in response to creaturely behavior." His plan must be "flexible," because he "must 'improvise' as circumstances change if He wishes to reach His objectives" (*God's Foreknowledge and Man's Free Will*, p. 63).

171. William Newton Clarke, *The Christian Doctrine of God*, p. 310.

says, "He chose us in Him before the foundation of the world, that we should be holy and blameless in Him. In love He predestined us to adoption as sons through Jesus Christ to Himself, according to the kind intention of His will" (Eph. 1:4-5). We have "been predestined according to His purpose who works all things after the counsel of His will" (Eph. 1:11). God's "eternal purpose" is "carried out in Christ Jesus our Lord" (Eph. 3:11). He has saved us "according to His own purpose and grace which was granted us in Christ Jesus from all eternity" (II Tim. 1:9). Hebrews 6:17 speaks specifically of "the unchangeableness of His purpose."

It is important to remember that the entrance of sin into the world did not change God's purpose for creating the world in the first place. Because he foreknew this contingency even before the initial creation, he was able to include the work of redemption in the eternal plan from the very beginning. Thus the plan in God's mind at the moment of creation is the same plan he is working out now. In his eternal and infinite wisdom he devised a way to carry it out despite the entrance of sin; this way is redemption through Jesus Christ. This does not mean that redemption itself was God's original purpose;[172] rather it is the eternally-devised *means* of achieving it. His eternal purpose is "carried out" in Christ (Eph. 3:11).

Immutability and Incarnation

This means that the incarnation of God the Logos in the person of Jesus of Nazareth was not a change in God's eternal purpose. Indeed, in a sense the incarnation is the "temporal moment in which this purpose is consummated," as Muller says. "The immutability of God and his purpose manifests incarnation as the fulfillment of what was promised steadfastly of old and as the redemptive blessing of which God can never repent in the future."[173] In this sense the incarnation is the

---

172. For a discussion of God's purpose in creating, see Jack Cottrell, *What the Bible Says About God the Creator*, pp. 120-128.

173. Richard Muller, "Incarnation, Immutability, and the Case for Classical Theism," p. 39. Muller errs, I think, in calling the incarnation "the purpose of God in the very act of creation itself" (ibid.). In the first place, God's purpose in Christ does not focus on the incarnation but on his death and resurrection; the incarnation is but a means to this end. Second, as stated above, the work of Christ in itself is not the "eternal purpose," but the means of achieving it.

supreme demonstration of the immutability of God. As Barth says, "God is constant, He does not alter, when He becomes and is one with the creature in Jesus Christ. For this happening is simply God Himself, His free life, in which He is . . . incapable of being diverted from His purpose."[174]

At the same time and ironically, how to reconcile the incarnation with the immutability of God has always been one of the more troublesome problems related to the subject. How was it possible for God to become man without some change occurring in the divine nature itself? Classical theism has defended the compatibility of the two, declaring that God does not change in the event of the incarnation. "There was no change in the divine nature of the Son when he assumed human nature," says Charnock.[175]

Not everyone within Christendom has agreed with this, however. Some have argued from Philippians 2:7 that the divine nature was in some sense reduced at the incarnation. This verse says that when he became man, the pre-existing Logos "emptied Himself." The verb here is kenoō, from which we get the noun kenosis. Some have taken this to mean that at the incarnation the Logos "emptied himself of his deity," or at least part of his deity. This view became prominent in the nineteenth century in what is known as "kenotic theology," represented especially by German theologians such as Gottfried Thomasius, I. A. Dorner, and Wolfgang Gess. These men "ventured to speak of a change in God in the incarnation in the sense that the eternal Son of God subjected himself to a radical self-limitation."[176] For example, Thomasius distinguished between two kinds of divine attributes: the immanent or internal, such as love, joy, and holiness; and the external, such as omnipotence and omnipresence. At the incarnation the Son divested himself of the latter attributes.[177] Such of course would be a radical change in the very essence of God.

In the more recent discussion of immutability, some are raising this question again, though not necessarily in such an extreme way. The

---

174. Karl Barth, *Church Dogmatics*, II/1, p. 515.
175. Stephen Charnock, *The Existence and Attributes of God*, p. 123.
176. Hendrikus Berkhof, *Christian Faith*, p. 144.
177. Stephen M. Smith, "Kenosis, Kenotic Theology," *Evangelical Dictionary of Theology*, ed. Walter A. Elwell (Grand Rapids: Baker Book House, 1984), p. 602.

question is again being asked, how is the incarnation possible without *some* kind of change in God? Attention is focused on John 1:14, "The Word became flesh." Does not *becoming* indicate change? Thus must we not give up one or the other, either incarnation or immutability? König advocates giving up the latter. One thing we learn from the incarnation, he says, "is that we cannot be satisfied here with a metaphysical concept of immutability. In Christ, God became man, and therefore changed, becoming what he was not previously." Thus the incarnation is "a decisive testimony against a barren view of unchangeability." God not only undergoes change, but a humiliating change. "Jesus is God emptied."[178] In his challenge to classical theism Pinnock also emphasizes the "becoming" aspect of the incarnation. "The fourth Gospel says that the Word *became* flesh in the incarnation," he says; and this is "one example of many texts which indicate God's ability to change in his glorious freedom."[179] Pinnock appeals to Barth's treatment of immutability in support of his view,[180] and Henry chastises Barth for certain questionable expressions in this connection, especially the comment that God "becomes a creature" in the incarnation.[181]

It is true that Barth makes this statement,[182] but it is not fair to Barth to say that he is affirming an incarnational change in the very nature of God. In fact Barth defends a very traditional view of the incarnation, namely, that it involves *no change in God's essence* or in his essential deity. He rejects the kenotic theology because of its "open abandonment of the presupposition common to all earlier theology . . . that the Godhead of the man Jesus remains intact and unaltered."[183] He affirms that "God is always God even in His humiliation. The divine being does not suffer any change, any diminution, any transformation into something else, any admixture with something else, let alone any cessation. The deity of Christ is the one unaltered because unalterable deity

---

178. Adrio König, *Here Am I!*, pp. 88-89.

179. Clark Pinnock, "The Need for a Scriptural, and Therefore a Neo-Classical Theism," p. 40.

180. Ibid., pp. 39, 42.

181. Carl F. H. Henry, *God, Revelation and Authority*, V:296.

182. "In Jesus Christ God Himself has become a creature" (Karl Barth, *Church Dogmatics*, II/1, p. 514). Cf. also IV/1, pp. 181, 185.

183. Karl Barth, *Church Dogmatics*, IV/1, pp. 182-183.

of God." There was no loss, "diminution or alteration of His Godhead."[184] Barth himself explains his statement that God "has become a creature" as meaning that "He has become one with the creature, with man. . . . Where this creature, the man Jesus Christ is, God Himself is present."[185]

This seems to me to be an adequate statement of the traditional view of classical theism, which I believe is quite correct on this point. In the incarnation God does *not* change in his divine nature; he does *not* give up any of his attributes; he does *not* "divest himself of his deity" either wholly or in part. He could not do so and still be God. Such a change in his essence is in fact an ontological impossibility. The "kenosis" in Philippians 2:7 was not a diminishing of his divine nature but a veiling of it, which consisted of a temporary suspension of the exercise of his prerogatives as God. "He did not cease to be God," says Charnock. "The glory of his divinity was not extinguished nor diminished, though it was obscured and darkened under the veil of our infirmities; but there was no more change in the hiding of it than there is in the body of the sun when it is shadowed by the interposition of a cloud."[186]

Thus we affirm with Paul that in Christ "all the fulness of Deity dwells in bodily form" (Col. 2:9). Unless this is so, i.e., unless the incarnation could take place without any change in the essence of the deity of the Logos, redemption itself is impossible. As Charnock well puts it,[187]

> . . . His blood, while it was pouring out from his veins, was the blood of God, Acts xx.28; and therefore, when he was bowing the head of his humanity upon the cross, he had the nature and perfections of God; for had he ceased to be God, he had been a mere creature. and his sufferings would have been of as little value and satisfaction as the sufferings of a creature.
>
> He could not have been a sufficient mediator had he ceased to be God; and he had ceased to be God had he lost any one perfection proper to the divine nature . . . .

---

184. Ibid., pp. 179-180. "God for His part is God in His unity with this creature . . . without ceasing to be God, without any alteration or diminution of His divine nature" (ibid., p. 183.).

185. Karl Barth, *Church Dogmatics*, II/1, p. 514.

186. Stephen Charnock, *The Existence and Attributes of God*, p. 124.

187. Ibid.

Barth agrees with this point: "Any subtraction or weakening of [the deity of the Logos] would at once throw doubt upon the atonement made in Him." Again: "If in Christ—even in the humiliated Christ born in a manger at Bethlehem and crucified on the cross of Golgotha—God is not unchanged and wholly God, then everything that we may say about the reconciliation of the world made by God in this humiliated One is left hanging in the air." Surely, "if God is not truly and altogether in Christ, what sense can there be in talking about the reconciliation of the world with God in Him?"[188]

What then does John 1:14 mean when it says "The Word became flesh?" Certainly it is going further than exegesis requires to insist that the word *became* must refer to some ontological alteration in God's own essence. In view of parallel expressions in Scripture, says Muller, it is sufficient to read this as meaning that the Word was "manifested in" or "present in" the flesh. He refers to I Timothy 3:16, "He who was revealed in the flesh"; and I John 4:2, "Jesus Christ has come in the flesh" (cf. 2 John 7).[189]

If the incarnation means that there was no change in the essence of God, does this mean that God experienced no change at all in this act? Not at all. We can agree with Berkhof that God "experienced a profound change when the Word became flesh."[190] But this has already been conceded by classical theists, except that they simply have been unwilling to speak of it as change. I am referring to the traditional notion that the incarnation was accomplished not by subtraction from the divine nature but by the adding or joining of human nature to the divine. Though it is true that this involved no alteration in the divine essence itself, it surely made a profound difference to God's own experience and consciousness and actions.

The key to the incarnation, then, is not that the Logos gave up anything, but that he *took* something. Philippians 2:7 calls it "taking the form of a bond-servant, and being made in the likeness of men." As Charnock says, "He assumed our nature without laying aside his own."[191]

---

188. Karl Barth, *Church Dogmatics*, pp. 180, 183.

189. Richard Muller, "Incarnation, Immutability, and the Case for Classical Theism," p. 35.

190. Hendrikus Berkhof, *Christian Faith*, p. 141.

191. Stephen Charnock, *The Existence and Attributes of God*, p. 124.

This is Barth's point as well: "All the older theology rightly stressed the fact that the incarnation of the Logos, the God-manhood of Jesus Christ, could not mean any alteration in the divine being . . . . For it consisted in the assumption of human nature." This is to say "that the incarnation not only does not mean any curtailment or compromising of the immutable divine nature, but that it means the revelation of it in its perfection."[192] Barth says,[193]

> . . . It was not to Him an inalienable necessity to exist only in that form of God, only to be God, and therefore only to be different from the creature, from man, as the reality which is distinct from God, only to be the eternal Word and not flesh. He was not committed to any such "only." In addition to His form in the likeness of God He could also . . . take the form of a servant. He could be like men. He could be found in fashion as a man. As God, therefore (without ceasing to be God) He could be known only to Himself, but unknown as such in the world and for the world. His divine majesty could be in this alien form. It could be a hidden majesty. He could, therefore, humble Himself in this form. . . .

In saying this Barth is well within the bounds of the traditional view as stated by Henry himself:[194]

> . . . The fact remains that Christ did not become *man* in lieu of his divinity, but that the divine person and nature added human nature and carried that nature in glorified form into eternity. The permanent inclusion even of this glorified human nature in the experience of the Godhead did not involve a new mode of deity, however . . . .

In conclusion to this section we may confidently affirm that the incarnation is completely consistent with the immutability of God as we have seen it taught in the Bible, namely, that God is unchangeable in his essence and character but subject to change in his experience and states of consciousness. One last quotation makes this point well:[195]

---

192. Karl Barth, *Church Dogmatics*, II/1, p. 515.
193. Karl Barth, *Church Dogmatics*, IV/1, p. 180. We strongly disagree with Barth, however, that the "form of a servant" was natural and proper for God; and that being humble, subordinate and obedient is an inherent part of the divine nature. Cf. ibid., pp. 193ff.
194. Carl F. H. Henry, *God, Revelation and Authority*, V:292-293.
195. C. Samuel Storms, *The Grandeur of God*, p. 108.

. . . The second person of the Trinity has taken unto Himself or assumed a human nature, yet without alteration or reduction of His essential deity. He is now what He has always been: very God. He is now what He once was not: very man. He is now—and forever will be—both: the God-man. It is a simplistic and ill-conceived doctrine of immutability that denies any part of this essential biblical verity. Thus, to say *without qualification* that God cannot change or that He can and often does change is at best unwise, at worst misleading. Our concept of immutability must be formulated in such a way that we do justice to every biblical asser- tion concerning both the "being" and "becoming" of God.

Immutability and Divine Suffering

We have said that the incarnation involved profound changes in God's experience and states of consciousness. If this were true in no other way, it would be eminently true with reference to the suffering ex- perienced by God in Jesus' propitiatory death for the sins of the world. However, this view of divine suffering stands in sharp contrast with traditional theism's affirmation of the *impassibility* of God. This term comes from the Latin *passus*, a participle form of *patior*, which means "to experience, to undergo, to suffer." From this we get the English word *passion*, which can mean any strong emotion or feeling, but in theological contexts usually refers to the suffering of Christ. Thus the word *impassible* can mean (generally) incapable of emotions as such, or (specifically) incapable of suffering. Gordon R. Lewis thus defines the doctrine of the impassibility of God as "the doctrine that God is not capable of being acted upon or affected emotionally by anything in crea- tion."[196] This would have special reference to his inability to suffer. As Owen says, "The word means particularly that he cannot experience sorrow, sadness or pain."[197] The idea is that a perfect God would always be in an inner state of supreme blessedness; suffering would contradict such blessedness; therefore it is impossible.

Impassibility in Classical Theism

The doctrine of impassibility was widely accepted by the Church

---

196. Gordon R. Lewis, "Impassibility of God," *Evangelical Dictionary of Theology*, ed. Walter A. Elwell (Grand Rapids: Baker Book House, 1984), p. 553.
197. H. P. Owen, *Concepts of Deity*, p. 23.

Fathers during the early centuries of Christianity. In agreement with the classical Greek view of God, they denied that God is capable of suffering. This should not be confused with the denial of the doctrine known as *patripassianism* (or "Father-suffering-ism," as Brown calls it).[198] This idea is associated with the Trinitarian heresy of modalism, which taught that it was the Father himself who became incarnate in Christ and suffered on the cross. One may deny patripassianism and still acknowledge that God the Father is capable of suffering, just as are God the Son and God the Holy Spirit. This latter view is sometimes called *theopaschitism* (or "God-suffering").[199] The fact is that as a rule the early Christian theologians denied both.

Examples of the teaching of impassibility include Ignatius, who describes the God who became incarnate for us as "the Invisible, who became visible for our sake" and "the Impassible, who suffered for our sake."[200] Justin Martyr refers to "the unbegotten and impassible God."[201] "God is uncreated, and, impassible," says Athenagoras.[202] Clement of Alexandria agrees that "it were wrong to conceive of God as subject to passions."[203] Bethune-Baker describes Hilary's attempts "to guard the impassibility of the Godhead in itself, while recognizing the sufferings of the Incarnate God in his human nature."[204] This last quotation indicates how the Fathers reconciled God's impassibility with the suffering of Christ: Christ suffered only in his human nature, not in his divine nature.

Such a view has been accepted by many throughout the history of

---

198. Harold O. J. Brown, *Heresies* (Garden City, N.Y.: Doubleday & Company, 1984), p. 85.

199. G. C. Berkouwer, *The Triumph of Grace*, p. 298.

200. Ignatius, "To Polycarp," VII:3, *The Apostolic Fathers*, ed. J. B. Lightfoot and J. R. Harmer (Grand Rapids: Baker Book House, 1962), p. 87.

201. Justin Martyr, "The First Apology," XXV, *The Ante-Nicene Fathers*, ed. Alexander Roberts and James Donaldson (New York: Charles Scribner's Sons, 1913), I:171.

202. Athenagoras, "A Plea for the Christians," VIII, tr. B. P. Pratten, *The Ante-Nicene Fathers*, ed. Alexander Roberts and James Donaldson (New York: Charles Scribner's Sons, 1913), II:132.

203. Clement of Alexandria, "The Stromata, or Miscellanies," V:4, *The Ante-Nicene Fathers*, ed. Alexander Roberts and James Donaldson (New York: Charles Scribner's Sons, 1913), II:450.

204. J. F. Bethune-Baker, *An Introduction to the Early History of Christian Doctrine*, 4 ed. (London: Methuen & Co., 1929), p. 298.

Christendom. An example from the period of Protestant scholasticism is Wendelin, who says, "It is Christ's human nature that suffered for us, not the divine which cannot suffer and die."[205] Bucanus agrees that "the *persona* which suffered is God and man, but not in the divine [which is impossible!] but in the human nature assumed, which was capable of suffering."[206] Charnock declares that "no proper grief can be imagined to be in God," for "we must not conclude him to have passions like us."[207] In modern times Berkouwer has argued strongly against theopaschitism. We cannot conclude the suffering of God from the fact that Jesus was "true God," he says. "We consider the theopaschitic 'conclusion' to be unacceptable."[208]

Impassibility Questioned

Not everyone has been content with the doctrine of God's impassibility, however. In his exposition of classical theism, Owen acknowledges that this is its "most questionable aspect."[209] There are two basic reasons for calling it into question. First, how can God be love and not suffer pain in the face of human suffering and evil?[210] It seems that he cannot. Moltmann says, "God's being is in suffering and the suffering is in God's being itself, because God is love."[211] This should not be understood in the sense of process thought, where God necessarily suffers because he necessarily participates in every human experience. "There are other forms of suffering between unwilling suffering as a result of an alien cause and being essentially unable to suffer, namely active suffering, the suffering of love, in which one voluntarily opens himself to the possibility of being affected by another." If God is incapable of suffering altogether, then he is incapable of love.[212]

The second reason for questioning the classical notion of impassibili-

---

205. In Heinrich Heppe, *Reformed Dogmatics*, ed. Ernst Bizer, tr. G. T. Thomson (London: Allen & Unwin, 1950), p. 465.

206. Ibid., p. 466.

207. Stephen Charnock, *The Existence and Attributes of God*, p. 125.

208. G. C. Berkouwer, *The Triumph of Grace*, p. 304.

209. H. P. Owen, *Concepts of Deity*, p. 24.

210. Ibid. Cf. Clark Pinnock, "God Limits His Knowledge," p. 155.

211. Jürgen Moltmann, *The Crucified God*, p. 227.

212. Ibid., p. 230. Cf. Lester Kuyper, "The Suffering and the Repentance of God," pp. 274ff.

ty is the reality of the incarnation itself. How is the incarnation real, i.e., how can we say that both the divine and the human were united in a single person, if the divine nature did not suffer when Jesus suffered? As Owen states it, "It is very hard to believe that if God fully became Man he did not experience any of the pains that his Manhood endured."[213]

Indeed, it is not only very hard, but impossible to believe. Though it is no doubt the case that there are some kinds of suffering that God cannot experience, as Owen notes,[214] we must reject the notion of his absolute impassibility. As has already been evident in this chapter, I believe that God can and does suffer as the result of his creation of free-will beings who have chosen to sin against him—a possibility that he freely chose to risk when he created the universe in the first place. For our sakes, out of love, he was willing to take this risk! I agree with Pinnock, that "God's ability to suffer and his willingness to do so, far from being a difficulty to explain, is the glory of the gospel. . . . The cross compels us to reject a metaphysics that does not permit God to suffer."[215]

God's Suffering in the Old Testament

It is not only the cross that compels us to accept the suffering of God, since the fact of his suffering is already seen in his dealings with sinful man in the Old Testament. We have noted how the word *nācham* sometimes refers to God's experience of the strong feeling of grief. This could not be more clear than in Genesis 6:6, which states God's reaction to the universal wickedness that had invaded his world: "The Lord was grieved that he had made man on the earth, and his heart was filled with pain" (NIV). The same word is used in Judges 2:18 to describe God's feelings toward Israel as they endured oppression from their enemies: "The Lord was moved to pity [*nācham*] by their groaning because of those who oppressed and afflicted them."

Adrio König is struck by the Old Testament picture of Yahweh as

---

213. H. P. Owen, *Concepts of Deity*, p. 24.

214. Ibid. E.g., physical pain, the pain of guilt, and the pain of fear.

215. Clark Pinnock, "The Need for a Scriptural, and Therefore a Neo-Classical Theism," p. 41. Pinnock refers to Moltmann, *The Crucified God*, pp. 267-278, where Moltmann says among other things that "to speak of a God who could not suffer would make God a demon" (p. 274). This is surely a bit extreme.

being "deeply disturbed" and "pained" by Israel's faithlessness. He notes that the lamentations of Jeremiah are no less than the lamentations of God himself, since Israel's apostasy causes him inward conflict, distress, and bitter disappointment. Their sin "really reached the Lord's heart, and he is deeply touched by it." All of this "hurt the Lord so deeply" because Judah was the beloved of his soul.[216] A similar picture is drawn by all the prophets, says König:[217]

> . . . The prophets do not proclaim a detached, remote, dispassionate, uninvolved and neutral God, but The God of Israel who was deeply engaged in Israel's joys and sorrows. The fate of the people involved him, and as the living God he lived with them, and among them. Their love and obedience gave him joy, their unfaithfulness pained him; he suffered with them in their captivity and exile.

As Isaiah 63:9-10 clearly shows, God suffered when Israel sinned against him, and he suffered when others sinned against Israel:

> In all their affliction He was afflicted, and the angel of His presence saved them; in His love and in His mercy He redeemed them; and He lifted them and carried them all the days of old. But they rebelled and grieved His Holy Spirit; therefore, He turned Himself to become their enemy, He fought against them.

As König says, "The Lord really suffered under the faithlessness of his people."[218]

It appears that Kazoh Kitamori was moved to develop his "theology of the pain of God" by two Old Testament passages, Jeremiah 31:20 and Isaiah 63:15.[219] These passages speak of God's bowels or heart or inward being; they speak of God as being somehow troubled in his heart. In Isaiah 63:15 the prophet cries out to God, "Where are Thy zeal and Thy mighty deeds? The stirrings of Thy heart and Thy compassion are restrained toward me." In Jeremiah 31:20 God speaks, "'Is Ephraim My dear son? Is he a delightful child? Indeed, as often as I have spoken against him, I certainly still remember him; therefore My heart

---

216. Adrio König. *Here Am I!*, pp. 74-77.
217. Ibid., p. 92.
218. Ibid., p. 99.
219. See Kazoh Kitamori. *Theology of the Pain of God*, pp. 151ff.

yearns for him; I will surely have mercy on him,' declares the Lord."
The verb used in these verses, hāmāh, "is a strong word, emphasizing
unrest, commotion, strong feeling, or noise." It is translated variously as
"cry aloud, mourn, rage, roar, sound; make noise, tumult; be
clamorous, disquieted, loud, moved, troubled, in an uproar."[220]
Kitamori says he noted that the Japanese version of Jeremiah 31:20
reads, "My heart is pained."[221] He also compared how the Old Testament writers used the verb hāmāh to describe the pain of their own
hearts (e.g., in Jer. 4:19; 48:36; Isa. 16:11; Pss. 38:8; 42:5; 43:5).
Thus he concluded that in Jeremiah 31:20, "Jeremiah must have seen
in God the same condition of the heart which the prophets and
psalmists themselves experienced. What kind of condition? The pain!
The pain of God!"[222] This pain is the result of the fact that God is both
love and wrath, and from the fact that both are directed toward the
same object. Without wrath there would be no pain. "God suffers pain
only when he tries to *love* us, the objects of his wrath." His love comes
to us with forgiveness for our sins, though we deserve his wrath. This is
the source of the pain of God. "The pain of God is the forgiveness of
sins."[223]

God's Suffering in the Work of Redemption

The suffering of God was thus a reality as soon as sin was a reality,
and perhaps from the time God foreknew the reality of sin. But the
climactic suffering of God took place in connection with his work of
redemption, as that was accomplished through the substitutionary
death of the incarnate Logos (as described in the last chapter). This
divine suffering took two forms. First, the divine nature of Christ himself
suffered when he took our sins and our penalty upon himself on the
cross. The incarnate Christ indeed had two natures, divine and human;
but he was *only one person*, one center of consciousness. Whatever experiences passed through the consciousness of Jesus of Nazareth passed through the consciousness of God the Son. When Jesus experienc-

---

220. Carl P. Weber, "hāmāh," *Theological Wordbook of the Old Testament*, ed. R.
Laird Harris et al. (Chicago: Moody Press, 1980), I:219.
221. Kazoh Kitamori, *Theology of the Pain of God*, p. 8.
222. Ibid., pp. 152-153.
223. Ibid., pp. 21-22, 27, 34-35, 40, 115.

ed suffering and death on the cross, God the Son experienced suffering and death.[224] "Although He was a Son, He learned obedience from the things which He suffered" (Heb. 5:8). Particularly poignant was "the pain of his God-forsakenness"[225] (Matt. 27:46).

The second form of divine suffering connected with the cross was the suffering of God the Father, the real pain he endured in sending his own Son to die on the cross. His own Son! This is how Romans 8:32 puts it: "He . . . did not spare His own Son, but delivered Him up for us all." König comments on the intense pain hidden just below the surface of this terse expression, "His own Son"! "This is no neutral, or objective report, but expresses astonishment: Did God do even this?"[226] One point must be made clear. In reference to the cross, the Father did not suffer *what* the Son suffered, but *because* the Son suffered. He was not experiencing the agonies of Calvary; only God the Son was experiencing those. The Father rather was experiencing the agonies of a *Father* as he watched his only begotten and only beloved Son go through an ordeal unlike anything eternity had ever seen or will ever see again.

Berkouwer objects to this whole line of thought, denying theopaschitism or the idea that God suffers as such, even in the incarnation. At stake, he thinks, is the integrity of Christ's role as Mediator between us and God. "When God *Himself* is the subject of the suffering in substitutionary self-surrender," the whole idea of mediatorship disappears. How can God be both the subject *and* the object of the curse, the wrath, and the forsaking? "How can *God* be forsaken of *God*?"[227] In my opinion this objection by Berkouwer misses the mark because it assumes that if God himself suffers on the cross, then God the Father and God the Son must be sharing the exact same suffering. If this were so, as it would be on the model of process thought, then Berkouwer would be

---

224. To say that he "experienced death" is not to say that he died; these are two different things. Technically speaking, in the death of a human being only the body dies; the spirit does not die but rather *experiences* that death. So in Jesus, on the cross his human body died, but his human spirit *and his divine nature* experienced death. It is not correct to say, as Moltmann does, that "God died on the cross of Christ" (*The Crucified God*, p. 216).

225. Hendrikus Berkhof, *Christian Faith*, p. 141.

226. Adrio König, *Here Am I!*, p. 100.

227. G. C. Berkouwer, *The Triumph of Grace*, pp. 304-305, 312. See also his discussion in *The Work of Christ*, pp. 264ff.

right; Christ's role as Mediator would be compromised. But, as indicated above, I do not believe that we should say that the Father and the Son suffer the same thing. The Son suffers the eternal wrath of the Father upon sin, and the Father suffers to see his Son having to endure it. In other words, the suffering of the Mediator is still unique. The basis for making this distinction is the concept of the economic Trinity.[228]

(It would seem that Kitamori does not make this proper and necessary distinction, and thus in the final analysis his view would be vulnerable before Berkouwer's criticism. He says, for example, "God the Father who hid himself in the death of God the Son is God in pain. Therefore the pain of God is neither merely the pain of God the Son, nor merely the pain of God the Father, but the pain of the two persons who are essentially one."[229] The same is true of Moltmann, who says, for example, "In the passion of the Son, the Father himself suffers the pains of abandonment. In the death of the Son, death comes upon God himself, and the Father suffers the death of his Son in his love for forsaken man."[230])

We conclude, then, that the doctrine of divine impassibility cuts the very nerve of the gospel of redemption and must be rejected. Kitamori is at least looking in the right direction when he says that the pain of God is "the heart of the gospel," that "in the gospel the final word is the *pain of God.*"[231] The only way for God to be true to both sides of his nature—his love and his wrath—is through the suffering of God the Son for the propitiation of the sins of the world. Thus the very nature of the atonement as understood here *requires* that God suffer as he did in the divine nature of Jesus Christ. Only if he suffered in his divine nature could his substitutionary suffering be *infinite* and thus equivalent to eternity in hell for the whole human race. God's ability to suffer is thus the very presupposition of the atonement.

---

228. Berkouwer seems to be assuming a concept of the Trinity that says anything experienced by one of the Trinitarian persons is automatically experienced by the other two. To separate the suffering of the Father from that of the Son, and vice versa, he calls "a mutilation of the mystery of the trinity" (*The Work of Christ*, p. 279). In my judgment this is an implicit rejection of the whole concept of the economic Trinity, however.

229. Kazoh Kitamori, *Theology of the Pain of God*, p. 115.

230. Jürgen Moltmann, *The Crucified God*, p. 192. Cf. p. 216.

231. Kazoh Kitamori, *Theology of the Pain of God*, pp. 19, 47.

Immutability as Divine Faithfulness

The main point of the doctrine of immutability has always been, as Davis says, "that God is not a fickle, capricious god like the gods of the pagans—he can be relied on because he is ever and eternally the same."[232] It was designed to preserve "the view that God is faithful in keeping his promises, that his basic benevolent nature remains the same."[233] In other words, the bottom line of the doctrine of immutability is the faithfulness of God. The immutable God is unchanging in his purposes and his commitments; he will ever be true to his word and to his promises. To use Barth's term, there is a constancy in God's nature and character and in his dealings with men that enables us to have the utmost confidence in him.

This has been the main emphasis of those (such as Davis) who are challenging the traditional doctrine of classical theism. Their point is that the Bible's teaching about divine immutability is more concerned with moral than ontological unchangeability. For example, Wolterstorff says that Biblical changelessness means that God "is steadfast in his redeeming intent and ever faithful to his children." E.g., Malachi 3:6 simply means that "God is faithful to his people Israel—that he is unchanging in his fidelity to the covenant he has made with them."[234] Hendrikus Berkhof says that it is correct to speak of immutability "if one means by it the unchangeableness of God's faithfulness. God is not unreliable or capricious. He adheres to his purpose and does not forsake the work of his hands."[235] As Pinnock says, "Although the Scriptures plainly teach God's constancy and reliability in the moral and religious sphere, nowhere do they teach or imply immutability in the strong metaphysical sense which was adopted in the classical tradition."[236]

This is true to an extent. We can agree that faithfulness *is* the *main point* of the doctrine of immutability. But we must be careful not to fall into the fallacy of false choice here, as some seem to have done. They

---

232. Stephen Davis, *Logic and the Nature of God*, p. 41.
233. Ibid., p. 47.
234. Nicholas Wolterstorff, "God Everlasting," pp. 182, 201.
235. Hendrikus Berkhof, *Christian Faith*, p. 140.
236. Clark Pinnock, "The Need for a Scriptural, and Therefore a Neo-Classical Theism," p. 38.

seem to be saying that all aspects of ontological or metaphysical immutability are illicit or irrelevant, and *only* the unchangeable faithfulness of God is important. This seems to be Berkhof's sole emphasis,[237] as well as that of König, with his preference for faithfulness as an alternative to immutability.[238] H. M. Hughes likewise sees the focus of immutability in God's unchanging holiness, righteousness and love, i.e., "His moral nature and purpose."[239] But it is false to assume that one must choose either one or the other, either the immutability of God's metaphysical nature or the immutability of his moral nature. In truth, these cannot be separated. We have stressed that God is unchanging in his nature and character, and we now assert that this is the very fact that makes him unchanging in his word and his ways with men. The one is the very ground or foundation of the other. Only a God who is unchanging in his basic nature can be depended upon with confidence. As Tozer says, "If He is unchanging, it follows that He could not be unfaithful."[240] Henry strongly disagrees with those who see in Hebrews 13:8 only a reference to Christ's faithfulness and not also his changelessness. "Because Christ is ontologically changeless his salvation is permanently reliable; a changing Christ is no sure ground of hope."[241]

The view we have presented here is that although God is changeable in his experiences, actions, and states of consciousness, nevertheless he is unchangeable in his essence and character. Grounded in this immutability of God's nature is his faithfulness: *He is faithful.* This is affirmed over and over in Scripture. "The word of the Lord is upright; and all His work is done in faithfulness" (Ps. 33:4). "Thy faithfulness reaches to the skies" (Ps. 36:5). "Thy faithfulness continues throughout all generations" (Ps. 119:90; cf. 100:5). "Great is Thy faithfulness" (Lam. 3:23). "God is faithful" (I Cor. 1:9; II Cor. 1:18). "Faithful is He who calls you" (I Thes. 5:24). "He who promised is faithful" (Heb. 10:23).

---

237. Hendrikus Berkhof, *Christian Faith*, pp. 140-147.
238. Adrio König, *Here Am I!*, p. 89; cf. pp. 84-102.
239. H. Maldwyn Hughes, *The Christian Idea of God* (London: Duckworth, 1936), p. 36.
240. A. W. Tozer, *The Knowledge of the Holy*, p. 84.
241. Carl F. H. Henry, *God, Revelation and Authority*, V:294.

But just what *is* faithfulness? What does it mean to say that God is faithful? In both testaments the word groups from which the term *faithful* comes ('āman; *pisteuō*) carry the root ideas of firmness, certainty, conviction, and confidence, and therefore trustworthiness, reliability, dependability, and faithfulness. Such an idea presupposes a personal commitment to an announced plan or purpose, or an agreement or covenant between two parties in which one promises to carry out a certain plan of action. A person may be deemed faithful if he can be depended upon to do what he has promised.

We can see immediately how important this idea is for our understanding of the nature of God, and especially for our understanding of his nature as Redeemer. Where our salvation is concerned, we are solely dependent upon God; it is altogether in his hands. If he should choose not to provide a way of redemption for us, there would be absolutely nothing we could do about it. Thus when he tells us that he *has* done something about it, that he has paid the price for our sins and conquered death through the incarnate Son of God, this is a matter of the utmost relief and rejoicing. But the question is, can we really *believe* that God has done this for us? Can we really *trust* him to carry through on his promises? He has given us his word, but can we count on it? YES WE CAN, because GOD IS FAITHFUL!

The essence of divine faithfulness is that God is true to his word. "The grass withers, the flower fades, but the word of our God stands forever" (Isa. 40:8; cf. I Peter 1:23-25). His word does not fail (Rom. 9:6). "As for God, his way is perfect; the word of the Lord is flawless" (Ps. 18:30; cf. Prov. 30:5; NIV). "Forever, O Lord, Thy word is settled in heaven. Thy faithfulness continues throughout all generations" (Ps. 119:89-90). In this last quotation the relation between God's faithfulness and the certainty of his word is clear.

When we say God is faithful, we mean first of all that he is faithful to himself and to his own nature. "He remains faithful; for He cannot deny Himself" (II Tim. 2:13). This is basically the essence of his righteousness, as we have already seen. His righteousness and faithfulness cannot be separated: "Thou hast fulfilled Thy promise, for Thou art righteous" (Neh. 9:8). "Righteousness will be the belt about His loins, and faithfulness the belt about His waist" (Isa. 11:5). But the main emphasis in faithfulness is that God is faithful to his creatures; he is faithful to those to whom he has made promises; he keeps his word to

519

his people.

The Truthfulness of God

The Bible's general teaching concerning God's faithfulness centers around the certainty of his word and thus his truthfulness. In fact, in the Old Testament there is very little difference between the concepts of faithfulness and truth. The Hebrew words for each ('ĕmūnāh and 'ĕmet, respectively) both come from the same verb, 'āman. They seem to be almost interchangeable, with either of them accepting either meaning. Thus the faithfulness of God is well expressed as his truthfulness.

God Speaks Truth. God and truth are practically synonymous in the Bible. "God is true," says John 3:33 (cf. Rom. 3:4). He is the "God of truth" (Ps. 31:5; Isa. 65:16; Jer. 10:10). Jesus claimed, "I am . . . the truth" (John 14:6). God abounds in truth (Ex. 34:6; Ps. 86:15). "The truth of the Lord is everlasting" (Ps. 117:2). "Thy words are truth" (II Sam. 7:28; cf. Ps. 119:160). "Thy word is truth" (John 17:17). His words are "faithful and true" (Rev. 21:5; 22:6). Spoken negatively, God "cannot lie" (Titus 1:2). "God is not a man, that He should lie" (Num. 23:19). "The Glory of Israel will not lie" (I Sam. 15:29). When making a promise, "it is impossible for God to lie" (Heb. 6:18). This is why he is faithful.

God Keeps His Promises. The element of truth or faithfulness is especially relevant to the promises of God. That God is a faithful God means that he is a promise-keeping God. In Hebrews 6:18 the "two unchangeable things, in which it is impossible for God to lie," are his promise and his oath. When God makes a promise, we can depend on him to keep it, "for He who promised is faithful" (Heb. 10:23; cf. 11:11). We believe he can keep his promises because he is omnipotent, but we believe he will keep them because he is faithful. As if his promise were not enough, as a concession to our weakness, God adds to it his oath. This he did in his promise concerning Abraham's many descendants: "By Myself I have sworn, declares the Lord," that "I will greatly bless you, and I will greatly multiply your seed" (Gen. 22:16-17). This is that to which Hebrews 6:17 refers, "In the same way God, desiring even more to show to the heirs of the promise the unchangeableness of His purpose, interposed with an oath." See also Psalms 89:35; 132:11; Isaiah 45:23; Acts 2:30.

God's promises sometimes take the form of a covenant, and his faithfulness is seen in the keeping of the covenant. As Moses told Israel, God "will not fail you nor destroy you nor forget the covenant with your fathers which He swore to them" (Deut. 4:31). "Know therefore that the Lord your God, He is God, the faithful God, who keeps His covenant and His lovingkindness to a thousandth generation" (Deut. 7:9). "I will never break My covenant with you," he said (Judg. 2:1). "My covenant I will not violate, nor will I alter the utterance of My lips" (Ps. 89:34). "My covenant of peace will not be shaken" (Isa. 54:10). See I Kings 8:23; Nehemiah 9:32; Psalm 89:28; Jeremiah 31:32; Daniel 9:4. The Old Testament notes again and again how God kept his covenant promises to the Fathers (Ex. 6:5; Josh. 21:45; 23:14; I Kings 8:56; Ps. 105:8ff.). Even when others failed or became unfaithful, God remained faithful to his promise (Neh. 9:33; Hosea 11:12; Rom. 3:3; II Tim. 2:13).

God Fulfills His Purposes. We have seen above how God has an eternal and unchanging purpose; he is faithful in that he carries out this purpose. He sticks to his plan. Isaiah 25:1 says, "O Lord, Thou art my God; I will exalt Thee, I will give thanks to Thy name; for Thou hast worked wonders, plans formed long ago, with perfect faithfulness." As Henry says, Scripture stresses God's "constancy and faithfulness and guarantees that he will undeviatingly carry through his plan. . . . God is not a vacillating human who backtracks on his word."[242]

God Is a Rock. A very common Old Testament descriptive title for God is "Rock," a term that stresses his utter dependability. Because God is faithful and true, we can stand upon him and his word and know that we are standing on the firmest possible foundation. The point is summed up in Deuteronomy 32:4, "The Rock! His work is perfect, for all His ways are just; a God of faithfulness and without injustice, righteous and upright is He." "There is no one besides Thee, nor is there any rock like our God" (I Sam. 2:2). "The Lord is my rock and my fortress and my deliverer, my God, my rock, in whom I take refuge" (Ps. 18:2). "He only is my rock and my salvation, my stronghold; I shall not be greatly shaken" (Ps. 62:2). "Trust in the Lord forever, for in God

---

242. Ibid., p. 302.

the Lord, we have an everlasting Rock" (Isa. 26:4).[243] When our Redeemer is called a "rock," says Ringgren, this means that he "is the reliable protector who never wavers."[244]

Faithfulness and Redemption

God is faithful and true in all his ways, but the area where this matters most to us is his work of redemption. This is indeed the area where the faithfulness of God is put to the severest test, and it is the area where he proves to be absolutely faithful in the most glorious fashion. In a very real sense, everything else we have said about God as Creator, Ruler and Redeemer will amount to nothing if we cannot have the utmost confidence that he will be true to his promises of redemption. But we need not fear, because God is unchanging in his mercy and grace toward us and in his purpose to save us. He will faithfully carry his plan of redemption through to the end.

The Old Testament emphasizes the fact that God's love is unchanging (Micah 7:18-20). The words for truth and faithfulness are often coupled with *chesed*, the word for God's lovingkindness. For example, Psalm 85:10 says, "Lovingkindness and truth have met together." God is "abundant in lovingkindness and truth" (Ps. 86:15). It is good, says Psalm 92:2, "to declare Thy lovingkindness in the morning, and Thy faithfulness by night." Such examples could be multiplied, but the point is that God is faithful in showing his love and his mercy to those in need of it. God promised salvation to Israel: "'For I am with you,' declares the Lord, 'to save you'" (Jer. 30:11). "The Lord's lovingkindnesses indeed never cease, for His compassions never fail. They are new every morning; great is Thy faithfulness" (Lam. 3:22-23). Many of the times when God is called a "rock," the emphasis is on salvation. He is "the Rock of salvation" (Deut. 32:15; Pss. 89:26; 95:1). He is "my rock and my Redeemer" (Ps. 19:14; cf. 78:35). "He only is my rock and my salvation" (Ps. 62:2, 6; cf. 18:46). He is completely dependable when it

---

243. Other references to God as a Rock include Deut. 32:15, 18, 30-31, 37; II Sam. 22:2-3, 32, 47; II Sam. 23:3; Pss. 18:31, 46; 19:14; 28:1; 31:2-3; 42:9; 62:6-7; 71:3; 78:35; 89:26; 92:15; 94:22; 95:1; Isa. 17:10; 44:8; I Cor. 10:4.

244. Helmer Ringgren, *"gā'al," Theological Dictionary of the Old Testament*, revised edition, ed. G. J. Botterweck and Helmer Ringgren, tr. John T. Willis (Grand Rapids: Eerdmans, 1977), II:355.

comes to salvation.

The Old Testament redemptive events in which God faithfully fulfilled his covenant promises to his people were almost entirely acts of temporal salvation. But the ultimate purpose and fulfilment of the Old Testament covenants went beyond the limits of the Old Testament itself and even beyond the limits of Israel. They pointed to a work of redemption that would have not temporal but eternal consequences, and not for just one nation but for all the nations of the earth. In other words the covenants with the Fathers and with Israel and with David all looked ahead to the coming of Jesus Christ and his death and resurrection for the redemption of the world. Thus the focal point of all of God's promise keeping and covenant faithfulness was the cross and the empty tomb. He kept his promises to the Fathers when he sent Jesus to be the propitiation for the sins of the whole world.

This was the goal of the Abrahamic covenant: "In you all the families of the earth shall be blessed" (Gen. 12:3). The same was repeated to Isaac and Jacob (Gen. 26:4; 28:14). God also promised King David that his throne would be occupied forever (II Sam. 7:16; Pss. 89:28-37; 132:11). The New Testament shows us that these covenants and promises were all fulfilled in Jesus Christ. In Acts 13:32-33 Paul declares, "And we preach to you the good news of the promise made to the fathers, that God has fulfilled this promise to our children in that He raised up Jesus." In Acts 3:25-26 Peter says, "It is you who are the sons of the prophets, and of the covenant which God made with your fathers, saying to Abraham, 'And in your seed all the families of the earth shall be blessed.' For you first, God raised up His Servant, and sent Him to bless you by turning every one of you from your wicked ways." See Acts 2:30; Rom. 4:16; Gal. 3:8-14. In Ephesians 3:1-11 Paul says that God's eternal purpose to unite the Jews and Gentiles together into one body, the church, has been "carried out in Christ Jesus our Lord" (v. 11). Jesus thus is God's covenant faithfulness personified.

God's faithfulness in redemption is also demonstrated in the fulfilment of the many prophecies of the coming Messiah, beginning with the one in Genesis 3:15. This gives us confidence to trust him regarding those promises and prophecies yet to be fulfilled.

For Christians today God's faithfulness in redemption is most important in connection with those promises directed toward us first in our sin and then in our Christian life. Wrapped up in these promises is "the hope of eternal life, which God, who cannot lie, promised long ages ago" (Titus 1:2). The following is a condensed listing of such promises: "Whoever will call upon the name of the Lord will be saved" (Rom. 10:13). "Believe in the Lord Jesus, and you shall be saved" (Acts 16:31). "If you confess with your mouth Jesus as Lord, and believe in your heart that God raised Him from the dead, you shall be saved" (Rom. 10:9). "He who has believed and has been baptized shall be saved" (Mark 16:16). "Repent, and let each of you be baptized in the name of Jesus Christ for the forgiveness of your sins; and you shall receive the gift of the Holy Spirit" (Acts 2:38). "I will never desert you, nor will I ever forsake you" (Heb. 13:5). "If we walk in the light as He Himself is in the light, we have fellowship with one another, and the blood of Jesus His Son cleanses us from all sin" (I John 1:7). "God is faithful, who will not allow you to be tempted beyond what you are able, but with the temptation will provide the way of escape also, that you may be able to endure it" (I Cor. 10:13). "The Lord is faithful, and He will strengthen and protect you from the evil one" (II Thes. 3:3). "Be faithful until death, and I will give you the crown of life" (Rev. 2:10).

These redemptive promises contain infinite treasure for those who will believe them and who will believe in the one who made them. Do we have grounds for such belief? Indeed we do, for the Redeemer who made these promises is unchanging; and because he is unchanging, he is utterly faithful.

THE IMMUTABLE GOD AND THE CHRISTIAN LIFE

As we close our study of God the Redeemer and our study of God in general, it is appropriate to ask concerning the value of the doctrine of immutability for our daily lives. What difference does it make whether God is immutable? Is this an important doctrine? Indeed it is, for without an unchanging God the very foundation of the most significant elements of the Christian life would be lost. Here we shall simply and briefly point out those things that rest upon his unchanging nature and character.

First, we reaffirm that God's immutability is the basis for our *trust* in him. "Trust in the Lord forever, for in God the Lord, we have an everlasting Rock," says Isaiah 26:4. "In Thee our fathers trusted; they trusted, and Thou didst deliver them" (Ps. 22:4). God's unchanging record of kept promises is grounds for our depending on him to keep his promises to us.

Second, God's changelessness is the basis for inner *peace of mind*; it gives us rest for our souls. This follows from the first point. Nothing else gives us peace of mind like being able to trust someone into whose care we have committed something of value. Who would want to leave his child with a baby-sitter who cannot be trusted? Who enjoys being treated by a physician whose competence is in doubt? We have committed our eternal destiny into the hands of God. Can we trust him? Yes, because he is an immutably faithful God. And because we can trust him, we have peace within. Tozer gives us the following reflections on the relation between immutability and peace:[245]

> In this world where men forget us, change their attitude toward us as their private interests dictate, and revise their opinion of us for the slightest cause, is it not a source of wondrous strength to know that the God with whom we have to do changes not? That His attitude toward us now is the same as it was in eternity past and will be in eternity to come?
>
> What peace it brings to the Christian's heart to realize that our Heavenly Father never differs from Himself. In coming to Him at any time we need not wonder whether we shall find Him in a receptive mood. He is always receptive to misery and need, as well as to love and faith. He does not keep office hours nor set aside periods when He will see no one. Neither does He change His mind about anything. Today, this moment, He feels toward His creatures, toward babies, toward the sick, the fallen, the sinful, exactly as He did when He sent His only-begotten Son into the world to die for mankind.
>
> God never changes moods or cools off in His affections or loses enthusiasm. His attitude toward sin is now the same as it was when He drove out the sinful man from the eastward garden, and His attitude toward the sinner the same as when He stretched forth His hands and cried, "Come unto me, all ye that labour and are heavy laden, and I will give you rest."

Third, God's immutability gives us a feeling of *security*, a knowledge that God's unchanging love and strength are giving us protection from our enemies. "He will cover you with His pinions, and under His wings you may seek refuge; His faithfulness is a shield and bulwark" (Ps.

---

245. A. W. Tozer, *The Knowledge of the Holy*, p. 59.

91:4). His faithfulness does not allow us to be tempted beyond what we are able to bear (I Cor. 10:13). "The Lord is faithful, and He will strengthen and protect you from the evil one" (II Thes. 3:3). Many of the "rock" passages present God as a rock of refuge. He is "my God, my rock, in whom I take refuge" (Ps. 18:2). "Thou art my rock and my fortress" (Ps. 31:3). "The Lord has been my stronghold, and my God the rock of my refuge" (Ps. 94:22). Paul tells us that nothing is strong enough "to separate us from the love of God, which is in Christ Jesus our Lord" (Rom. 8:39), who "is the same yesterday and today, yes and forever" (Heb. 13:8).

Fourth, the immutability of God gives us *courage* to be strong in the Lord even when circumstances around us keep changing and even when they are grim. At the threshold of Canaan when the Israelites faced many enemies Moses told them, "Be strong and courageous, do not be afraid or tremble at them, for the Lord your God is the one who goes with you. He will not fail you or forsake you." So "do not fear, or be dismayed" (Deut. 31:6-8). Peter admonishes those Christians facing adversity, "Therefore, let those also who suffer according to the will of God entrust their souls to a faithful Creator in doing what is right" (I Peter 4:19). We can have courage even in dire circumstances because we know that God himself has not turned against us. As the song says, "When darkness veils his lovely face, I rest on his unchanging grace."

Fifth, the immutability of God is an essential part of the foundation for our *worship*. How could we be comfortable worshiping a changing god? As Charnock asks, "What comfort could it be to pray to a god, that, like the chameleon, changed colours every day, every moment?[246] Henry rightly says,[247]

> . . . A creator and sustainer of the world who is vulnerable to mutability, a redeemer and judge of mankind whose essential nature might waver and whose purpose may vacillate, is not a deity in whom we can ever be religiously at rest. The gods of change and caprice belong to the world of paganism. A deity of shifting whims and moods is too much like mere mortals to merit worship.

But an unchanging God is truly worthy of worship, and can be praised

---

246. Stephen Charnock, *The Existence and Attributes of God*, p. 131.
247. Carl F. H. Henry, *God, Revelation and Authority*, V:288.

in the words of Deuteronomy 32:3-4, "For I proclaim the name of the Lord; ascribe greatness to our God! The Rock! His work is perfect, for all His ways are just; a God of faithfulness and without injustice, righteous and upright is He."

Sixth, we find the immutability of God's moral nature in the sense of his faithfulness to be a model for our *imitation*. In II Corinthians 1:18, when Paul affirms that God is faithful, he sets this forth as a virtue to be imitated by us in our relationships with one another. "But as God is faithful, our word to you is not yes and no." That is, we should set our minds firmly upon one course of action and stick to it, namely, that course marked by righteousness and truth. We should not vacillate back and forth in uncertainty. (See vv. 15-17 for the situation that occasioned this remark by Paul.)

Finally, the unchangeable nature of God is the firm ground for our *hope* for the future. There is a dark side to God's immutability, as Pink notes: "It insures the execution of His threatenings, as well as the performance of His promises."[248] Christians do not dwell on this dark side, however, but in the light of God's unchanging promises. Thus we know, as Clarke says, that "such immutability is the hope of the universe."[249] Our personal hope depends upon it. God gives us his promise and his oath, "in order that by two unchangeable things, in which it is impossible for God to lie, we may have strong encouragement, we who have fled for refuge in laying hold of the hope set before us" (Heb. 6:18). So "let us hold fast the confession of our hope without wavering, for He who promised is faithful" (Heb. 10:23). "Faithful is He who calls you, and He also will bring it to pass" (I Thess. 5:24). Tozer says, "Upon God's faithfulness rests our whole hope of future blessedness. Only as He is faithful will His covenants stand and His promises be honored. Only as we have complete assurance that He is faithful may we live in peace and look forward with assurance to the life to come."[250]

I believe it would be appropriate to close this study of the doctrine of

---

248. Arthur W. Pink, *The Attributes of God* (Swengel, Pa.: Reiner Publications, n.d.), p. 35.

249. William Newton Clarke, *The Christian Doctrine of God*, p. 311.

250. A. W. Tozer, *The Knowledge of the Holy*, p. 87.

God at this place with the prayer of Psalm 19:14,

> *Let the words of my mouth*
> *and the meditation of my heart*
> *Be acceptable in Thy sight,*
> *O LORD, MY ROCK AND MY REDEEMER.*

BIBLIOGRAPHY

Abe, Masao. "Buddhist *Nirvana:* Its Significance in Contemporary Thought and Life," *Living Faiths and Ultimate Goals,* ed. S.J. Samartha. Geneva: World Council of Churches, 1974. Pp. 12-22.

Achtemeier, E.R. "Righteousness in the OT," *The Interpreter's Dictionary of the Bible,* ed. George A. Buttrick. Nashville: Abingdon Press, 1962. IV:80-85.

Achtemeier, P.J. "Righteousness in the NT," *The Interpreter's Dictionary of the Bible,* ed. George A. Buttrick. Nashville: Abingdon Press, 1962. IV:91-99.

Anselm. *Cur Deus Homo.* Edinburgh: John Grant, 1909.

Armstrong, Herbert W., ed. Ambassador College Correspondence Course. Pasadena: Ambassador College, 1977.

Askari, Hasan. "Unity and Alienation in Islam," *Living Faiths and Ultimate Goals,* ed. S.J. Samartha. Geneva: World Council of Churches, 1974. Pp. 45-55.

Athenagoras. "A Plea for the Christians," tr. B.P. Pratten, *The Ante-Nicene Fathers,* ed. Alexander Roberts and James Donaldson. New York: Charles Scribner's Sons, 1913. II:129-148.

Atkins, Gaius Glenn, and Charles S. Braden. *Procession of the Gods.* 3 ed. New York: Harper & Brothers, 1948.

Aulén, Gustaf. *Christus Victor: An Historical Study of the Three Main Types of the Idea of Atonement,* tr. A.G. Hebert. New York: Macmillan, 1951.

_____ . *The Faith of the Christian Church,* tr. Eric H. Wahlstrom and G.E. Arden. Philadelphia: Muhlenberg Press, 1948.

Bales, James D. *Communism: Its Faith and Fallacies.* Grand Rapids: Baker Book House, 1962.

Barclay, William. *New Testament Words.* Philadelphia: Westminster Press, 1974.

Barth, Karl. "Church and Culture," in *Theology and Church: Shorter Writings, 1920-1928,* tr. Louise P. Smith. London: S.C.M. Press, 1962. Pp. 334-354.

_____ . *Church Dogmatics, Volume I: The Doctrine of the Word of God, Part 1,* tr. G.T. Thomson, Edinburgh: T. & T. Clark, 1936.

————— . *Church Dogmatics, Volume II: The Doctrine of God, Part 1*, ed. G.W. Bromiley and T.F. Torrance, tr. T. H.L. Parker et al. Edinburgh: T. & T. Clark, 1957.

————— . *Church Dogmatics, Volume II: The Doctrine of God, Part 2*, ed. G.W. Bromiley and T.F. Torrance, tr. G.W. Bromiley et al. Edinburgh: T. & T. Clark, 1957.

————— . *Church Dogmatics, Volume III: The Doctrine of Creation, Part 1*, tr. J.W. Edwards et al. Edinburgh: T. & T. Clark, 1958.

————— . *Church Dogmatics, Volume IV: The Doctrine of Reconciliation, Part 1*, ed. G.W. Bromiley and T.F. Torrance, tr. G.W. Bromiley. Edinburgh: T. & T. Clark, 1956.

Bates, William. *The Harmony of the Divine Attributes.* Philadelphia: Presbyterian Board of Publication, n.d.

Bavinck, Herman. *The Doctrine of God*, ed. and tr. William Hendriksen. Grand Rapids: Eerdmans, 1951.

Bennett, John C. *Christianity and Communism Today.* New York: Association Press, 1960.

Berdyaev, Nicholas. *Freedom and the Spirit.* London, 1944.

Berkhof, Hendrikus. *Christian Faith: An Introduction to the Study of the Faith*, tr. Sierd Woudstra. Grand Rapids: Eerdmans, 1979.

————— . "The (Un)changeability of God," *Grace Upon Grace: Essays in Honor of Lester J. Kuyper*, ed. James I. Cook. Grand Rapids: Eerdmans, 1975. Pp. 21-29.

Berkhof, Louis. *Systematic Theology.* London: Banner of Truth Trust, 1939.

Berkouwer, G.C. *The Triumph of Grace in the Theology of Karl Barth*, tr. Harry R. Boer. Grand Rapids: Eerdmans, 1956.

————— . *The Work of Christ*, tr. Cornelius Lambregtse. Grand Rapids: Eerdmans, 1965.

Bethune-Baker, J.F. *An Introduction to the Early History of Christian Doctrine.* 4 ed. London: Methuen & Co., 1929.

Bilaniuk, Petro B.T. "The Holiness of God in Eastern Orthodoxy," *God: The Contemporary Discussion*, ed. Frederick Sontag and M. Darrol Bryant. New York: Rose of Sharon Press, 1982. Pp. 43-66.

Bishop, Jim. *The Day Christ Died*. New York: Pocket Books, 1969.

Bloesch, Donald G. *Essentials of Evangelical Theology, Volume One: God, Authority, and Salvation*. San Francisco: Harper and Row, 1978.

Bockmuehl, Klaus. *The Challenge of Marxism: A Christian Response*. Downers Grove: InterVarsity Press, 1980.

Boettner, Loraine. *Studies in Theology*. 3 ed. Grand Rapids: Eerdmans, 1953.

Boice, James M. *Foundations of the Christian Faith, Volume I: The Sovereign God*. Downers Grove: InterVarsity Press, 1978.

_____ . *Foundations of the Christian Faith, Volume II: God the Redeemer*. Downers Grove: InterVarsity Press, 1978.

Bonhoeffer, Dietrich. *Letters and Papers from Prison*, enlarged edition, ed. Eberhard Bethge, tr. Reginald Fuller et al. New York: Macmillan, 1972.

Borland, James A. *Christ in the Old Testament*. Chicago: Moody Press, 1978.

Bowling, Andrew. "*tōb,*" *Theological Wordbook of the Old Testament*, ed. R. Laird Harris et al. Chicago: Moody Press, 1980. I:345-346.

Braden, Charles S. *Man's Quest for Salvation*. Chicago: Willett, Clark & Company, 1941.

Brandon, S. G. F. *The Judgment of the Dead*. New York: Charles Scribner's Sons, 1967.

_____ . "Redemption in Ancient Egypt and Early Christianity," *Types of Redemption*, ed. R.J. Zwi Werblowsky and C.J. Bleeker. Leiden: E.J. Brill, 1970. Pp. 36-45.

Bravo, Francisco. *Christ in the Thought of Teilhard de Chardin*, tr. Cathryn B. Larme. Notre Dame: University of Notre Dame Press, 1967.

Brinsmead, Robert D. "The Scandal of God's Justice – Part 1," *The Christian Verdict* (Essay 6, 1983). Pp. 2-10.

_____ . "The Scandal of God's Justice – Part 2," *The Christian Verdict*

(Essay 7, 1983). Pp. 2-10.

_____ . "The Triumph of God's Justice," *The Christian Verdict* (Essay 8, 1983). Pp. 7-11.

Brown, Colin. "Redemption" (part), *The New International Dictionary of New Testament Theology,* ed. Colin Brown. Grand Rapids: Zondervan, 1978. III:177-223.

_____ . "Righteousness, Justification" (part), *The New International Dictionary of New Testament Theology,* ed. Colin Brown. Grand Rapids: Zondervan, 1978. III:352-377.

Brown, Harold O.J. *Heresies.* Garden City, N.Y.: Doubleday, 1984.

Brown, William Adams. *Christian Theology in Outline.* New York: Charles Scribner's Sons, 1906.

Brumback, Carl. *God in Three Persons.* Cleveland, Tenn.: Pathway Press, 1959.

Brunner, Emil. *The Christian Doctrine of God: Dogmatics, Volume I,* tr. Olive Wyon. Philadelphia: Westminster Press, 1950.

Bryson, Harold T. *Yes, Virginia, There Is a Hell.* Nashville: Broadman, 1975.

Büchsel, Friedrich. "λύω, etc." (part), *Theological Dictionary of the New Testament,* ed. Gerhard Kittel, tr. Geoffrey W. Bromiley. Grand Rapids: Eerdmans, 1967. IV:328-356.

Bushnell, Horace, *Forgiveness and Law.* New York: Scribner, Armstrong & Co., 1874.

Buswell, James Oliver, Jr. *A Systematic Theology of the Christian Religion.* 2 vols. Grand Rapids: Zondervan, 1962.

Calvin, John. *Institutes of the Christian Religion,* ed. John T. McNeill, tr. Ford Lewis Battles. 2 vols. "Library of Christian Classics," Volumes XX-XXI. Philadelphia: Westminster Press, 1960.

Campbell, Alexander. *The Christian System.* Cincinnati: Standard Publishing, n.d.

Cauthen, Kenneth, *The Impact of American Religious Liberalism.* New York: Harper & Row, 1962.

Charnock, Stephen. *The Existence and Attributes of God.* Grand Rapids: Kregel reprint, 1958.

Chatterjee, Satis Chandra. "Hindu Religious Thought," *The Religion of the Hindus,* ed. Kenneth W. Morgan. New York: Ronald Press, 1953. Pp. 206-261.

Clark, Don. "A Custom of Cruelty," *Christian Standard* (March 22, 1969), 104:3-4.

Clark, Gordon H. *The Trinity.* Jefferson, Md.: The Trinity Foundation, 1985.

Clarke, W. Norris. "A New Look at the Immutability of God," *God, Knowable and Unknowable,* ed. Robert Roth. New York: Fordham University Press, 1973.

_____ . *The Philosophical Approach to God: A Neo-Thomist Perspective.* Winston-Salem: Wake Forest University, 1979.

Clarke, William Newton. *The Christian Doctrine of God.* Edinburgh: T. & T. Clark, 1909.

Clement of Alexandria. "The Stromata, or Miscellanies," *The Ante-Nicene Fathers,* ed. Alexander Roberts and James Donaldson. New York: Charles Scribner's Sons, 1913. II:299-568.

Clement of Rome. "To the Corinthians," *The Apostolic Fathers,* ed. J.B. Lightfoot and J.R. Harmer. Grand Rapids: Baker Book House, 1962. Pp. 13-41.

Colwell, E.C. "A Definite Rule for the Use of the Article in the Greek New Testament," *Journal of Biblical Literature* (January 1933), 52:13.

Conzelmann, Hans. "χάρις, etc." (part), *Theological Dictionary of the New Testament,* ed. Gerhard Friedrich, tr. Geoffrey W. Bromiley. Grand Rapids: Eerdmans, 1974. IX:372-415.

Copleston, Frederick. *A History of Philosophy, Volume I: Greece and Rome.* New revised edition, in two parts. Garden City, N.Y.: Doubleday Image, 1962.

Coppes, Leonard J. "rācham," *Theological Wordbook of the Old Testament,* ed. R. Laird Harris et al. Chicago: Moody Press, 1980. II:841-843.

Cote, Richard G. *Universal Grace: Myth or Reality?* Maryknoll, N.Y.: Orbis

Books, 1977.

Cottrell, Jack. "Faith, History, and the Resurrection Body of Jesus," *The Seminary Review* (December 1982), 28:143-160.

—————— . *His Truth*. Cincinnati: Standard Publishing, 1980.

—————— . *Tough Questions – Biblical Answers, Part Two*. Joplin, Mo.: College Press, 1986 reprint of 1982 edition entitled *The Bible Says*.

—————— . *What the Bible Says About God the Creator*. Joplin, Mo.: College Press, 1983.

—————— . *What the Bible Says About God the Ruler*. Joplin, Mo.: College Press, 1984.

Cox, Harvey. *The Secular City*, revised ed. New York: Macmillan, 1966.

Crespy, Georges. *From Science to Theology: An Essay on Teilhard de Chardin*, tr. George H. Shriver. Nashville: Abingdon Press, 1968.

Crossley, Robert. *The Trinity*. Downers Grove: InterVarsity Press, 1977.

Crouch, Owen L. "The Wrath of God!", *Christian Standard* (September 7, 1975), 110:13-14.

Cullman, Oscar, *The Christology of the New Testatment*, tr. Shirley C. Guthrie and Charles A.M. Hall. Revised ed. Philadelphia: Westminster Press, 1959.

Culver, Robert D. *"shāpat," Theological Wordbook of the Old Testament*, ed. R. Laird Harris et al. Chicago: Moody Press, 1980. II:947-949.

Daane, James. *The Freedom of God*. Grand Rapids: Eerdmans, 1973.

Davis, Stephen T. *Logic and the Nature of God*. Grand Rapids: Eerdmans, 1983.

de Silva, Lynn A. *Creation, Redemption, Consummation in Christian and Buddhist Thought*. Chengmai: Thailand Theological Seminary, 1964.

Dekoster, Lester. *Communism and Christian Faith*. Grand Rapids: Eerdmans, 1962.

Dewart, Leslie. *The Future of Belief: Theism in a World Come of Age*. New York: Herder and Herder, 1966.

DeWolf, L. Harold. *A Theology of the Living Church.* New York: Harper & Brothers, 1953.

Dickinson, Curtis. "Love and Judgment," *The Witness* (January 1983), 23:1-2.

Ditmanson, Harold H. *Grace in Experience and Theology.* Minneapolis: Augsburg, 1977.

The Doctrine of Grace, ed. W.T. Whitley, London: SCM Press, 1932.

Documents of the Christian Church, ed. Henry Bettenson. 2 ed. London: Oxford University Press, 1963.

Dodd, C.H. *The Bible and the Greeks.* London: Hodder & Stoughton, 1935.

_____ . *The Epistle of Paul to the Romans.* New York: Harper & Brothers, 1932.

Donceel, Joseph F. *The Searching Mind: An Introduction to a Philosophy of God.* Notre Dame: University of Notre Dame Press, 1979.

Dumoulin, H. "Grace and Freedom in the Way of Salvation in Japanese Buddhism," *Types of Redemption,* ed. R.J. Zwi Werblowsky and C.J. Bleeker. Leiden: E.J. Brill, 1970. Pp. 98-104.

Eichrodt, Walther. *Theology of the Old Testament,* tr. J.A. Baker. 2 vols. Philadelphia: Westminster Press, 1961, 1967.

Erickson, Millard J. *Christian Theology.* 3 vols. Grand Rapids: Baker Book House, 1983-1985.

Esser, Hans-Helmut. "Grace, Spiritual Gifts," *The New International Dictionary of New Testament Theology,* ed. Colin Brown. Grand Rapids: Zondervan, 1976. II:115-124.

_____ . "Law, Custom, Elements," *The New International Dictionary of New Testament Theology,* ed. Colin Brown. Grand Rapids: Zondervan, 1976. II:436-456.

_____ . "Mercy, Compassion," *The New International Dictionary of New Testament Theology,* ed. Colin Brown. Grand Rapids: Zondervan, 1976. II:593-601.

Evans, William. "Wrath," *International Standard Bible Encyclopedia,* ed. James Orr. Chicago: Howard-Severance, 1915. V:3113.

Farley, Edward. *The Transcendence of God: A Study in Contemporary Philosophical Theology.* Philadelphia: Westminster Press, 1960.

Ferre, Nels F.S. *The Christian Understanding of God.* New York: Harper

& Brothers, 1951.

Fichtner, Johannes. "ὀργή, etc." (part), *Theological Dictionary of the New Testament*, ed. Gerhard Friedrich, tr. Geoffrey W. Bromiley. Grand Rapids: Eerdmans, 1967. V:382-447.

Foerster, Werner. "σῴζω, etc." (part), *Theological Dictionary of the New Testament*, ed. Gerhard Friedrich, tr. Geoffrey W. Bromiley. Grand Rapids: Eerdmans, 1971. VII:965-1024.

Fortman, Edmund J. *The Triune God: A Historical Study of the Doctrine of the Trinity*. Grand Rapids: Baker Book House, 1982.

Fox, Douglas A. *Buddhism, Christianity and the Future of Man*. Philadelphia: Westminster Press, 1972.

France, R.T. *The Living God*. Downers Grove: InterVarsity Press, 1970.

Franks, Robert S. *The Doctrine of the Trinity*. London: Duckworth, 1953.

Freedman, D.N. "YHWH" (Part), *Theological Dictionary of the Old Testament*, ed. G.J. Botterweck and Helmer Ringgren, tr. David E. Green. Grand Rapids: Eerdmans, 1986. V:500-521.

Fulton, William. "Trinity," *Encyclopedia of Religion and Ethics*, ed. James Hastings. New York: Charles Scribner's Sons, 1922. XII:458-462.

Galloway, Allan D. *The Cosmic Christ*. London: Nisbet & Co., 1951.

Geden, A.S. "Salvation (Hindu)," *Encyclopedia of Religion and Ethics*, ed. James Hastings. New York: Charles Scribner's Sons, 1921. XI:132-137.

Gilkey, Langdon. *Maker of Heaven and Earth*. Garden City, N.Y.: Doubleday Anchor, 1965.

Girdlestone, Robert B. *Synonyms of the Old Testament*. Grand Rapids: Eerdmans, 1951 reprint of 1897 edition.

Gleason, Robert W. *Yahweh: The God of the Old Testament*. Englewood Cliffs, N.J.: Prentice-Hall, 1964.

Glueck, Nelson. *Hesed in the Bible*, tr. Alfred Gottschalk. Cincinnati: Hebrew Union College Press, 1967.

Grant, Robert M. *The Early Christian Doctrine of God*. Charlottesville:

University Press of Virginia, 1966.

Graves, Robert Brent. *The God of Two Testaments*. Hazelwood, Mo.: Pentecostal Publishing House, 1977.

Green, E.M.B. *The Meaning of Salvation*. Philadelphia: Westminster Press, 1965.

Gregory of Nyssa, "An Address on Religious Instruction," *Christology of the Later Fathers*, ed. Edward R. Hardy. "Library of Christian Classics," Vol. III. Philadelphia: Westminster Press, n.d. Pp. 268-325.

Grether, Oskar, and Johannes Fichtner, "ὀργή, etc." (part), *Theological Dictionary of the New Testament*, ed. Gerhard Friedrich, tr. Geoffrey W. Bromiley. Grand Rapids: Eerdmans, 1967. V:382-447.

Griffith, G.O. *St. Paul's Gospel to the Romans*. Oxford, 1949.

Grotius, Hugo. *A Defence of the Catholic Faith Concerning the Satisfaction of Christ*, tr. Frank Hugh Foster. Andover: Warren F. Draper, 1889.

Gruenler, Royce Gordon. *The Inexhaustible God: Biblical Faith and the Challenge of Process Theism*. Grand Rapids: Baker Book House, 1983.

Gruss, Edmond C. *Apostles of Denial*. Grand Rapids: Baker Book House, 1970.

Guillebaud, H.E. *Why the Cross?* 2 ed. London: Inter-Varsity Fellowship, 1946.

Günther, Walther, and Hans-Georg Link, "Love" (part), *The New International Dictionary of New Testament Theology*, ed. Colin Brown. Grand Rapids: Zondervan, 1976. II:538-551.

Gutbrod, W. "νόμος, etc.," *Theological Dictionary of the New Testament*, ed. Gerhard Kittel, tr. Geoffrey W. Bromiley. Grand Rapids: Eerdmans, 1967. IV:1022-1091.

Guiterrez, Gustavo. *A Theology of Liberation*, tr. Caridad Inda and John Eagleson. Maryknoll, N.Y.: Orbis Books, 1973.

Hahn, H.C. "Anger, Wrath" (part), *The New International Dictionary of New Testament Theology*, ed. Colin Brown. Grand Rapids: Zondervan, 1975. I: 105-113.

Haight, Roger. *An Alternative Vision: An Interpretation of Liberation Theology*. New York: Paulist Press, 1985.

Haley, John W. *An Examination of the Alleged Discrepancies of the Bible.* Nashville: Gospel Advocate, 1951 reprint of 1874 edition.

Hals, Ronald M. *Grace and Faith in the Old Testament.* Minneapolis: Augsburg, 1980.

Hanson, R.P.C. *The Attractiveness of God: Essays in Christian Doctrine.* Richmond: John Knox Press, 1973.

Harnack, Adolph. *History of Dogma*, tr. Neil Buchanan. 7 vols. in 4. New York: Dover Publications, 1961.

Harris, R. Laird, *"chesed," Theological Wordbook of the Old Testament*, ed. R. Laird Harris et al. Chicago: Moody Press, 1980. I:305-307.

_____ . Editorial note, J. Barton Payne, *"hāwāh," Theological Wordbook of the Old Testament*, ed. R. Laird Harris et al. Chicago: Moody Press, 1980. I:210-212.

_____ . *"gā'al," Theological Wordbook of the Old Testament*, ed. R. Laird Harris et al. Chicago: Moody Press, 1980. I:144-145.

Hartshorne, Charles. *The Divine Relativity: A Social Conception of God.* New Haven: Yale University Press, 1948.

_____ . *Omnipotence and Other Theological Mistakes.* Albany: State University of New York, 1984.

Heim, Karl. *Jesus the World's Perfecter*, tr. D.H. van Daalen. Edinburgh: Oliver and Boyd, 1959.

Henry, Carl F.H. *Aspects of Christian Social Ethics.* Grand Rapids: Eerdmans, 1964.

_____ . *God, Revelation and Authority, Volume II: God Who Speaks and Shows, Fifteen Theses, Part One.* Waco: Word Books, 1976.

_____ . *God, Revelation and Authority, Volume IV: God who Speaks and Shows, Fifteen Theses, Part Three.* Waco: Word Books, 1979.

_____ . *God, Revelation and Authority, Volume V: God Who Stands and Stays, Part One.* Waco: Word Books, 1982.

_____ . *God, Revelation and Authority, Volume VI: God Who Stands and Stays, Part Two.* Waco: Word Books, 1983.

Heppe, Heinrich. *Reformed Dogmatics*, ed. Ernst Bizer, tr. G.T. Thomson. London: Allen & Unwin, 1950.

Hodge, Charles. *Systematic Theology*. 3 vols. Grand Rapids: Eerdmans reprint, n.d.

Hoekema, Anthony, *Mormonism*. Grand Rapids: Eerdmans, 1963.

Hughes, H. Maldwyn. *The Christian Idea of God*. London: Duckworth, 1936.

Humanist Manifestos I and II. Buffalo: Prometheus Books, 1973.

"I Believe: A 1,600-year-old Confession of Faith," *Christianity Today* (December 11, 1981), 25:10-13.

Ignatius. "To Polycarp," *The Apostolic Fathers*, ed. J.B. Lightfoot and J.R. Harmer. Grand Rapids: Baker Book House, 1962. Pp. 86-88.

—————— . "To the Magnesians," *The Apostolic Fathers*, ed. J.B. Lightfoot and J.R. Harmer. Grand Rapids: Baker Book House, 1962. Pp. 69-72.

Irenaeus. "Against Heresies," tr. Alexander Roberts. *The Ante-Nicene Fathers*, ed. Alexander Roberts and James Donaldson. New York: Charles Scribner's Sons, 1913. I:315-567.

Ishizu, Teruji. "The Basis of the Idea of Redemption in Japanese Religions," *Types of Redemption*, ed. R.J. Werblowsky and C.J. Bleeker. Leiden: E.J. Brill, 1970. Pp. 88-97.

James, Stephen A. "Divine Justice and the Retributive Duty of Civil Government," *Trinity Journal* (Autumn 1985; new series), 6:199-210.

Jenkins, David. "What Does Salvation Mean to Christians Today?", *Living Faiths and Ultimate Goals*, ed. S.J. Samartha. Geneva: World Council of Churches, 1974. Pp. 34-44.

Jeremias, Joachim. *The Central Message of the New Testament*. London: SCM Press, 1965.

Johnston, Robert K. *Evangelicals at an Impasse: Biblical Authority in Practice*. Atlanta: John Knox Press, 1979.

Jonas, Hans. "Gnosticism," *The Encyclopedia of Philosophy*, ed. Paul Edwards. New York: Macmillan, 1967. III:336-342.

Jones, A.B. "Consciousness and Its Relation to the Holy Spirit," in *A Symposium on the Holy Spirit*, by A.B. Jones et al. Joplin, Mo.: College Press, 1966 reprint.

Joseph, Morris. "Salvation (Jewish)," *Encyclopedia of Religion and Ethics*, ed. James Hastings. New York: Charles Scribner's Sons, 1921. XI:138-148.

Justin Martyr. "Dialogue of Justin, Philosopher and Martyr, with Trypho, A Jew," *The Ante-Nicene Fathers*, ed. Alexander Roberts and James Donaldson. New York: Charles Scribner's Sons, 1913. I:194-270.

———. "The First Apology," *The Ante-Nicene Fathers*, ed. Alexander Roberts and James Donaldson. New York: Charles Scribner's Sons, 1913. I:163-187.

Kaiser, Christopher B. *The Doctrine of God: An Historical Survey*. Westchester, Ill.: Crossway Books, 1982.

Kasper, Walter. *The God of Jesus Christ*, tr. Matthew J. O'Connell. New York: Crossroad Publishing Co., 1984.

Keil, C.F., and F. Delitzsch. *Biblical Commentary on the Old Testament: The Books of Ezra, Nehemiah, and Esther*, tr. Sophia Taylor. Grand Rapids: Eerdmans, 1950 reprint.

Kelly, J. N. D. *Early Christian Doctrines*. Revised ed. San Francisco: Harper & Row, 1978.

Kilpatrick, T.B. "Salvation (Christian)," *Encyclopedia of Religion and Ethics*, ed. James Hastings. New York: Charles Scribner's Sons, 1921. XI:110-131.

Kitamori, Kazoh. *Theology of the Pain of God*. Richmond: John Knox Press, 1965.

Kleinknecht, Hermann. "θεός, etc." (part), *Theological Dictionary of the New Testament*, ed. Gerhard Kittel, tr. Geoffrey W. Bromiley. Grand Rapids: Eerdmans, 1965. III:65-123.

Kliever, Lonnie D. *The Shattered Spectrum: A Survey of Comtemporary Theology*. Atlanta: John Knox Press, 1981.

Knudson, Albert C. *The Doctrine of God*. Nashville: Abingdon-Cokesbury Press, 1930.

König, Adrio. *Here Am I! A Christian Reflection on God.* Grand Rapids: Eerdmans, 1982.

Koran, The, tr. George Sale. London: Frederick Warne and Co., 1890.

Küng, Hans. *Does God Exist? An Answer for Today,* tr. Edward Quinn. Garden City, N.Y.: Doubleday, 1980.

Kuyper, Lester J. "The Suffering and the Repentance of God," *Scottish Journal of Theology* (September 1969), 22:257-277.

Ladd, George E. *A Theology of the New Testament.* Grand Rapids: Eerdmans, 1974.

Lamont, Corliss. *The Philosophy of Humanism.* 5 ed. New York: Frederick Unger, 1965.

Lawlor, George. *When God Became Man.* Chicago: Moody Press, 1978.

Lazarus-Yafeh, Hava. "Is There a Concept of Redemption in Islam?", *Types of Redemption,* ed. R.J. Werblowsky and C.J. Bleeker. Leiden: E.J. Brill, 1970. Pp. 168-180.

Lee, Francis Nigel. *Communist Eschatology.* Nutley, N.J.: Craig Press, 1974.

Lehmann, Paul L. *Ethics in a Christian Context.* New York: Harper & Row, 1963.

Lewis, C.S. *The Four Loves.* London: Geoffrey Bles, 1960.

——————— . *Mere Christianity.* New York: Macmillan, 1960.

Lewis, Gordon R. "Impassibility of God," *Evangelical Dictionary of Theology,* ed. Walter A. Elwell. Grand Rapids: Baker Book House, 1984. Pp. 553-554.

Lightner, Robert P. "Hate," *Evangelical Dictionary Of Theology,* ed. Walter A. Elwell. Grand Rapids: Baker Book House, 1984. Pp. 495-496.

Lonergan, Bernard J.F. "The Dehellenization of Dogma," *The Future of Belief Debate,* ed. Gregory Baum. New York: Herder and Herder, 1967. Pp. 69-91.

MacDonald, William G. " '...The Spirit of Grace' (Heb. 10:29)," *Grace Unlimi-*

ted, ed. Clark H. Pinnock. Minneapolis: Bethany Fellowship, 1975. Pp. 174-194.

MacIntyre, Alasdair. "Existentialism," *The Encyclopedia of Philosophy,* ed. Paul Edwards. New York: Macmillan, 1967. III:147-154.

Macquarrie, John. *Existentialism.* Philadelphia: Westminster Press, 1972.

Martensen, H. *Christian Dogmatics,* tr. William Urwick. Edinburgh: T. & T. Clark, 1898.

Mascall, E.L. *He Who Is: A Study in Traditional Theism.* London: Darton, Longman & Todd Libra edition, 1966.

Masutani, Fumio. *A Comparative Study of Buddhism and Christianity.* 7 ed. Tokyo: Bukkyo Dendo Kyokai, 1967.

Matthews, W. R. *God in Christian Experience.* New York: Harper & Brothers, 1930.

Maurer, Christian. " ὑπόδικος ," *Theological Dictionary of the New Testament,* ed. Gerhard Friedrich, tr. Geoffrey W. Bromiley. Grand Rapids: Eerdmans, 1957. VIII:557-558.

McGiffert, A.C. *A History of Christian Thought.* 2 vols. New York: Charles Scribner's Sons, 1932.

Menninger, Karl. *Whatever Became of Sin?* New York: Hawthorn Books, 1973.

Metzger, Bruce M. "The Punctuation of Rom. 9:5," *Christ and Spirit in the New Testament,* ed. Barnabas Lindars and Stephen Smalley. Cambridge: University Press, 1973. Pp. 95-112.

Migliore, Daniel. *The Power of God.* Philadelphia: Westminster Press, 1983.

Mikolaski, Samuel J. *The Grace of God.* Grand Rapids: Eerdmans, 1966.

Miller, William McElwee. *A Christian's Response to Islam.* Nutley, N.J.: Presbyterian and Reformed, 1977.

Miranda, José P. *Marx and the Bible: A Critique of the Philosophy of Oppression,* tr. John Eagleson. Maryknoll, N.Y.: Orbis Books, 1974.

Moffatt, James. *Grace in the New Testament.* New York: Ray Long & Richard

R. Smith, 1932.

Moltmann, Jürgen. *The Crucified God*, tr. R.A. Wilson and John Bowden. New York: Harper & Row, 1974.

Morris, Leon. *The Apostolic Preaching of the Cross*. 2 ed. Grand Rapids: Eerdmans, 1960.

——————. *Testaments of Love*. Grand Rapids: Eerdmans, 1981.

Mott, Stephen Charles. *Biblical Ethics and Social Change*. New York: Oxford University Press, 1982.

Motyer, J.A. "Atonement, Day of," *Evangelical Dictionary of Theology*, ed. Walter A. Elwell. Grand Rapids: Baker Book House, 1984. Pp. 97-98.

Muller, Richard A. "Incarnation, Immutability, and the Case for Classical Theism," *Westminster Theological Journal* (Spring 1983), 45:22-40.

Murti, T.R.V. "The Concept of Freedom as Redemption," *Types of Redemption*, ed. R.J. Zwi Werblowsky and C.J. Bleeker. Leiden: E.J. Brill, 1970. Pp. 213-222.

Nash, Ronald H. *The Concept of God*. Grand Rapids: Zondervan, 1983.

Neville, Robert C. "Creation and the Trinity," *Theological Studies* (1969), 30:3ff.

Nicole, Roger. "C.H. Dodd and the Doctrine of Propitiation," *Westminster Theological Journal* (1955), 17:117-157.

——————. "The Meaning of the Trinity," *One God in Trinity*, ed. Peter Toon and James D. Spiceland. Westchester, Ill.: Cornerstone Books, 1980.

Noss, John B. *Man's Religions*. New York: Macmillan, 1949.

Núñez C., Emilio A. *Liberation Theology*, tr. Paul E. Sywulka. Chicago: Moody Press, 1985.

Nygren, Anders. *Agape and Eros*, tr. Philip Watson. Philadelphia: Westminster Press, 1953.

O'Leary, Joseph S. *Questioning Back: The Overcoming of Metaphysics in Christian Tradition*. Minneapolis: Winston Press, 1985.

Origen. "De Principiis," tr. Frederick Crombie. *The Ante-Nicene Fathers,* ed. Alexander Roberts and James Donaldson. New York: Charles Scribner's Sons, 1913. IV:239-382.

Owen, H.P. *Concepts of Deity.* New York: Herder and Herder, 1971.

Packer, J.I. *Knowing God.* Downer's Grove: InterVarsity Press, 1973.

Panikkar, R. "The Myth of Incest as Symbol for Redemption in Vedic India," *Types of Redemption,* ed R.J. Zwi Werblowsky and C.J. Bleeker. Leiden: E.J. Brill, 1970. Pp. 130-143.

Payne, J. Barton. *"hāwāh,"* Theological Wordbook of the Old Testament, ed. R. Laird Harris et al. Chicago: Moody Press, 1980. I:210-212.

Pink, Arthur W. *The Attributes of God.* Swengel, Pa.: Reiner Publications, 1968.

Pinnock, Clark. "God Limits His Knowledge," *Predestination and Free Will,* ed. David Basinger and Randall Basinger. Downers Grove: InterVarsity Press, 1986. Pp. 143-162.

————— . "Liberation Theology: The Gains, the Gaps," *Christianity Today* (January 16, 1976), 20:13-15.

————— . "The Need for a Scriptural, and Therefore a Neo-Classical Theism," *Perspectives on Evangelical Theology,* ed. Kenneth Kantzer and Stanley Gundry. Grand Rapids: Baker Book House, 1979. Pp. 37-42.

Pohle, Joseph. *Grace Actual and Habitual,* ed. Arthur Preuss. St. Louis: B. Herder, 1912.

Pope, William Burt. *A Compendium of Christian Theology.* 3 ed., 3 vols. Cleveland: Thomas and Mattell, n.d.

Prenter, Regin. *Creation and Redemption,* tr. Theodor I. Jensen. Philadelphia: Fortress Press, 1967.

Presler, Henry H. "Indian Aborigine Contributions to Hindu Ideas of Mukti Libation," *Types of Redemption,* ed. R.J. Zwi Werblowsky and C.J. Bleeker. Leiden: E.J. Brill, 1970. Pp. 144-167.

Prestige, G.L. *Fathers and Heretics.* London: S.P.C.K., 1963.

Procksch, Otto. "ἄγιος, etc.," *Theological Dictionary of the New Testament,* ed.

Gerhard Kittel, tr. Geoffrey W. Bromiley. Grand Rapids: Eerdmans, 1964. I:88-115.

————— . "λύω, etc.," *Theological Dictionary of the New Testament,* ed. Gerhard Kittel, tr. Geoffrey W. Bromiley. Grand Rapids: Eerdmans, 1967. IV:328-335.

Quell, Gottfried. "ἀγαπάω, etc." (part), *Theological Dictionary of the New Testament,* ed. Gerhard Kittel, tr. Geoffrey W. Bromiley. Grand Rapids: Eerdmans, 1964. I:21-55.

————— . "δίκη: The Concept of Law in the OT," *Theological Dictionary of the New Testament,* ed. Gerhard Kittel, tr. Geoffrey W. Bromiley. Grand Rapids: Eerdmans, 1964. II:174-178.

Rahner, Karl. *Do You Believe in God?* New York: Paulist Press, 1969.

————— . *The Trinity,* tr. Joseph Donceel. London: Burns and Oates, 1979.

Rall, Harris Franklin. *Religion as Salvation.* Nashville: Abingdon-Cokesbury Press, 1953.

Randall, John Herman, Jr. *Hellenistic Ways of Deliverance and the Making of the Christian Synthesis.* New York: Columbia University Press, 1970.

Rauschenbusch, Walter. *A Theology for the Social Gospel.* New York: Macmillan, 1918.

Raymond, Miner. *Systematic Theology.* 3 vols. Cincinnati: Walden and Stowe, 1877.

Rengstorff, K.H. "Jesus Christ," *The New International Dictionary of New Testament Theology,* ed. Colin Brown. Grand Rapids: Zondervan, 1976. II:330-348.

Reumann, John. *Creation and New Creation.* Minneapolis: Augsburg, 1973.

Rhys Davids, C.A.F. "Salvation (Buddhist)," *Encyclopedia of Religion and Ethics,* ed. James Hastings. New York: Charles Scribner's Sons, 1921. XI:110.

Rice, Richard. *God's Foreknowledge and Man's Free Will.* Minneapolis: Bethany House, 1985 reprint of 1980 edition entitled *The Openness of God.*

Ringgren, Helmer. "gā'al," *Theological Dictionary of the Old Testament,* revised edition, ed. G.J. Botterweck and Helmer Ringgren, tr. John T. Willis,

Grand Rapids: Eerdmans, 1977. II:350-355.

Roark, Dallas. *The Christian Faith: An Introduction to Christian Thought.* Grand Rapids: Baker Book House, 1977 reprint of 1969 edition.

Robinson, John A.T. *Honest to God.* London: S.C.M. Press, 1963.

Robinson, William Childs. "Wrath of God," *Evangelical Dictionary of Theology,* ed. Walter A. Elwell. Grand Rapids: Baker Book House, 1984. Pp. 1196-1197.

Roy, Ajit. "A Marxist View of Liberation," *Living Faiths and Ultimate Goals,* ed. S.J. Samartha. Geneva: World Council of Churches, 1974. Pp. 56-67.

Schmid, Heinrich. *The Doctrinal Theology of the Evangelical Lutheran Church,* tr. Charles A. Hay and Henry E. Jacobs. 3 ed. Minneapolis: Augsburg, 1961 reprint of 1899 edition.

Scholem, G. "Opening Address," *Types of Redemption,* ed. R.J. Zwi Werblowsky and C.J. Bleeker. Leiden: E.J. Brill, 1970. Pp. 5-12.

Schrenk, Gottlob. "δίκη, δίκαιος , etc." *Theological Dictionary of the New Testament,* ed. Gerhard Kittel, tr. Geoffrey W. Bromiley. Grand Rapids: Eerdmans, 1964. II:174-225.

Sell, Edward. "Salvation (Muslim)," *Encyclopedia of Religion and Ethics,* ed. James Hastings. New York: Charles Scribner's Sons, 1921. XI:148-149.

Shedd, William G.T. *Dogmatic Theology.* 3 vols. Grand Rapids: Zondervan, 1969 reprint of 1888 edition.

Sheed, F.J. *Communism and Man.* New York: Sheed and Ward, 1949.

Sivaraman, K. "The Meaning of *Moksha* in Contemporary Hindu Thought and Life," *Living Faiths and Ultimate Goals,* ed. S.J. Samartha. Geneva: World Council of Churches, 1974. Pp. 2-11.

Skard, Bjarne. *The Incarnation: A Study of the Christology of the Ecumenical Creeds,* tr. Herman E. Jorgensen. Minneapolis: Augsburg, 1960.

Smart, Ninian. "Buddhism," *The Encyclopedia of Philosophy,* ed. Paul Edwards. New York: Macmillan, 1967. I:416-420.

Smith, Joseph. *Doctrine and Covenants* and *The Pearl of Great Price.* Salt Lake City: The Church of Jesus Christ of Latter-day Saints, 1973.

Smith, Mont W. *What the Bible Says About Covenant.* Joplin, Mo.: College Press, 1981.

Smith, Stephen M. "Kenosis, Kenotic Theology," *Evangelical Dictionary of Theology,* ed. Walter A. Elwell. Grand Rapids: Baker Book House, 1984. Pp. 600-602.

Snaith, Norman H. *The Distinctive Ideas of the Old Testament.* New York: Schocken Books, 1964.

Song, Choan-seng. "New China and Salvation History – A Methodological Enquiry," *Living Faiths and Ultimate Goals,* ed. S.J. Samartha. Geneva: World Council of Churches, 1974. Pp. 68-89.

Sproul, R.C. *The Holiness of God.* Wheaton: Tyndale House, 1985.

Stählin, Gustav. "ὀργή, etc." (part), *Theological Dictionary of the New Testament,* ed. Gerhard Friedrich, tr. Geoffrey W. Bromiley. Grand Rapids: Eerdmans, 1967. V.:382-447.

Stauffer, Ethelbert. "ἀγαπάω, etc." (part), *Theological Dictionary of the New Testament,* ed. Gerhard Kittel, tr. Geoffrey W. Bromiley. Grand Rapids: Eerdmans, 1964. I:21-55.

————. *New Testament Theology,* tr. John Marsh. London: S.C.M. Press, 1955.

Stigers, Harold G. "tsādeq," *Theological Wordbook of the Old Testament,* ed. R. Laird Harris et al. Chicago: Moody Press, 1980. II:752-755.

Storms, C. Samuel. *The Grandeur of God.* Grand Rapids: Baker Book House, 1984.

Strong, Augustus H. *Systematic Theology.* 3 volumes in 1. Valley Forge: Judson Press, 1907.

Tasker, R. V.G. *The Biblical Doctrine of the Wrath of God.* London: The Tyndale Press, 1951.

The Teaching of Buddha. 265 revised ed. Tokyo: Buddhist Promoting Foundation, 1982.

The Teachings of the Compassionate Buddha, ed. E.A. Burtt. New York: New American Library, 1955.

Tertullian. "Against Praxeas," tr. Peter Holmes. *The Ante-Nicene Fathers*, ed. Alexander Roberts and James Donaldson. New York: Charles Scribner's Sons, 1908. III:597-627.

Theophilus. "To Autolycus," tr. Marcus Dods. *The Ante-Nicene Fathers*, ed. Alexander Roberts and James Donaldson. New York: Charles Scribner's Sons, 1913. II:89-121.

Todrank, Gustave H. *The Secular Search for a New Christ*. Philadelphia: Westminster Press, 1969.

Tozer, A.W. *The Knowledge of the Holy*. London: James Clarke & Co., 1965.

Trench, Richard C. *Synonyms of the New Testament*. Grand Rapids: Eerdmans, 1958 reprint of 1880 ed.

Van Dusen, Henry P. *Spirit, Son and Father*. New York: Charles Scribner's Sons, 1958.

Van Groningen, Gerard. "*ka'as*," *Theological Wordbook of the Old Testament*, R. Laird Harris et al. Chicago: Moody Press, 1980. I:451.

─────── . "*qātsap*," *Theological Wordbook of the Old Testament*, ed. R. Laird Harris et al. Chicago: Moody Press, 1980. II:808-809.

─────── . "*sānē'*," *Theological Wordbook of the Old Testament*, ed. R. Laird Harris et al. Chicago: Moody Press, 1980. II:879-880.

Van Til, Cornelius. *Common Grace*. Philadelphia: Presbyterian and Reformed, 1947.

Vos, Geerhardus. *The Self-Disclosure of Jesus*, ed. Johannes Vos. Grand Rapids: Eerdmans, 1954.

Wainwright, Arthur W. *The Trinity in the New Testament*. London: S.P.C.K., 1962.

Warfield, B.B. "The Biblical Doctrine of the Trinity," *Biblical and Theological Studies*, by B.B. Warfield, ed. Samuel G. Craig. Nutley, N.J.: Presbyterian and Reformed, 1952. Pp. 22-59.

─────── . "The Chief Theories of the Atonement," *The Person and Work of Christ*, by B.B. Warfield, ed. Samuel G. Craig. Nutley, N.J.: Presbyterian and Reformed, 1950. Pp. 351-369.

——————— . "The Divine Messiah in the Old Testament," *Biblical and Theological Studies,* by B.B. Warfield, ed. Samuel G. Craig. Nutley, N.J.: Presbyterian and Reformed, 1952. Pp. 79-126.

——————— . "The New Testament Terminology of 'Redemption,' " *The Person and Work of Christ,* by B.B. Warfield, ed. Samuel G. Craig. Nutley, N.J.: Presbyterian and Reformed, 1950. Pp. 429-475.

Warren, Virgil. *What the Bible Says About Salvation.* Joplin, Mo.: College Press, 1982.

Weber, Carl P. *"hāmāh,"* *Theological Wordbook of the Old Testament,* ed. R. Laird Harris et al. Chicago: Moody Press, 1980. I:219-220.

Welch, Claude. *In This Name: The Doctrine of the Trinity in Contemporary Theology.* New York: Charles Scribner's Sons, 1952.

Wells, David F. *The Person of Christ.* Westchester, Ill.: Crossway Books, 1984.

Westermann, Claus. *What Does the Old Testament Say About God?* ed. Friedemann W. Golka. Atlanta: John Knox Press, 1979.

White, R.E.O. "Savior," *Evangelical Dictionary of Theology,* ed. Walter A. Elwell. Grand Rapids: Baker Book House, 1984. P. 975.

——————— . "Vengeance," *Evangelical Dictionary of Theology,* ed. Walter A. Elwell. Grand Rapids: Baker Book House, 1984. Pp. 1137-1138.

Wildiers, N.M. *An Introduction to Teilhard de Chardin,* tr. Hubert Hoskins. New York: Harper & Row, 1968.

Wiley, H. Orton. *Christian Theology.* 3 vols. Kansas City, Mo.: Beacon Hill Press, 1940.

Willems, Boniface A. *The Reality of Redemption.* New York: Herder and Herder, 1970.

Williams, Colin W. *What in the World?* New York: National Council of the Churches of Christ, 1964.

Wilson, Marvin R. *"nācham,"* *Theological Wordbook of the Old Testament,* ed. R. Laird Harris et al. Chicago: Moody Press, 1980. II:570-571.

Wolterstorff, Nicholas. "God Everlasting," *God and the Good: Essays in Honor of Henry Stob,* ed. Clifton Orlebeke and Lewis Smedes. Grand Rapids:

Eerdmans, 1975. Pp. 181-203.

Wood, Leon J. *"chāpēts," Theological Wordbook of the Old Testament,* ed. R. Laird Harris et al. Chicago: Moody Press, 1980. I:310-311.

Wood, Nathan R. *The Secret of the Universe.* 10 ed. Grand Rapids: Eerdmans, 1955.

Young, Norman. *Creator, Creation and Faith.* Philadelphia: Westminster Press, 1976.

Zaehner, R.C. *Hinduism.* 2 ed. New York: Oxford University Press, 1966.

Ziesler, J.A. "Righteousness," *The Westminster Dictionary of Christian Theology,* ed. Alan Richardson and John Bowden. Philadelphia: Westminster Press, 1983. Pp. 507-508.

Zimmerli, Walther. "χάρις , etc." (part), *Theological Dictionary of the New Testament,* ed. Gerhard Friedrich, tr. Geoffrey W. Bromiley. Grand Rapids: Eerdmans, 1974. IX:372-415.

Index of Names

Index of Bible Names

Index of Subjects

WHAT THE BIBLE SAYS ABOUT GOD THE REDEEMER

Index of Scriptures

(Jeremiah)

(Jeremiah)

Lamentations

(Lamentations)

Ezekiel

(Ezekiel)

Daniel

Hosea

(Romans)

Reference	Page
3:28-29	136
4:3	202
4:4	384
4:5	202,453
4:7-8	371
4:9	202
4:15	265,285
4:16	459,523
4:17	36,444,458
4:22	202
5:1	436
5:7	205
5:8	331,332,340
5:9	186,302,435
5:10	286
5:12	295,442
5:12ff.	31
5:14	448
5:15	367
5:15-16	367
5:17	367
5:18	453
5:19	202
5:20	266,272
6:3-4	447
6:3-5	35,172
6:4	40
6:9	444,445
6:16-18	439
6:17	404
6:19	259
6:22	259
6:23	265,288,367,370 376,442
7:5	268
7:7	267
7:8	268-69
7:10	268,272
7:12	213,265
7:14	265
7:16	265

(Romans)

Reference	Page
8:1	453
8:6	268
8:7	270
8:10	407,442
8:10-11	35
8:11	458
8:13	259
8:15	343
8:19-22	40,407
8:19-23	31,39
8:20	450
8:21	450
8:22-23	450
8:23	39,41,438,449
8:26	171
8:27	129
8:29	160,446,449
8:32	370,515
8:35	325
8:39	526
9:3-5	423
9-11	394
9:5	124,127
9:6	519
9:13	287,333
9:15	353,364
9:18	353
9:22	299-300
9:22-23	358
10:3	452
10:9	121,128,399,449, 524
10:13	128,524
11:22	256,313
11:26	14,18
11:28	333
12:1	353,354
12:3	366
12:6	366
12:10	327
12:19	290